W9-CDL-818

SCHOLASTIC ATLAS OF THE WORLD

SCHOLASTIC ATLAS OF THE WORLD

SCHOLASTIC REFERENCE

Library of Congress Cataloging-in-Publication Data
Steele, Philip, 1948–
Scholastic atlas of the world/by Philip Steele
p.cm.
Includes index.
1. Atlases [1.Atlases. 2. Geography.] I. Title.
G1021.S687 2001
912—dc21   00-030064

ISBN 0-439-08795-3

MiLeS
KeLLy
PUBLISHING

Produced by Miles Kelly Publishing Ltd
Bardfield Centre, Great Bardfield, Essex, CM7 4SL, UK

Project Manager: Anne Marshall
Design: Jo Brewer, Alex Charles, Digital Wisdom
Design Assistance: Andy Knight
Cartography: Digital Wisdom (Nicholas Rowland)
Consultants: Clive Carpenter, Keith Lye

Text: Philip Steele, Jane Walker
Editors: Neil de Cort, Belinda Gallagher
Assistant Editors: Mark Darling, Helen Parker, Liz Tortice

Proofreader: Sarah Doughty
Statistics: Clive Carpenter, Luke Seaber
Index: Jane Parker, Textype Typesetters
Picture Research: Lesley Cartlidge, Kate Miles, Liberty Newton
Artwork Commissioner: Janice Bracken
Publishing Director: Jim Miles

Color reproduction: DPI Colour, Saffron Walden, Essex, UK

10 9 8 7 6 5 4 3 2 1   01 02 03 04 05

Printed in the U.S.A.   23
First printing, August 2001

Scholastic Reference Staff

Editorial Director: Wendy Barish
Associate Editor: Mary Varilla Jones
Editorial Assistant: Elysa Jacobs
Curriculum Consultant: Bob Stremme
Flag Consultant: Dr. Whitney Smith, Flag Research Center

Creative Director: David Saylor
Art Director: Nancy Sabato

Managing Editor: Manuela Soares
Associate Production Editor: Victoria Washington Maher

Manufacturing Vice President: Angela Biola
Manufacturing Manager: Alison Forner

Population and life expectancy figures used in this book are from the International Database of the U.S. Census Bureau. The source used to identify area, language, and religion was the *CIA World Factbook*. Statistics on motor vehicle use were obtained from the American Automobile Manufacturer's Association.

The population statistics for the United States are the numbers released from the U.S. Census Bureau from Census 2000. The life facts statistics for the United States are based on the U.S. Census Bureau population projections for the year 2000.

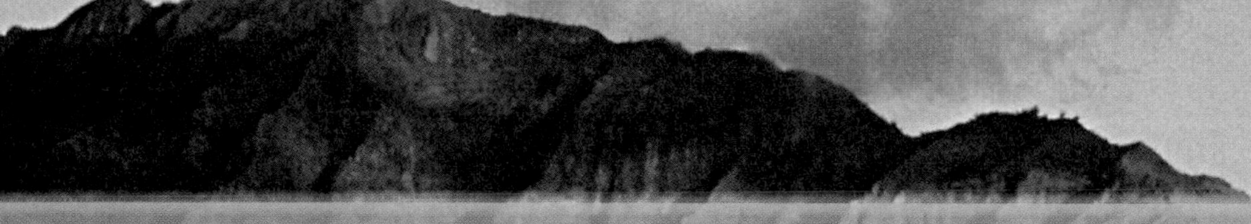

Countries

Contents

How to Use this Atlas

The *Scholastic Atlas of the World* presents information in a new and exciting way. Comparisons are made between countries and the United States—land area, time difference, life expectancy, car ownership, how long it takes to travel between distant cities—and many more features. How does the height of Mount McKinley, the highest mountain in the United States, compare with other mountains around the world? How does the length of different rivers compare? All these exciting and unique features are contained within this atlas.

Understanding the maps

This key shows the different features, labels, and symbols included in the maps, and helps you to read and understand them.

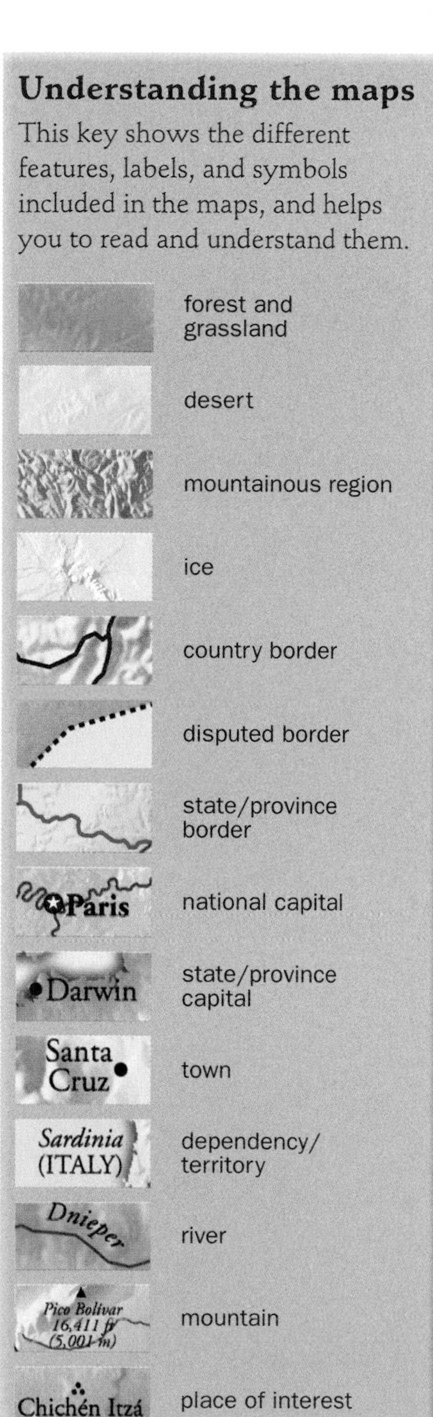

forest and grassland
desert
mountainous region
ice
country border
disputed border
state/province border
Paris
national capital
Darwin
state/province capital
Santa Cruz
town
Sardinia (ITALY)
dependency/ territory
Dnieper
river
Pico Bolívar 16,411 ft (5,001 m)
mountain
Chichén Itzá
place of interest

The projection used for these maps is cylindrical—see page 11.

Continent tabs

The world maps are arranged within continents (see page 16), shown by these index tabs. Each continent has its own page background color.

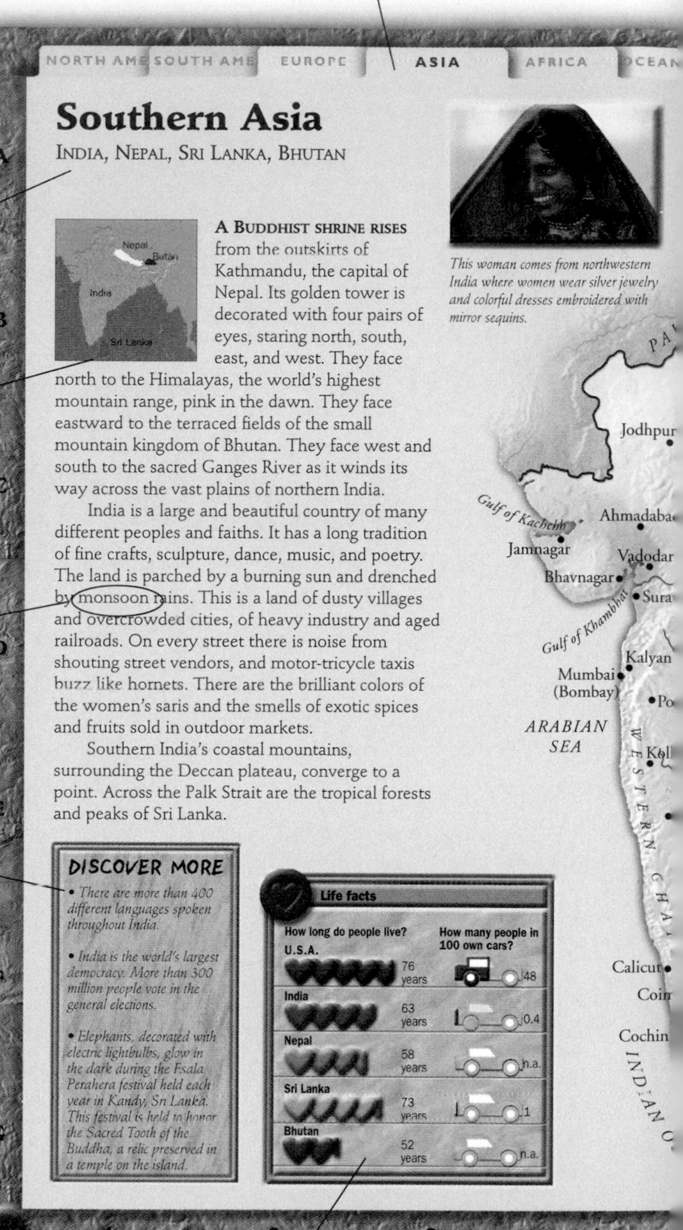

NORTH AME
SOUTH AME
EUROPE
ASIA
AFRICA
OCEAN
Southern Asia
INDIA, NEPAL, SRI LANKA, BHUTAN
A BUDDHIST SHRINE RISES from the outskirts of Kathmandu, the capital of Nepal. Its golden tower is decorated with four pairs of eyes, staring north, south, east, and west. They face north to the Himalayas, the world's highest mountain range, pink in the dawn. They face eastward to the terraced fields of the small mountain kingdom of Bhutan. They face west and south to the sacred Ganges River as it winds its way across the vast plains of northern India.
India is a large and beautiful country of many different peoples and faiths. It has a long tradition of fine crafts, sculpture, dance, music, and poetry. The land is parched by a burning sun and drenched by monsoon rains. This is a land of dusty villages and overcrowded cities, of heavy industry and aged railroads. On every street there is noise from shouting street vendors, and motor-tricycle taxis buzz like hornets. There are the brilliant colors of the women's saris and the smells of exotic spices and fruits sold in outdoor markets.
Southern India's coastal mountains, surrounding the Deccan plateau, converge to a point. Across the Palk Strait are the tropical forests and peaks of Sri Lanka.
This woman comes from northwestern India where women wear silver jewelry and colorful dresses embroidered with mirror sequins.
DISCOVER MORE
• There are more than 400 different languages spoken throughout India.
• India is the world's largest democracy. More than 300 million people vote in the general elections.
• Elephants, decorated with electric lightbulbs, glow in the dark during the Esala Perahera festival held each year in Kandy, Sri Lanka. This festival is held to honor the Sacred Tooth of the Buddha, a relic preserved in a temple on the island.
Life facts
How long do people live?
How many people in 100 own cars?
U.S.A. 76 years 48
India 63 years 0.4
Nepal 58 years n.a.
Sri Lanka 73 years 1
Bhutan 52 years n.a.
Jodhpur
Ahmadaba
Jamnagar
Vadodar
Bhavnagar
Gulf of Kachchh
Gulf of Khambhat
Kalyan
Mumbai (Bombay)
ARABIAN SEA
Calicut
Cochin
A
B
C
D
E
F
G
1
2
3
4

Country listing

Countries featured on the page are listed in order of their physical size.

Political map

This shows the countries and how they relate to the surrounding land area.

Important words

Difficult words that need more explanation are listed in the glossary on page 206.

Discover more

Did you know that Europe has a longer coastline than anywhere else in the world or that the Dead Sea is actually a lake? Find out more fascinating world facts in these boxes.

Abbreviations

FED.	Federation
Gt	Great
I.	island
Is/IS	islands
L.	lake
Mt	Mount
MTS	mountains
n.a.	not available
St.	Saint
cm	centimeter
cu	cubic
ft	feet
in	inch
l	liter
lb	pound
kg	kilogram
km	kilometer
m	meter
mi	mile
mm	millimeter
sq	square
t	metric ton

Life facts

How does life in the United States compare with the rest of the world? How long does the average person expect to live? How many people own cars? Find out here.

In the North American section of this atlas on pages 40–67, state and province facts are compared (as on the right). Find out how populated each state is and who lives there.

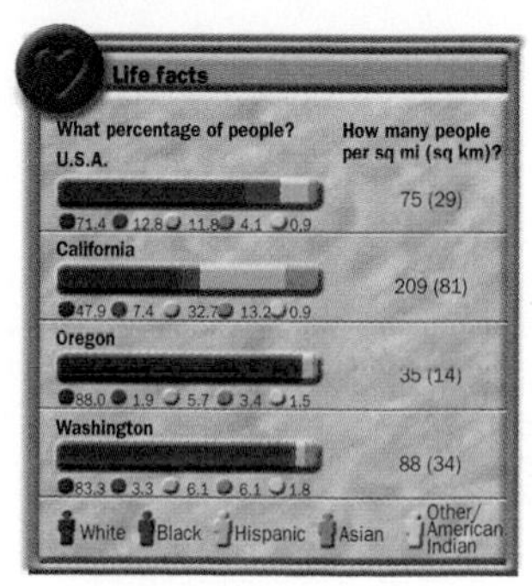

Life facts
What percentage of people?
How many people per sq mi (sq km)?
U.S.A.
75 (29)
California
209 (81)
Oregon
35 (14)
Washington
88 (34)
White
Black
Hispanic
Asian
Other/ American Indian

(Note: Figures in the Life facts boxes do not always add up to 100 because some people fall into more than one type. The term American Indian is used in line with the U.S. Census Bureau figures.)

Scale and compass rose

The scale allows you to find out how large an area on a map is (see page 12). The compass rose helps you to find north.

Highest mountains

The world's tallest mountains are compared with Mount McKinley, the tallest in the United States. The symbol is used on the map to show where the featured mountain is situated.

Where in the world?

Look at

the area of the United States compared with that of other country groupings.

the time difference between Washington, DC, the featured city, and GMT (Greenwich mean time, see page 15).

Find out

where the featured countries are on the globe (highlighted in red).

latitude (drawn in a west–east direction and shown in blue) and longitude (drawn between the North Pole and the South Pole and shown in red) lines that pinpoint the featured city (see page 13).

how far away the featured city is from Washington, DC, and how long it takes to fly there, traveling at 520 mph (835 km).

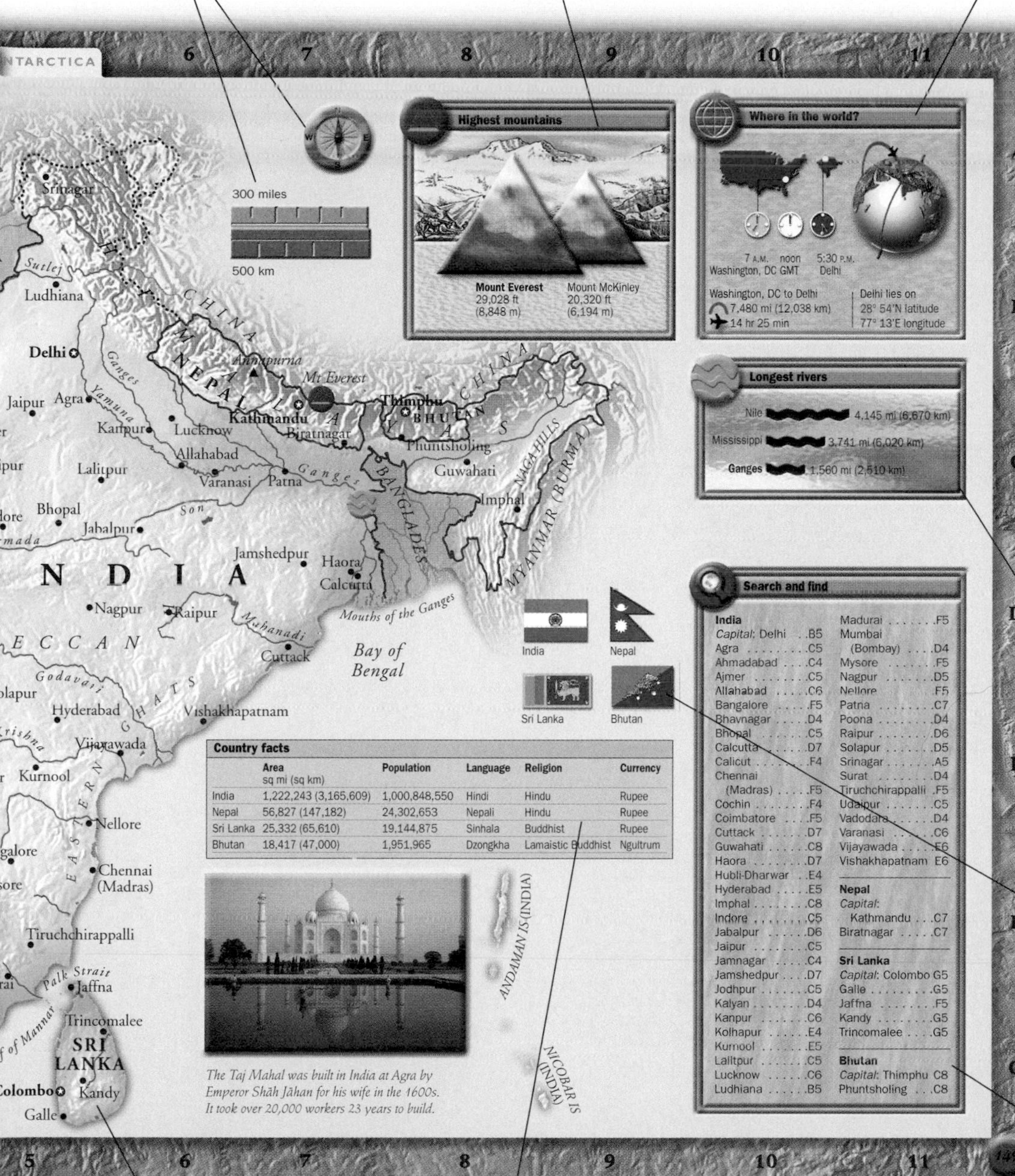

300 miles
500 km
Highest mountains
Mount Everest 29,028 ft (8,848 m)
Mount McKinley 20,320 ft (6,194 m)
Where in the world?
7 A.M. Washington, DC
noon GMT
5:30 P.M. Delhi
Washington, DC to Delhi 7,480 mi (12,038 km) 14 hr 25 min
Delhi lies on 28° 54'N latitude 77° 13'E longitude
Longest rivers
Nile 4,145 mi (6,670 km)
Mississippi 3,741 mi (6,020 km)
Ganges 1,560 mi (2,510 km)
INDIA
NEPAL
CHINA
BHUTAN
BANGLADESH
MYANMAR (BURMA)
SRI LANKA
Bay of Bengal
India
Nepal
Sri Lanka
Bhutan
Country facts
	Area sq mi (sq km)	Population	Language	Religion	Currency
India	1,222,243 (3,165,609)	1,000,848,550	Hindi	Hindu	Rupee
Nepal	56,827 (147,182)	24,302,653	Nepali	Hindu	Rupee
Sri Lanka	25,332 (65,610)	19,144,875	Sinhala	Buddhist	Rupee
Bhutan	18,417 (47,000)	1,951,965	Dzongkha	Lamaistic Buddhist	Ngultrum
Search and find
India
Capital: Delhi . . B5
Agra C5
Ahmadabad C4
Ajmer C5
Allahabad C6
Bangalore F5
Bhavnagar D4
Bhopal C5
Calcutta D7
Calicut F4
Chennai (Madras) F5
Cochin F4
Coimbatore F5
Cuttack D7
Guwahati C8
Haora D7
Hubli-Dharwar . . E4
Hyderabad E5
Imphal C8
Indore C5
Jabalpur D6
Jaipur C5
Jamnagar C4
Jamshedpur D7
Jodhpur C5
Kalyan D4
Kanpur C6
Kolhapur E4
Kurnool E5
Lalitpur C5
Lucknow C6
Ludhiana B5
Madurai F5
Mumbai (Bombay) D4
Mysore F5
Nagpur D5
Nellore F5
Patna C7
Poona D4
Raipur D6
Solapur D5
Srinagar A5
Surat D4
Tiruchchirappalli . F5
Udaipur C5
Vadodara D4
Varanasi C6
Vijayawada E6
Vishakhapatnam E6
Nepal
Capital: Kathmandu . . . C7
Biratnagar C7
Sri Lanka
Capital: Colombo G5
Galle G5
Jaffna F5
Kandy G5
Trincomalee . . . G5
Bhutan
Capital: Thimphu C8
Phuntsholing . . . C8
The Taj Mahal was built in India at Agra by Emperor Shāh Jāhan for his wife in the 1600s. It took over 20,000 workers 23 years to build.

Longest rivers

Some of the countries' longest rivers are compared with the Nile (the world's longest) and the Mississippi (the longest in the United States). The symbol is used on the map to show you where the featured river is situated.

Flags

Each country has its own flag. In the United States and Canada, the state and province flags are also shown.

Search and find

Here you can find the cities and towns featured on the map. Use the grid references to locate their exact position.

Physical maps

The key on the left will help you to identify the different towns, land features, and borders included on each map. Towns where most people live have been included as well as those places that are important for other reasons, such as trade and tourism. The longest rivers, the highest mountains, and the most notable physical features are shown.

Fact box

Find out more about each country—its area, population, language, religion, and currency. On continent spreads you will also find the largest country by area and population within that continent. For the United States and Canada, state and province information, such as the state flower, is given. (Sources for the statistics can be found on the copyright page.)

Map grid references

The letters and numbers that are contained within this border help you to find places on the map. For example, look for Calcutta in the Search and find—its grid reference is D7. Trace with your finger a line across from D and down from 7 and you will find Calcutta on the map. The index at the back of the book lists the grid references of all towns, cities, rivers, mountains, and other map features. Using this method you can find any of them on the maps.

Making Maps

About 4,500 years ago a skilled worker in Babylon was making detailed markings on a clay tablet. The markings he made probably showed some buildings in a nearby river valley. The worker was making one of the very first maps.

The ancient Egyptians and Greeks made maps, too. One Egyptian-Greek astronomer who was named Ptolemy (365–283 B.C.) wrote down everything that was known about the world, and drew maps to illustrate his words, in a huge book called *Geography*. Later, during the Middle Ages, the mapmaking skills of Chinese and Arab scholars were ahead of the rest of the world. The first map ever to be printed appeared in a Chinese encyclopedia in about 1155—more than 300 years before Europeans knew how to print.

Maps became more available in the 1500s. At this time Europeans were discovering new areas of the world. In 1492, when Columbus set sail and discovered the New World, the latest world map did not even show North or South America. After the invention of the printing press, probably by Johann Gutenberg in the mid–1400s, maps were produced more cheaply.

As people discovered new places, they needed new maps. Trail maps were made for the pioneers who traveled west across America in the late 1700s and early 1800s. During the world wars, the invention of the airplane helped armies, because accurate maps could be drawn using photos taken from the air.

Today, most of our maps are produced by computers. Material is collected from surveys of Earth, and aerial photos and satellite images. Computers arrange this material to draw the highly accurate maps you use today.

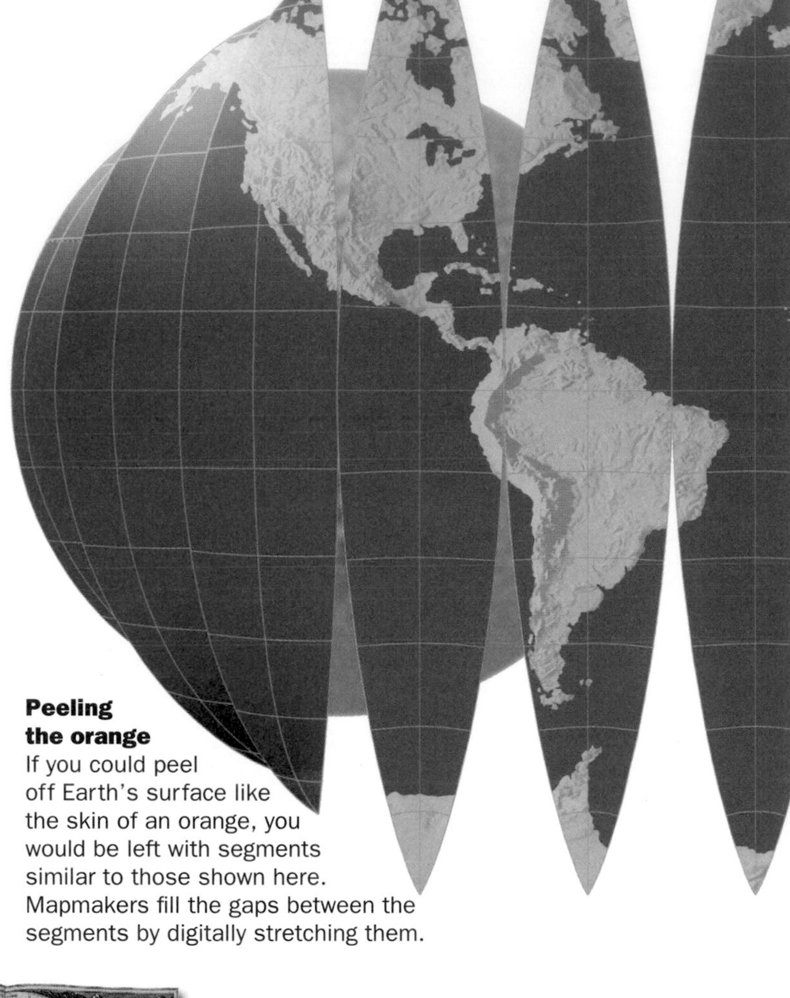

Peeling the orange
If you could peel off Earth's surface like the skin of an orange, you would be left with segments similar to those shown here. Mapmakers fill the gaps between the segments by digitally stretching them.

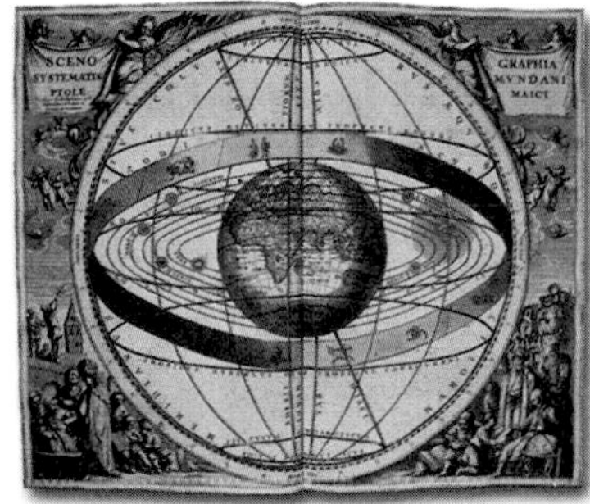

▲ *Ptolemy's map of the world first appeared in about A.D. 150 in ancient Egypt. Over 1,300 years later it was finally printed in an atlas in Germany.*

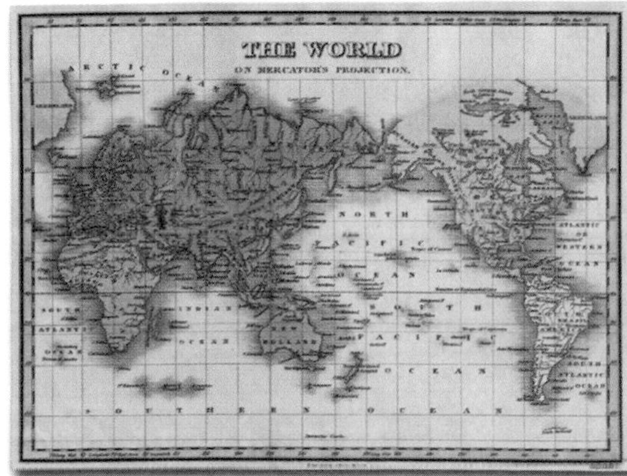
THE WORLD
ON MERCATOR'S PROJECTION.

▶ *Gerardus Mercator was a mapmaker from Flanders (in modern Belgium). In 1569 he drew Earth's surface onto a flat sheet of paper. It was easier for sailors to navigate by this kind of map or chart.*

Map of the 13 colonies
In the 1600s and 1700s, 13 colonies were set up along the east coast of North America by people arriving mainly from England. These 13 colonies eventually became the founding states of the United States of America.

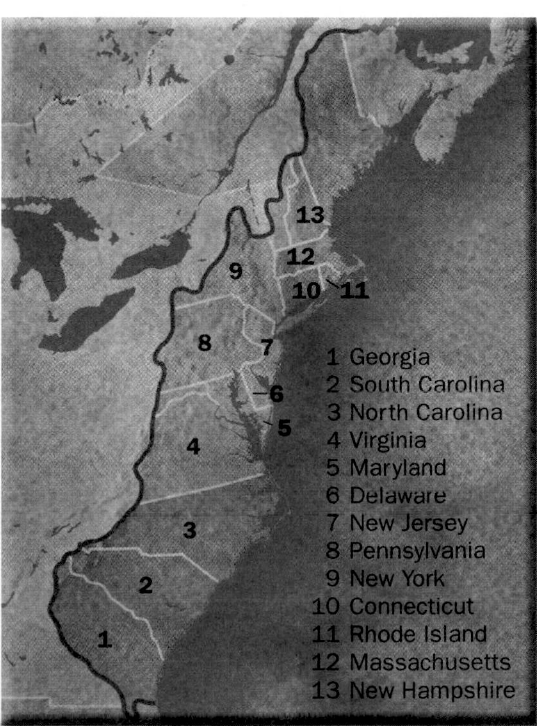
13
12
9
10
11
8
7
6
5
4
3
2
1
1 Georgia
2 South Carolina
3 North Carolina
4 Virginia
5 Maryland
6 Delaware
7 New Jersey
8 Pennsylvania
9 New York
10 Connecticut
11 Rhode Island
12 Massachusetts
13 New Hampshire

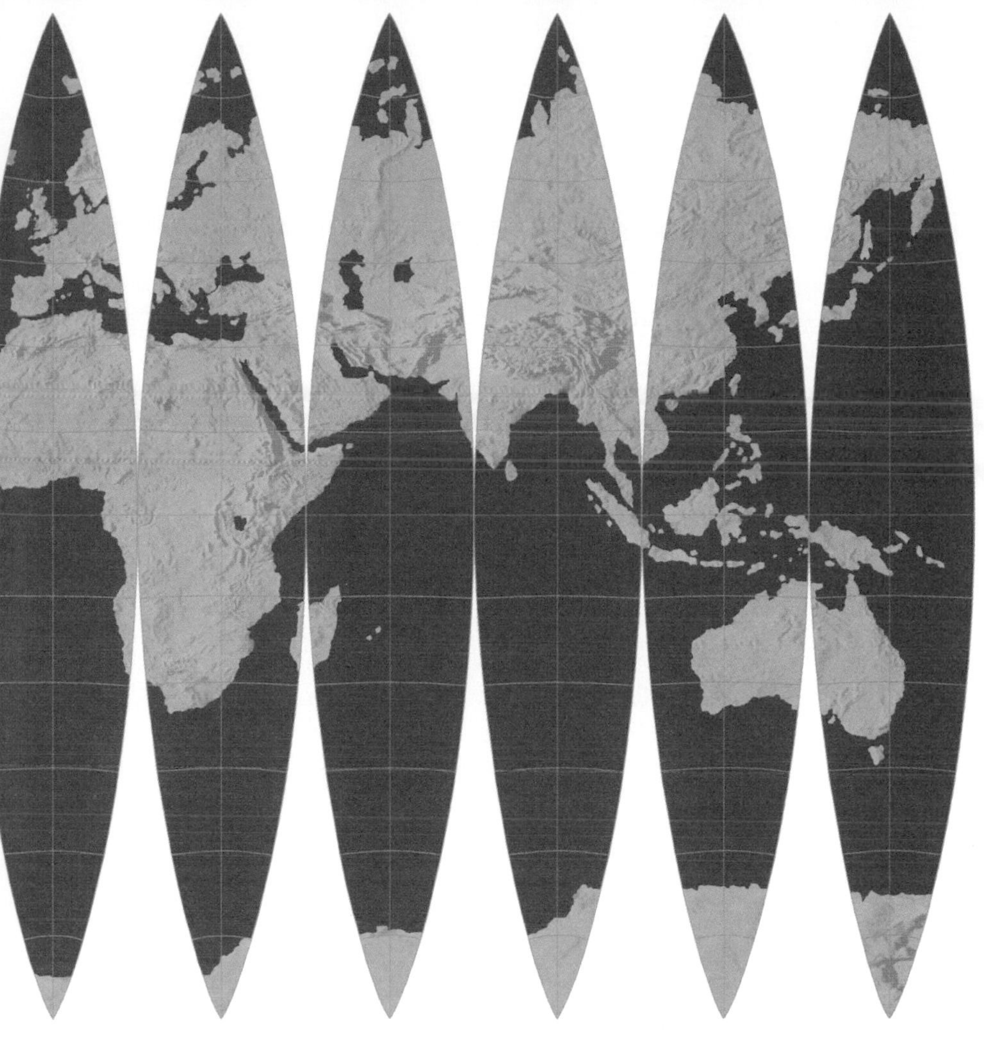

Boundaries in Europe

A political map shows the boundaries of different states and countries. The maps below show the same area of land, but the boundaries are very different. The map on the left shows Europe in 1980. The one on the right shows the same area in 1999. By this time Czechoslovakia and Yugoslavia had broken up, but East and West Germany had united to form the new Germany.

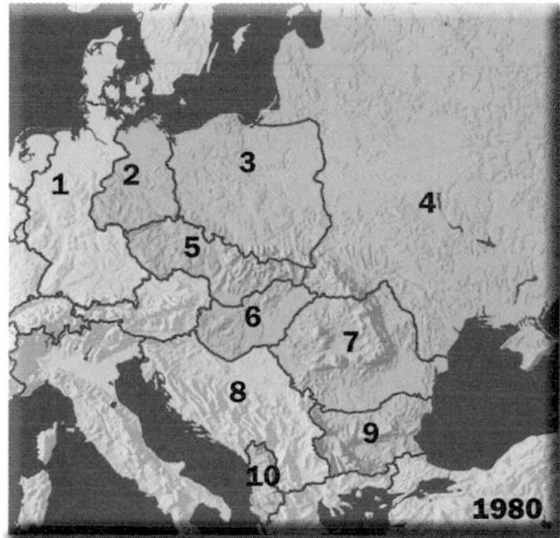
1980

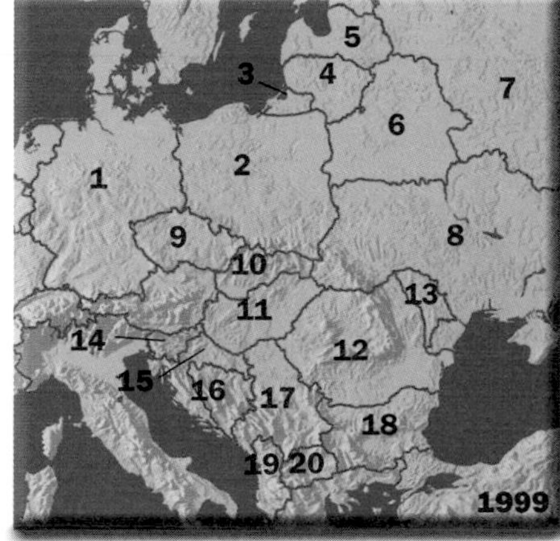
1999

1 West Germany
2 East Germany
3 Poland
4 USSR
5 Czechoslovakia
6 Hungary
7 Romania
8 Yugoslavia
9 Bulgaria
10 Albania

1 Germany
2 Poland
3 Kaliningrad
4 Lithuania
5 Latvia
6 Belarus
7 Russian Federation
8 Ukraine
9 Czech Republic
10 Slovakia
11 Hungary
12 Romania
13 Moldova
14 Slovenia
15 Croatia
16 Bosnia-Herzegovina
17 Yugoslavia
18 Bulgaria
19 Albania
20 Macedonia

What is a projection?

Because the earth is round, mapmakers have a difficult job representing it on a flat map. The earth has to be stretched and distorted to make it appear flat on a page. The way in which the earth is stretched is called a map projection, and each projection stretches the image of the earth in a different way. There are several different types of projection, and the ones shown below are most commonly used. Some projections show the shape of the land accurately but their size is incorrect. With others, the opposite is true. However, no projection is completely accurate, and all distort to some extent.

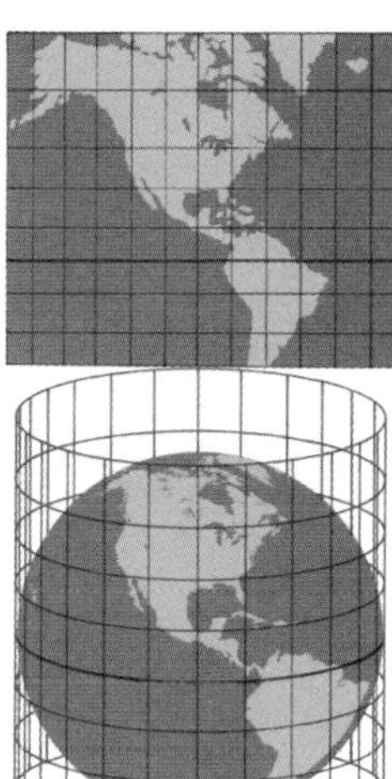

Cylinder shaped
Imagine wrapping a sheet of paper around a lit-up globe of the world and projecting the lines of latitude and longitude (page 13) onto the paper. Unwrap the paper and spread it flat to produce the kind of flat map often used by sailors.

Cone shaped
Imagine placing a paper cone over a lit-up globe, and projecting the lines of latitude and longitude onto the cone. Unwrap and flatten the paper to produce the kind of map that often shows wide areas of land such as the United States or Russian Federation.

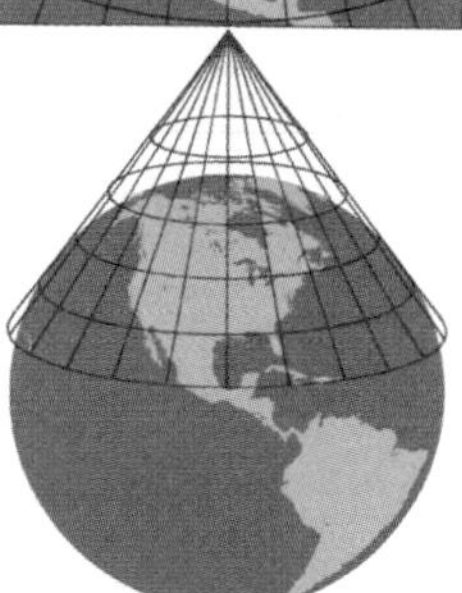

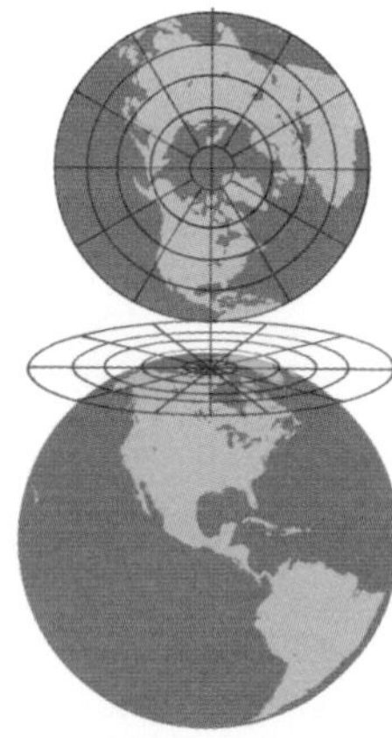

Plane shaped
Imagine holding a sheet of paper so that it touches one place on a lit-up globe. Project the lines of latitude and longitude onto the paper and then lay it on a flat surface. This kind of map is often used to show the world's polar regions.

Using Maps

A MAP IS A PICTURE OF AN AREA ON EARTH'S surface. It uses lines, colors, and symbols to give you information about that area. It may be a picture of the whole world or of a small area in a city or town. Maps tell you many different things—the location of countries, cities, and towns; the features of the landscape, the distribution of the population, or the climate of a particular region.

Different maps

People choose a type of map that best suits how they are going to use it. A hiker, for example, needs a different kind of map from one that is needed by someone driving a car. The hiker needs a physical map showing the height and shape of the land, the course of rivers and streams, where bridges are, the route of footpaths, and so on. The driver, on the other hand, needs a road map which shows highways and other main roads, scenic routes, parks, and nature preserves, as well as the location of highway services and intersections.

All about scale

The area shown on a map is, of course, much bigger than it appears on the printed page—this is because the map is drawn to scale. A map of the world shows us only a small amount of detail—we call it a small-scale map. A street map may show details of every building—it is called a large-scale map.

ARIZONA

MONTANA

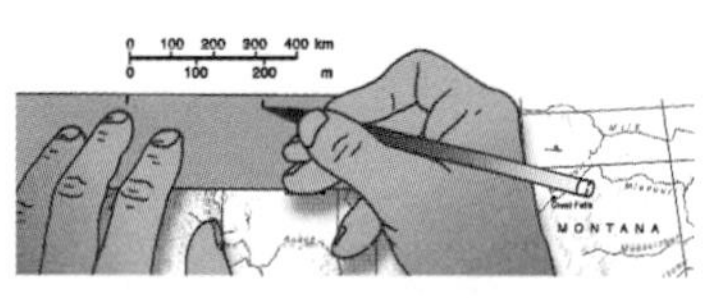
MONTANA

How to use a map scale

1 To measure the distance between two cities, first mark the positions of the city dots onto the edge of a small piece of paper.

2 Place the paper along the map's scale, with the left-hand mark against the 0. If the scale is shorter than the distance you want to measure, mark where the scale ends, say 200 miles (320 km). Note the distance already measured. Place this new mark against the 0.

3 Repeat this last step until you have reached the mark for the second city. Then add up each of the distances. This will give you the correct total of the number of miles between the two cities.

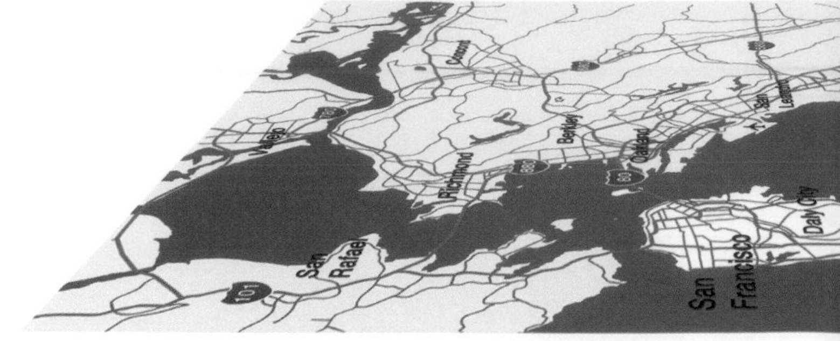
San Rafael
Richmond
San Francisco
Daly City

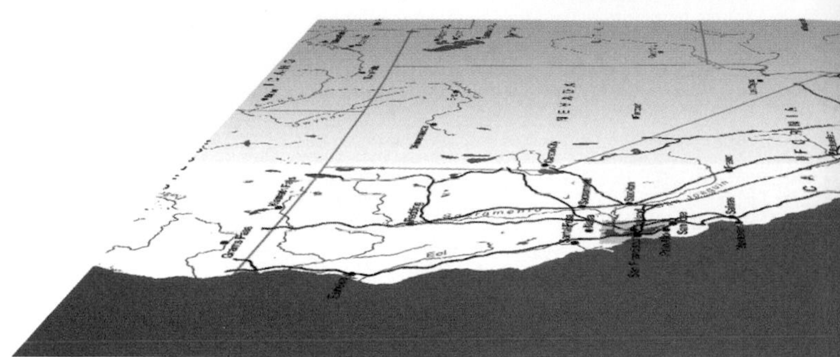
NEVADA
CALIFORNIA

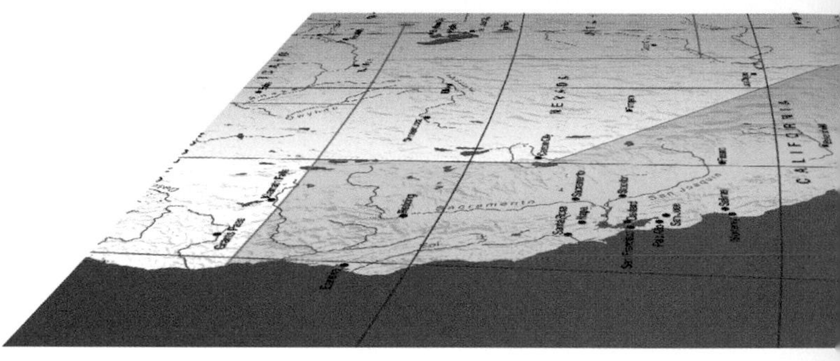
NEVADA
CALIFORNIA

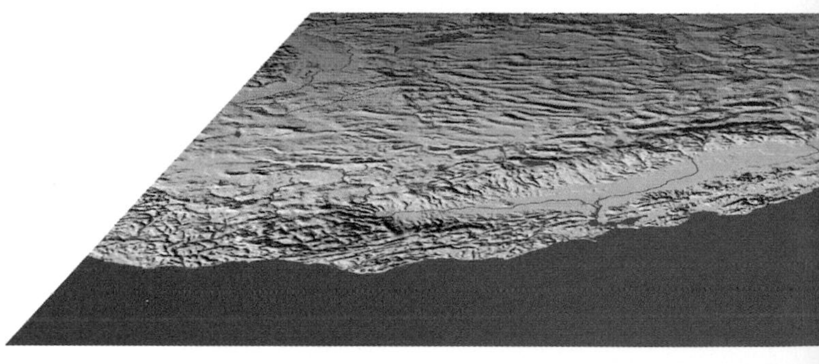

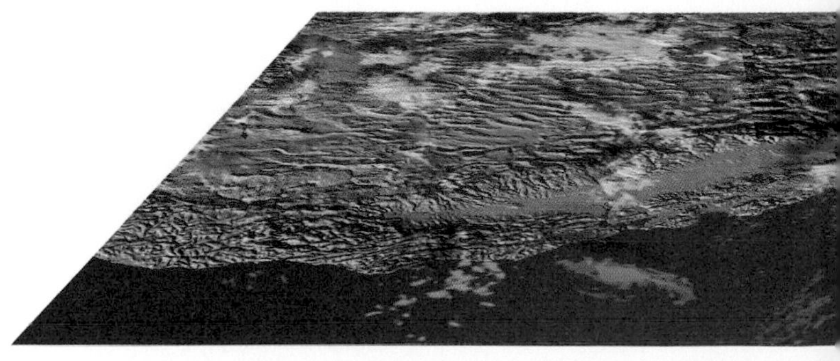

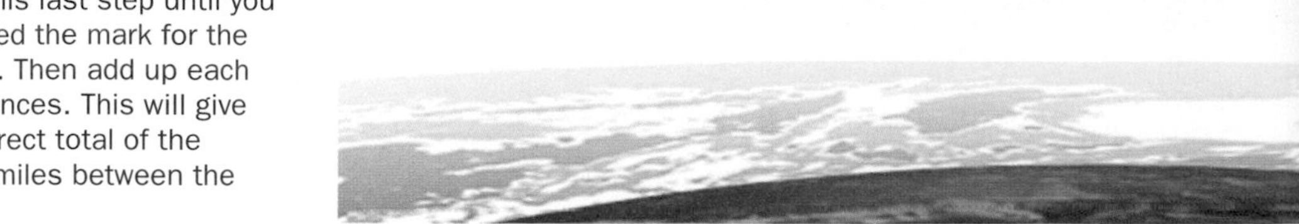

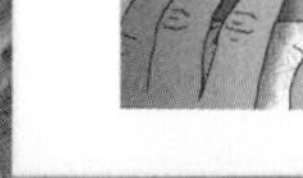

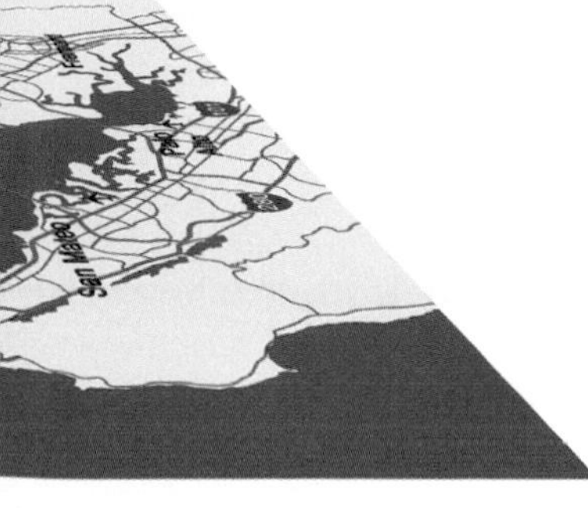

Street map
You use a street map to find your way around a city. This street map shows, in detail, an area of the city of San Francisco, California.

Road map
Here is a road map showing the main U.S. highways, intersections, four-lane roads, scenic routes, and some minor roads in California.

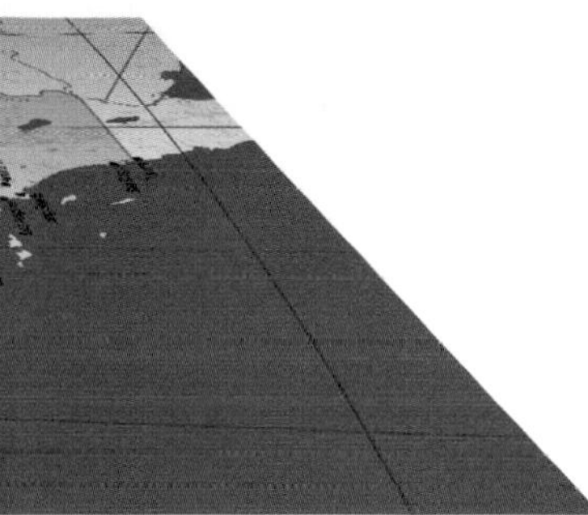

Political map
This political map shows the state and county boundaries of California, its neighboring states, the state capital, and the names and locations of major cities and towns.

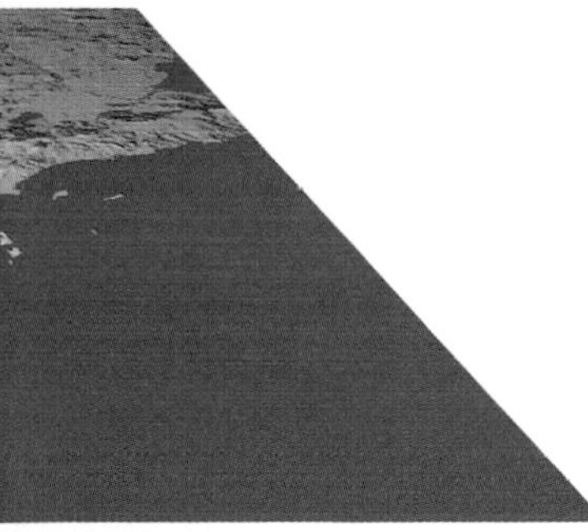

Physical map
The natural features of California are shown in this physical map—the highland and lowland areas, deserts, lakes, rivers, and the shape of the coastline.

Satellite image
This shows the area of Earth's surface that makes up the state of California.

The Earth in space
Satellite photographs can be taken from space. They show sections of Earth's surface.

Finding the location of a place

Maps are marked with a system of lines to help you describe and find the location of a certain place. The horizontal lines are called lines of latitude, and the vertical ones are lines of longitude. Latitude and longitude are measured in degrees (°).

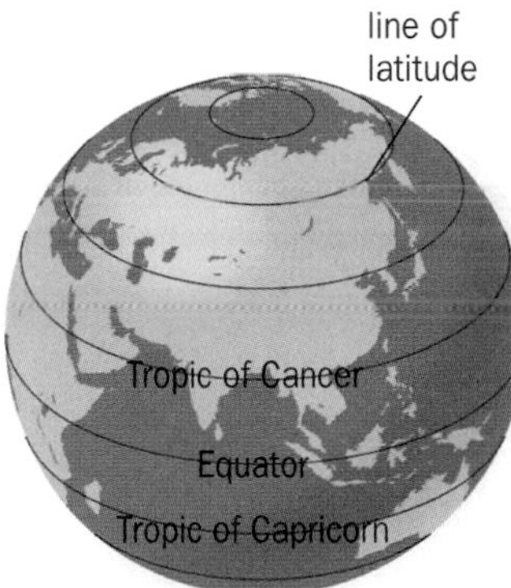
line of latitude
Tropic of Cancer
Equator
Tropic of Capricorn

Lines of latitude
These are imaginary lines that circle the world in an east–west direction. They tell you how far north or south a place is from the Equator, a line drawn at 0° latitude. They are drawn parallel to the Equator. Two special lines of latitude are the Tropic of Cancer and the Tropic of Capricorn. The Tropic of Cancer marks the northern boundary of the tropics. The Tropic of Capricorn marks the southern boundary. Because these regions lie close to the Equator, it is very hot, as the Sun shines directly overhead.

Lines of longitude
These are imaginary lines that run across Earth's surface in a north–south direction, from the North Pole to the South Pole. We start counting lines of longitude to the east and the west of the Greenwich Meridian, the 0° line of longitude that passes through the borough of Greenwich in London, England.

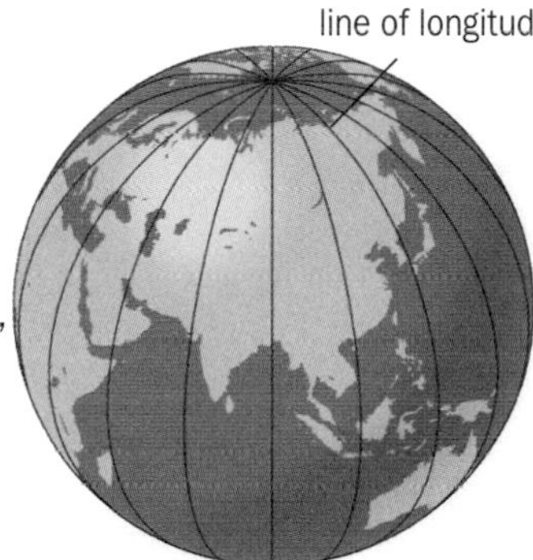
line of longitude

Hemispheres

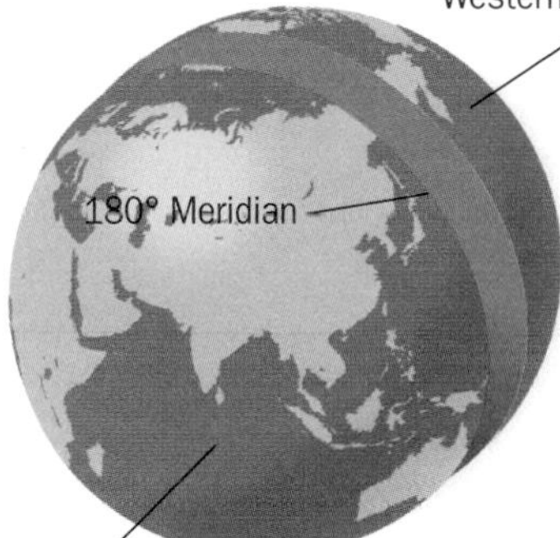
Western Hemisphere
180° Meridian
Eastern Hemisphere

The Greenwich Meridian and the 180° Meridian divide the world into two halves called the Eastern Hemisphere and the Western Hemisphere—each hemisphere has 180 degrees of longitude.

Northern Hemisphere
Equator
Southern Hemisphere

The Equator divides the world into two halves called the Northern Hemisphere and the Southern Hemisphere—each hemisphere has 90 degrees of latitude.

On a map you can find any place on Earth's surface if you know its latitude and its longitude. For example, the exact location of the city of Philadelphia (Pennsylvania) is as follows: 40°N, 75°W. In other words, Philadelphia lies on the line of latitude which is 40 degrees north of the Equator, and on the line of longitude 75 degrees west of the Greenwich Meridian.

The Earth in Space

Earth is part of a family of planets, moons, comets, asteroids, and other space material traveling around the Sun. We call this family the Solar System (after the Latin word *sol*, which means the Sun). The Sun is a small star, one of millions in an enormous star group called the Milky Way. We belong to this galaxy, which is just one of millions of others in the vast Universe.

Each of the nine known planets moving around the Sun travels along an oval-shaped path called an orbit. The planets take different amounts of time to make a complete orbit around the Sun. Earth takes $365\frac{1}{4}$ days, or one year. Mercury, the planet closest to the Sun, takes just 88 days to orbit it. Pluto, which is usually the planet farthest from the Sun, takes almost 248 years to complete its orbit.

Pluto
Neptune
Uranus
Saturn

The moving Earth

Earth turns around on its axis like a spinning top. This axis is an imaginary line between the North and South poles. It takes 24 hours for Earth to spin all the way around, giving us day and night. As Earth spins, it is daytime in places facing the Sun, and nighttime in places facing away from the Sun. At the same time, Earth is also moving around the Sun. The axis of the moving Earth is not in an upright position—it tilts by $23\frac{1}{2}°$ away from the vertical. It is this tilt which gives us our seasons. In summer, for example, a place may have more hours of daylight, and in winter, it may have less.

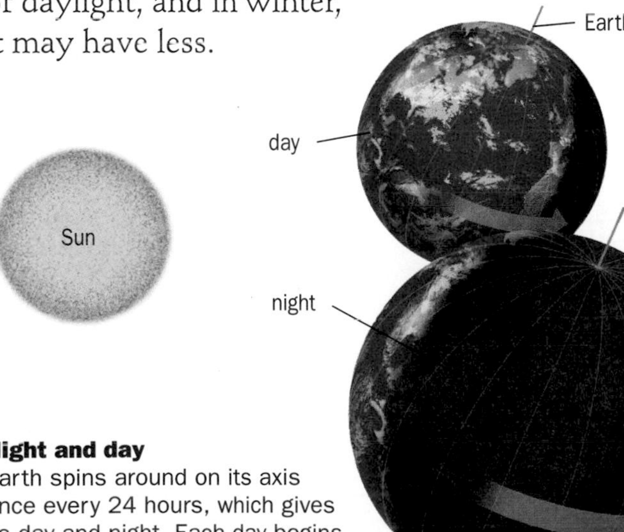
Earth's axis
day
Sun
night
Earth revolving on its axis

Night and day
Earth spins around on its axis once every 24 hours, which gives us day and night. Each day begins when the Sun rises in the east, and night begins when the Sun sets in the west. Noon is when the Sun is at its highest point in the sky.

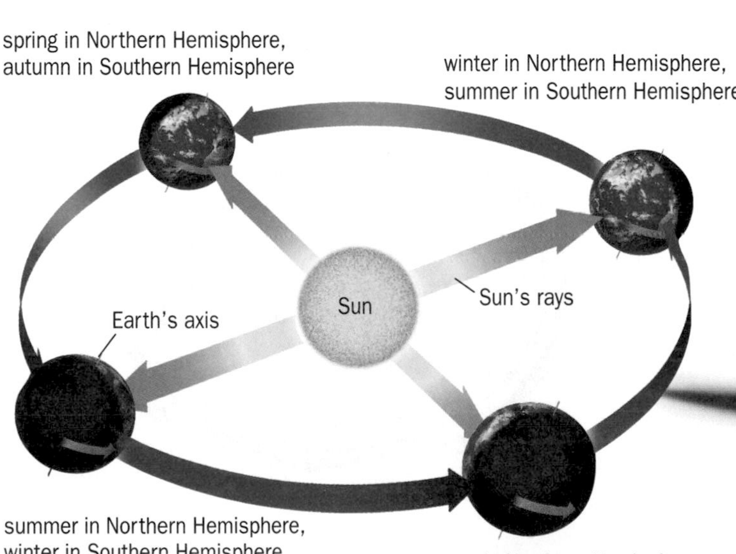
spring in Northern Hemisphere, autumn in Southern Hemisphere
winter in Northern Hemisphere, summer in Southern Hemisphere
Sun
Sun's rays
Earth's axis
summer in Northern Hemisphere, winter in Southern Hemisphere
autumn in Northern Hemisphere, spring in Southern Hemisphere

Earth's orbit
The tilted angle of Earth's axis and Earth's orbit around the Sun give us our seasons. From March to September, Earth's Northern Hemisphere is tilted toward the Sun. Places in the Northern Hemisphere have spring, followed by summer. At the same time, places in the Southern Hemisphere have fall, followed by winter. From September to March the Southern Hemisphere is tilted toward the Sun. Places in the south have spring and summer, while those in the north have fall and winter.

▶ *This dramatic photo was taken by the Hubble Space Telescope (HST). It shows the clouds of gas around a dying star. First launched into space in 1990, the HST has produced the clearest, most detailed pictures of space ever seen. Every few years astronauts from the space shuttle repair and maintain the telescope.*

International Date Line
Greenwich Meridian
1 2 3 4 5 6 7 8 9 10 11 12 1 2 3 4 5 6 7 8 9 10 11 12
A.M.
TIME
P.M.
Jupiter
Mars
Sun
Venus
Earth
Mercury

Time zones

To make it easier for travelers, the world is divided into 24 time zones. The zones are numbered from the Greenwich Meridian, the line of longitude at 0°, and each zone measures about 15° of longitude. There are 23 full time zones, and two half zones, one on each side of the International Date Line. This is an imaginary line at 180°, exactly halfway around the world from the Greenwich Meridian. Each time zone is one hour ahead of its neighboring zone to the west, and one hour behind its neighboring zone to the east.

So if you travel east across two time zones, you have to put your watch forward two hours. If you travel west across one time zone, you put your watch back one hour.

The planets

Some of the planets, such as Earth and Mars, are made mainly of rock. Others are made of gas and are much bigger than our planet Earth. We sometimes call them the gas giants. Pluto, the smallest planet, is a mixture of ice and rock. Earth is the only one of the nine planets on which we know for sure that life exists.

Our Planet Earth

A DESERT COVERING ALMOST ONE-THIRD OF THE huge African continent, a waterfall with a drop of over 3,000 feet (914 m)—that's almost three times the height of the Empire State Building—and an underground cave system stretching around 345 miles (555 km). These are just three of the natural features that you can find on our amazing, and totally unique, planet Earth.

About 73 percent of our planet is covered with water. The Pacific Ocean, the largest body of water, covers almost one-third of Earth's surface. The remaining land is divided up into today's seven great continents—from largest to smallest: Asia, Africa, North America, South America, Antarctica, Europe, and Oceania. The landscape is dotted with a huge variety of wonderful natural features: towering mountains and hot, dry deserts, fast-flowing rivers and large lakes, majestic volcanoes and steep-sided valleys, caves and caverns many miles underground, huge rivers of ice called glaciers, and vast ice sheets.

There are now more than six billion people living on Earth, and we inhabit almost every corner of the globe. We share this natural world with more than two million species of living things, ranging in size from giant sequoia trees and huge blue whales to tiny organisms that you can see only with the help of a powerful microscope.

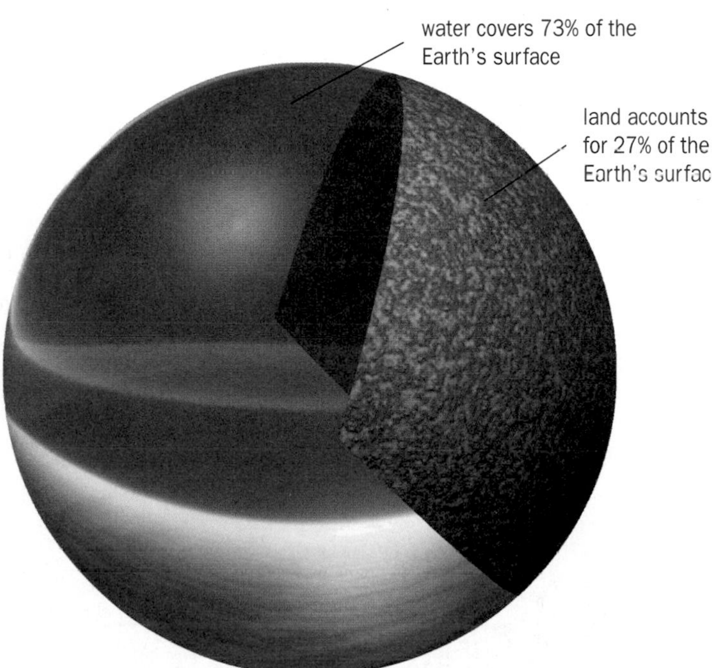
water covers 73% of the Earth's surface
land accounts for 27% of the Earth's surface

Water on Earth
The oceans and seas contain 97 percent of all the water on Earth. The remaining 3 percent is either frozen in ice caps and glaciers or in lakes, rivers, and under the ground.

Country populations
Around half the world's population is concentrated in just five countries: China, India, the United States, Indonesia, and Brazil.

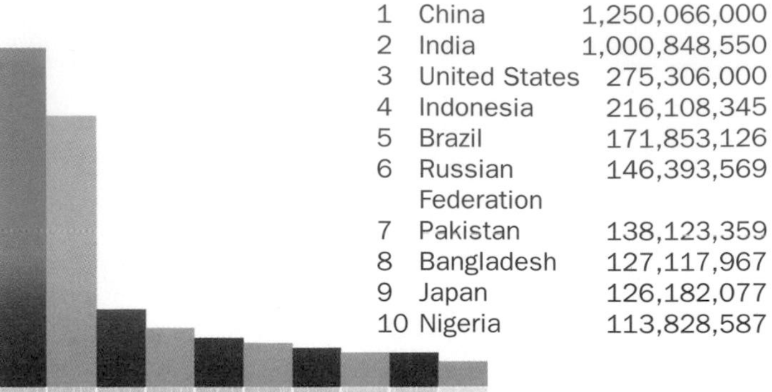
1
2
3
4
5
6
7
8
9
10

1	China	1,250,066,000
2	India	1,000,848,550
3	United States	275,306,000
4	Indonesia	216,108,345
5	Brazil	171,853,126
6	Russian Federation	146,393,569
7	Pakistan	138,123,359
8	Bangladesh	127,117,967
9	Japan	126,182,077
10	Nigeria	113,828,587

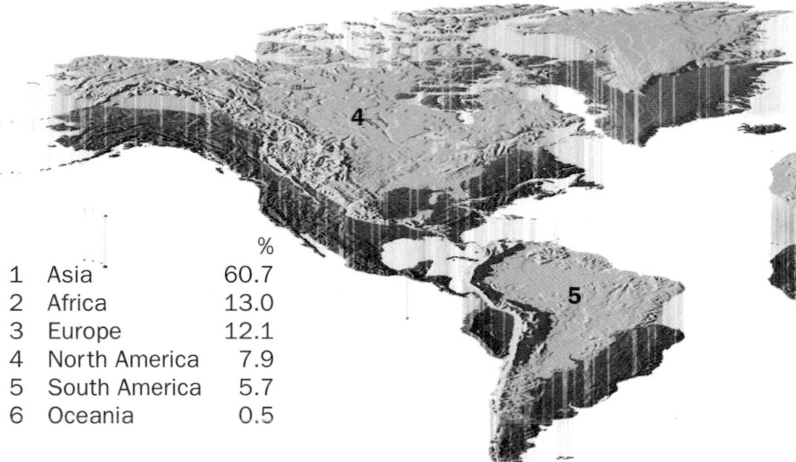
4
5

		%
1	Asia	60.7
2	Africa	13.0
3	Europe	12.1
4	North America	7.9
5	South America	5.7
6	Oceania	0.5

◀ ***Highest mountain***
Mount Everest is on the border of Nepal and China. Scientists have recently discovered that it's even bigger than they previously thought! In November 1999 the mountain's official height was changed to 29,028 ft (8,848 m)—that's 7 ft (2 m) more than its previous official height.

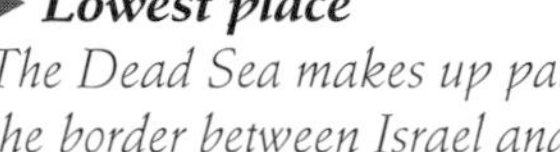

▶ ***Lowest place***
The Dead Sea makes up part of the border between Israel and Jordan. It lies at 1,312 ft (400 m) below sea level. It is called the Dead Sea because no fish and only a few kinds of plants can survive in its very salty waters.

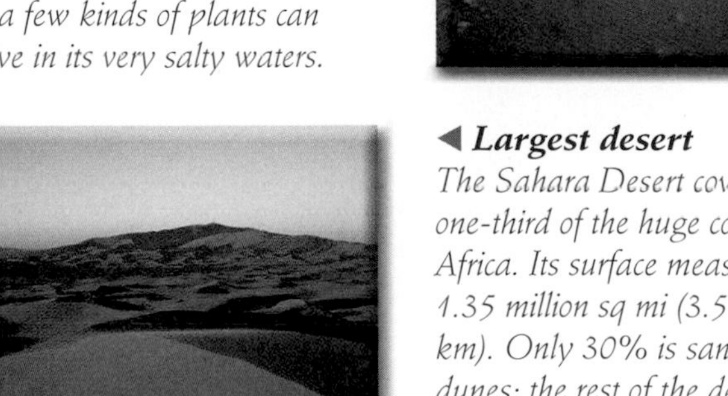

◀ ***Largest desert***
The Sahara Desert covers almost one-third of the huge continent of Africa. Its surface measures 1.35 million sq mi (3.5 million sq km). Only 30% is sand and sand dunes; the rest of the desert consists of broad flat areas of small rocks and gravel.

Highest population

The diagram below shows the populated continents of the world peeled back from Earth's surface in layers. Asia, the most heavily populated continent, is shown as the highest layer.

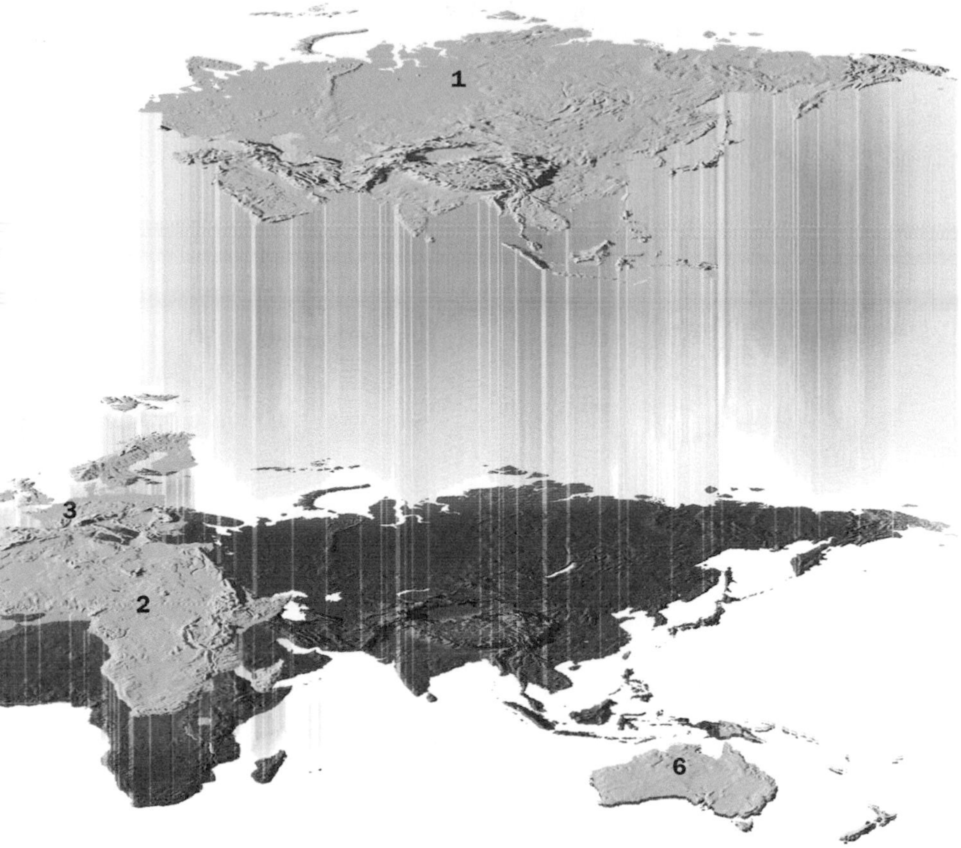
1
3
2
6

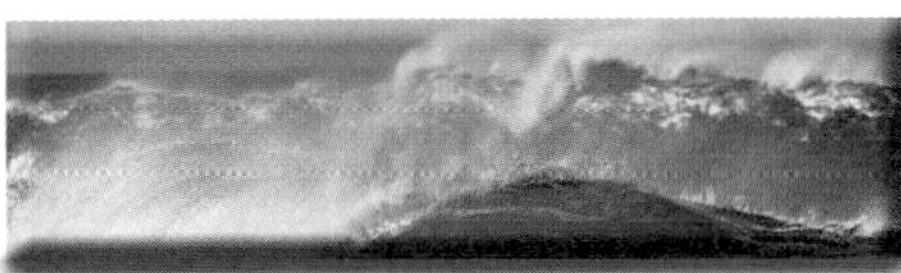

◀ ***Largest ocean***

The Pacific Ocean is almost double the size of the Atlantic, covering 64,186,300 sq mi (1,662,425,000 sq km).

▶ ***Largest island***

Greenland is more than four times the size of the second-largest island, Papua New Guinea. The ice-cold land of Greenland covers an area of 840,000 sq mi (2,175,600 sq km). It is a province of Denmark and is about 50 times bigger than Denmark itself.

◀ ***Largest lake***

Asia's Caspian Sea covers an area of 152,239 sq mi (394,299 sq km). Although it is landlocked, which means it is surrounded by land on all sides, the Romans called it a "sea" because its waters are salty. The largest freshwater lake is Lake Superior, one of North America's five Great Lakes.

▶ ***Longest river***

Africa's mighty Nile River flows for 4,145 mi (6,670 km) from its source near Lake Victoria northward to the Mediterranean Sea. By contrast, the world's shortest recorded river is the Roe in the state of Montana—it's just 201 ft (64 m) long!

Population explosion

The world's population is on average growing by 212,000 people every day. However, the population is not evenly distributed as some larger countries have small populations.

Area and population

Australia covers almost 3 million square miles (7.8 million sq km). Yet it has a population of just 18.8 million. The Netherlands is just 16,033 square miles (41,525 sq km), yet its population is almost as big as that of Australia—15.8 million.

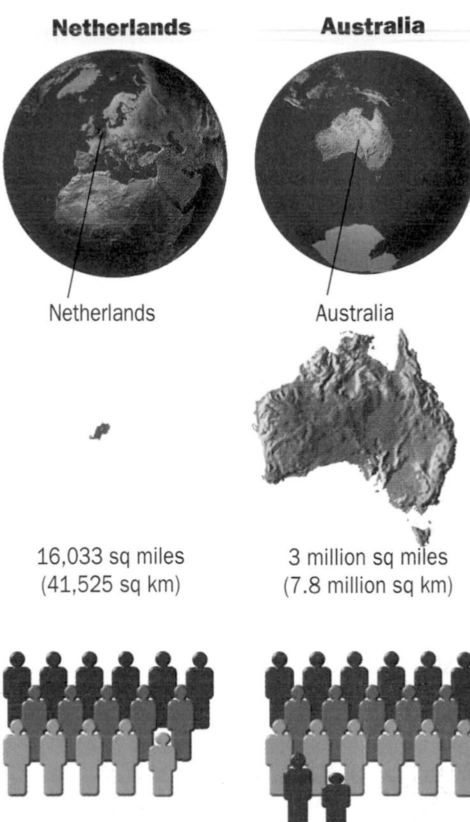
Netherlands
Australia
Netherlands
Australia
16,033 sq miles
(41,525 sq km)
3 million sq miles
(7.8 million sq km)
15.8 million people
18.8 million people

Population density

Few people live in the huge desert areas and dry plains of Australia's interior; most of the population lives on or near the cooler coastal regions where there is more rainfall. On average, this sparsely populated country has no more than 6 people living in every square mile (2.3 per sq km). The tiny Netherlands, on the other hand, has 985 people in every square mile (380 per sq km). Bangladesh, in southern Asia, is one of the most densely populated countries with an average of 2,286 people living in every square mile (883 per sq km).

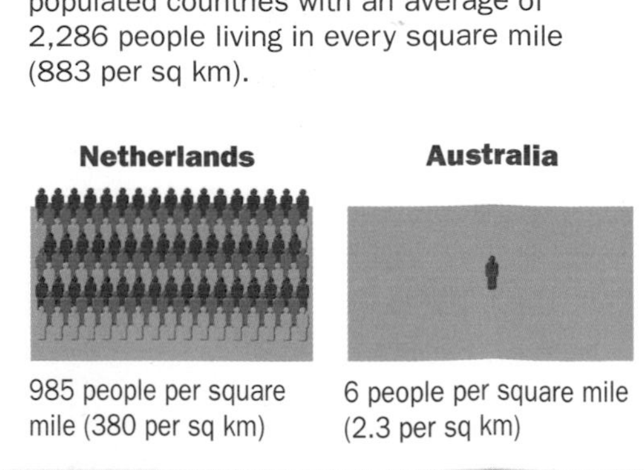
Netherlands
Australia
985 people per square mile (380 per sq km)
6 people per square mile (2.3 per sq km)

The Moving Earth

EARTH IS A HUGE ROCKY BALL. LARGE CHUNKS of land called continents and vast expanses of ocean cover its surface. They are part of the hard "skin," or crust, that surrounds the whole Earth. This rocky outer layer is thicker under the continents, where it is up to 25 miles (40 km) thick, than under the oceans, where it is about 5 miles (8 km) thick.

Beneath this crust are layers of hot rocks and metals, some of them solid and some liquid. Immediately below the crust is a layer of hard rock reaching down about 1,800 miles (2,900 km). We call this layer the mantle. Its rocks are made up of different materials: silicon, aluminum, magnesium, iron, and oxygen. Below the mantle is the next layer, called the outer core. Here it is so hot that the rocks of iron and nickel have melted and become liquid. The temperature in the outer core can be as hot as 9,000° F (5,000° C)—that's 500 times hotter than boiling water!

Farther down still, at the very center of Earth, lies a ball of solid iron and nickel—the inner core. Its center is about 4,000 miles (6,400 km) from the surface. Scientists learn about Earth's interior by studying how earthquake waves travel.

crust

mantle

outer core of molten metal

solid metal inner core

Inside the Earth
The part of Earth's crust that lies beneath the continents is known as continental crust. Oceanic crust lies beneath the oceans and seas. As you move down through the thick, rocky mantle the temperature increases. We can only imagine what the outer and inner cores are like. Scientists have never seen them, nor obtained any samples from them, but guess that the outer core may be made from liquid iron and nickel, while the inner core may be solid metal.

A moving jigsaw
Earth's crust is divided into 16 huge pieces, called plates. Each one is made up of rock and a section of the upper mantle. The plates float on the hot liquid rocks below them, while the currents in these rocks keep the plates moving all the time. You cannot feel the land beneath your feet shifting because the plates move very slowly—between about ½ and 4 inches (1.25 and 10 cm) a year. There is more likely to be volcanic and earthquake activity where the plates meet.

▲ major volcanoes
● major earthquake sites
plate boundaries

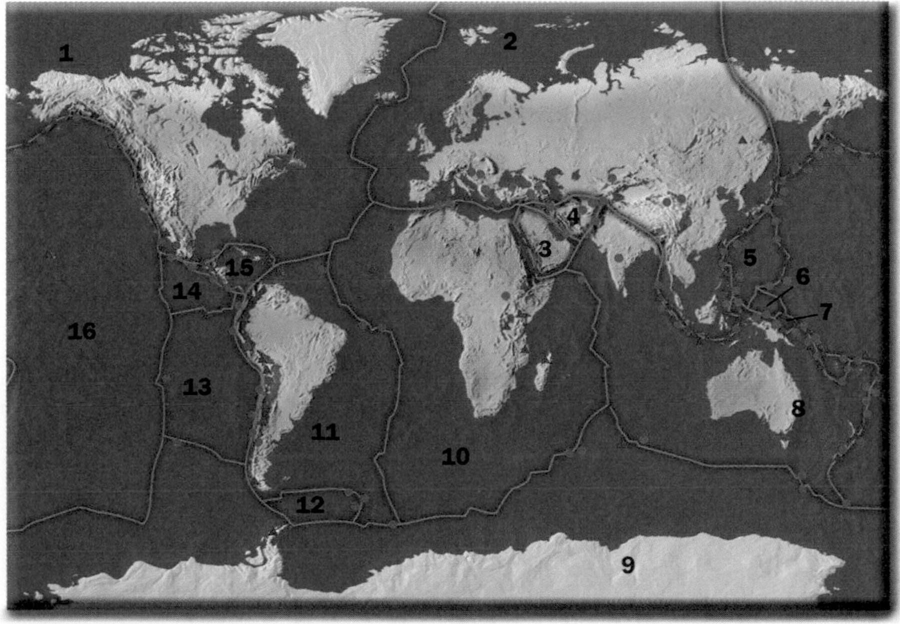
1
2
3
4
5
6
7
8
9
10
11
12
13
14
15
16

Plates
1 North American
2 Eurasian
3 Arabian
4 Iranian
5 Philippine
6 Caroline
7 Fiji
8 Indo-Australian
9 Antarctic
10 African
11 South American
12 Scotia
13 Nazca
14 Cocos
15 Caribbean
16 Pacific

Plate movement

The plates that make up Earth's crust sometimes move away from each other, and sometimes toward each other. They also slide past each other. When two plates collide, one plate may pile up against the other to form a great mountain range, such as the Andes in South America. This mountain building does not happen quickly, though—it takes millions of years. After a collision, one plate might be forced down below the other to form a deep trench on the ocean floor.

The boundary between two sliding plates is called a fault line. Where plates slide past each other, this movement often strains the rocks on each side of the fault line. If the strain becomes too great, the rocks snap and jerk, and an earthquake happens.

fault line
sliding motion causes rocks to strain

◀ *A devastating earthquake in 1999 destroyed the homes of thousands of Turkish people.*

Fiery volcanoes

When one plate is pushed below another, the hard rocks of the crust melt in the hot mantle. Sometimes this melted rock forces its way back upward and bursts through the surface, forming a volcano.

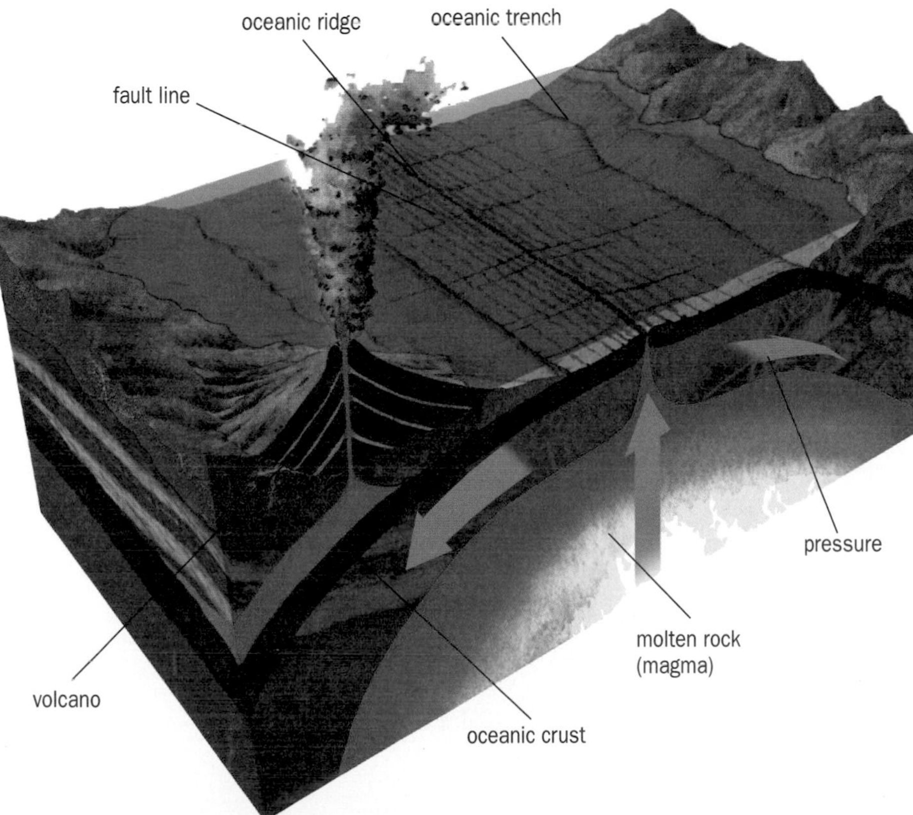
oceanic ridge
oceanic trench
fault line
pressure
molten rock (magma)
volcano
oceanic crust

The changing Earth

200 million years ago

The world consisted of a huge single land mass, Pangaea, which began to break apart slowly. The very biggest dinosaurs roamed the land, and the first birds appeared. Shelled squid, snails, and many kinds of fish lived in the warm seas.

120 million years ago

The breakup of the supercontinent Pangaea produced two smaller landmasses—Laurasia to the north and Gondwanaland to the south. The first flowering plants appeared on the land, and dinosaurs developed spiky horns and body armor.

60 million years ago

Laurasia and Gondwanaland eventually broke up to form the seven continents we know today. By this time the last dinosaurs had died out and warm-blooded mammals were becoming common.

Oceans and Seas

SALT WATER COVERS MORE THAN TWO-THIRDS OF Earth's surface. It is contained in the four great oceans (the Pacific, the Atlantic, the Indian, and the Arctic) and in smaller areas of water called seas, as well as in many gulfs and bays.

Teeming with life

The oceans are teeming with life. The huge variety of creatures living in them ranges from the microscopic plankton that float on the water's surface to the mighty blue whale, the largest creature alive today: An adult male can grow up to 100 feet (30 m) long. Most marine life lives near the surface where food supplies are plentiful—only a few creatures survive in the cold, dark depths and on the ocean floor itself.

A moving ocean floor

Oceanographers are scientists who study the sea. They have found that the ocean floor is actually on the move. It is slowly shifting by between 1/2 and 4 inches (1.25 and 10 cm) a year. This movement happens because the huge plates that form Earth's crust are constantly on the move, carrying the ocean floor with them. Sometimes the plates drift slowly apart, and new ocean floor forms between them. The floor of the Atlantic Ocean, for instance, is growing wider by about 1 inch (2.5 cm) every year. Something different is happening in the Pacific Ocean—it's shrinking a little each year as two plates collide and one is forced under the other.

▲ *In warm tropical seas a coral reef is packed with brightly colored coral formations in a mass of different shapes and sizes. The reef itself is formed from the skeletons of the tiny coral animals.*

▲ *Strange-looking giant tube worms cluster around hydrothermal vents on the ocean floor. Hot, black water heated by the hot rocks below the ocean floor pours out of these chimney-like vents on the ocean floor.*

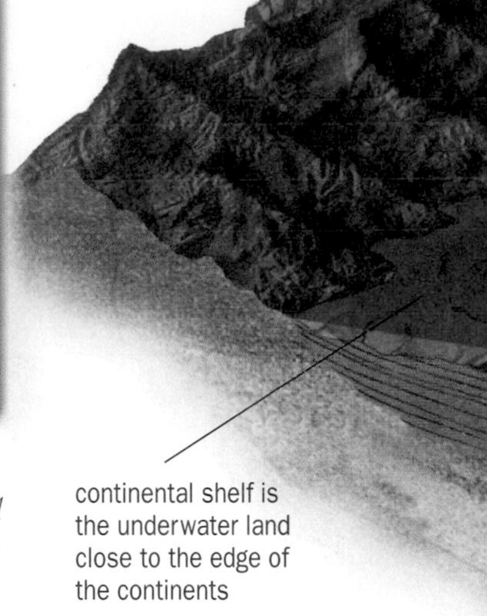
continental shelf is the underwater land close to the edge of the continents

What are tides?
When the sea rises up the beach, it is called high tide; when it falls back down the beach, it is known as low tide. In most places there are two high tides and two low tides in every 24-hour period. Tides are caused by the Moon's gravity pulling on Earth and its oceans and seas. This gravity pulls the water upward at places directly below the Moon to create a bulge. At the same time a second bulge forms on the opposite side of Earth. High tide occurs at these two bulges, while at the same time, places in between the bulges have low tide. These two bulges always stay in the same place, one under the Moon and the other on the opposite side of Earth. As Earth is constantly rotating, these tides occur at different places at different times of the day.

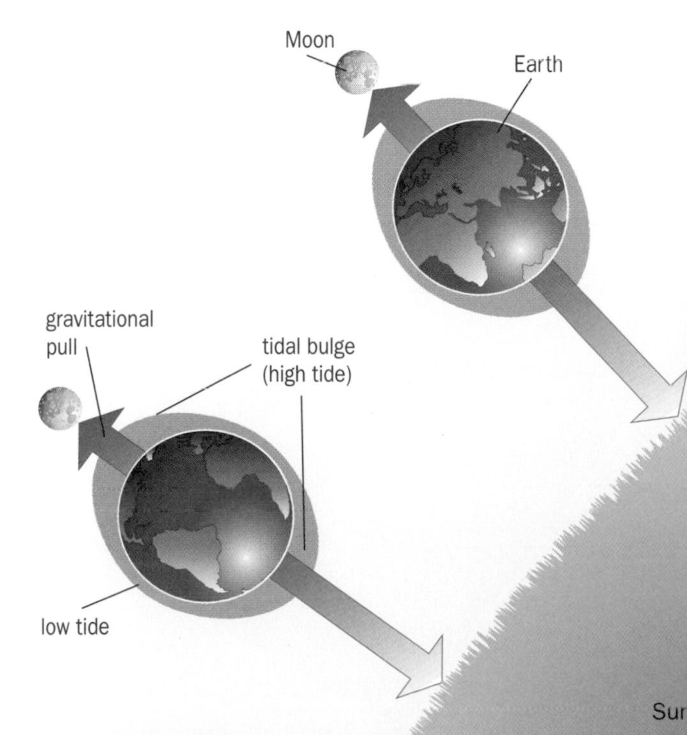
Moon
Earth
gravitational pull
tidal bulge (high tide)
low tide
Sun

Underwater landscape

The floor of the ocean has its own landscape, with features similar to those on land: wide, flat areas called abyssal plains, erupting volcanoes, underwater mountains called seamounts, and deep, narrow valleys, called trenches. Some underwater peaks are so tall that they rise above the water's surface, creating islands such as the Azores, off the coast of northwest Africa.

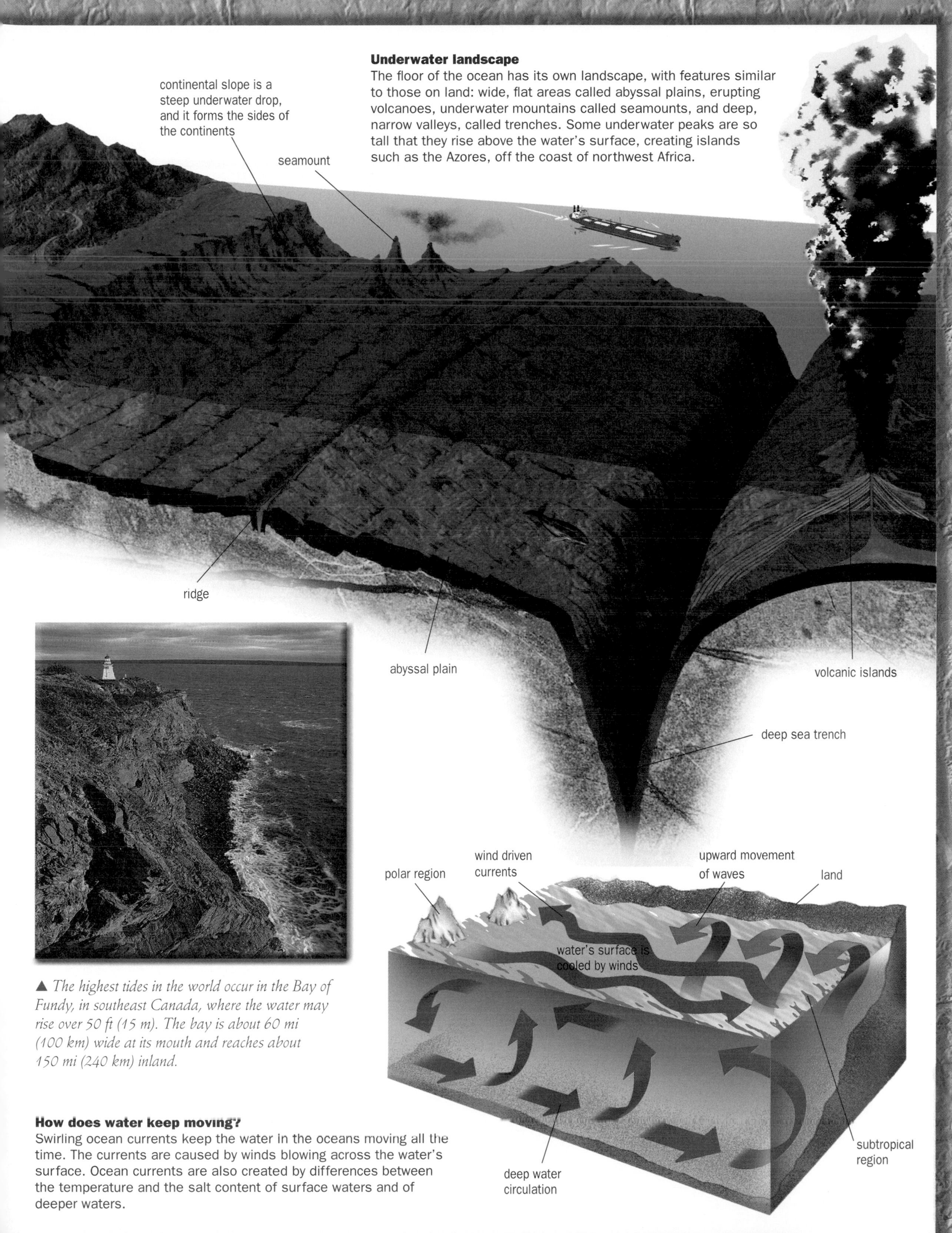

continental slope is a steep underwater drop, and it forms the sides of the continents
seamount
ridge
abyssal plain
volcanic islands
deep sea trench
polar region
wind driven currents
upward movement of waves
land
water's surface is cooled by winds
subtropical region
deep water circulation

▲ *The highest tides in the world occur in the Bay of Fundy, in southeast Canada, where the water may rise over 50 ft (15 m). The bay is about 60 mi (100 km) wide at its mouth and reaches about 150 mi (240 km) inland.*

How does water keep moving?

Swirling ocean currents keep the water in the oceans moving all the time. The currents are caused by winds blowing across the water's surface. Ocean currents are also created by differences between the temperature and the salt content of surface waters and of deeper waters.

Weather and Climate

WILL IT RAIN AT TOMORROW'S BASEBALL GAME? How hot will it be at the beach? Will there be enough wind to fly a kite this afternoon? All these are questions about the weather, such as the rain, sunshine, snow, wind, and storms that can affect our lives from day to day. The place we live in usually has the same pattern of weather over a longer period of time. However, it may have hot, dry weather in summer and warm, wet weather in winter. This usual, or average, pattern of weather over a longer period of time is called climate.

Climates of the world

What's the climate like where you live? If you live near the Equator, your climate will be warm or hot. If you live in the far north of the world, you will have a cold climate. The position of a place north or south of the Equator—its latitude—affects its climate. The height of a place above sea level—its altitude—and its distance from the ocean also affect its climate.

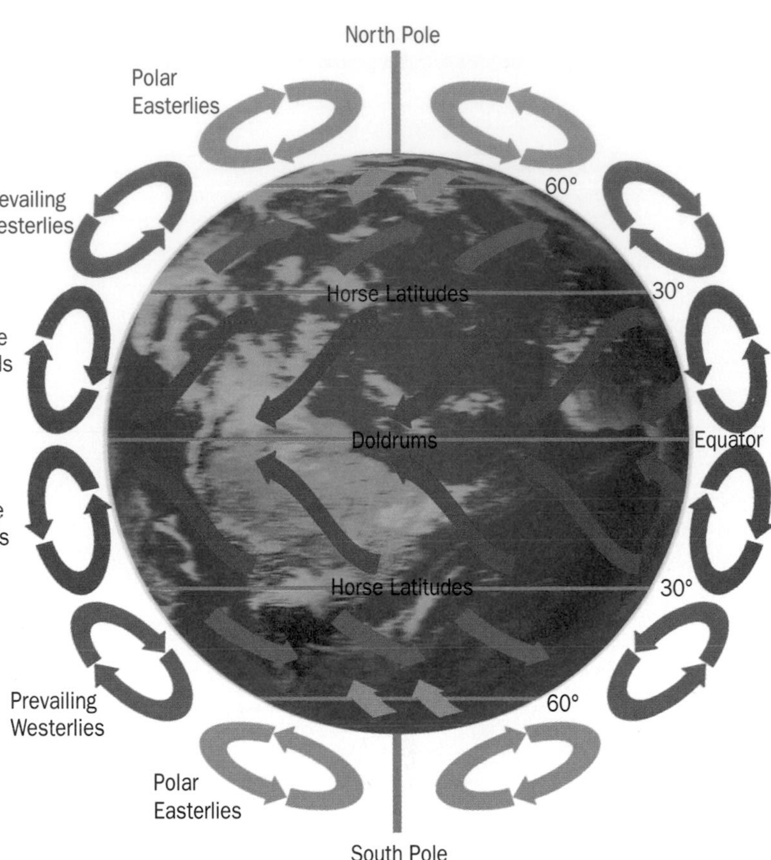

North Pole
Polar Easterlies
Prevailing Westerlies
60°
Horse Latitudes
30°
Trade Winds
Doldrums
Equator
Trade Winds
Horse Latitudes
30°
Prevailing Westerlies
60°
Polar Easterlies
South Pole

Moving air
The Sun heats the ground unevenly. The air above heated areas rises, and cooler air flows in to replace the rising hot air. This movement, or circulation, of air produces winds. Six main belts of winds blow over large areas of Earth's surface. However there are areas where there is very little or no wind at all. The doldrums is an area around the Equator where air only rises instead of moving across Earth. At 30 degrees north and south of the Equator lie other areas of very little wind movement. These are the horse latitudes, so called because many horses died on board sailing ships that were stalled by lack of wind.

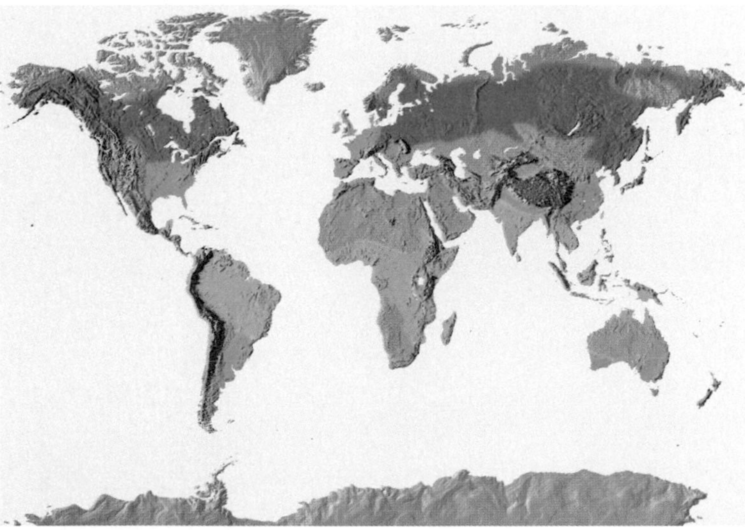

Different types of climate
Every place on Earth has its own climate. Sometimes places with the same kind of climate are far away from each other. For instance, you can find places where it is hot and rainy all year round in Brazil, in central Africa, and in southeast Asia. Scientists have given names to the different types of climate found across the world. The main types are: polar, wet temperate, dry temperate, desert, tropical, and mountain.

- polar
- wet temperate
- dry temperate
- desert
- tropical
- mountain

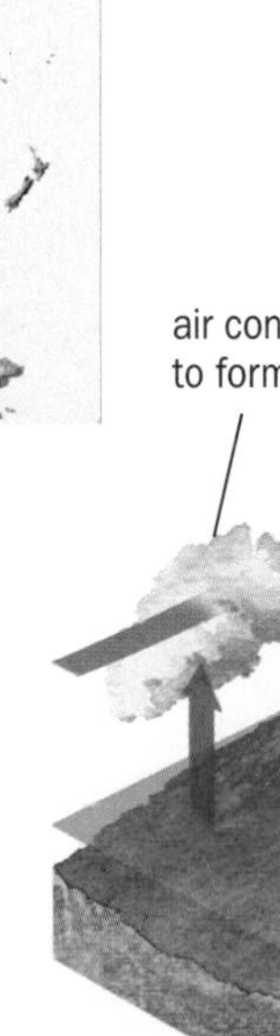

rain falls to Earth
air condenses to form clouds
moist air rises from the ocean and vegetation

How rain forms
Warm, moist air rises from the oceans and seas. When it cools down, the water vapor condenses into droplets of water and forms clouds. The water droplets fall back down to the ground as rain, sleet, or snow.

Heat from the Sun

Because the Earth is curved, different places receive different intensities of heat from the Sun. In tropical places near the Equator, the Sun's rays shine down almost directly overhead, providing lots of heat. As Earth curves round to the north or south, the Sun's rays have to travel farther, and the intensity of heat is reduced. This is why the farther from the Equator you go, the colder it becomes.

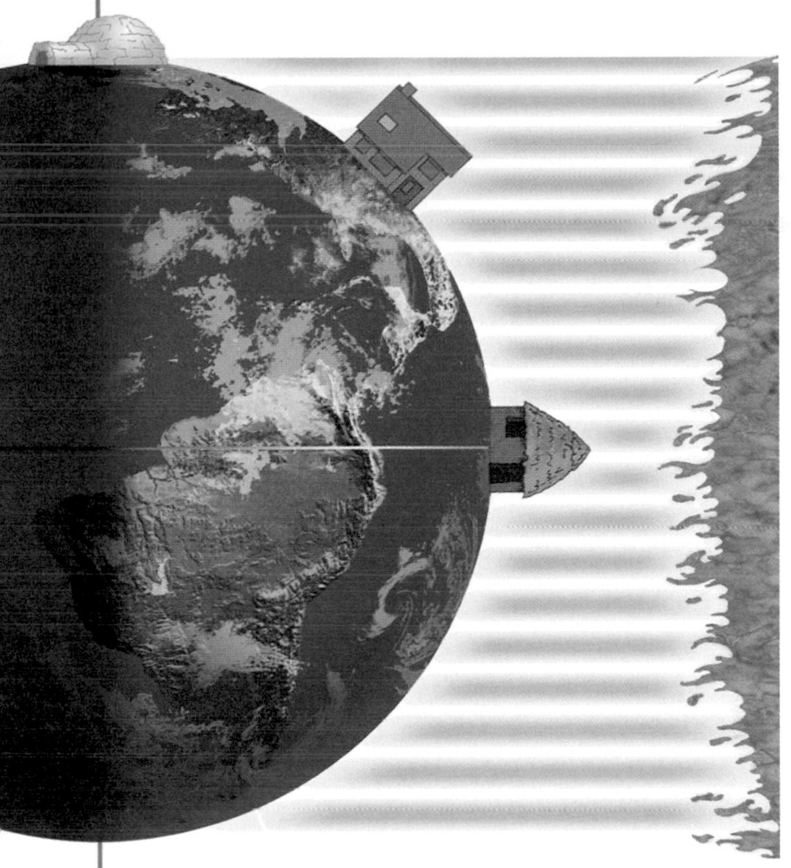

Arctic zone
The Sun's rays are weaker when they reach this region in the far north.

Temperate zone
At this angle of Earth's curve, the Sun's rays are more direct.

Tropical zone
The Sun shines almost directly overhead all year round.

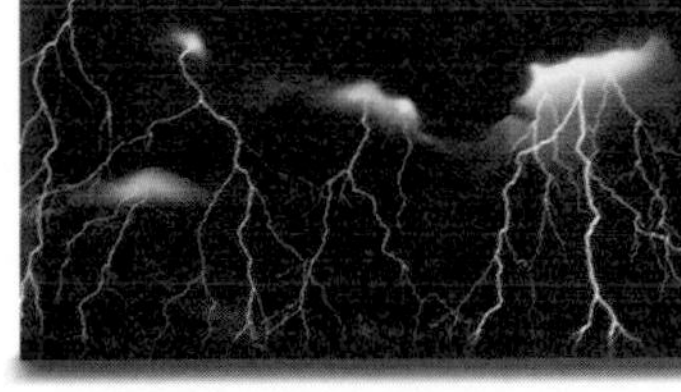

▲ *Lightning, a giant spark of electricity, flashes across a dark sky during a thunderstorm.*

◀ *The violent, twisting winds of a tornado can uproot trees, destroy buildings, and suck up large objects such as automobiles, carrying them for hundreds of feet.*

The atmosphere

The atmosphere is the layer of gases that surrounds Earth. It contains the gases nitrogen and oxygen, which make up about 99 percent of the atmosphere. The other one percent consists of tiny amounts of argon, carbon dioxide, water vapor, hydrogen, and other gases. The atmosphere protects us from the Sun's harmful rays. At the same time it helps to keep us warm by trapping some of the Sun's heat. Scientists divide the atmosphere into four layers: the troposphere, the stratosphere, the mesosphere, and the thermosphere.

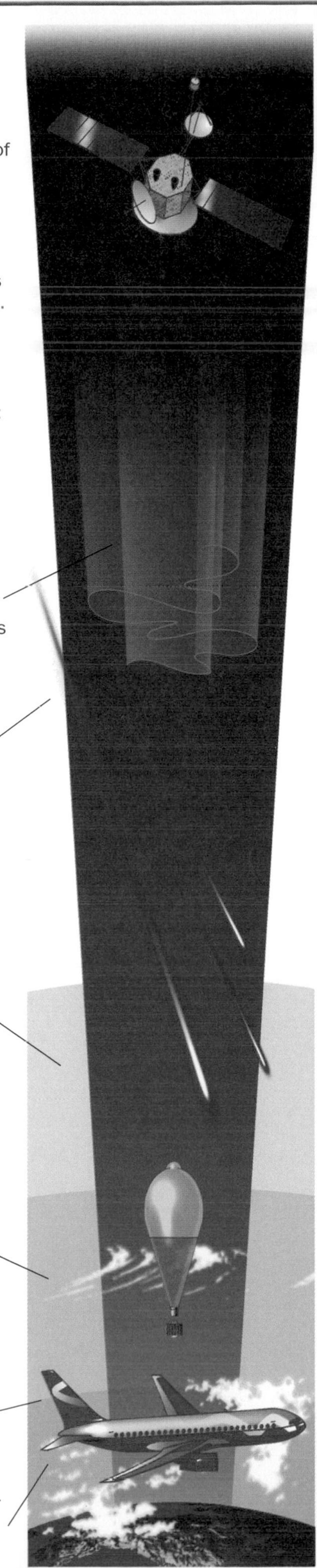

Auroras are flashes of light that occur hundreds of miles above the Earth's surface.

The thermosphere is the upper layer of the atmosphere. Beyond it lies the beginning of space.

The mesosphere reaches about 50 miles (80 km) above Earth's surface. You can see the trails left by meteors, or shooting stars, in this layer.

Within the stratosphere is the ozone layer, which absorbs the Sun's dangerous ultraviolet rays.

The stratosphere reaches about 30 miles (48 km) above the ground. Jet planes fly in this layer to avoid the weather in the troposphere below.

The troposphere is the layer closest to Earth. Most of our weather happens here.

Shaping the Land

THE LANDSCAPE AROUND US IS CONTINUALLY changing—but so slowly that we do not notice. All the time new mountains are being formed, existing ones are changing shape, rocks are being worn away, and new valleys are taking shape.

Making mountains

The giant slow-moving plates of Earth's crust sometimes collide, pushing a section of crust up to form a mountain range. At other times, the crust is squeezed into folds of land thousands of feet high. Many mountain ranges were made hundreds of millions of years ago. The Appalachian Mountains in the United States first formed over 400 million years ago—before the first dinosaurs appeared. The European Alps, in contrast, are young mountains which were still forming just 15 million years ago.

Changing shape

The shape and size of a mountain depend on its age and how it was formed. The shape also depends on how much of it is being worn away.

The land is continually reshaped as rocks are broken up by water, ice, and chemicals in water. This is "weathering." The pieces of rock are then carried from place to place by wind, water, or glaciers. As this material moves, it wears away mountain slopes, changes the shape of rock formations, widens river valleys, and carves out new ones. Rivers and streams carry rock pieces over long distances, wearing away rocks as they flow. In the Grand Canyon, the Colorado River has cut through layers of rocks over millions of years to create a valley which is over one mile (1.6 km) deep in places.

active volcano
vent
layers of lava and ash

Volcanic mountains form when hot molten rock from deep inside Earth bursts through the surface. It cools and becomes solid rock, eventually forming a mountain. Two very famous examples of volcanic mountains are Mount Kilimanjaro in Tanzania and Mount Fuji in Japan.

Fold mountains are created when two plates of Earth's crust collide. The rocky layers crumple and wrinkle, creating wave-like folds of mountains. The Himalayas and the Rocky Mountains were formed in this way.

compression

layers of rock buckle

compression

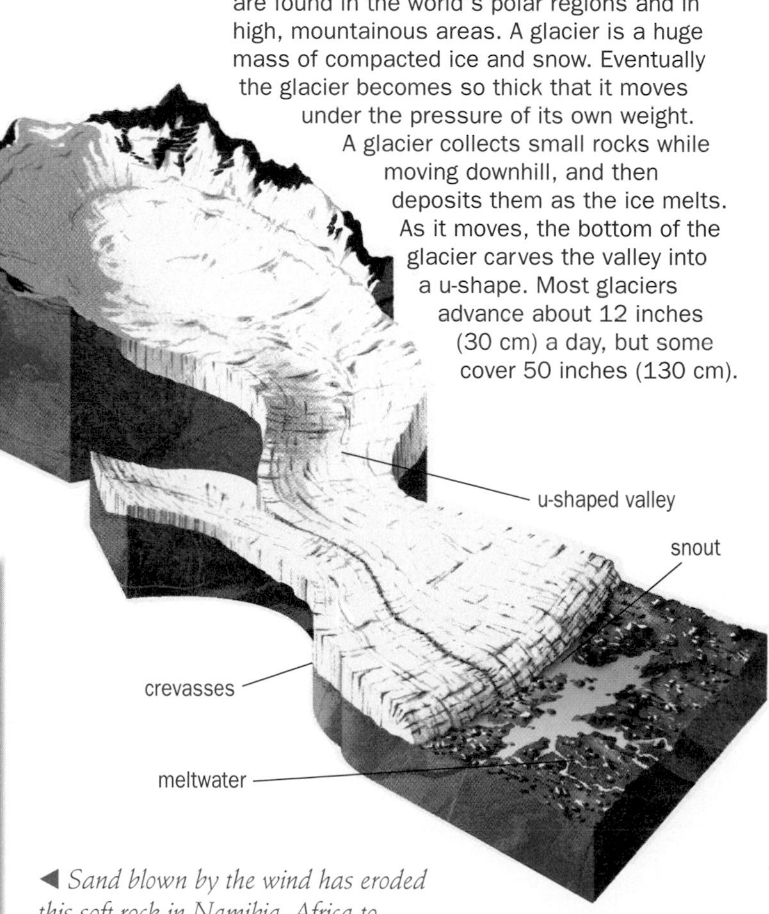
u-shaped valley
snout
crevasses
meltwater

Glaciers are found in the world's polar regions and in high, mountainous areas. A glacier is a huge mass of compacted ice and snow. Eventually the glacier becomes so thick that it moves under the pressure of its own weight. A glacier collects small rocks while moving downhill, and then deposits them as the ice melts. As it moves, the bottom of the glacier carves the valley into a u-shape. Most glaciers advance about 12 inches (30 cm) a day, but some cover 50 inches (130 cm).

◀ *Sand blown by the wind has eroded this soft rock in Namibia, Africa to create this strange-looking rock shape.*

Block mountains form when a large block-like area of crust is forced upward along a fault line or between two separate fault lines. This is how California's Sierra Nevada was formed.

fault
tension
block forced up
block forced down

Dome mountains are made when a section of Earth's crust is pushed up into a dome-shaped bulge. The Black Hills in South Dakota are a good example of dome mountains.

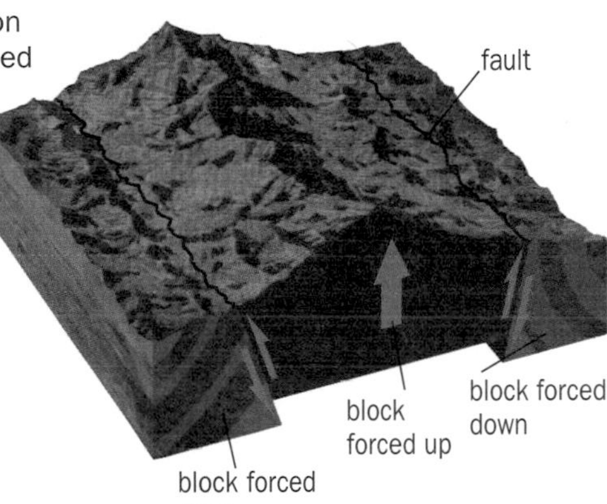
fault
block forced down
block forced up
block forced down

▲ *Young mountains, such as the Alps in central Europe, have towering, jagged peaks, not yet showing signs of erosion.*

▲ *Old mountains usually are more rounded in shape, with gentler and lower slopes. They have been worn down by millions of years of erosion.*

Rock types

Three kinds of rock make up Earth's hard outer layer: igneous rock, sedimentary rock, and metamorphic rock. Although all three kinds are made from the same basic materials, they were formed in different ways.

Igneous

Liquid rock from deep inside Earth slowly cools and hardens to form igneous rock. Sometimes the melted rock bursts onto Earth's surface as lava during a volcanic eruption, before cooling and hardening in the same way.

Granite is an igneous rock made of lots of coarse, colorful grains. Some forms are a pinkish color. Granite is a very strong rock and is often used in buildings—the large number of rosy-pink granite buildings in the Scottish city of Aberdeen have earned it the nickname "Granite City."

granite

basalt

Dark-colored basalt is the most common igneous rock on the Earth. It's even found on the flat parts of the Moon's surface!

Sedimentary

Sedimentary rocks form from the remains of plants and animals that lived on the ocean floor long ago, or from the sand and mud remains of ancient rocks. These remains build up in layers and eventually harden to form solid rock.

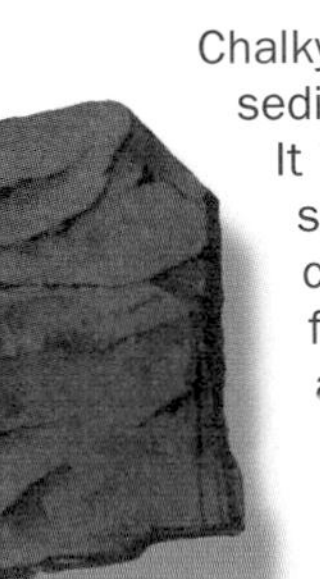

Chalky limestone is a sedimentary rock. It is common in seaside cliffs. You can often see the fossilized skeletons and shells of tiny sea creatures in its rocky layers.

limestone

Shale is a fine-grained sedimentary rock formed when mud and clay are squeezed together. We break up shale and use it to make cement and bricks.

shale

Metamorphic

Metamorphic rocks are igneous and sedimentary rocks that have been changed by heat, pressure, or heat and pressure together inside Earth's crust.

Slate is a metamorphic rock formed from shale. It can be split into smooth, thin sheets and used for roof tiles.

slate

Marble is a metamorphic rock formed from limestone. It has many beautiful color variations and is a prized material for buildings, sculptures, monuments, and decorative ornaments.

marble

Water on the Move

RIVERS CONTAIN LESS THAN ONE PERCENT OF ALL the water on Earth's surface, and yet they are an important natural feature. Since ancient times, rivers have supplied us with water for drinking and washing, and watering our crops. They have also provided vital transportation routes, by linking coasts and inland areas. Many towns and cities grew up where bridges had been built to cross the local river. A fast-flowing river can also be used to generate electricity.

Rivers are a powerful force shaping our landscape. During its journey a river erodes the rocks over which it flows, changing the shape of valleys and cutting deep gorges in the land.

From beginning to end

Most rivers have their source, or beginning, in mountains or hills where rain and melted snows collect. Sometimes a number of small streams come together to form a river. Other rivers start where natural underground springs bubble up to the surface, or where the thick ice of a glacier melts. At the beginning, the river is quite shallow, and it may have several steep waterfalls and fast-flowing rapids. The water flows at its fastest speed here, continuously eroding and cutting out a V-shaped valley with steep sides.

Further from the source, the river flows more slowly across a fairly flat area called the floodplain. It snakes from one side of the plain to the other in wide curves called meanders. As the river reaches the sea, it becomes wider and its waters flow even more slowly. Where it joins the sea, huge quantities of transported material are deposited to form a delta, such as the Mississippi Delta.

◀ *Huge dams of stone, concrete, or earth are constructed to create artificial lakes, such as Egypt's Lake Nasser. Water from Lake Nasser is used to irrigate farmland and generate electricity.*

▲ *Tons of silt and sand are carried along by the Colorado River on its 1,450-mi (2,333-km) long course from the Rocky Mountains of Colorado to the Gulf of California.*

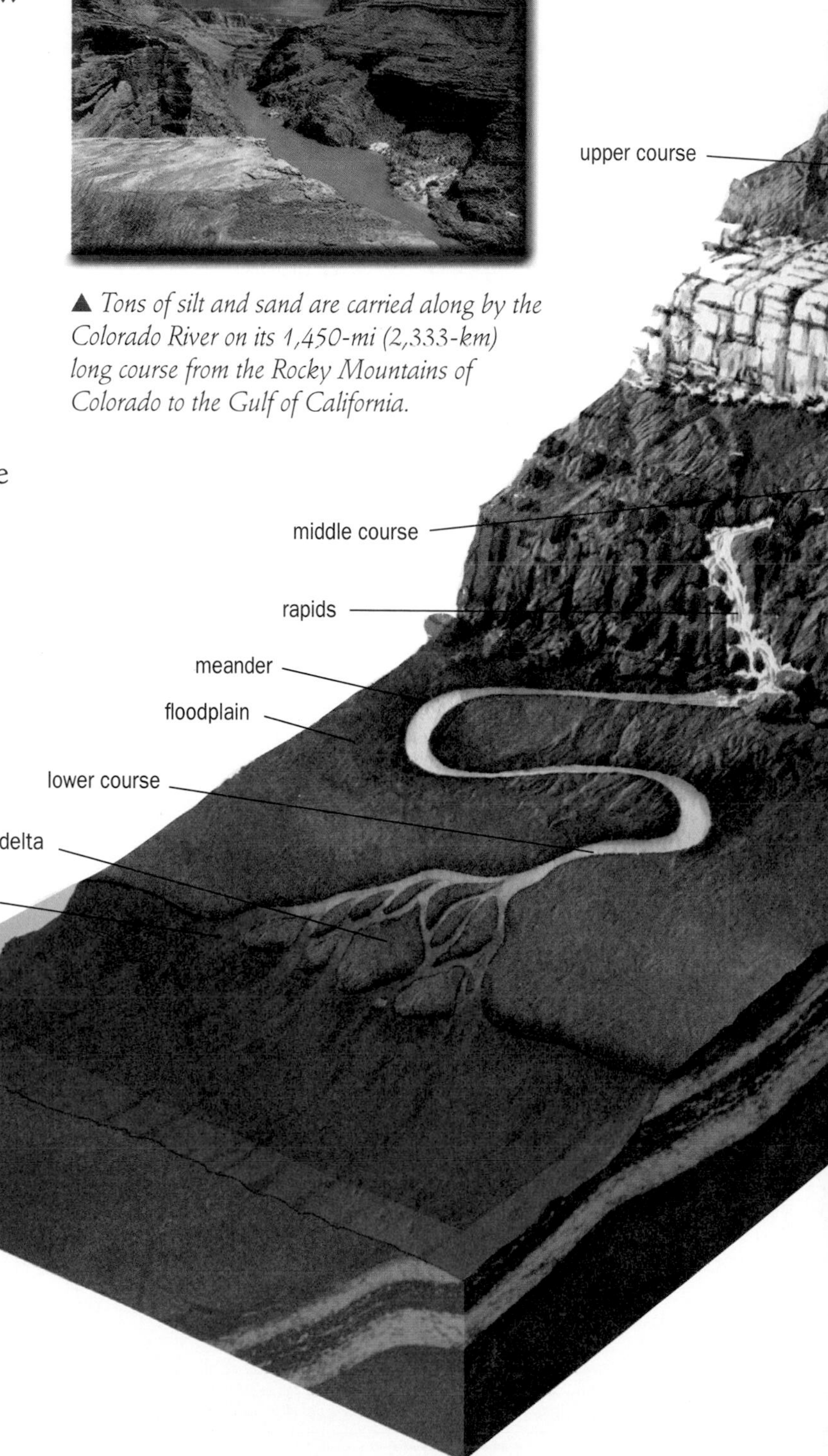
upper course
middle course
rapids
meander
floodplain
lower course
delta
mouth

◀ *A powerful tugboat pushes huge barges on the Mississippi River. These barges carry agricultural products, coal, petroleum, and steel goods.*

The river's journey

A river makes a journey, or course, from its source to its mouth, where it finally joins the sea, a lake, or a larger river. The river is fast flowing in the upper course, but it flows more slowly and smoothly during the middle and lower courses.

The Great Lakes

The biggest group of freshwater lakes in the world—the Great Lakes—make up part of the border between Canada and the United States. The group consists of five lakes. Lake Superior is the world's largest freshwater lake.

Depth of lakes

Superior	1,330 ft (405 m)
Michigan	923 ft (281 m)
Ontario	802 ft (244 m)
Huron	750 ft (229 m)
Erie	210 ft (64 m)

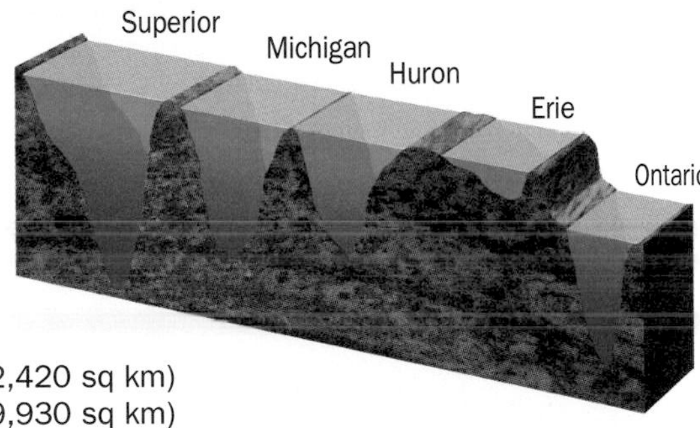
Superior
Michigan
Huron
Erie
Ontario

Area of lakes

1 Superior	31,700 sq mi (82,420 sq km)
2 Huron	23,050 sq mi (59,930 sq km)
3 Michigan	22,300 sq mi (57,980 sq km)
4 Erie	9,910 sq mi (25,766 sq km)
5 Ontario	7,550 sq mi (19,630 sq km)

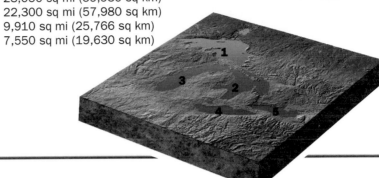

glacier
stream
sinkhole
stalactite
stalagmite
underground stream

Limestone caves

Caves form in areas where the rock is made mostly of limestone. Over thousands of years, water makes its way through cracks in the rock and slowly dissolves the limestone. Underground streams also eat away at the limestone until eventually a hollow cave is created. Stalactites are formations of crystals that hang from the roof of a cave. Stalagmites are pillars of crystallized material that rise up from a cave floor.

▶ *Venezuela's spectacular Angel Falls, flows into the Churún River. It has the longest unbroken drop in the world—a staggering 3,212 ft (979 m).*

What kind of delta?

The Nile Delta forms where the Nile River joins the Mediterranean Sea. (The name comes from the triangle-shaped Greek letter, Δ delta.)

the Nile Delta is shaped like a triangle

At the end of its course the Mississippi River joins the Gulf of Mexico. It divides into several smaller channels, forming a delta shaped like a bird's foot.

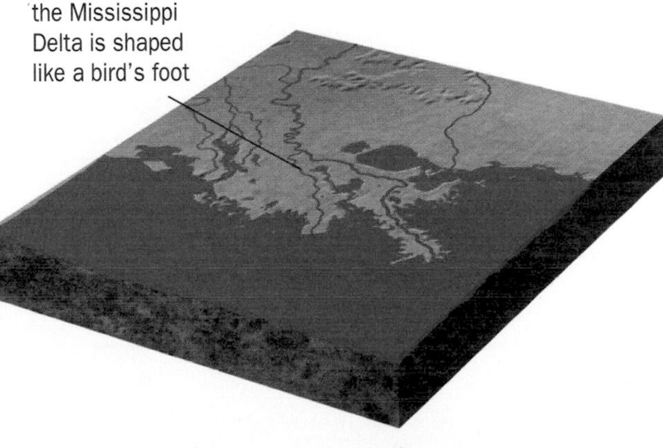
the Mississippi Delta is shaped like a bird's foot

Islands and Coastlines

ISLANDS COME IN MANY DIFFERENT SIZES, FROM THE huge ice-capped island of Greenland to tiny uninhabited fragments of rock dotted around the oceans. Although Australia is an island, we usually refer to it as a country, because it is so big. Some countries, such as the Philippines and Indonesia, are made up of thousands of separate islands. Every island is a piece of land surrounded by water.

▲ *When the volcanic eruptions that created Surtsey finally stopped, the island's tip reached more than 644 ft (170 m) above the sea. Surtsey is named after an Icelandic god of fire.*

▲ *More than 40% of the Netherlands was at one time covered by the sea. The Dutch have pumped out the water to "reclaim" the land.*

An island is born

Many islands were formed thousands or even millions of years ago. Some were joined onto a larger piece of land but became separated when the sea level rose—this is how the British Isles were cut off from continental Europe more than 10,000 years ago. Some islands are fragments of land that broke off from continents. Some were formed when the land connecting the island to a continent was worn away—either by waves or by rivers and streams.

Other islands appeared much more recently—and new ones are still made from time to time. In 1963, a new island appeared off the coast of Iceland. The island, called Surtsey, is made of the cooled, hardened lava from a volcano erupting on the seabed. The lava built up in layers until eventually it rose above the water and formed an island.

Continental island
A continental island, such as Greenland, was at some time joined onto a continent.

Volcanic island
A volcanic island is built up from layers of lava deposited on the ocean floor. A curving row of these islands, such as Japan, is known as an island arc.

The changing coast

Around the edges of every piece of land, whether a huge continent or a small island, the action of the sea is constantly changing and reshaping the coastline. Waves cut away rocks that line the shore to form cliffs. In places, so much rock is worn away at the base of a sea cliff that a cave forms. Besides being destructive, the sea can also create. Waves carry broken rocks and sand and deposit them to form ridges of shingle, or small pebbles, called spits.

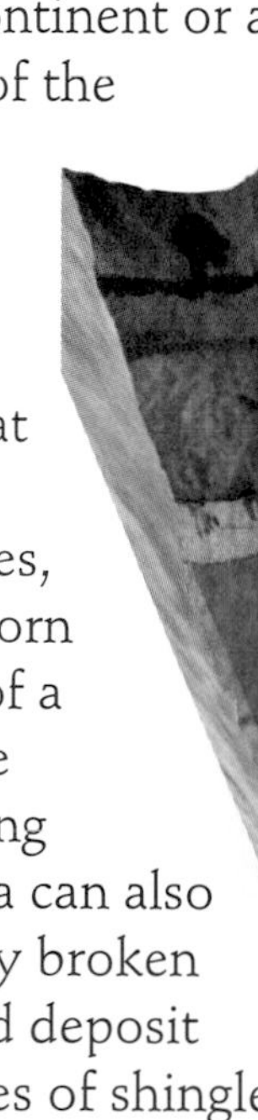

shingle spit
sand dune
sand bar
stack (rock eroded on either side)
arch through eroded cliff
cave

How an atoll is formed
In warm seas, coral islands are made from the limestone skeletons of millions of tiny coral animals. The skeletons are packed together to form a coral reef. Sometimes a reef grows around the rim of a sinking volcano. Eventually the reef is a complete ring, called an atoll, surrounding an area of water known as a lagoon. Over time, soil collects on parts of the coral reef and plants begin to grow there. The atoll gradually breaks up into small coral islands.

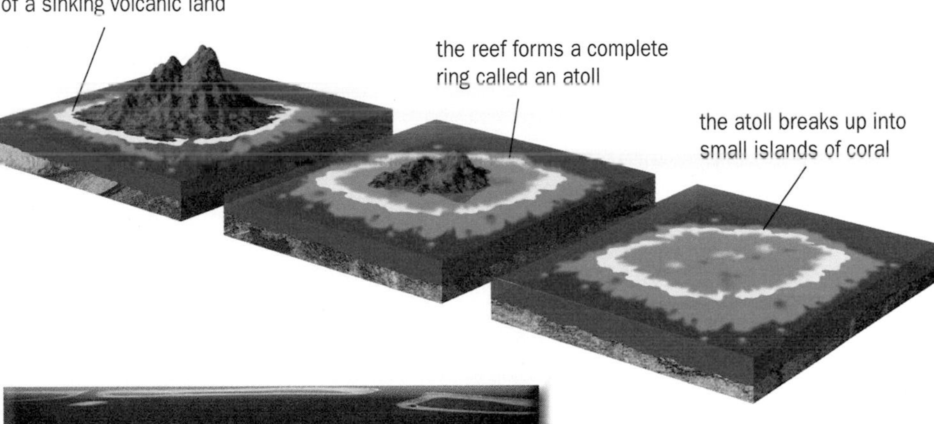
a coral reef grows around the rim of a sinking volcanic land
the reef forms a complete ring called an atoll
the atoll breaks up into small islands of coral

◀ *Some coral islands of the Maldives, in the Indian Ocean, are less than 6 ft (1.8 m) above sea level. If the sea levels around the world were to rise slightly, most of these islands would disappear beneath the ocean.*

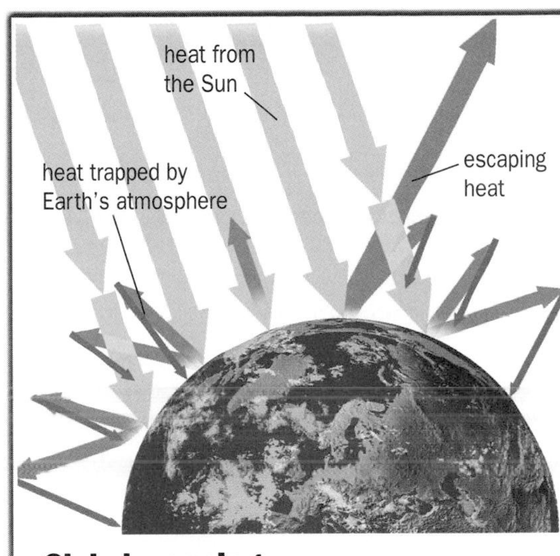
heat from the Sun
escaping heat
heat trapped by Earth's atmosphere

Global warming
Scientists who study Earth's climate have observed that temperatures around the world are gradually increasing. During the 21st century, the temperature of Earth may rise by between 1.8° and 7°F (1°and 3.5°C) above average. Why is this happening?

The gases in the atmosphere help to keep Earth warm by trapping some of the Sun's heat. However, human activities such as burning fossil fuels—coal, oil, and gas—have increased the levels of these gases. The increased gas levels are trapping too much heat, causing Earth's temperature to rise. A hotter planet might cause areas of farmland to turn to desert, and the ice caps around the poles might melt, making sea levels rise—this would flood some islands and low-lying coastal areas.

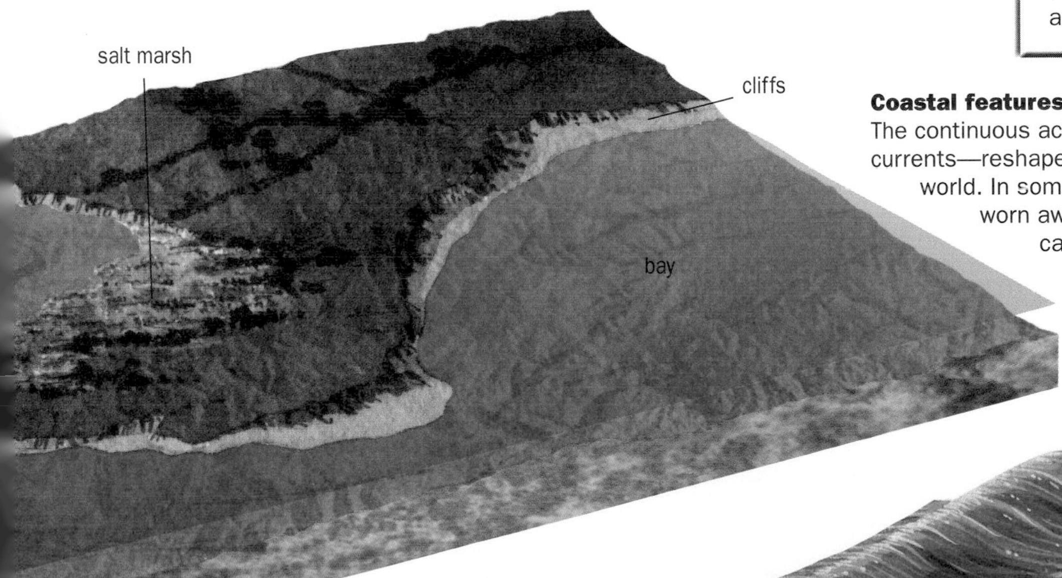

salt marsh

cliffs

bay

Coastal features
The continuous action of the oceans—their waves, tides, and currents—reshapes and rebuilds every coastline around the world. In some places material is added, while in others it is worn away. The ocean erodes rocks to form cliffs and caves, and in other places builds up reefs and shingle spits.

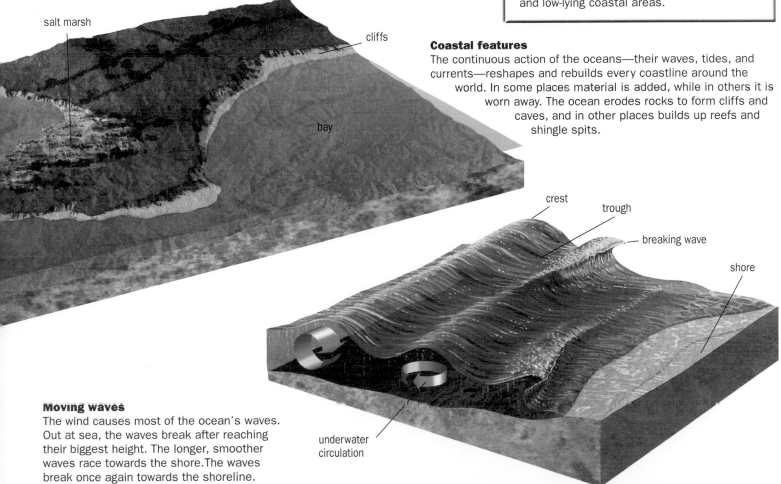

crest

trough

breaking wave

shore

underwater circulation

Moving waves
The wind causes most of the ocean's waves. Out at sea, the waves break after reaching their biggest height. The longer, smoother waves race towards the shore.The waves break once again towards the shoreline.

Natural Regions

ALL THE PLANTS AND ANIMALS FOUND ON EARTH make up our living world. We already know about more than two million different kinds, or species, of animals and plants—and there may be millions more that we have not yet discovered! The land can be divided into a series of natural regions. Each type of region has its own particular landscape and climate, and the plants and animals found there are typical of that region.

The animals and plants of a particular region have adapted over many, many thousands of years to suit their surroundings. In hot deserts, for example, plants such as the cactus grow thick, fleshy stems that can store water. On cold mountaintops, the thick, hairy coats and sure-footed hooves of wild goats help them to survive in harsh, rugged conditions.

Key to the world's natural regions

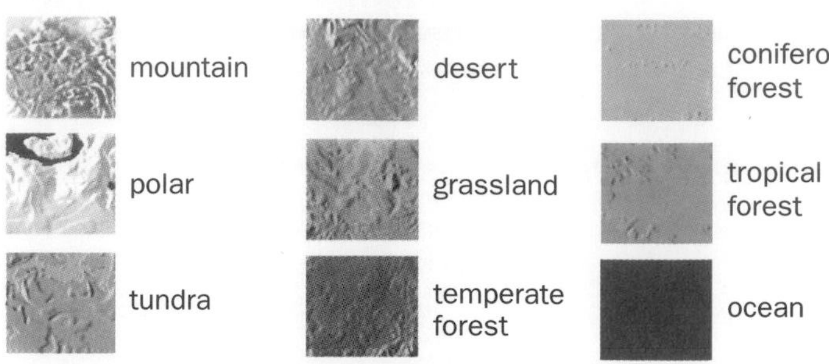
mountain
desert
coniferous forest
polar
grassland
tropical forest
tundra
temperate forest
ocean

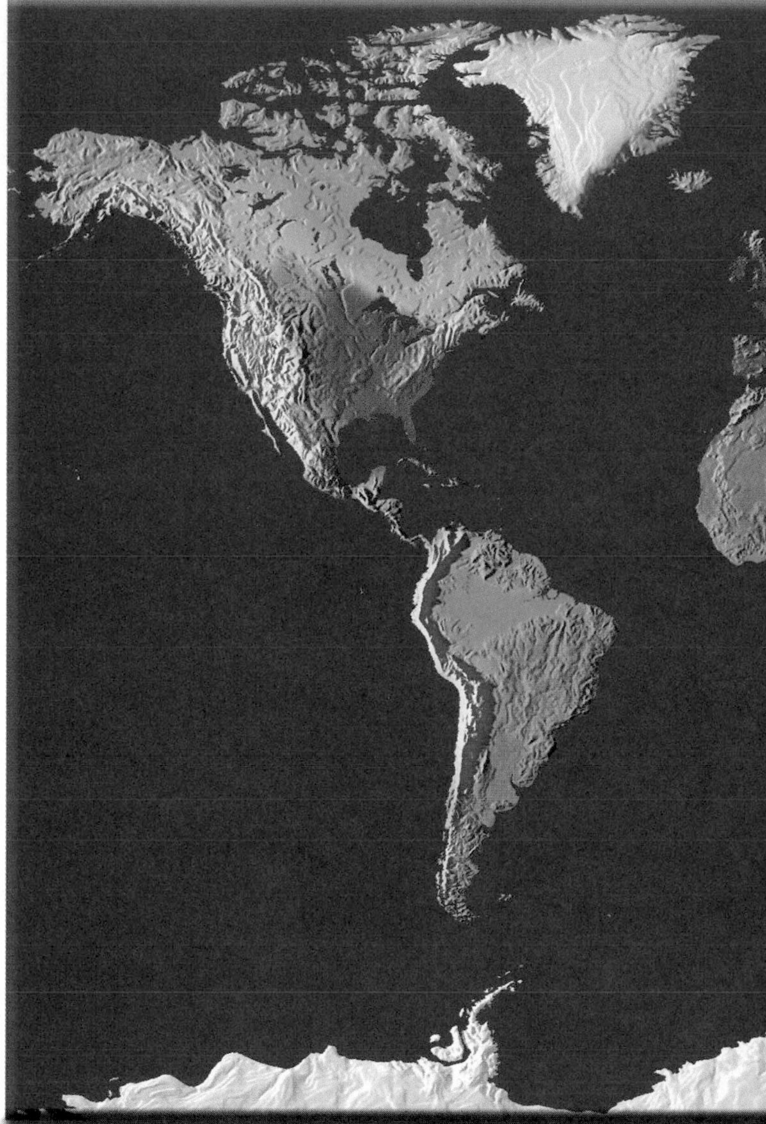

◀ ***Mountain***
The higher you climb a mountain, the colder it becomes. Above a certain height, which is called the tree line, it becomes too cold even for trees to grow. Many mountain animals have thick fur coats to protect their bodies from the cold surroundings.

▼ ***Polar***
These regions are bitterly cold all year round. Very few animals live in these areas, but those that do are perfectly adapted to their environment.

▶ ***Tundra***
These are very cold areas where the summers are short. Few land animals live here, where the land stays frozen for much of the year. No trees grow, but some mosses, low shrubs, and small wildflowers survive.

▶ Ocean
The ocean is home to more than 13,000 different kinds of fishes, as well as many other animals, from tiny shrimps to large sea mammals, such as seals and whales. Marine plants, which include seaweed, live in the sunlit waters near the surface.

◀ Tropical forest
In tropical rain forests, tall trees grow so close together that little sunlight reaches the forest floor. More kinds of plants and animals live here than in any other kind of natural region.

▼ Coniferous forest
These are made up of evergreen trees, which keep their leaves all year round. In the cold winter months some animals hibernate, which means they sleep much of the winter.

▶ Temperate forest
Most of the trees in a temperate forest are deciduous, which means they lose their leaves in places with cold winters. Some animals hibernate and some survive on stored food during the cold winters, while others travel to warmer places to find food.

▼ Grassland
These are large, open areas where different kinds of grasses grow, providing food for grazing animals. Many grassland areas are now used for growing crops.

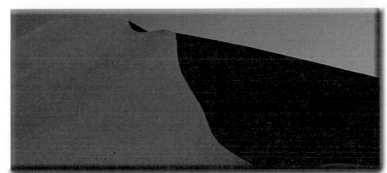

▲ Desert
Deserts are usually very hot, dry areas where animals have to find shade to escape from the extreme daytime heat.

The Earth's Resources

The Earth provides us with everything we need to live on this planet. It gives us fresh water for drinking and washing, and for watering our crops. It provides plants for us to eat and feed for our animals. It gives us materials such as timber and cotton as well as animals to give us milk, meat, wool, and other products. All these are natural resources that should never run out if we look after them carefully—they are renewable. The Earth provides us with other natural resources, too, such as coal, oil, and gas fuels; metals; and precious stones such as diamonds and emeralds. These resources are non-renewable—they do not regrow or reappear, and one day supplies of them will be used up.

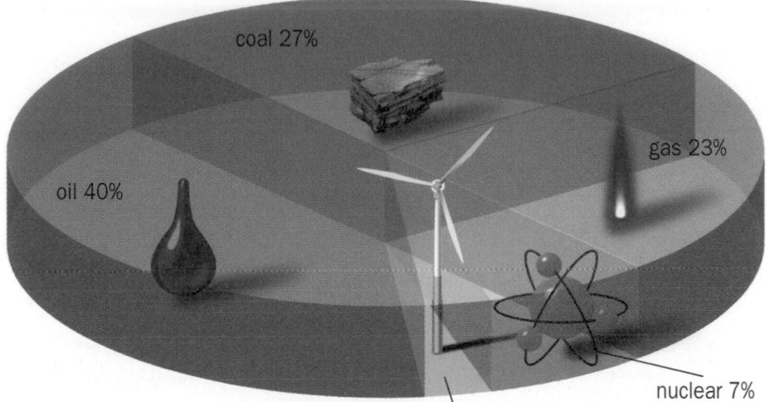
coal 27%
gas 23%
oil 40%
nuclear 7%
hydroelectric/alternative sources 3%

World energy
Fossil fuels such as oil, coal, and gas will eventually run out. Alternative energy sources are constantly being tested. The pie chart above shows how much of our energy still comes from fossil fuels, and how little is supplied by other sources.

The world's energy

Energy resources are some of our most important natural resources. Without them we could not heat and light our homes, travel by train, plane, ship, or automobile, operate machines, have plastic products, and so on. Most of the world's energy comes from coal, oil, and gas. We call these fossil fuels, because they are made from the remains of plants and animals that lived millions of years ago.

Supplies of fossil fuels will run out one day and burning fossil fuels causes serious pollution and contributes to global warming (see page 29). So, people are looking for ways to obtain energy from renewable resources such as solar power, wind power, and hydroelectric power—the energy obtained from flowing water. As supplies of fossil fuels run out, these renewable and less polluting resources will become more and more important.

Energy distribution
The map below shows the distribution of fossil fuels around the world.

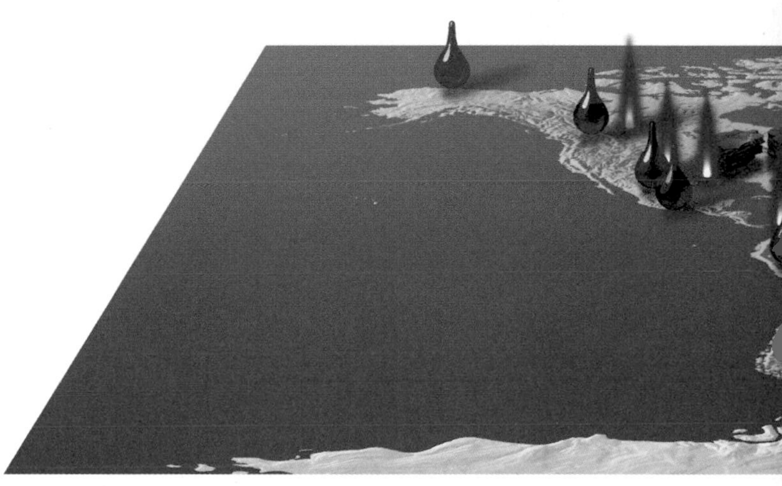

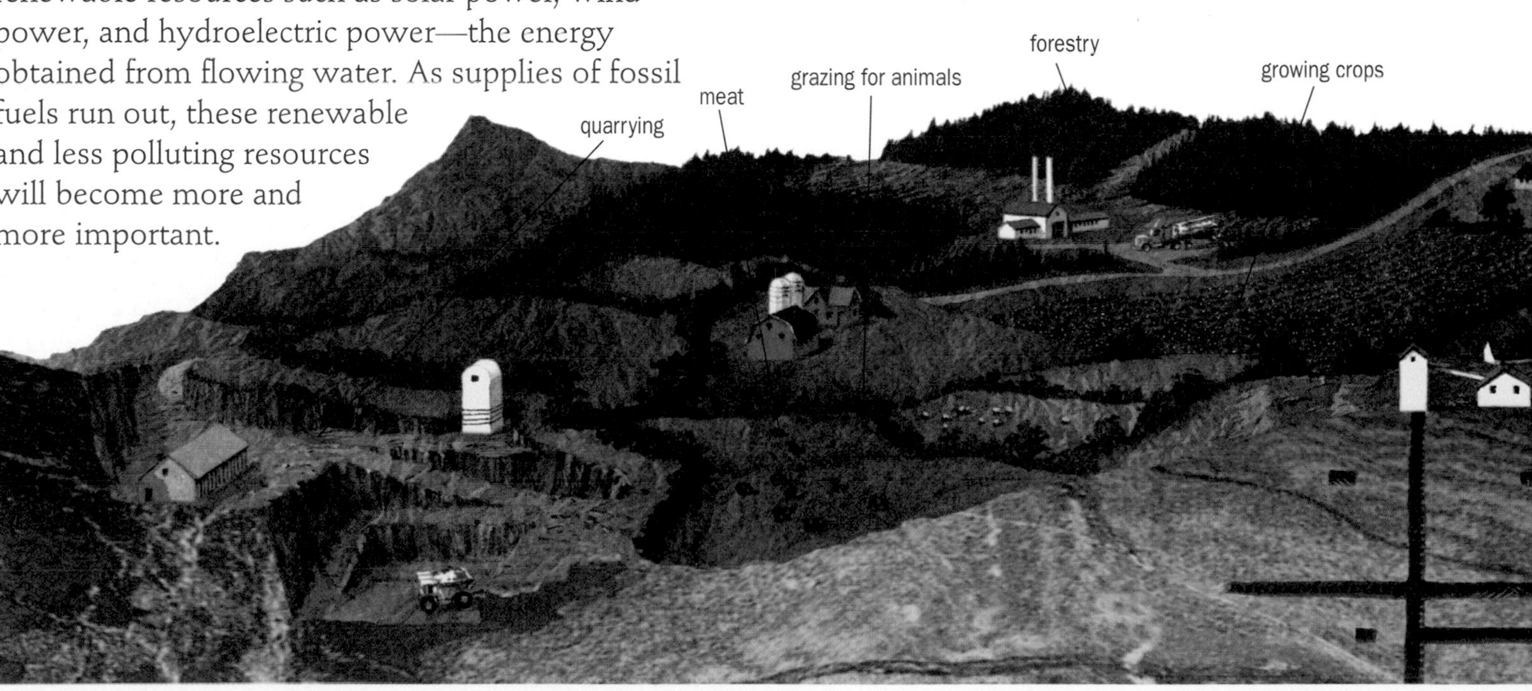
forestry
grazing for animals
growing crops
meat
quarrying

▲ *Some natural resources, such as salt, are obtained from the sea. Salt mining is a cost-effective way of making use of the sea.*

▲ *Panels of solar cells on the roof of this house turn sunlight into electricity for use in the home and to provide hot water.*

▲ *Large numbers of tall wind turbines, which drive the generators that produce electricity, combine to create a "wind farm."*

▲ *The fertile soils of the prairies of North America have been used to create rich farmland for grazing animals and for growing crops.*

How coal is formed

Dead plant remains collect on the floor of swampy areas. They slowly build up and harden into a thick layer of peat.

The peat layers are buried under deposits of sand and minerals. These sediments press down on the peat.

As more and more layers compress the peat, some of the sediments turn into rock called lignite. The extra pressure from the rocky layers eventually turns the peat into coal.

swamp
peat
lignite
coal

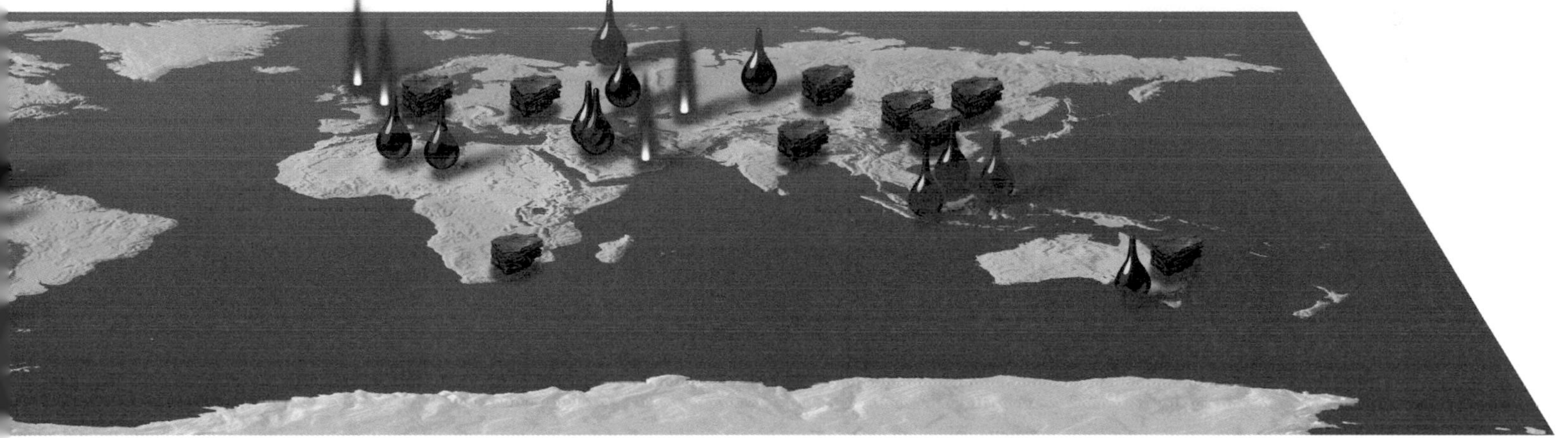

Using the land

The land provides us with a wealth of different natural resources. We should take care to preserve the resources available to us for as long as we can.

mining
wind farms
fishing

World in a Day

ONE WHOLE DAY AND ONE WHOLE NIGHT LAST FOR a total of 24 hours. What happens to you during that time? You get out of bed each morning, go to school, eat your meals, come home and play or watch TV, and then finally go to bed and sleep—all in one 24-hour period. But what is happening in the world around you at the same time? Some truly amazing things can take place on the planet Earth in 24 hours—here are just a few of the things that happen in the world in a day.

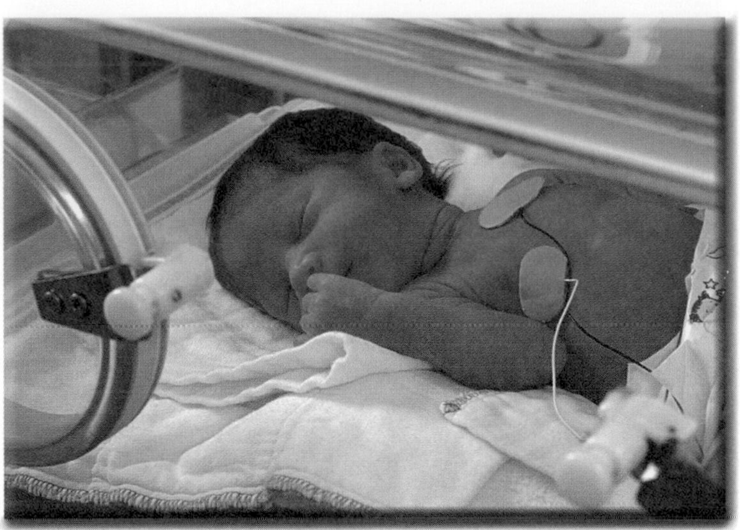

▲ *360,187 babies are born and 148,348 people die.*
At least another 25 babies will be born while you are reading this sentence.

◀ *The world's population increases by 211,839.*
The world's population is growing all the time—it has more than doubled in the past 50 years.

▼ *8.5 million tons (7.7 million t) of water evaporate from the Dead Sea, on the border between Israel and Jordan.*
The Dead Sea, the lowest place on the earth's surface, is in fact a lake. This girl, floating in the Dead Sea, is unable to sink because the water is at least nine times more salty than seawater, making it very buoyant.

▲ *1,000 very minor earthquakes occur.*
A "very minor earthquake" measures between 2 and 3 on the scale used to describe the strength of earthquakes, but a "major earthquake" may measure between 7 and 8 and be up to 60 times more powerful.

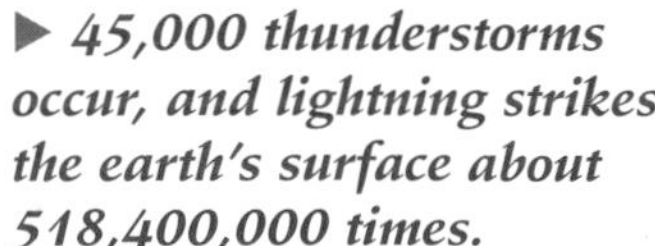

▶ *45,000 thunderstorms occur, and lightning strikes the earth's surface about 518,400,000 times.*
During a thunderstorm, bright flashes of lightning usually appear in the sky—they are really giant sparks of electricity. Although thunderstorms occur all over the world, they are most frequent in tropical areas.

◀ *102,240 million gallons (464,790 million l) flow over the Victoria Falls.*
Water drops 343 ft (105 m) at the center of the spectacular falls on the Zambezi River, between Zambia and Zimbabwe, southern Africa.

▼ *A bamboo plant can grow 18 in (46 cm).*
Bamboo, much loved by pandas, is a kind of giant grass with strong, hollow stems. In tropical countries it is used to make houses, furniture, mats, and rafts.

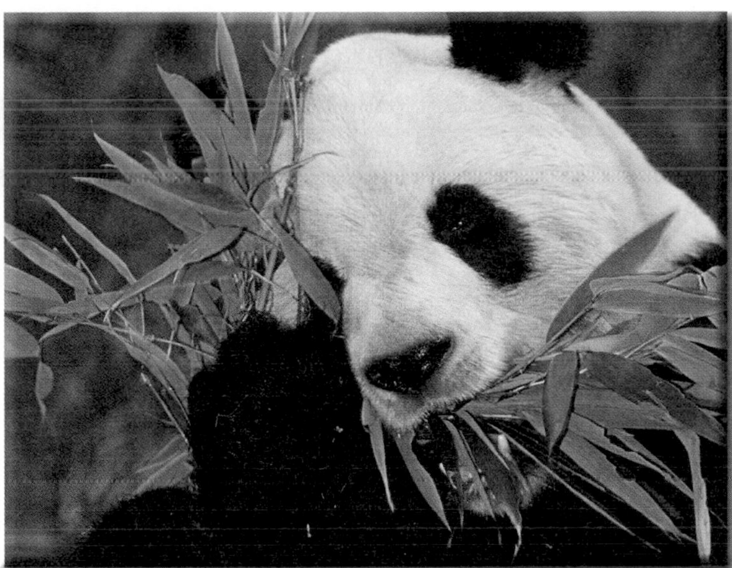

▼ *More than 2,000 planes land and take off at Chicago's O'Hare International Airport, one of the busiest in the world, and more than 54,200 Americans travel abroad.*
Passengers can fly from New York to London, for example, in about seven hours—just 60 years ago the same journey took about 24 hours!

UNITED AIRLINES

▼ *About 2,000 lb (900 kg) of space dust and debris fall onto the earth's surface.*
The dust and debris are probably tiny leftover pieces of the material that originally formed the Moon and the planets.

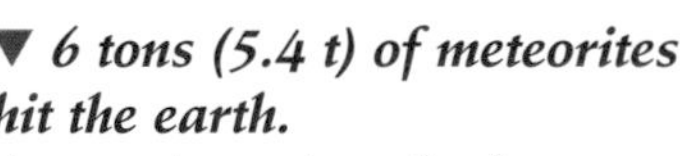

▼ *6 tons (5.4 t) of meteorites hit the earth.*
A meteorite, a piece of rocky or metallic material from space, has created this giant meteor crater.

▲ *The average person watches four hours of television.*
Americans own more than 220 million TV sets. In our homes, the television is switched on for an average of seven hours each day.

Countries of the World

Greenland
(DENMARK)
Alaska (U.S.A.)
C A N A D A
Newfoundland
St. Pierre & Miquelon
(FRANCE)
Azores
(PORTUGA
UNITED STATES OF AMERICA
Bermuda
(U.K.)
Virgin Is
(U.S.A. & U.K.)
BAHAMAS
DOMINICAN
REPUBLIC
ST. KITTS & NEVIS
ANTIGUA & BARBUDA
Guadeloupe (FRANCE)
DOMINICA
Martinique (FRANCE)
BARBADOS
ST. VINCENT &
THE GRENADINES
TRINIDAD
& TOBAGO
ST. LUCIA
GRENADA
Puerto Rico (U.S.A.)
CUBA
HAITI
JAMAICA
MEXICO
BELIZE
GUATEMALA
HONDURAS
EL SALVADOR
NICARAGUA
COSTA RICA
PANAMA
CAPE
VERDE
Hawaiian Is
(U.S.A.)
Clipperton I.
(FRANCE)
VENEZUELA
GUYANA
SURINAME
FRENCH
GUIANA
COLOMBIA
Galápagos Is
(ECUADOR)
ECUADOR
PERU
B R A Z I L
French
Polynesia
(FRANCE)
Cook Is
(NEW ZEALAND)
Pitcairn I.
(U.K.)
BOLIVIA
Martin Va
(BRAZI
CHILE
PARAGUAY
Easter I.
(CHILE)
Juan Fernandez Is
(CHILE)
URUGUAY
ARGENTINA
Falkland Is
(U.K.)
South Georgia
(U.K.)
South
Sandwich Is
(U.K.)

KEY

1 ALBANIA
2 ANDORRA
3 BOSNIA-HERZEGOVINA
4 CROATIA
5 LIECHTENSTEIN
6 LUXEMBOURG
7 MACEDONIA
8 MOLDOVA
9 MONACO
10 NETHERLANDS
11 SAN MARINO
12 VATICAN CITY
13 SLOVENIA
14 SWITZERLAND
15 YUGOSLAVIA
16 ARMENIA
17 AZERBAIJAN
18 UNITED ARAB EMIRATES
19 KALININGRAD (RUSSIAN FEDERATION)

DISCOVER MORE

• Political maps show the borders of countries, states, or counties. They show capital cities and major centers of population. They may show transportation networks as well. On political maps, coloring may be used to separate one country or region from another.

World facts

Number of countries	**Number of dependencies**	**Largest country by area** sq mi (sq km)	**Largest country by population**
194	64	Russian Federation 6,592,735 (17,075,184)	China 1,250,066,000

This map of the world is a cylindrical projection

Svalbard
(Norway)
Franz Josef Land
Severnaya Zemlya
Novaya Zemlya
New Siberian Is
Jan Mayen I.
(Norway)
Faroe Is
(Denmark)
SWEDEN
FINLAND
NORWAY
ESTONIA
LATVIA
LITHUANIA
DENMARK
UNITED KINGDOM
IRELAND
BELARUS
POLAND
GERMANY
BELGIUM
CZECH REPUBLIC
SLOVAKIA
UKRAINE
AUSTRIA
HUNGARY
FRANCE
ROMANIA
ITALY
BULGARIA
SPAIN
PORTUGAL
GREECE
MALTA
GEORGIA
TURKEY
CYPRUS
SYRIA
LEBANON
ISRAEL
IRAQ
IRAN
JORDAN
KUWAIT
BAHRAIN
QATAR
SAUDI ARABIA
OMAN
YEMEN
RUSSIAN FEDERATION
KAZAKHSTAN
UZBEKISTAN
KYRGYZSTAN
TURKMENISTAN
TAJIKISTAN
AFGHANISTAN
PAKISTAN
MONGOLIA
CHINA
NORTH KOREA
SOUTH KOREA
JAPAN
NEPAL
BHUTAN
BANGLADESH
INDIA
MYANMAR (Burma)
LAOS
THAILAND
VIETNAM
CAMBODIA
TAIWAN
PHILIPPINES
MOROCCO
TUNISIA
ALGERIA
LIBYA
EGYPT
MALI
NIGER
CHAD
SUDAN
ERITREA
DJIBOUTI
ETHIOPIA
SOMALIA
BURKINA FASO
GUINEA
NIGERIA
SIERRA LEONE
LIBERIA
IVORY COAST
GHANA
TOGO
BENIN
CAMEROON
CENTRAL AFRICAN REPUBLIC
EQUATORIAL GUINEA
SÃO TOMÉ & PRÍNCIPE
GABON
REPUBLIC OF CONGO
DEMOCRATIC REPUBLIC OF CONGO
UGANDA
KENYA
RWANDA
BURUNDI
TANZANIA
SEYCHELLES
COMOROS
Mayotte
(FRANCE)
ANGOLA
ZAMBIA
MALAWI
MOZAMBIQUE
ZIMBABWE
NAMIBIA
BOTSWANA
MADAGASCAR
MAURITIUS
Réunion
(FRANCE)
SWAZILAND
LESOTHO
SOUTH AFRICA
Ascension I.
(St. Helena)
St. Helena
(U.K.)
Laccadive Is
(INDIA)
Andaman Is
(INDIA)
SRI LANKA
Nicobar Is
(INDIA)
MALDIVES
British Indian Ocean Territory
(U.K.)
Cocos Is
(AUSTRALIA)
Christmas I.
(AUSTRALIA)
MALAYSIA
BRUNEI
SINGAPORE
Sumatra
Borneo
Celebes
Java
INDONESIA
Irian Jaya
EAST TIMOR
PAPUA NEW GUINEA
Midway Is
(U.S.A.)
Northern Mariana Is
(U.S.A.)
MARSHALL ISLANDS
Guam (U.S.A.)
MICRONESIA
PALAU
FED. STATES OF MICRONESIA
MELANESIA
NAURU
KIRIBATI
SOLOMON ISLANDS
TUVALU
Tokelau
SAMOA
Wallis & Futuna
(FRANCE)
American Samoa
(U.S.A.)
VANUATU
FIJI
Niue
(N.Z.)
TONGA
New Caledonia
(FRANCE)
AUSTRALIA
Norfolk I.
(AUSTRALIA)
Kermadec Is
(NEW ZEALAND)
NEW ZEALAND
Tasmania
Chatham Is
(NEW ZEALAND)
Amsterdam Is
(FRANCE)
St. Paul Is
(FRANCE)
Crozet Is
(FRANCE)
Kerguelen Is
(FRANCE)
Prince Edward Is
(SOUTH AFRICA)
Heard & McDonald Is
(AUSTRALIA)
Auckland Is
(NEW ZEALAND)
Macquarie I.
(AUSTRALIA)
ANTARCTICA

The Physical World

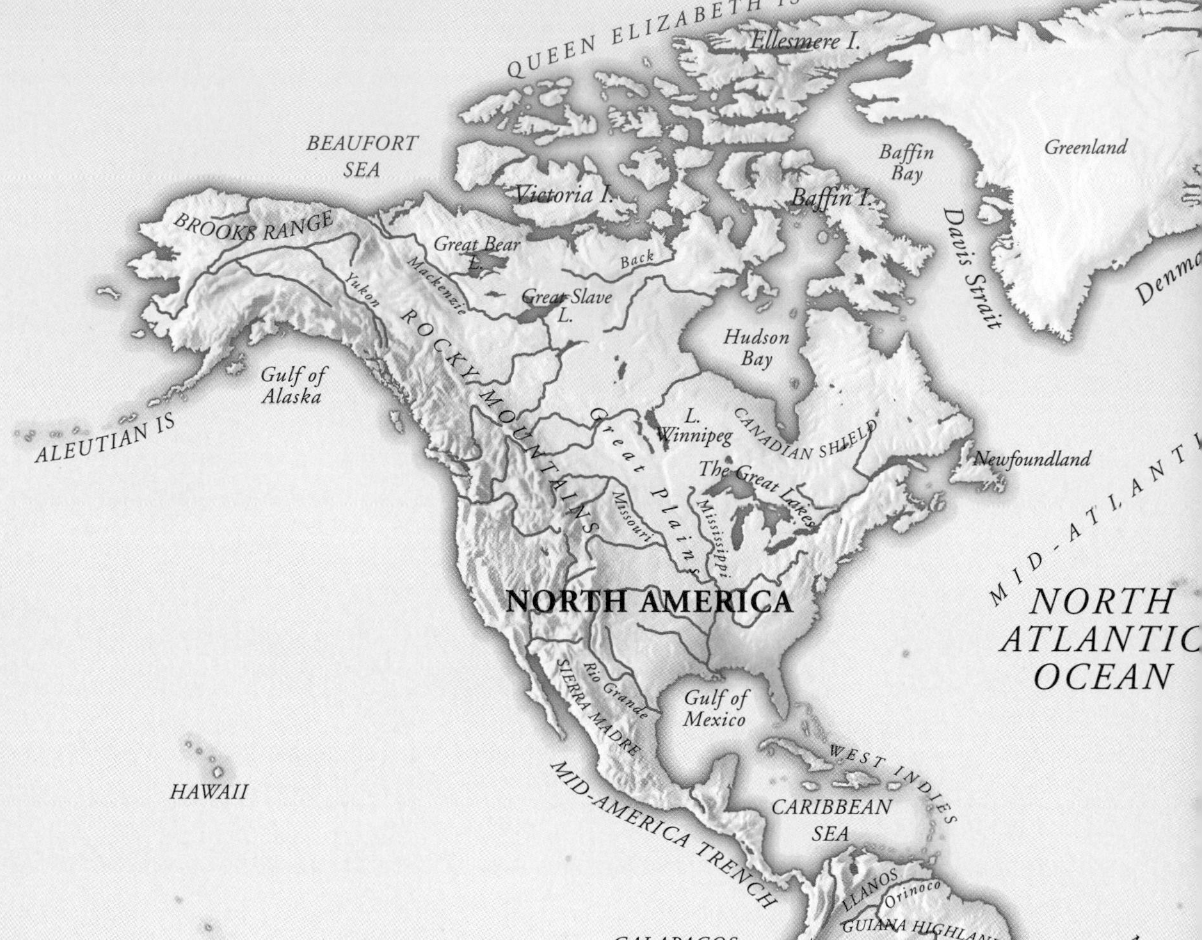
QUEEN ELIZABETH IS
Ellesmere I.
BEAUFORT SEA
Baffin Bay
Greenland
Victoria I.
Baffin I.
Davis Strait
Denma
BROOKS RANGE
Great Bear L.
Back
Yukon
Mackenzie
Great Slave L.
Hudson Bay
ROCKY MOUNTAINS
Gulf of Alaska
ALEUTIAN IS
L. Winnipeg
CANADIAN SHIELD
Great Plains
Newfoundland
The Great Lakes
Missouri
Mississippi
MID-ATLANTI
NORTH AMERICA
NORTH ATLANTIC OCEAN
Rio Grande
SIERRA MADRE
Gulf of Mexico
WEST INDIES
HAWAII
MID-AMERICA TRENCH
CARIBBEAN SEA
LLANOS
Orinoco
GUIANA HIGHLANDS
GALAPAGOS IS
ANDES
Amazon
Amazon Basin
PACIFIC OCEAN
SOUTH AMERICA
Selvas
PERU-CHILE TRENCH
GRAN CHACO
BRAZILIAN HIGHLANDS
ANDES
Pampas
FALKLAND IS
Cape Horn

DISCOVER MORE

• Physical maps can include many details. They show the relief of the land—its height above or below sea level. They show mountain ranges, with the altitude of the highest peaks. They show plains and the courses of rivers. They show coastlines, lakes, islands, and oceans. Coloring may help to indicate the nature of the landscape, with deserts in yellow, or rain forests in dark green.

World facts

Circumference of Earth mi (km)	**Area of water** sq mi (sq km)	**Area of land** sq mi (sq km)	**Largest continent** sq mi (sq km)
24,902 (40,075)	139,782,000 (362,033,000)	57,151,000 (148,021,000)	Asia 17,400,000 (45,066,000)

Antarctic Peninsula

This map of the world is a cylindrical projection

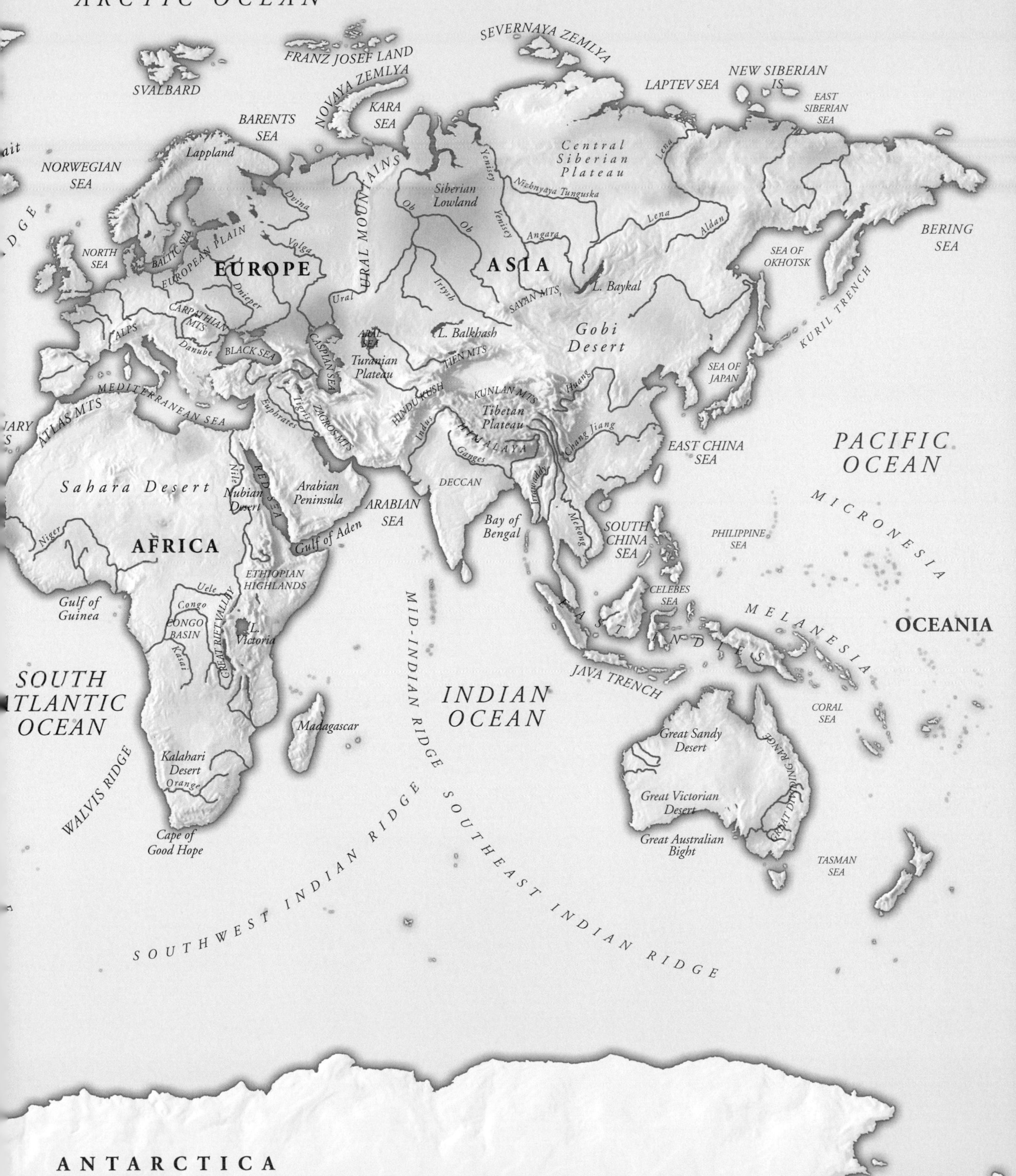

ARCTIC OCEAN
SVALBARD
FRANZ JOSEF LAND
NOVAYA ZEMLYA
SEVERNAYA ZEMLYA
BARENTS SEA
KARA SEA
LAPTEV SEA
NEW SIBERIAN IS.
EAST SIBERIAN SEA
NORWEGIAN SEA
Lappland
URAL MOUNTAINS
Central Siberian Plateau
Siberian Lowland
Dvina
Yenisey
Lena
Nizhnyaya Tunguska
Ob
Aldan
Angara
NORTH SEA
BALTIC SEA
EUROPEAN PLAIN
Volga
EUROPE
ASIA
BERING SEA
SEA OF OKHOTSK
KURIL TRENCH
Dnieper
Ural
Irtysh
SAYAN MTS.
L. Baykal
CARPATHIAN MTS
ALPS
Danube
BLACK SEA
CASPIAN SEA
ARAL SEA
L. Balkhash
Gobi Desert
Turanian Plateau
TIEN MTS
SEA OF JAPAN
MEDITERRANEAN SEA
ATLAS MTS
Tigris
Euphrates
ZAGROS MTS
HINDU KUSH
KUNLAN MTS
Tibetan Plateau
Huang
HIMALAYA
Indus
Ganges
Chang Jiang
EAST CHINA SEA
PACIFIC OCEAN
Sahara Desert
Nile
Nubian Desert
RED SEA
Arabian Peninsula
ARABIAN SEA
DECCAN
Irrawaddy
Mekong
Bay of Bengal
SOUTH CHINA SEA
MICRONESIA
PHILIPPINE SEA
Niger
AFRICA
Gulf of Aden
ETHIOPIAN HIGHLANDS
Uele
Gulf of Guinea
Congo
CONGO BASIN
Kasai
GREAT RIFT VALLEY
L. Victoria
MID-INDIAN RIDGE
CELEBES SEA
EAST INDIES
MELANESIA
OCEANIA
JAVA TRENCH
SOUTH
OCEAN
INDIAN OCEAN
Madagascar
CORAL SEA
Great Sandy Desert
GREAT DIVIDING RANGE
WALVIS RIDGE
Kalahari Desert
Orange
Great Victorian Desert
Great Australian Bight
Cape of Good Hope
SOUTHWEST INDIAN RIDGE
SOUTHEAST INDIAN RIDGE
TASMAN SEA
ANTARCTICA

North America

One sign of spring in the United States is the honking of Canada geese flying northward toward the Arctic Circle in wedge-shaped formations. There, in their breeding grounds on the treeless tundra of the far north, the snow and ice are beginning to melt after the long, bitter winter. The flight paths of many migrating birds cross over this continent from the hot, humid Gulf of Mexico to the glaciers of Greenland.

The world's third largest continent includes Canada, the United States of America (with the separate state of Alaska in the northwest), Mexico, and the seven small nations of Central America. It also includes the Danish territory of Greenland (the world's biggest island), and the minuscule French islands of St. Pierre and Miquelon.

From Pacific shore to Atlantic shore, west to east, the land surface crumples. First, there are coastal mountain ranges—Coast, Cascade, Sierra Nevada. Then there is the Great Basin, a strange land of salt lakes and eroded rocks, with deserts extending into Mexico. The massive ranges of the Rockies drop to the Great Plains and the Mississippi–Missouri river system.

Mountains continue southward, with Mexico's Sierra Madre range converging to join the rocky spine that runs through Central America. Northern deserts give way to a natural rain forest zone, which in many areas has been cleared by farmers and ranchers.

ARCTIC
BEAUFORT SEA
Alaska (U.S.A.)
Aleutian Is
Kodiak I.
Gulf of Alaska
Juneau
Queen Charlotte Is
CA
PACIFIC OCEAN
UNITED
Hawaii (U.S.A.)
Gulf of California

DISCOVER MORE

- *Lake Superior, between Canada and the United States, is the largest body of freshwater in the world. About 200 rivers drain into the lake, and it covers an area of 32,483 sq mi (84,131 sq km).*
- *The lowest point in North America is Badwater, in Death Valley, California. It lies at 282 ft (86 m) below sea level.*

The rocks of the Grand Canyon, in Arizona, have been eroded for a billion years. The world's biggest gorge has been carved out by the Colorado River.

Continent facts

	Area sq mi (sq km)	% of Earth's area	Population	Largest country by area sq mi (sq km)	Largest country by population
North America	9,400,000 (24,346,000)	16.2	475,815,000	Canada 3,851,800 (9,976,162)	U.S.A. 281,421,906

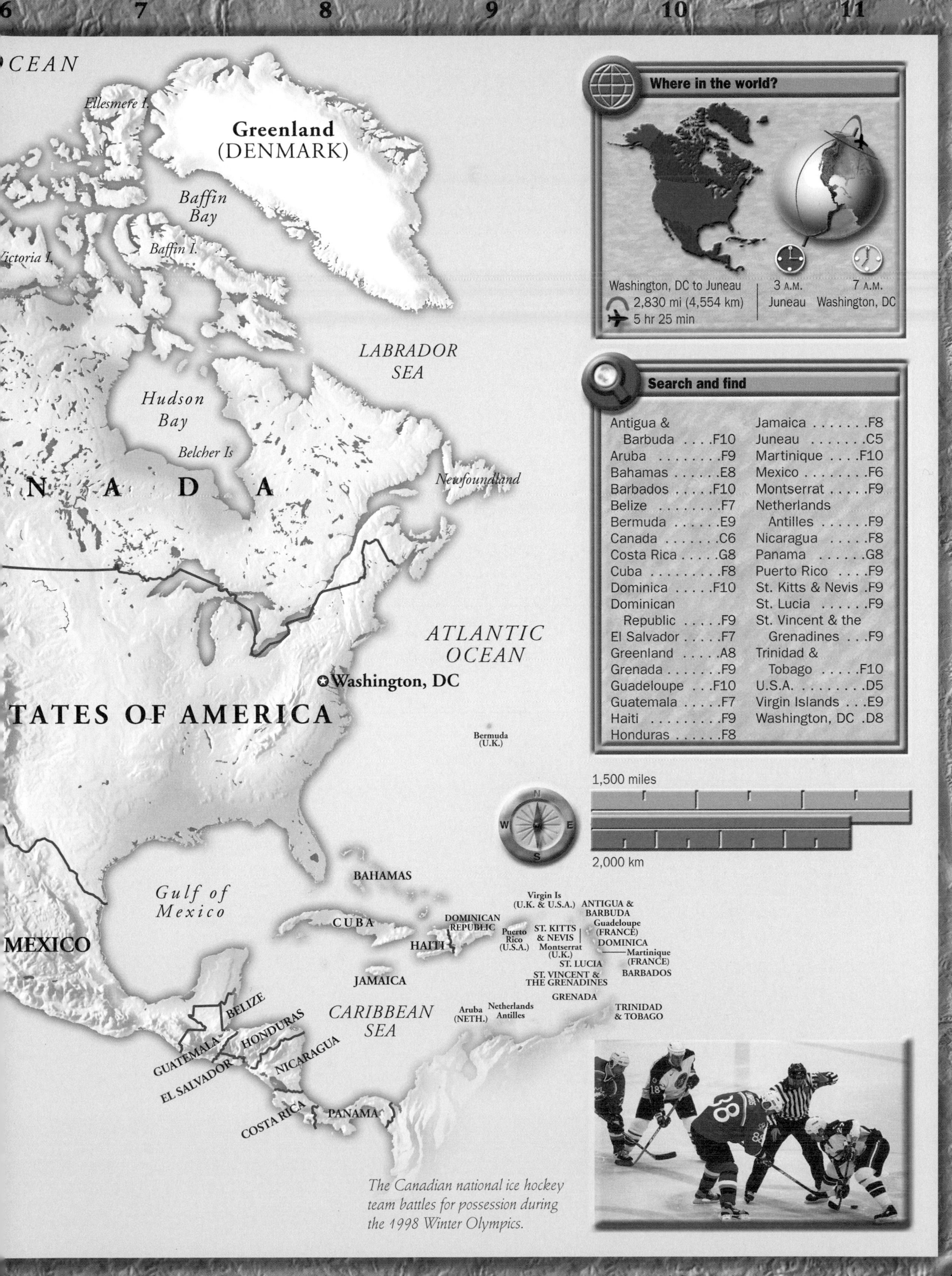

6 7 8 9 10 11
A B C D E F G
OCEAN
Ellesmere I.
Greenland
(DENMARK)
Baffin Bay
Baffin I.
Victoria I.
LABRADOR SEA
Hudson Bay
Belcher Is
Newfoundland
CANADA
ATLANTIC OCEAN
Washington, DC
TATES OF AMERICA
Bermuda (U.K.)
Gulf of Mexico
MEXICO
BAHAMAS
CUBA
HAITI
DOMINICAN REPUBLIC
Puerto Rico (U.S.A.)
Virgin Is (U.K. & U.S.A.)
ANTIGUA & BARBUDA
ST. KITTS & NEVIS
Guadeloupe (FRANCE)
Montserrat (U.K.)
DOMINICA
Martinique (FRANCE)
ST. LUCIA
ST. VINCENT & THE GRENADINES
BARBADOS
GRENADA
JAMAICA
CARIBBEAN SEA
Aruba (NETH.)
Netherlands Antilles
TRINIDAD & TOBAGO
BELIZE
HONDURAS
GUATEMALA
EL SALVADOR
NICARAGUA
COSTA RICA
PANAMA
Where in the world?
Washington, DC to Juneau
2,830 mi (4,554 km)
5 hr 25 min
3 A.M. Juneau
7 A.M. Washington, DC
Search and find
Antigua & Barbuda F10
Aruba F9
Bahamas E8
Barbados F10
Belize F7
Bermuda E9
Canada C6
Costa Rica G8
Cuba F8
Dominica F10
Dominican Republic F9
El Salvador F7
Greenland A8
Grenada F9
Guadeloupe . . .F10
Guatemala F7
Haiti F9
Honduras F8
Jamaica F8
Juneau C5
Martinique F10
Mexico F6
Montserrat F9
Netherlands Antilles F9
Nicaragua F8
Panama G8
Puerto Rico F9
St. Kitts & Nevis .F9
St. Lucia F9
St. Vincent & the Grenadines . . .F9
Trinidad & Tobago F10
U.S.A. D5
Virgin Islands . . .E9
Washington, DC .D8
1,500 miles
2,000 km
N S E W

The Canadian national ice hockey team battles for possession during the 1998 Winter Olympics.

United States of America

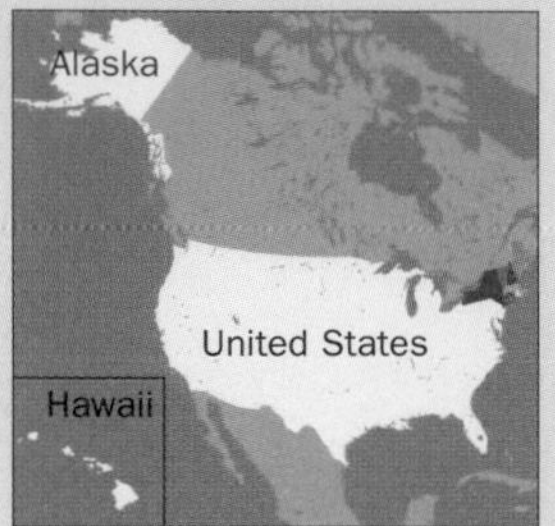
Alaska
United States
Hawaii

THE UNITED STATES OF AMERICA is a country that is on the move. Departure boards in airports and bus stations display the names of American towns and cities across six time zones.

The endless traffic flows through the great cities of the east before spreading out along the interstate highway network. Here are the huge green-and-yellow patchwork fields of Nebraska, under a thundery sky. Drivers draw up at a truck stop for a doughnut and a pot of coffee. There are the hills of Wyoming in pale moonlight and the shimmering desert highways of Arizona. And here on the West Coast, traffic crosses San Francisco's Golden Gate Bridge and the freeways of Los Angeles.

Although the United States is the most populous country in the Americas, it still has many areas of wilderness. It is bordered to the east by the Atlantic Ocean and to the west by the Pacific Ocean. To the south, its border with Mexico follows the Rio Grande, whereas most of the northern border with Canada is a straight line ruled straight across the map, rather than a natural feature. Alaska, in the northwest, forms an Arctic outpost, while the volcanic islands of Hawaii lie far to the west in the Pacific Ocean.

The 50 states are home to many different peoples. There are Inuits, Native Americans, and many people with African, European, Asian, or Polynesian roots. English is the first language, but Spanish is widely spoken, and other languages may also be heard.

The Caribbean island of Puerto Rico is self-governing but has especially close links with the United States and is called a Commonwealth Territory.

RUSSIAN FEDERATION
ALASKA
CANADA
BERING SEA
Gulf of Alaska
Aleutian Is
1 inch to 800 miles
CANADA
WASHINGTON
ROCKY MOUNTAINS
Missouri
MONTANA
NORTH DAKOTA
OREGON
SOUTH DAKOTA
IDAHO
WYOMING
NEBRASKA
NEVADA
UTAH
COLORADO
KANSAS
PACIFIC OCEAN
CALIFORNIA
OKLAHOMA
ARIZONA
NEW MEXICO
TEXAS
MEXICO
Rio Grande
HAWAII
Kauai
Niihau
Kauai Channel
Oahu
Molokai
Maui
Lanai
Kahoolawe
Hawaii
PACIFIC OCEAN
1 inch to 140 miles

DISCOVER MORE

- *A road trip across the United States, from the coast of New York to the coast of California, is approximately 3,000 mi (4,828 km).*
- *Nearly one-third of land in the U.S. is protected by the government, including national parks, forests, seashores, and wildlife refuges.*

Country facts

	Area sq mi (sq km)	Population	Language	Religion	Currency
United States	3,717,796 (9,629,092)	281,421,906	English	Protestant/Catholic	Dollar

United States of America

The impressive dome of the Capitol towers over Washington, DC. On its base are inscribed the Latin words E Pluribus Unum*—which means "Out of the Many, One."*

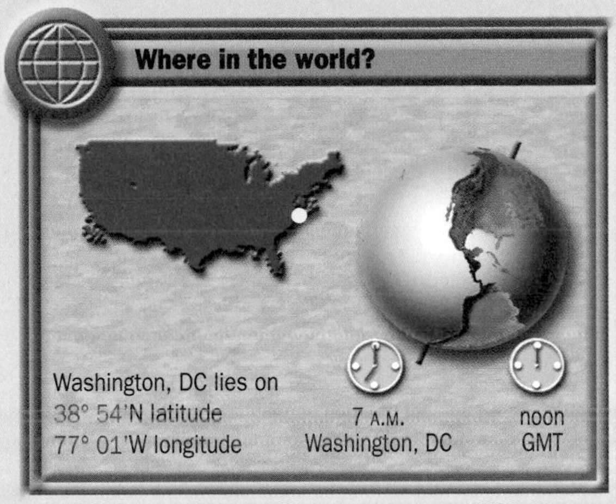

Where in the world?
Washington, DC lies on
38° 54'N latitude
77° 01'W longitude
7 A.M.
Washington, DC
noon
GMT

MAINE
VERMONT
NEW HAMPSHIRE
MASSACHUSETTS
RHODE ISLAND
CONNECTICUT
NEW YORK
MINNESOTA
MICHIGAN
WISCONSIN
Mississippi
IOWA
Missouri
PENNSYLVANIA
OHIO
NEW JERSEY
DELAWARE
Washington, DC
INDIANA
ILLINOIS
WEST VIRGINIA
MARYLAND
VIRGINIA
ATLANTIC OCEAN
MISSOURI
KENTUCKY
NORTH CAROLINA
ARKANSAS
TENNESSEE
SOUTH CAROLINA
ALABAMA
GEORGIA
MISSISSIPPI
LOUISIANA
Cape Canaveral
FLORIDA
Gulf of Mexico
Florida Keys

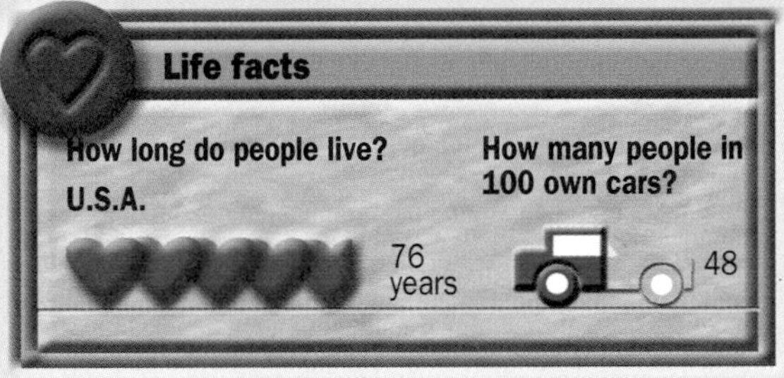

Life facts
How long do people live?
U.S.A.
76 years
How many people in 100 own cars?
48

Search and find

U.S.A.
Capital:
Washington, DC .C8
Alabama D7
Alaska A5
Arizona D4
Arkansas D7
California D4
Colorado D4
Connecticut C9
Delaware C8
Florida E8
Georgia E8
Hawaii F4
Idaho C4
Illinois D7
Indiana C7
Iowa C7
Kansas D6
Kentucky D7
Louisana E7
Maine B9
Maryland D8
Massachusetts .C9
Michigan C7
Minnesota C6
Mississippi E7
Missouri D7
Montana C5
Nebraska C6
Nevada D4
New Hampshire .C9
New Jersey C8
New Mexico D5
New York C8
North Carolina . .D8
North Dakota . . .C6
Ohio C8
Oklahoma D6
Oregon C4
Pennsylvania . . .C8
Rhode Island . . .C9
South Carolina . .D8
South Dakota . .C6
Tennessee D7
Texas E6
Utah D4
Vermont C8
Virginia D8
Washington C4
West Virginia . . .D8
Wisconsin C7
Wyoming C5

N
W
E
S
1,000 miles
1,500 km

Since 1886 the Statue of Liberty, a gift to the United States from France, has held her torch high above New York City's harbor. Inside, steps allow visitors to climb up to the head.

United States: The Northeast

NEW YORK, MAINE, VERMONT, NEW HAMPSHIRE, MASSACHUSETTS, CONNECTICUT, RHODE ISLAND

Alaska
United States
Hawaii

NEW YORK CITY HAS MORE skyscrapers than any other city in the world. Their sheer walls divide the island of Manhattan, flanked by the East River and the Hudson River, into canyons of glass and steel. Here is Wall Street, the financial center of the United States, and also the theater lights of Broadway. In winter the streets may be filled with swirling snow, in summer they may swelter in a heat wave. New York City is home to 7.4 million people. To the west lies the rolling green farmland of New York State, bordered to the west by two of the Great Lakes, Ontario and Erie.

The northeastern states take in the Allegheny Mountains, one of the Appalachian ranges, and the rocky coasts of the North Atlantic Ocean. Large areas are covered with birch and maple forests, which are spectacular in the fall as the leaves turn to red and gold. The six most northeasterly states are often referred to as New England. They extend from the forests and tidal pools of Maine to the trim wooden houses and white churches of historical Massachusetts and the city of Boston, to the shores of Rhode Island and Connecticut.

New Hampshire and Vermont sit between these states, and are both known for their scenic beauty. Their snow-covered mountains attract thousands of skiers during the winter months.

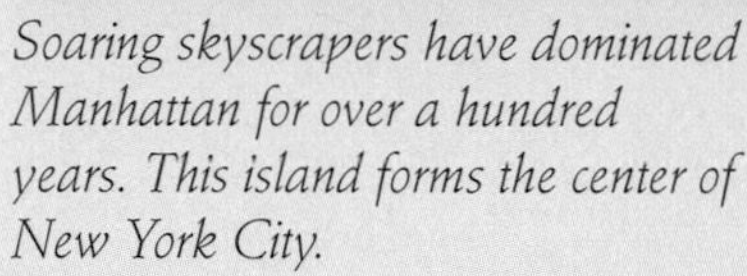
Soaring skyscrapers have dominated Manhattan for over a hundred years. This island forms the center of New York City.

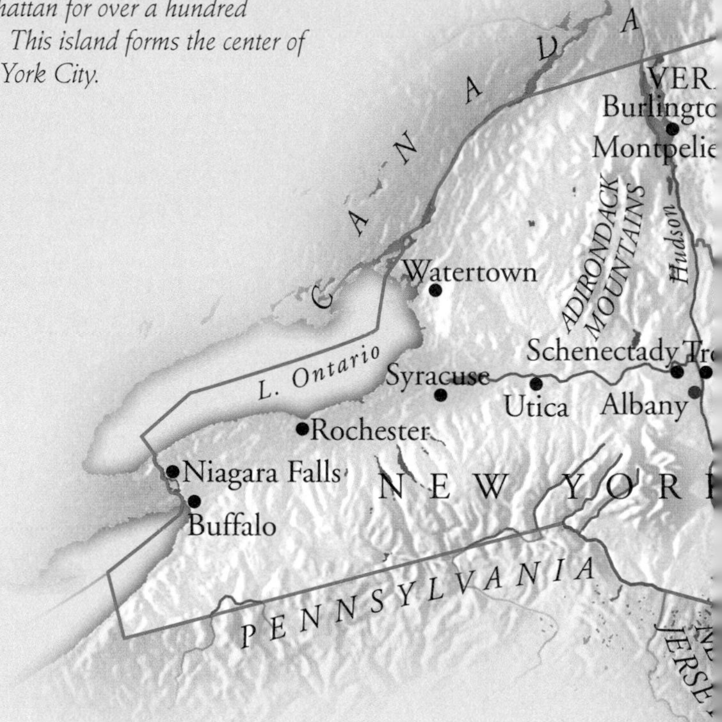
C A N A D A
Burlington
Montpelier
ADIRONDACK MOUNTAINS
Hudson
Watertown
L. Ontario
Syracuse
Schenectady
Utica
Albany
Rochester
Niagara Falls
Buffalo
N E W Y O R K
P E N N S Y L V A N I A

DISCOVER MORE

- *Each day in the United States begins in Maine. As the easternmost American state, it is always the first to see the sunrise.*
- *Approximately 202,000 cu ft (5,720 cu m) per second of water is harnessed to generate electricity at the American and the Horseshoe falls on the Niagara River in Canada.*

New York

Maine

Vermont

New Hampshire

Massachusetts

Connecticut

Rhode Island

State facts

	Area sq mi (sq km)	Population	Flower	Tree	Bird
New York	53,989 (139,832)	18,976,457	Rose	Sugar maple	Bluebird
Maine	33,741 (87,389)	1,274,923	White pinecone/tassel	Eastern white pine	Chickadee
Vermont	9,615 (24,903)	608,827	Red clover	Sugar maple	Hermit thrush
New Hampshire	9,283 (24,043)	1,235,786	Purple lilac	White birch	Purple finch
Massachusetts	9,241 (23,934)	6,349,097	Mayflower	American elm	Chickadee
Connecticut	5,544 (14,359)	3,405,565	Mountain laurel	White oak	Robin
Rhode Island	1,231 (3,188)	1,048,319	Violet	Red maple	Rhode Island red

Many lighthouses were built to guide shipping through shoals off Cape Cod, Massachusetts.

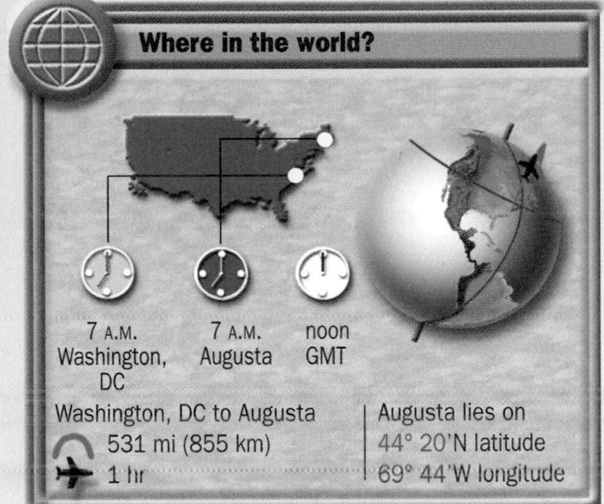
Where in the world?
7 A.M. Washington, DC
7 A.M. Augusta
noon GMT
Washington, DC to Augusta
531 mi (855 km)
1 hr
Augusta lies on
44° 20'N latitude
69° 44'W longitude

200 miles
300 km
N
W
E
S

The lush New England landscape of Vermont is the perfect environment for cattle farming. Cattle are kept for meat and milk.

Presque Isle
MAINE
Penobscot
Bangor
Mt Washington 6,288 ft (1,917 m)
Augusta
Lewiston
Portland
NORTH ATLANTIC OCEAN
NEW HAMPSHIRE
Concord
Portsmouth
Manchester
Nashua
Salem
Boston
Cape Cod
Worcester
MASSACHUSETTS
Providence
Hartford
RHODE ISLAND
New Haven
CONNECTICUT
Bridgeport
Long I.
New York City

Acadia National Park lies on the Atlantic coast of Maine. This is a wild land of forests, lakes, and tidal pools.

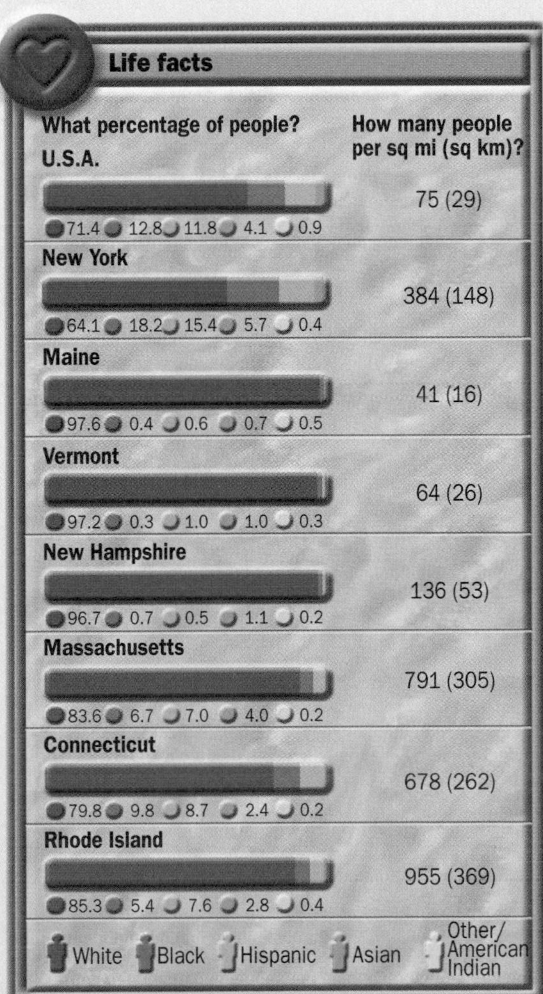

Life facts

What percentage of people?	White	Black	Hispanic	Asian	Other/American Indian	How many people per sq mi (sq km)?
U.S.A.	71.4	12.8	11.8	4.1	0.9	75 (29)
New York	64.1	18.2	15.4	5.7	0.4	384 (148)
Maine	97.6	0.4	0.6	0.7	0.5	41 (16)
Vermont	97.2	0.3	1.0	1.0	0.3	64 (26)
New Hampshire	96.7	0.7	0.5	1.1	0.2	136 (53)
Massachusetts	83.6	6.7	7.0	4.0	0.2	791 (305)
Connecticut	79.8	9.8	8.7	2.4	0.2	678 (262)
Rhode Island	85.3	5.4	7.6	2.8	0.4	955 (369)

Search and find

New York
State Capital:
Albany D6
Buffalo D4
New York City . . .E6
Niagara Falls . . .D4
Rochester D4
Schenectady . . .D6
Syracuse D5
Troy D6
Utica D5
Watertown D5

Maine
State Capital:
Augusta C7
Bangor C7
Lewiston C7
Portland C7
Presque Isle . . .B7

Vermont
State Capital:
Montpelier . . .C6
Burlington C6

New Hampshire
State Capital:
Concord D7
Manchester D7
Nashua D7
Portsmouth D7

Massachusetts
State Capital:
Boston D7
Salem D7
Springfield D6
Worcester D7

Connecticut
State Capital:
Hartford D6
Bridgeport E6
New Haven D6

Rhode Island
State Capital:
Providence . . .D7

A

United States: Mid-Atlantic

PENNSYLVANIA, MARYLAND, NEW JERSEY, DELAWARE, WASHINGTON, DC

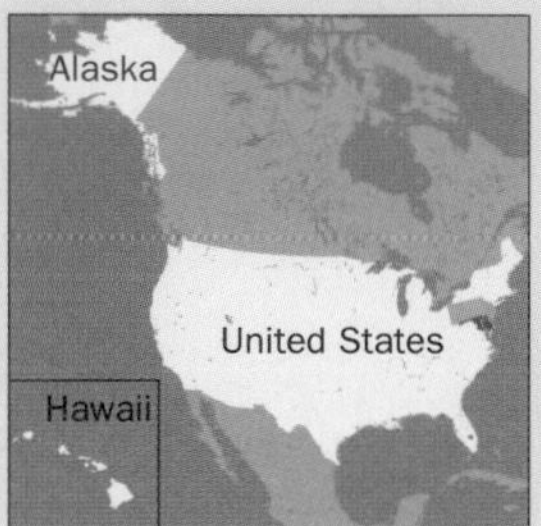
Alaska
United States
Hawaii

SOUTH OF NEW YORK STATE, the New Jersey coastline is surrounded by sand dunes and wetlands. The eastern part is densely populated, with major cities such as Trenton and Newark.

B

The coastal plain rises, continuing into neighboring Pennsylvania, beyond the Delaware River. This land of woods and waterways became one of the first industrial states, a great center of coal mining and steel manufacturing. Its chief cities are the industrial center of Pittsburgh and historic Philadelphia, the great seaport where the original thirteen colonies declared their independence from Britain in 1776.

C

On the Atlantic seaboard, Maryland is a small state bordering the Chesapeake Bay, which bites deep into the coastal plain, creating the long Delmarva peninsula (shared by the small states of Delaware, Maryland, and Virginia). This coast is famous for its clams and crabs. Its chief port is Baltimore.

D

The federal capital, Washington, occupies its own territory on the Potomac River, the District of Columbia (DC). It is dominated by the great dome of the Capitol building, the meeting place for Congress. Here, too, is the White House, the official residence of the President.

E

A Pittsburgh welder sets the sparks flying. In the 1800s, Pittsburgh was the world's biggest steel-producing city. It remains a major industrial center, but many of its mills and chimneys have been replaced by modern skyscrapers and green parkland.

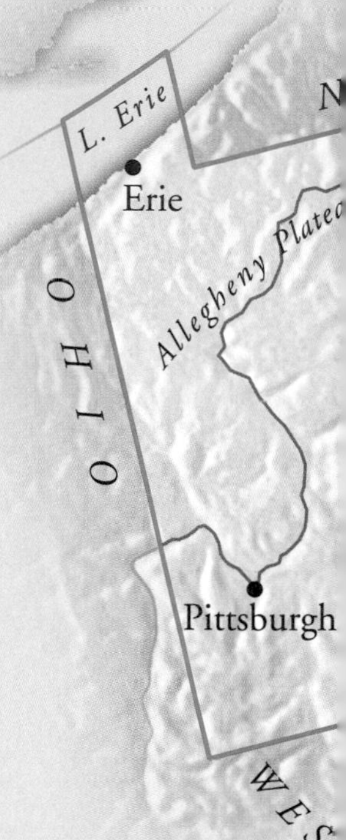
L. Erie
Erie
N
Allegheny Plate
OHIO
Pittsburgh
WES

The Amish live in Pennsylvania and the Midwest where they farm land in the traditional way and use no modern machinery.

Pennsylvania

Maryland

New Jersey

Delaware

Washington, DC

F

DISCOVER MORE

- *Maryland has one of the most irregular state borders in the whole country. It runs across a peninsula, around headlands and coastal inlets, and follows the course of winding rivers.*
- *The world's biggest library is in Washington, DC. The Library of Congress has more than 95 million books.*

G

State facts

	Area sq mi (sq km)	Population	Flower	Tree	Bird
Pennsylvania	46,058 (119,290)	12,281,054	Mountain laurel	Hemlock	Ruffed grouse
Maryland	12,297 (31,849)	5,296,486	Black-eyed Susan	White oak	Baltimore oriole
New Jersey	8,215 (21,277)	8,414,350	Purple violet	Red oak	Eastern goldfinch
Delaware	2,396 (6,206)	783,600	Peach blossom	American holly	Blue hen chicken
Washington, DC	70 (181)	572,059	Western rhododendron	Western hemlock	Willow goldfinch

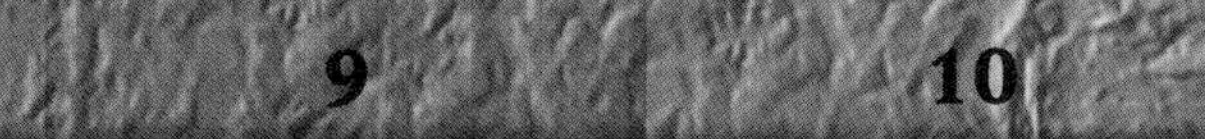

6
7
8
9
10
11

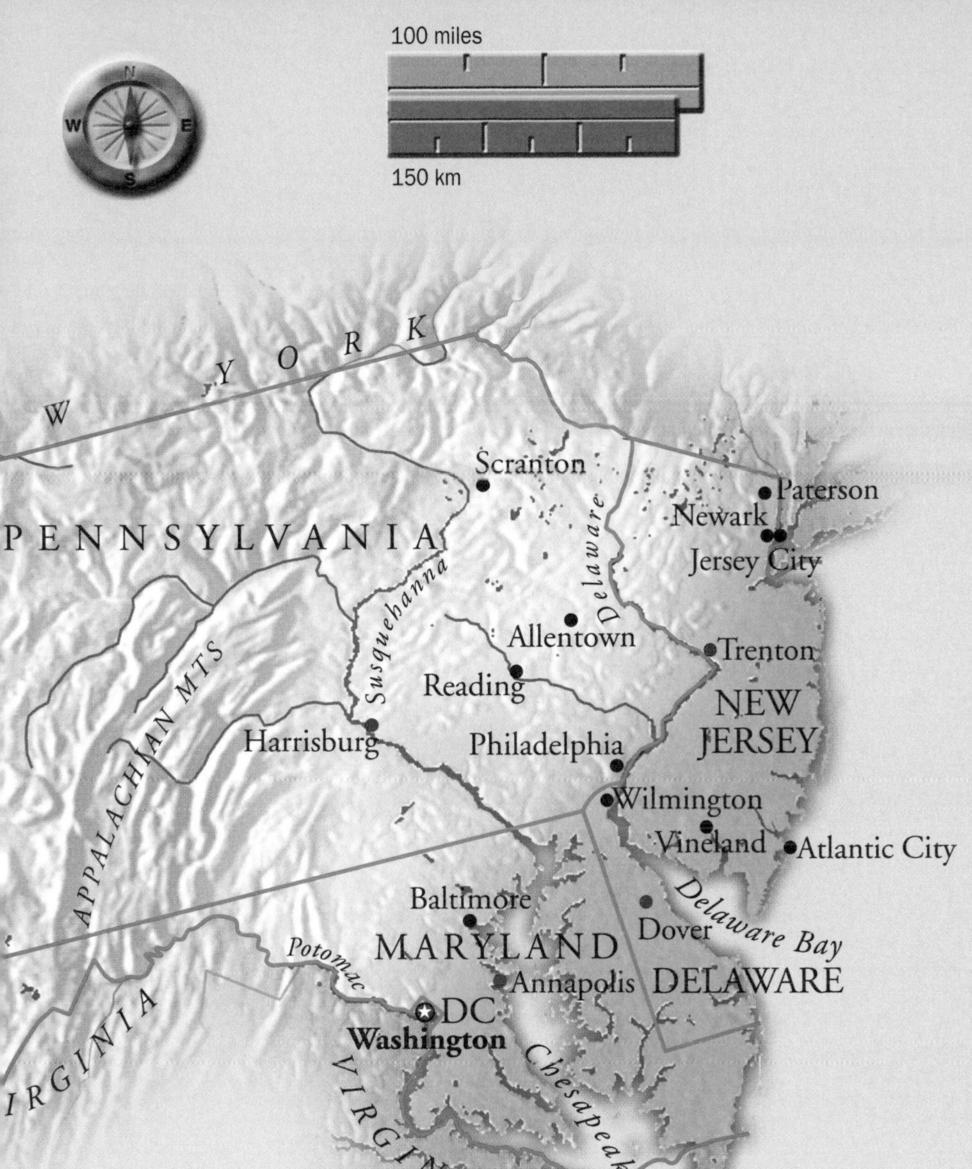

100 miles
150 km
N
W
E
S
NEW YORK
PENNSYLVANIA
APPALACHIAN MTS
Susquehanna
Delaware
Scranton
Paterson
Newark
Jersey City
Allentown
Trenton
Reading
Harrisburg
Philadelphia
NEW JERSEY
Wilmington
Vineland
Atlantic City
Baltimore
Dover
Delaware Bay
MARYLAND
Potomac
Annapolis
DELAWARE
DC
Washington
Chesapeake Bay
VIRGINIA

The lights of Baltimore's skyline and inner harbor seen at dusk. It is one of the country's busiest ports.

The Delaware River winds through a wooded valley in Pennsylvania and mountains in New Jersey. The Delaware Water Gap is a popular recreation area.

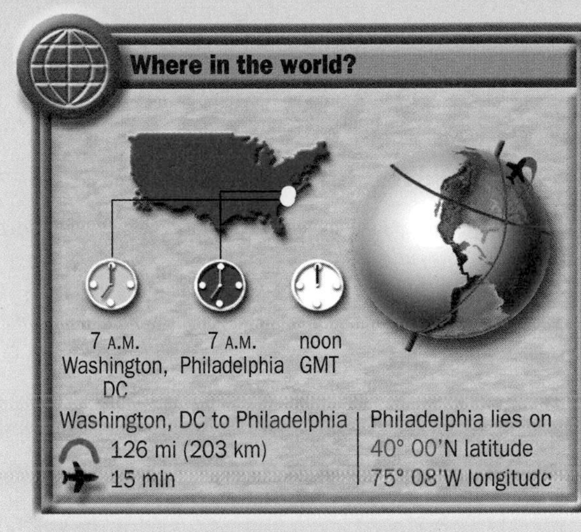

Where in the world?
7 A.M. Washington, DC
7 A.M. Philadelphia
noon GMT
Washington, DC to Philadelphia
126 mi (203 km)
15 min
Philadelphia lies on
40° 00'N latitude
75° 08'W longitude

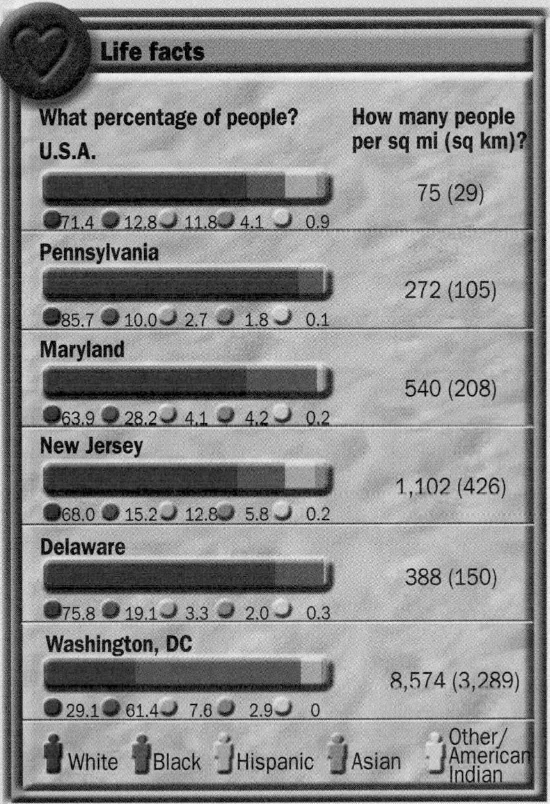

Life facts
What percentage of people?
How many people per sq mi (sq km)?
U.S.A.
71.4 12.8 11.8 4.1 0.9
75 (29)
Pennsylvania
85.7 10.0 2.7 1.8 0.1
272 (105)
Maryland
63.9 28.2 4.1 4.2 0.2
540 (208)
New Jersey
68.0 15.2 12.8 5.8 0.2
1,102 (426)
Delaware
75.8 19.1 3.3 2.0 0.3
388 (150)
Washington, DC
29.1 61.4 7.6 2.9 0
8,574 (3,289)
White
Black
Hispanic
Asian
Other/ American Indian

Search and find

Pennsylvania
State Capital:
Harrisburg . . .C7
Allentown C8
Erie B5
Philadelphia C8
Pittsburgh C6
Reading C8
Scranton B8

Maryland
State Capital:
Annapolis D8
Baltimore D8

New Jersey
State Capital:
Trenton C9
Atlantic City C9
Jersey City B9
Newark B9
Paterson B9
Vineland C9

Delaware
State Capital:
Dover D8
Wilmington C8

District of Columbia
Capital:
Washington . .D8

United States: The South

FLORIDA, GEORGIA, ARKANSAS, NORTH CAROLINA, ALABAMA, LOUISIANA, MISSISSIPPI, VIRGINIA, TENNESSEE, KENTUCKY, SOUTH CAROLINA, WEST VIRGINIA

Alaska
United States
Hawaii

SOUTH OF THE CHESAPEAKE Bay, the pounding of Atlantic breakers has created a long chain of sandy beaches, flanked by offshore islands and lagoons, that extend from Virginia to the Florida Keys. Coastal plains and plateaus rise to form the ranges of the Appalachian Mountains.

The estuaries of four rivers cut through the state of Virginia, which has large industrial centers in Richmond and Norfolk. Beyond the mountains lies West Virginia, a land of whitewater rivers and forests.

Farther south, the Atlantic coast passes through the humid lands of North and South Carolina, and Georgia. Hills, waterways, and woodlands stretch west through Tennessee and Kentucky. The fertile farmland of the South produces peanuts, tobacco, and cotton. Atlanta, Georgia, is a major business center.

The sunny, palm-fringed state of Florida stretches south to Key West, attracting tourists from all over the world. Alligators and snakes are among the creatures that live in the wetlands of The Everglades.

The southernmost states line the oil-rich Gulf of Mexico. This thundery coastline is indented by creeks, bayous, and the maze of the Mississippi Delta. New Orleans, Louisiana, lies on the east bank of the Mississippi River, shielded from floodwater by high walls, called levees. About half of the land in Louisiana is covered by forests.

Wheeling
OHIO
WEST VIRGINIA
Charleston
Huntington
INDIANA
ILLINOIS
Frankfort
Louisville
Lexington
KENTUCKY
Owensboro
Paducah
Nashville
Johnson City
Clarksville
Knoxville
MISSOURI
TENNESSEE
APPALACHIAN
OKLAHOMA
ARKANSAS
Chattanooga
Greenville
Fort Smith
Memphis
Arkansas
Little Rock
Tennessee
Huntsville
Atlanta
Hot Springs
Birmingham
Augusta
Pine Bluff
MISSISSIPPI
Macon
El Dorado
Mississippi
Greenville
ALABAMA
Columbus
Montgomery
Yazoo
Meridian
GEORGIA
TEXAS
Shreveport
Jackson
Alabama
Albany
LOUISIANA
Hattiesburg
Red
Natchez
Tallahassee
Alexandria
Biloxi
Mobile
Pensacola
Baton Rouge
Lafayette
Cape St. George
New Orleans
Lake Charles
Mississippi Delta
Clearwater
Gulf of Mexico

Florida

Georgia

Arkansas

North Carolina

Alabama

Louisiana

Mississippi

Virginia

Tennessee

Kentucky

South Carolina

West Virginia

State facts

	Area sq mi (sq km)	Population	Flower	Tree	Bird
Florida	59,928 (155,214)	15,982,378	Orange blossom	Sabal palmetto palm	Mockingbird
Georgia	58,977 (152,750)	8,186,453	Cherokee rose	Live oak	Brown thrasher
Arkansas	53,182 (137,741)	2,673,400	Apple blossom	Pine	Mockingbird
North Carolina	52,672 (136,420)	8,049,313	Dogwood	Pine	Cardinal
Alabama	52,237 (135,294)	4,447,100	Camellia	Southern longleaf pine	Yellowhammer
Louisiana	49,651 (128,596)	4,468,976	Magnolia	Cypress	Eastern brown pelican
Mississippi	48,286 (125,061)	2,844,658	Magnolia	Magnolia	Mockingbird
Virginia	42,326 (109,624)	7,078,515	Dogwood	Dogwood	Cardinal
Tennessee	42,146 (109,158)	5,689,283	Iris	Tulip poplar	Mockingbird
Kentucky	40,411 (104,664)	4,041,769	Goldenrod	Tulip poplar	Cardinal
South Carolina	31,189 (80,780)	4,012,012	Yellow jessamine	Palmetto	Carolina wren
West Virginia	24,231 (62,758)	1,808,344	Big rhododendron	Sugar maple	Cardinal

DISCOVER MORE

• Giant dunes and huge waves are a feature of the Outer Banks, a long spit of sand on the North Carolina coast. This part of the coast has seen so many shipwrecks that it is sometimes called "the Graveyard of the Atlantic."

PENNSYLVANIA
MARYLAND
Morgantown
Richmond
VIRGINIA
Norfolk
Roanoke
Greensboro
Durham
Raleigh
Winston-Salem
Outer Banks
Cape Hatteras
NORTH CAROLINA
Charlotte
Wilmington
Columbia
Cape Fear
SOUTH CAROLINA
Charleston
Savannah
ATLANTIC OCEAN
Jacksonville
St. Augustine
Daytona Beach
Orlando
Cape Canaveral
FLORIDA
Tampa
L. Okeechobee
St. Petersburg
West Palm Beach
Fort Lauderdale
Fort Myers
The Everglades
Miami
Naples
Florida Keys
Key West
Straits of Florida

N
W
E
S

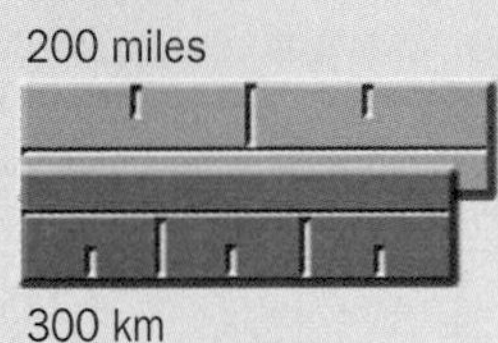
200 miles
300 km

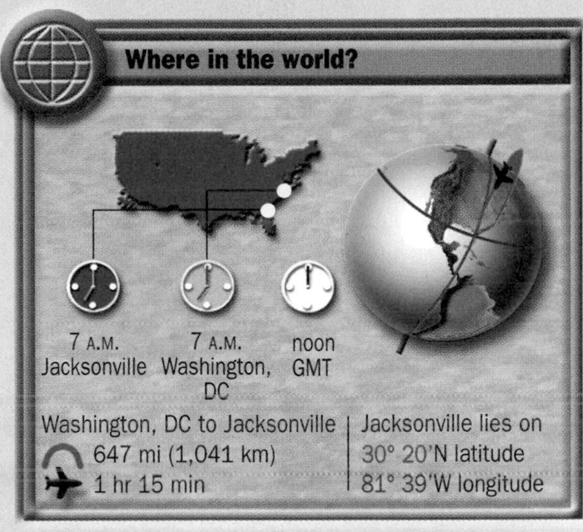
Where in the world?
7 A.M.
Jacksonville
7 A.M.
Washington, DC
noon
GMT
Washington, DC to Jacksonville
647 mi (1,041 km)
1 hr 15 min
Jacksonville lies on
30° 20'N latitude
81° 39'W longitude

Search and find

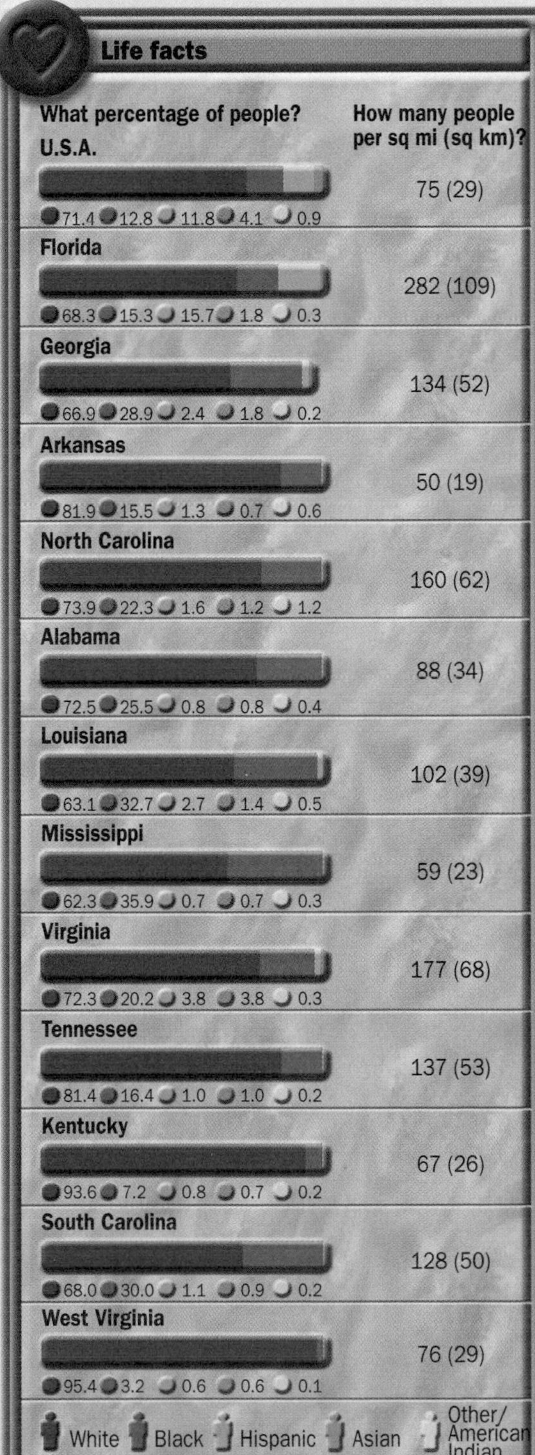

Life facts

	What percentage of people? (White / Black / Hispanic / Asian / Other/American Indian)	How many people per sq mi (sq km)?
U.S.A.	71.4 / 12.8 / 11.8 / 4.1 / 0.9	75 (29)
Florida	68.3 / 15.3 / 15.7 / 1.8 / 0.3	282 (109)
Georgia	66.9 / 28.9 / 2.4 / 1.8 / 0.2	134 (52)
Arkansas	81.9 / 15.5 / 1.3 / 0.7 / 0.6	50 (19)
North Carolina	73.9 / 22.3 / 1.6 / 1.2 / 1.2	160 (62)
Alabama	72.5 / 25.5 / 0.8 / 0.8 / 0.4	88 (34)
Louisiana	63.1 / 32.7 / 2.7 / 1.4 / 0.5	102 (39)
Mississippi	62.3 / 35.9 / 0.7 / 0.7 / 0.3	59 (23)
Virginia	72.3 / 20.2 / 3.8 / 3.8 / 0.3	177 (68)
Tennessee	81.4 / 16.4 / 1.0 / 1.0 / 0.2	137 (53)
Kentucky	93.6 / 7.2 / 0.8 / 0.7 / 0.2	67 (26)
South Carolina	68.0 / 30.0 / 1.1 / 0.9 / 0.2	128 (50)
West Virginia	95.4 / 3.2 / 0.6 / 0.6 / 0.1	76 (29)

White · Black · Hispanic · Asian · Other/American Indian

A space shuttle is attached to the rocket's side as it takes off from John F. Kennedy Space Center, on Florida's Cape Canaveral.

United States: The Southwest

TEXAS, NEW MEXICO, ARIZONA, OKLAHOMA

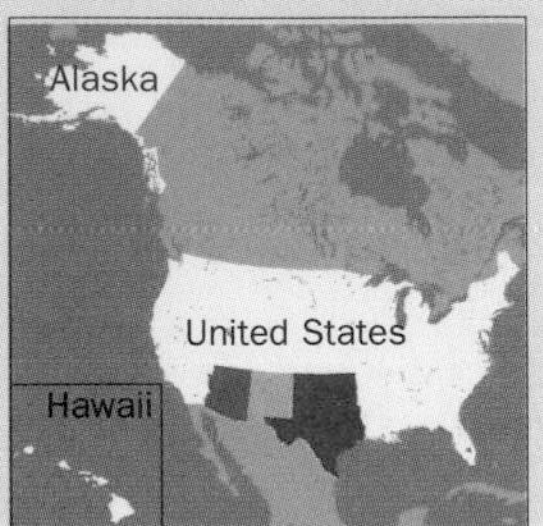
Alaska
United States
Hawaii

TEXAS IS THE BIGGEST AMERICAN state after Alaska. It borders the steamy Gulf of Mexico, the Rio Grande, and the hot, dusty, short-grass plain, which extends into New Mexico. Some Texans have become wealthy through the production of oil and by running cattle ranches. Many Texans wear traditional cowboy boots, belt, and a broad-brimmed Stetson hat, even though they may live in a large, modern city such as San Antonio, Houston, or Dallas.

North across the Red River lies Oklahoma, another state that built its economy on cattle and oil. Most of its population work as farmers, and wheat is the chief crop.

Neighboring New Mexico is a sunny state with deserts of glistening white sand in the south and mountains in the north. Many people work in the mining industry.

Westward again, the climate becomes hotter and drier, but dams and irrigation systems make it possible to grow cotton, grains, and fruit in some areas. Southern Arizona is a land covered in thorny scrub and saguaro, the world's biggest cactus. Ancient rock dwellings may still be seen across this land. They were once inhabited by a Native American people known as the Anasazi. South of Phoenix, in Arizona, desert stretches over the Mexican border.

The southwestern states are home to many people of Mexican origin and to Native American peoples such as the Apache and the Navajo.

NEVADA
UTAH
Hoover Dam
Grand Canyon
Colorado Plateau
Farmington
Humphreys Peak 12,634 ft (3,851 m)
Winslow
Gallup
Flagstaff
Albuquerque
Prescott
ARIZONA
CALIFORNIA
Colorado
Phoenix
Mesa
Gila
Silver City
Rio Grande
Yuma
Tucson
Deming
Douglas

Much of the Arizona landscape is arid. Annual rainfall at Yuma is just 3 in (7.5 cm) compared to Hawaii which receives as much as 200 in (508 cm) on the mountaintops and 25 in (64 cm) on the lowlands.

DISCOVER MORE

- *The Carlsbad Caverns in New Mexico are home to millions of bats. At sundown they swarm out of Bat Cave, forming a great, dark cloud.*
- *The Grand Canyon is the world's largest gorge, eroded from the plateau lands of northern Arizona by the Colorado River. It is 217 mi (349 km) long, between 3 and 15 mi (8 and 25 km) wide, and in places drops 6,230 ft (1,900 m).*

Texas

New Mexico

Arizona

Oklahoma

State facts

	Area sq mi (sq km)	Population	Flower	Tree	Bird
Texas	267,277 (692,247)	20,851,820	Bluebonnet	Pecan	Mockingbird
New Mexico	121,598 (314,939)	1,819,046	Yucca	Piñon	Roadrunner
Arizona	114,006 (295,276)	5,130,632	Blossom of the saguaro cactus	Paloverde	Cactus wren
Oklahoma	69,903 (181,049)	3,450,654	Mistletoe	Redbud	Scissor-tailed flycatcher

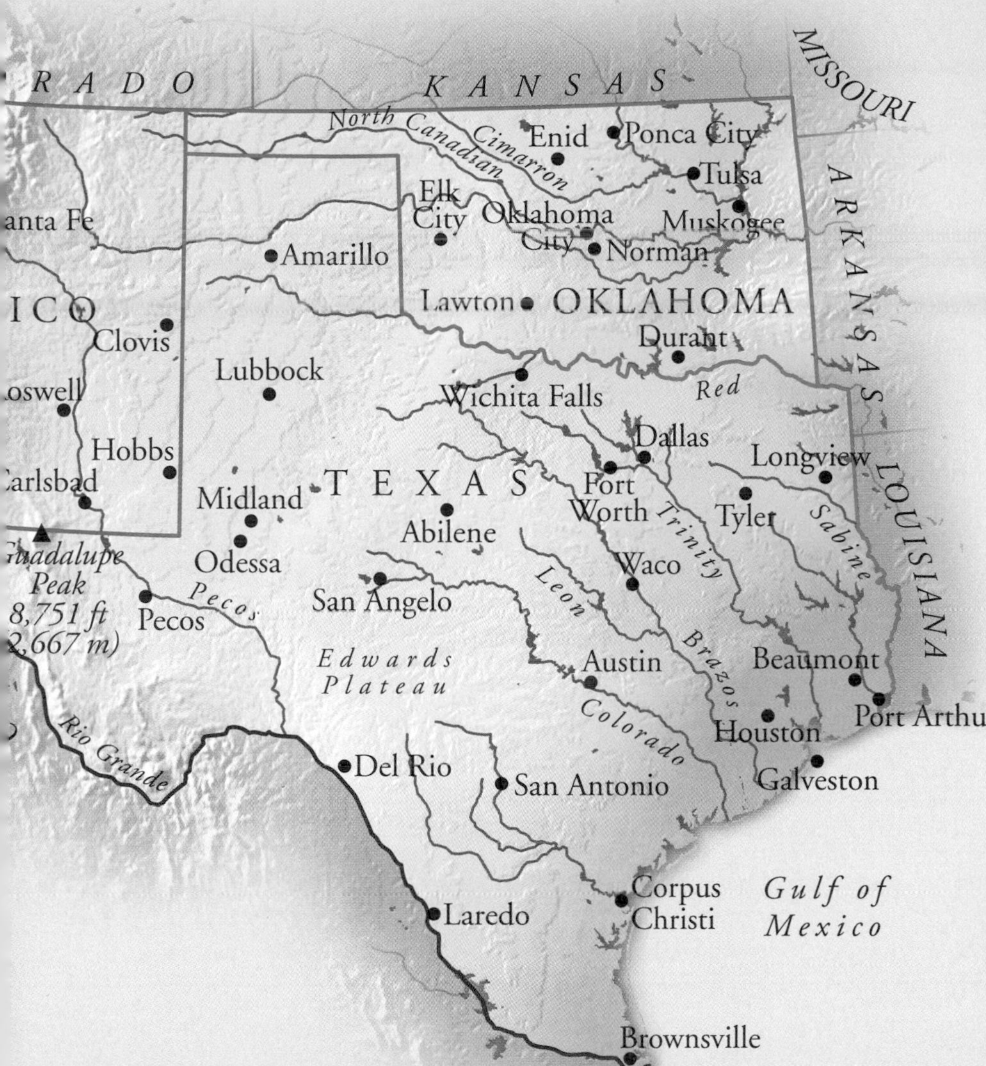
RADO
KANSAS
MISSOURI
North Canadian
Cimarron
Enid
Ponca City
Tulsa
Elk City
Oklahoma City
Muskogee
Norman
anta Fe
Amarillo
ARKANSAS
Lawton
OKLAHOMA
ICO
Clovis
Durant
Lubbock
Red
oswell
Wichita Falls
Hobbs
Dallas
Longview
arlsbad
Midland
TEXAS
Fort Worth
Trinity
Tyler
Sabine
LOUISIANA
Abilene
Guadalupe Peak 8,751 ft (2,667 m)
Odessa
Pecos
Leon
Waco
San Angelo
Pecos
Brazos
Edwards Plateau
Austin
Beaumont
Colorado
Port Arthur
Rio Grande
Houston
Del Rio
San Antonio
Galveston
Corpus Christi
Gulf of Mexico
Laredo
Brownsville

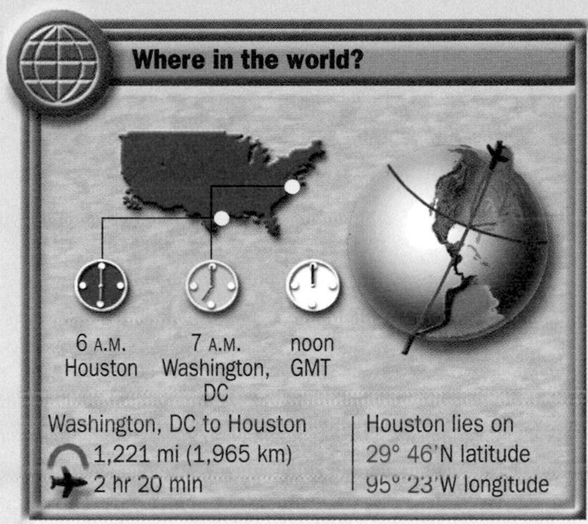
Where in the world?
6 A.M. Houston
7 A.M. Washington, DC
noon GMT
Washington, DC to Houston
1,221 mi (1,965 km)
2 hr 20 min
Houston lies on
29° 46'N latitude
95° 23'W longitude

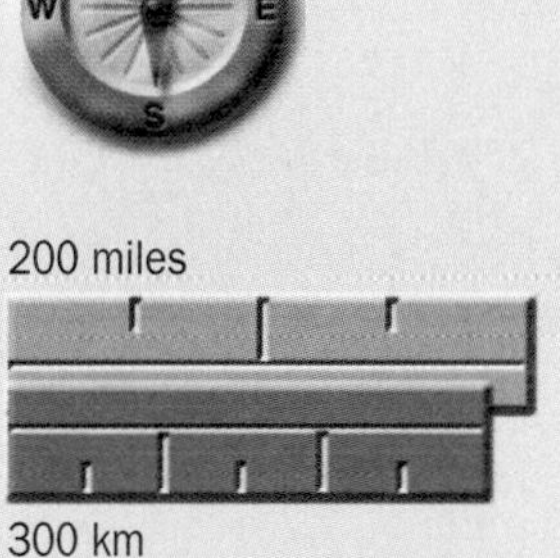
N
W
E
S
200 miles
300 km

Texas has become rich producing more oil than any other state in the United States.

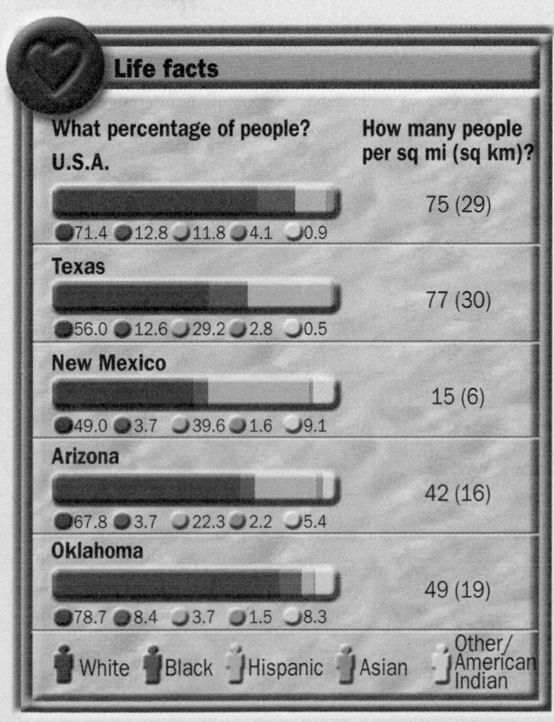
Life facts
What percentage of people?
How many people per sq mi (sq km)?
U.S.A.
71.4 12.8 11.8 4.1 0.9
75 (29)
Texas
56.0 12.6 29.2 2.8 0.5
77 (30)
New Mexico
49.0 3.7 39.6 1.6 9.1
15 (6)
Arizona
67.8 3.7 22.3 2.2 5.4
42 (16)
Oklahoma
78.7 8.4 3.7 1.5 8.3
49 (19)
White
Black
Hispanic
Asian
Other/American Indian

Search and find

Texas
State Capital:
Austin C8
Abilene C8
Amarillo B7
Beaumont C9
Brownsville E8
Corpus Christi . . D8
Dallas C8
Del Rio D7
El Paso C6
Fort Worth C8
Galveston D9
Houston C9
Laredo D8
Longview C9
Lubbock B7
Midland C7
Odessa C7
Pecos C7
Port Arthur C9
San Angelo C7
San Antonio D8
Tyler C9
Waco C8
Wichita Falls . . . B8

New Mexico
State Capital:
Santa Fe B6
Albuquerque . . . B6
Carlsbad C6
Clovis B7
Deming C5
Farmington A5
Gallup B5
Hobbs C7
Las Cruces C6
Los Alamos B6
Roswell B6
Silver City C5

Arizona
State Capital:
Phoenix B4
Douglas C5
Flagstaff B5
Mesa B4
Prescott B4
Tucson C5
Winslow B5
Yuma B4

Oklahoma
State Capital:
Oklahoma City B8
Durant B8
Elk City B8
Enid B8
Lawton B8
Muskogee B9
Norman B8
Ponca City B8
Tulsa B8

United States: The Midwest

MINNESOTA, KANSAS, NEBRASKA, SOUTH DAKOTA, NORTH DAKOTA, MISSOURI, IOWA

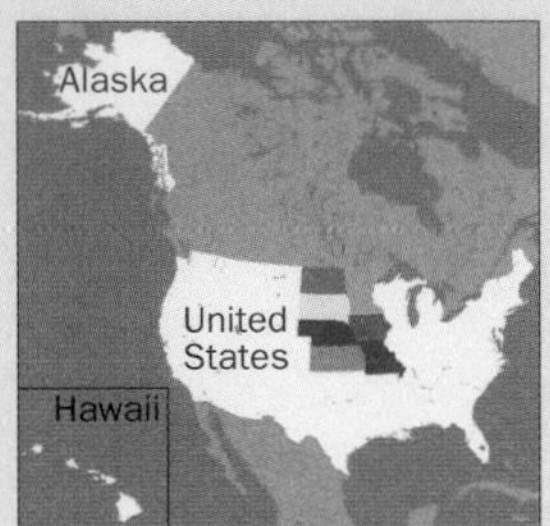

Alaska
United States
Hawaii

A PICKUP TRUCK BOUNCES along a farm track, crossing wide, flat fields planted with soybeans and corn. The farmer eyes the sky anxiously, for it is early summer, and the radio forecasts twisters. These tornadoes are dark, funnel-like whirlwinds that can lift the roof off a barn. Summers are hot but stormy. Winters can be very cold, with heavy snowfalls.

From the Mississippi River west to Wyoming and Montana is a vast, sloping plateau called the Great Plains. Short grasses are the natural vegetation of the dry west, but longer grasses have always grown in the east, where the rainfall is higher. The grasslands, which form part of the North American prairies, extend northward across Canada and have become one of the world's "breadbaskets," or key grain-producing regions. The prairie is rich with wildlife, such as the North American bison (or buffalo) and burrowing rodents called prairie dogs.

In St. Louis, Missouri, is the Midwest's most famous landmark, a graceful 630-feet (192-m) high arc of steel called the Gateway Arch. Westward lie the agricultural states of Iowa, Kansas, and Nebraska.

Minnesota, on the shores of Lake Superior, is known for its dairy farms and is one of the country's main milk-producers. On the sparsely populated prairies of North and South Dakota, cattle are raised.

CANADA
Red Lake
MINNE
Williston
Minot
Grand Forks
Red
L. Sakakawea
NORTH DAKOTA
Fargo
Moorhead
Bismarck
Jamestown
Mississippi
MONTANA
Missouri
Aberdeen
James
SOUTH DAKOTA
Minneapol
Watertown
Minnesota
Rapid City
Cheyenne
Pierre
Sioux Falls
Mount Rushmore
White
Missouri
Des Moi
WYOMING
Sioux City
NEBRASKA
North Platte
North Platte
Omaha
Council Bluffs
Grand Island
Platte
Lincoln
Republican
St. Josep
COLORADO
Kansas
Kans City
Hays
Salina
Topeka
KANSAS
Arkansas
Hutchinson
Dodge City
Wichita
Cimarron
OKLAHOMA

DISCOVER MORE

• In most years, the United States can expect over 900 tornadoes, or "twisters." They are created by warm air from the Gulf of Mexico meeting cool air from the Rocky Mountains over the Great Plains. Front-line states in "Tornado Alley" include Kansas, Nebraska, Iowa, Missouri, and many in the South and Southwest.

St. Louis's Gateway Arch rises above the lights of the city reflected in the water at night.

Mount Rushmore, in South Dakota, has been carved into gigantic rock face portraits of U.S. presidents—George Washington, Thomas Jefferson, Theodore Roosevelt, and Abraham Lincoln.

T A
uluth
WISCONSIN
Paul
ochester
Mississippi
A
Waterloo
Cedar Rapids
Cedar
Davenport
es Moines
ILLINOIS
Mississippi
Columbia
St. Louis
fferson City
MISSOURI
Cape Girardeau
Springfield
ARKANSAS

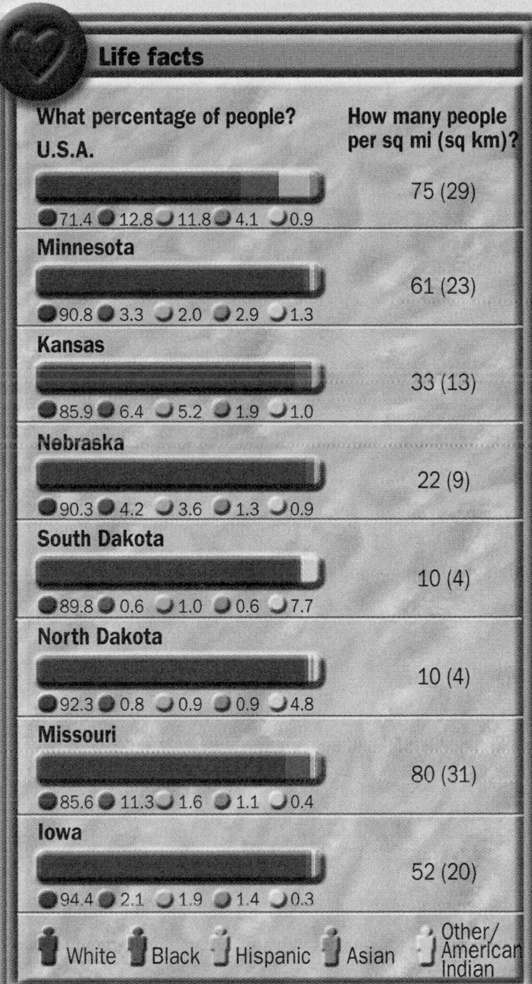

Life facts
What percentage of people?
How many people per sq mi (sq km)?
U.S.A.
71.4 12.8 11.8 4.1 0.9
75 (29)
Minnesota
90.8 3.3 2.0 2.9 1.3
61 (23)
Kansas
85.9 6.4 5.2 1.9 1.0
33 (13)
Nebraska
90.3 4.2 3.6 1.3 0.9
22 (9)
South Dakota
89.8 0.6 1.0 0.6 7.7
10 (4)
North Dakota
92.3 0.8 0.9 0.9 4.8
10 (4)
Missouri
85.6 11.3 1.6 1.1 0.4
80 (31)
Iowa
94.4 2.1 1.9 1.4 0.3
52 (20)
White
Black
Hispanic
Asian
Other/ American Indian

N
W
E
S

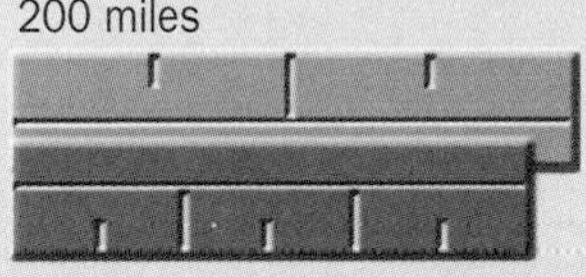

200 miles
300 km

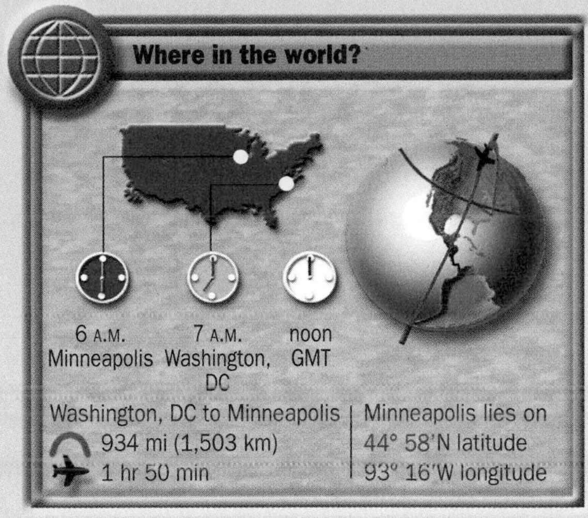

Where in the world?
6 A.M. Minneapolis
7 A.M. Washington, DC
noon GMT
Washington, DC to Minneapolis
934 mi (1,503 km)
1 hr 50 min
Minneapolis lies on
44° 58′N latitude
93° 16′W longitude

Search and find
Minnesota
State Capital:
St. Paul B6
Duluth B6
Minneapolis B6
Moorhead B5
Rochester C6
Kansas
State Capital:
Topeka D6
Dodge City E4
Hays D5
Hutchinson E5
Salina D5
Wichita E5
Nebraska
State Capital:
Lincoln D5
Grand Island . . . D5
North Platte D4
Omaha D5
South Dakota
State Capital:
Pierre C4
Aberdeen B5
Rapid City C4
Sioux Falls C5
Watertown C5
North Dakota
State Capital:
Bismarck B4
Fargo B5
Grand Forks B5
Jamestown B5
Minot B4
Williston B4
Missouri
State Capital:
Jefferson City . D7
Cape Girardeau . E7
Columbia D7
Kansas City D6
Springfield E6
St. Joseph D6
St. Louis D7
Iowa
State Capital:
Des Moines . . D6
Cedar Rapids . . . C7
Council Bluffs . . D7
Davenport C7
Sioux City C5
Waterloo C6

Minnesota

KANSAS

Kansas

Nebraska

South Dakota

North Dakota

Missouri

IOWA

Iowa

State facts

	Area sq mi (sq km)	Population	Flower	Tree	Bird
Minnesota	86,943 (225,182)	4,919,479	Pink and white lady's slipper	Red pine	Common loon
Kansas	82,282 (213,110)	2,688,418	Native sunflower	Cottonwood	Western meadowlark
Nebraska	77,358 (200,357)	1,711,263	Goldenrod	Cottonwood	Western meadowlark
South Dakota	77,121 (199,743)	754,844	Pasqueflower	Black Hills spruce	Chinese red-necked pheasant
North Dakota	70,704 (183,123)	642,200	Wild prairie rose	American elm	Western meadowlark
Missouri	69,709 (180,546)	5,959,211	Hawthorn	Dogwood	Bluebird
Iowa	56,276 (145,755)	2,926,324	Wild rose	Oak	Eastern goldfinch

United States: Great Lakes

MICHIGAN, WISCONSIN, ILLINOIS, OHIO, INDIANA

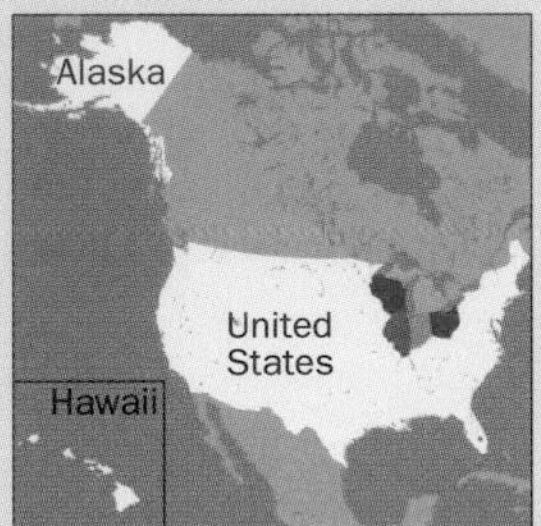
Alaska
United States
Hawaii

CHICAGO IS CALLED "THE Windy City" because strong winds blowing off Lake Michigan are funneled around its gigantic skyscrapers. The Great Lakes form a body of water about 98,185 square miles (245,300 sq km) in area. They were scooped out of the continent by movements of ice in prehistoric times. Michigan is the only lake lying entirely within the United States. Superior, Huron, Erie, and Ontario all form part of the U.S.-Canadian border.

The shores of the Great Lakes include bluffs topped by sand dunes, weathered rocks, forest, and farmland. Here, too, are large industrial cities such as Detroit, nicknamed "Motor City" for being the center of the U.S. automobile industry, and the port of Cleveland.

Ohio has long been a center of manufacturing, but the western part of the state consists largely of wooded countryside and farmland. In Indiana there are steel mills along the shores of Lake Michigan, wide fields of corn, and rolling hills on the Kentucky border. Wisconsin is crossed by rivers and streams and dotted with thousands of small lakes. It is a major center of dairy farming, producing milk, butter, and cheese.

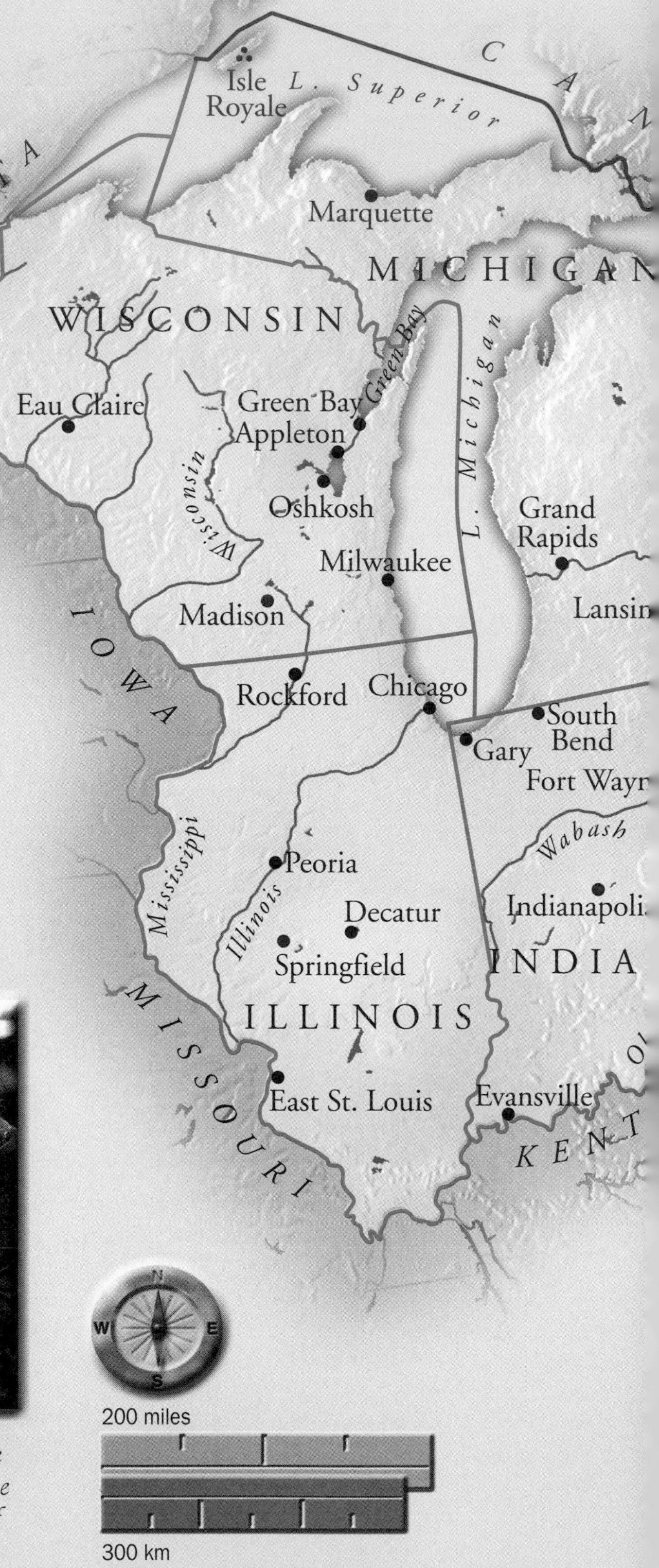
Isle Royale
L. Superior
MINNESOTA
Marquette
MICHIGAN
WISCONSIN
Green Bay
Eau Claire
Green Bay
Appleton
Wisconsin
Oshkosh
L. Michigan
Grand Rapids
Milwaukee
Madison
IOWA
Rockford
Chicago
South Bend
Gary
Fort Wayne
Wabash
Peoria
Mississippi
Illinois
Decatur
Indianapolis
Springfield
INDIANA
ILLINOIS
MISSOURI
East St. Louis
Evansville
KENTUCKY
N
W
E
S
200 miles
300 km

The Great Lakes region has been the center of the U.S. car industry since its early days. It was in the factories of Detroit that production-line methods of manufacturing were first developed.

DISCOVER MORE

- *Winds in Illinois can change temperatures by as much as 20°F (11°C) in an hour.*
- *Isle Royale is the largest island in Lake Superior, and the wildest spot in the region, home to timber wolves, moose, and beaver.*

State facts

	Area sq mi (sq km)	Population	Flower	Tree	Bird
Michigan	96,705 (250,465)	9,938,444	Apple blossom	White pine	Robin
Wisconsin	65,499 (169,642)	5,363,675	Wood violet	Sugar maple	Robin
Illinois	57,918 (150,007)	12,419,293	Native violet	White oak	Cardinal
Ohio	44,828 (116,104)	11,353,140	Scarlet carnation	Buckeye	Cardinal
Indiana	36,420 (94,327)	6,080,485	Peony	Tulip poplar	Cardinal

The Chicago River, an inlet of Lake Michigan, runs through the heart of the city. It is crossed by a series of bridges and tunnels. It divides Chicago into a North Side, a West Side, and a South Side.

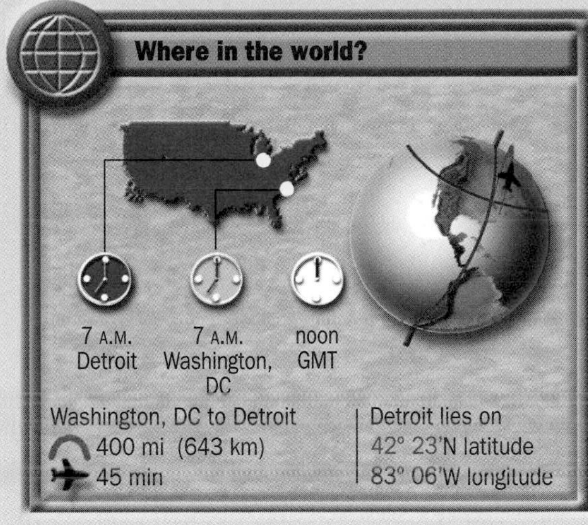

Where in the world?
7 A.M. Detroit
7 A.M. Washington, DC
noon GMT
Washington, DC to Detroit
400 mi (643 km)
45 min
Detroit lies on
42° 23'N latitude
83° 06'W longitude

Huron
Port Huron
Flint
Ann Arbor
Toledo
Cleveland
Akron
L. Erie
PENNSYLVANIA
OHIO
Columbus
Dayton
Cincinnati
Ohio
WEST VIRGINIA

The Ohio River forms the southern borders of Ohio, Indiana, and Illinois, and the northern borders of West Virginia and Kentucky.

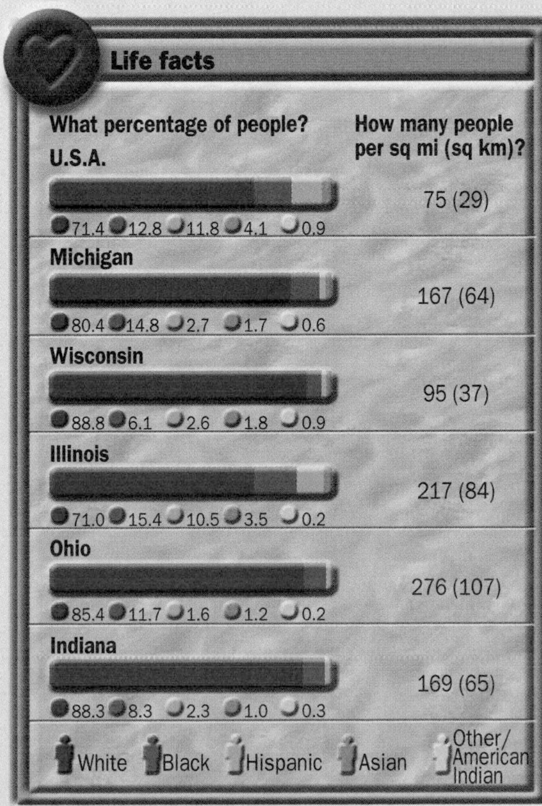

Life facts
What percentage of people?
How many people per sq mi (sq km)?
U.S.A.
71.4 12.8 11.8 4.1 0.9
75 (29)
Michigan
80.4 14.8 2.7 1.7 0.6
167 (64)
Wisconsin
88.8 6.1 2.6 1.8 0.9
95 (37)
Illinois
71.0 15.4 10.5 3.5 0.2
217 (84)
Ohio
85.4 11.7 1.6 1.2 0.2
276 (107)
Indiana
88.3 8.3 2.3 1.0 0.3
169 (65)
White
Black
Hispanic
Asian
Other/American Indian

Search and find
Michigan
State Capital:
Lansing C6
Ann Arbor C6
Detroit C6
Flint C6
Grand Rapids . . .C6
Marquette B5
Port Huron C7
Saginaw C6
Wisconsin
State Capital:
Madison C5
Appleton C5
Eau Claire B4
Green Bay B5
Milwaukee C5
Oshkosh C5
Illinois
State Capital:
Springfield . . .D5
Chicago C5
Decatur D5
East St. Louis . .E5
Peoria D5
Rockford C5
Ohio
State Capital:
Columbus D7
Akron C7
Cincinnati D6
Cleveland C7
Dayton D6
Toledo C6
Indiana
State Capital:
Indianapolis . .D6
Evansville E5
Fort Wayne D6
Gary D5
South Bend C5

Michigan

WISCONSIN
1848

Wisconsin

ILLINOIS

Illinois

Ohio

Indiana

United States: Mountain

Montana, Nevada, Colorado, Wyoming, Utah, Idaho

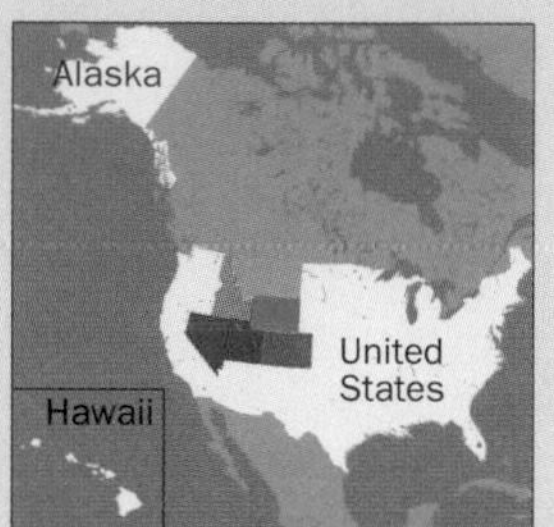
Alaska
United States
Hawaii

Beneath blue skies and white clouds, jagged peaks of granite streaked with snow tower over dark pines and aspens that shiver in the wind. The massive Rocky Mountains, home of bighorn sheep, goats, deer, and grizzly bears, run north to south in the western part of the region, from the Canadian border to New Mexico. The Rockies include a series of mountain chains.

This dramatic scenery attracts many backpackers and tourists to national parks such as Yellowstone, and Colorado is a center for winter sports. The mountains are rich in minerals. They are flanked to the east by the short grass prairie of the Great Plains, well known as cattle-ranching country.

To the west of the Rockies lies the Great Basin, a vast inland area drained by westward-flowing rivers. Here are vast salt lakes, deserts, mesas, buttes, and canyons, rocks that have been eroded by wind and water into arches and pinnacles. Large cities have grown up around these extraordinary landscapes, such as Salt Lake City, heart of the Mormon faith, and Las Vegas, a neon-lighted sprawl of casinos, gambling arcades, theaters, and hotels in the Nevada desert.

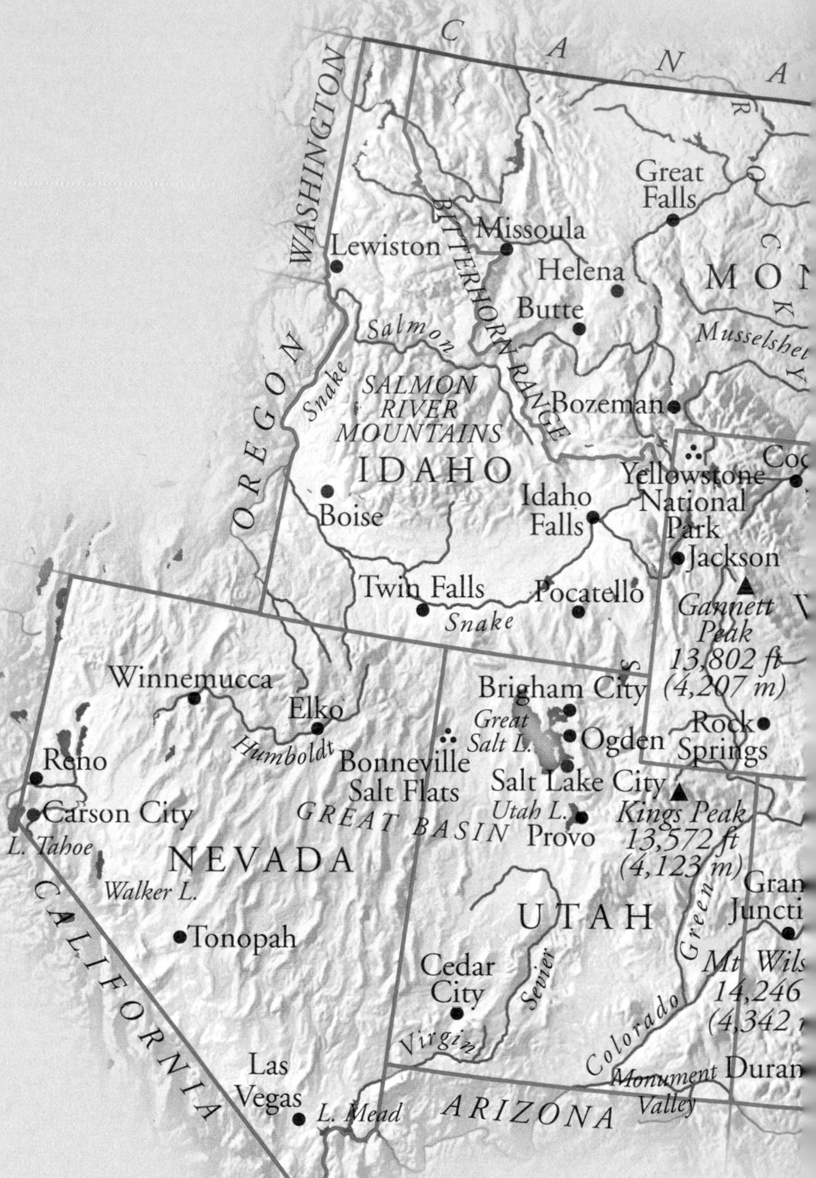
CANADA
WASHINGTON
OREGON
CALIFORNIA
IDAHO
NEVADA
UTAH
ARIZONA
Great Falls
Lewiston
Missoula
Helena
Butte
Bozeman
BITTERROOT RANGE
SALMON RIVER MOUNTAINS
Salmon
Snake
Musselshell
Yellowstone National Park
Idaho Falls
Boise
Jackson
Twin Falls
Pocatello
Gannett Peak 13,802 ft (4,207 m)
Winnemucca
Elko
Humboldt
Brigham City
Great Salt L.
Ogden
Rock Springs
Reno
Bonneville Salt Flats
Salt Lake City
Carson City
L. Tahoe
GREAT BASIN
Utah L.
Provo
Kings Peak 13,572 ft (4,123 m)
Walker L.
Tonopah
Cedar City
Sevier
Green
Virgin
Colorado
Mt Wils 14,246 (4,342
Monument Valley
Las Vegas
L. Mead

N
W
E
S

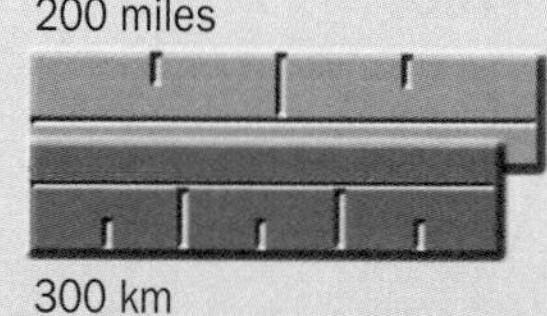
200 miles
300 km

DISCOVER MORE

- *The world's tallest active geyser is the Steamboat, in Yellowstone National Park, Wyoming. Geysers are jets of water heated by volcanic activity deep beneath the Earth. Steamboat sends up jets between 195 to 375 ft (60 to 115 m) high.*
- *Empty, flat wildernesses, such as Bonneville Salt Flats in Utah, are ideal places for trying to break land speed records.*

State facts

	Area sq mi (sq km)	Population	Flower	Tree	Bird
Montana	147,046 (380,849)	902,195	Bitterroot	Ponderosa pine	Western meadowlark
Nevada	110,567 (286,369)	1,711,263	Sagebrush	Single-leaf piñon and Bristle-cone pine	Mountain bluebird
Colorado	104,100 (269,619)	4,301,261	Rocky Mountain columbine	Colorado blue spruce	Lark bunting
Wyoming	97,818 (253,349)	493,782	Indian paintbrush	Plains cottonwood	Western meadowlark
Utah	84,904 (219,901)	2,233,169	Sego lily	Blue spruce	Seagull
Idaho	83,574 (216,457)	1,293,953	Syringa	White pine	Mountain bluebird

6
7
8
9
10
11

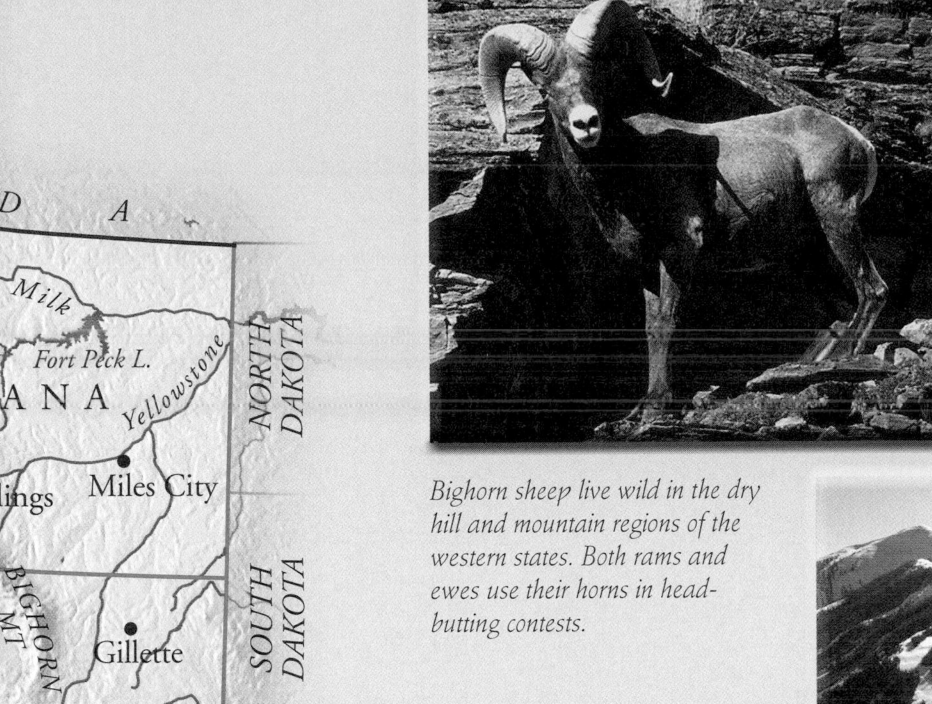
D A
Milk
Fort Peck L.
ANA
Yellowstone
NORTH DAKOTA
Miles City
lings
SOUTH DAKOTA
BIGHORN MT
Gillette
OMING
Casper
NEBRASKA
Laramie
Cheyenne
Fort Collins
Sterling
Greeley
South Platte
Boulder
Aspen
Denver
Mt Elbert 14,432 ft (4,399 m)
Colorado Springs
Arkansas
Pueblo
Lamar
KANSAS
COLORADO
NEW MEXICO

Where in the world?

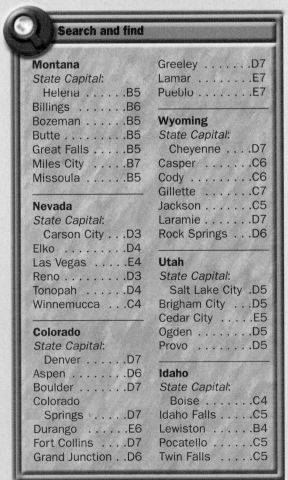

4 A.M. Las Vegas	7 A.M. Washington, DC	noon GMT

Washington, DC to Las Vegas
2,091 mi (3,365 km)
4 hr

Las Vegas lies on
36° 12'N latitude
115° 13'W longitude

Bighorn sheep live wild in the dry hill and mountain regions of the western states. Both rams and ewes use their horns in head-butting contests.

Many people travel to ski on the spectacular snow-covered mountains in Colorado.

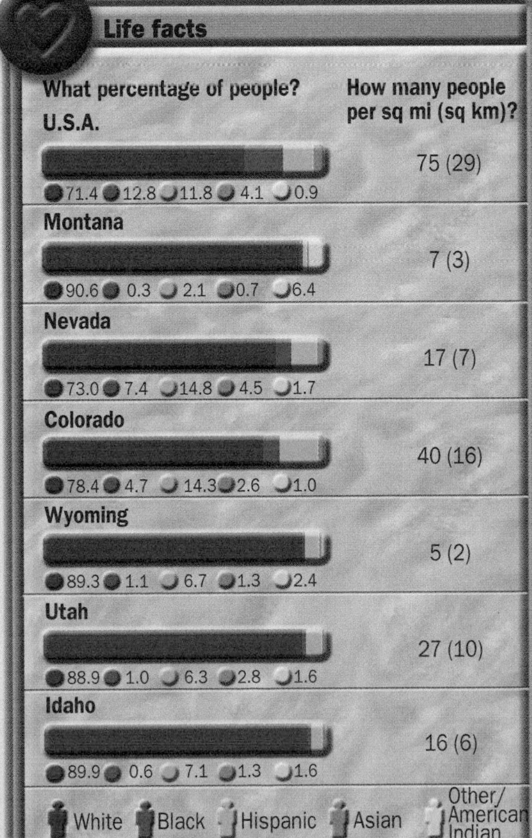

Life facts

What percentage of people?	White	Black	Hispanic	Asian	Other/American Indian	How many people per sq mi (sq km)?
U.S.A.	71.4	12.8	11.8	4.1	0.9	75 (29)
Montana	90.6	0.3	2.1	0.7	6.4	7 (3)
Nevada	73.0	7.4	14.8	4.5	1.7	17 (7)
Colorado	78.4	4.7	14.3	2.6	1.0	40 (16)
Wyoming	89.3	1.1	6.7	1.3	2.4	5 (2)
Utah	88.9	1.0	6.3	2.8	1.6	27 (10)
Idaho	89.9	0.6	7.1	1.3	1.6	16 (6)

Search and find

Montana
State Capital:
Helena B5
Billings B6
Bozeman B5
Butte B5
Great Falls B5
Miles City B7
Missoula B5

Nevada
State Capital:
Carson City . . . D3
Elko D4
Las Vegas E4
Reno D3
Tonopah D4
Winnemucca . . . C4

Colorado
State Capital:
Denver D7
Aspen D6
Boulder D7
Colorado Springs D7
Durango E6
Fort Collins D7
Grand Junction . . D6
Greeley D7
Lamar E7
Pueblo E7

Wyoming
State Capital:
Cheyenne D7
Casper C6
Cody C6
Gillette C7
Jackson C5
Laramie D7
Rock Springs . . . D6

Utah
State Capital:
Salt Lake City . D5
Brigham City . . . D5
Cedar City E5
Ogden D5
Provo D5

Idaho
State Capital:
Boise C4
Idaho Falls C5
Lewiston B4
Pocatello C5
Twin Falls C5

Montana Nevada
Colorado Wyoming
Utah Idaho

United States: West Coast

California, Oregon, Washington

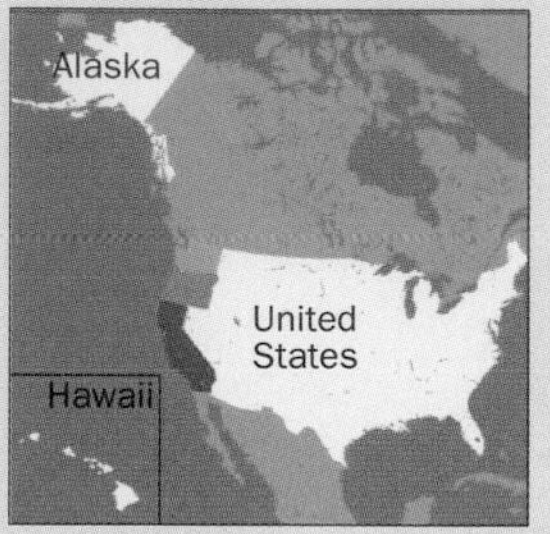
Alaska
United States
Hawaii

San Francisco, California, is one of North America's most beautiful cities. Its steep streets, lined with fine old frame houses, look out over a wide bay, sparkling blue on a fresh spring morning, or shrouded in a white sea mist. Downtown are high-rise office buildings, old waterfronts, and the bustling streets of Chinatown.

South of San Francisco, the climate is dry and warm. Ocean spray crashes over sea lions as they emerge onto sun-baked rocks offshore. Warm sunshine fills the air with the scent of pines. Moving south, highways converge on Los Angeles, the second most populated city and the largest in area in the United States. Freeways cut through sprawling suburbs, often dense with smog, to palm-lined avenues, theme parks, and the film and television studios of Hollywood.

Eastern California takes in the Sierra Nevada mountains, the rock faces of Yosemite, and forests of gigantic sequoia trees. To the southeast lie the arid wildernesses of Death Valley and the Mojave Desert.

To the north of California are the states of Oregon and Washington, with major ports at Portland and Seattle. The economy here depends on technology, fruit and vegetable crops, timber, and fishing. Winds from the Pacific Ocean shed heavy rain and snow on the windward slopes of the Cascade Range. Foggy forests fringe the slopes of snowy peaks, some of them active volcanoes. The whole Pacific coast is a danger zone for earthquakes and volcanic activity.

Water plunges for 2,424 ft (739 m) over Yosemite Falls, swollen by melting snow in the spring. Situated in Yosemite National Park, it is the world's second-highest waterfall.

Mount Rainier towers over Washington, to a height of 14,409 ft (4,392 m) above sea level. It is a volcano that experiences heavy snowfalls.

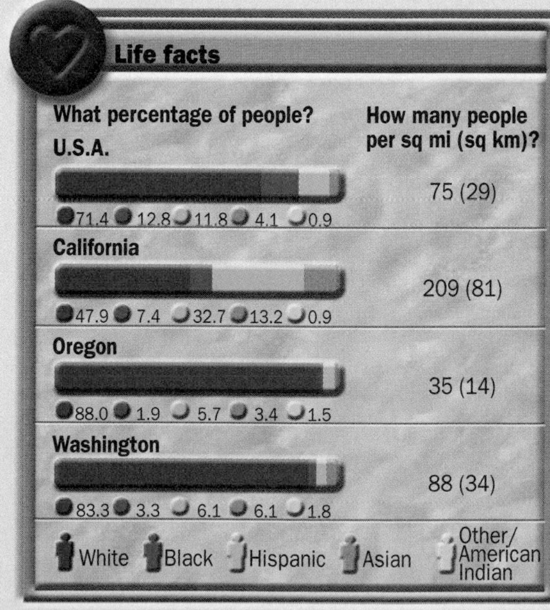
Life facts
What percentage of people?
How many people per sq mi (sq km)?
U.S.A.
71.4 12.8 11.8 4.1 0.9
75 (29)
California
47.9 7.4 32.7 13.2 0.9
209 (81)
Oregon
88.0 1.9 5.7 3.4 1.5
35 (14)
Washington
83.3 3.3 6.1 6.1 1.8
88 (34)
White
Black
Hispanic
Asian
Other/American Indian

DISCOVER MORE

- *The highest temperature ever recorded in the United States—134°F (57°C)—was measured in Death Valley in California on July 10, 1913.*
- *Washington's nickname, the "Evergreen State," comes from the many evergreen trees that grow in the state. It has large areas of thick forests.*

CALIFORNIA REPUBLIC

California

STATE OF OREGON
1859

Oregon

Washington

State facts

	Area sq mi (sq km)	Population	Flower	Tree	Bird
California	158,869 (411,471)	33,871,648	Golden poppy	California redwood	California valley quail
Oregon	97,132 (251,572)	3,421,399	Oregon grape	Douglas fir	Western meadowlark
Washington	70,637 (182,949)	5,894,121	Western rhododendron	Western hemlock	Willow goldfinch

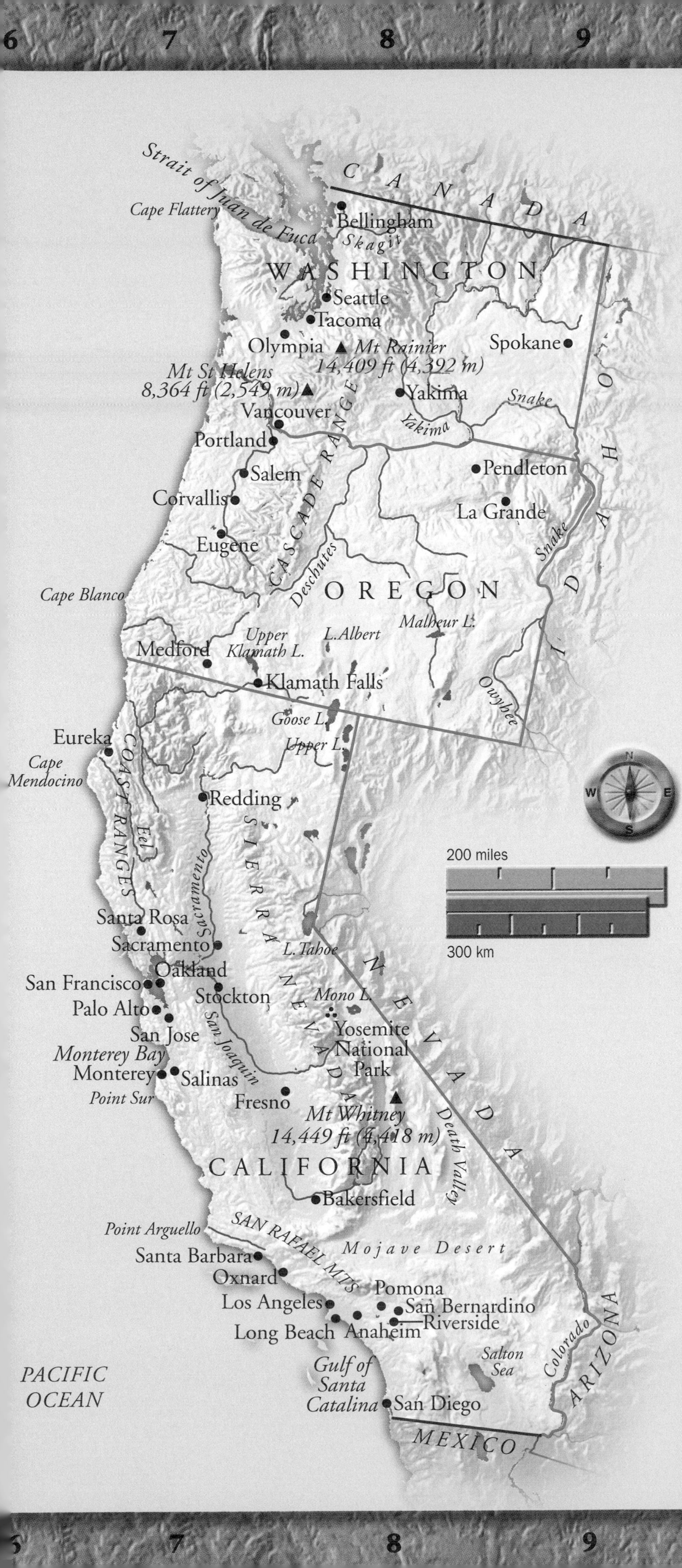

CANADA
Strait of Juan de Fuca
Cape Flattery
Bellingham
Skagit
WASHINGTON
Seattle
Tacoma
Olympia
Mt Rainier 14,409 ft (4,392 m)
Mt St Helens 8,364 ft (2,549 m)
Spokane
Yakima
Vancouver
Portland
Salem
Corvallis
Eugene
CASCADE RANGE
Snake
Yakima
Pendleton
La Grande
Deschutes
OREGON
Cape Blanco
Malheur L.
L. Albert
Upper Klamath L.
Medford
Klamath Falls
Owyhee
IDAHO
Goose L.
Upper L.
Eureka
Cape Mendocino
COAST RANGES
Eel
Redding
SIERRA NEVADA
Sacramento
Santa Rosa
Sacramento
Oakland
San Francisco
Palo Alto
San Jose
Stockton
L. Tahoe
Mono L.
Yosemite National Park
San Joaquin
Monterey Bay
Monterey
Salinas
Point Sur
Fresno
Mt Whitney 14,449 ft (4,418 m)
NEVADA
Death Valley
CALIFORNIA
Bakersfield
Point Arguello
SAN RAFAEL MTS
Mojave Desert
Santa Barbara
Oxnard
Pomona
Los Angeles
San Bernardino
Riverside
Long Beach
Anaheim
Salton Sea
Colorado
ARIZONA
PACIFIC OCEAN
Gulf of Santa Catalina
San Diego
MEXICO

200 miles
300 km

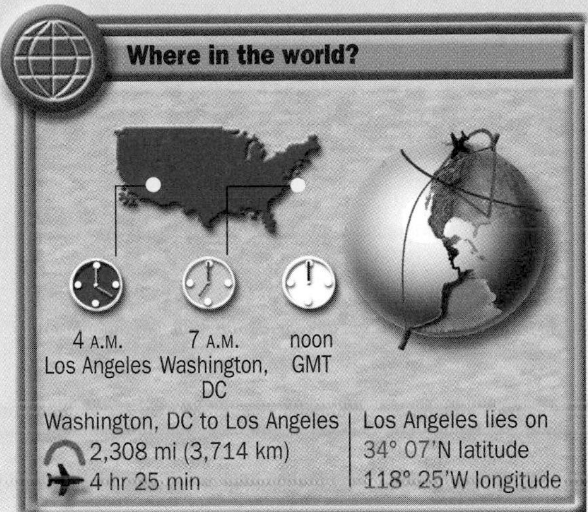

Where in the world?
4 A.M. Los Angeles
7 A.M. Washington, DC
noon GMT
Washington, DC to Los Angeles
2,308 mi (3,714 km)
4 hr 25 min
Los Angeles lies on
34° 07′N latitude
118° 25′W longitude

The blue skies of Oregon are reflected in Crater Lake, the deepest inland body of water in the United States, situated in the Cascade Mountains of Oregon. It was formed nearly 7,000 years ago, when a volcano collapsed inward after a massive eruption.

Search and find

California		Oregon		Washington	
State Capital: Sacramento	E7	*State Capital*: Salem	B7	*State Capital*: Olympia	B8
Anaheim	G8	Corvallis	C7	Bellingham	A8
Bakersfield	F8	Eugene	C7	Seattle	B8
Eureka	D7	Klamath Falls	C7	Spokane	B9
Fresno	E8	La Grande	C9	Tacoma	B8
Long Beach	G8	Medford	C7	Vancouver	B8
Los Angeles	F8	Pendleton	B8	Yakima	B8
Monterey	E7	Portland	B7		
Oakland	E7				
Oxnard	F8				
Palo Alto	E7				
Pomona	F8				
Redding	D7				
Riverside	G8				
Salinas	E7				
San Bernardino	G8				
San Diego	G8				
San Francisco	E7				
San Jose	E7				
Santa Barbara	F7				
Santa Rosa	E7				
Stockton	E7				

United States: Pacific States

ALASKA, HAWAII

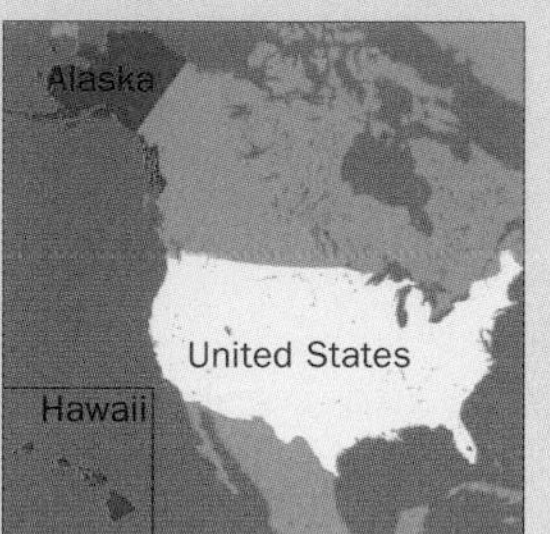
Alaska
United States
Hawaii

EAST MEETS WEST AT THE Bering Strait, where the coastline of Alaska is just 55 mi (90 km) from Asia and the Russian Federation. To the south, the Aleutian Islands emerge from the Pacific Ocean. Alaska has coasts on both the Pacific and Arctic oceans, each full of countless islands, sounds and straits, deltas and bays. Glaciers descend to foggy waters cruised by great whales. Most Alaskans live in the milder south, in cities such as Anchorage. The state's interior is largely a wilderness of snowy forests, icy mountains, and bare tundra, stretching far into the arctic. It is roamed by caribou, wolves, and bears. The far north is home to isolated Inuit communities and the oil workers of Point Barrow. Oil is piped south across the tundra.

The Hawaiian Islands lie in the ocean swell of the mid-Pacific Ocean. Small wonder that surfing was invented here. There are eight major islands. Their original inhabitants are the Hawaiians, a Polynesian people. Today, Hawaii's busy state capital, Honolulu, on the island of Oahu, has been settled by many people from Asia and the mainland United States. Honolulu is a popular tourist destination. The islands are lush and green, surrounded by deep-blue seas. There are brilliantly colored flowers, cascading waterfalls, and palm trees. Sugar cane is Hawaii's most important crop, and pineapples are also grown.

Oil and natural gas provide the state of Alaska with 80 percent of its wealth. A pipeline carries oil across the state from Prudhoe Bay, in the far north, to the southern tanker terminal at Valdez, on Port William Sound.

ARCTIC
CHUKCHI SEA
Point Hope
RUSSIAN FEDERATION
Bering Strait
Nome
Gambell
Norton
St. Lawrence I.
Alakanuk
BERING SEA
Hooper Bay
St. Matthew I.
Nunivak I.
Cape New
St. Paul I.
St. George I.
Unimak I.
Near Is
ALEUTIAN IS
Fox Is
Dutch Harbor
Rat Is
Andreanof Is
Kauai
Mt Kawaikini 5,243 ft (1,598 m)
Kapaa
Puuwai
Lihue
Niihau
Kauai Channel
Oahu
Waialua
Wahiawa
Waipahu
Honolulu
HAW

Kilauea Crater on Hawaii Island belches out red-hot lava and smoke. The volcanic activity that created the Hawaiian islands is still shaping them today.

DISCOVER MORE

- *At 20,320 ft (6,194 m) Mount McKinley, in Alaska's Denali National Park, is the highest peak in North America.*
- *Mount Waialeale on Kauai Island has had 350 days of rain in a single year—which makes it one of the wettest places on Earth.*

Alaska

Hawaii

State facts

	Area sq mi (sq km)	Population	Flower	Tree	Bird
Alaska	615,230 (1,593,446)	626,932	Forget-me-not	Sitka spruce	Willow ptarmigan
Hawaii	6,459 (16,729)	1,211,537	Yellow hibiscus	Kukui (candlenut)	Hawaiian goose

6
7
8
9
10
11

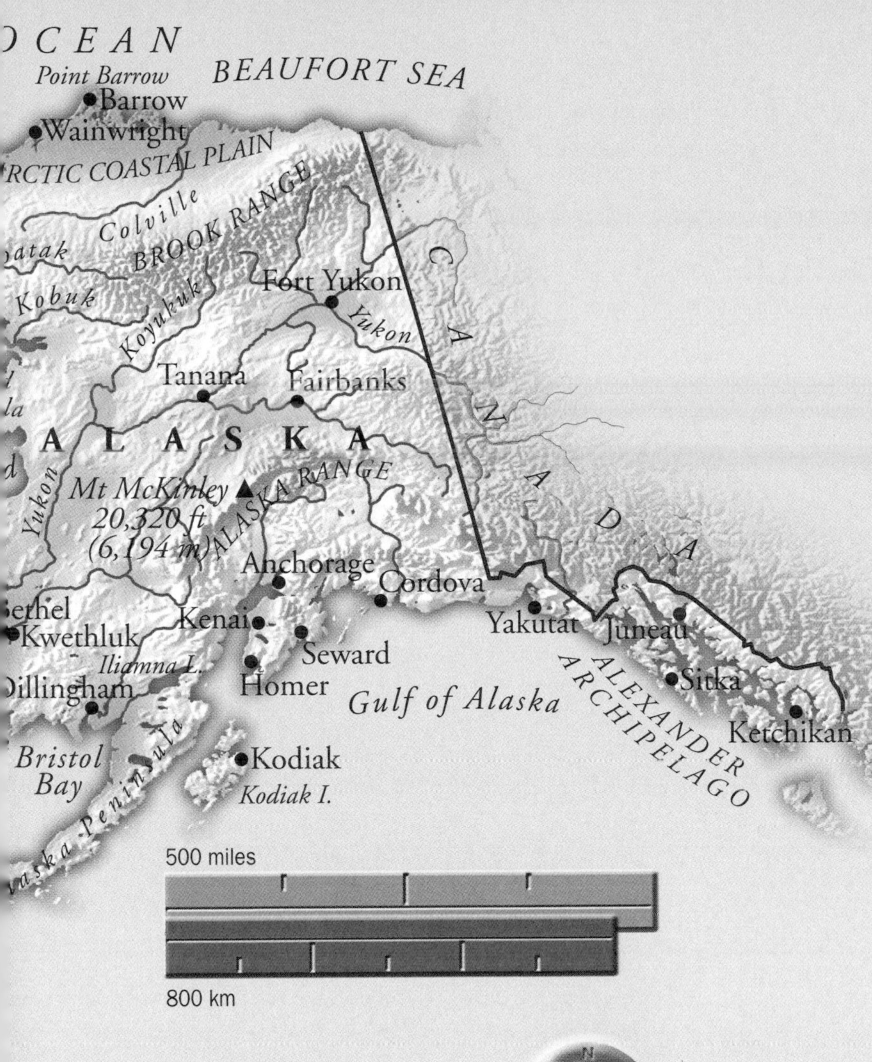

OCEAN
Point Barrow
Barrow
BEAUFORT SEA
Wainwright
ARCTIC COASTAL PLAIN
Colville
BROOK RANGE
Kobuk
Koyukuk
Fort Yukon
Yukon
CANADA
Tanana
Fairbanks
ALASKA
Yukon
Mt McKinley
20,320 ft
(6,194 m)
ALASKA RANGE
Anchorage
Cordova
Bethel
Kwethluk
Kenai
Iliamna L.
Seward
Homer
Yakutat
Juneau
Sitka
Ketchikan
Dillingham
Gulf of Alaska
ALEXANDER ARCHIPELAGO
Bristol Bay
Alaska Peninsula
Kodiak
Kodiak I.
500 miles
800 km

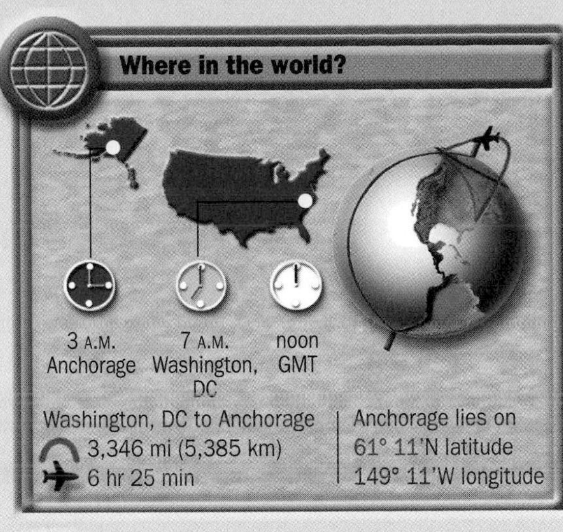

Where in the world?
3 A.M.
Anchorage
7 A.M.
Washington, DC
noon
GMT
Washington, DC to Anchorage
3,346 mi (5,385 km)
6 hr 25 min
Anchorage lies on
61° 11'N latitude
149° 11'W longitude

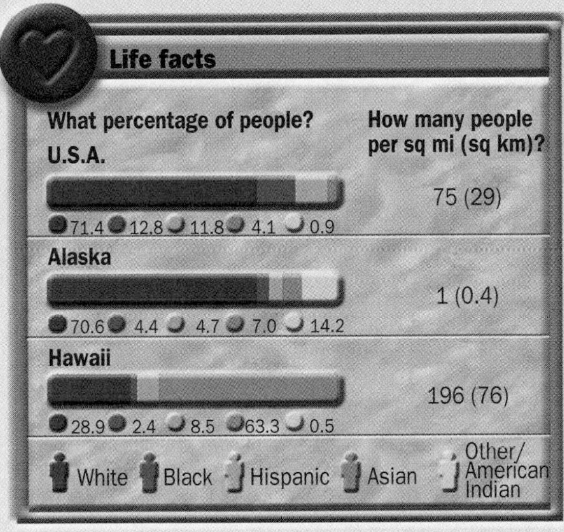

Life facts
What percentage of people?
How many people per sq mi (sq km)?
U.S.A.
71.4 12.8 11.8 4.1 0.9
75 (29)
Alaska
70.6 4.4 4.7 7.0 14.2
1 (0.4)
Hawaii
28.9 2.4 8.5 63.3 0.5
196 (76)
White
Black
Hispanic
Asian
Other/ American Indian

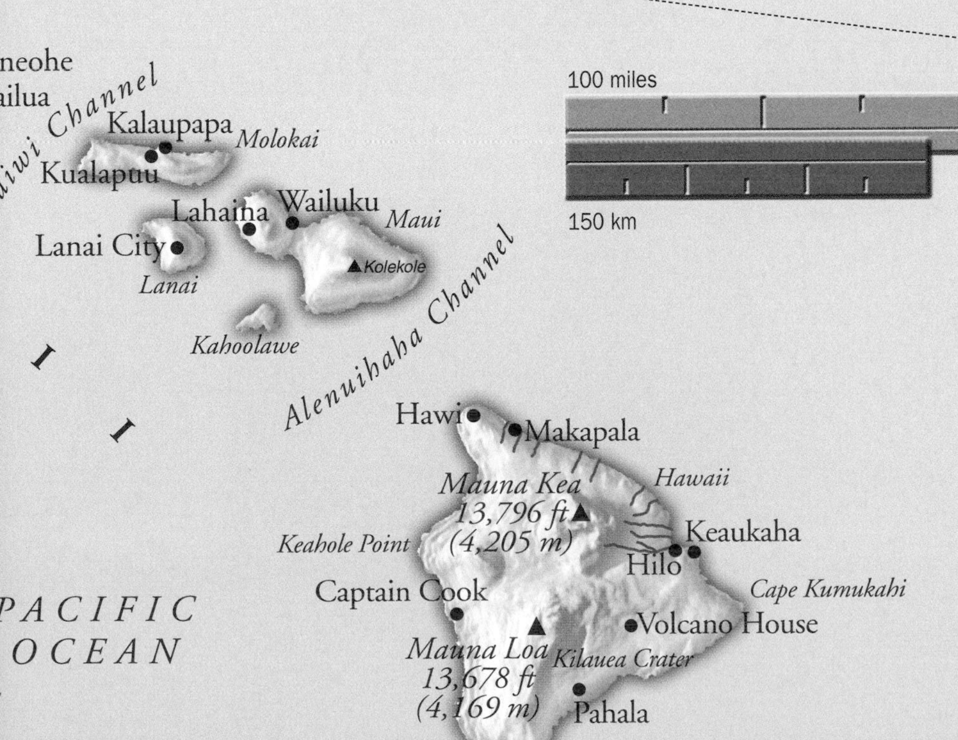

Kaneohe
Kailua
Kaiwi Channel
Kalaupapa
Molokai
Kualapuu
Lahaina
Wailuku
Maui
Lanai City
Kolekole
Lanai
Kahoolawe
Alenuihaha Channel
100 miles
150 km
Hawi
Makapala
Mauna Kea
13,796 ft
(4,205 m)
Hawaii
Keahole Point
Keaukaha
Hilo
Captain Cook
Cape Kumukahi
PACIFIC OCEAN
Volcano House
Mauna Loa
13,678 ft
(4,169 m)
Kilauea Crater
Pahala
Ka Lea

Search and find

Alaska		Hawaii	
State Capital:		*State Capital*:	
Juneau	C9	Honolulu	E6
Alakanuk	B6	Captain Cook	G8
Anchorage	B7	Hawi	F8
Barrow	A7	Hilo	G8
Bethel	C7	Kailua	E6
Cordova	C7	Kalaupapa	E7
Dillingham	C7	Kaneohe	E6
Dutch Harbor	D6	Kapaa	D5
Fairbanks	B7	Keaukaha	G8
Fort Yukon	A7	Kualapuu	E7
Gambell	B6	Lahaina	F7
Homer	C7	Lanai City	F7
Hooper Bay	B6	Lihue	E5
Kenai	C7	Makapala	F8
Ketchikan	C9	Pahala	G8
Kodiak	C7	Puuwai	E4
Kwethluk	C6	Volcano House	G8
Nome	B6	Wahiawa	E6
Point Hope	A6	Waialua	E6
Seward	C7	Wailuku	F7
Sitka	C8	Waipahu	E6
Tanana	B7		
Wainwright	A6		
Yakutat	C8		

Canada

Canada

CANADA STRETCHES NORTH from the Great Lakes to the Arctic Ocean, taking in broad bands of treeless tundra, forests of spruce and birch, and in the milder south, sugar maple. It is a land of lakes and rivers, big skies, and empty spaces. The west rises to a series of high mountain ranges, including the northern limits of the Rockies. In the east, ice has carved out the sweep of Hudson Bay.

Canada is the world's second-largest country, but its population is only 11 percent of that of the United States, its neighbor to the south and west. Because of the icy northern climate, about three-quarters of all Canadians live in towns and cities near the southern border. The close ties between Canada and the United States stretch back to their shared history.

Canadians, however, are an independent-minded people with a strong sense of their own identity. That identity varies greatly from one part of Canada to another, from English-speaking Toronto to French-speaking Montreal, from the fishing villages of Newfoundland on the east coast to the central prairies, and from the city streets of Vancouver in the west to the Inuit settlements of the Arctic north.

DISCOVER MORE

- *At 1,820 ft (555 m), Toronto's CN Tower, on the shores of Lake Ontario, is the world's tallest telecommunications tower.*
- *Compass needles do not point due north, but spin toward a point called the Magnetic North Pole, which is located in the Canadian Arctic. Its precise position varies from year to year, reflecting changes in the earth's magnetic field.*

The Royal Canadian Mounted Police force has a history dating back to 1873. Mounties still wear their traditional uniform for ceremonial occasions.

Country facts

	Area sq mi (sq km)	Population	Language	Religion	Currency
Canada	3,851,800 (9,976,162)	31,006,347	English/French	Catholic/Protestant	Dollar

Canada

6 7 8 9 10 11
A B C D E F G
Ellesmere I.
Greenland (DENMARK)
Devon I.
Baffin Bay
Baffin I.
Davis Strait
NAVUT
Foxe Basin
Iqaluit
Southampton I.
Hudson Strait
LABRADOR SEA
Coats I.
Mansel I.
Ungava Peninsula
ADA
Churchill
Hudson Bay
NEWFOUNDLAND
Gander
Newfoundland
St. John's
Belcher Is
James Bay
QUEBEC
Severn
Albany
Fort Albany
PRINCE EDWARD I.
Charlottetown
NEW BRUNSWICK
NOVA SCOTIA
ONTARIO
Quebec
L. Nipigon
Fredericton
Halifax
Thunder Bay
Montreal
L. Superior
ATLANTIC OCEAN
Ottawa
L. Huron
Toronto
L. Ontario
L. Erie

The Canadian national parliament meets in Ottawa, a city in Ontario with about 314,000 inhabitants. The parliament buildings tower above the Ottawa River.

Where in the world?

7 A.M. Washington, DC — 7 A.M. Ottawa — noon GMT

Washington, DC to Ottawa
455 mi (732 km)
55 min

Ottawa lies on
45° 25'N latitude
75° 40'W longitude

Life facts

	How long do people live?	How many people in 100 own cars?
U.S.A.	76 years	48
Canada	79 years	43

Dense fur, covered by long hair, keeps the musk ox warm in the Canadian Arctic. It is not a true ox, but a relative of sheep and goats. However, at 1,100 lb (500 kg), it is no lightweight.

Search and find

Canada

Capital: Ottawa	E8	Prince George	D4
Calgary	E5	Prince Rupert	D3
Charlottetown	E9	Quebec	E8
Churchill	D6	Regina	E5
Dawson	C4	Saskatoon	E5
Edmonton	D5	St. John's	D10
Fort Albany	E7	Thunder Bay	E6
Fredericton	E9	Toronto	F8
Gander	D10	Vancouver	E4
Halifax	E9	Victoria	E4
Iqaluit	C8	Whitehorse	C4
Medicine Hat	E5	Winnipeg	E6
Montreal	E8	Yellowknife	C5

The Canadian Rockies form some of the most spectacular mountain scenery in the world. The jagged rocks and snowcapped peaks attract many climbers.

Canada: The East

QUEBEC, ONTARIO, NEWFOUNDLAND, NEW BRUNSWICK, NOVA SCOTIA, PRINCE EDWARD ISLAND

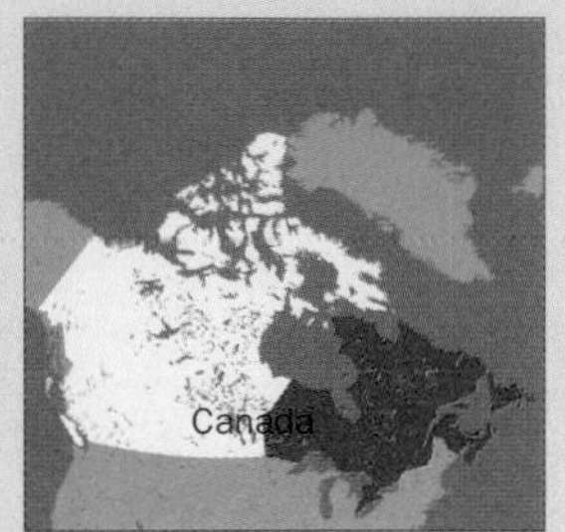
Canada

IT'S WINTER IN SNOWY OTTAWA. Skaters link arms on the frozen waters of the Rideau Canal, their breath turning to mist in the cold air. Some stop to warm themselves with a cup of hot chocolate. On the skyline are the towers of the parliament buildings, for Ottawa is the capital of Canada.

The biggest city is Toronto, in Ontario. A center of business, it bristles with skyscrapers, rising from the shores of Lake Ontario. Montreal is a historic city on the St. Lawrence River. It is in Quebec province, which extends northward along Hudson Bay. Most Canadians live in the southeast of the country.

Parts of the St. Lawrence have been turned into canals to form a seaway that links the Great Lakes with the Atlantic Ocean. The seaway passes through farmland and woods of maple and birch, meeting the sea opposite the foggy island of Newfoundland. Labrador, on the mainland, is a region of bogs, lakes, and forests. Southward lie three small provinces of farms and forests, known as the Maritimes—Nova Scotia, New Brunswick, and Prince Edward Island.

Canada's eastern provinces are populated by First Peoples such as the Innu and Mohawk, and by people of Asian, African, and European descent. The Europeans are divided between English speakers, including many of Scottish and Irish descent, and French speakers. Most French Canadians live in Quebec Province and parts of New Brunswick.

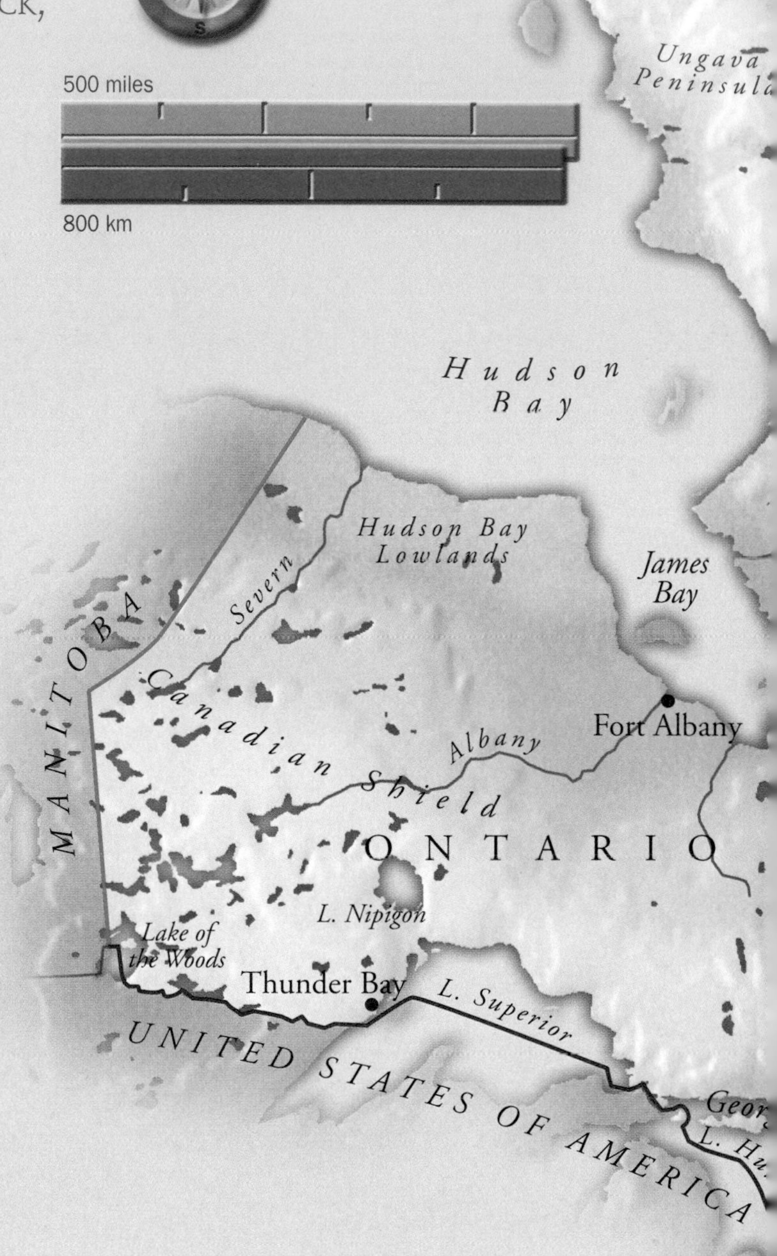
500 miles
800 km
Hudson Bay
Ungava Peninsula
Hudson Bay Lowlands
James Bay
Severn
MANITOBA
Canadian Shield
Albany
Fort Albany
ONTARIO
L. Nipigon
Lake of the Woods
Thunder Bay
L. Superior
UNITED STATES OF AMERICA
L. Huron
Windsor

DISCOVER MORE

- *The largest of Canada's provinces is Quebec, which is slightly bigger than Alaska. The smallest is Prince Edward Island, which is about the size of Delaware.*
- *The Bay of Fundy between New Brunswick and Nova Scotia experiences the highest tides in the world. The record stands at 54 ft (16.6 m).*

Quebec

Ontario

Newfoundland

New Brunswick

Nova Scotia

Prince Edward Island

Province facts

	Area sq mi (sq km)	Population	Flower
Quebec	594,860 (1,540,687)	7,138,795	White garden lily
Ontario	412,581 (1,068,585)	10,753,573	White trillium
Newfoundland	156,649 (405,721)	551,792	Pitcher plant
New Brunswick	28,355 (73,439)	738,133	Violet
Nova Scotia	21,425 (55,490)	909,282	Trailing arbutus
Prince Edward Island	2,185 (5,659)	134,557	Lady's slipper

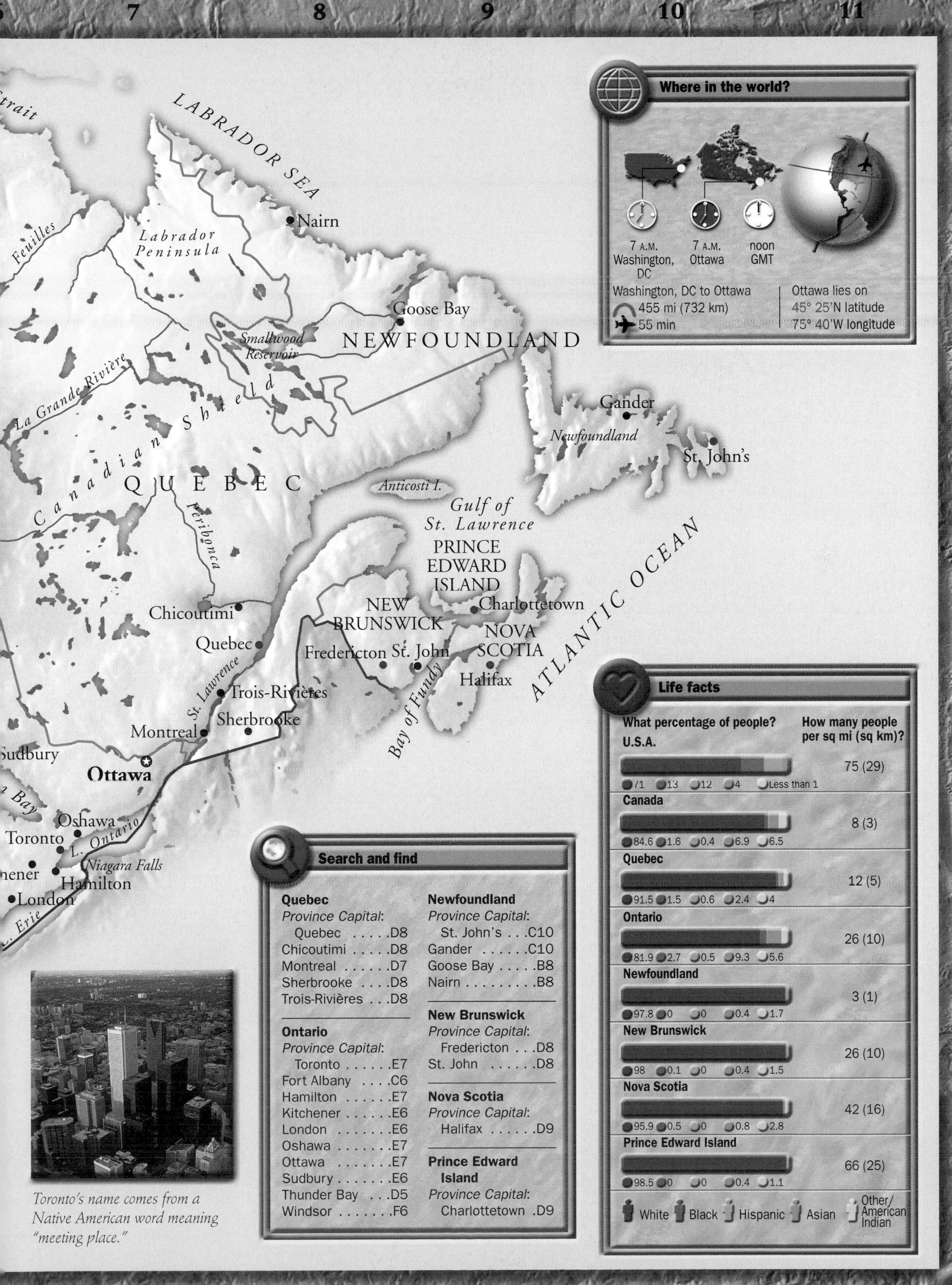

LABRADOR SEA
Strait
Nairn
Feuilles
Labrador Peninsula
Goose Bay
Smallwood Reservoir
NEWFOUNDLAND
La Grande Rivière
Canadian Shield
Gander
Newfoundland
St. John's
QUEBEC
Anticosti I.
Gulf of St. Lawrence
Peribonca
PRINCE EDWARD ISLAND
Charlottetown
ATLANTIC OCEAN
Chicoutimi
NEW BRUNSWICK
NOVA SCOTIA
Quebec
Fredericton
St. John
Halifax
St. Lawrence
Trois-Rivières
Bay of Fundy
Sherbrooke
Montreal
Sudbury
Ottawa
Oshawa
Toronto
L. Ontario
Niagara Falls
Hamilton
London
L. Erie
Where in the world?
7 A.M. Washington, DC
7 A.M. Ottawa
noon GMT
Washington, DC to Ottawa
455 mi (732 km)
55 min
Ottawa lies on
45° 25'N latitude
75° 40'W longitude
Life facts
What percentage of people?
How many people per sq mi (sq km)?
U.S.A. 71 13 12 4 Less than 1 — 75 (29)
Canada 84.6 1.6 0.4 6.9 6.5 — 8 (3)
Quebec 91.5 1.5 0.6 2.4 4 — 12 (5)
Ontario 81.9 2.7 0.5 9.3 5.6 — 26 (10)
Newfoundland 97.8 0 0 0.4 1.7 — 3 (1)
New Brunswick 98 0.1 0 0.4 1.5 — 26 (10)
Nova Scotia 95.9 0.5 0 0.8 2.8 — 42 (16)
Prince Edward Island 98.5 0 0 0.4 1.1 — 66 (25)
White Black Hispanic Asian Other/American Indian
Search and find
Quebec
Province Capital:
Quebec D8
Chicoutimi D8
Montreal D7
Sherbrooke D8
Trois-Rivières . . .D8
Ontario
Province Capital:
Toronto E7
Fort Albany C6
Hamilton E7
Kitchener E6
London E6
Oshawa E7
Ottawa E7
Sudbury E6
Thunder Bay . . .D5
Windsor F6
Newfoundland
Province Capital:
St. John's . . .C10
Gander C10
Goose Bay B8
Nairn B8
New Brunswick
Province Capital:
Fredericton . . .D8
St. John D8
Nova Scotia
Province Capital:
Halifax D9
Prince Edward Island
Province Capital:
Charlottetown .D9

Toronto's name comes from a Native American word meaning "meeting place."

Canada: The North and West

Nunavut, Northwest Territories, British Columbia, Alberta, Saskatchewan, Manitoba, Yukon Territory

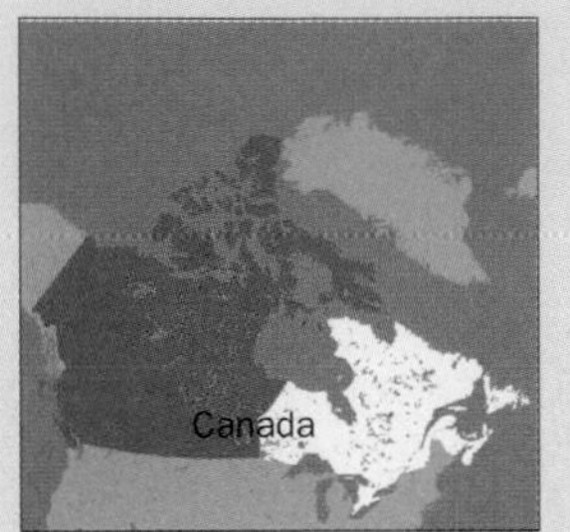
Canada

A SEA OF WHEAT RIPPLING IN THE wind awaits the line of harvesters. Storage elevators line the railroad track. These are Canada's prairie provinces—Manitoba, Saskatchewan, and Alberta—and they help to feed the world. Cattle graze grasslands, and large cities have grown up based on farming, food processing, and the oil wealth of Alberta. Towering over the Alberta landscape are the Canadian Rockies, a breathtaking panorama of high peaks and ridges.

British Columbia is a land of misty forests and mountains, bordering the Pacific Ocean. The province's biggest city is Vancouver, a major seaport and industrial center.

Northern Canada is a sparsely populated land of snowy mountains and dark conifer forests, where beavers build dams and loons call across lonely lakes. In the far north, beyond the frozen tundra, thousands of islands are locked in permanent ice. The wilderness is divided into territories instead of provinces. They are the Yukon, in the western mountains, Northwest Territories, around Great Slave Lake, and Nunavut, an Inuit homeland that stretches from Coppermine to Ellesmere and Baffin islands.

First Peoples of the region include the Inuit of Nunavut, the Déné of the northern forests, the Kwakiutl of British Columbia, and the Cree and Ojibway of the prairies. Vancouver has many people of British descent and is home to a large Asian population, while many farmers on the prairies are of Ukrainian, German, or Scandinavian descent.

DISCOVER MORE

- *Nunavut territory occupies one-fifth of all Canada, yet it is home to just 26,000 people—and quite a few polar bears.*
- *The Saskatchewan River takes its name from the Cree language.* Kis-is-ska-tche-wan *means "swift-flowing." Saskatchewan is now the name of the whole province.*

Province facts

	Area sq mi (sq km)	Population	Flower
Nunavut	818,959 (2,121,104)	26,000	Arctic poppy
Northwest Territories	503,951 (1,305,233)	39,672	Mountain avens
British Columbia	365,948 (947,805)	3,724,500	Pacific dogwood
Alberta	255,287 (661,193)	2,696,826	Wild rose
Saskatchewan	251,866 (652,333)	990,237	Prairie lily
Manitoba	250,947 (649,953)	1,113,898	Pasqueflower
Yukon Territory	186,661 (483,452)	30,766	Fireweed

Nunavut

Northwest Territories

British Columbia

500 miles
1,000 km
Ellesmere I.
Axel Heiberg I.
Bathurst I.
Devon I.
Baffin Bay
Prince of Wales I.
Baffin I.
Davis Strait
Cambridge Bay (Iqaluktuutiak)
N U N A V U T
Foxe Basin
Iqaluit
Southampton I.
Coral Harbour (Salliq)
Hudson Strait
Dubawnt L.
Rankin Inlet (Kangiqtiniq)
Coats I.
Mansel I.
Arviat
Hudson Bay

Churchill
Churchill
Nelson
MANITOBA
ONTARIO
L. Winnipegosis
L. Winnipeg
L. Manitoba
Winnipeg
Brandon

Where in the world?
7 A.M. Washington, DC
4 A.M. Vancouver
noon GMT
Washington, DC to Vancouver
2,361 mi (3,799 km)
4 hr 30 min
Vancouver lies on
49° 15′N latitude
123° 05′W longitude

The skyscrapers of downtown Vancouver rise from a narrow strip of land.

Life facts
What percentage of people?
How many people per sq mi (sq km)?
U.S.A.
71 13 12 4 Less than 1
75 (29)
Canada
84.6 1.6 0.4 6.9 6.5
8 (3)
British Columbia
76.9 0.3 0.3 14.7 7.8
10 (4)
Alberta
82.1 0.6 0.4 6.8 10.1
11 (4)
Saskatchewan
81.7 0.2 0.1 1.7 16.3
4 (2)
Manitoba
78.8 0.7 0.3 4.6 15.6
4 (2)
Yukon Territory
80.4 0.1 0.1 1.8 17.6
0.2 (0.06)
White Black Hispanic Asian Other/American Indian
Nunavut and Northwest Territories—not available

Search and find

Nunavut
Territory Capital:
Iqaluit D9
Arviat D7
Cambridge Bay (Iqaluktuutiak) .C6
Coral Harbour (Salliq) D8
Kugluktuk (Coppermine) .C5
Rankin Inlet (Kangiqtiniq) . .D6

Northwest Territories
Territory Capital:
Yellowknife . . .D5
Fort Resolution .D5
Fort Smith D5
Inuvik C4
Norman Wells . .C5

British Columbia
Province Capital:
Victoria F4
Hazelton E4
Kamloops F4
Prince George . .E4
Prince Rupert . . .E4
Vancouver F4

Alberta
Province Capital:
Edmonton E5
Calgary F5
Grande Prairie . .E5
Lethbridge F5
Medicine Hat . . .F5
Peace River E5

Saskatchewan
Province Capital:
Regina F6
Moose Jaw F6
Prince Albert . . .F6
Saskatoon F6

Manitoba
Province Capital:
Winnipeg F7
Brandon F7
Churchill E7

Yukon Territory
Territory Capital:
Whitehorse . . .D4
Dawson C4

Alberta Saskatchewan

Manitoba Yukon Territory

A B C D E F G

Mexico

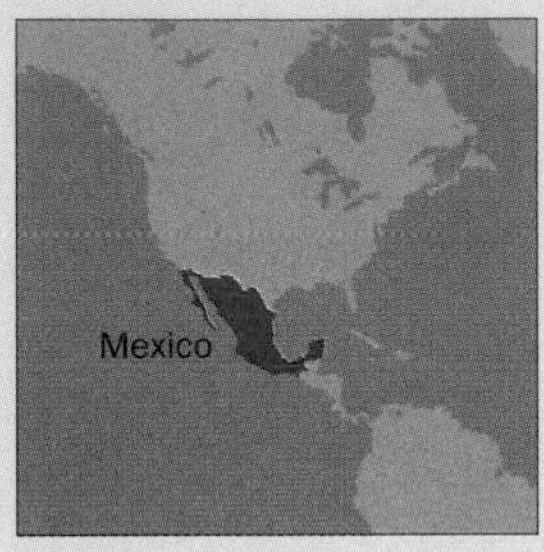
Mexico

A COUNTRY BUS strains its way up a rough mountain road, its windshield bordered with colored lights. Lightning forks across the dark sky, and heavy rain drums on the roof. The bus pulls into a small town square, in front of an ornate, twin-towered church and dripping palm trees. The next morning, the sun shines brightly in a clear blue sky and the intense heat returns. This is market day. There are crates of oranges for sale, heaps of onions and fiery chili peppers, brightly colored bottled drinks, and tasty snacks wrapped in pancakes called *tortillas*.

Mexico's national flag shows an eagle on a cactus grasping a snake, a suitable emblem for this land of deserts and volcanoes. The flag recalls an old myth of the Aztec people, who believed that this sight was a sign from their gods to start building the city of Tenochtitlán. In 1521 the Spanish invaded and destroyed the Aztec civilization. Today, most Mexicans are of Spanish, indigenous, or mixed descent. Tenochtitlán has become the vast sprawl of Mexico City, one of the world's biggest, liveliest, and most polluted cities—which is not surprising, since the city has more than 130,000 factories. Mexico's industry is based on oil, mining, machinery, textiles, and foods.

UNITED STATES OF
Tijuana
Mexicali
Ensenada
Ciudad Juárez
Guadalupe I.
Baja California
Gulf of California
Cedros I.
Eugenie Point
Hermosillo
Chihuahua
SIERRA MADRE OCCIDENTAL
Ciudad Obregón
MEXIC
Torreón
Culiacán
Durango
Mazatlán
PACIFIC OCEAN
Marías Is
Tepic
Guadalajara
Cape Corrientes
L. Chapa
Paricu
Volca
9,213
(2,808
Socorro I.

DISCOVER MORE

- *In 1943, a new volcano suddenly appeared in Mexico. It was given the name Paricutín. Red-hot lava continued to pour out of the ground on this spot. Within a year the volcano had risen to more than 980 ft (300 m) high.*

Flowers add color to a market in southern Mexico. The sellers are Zapotecs, a people who live by farming the slopes and valleys of the Southern Sierra Madre Mountains.

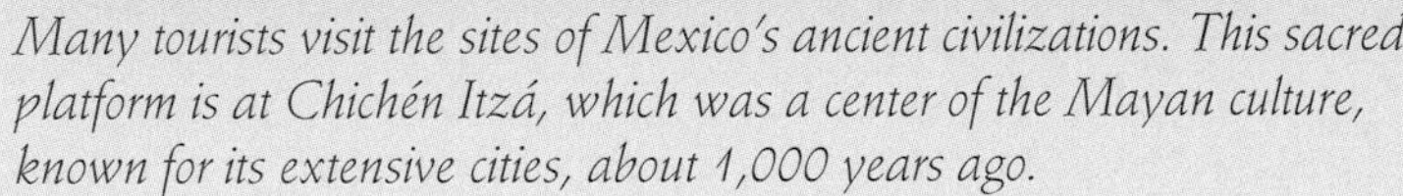

Many tourists visit the sites of Mexico's ancient civilizations. This sacred platform is at Chichén Itzá, which was a center of the Mayan culture, known for its extensive cities, about 1,000 years ago.

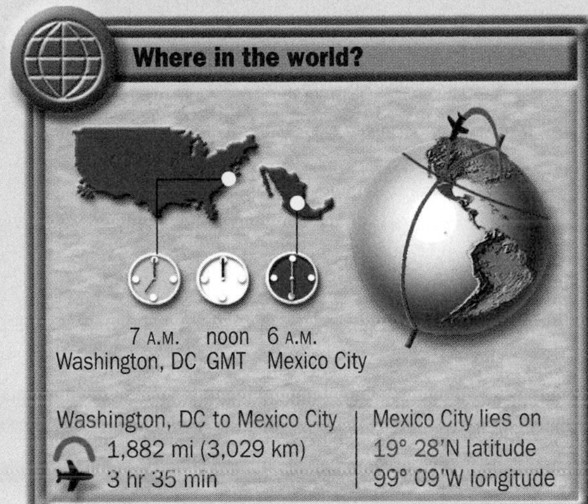
Where in the world?
7 A.M.
Washington, DC
noon
GMT
6 A.M.
Mexico City
Washington, DC to Mexico City
1,882 mi (3,029 km)
3 hr 35 min
Mexico City lies on
19° 28'N latitude
99° 09'W longitude

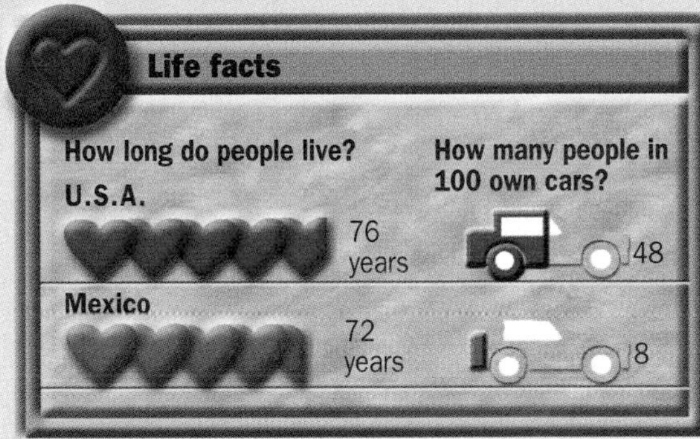
Life facts
How long do people live?
U.S.A.
76 years
Mexico
72 years
How many people in 100 own cars?
48
8

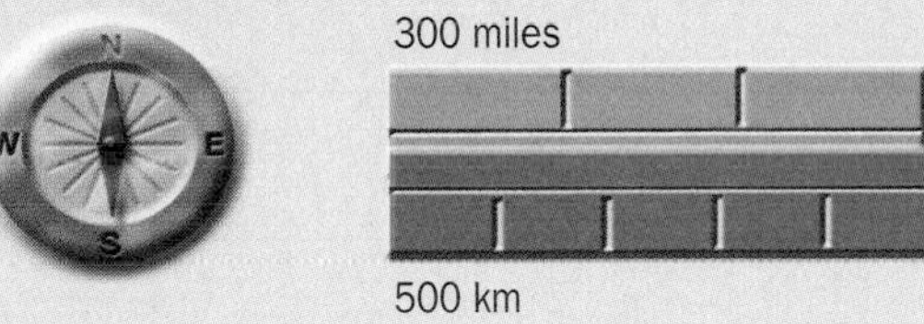
N
W
E
S
300 miles
500 km

A M E R I C A
Nuevo Laredo
Monterrey
Matamoros
SIERRA MADRE ORIENTAL
GULF OF MEXICO
San Luis Potosí
Tampico
Aguascalientes
León
Bay of Campeche
Orizaba 18,701 ft (5,700 m)
Morelia
Mexico City
Puebla
Veracruz
Mérida
Cancún
Cozumel I.
Chichén Itzá
Yucatán Peninsula
Terminos Lagoon
Villahermosa
Coatzacoalcos
Oaxaca
Acapulco
SIERRA MADRE DEL SUR
Gulf of Tehuantepec
GUATEMALA
BELIZE

Search and find

Mexico		Mazatlán	D5
Capital:		Mérida	D9
Mexico City	E7	Mexicali	B3
Acapulco	E7	Monterrey	C6
Aguascalientes	D6	Morelia	E6
Cancún	D9	Nuevo Laredo	C7
Chihuahua	C5	Oaxaca	E7
Ciudad Juárez	B5	Puebla	E7
Ciudad Obregón	C4	Saltillo	D6
Coatzacoalcos	E8	San Luis Potosí	D6
Culiacán	C5	Tampico	D7
Durango	D5	Tepic	D5
Ensenada	B3	Tijuana	B3
Guadalajara	E6	Torreón	D6
Hermosillo	C4	Veracruz	E7
León	D6	Villahermosa	E8
Matamoros	C7		

Mexico

Country facts

	Area sq mi (sq km)	Population	Language	Religion	Currency
Mexico	756,066 (1,958,211)	100,294,036	Spanish	Catholic	New Peso

Central America

Nicaragua, Honduras, Guatemala, Panama, Costa Rica, Belize, El Salvador

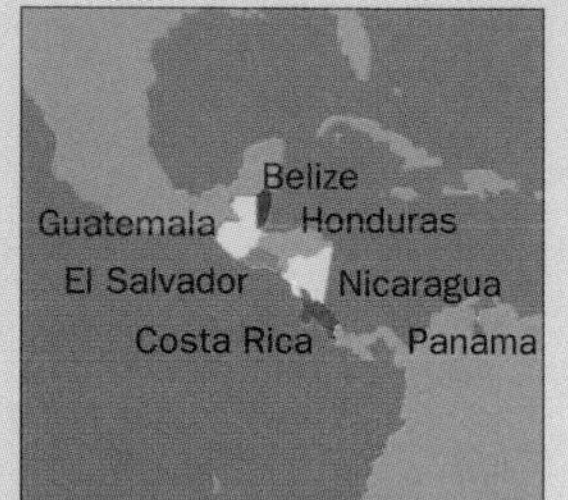
Belize
Guatemala
Honduras
El Salvador
Nicaragua
Costa Rica
Panama

A Mayan woman, her black, shiny hair tied in a single braid, kneels in front of a tree. A strap tied around her waist is joined to a loom, lengths of thread attached by a bar to a tree branch. In and out of the threads she passes a wooden shuttle, weaving patterns of brilliant scarlet and blue stripes. She is making a loose shirt called a *huipil*, to wear in the Holy Week procession before Easter. Each Guatemalan village has its own traditional weaving patterns.

The seven small countries of Central America are lands of rugged mountains, lakes, tropical forests, and steamy coastal plains, producing coffee, bananas, and sugarcane. Central America lies in an earthquake zone, and its eastern shores are regularly battered by hurricanes. The region's inhabitants are mostly descended from indigenous peoples and from the Spanish, who conquered these lands in the 1500s. There are also people of African descent. Spanish is the most common language.

MEXICO
Belize City
Belmopan
BELIZE
Gulf of Honduras
La Ceiba
San Pedro Sula
Patuca
HONDURAS
Volcán Tajmulco 13,845 ft (4,220 m)
GUATEMALA
Chichicastenango
Motagua
Quetzaltenango
Guatemala City
Tegucigalpa
Santa Ana
EL SALVADOR
San Salvador
San Miguel
NICA
Chinandega
León
L. Managua
Managua
L. Nicaragu
PACIFIC OCEAN

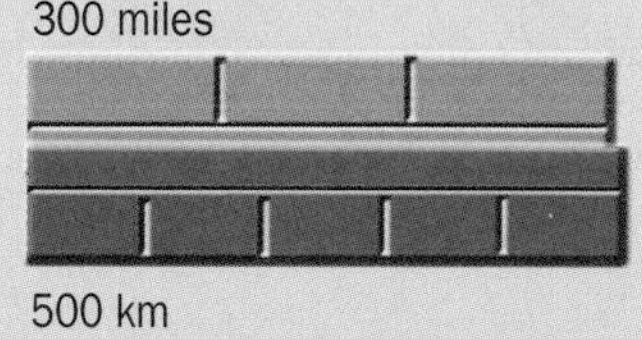
300 miles
500 km

DISCOVER MORE

- *The Panama Canal is one of the world's engineering marvels. It is 40 mi (64 km) long and cuts through the continent at its narrowest part. Opened in 1914, it soon became one of the world's most important shipping routes, linking the Atlantic and Pacific oceans.*
- *Where can you see the Pacific and Atlantic oceans at the same time? One such spot—when the clouds permit—is the volcanic crater of Irazú, in Costa Rica, 11,260 ft (3,432 m) above sea level.*

The great cinder cone of the Santa Ana volcano towers over the landscape of western El Salvador.

Nicaragua

Honduras

Guatemala

Panama

Costa Rica

Belize

El Salvador

A Mayan weaver passes her shuttle through the stretched threads of a backstrap loom in the market town of Chichicastenango, north of Guatemala City.

Mosquito Coast
GUA
Grande
Mosquito Coast
CARIBBEAN SEA
A RICA
Alajuela
Limón
San José
Colón
Panama Canal
Panama City
PANAMA
David
Gulf of Panama
Azuero Peninsula
Coiba I.
COLOMBIA

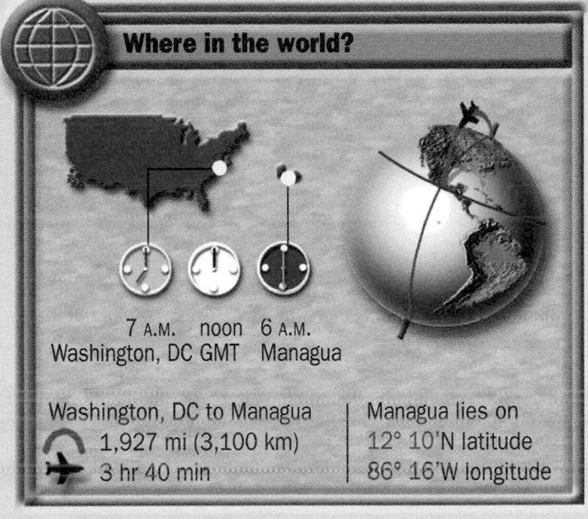

Where in the world?
7 A.M. Washington, DC
noon GMT
6 A.M. Managua
Washington, DC to Managua
1,927 mi (3,100 km)
3 hr 40 min
Managua lies on
12° 10'N latitude
86° 16'W longitude

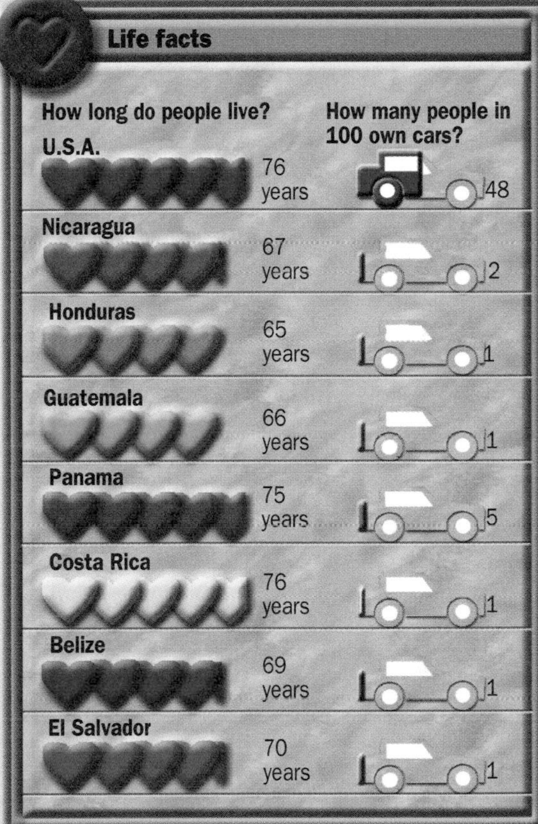

Life facts
How long do people live?
How many people in 100 own cars?
U.S.A. 76 years 48
Nicaragua 67 years 2
Honduras 65 years 1
Guatemala 66 years 1
Panama 75 years 5
Costa Rica 76 years 1
Belize 69 years 1
El Salvador 70 years 1

Search and find

Nicaragua
Capital: Managua D5
Chinandega C5
León D5

Honduras
Capital:
Tegucigalpa . .C5
La Ceiba B5
San Pedro Sula .B5

Guatemala
Capital:
Guatemala City C4
Chichicastenango C3
Quetzaltenango .C3

Panama
Capital: Panama City .E8
Colón D8
David E7

Costa Rica
Capital:
San José D6
Alajuela D6
Limón D7

Belize
Capital:
Belmopan B4
Belize City A4

El Salvador
Capital:
San Salvador .C4
San Miguel C5
Santa Ana C4

Country facts

	Area sq mi (sq km)	Population	Language	Religion	Currency
Nicaragua	50,893 (131,813)	4,717,132	Spanish	Catholic	Córdoba
Honduras	43,278 (112,090)	5,997,327	Spanish	Catholic	Lempira
Guatemala	42,042 (108,889)	11,800,000	Spanish	Catholic	Quetzal
Panama	30,193 (78,200)	2,778,526	Spanish	Catholic	Balboa/US Dollar
Costa Rica	19,730 (51,101)	3,674,490	Spanish	Catholic	Colón
Belize	8,865 (22,960)	235,789	English/Creole	Catholic	Dollar
El Salvador	8,124 (21,041)	5,839,079	Spanish	Catholic	Colón

Caribbean Islands

CUBA, DOMINICAN REP., HAITI, BAHAMAS, JAMAICA, TRINIDAD & TOBAGO, DOMINICA, ST. LUCIA, ANTIGUA & BARBUDA, BARBADOS, ST. VINCENT & THE GRENADINES, GRENADA, ST. KITTS & NEVIS

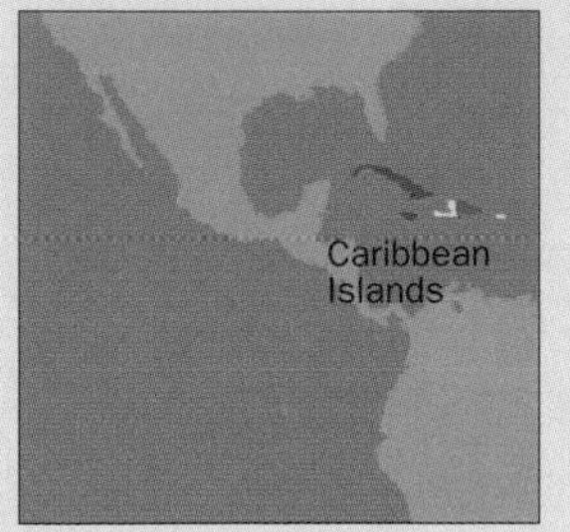
Caribbean Islands

THE CARIBBEAN SEA IS A western arm of the Atlantic Ocean, cradling chains of coral reefs and palm-fringed tropical islands; some are steep volcanoes blanketed in lush, green vegetation. The region is a mixture of peoples and cultures. Some islands have a predominantly Hispanic heritage, while others have African heritage. There are Asian and European minorities. Languages include Spanish and dialects of English, French, and Dutch.

Cuba is the largest island. Cubans love Latin dance music, such as salsa, and sports such as baseball. On Jamaica, the main sports are soccer and cricket, and the music is a thumping reggae. On Trinidad, Carnival is the biggest event of the year—featuring colorful costumes and dancing to the lilting music of steel drums.

Many Caribbean islands, such as Haiti, are desperately poor, and their plight is often made worse by the hurricanes that sweep the region causing destruction in late summer and fall.

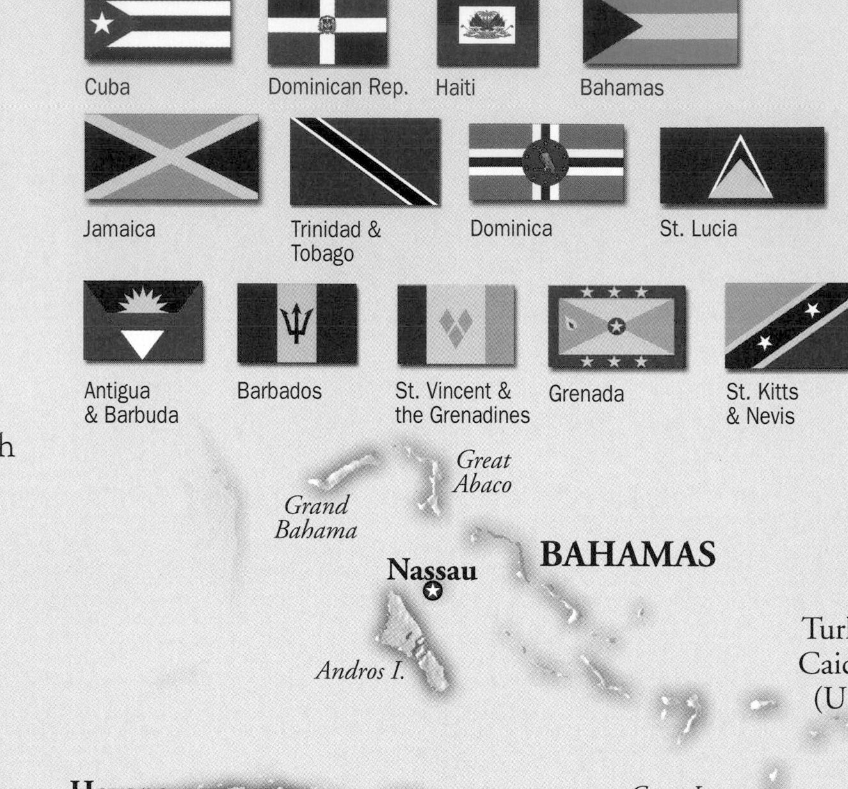
Cuba
Dominican Rep.
Haiti
Bahamas
Jamaica
Trinidad & Tobago
Dominica
St. Lucia
Antigua & Barbuda
Barbados
St. Vincent & the Grenadines
Grenada
St. Kitts & Nevis
Great Abaco
Grand Bahama
Nassau
BAHAMAS
Andros I.
Turks & Caicos (U.K.)
Great Inagua
Havana
Santa Clara
Pinar del Rio
Cienfuegos
CUBA
Camagüey
Holguín
Guantánamo
Cap Haïtien
HAITI
Port-au-Prince
Isle of Youth
Santiago de Cuba
GREATER AN
Cayman Is (U.K.)
Montego Bay
Kingston
JAMAICA

DISCOVER MORE

- *One of the strangest sights in the Caribbean is Trinidad's Pitch Lake. This lake does not contain water. In fact, it is sometimes possible to walk over it. It contains hot, sticky, black tar, which covers about 140 acres (57 hectares), to a depth of 135 ft (41 m).*
- *The Caribbean Sea is famous for beaches of white sand, but on the island of Montserrat they are gray, brown, or black. The grains of sand are formed from volcanic rock.*

Country facts

	Area sq mi (sq km)	Population	Language	Religion	Currency
Cuba	42,803 (110,860)	11,096,395	Spanish	NR*	Cuban Peso
Dominican Rep.	18,815 (48,731)	8,129,734	Spanish	Catholic	Peso
Haiti	10,714 (27,749)	6,884,264	Haitian Creole	Catholic/Voodoo	Gourde
Bahamas	5,382 (13,939)	283,705	English	Baptist/NR/C**	Dollar
Jamaica	4,243 (10,989)	2,652,443	English	Pentecostal/NR/C**	Dollar
Trinidad & Tobago	1,981 (5,131)	1,102,096	English	Catholic/Hindu	Dollar
Dominica	290 (751)	64,881	FC***/English	Catholic	East Caribbean Dollar
St. Lucia	239 (619)	154,020	English/FC***	Catholic	East Caribbean Dollar
Antigua & Barbuda	170 (440)	64,246	English	Anglican	East Caribbean Dollar
Barbados	166 (430)	259,191	English	Anglican/Pentecostal	Dollar
St. Vin. & Gren.	150 (389)	120,519	English	NR/Anglican	East Caribbean Dollar
Grenada	131 (339)	97,008	English	Catholic	East Caribbean Dollar
St. Kitts & Nevis	104 (269)	42,838	English	Anglican/Methodist	East Caribbean Dollar

*Non-religious **Non-religious/Catholic ***French Creole

Dunn's River Falls are a major attraction on the island of Jamaica. The waterfall has a drop of 600 ft (181 m) and rushes over rocky terraces on its way to the sea.

Search and find

Cuba
Capital: Havana D3
Camagüey D4
Cienfuegos D4
Guantánamo . . .D5
Holguín D5
Pinar del Rio . . .D3
Santa Clara D4
Santiago de Cuba E5

Dominican Republic
Capital:
Santo Domingo E6
Santiago D6

Haiti
Capital:
Port-au-Prince .E6
Cap Haïtien D6

Bahamas
Capital: Nassau .C4

Jamaica
Capital:
Kingston E5
Montego Bay . . .E4

Trinidad & Tobago
Capital:
Port of Spain . . .F9

Dominica
Capital: Roseau .E8

St. Lucia
Capital: Castries E9

Antigua & Barbuda
Capital:
St. John's D8

Barbados
Capital: Bridgetown E9

St. Vincent & the Grenadines
Capital: Kingstown E9

Grenada
Capital:
St. George's . .F9

St. Kitts & Nevis
Capital:
Basseterre . . .D8

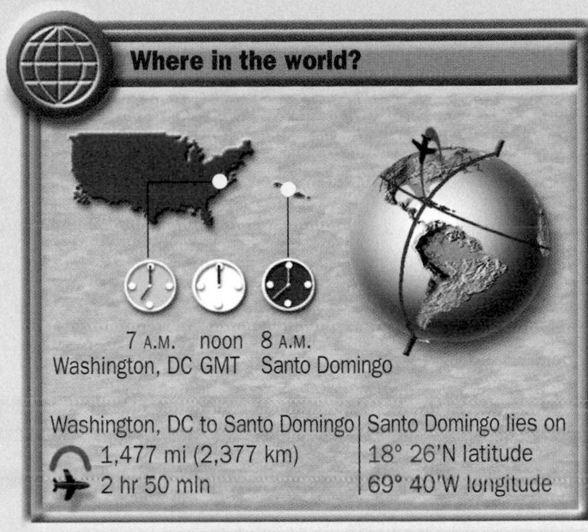
Where in the world?
7 A.M. Washington, DC
noon GMT
8 A.M. Santo Domingo
Washington, DC to Santo Domingo
1,477 mi (2,377 km)
2 hr 50 min
Santo Domingo lies on
18° 26'N latitude
69° 40'W longitude

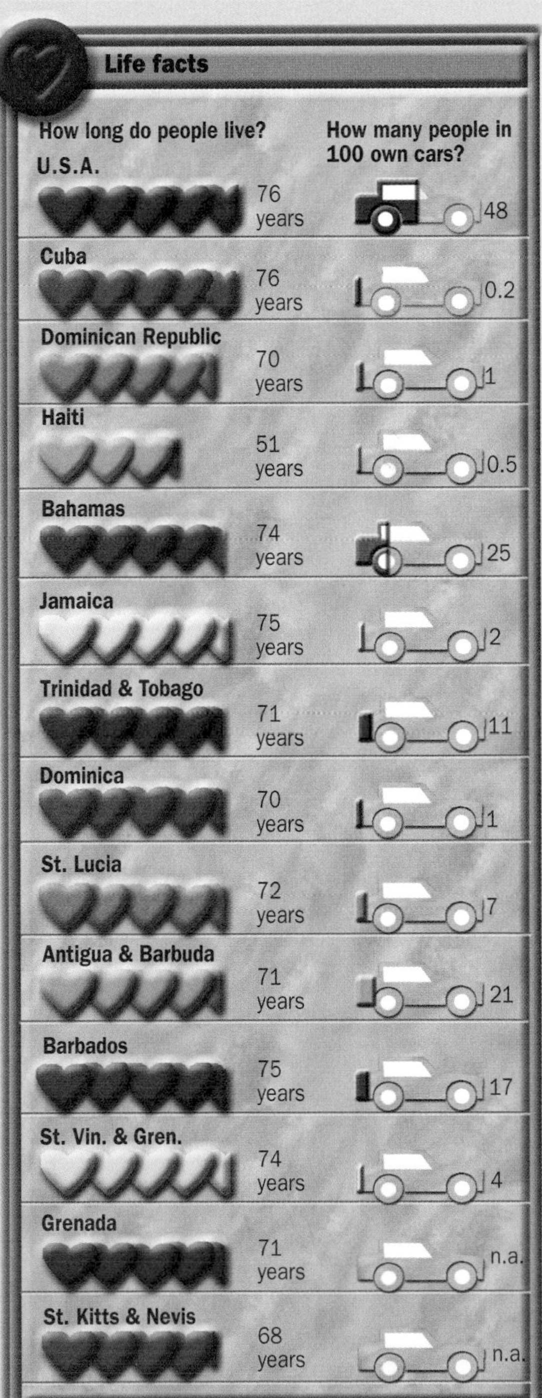

Life facts

	How long do people live?	How many people in 100 own cars?
U.S.A.	76 years	48
Cuba	76 years	0.2
Dominican Republic	70 years	1
Haiti	51 years	0.5
Bahamas	74 years	25
Jamaica	75 years	2
Trinidad & Tobago	71 years	11
Dominica	70 years	1
St. Lucia	72 years	7
Antigua & Barbuda	71 years	21
Barbados	75 years	17
St. Vin. & Gren.	74 years	4
Grenada	71 years	n.a.
St. Kitts & Nevis	68 years	n.a.

Virgin Is (U.S.A. & U.K.)
OMINICAN REPUBLIC
Santiago
Santo Domingo
San Juan
Puerto Rico (U.S.A.)
Basseterre
ST. KITTS & NEVIS
ANTIGUA & BARBUDA
St. John's
Guadeloupe (FRANCE)
Montserrat (U.K.)
DOMINICA
Roseau
Martinique (FRANCE)
T I L L E S
Castries
ST. LUCIA
BARBADOS
Bridgetown
Kingstown
ST. VINCENT & THE GRENADINES
GRENADA
St. George's
Tobago
TRINIDAD & TOBAGO
Port of Spain
Trinidad
Aruba (NETH.)
Netherlands Antilles
Curaçao
Bonaire
V E N E Z U E L A

N
W
E
S

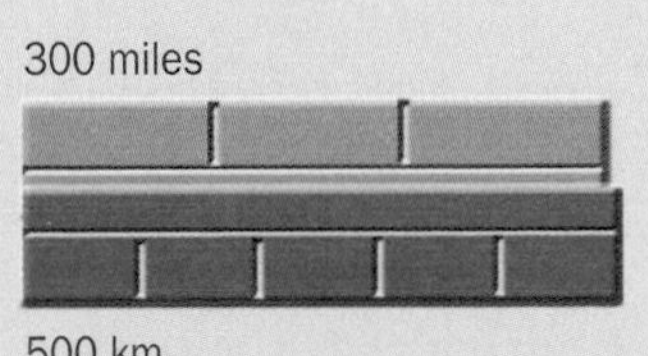
300 miles
500 km

White sands, blue seas, and palm trees attract tourists to the island of Barbados.

A B C D E F G

South America

STRETCHING FROM THE WARM CARIBBEAN SEA TOWARD cold Antarctic waters, South America is the world's fourth-largest continent. It is attached to Central America by the Isthmus of Panama, a narrow strip of land. To the west of South America is the South Pacific Ocean and to the east is the South Atlantic Ocean.

Stresses and strains within the earth's crust have pushed up the massive ridges and plateaus of the Andes Mountains, which run from the north to the south down the western side of the continent. To the west of the mountains is a narrow coastal plain, partly fertile, partly barren desert. To the east is the Amazon rain forest, the largest tropical rain forest on earth, which drains into the surging, muddy flow of the Amazon River on its way to the Atlantic Ocean.

South of the rain forest, scrub, swamp, and grasslands called the pampas give way to the bleak valleys of Patagonia. Beyond the Strait of Magellan, the southern island of Tierra del Fuego has been shaped by ice, wind, and rain.

The indigenous peoples of South America developed ancient civilizations in the Andes and Pacific regions. Today's South Americans are of European, African, and Asian, as well as indigenous, descent.

The chief European languages of the continent are Spanish and Portuguese (spoken in Brazil). Indigenous languages are still spoken in many regions. The great majority of South Americans are Roman Catholics, but there are a growing number of Protestants, too. South America is a meeting point for many different peoples and cultures.

CARIBBEAN SEA
Lesser Antilles
Isthmus of Panama
VENEZUELA
COLOMBIA
ECUADOR
PERU
BOLIVIA
SOUTH PACIFIC OCEAN
CHILE
ARGENTINA
N
W
E
S
1,000 miles
1,500 km
Chiloé I.
Tierra del Fuego

DISCOVER MORE

- *The widest point of South America is between Pariñas Point in Peru and Coqueiros Point in Brazil, a distance of 3,180 mi (5,120 km).*
- *The largest freshwater island on earth is Marajó in the Amazon River's estuary, in northeastern Brazil. It covers an area of about 15,500 sq mi (40,150 sq km).*

These parrots, called macaws, live in the canopy, or treetops, of the Amazon rain forest. Their powerful beaks are used for eating wild fruits and berries. Their brilliantly colored plumage is used to make headdresses by some of the forest peoples.

6
7
8
9
10
11

GUYANA
SURINAME
FRENCH GUIANA

NORTH ATLANTIC OCEAN

Fernando de Noronha I.

BRAZIL

PARAGUAY

Rio de Janeiro

SOUTH ATLANTIC OCEAN

URUGUAY

f San Matias

an Jorge

Falkland Is (U.K.)

South Georgia (U.K.)

SCOTIA SEA

A

B

C

D

E

F

G

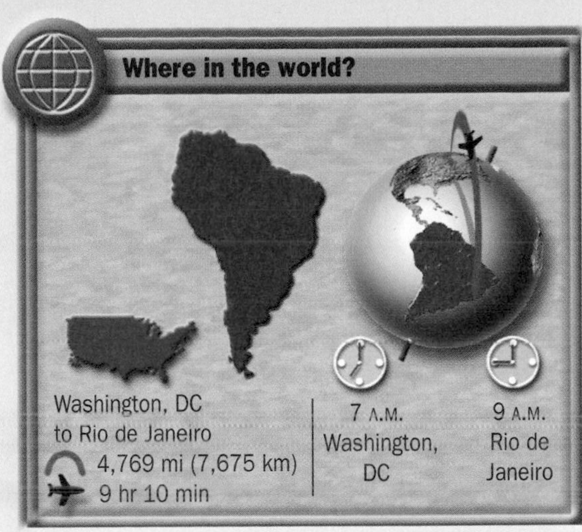

Where in the world?
Washington, DC to Rio de Janeiro
4,769 mi (7,675 km)
9 hr 10 min
7 A.M. Washington, DC
9 A.M. Rio de Janeiro

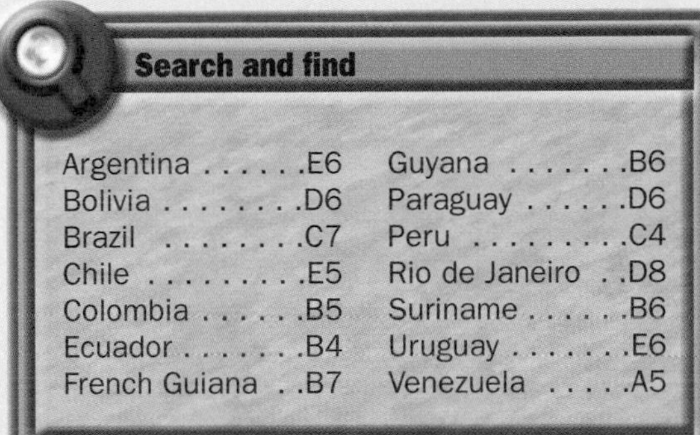

Search and find

Argentina E6
Bolivia D6
Brazil C7
Chile E5
Colombia B5
Ecuador B4
French Guiana . . B7
Guyana B6
Paraguay D6
Peru C4
Rio de Janeiro . . D8
Suriname B6
Uruguay E6
Venezuela A5

In the dense forests of southeastern Venezuela, the Carrao River, a tributary of the Caroní, plunges over a sheer cliff to form the world's highest waterfall. Known locally as Cherun-Meru, its international name is Angel Falls. This name comes from a U.S. pilot named Jimmy Angel, who sighted the falls in 1933.

Continent facts

	Area sq mi (sq km)	% of Earth's area	Population	Largest country by area sq mi (sq km)	Largest country by population
South America	6,900,000 (17,871,000)	11.9	343,294,000	Brazil (8,511,957)	Brazil 171,853,126

Colombia and Venezuela

Venezuela
Colombia

The Andes Mountains form a long spine down the western South American continent. The northern end of this range splits into three chains; the eastern chain reaches into northwest Venezuela. These mountains drop to fertile valleys, hot and humid coastal plains, the cattle country of Venezuela's Llanos grasslands, and vast tracts of rain forest. Through this winds the Orinoco River, dividing into a delta on the east coast.

Colombia produces some of the world's finest coffee and is rich in emeralds and gold. In Venezuela, oil derricks rise from the shallow waters of Lake Maracaibo. Colombians and Venezuelans are descended mainly from indigenous peoples, Spanish colonists, and African slaves.

The soaring towers of Bogotá, the Colombian capital, rise from a plain against a backdrop of hills and mountains. The city's modern business districts and wealthy suburbs give way to shantytowns of poor shacks. Far from the bustle of the big city, Colombia's southern highlands present a different scene. Sheep graze on green pastures in the cool mountain air. A family of the Guambiano people walk to market, dressed in cloaks, called ponchos, and round felt hats, the women in long blue skirts.

In Venezuela, most people live in the towns and cities. Poor workers from other parts of Latin America have joined local people to seek employment in the factories of the busy capital, Caracas. Rural populations include llaneros (cowboys of the Llanos) and native peoples such as the Yanomami, who live in the remote rain forests.

CARIBBEAN S
Point Gallinas
Gulf of Venezuela
Barranquilla
Pico Cristóbal Colón
18,947 ft
(5,775 m)
Cartagena
Maracaibo
L. Maracaibo
Pico Bolíva
16,411 ft
(5,001 m)
ANDES MTS
Cauca
Magdalena
Medellín
Cape Corrientes
Manizales
Pereira
Meta
Bogotá
Armenia
Ibagué
Cali
COLOMBIA
Nevado del Huila
18,865ft (5,749 m)
Vaupés
ECUADOR
Apaporis
Caquetá
Putumay
PERU

DISCOVER MORE

• A lake in the Colombian Andes is believed to contain priceless gold and emeralds thrown into its waters long ago by the Chibcha people. Legends of their ruler, the fabulous "golden man" or El Dorado, lured Spanish invaders to the region in the 16th century.

Caracas, capital of Venezuela, stretches for more than 9 mi (15 km) along the floor of a basin.

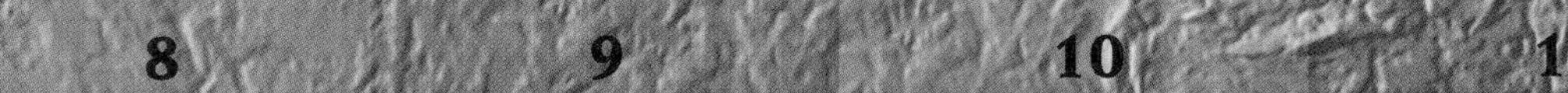

LESSER ANTILLES

Caracas
Valencia
Barquisimeto
Barcelona
Orinoco Delta
Orinoco
Ciudad Bolivar
Ciudad Guayana
VENEZUELA
Angel Falls
GUYANA
Gauviare
Orinoco
BRAZIL

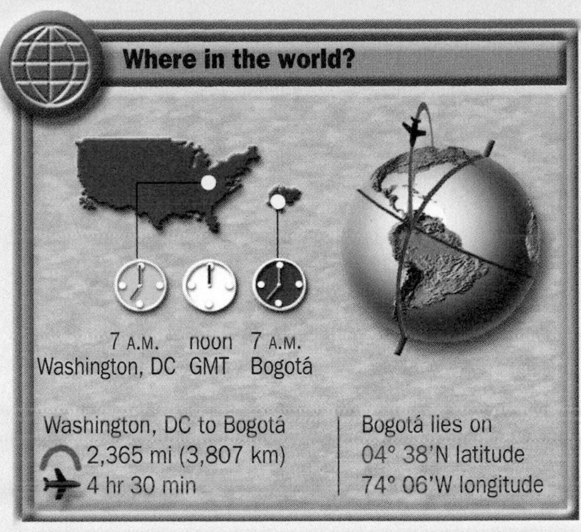
Where in the world?
7 A.M. Washington, DC
noon GMT
7 A.M. Bogotá
Washington, DC to Bogotá
2,365 mi (3,807 km)
4 hr 30 min
Bogotá lies on
04° 38'N latitude
74° 06'W longitude

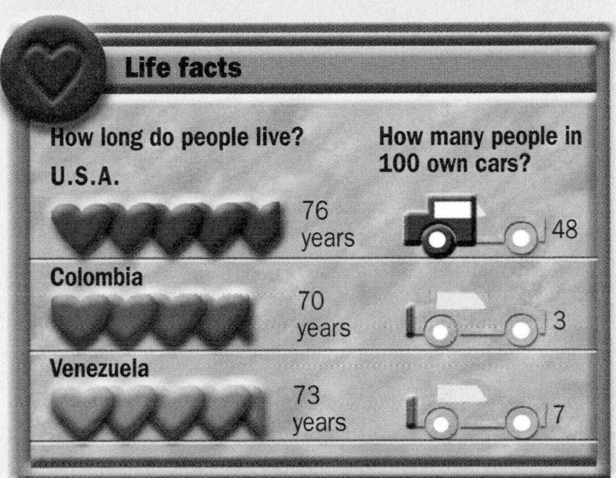
Life facts
How long do people live?
How many people in 100 own cars?
U.S.A.
76 years
48
Colombia
70 years
3
Venezuela
73 years
7

Linked by interweaving scarves, men and women dance through the streets of Medellín, Colombia. They are celebrating the Festival of Flowers, which is held in the city each August. The city exports flowers and is famous for its orchids.

N
W
E
S

300 miles
500 km

Search and find

Colombia		**Venezuela**	
Capital: Bogotá	C5	*Capital*: Caracas	B7
Armenia	C4	Barcelona	B8
Barranquilla	B5	Barquisimeto	B6
Cali	D4	Ciudad Bolivar	B8
Cartagena	B4	Ciudad Guayana	B8
Ibagué	C4	Maracaibo	B5
Manizales	C4	Valencia	B7
Medellín	C4		
Pereira	C4		

Colombia

Venezuela

Country facts

	Area sq mi (sq km)	Population	Language	Religion	Currency
Colombia	440,762 (1,141,574)	39,309,422	Spanish	Catholic	Peso
Venezuela	352,143 (912,054)	23,203,466	Spanish	Catholic	Bolivar

The Guianas

GUYANA, SURINAME, FRENCH GUIANA

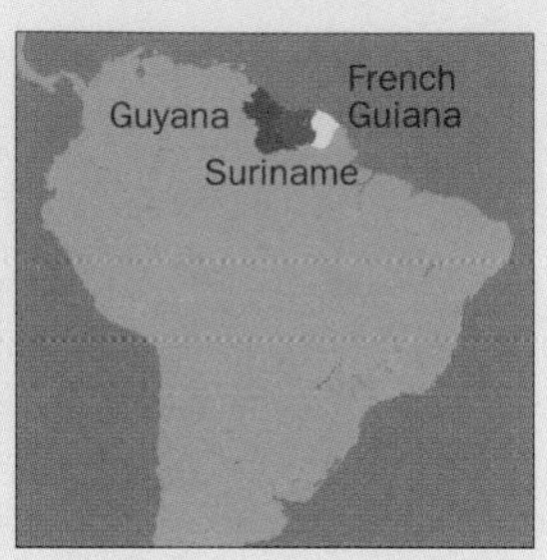
Guyana
French Guiana
Suriname

THE GUIANA HIGHLANDS RUN across the northeast of the South American continent, their mountain ridges clad in dense, tropical rain forest. Rivers drain the northern slopes, plunging down as spectacular waterfalls before crossing a hot, humid coastal plain. From here they flow into the Atlantic Ocean.

Most people live in the coastal region. The streets of Paramaribo, capital of Suriname, are lined with white wooden houses with balconies and porches, buildings in the old Dutch style, mosques, churches, and Hindu temples. Such contrasts are common in the region, for these three lands are inhabited by a mixture of peoples, partly of indigenous origin, partly descended from Africans, the British, Dutch, French, Portuguese, Chinese, Indians, and Southeast Asians. The result is one of the most exciting blends of cultures and languages in the Americas.

Lowland regions are fertile and enjoy a high rainfall. Many people work in sugarcane plantations, or farm rice and other tropical crops. Others work in mines, for the Guianas are rich in bauxite, the ore used to make aluminum.

In the remote forests of the interior, communities still live by hunting, fishing in the rivers, or growing crops such as cassava. This root produces a flour, which is made into starchy pancakes.

ATLANTIC OCEAN
VENEZUELA
Charity
Cuyuni
Georgetown
New Amsterda
Linden
Corriverton
GUYANA
PAKARAIMA MTS
Mt Roraima 9,094 ft (2,772 m)
S
Apoteri
KANUKU MOUNTAINS
Essequibo
B

DISCOVER MORE

- *Red-hot cayenne peppers are named after the capital of French Guiana.*
- *The name Guiana or Guyana means "land of many waters." Many rivers flow across these lands.*

A statue of Queen Victoria (1819–1901) looks out over Georgetown, capital of Guyana. The country was ruled by Britain from 1831 to 1966. Today it is an independent republic.

6 7 8 9 10 11

A fisherman hauls in a heavyweight catch from muddy waters in the forests of French Guiana.

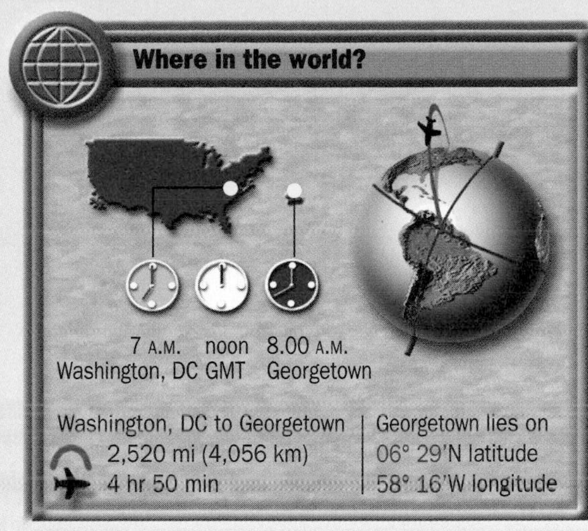

Where in the world?
7 A.M. Washington, DC
noon GMT
8.00 A.M. Georgetown
Washington, DC to Georgetown
2,520 mi (4,056 km)
4 hr 50 min
Georgetown lies on
06° 29'N latitude
58° 16'W longitude

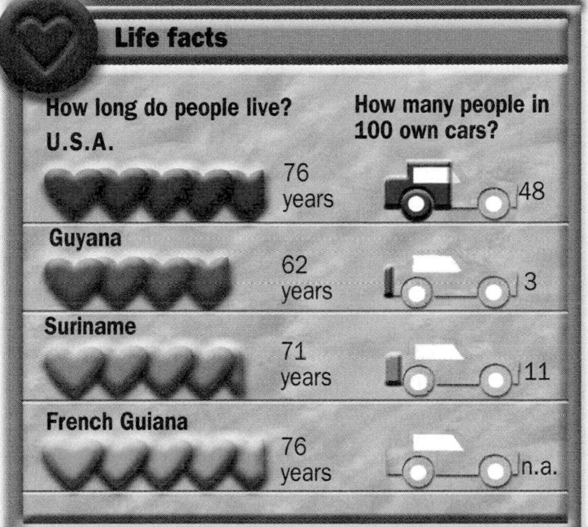

Life facts
How long do people live?
How many people in 100 own cars?
U.S.A.
76 years
48
Guyana
62 years
3
Suriname
71 years
11
French Guiana
76 years
n.a.

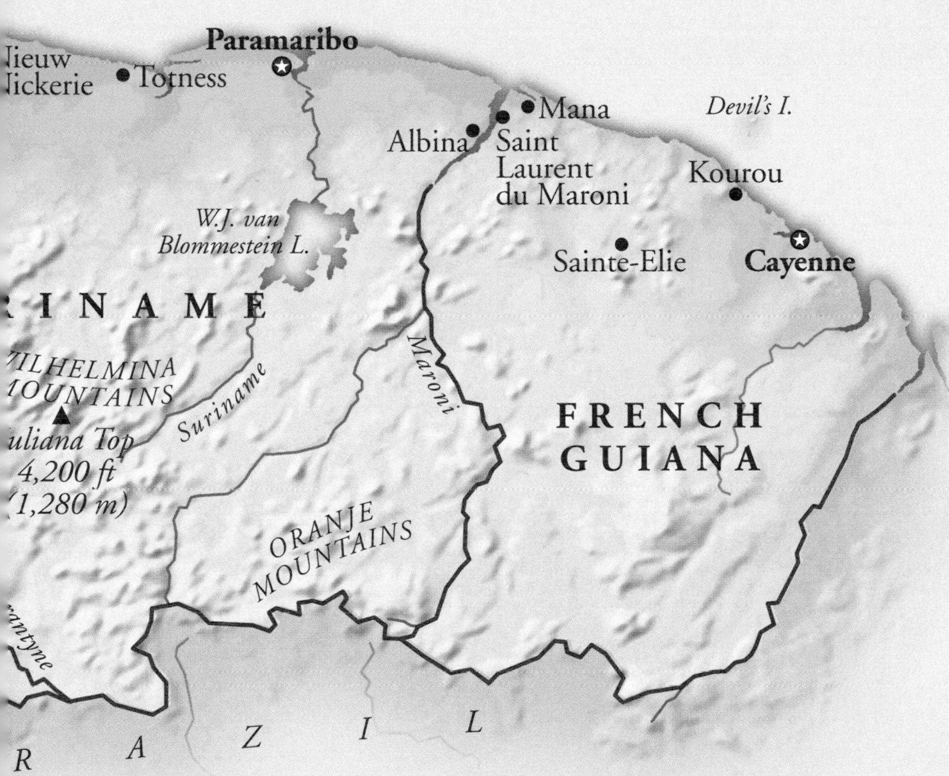

Nieuw Nickerie
Totness
Paramaribo
Albina
Mana
Saint Laurent du Maroni
Devil's I.
Kourou
W.J. van Blommestein L.
Sainte-Elie
Cayenne
INAME
ILHELMINA MOUNTAINS
Suriname
Maroni
uliana Top 4,200 ft (1,280 m)
FRENCH GUIANA
ORANJE MOUNTAINS
R A Z I L

Search and find
Guyana
Capital:
Georgetown . . .C5
Apoteri D5
Charity B5
Corriverton C6
Linden C5
New Amsterdam .C6
Suriname
Capital:
Paramaribo . . . C7
Albina C8
Nieuw Nickerie .C6
Totness C7
French Guiana
Capital:
Cayenne D9
Kourou D9
Mana C8
Sainte-Elie D8
Saint Laurent du Maroni C8

N
W
E
S

Guyana

Suriname

French Guiana

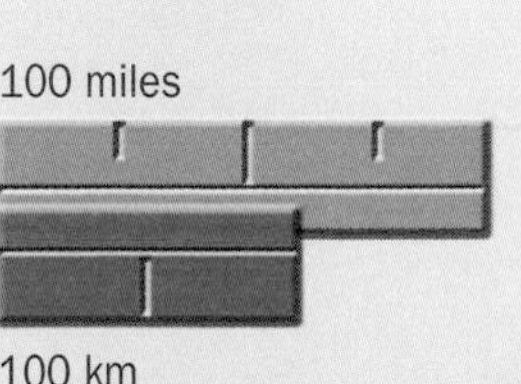

100 miles
100 km

Country facts

	Area sq mi (sq km)	Population	Language	Religion	Currency
Guyana	83,000 (214,970)	705,156	English/Creole	Hindu/Protestant	Dollar
Suriname	63,039 (163,271)	431,156	Dutch/Sranan/Hindu	Hindu/Catholic/Sunni Muslim	Suriname Guilder
French Guiana	33,399 (86,503)	167,982	French	Catholic	French Franc

A B C D E F G

6 7 8 9 10 11

Brazil

Brazil

A light aircraft bumps onto a red-dirt landing strip, cleared from remote rain forest near Brazil's border with Venezuela. This is the territory of the Yanomami people. Inside large, circular, palm-thatched huts, children play on floors of beaten earth. Several families live in the same building, each with their own hearth, where they cook fish or a starchy root called cassava. Hunters rest on hammocks slung between the hut's timbers.

Tens of thousands of streams feed the broad, muddy Amazon River as it winds eastward to the Atlantic Ocean. On the coast, large, modern cities such as Rio de Janeiro and São Paulo rise behind long, sandy beaches. The downtown skyscrapers and rich suburbs are fringed by *favelas* (slums). Most Brazilians, whether rich or poor, whether of African, Portuguese, or mixed descent, love sport (especially soccer), music, and dance, especially the samba. Rio's five days of carnival must be seen to be believed.

The great rain forests of Brazil take up one-third of the country. The northeast is mostly a dry land of woodland and scrub.

200 miles

300 km

DISCOVER MORE

- *Do you like your coffee sweet? Brazil produces more sugarcane and more coffee than any other country in the world.*
- *Brazil has won soccer's World Cup four times, more than any other country.*
- *The Amazon is the world's second longest river and drains an area of more than 2.7 million sq mi (7 million sq km).*

N
W
E
S

The sloth, a slow-moving creature of the Amazon rain forest, hangs upside down from the branches of trees.

The city of São Paulo has the largest population in South America—more than 17 million. It lies on the rim of a rich agricultural and industrial region, whose inhabitants are known as Paulistas.

Marajó Bay
Marajó I.
Belém
Tocantins
São Marcos Bay
São Luís
Fortaleza
Fernando de Noronha I.
Teresina
Cape São Roque
Natal
SERTÃO
Recife
Araguaia
Parnaíba
Sobradinho Reservoir
São Francisco
Maceió
AZIL
Salvador
ROSSO
EAU
Brasília
BRAZILIAN HIGHLANDS
ATLANTIC OCEAN
Goiânia
Uberlândia
Belo Horizonte
Campos
Cape São Tomé
São Paulo
Rio de Janeiro
Santos
SERRA DO MAR
Curitiba
Florianópolis
Pôrto Alegre
Patos Lagoon

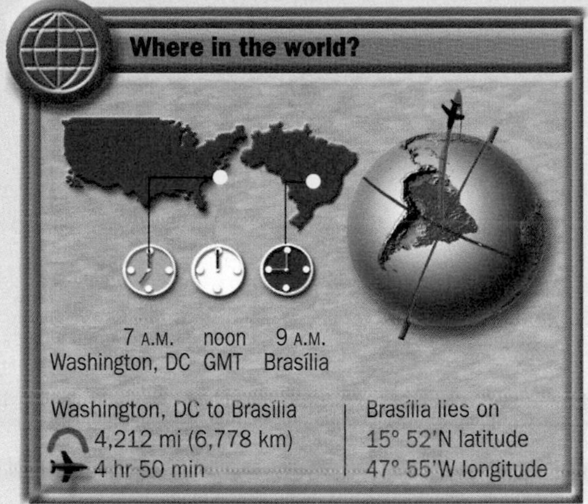

Where in the world?
7 A.M. Washington, DC
noon GMT
9 A.M. Brasília
Washington, DC to Brasília
4,212 mi (6,778 km)
4 hr 50 min
Brasília lies on
15° 52'N latitude
47° 55'W longitude

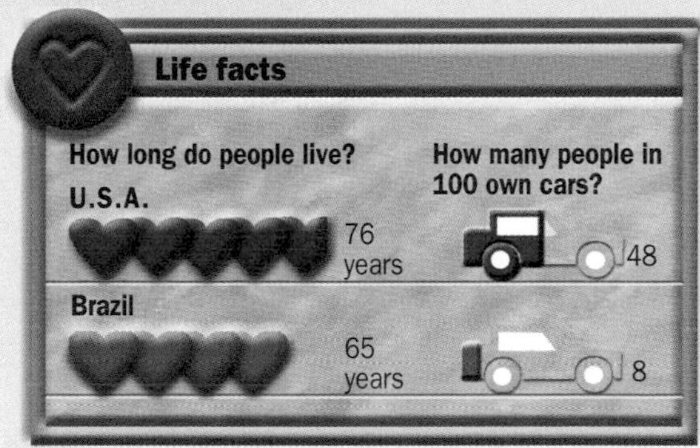

Life facts
How long do people live?
How many people in 100 own cars?
U.S.A.
76 years
48
Brazil
65 years
8

A canoe is paddled out from a village hut on the shores of the Amazon River. This broad, muddy river flows through the world's largest rain forest. Its waters are inhabited by fierce, flesh-eating piranha fish.

Longest rivers

Nile	4,145 mi (6,670 km)
Amazon	4,000 mi (6,437 km)
Mississippi	3,741 mi (6,020 km)

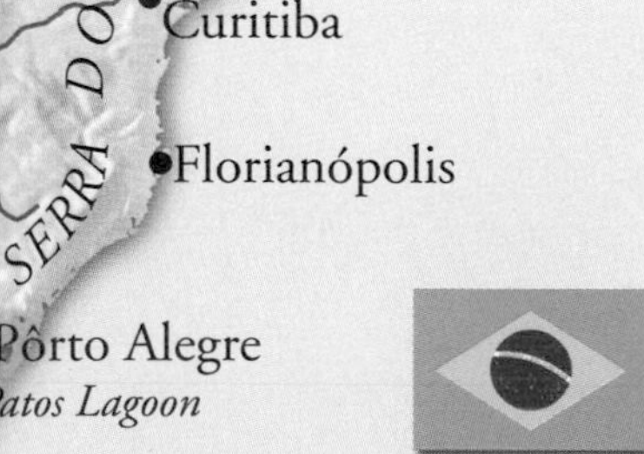

Brazil

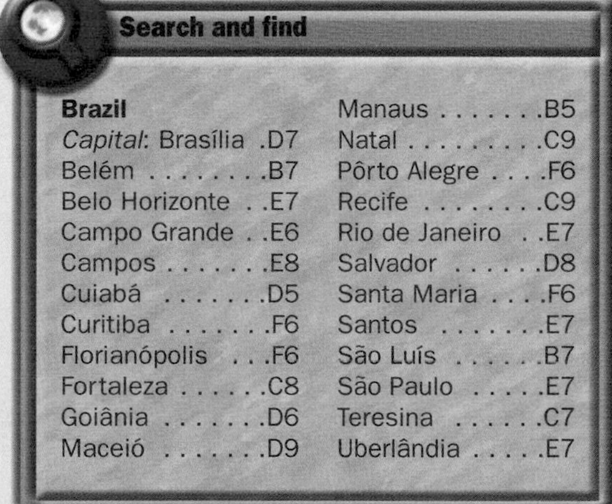

Search and find
Brazil
Capital: Brasília .D7
Belém B7
Belo Horizonte . .E7
Campo Grande . .E6
Campos E8
Cuiabá D5
Curitiba F6
Florianópolis . . .F6
Fortaleza C8
Goiânia D6
Maceió D9
Manaus B5
Natal C9
Pôrto Alegre F6
Recife C9
Rio de Janeiro . .E7
Salvador D8
Santa Maria F6
Santos E7
São Luís B7
São Paulo E7
Teresina C7
Uberlândia E7

Country facts

	Area sq mi (sq km)	Population	Language	Religion	Currency
Brazil	3,286,470 (8,511,957)	171,853,126	Portuguese	Catholic	Real

Middle Andes

PERU, ECUADOR

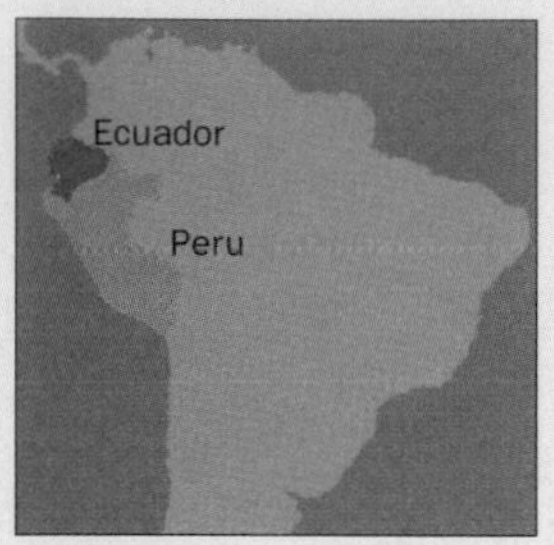
Ecuador
Peru

A YOUNG BOY PLAYS ON A SIMPLE flute as he herds llamas. They pass between ancient stone walls and terraced fields built by the Inca people, who ruled most of the Andes Mountains before Spanish invaders conquered Peru in 1532. Sheer, forested peaks climb into the mist.

In Ecuador and Peru, the snowcapped peaks of the Andes soar to more than 20,000 feet (6,000 m) above sea level, a long chain of peaks, volcanoes, and glaciers. They tower over sweeping plateaus and cool lakes, which reflect blue skies. Potatoes are grown at these high altitudes and left for the sun and frost to freeze-dry them. They will be boiled later to make vegetable stew.

In the east, mountain streams drain into the brimming waterways of the hot and sticky Amazon rain forest. In the west, the foothills of the Andes drop to a narrow plain along the Pacific coast, a hot, dry region broken by fertile river valleys. Here are farms, fishing villages, and large, modern cities such as Lima, with its port of Callao. Ecuador also includes the distant Pacific islands of the Galápagos, where unique giant tortoises live.

Spanish is spoken throughout the region, but local languages such as Quechua or Aymara are also widespread. About 90 percent of the population is Roman Catholic, and religious festivals are marked with colorful processions and pilgrimages.

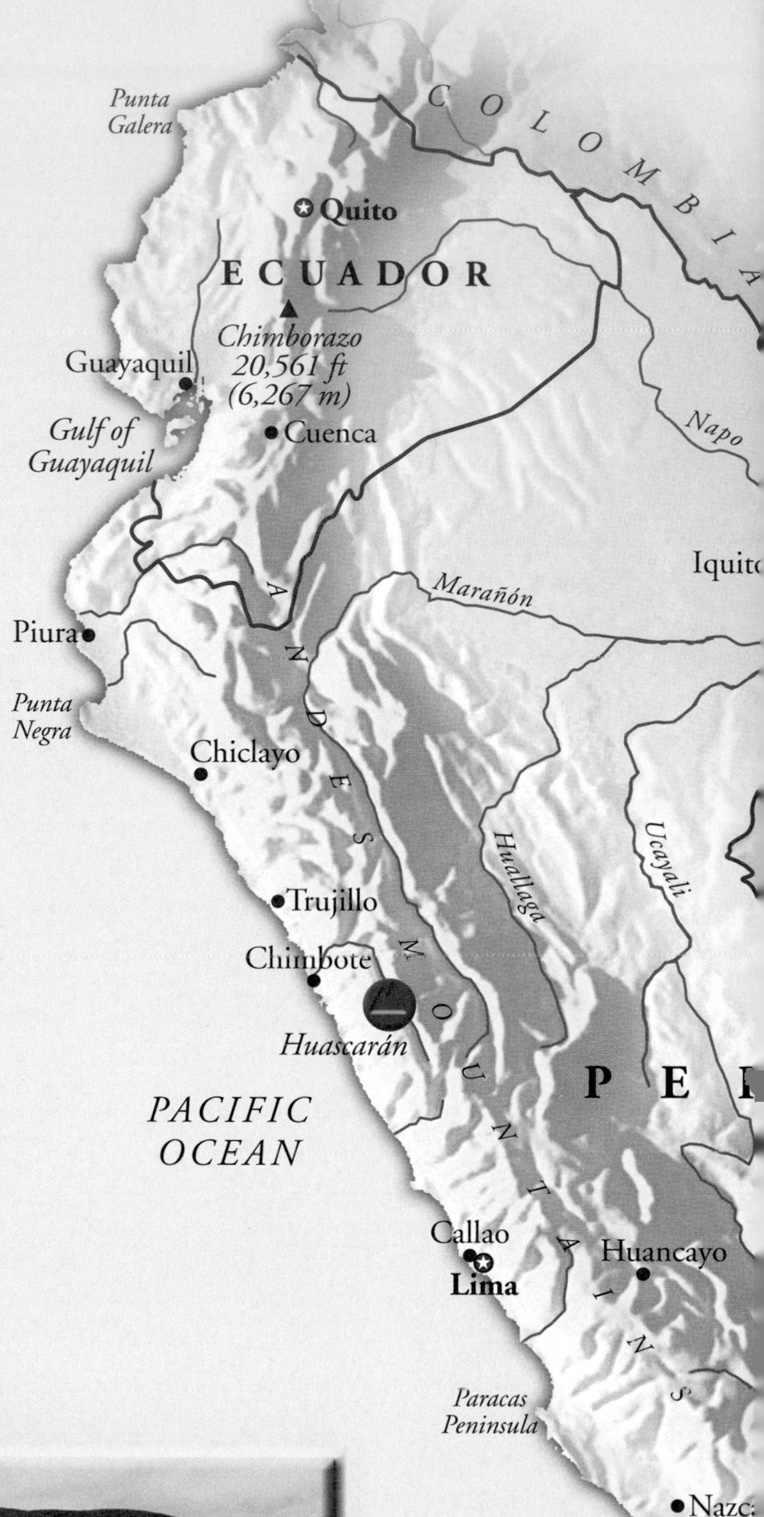
Punta Galera
COLOMBIA
Quito
ECUADOR
Chimborazo 20,561 ft (6,267 m)
Guayaquil
Gulf of Guayaquil
Cuenca
Napo
Iquito
Marañón
Piura
Punta Negra
ANDES MOUNTAINS
Chiclayo
Huallaga
Ucayali
Trujillo
Chimbote
Huascarán
PACIFIC OCEAN
PER
Callao
Lima
Huancayo
Paracas Peninsula
Nazca

DISCOVER MORE

* *Ecuador takes its name from the equator, on which it lies. However, its capital, Quito, is located so high above the hot lowlands that the climate there is mild all year round.*
* *The Peruvian railroad reaches 15,846 ft (4,830 m) in the Andes—the highest track anywhere in the world.*

Long lines are scraped from the desert floor of the Nazca region in southern Peru. They are in the shapes of animals, birds, spirals, and other patterns. Many are best viewed from the air, and yet they were created more than 2,000 years ago. They probably marked routes for religious processions.

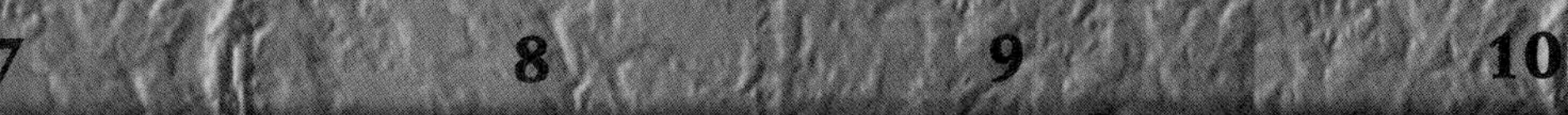

Highest mountains

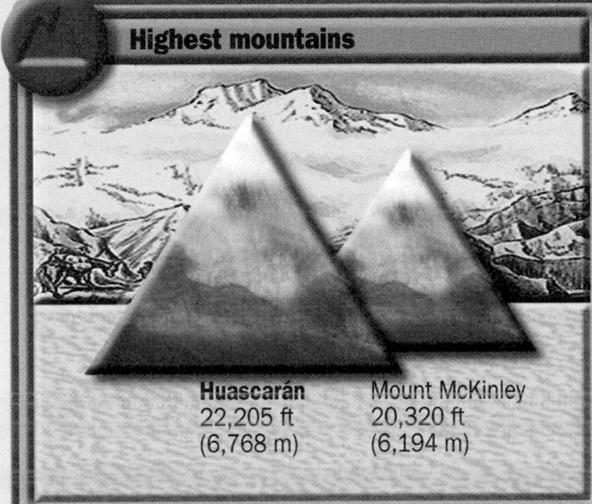
Huascarán
22,205 ft
(6,768 m)
Mount McKinley
20,320 ft
(6,194 m)

Where in the world?

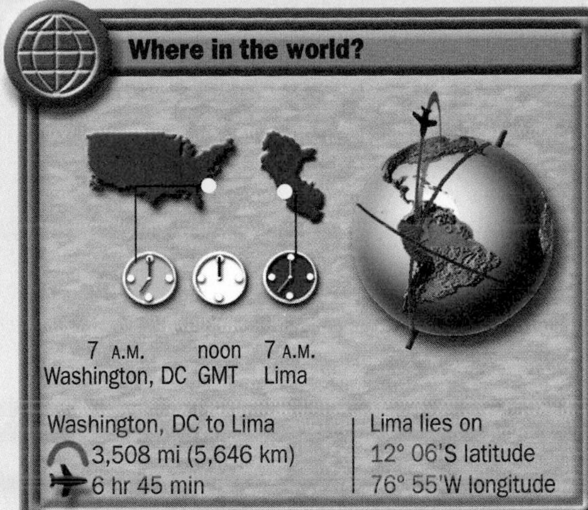
7 A.M.
Washington, DC
noon
GMT
7 A.M.
Lima
Washington, DC to Lima
3,508 mi (5,646 km)
6 hr 45 min
Lima lies on
12° 06'S latitude
76° 55'W longitude

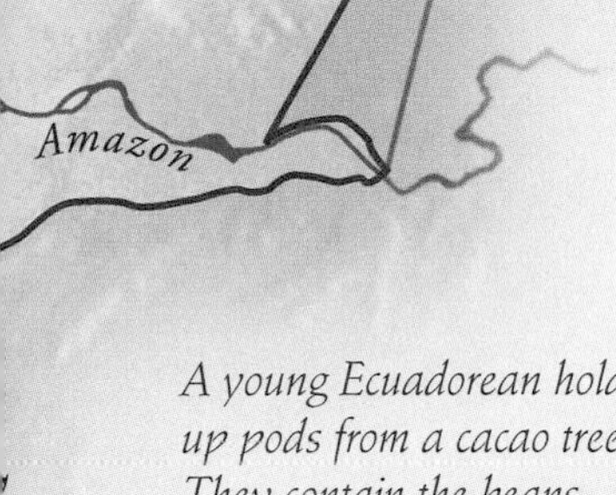
Amazon

A young Ecuadorean holds up pods from a cacao tree. They contain the beans that are used to make chocolate. Cacao is a native plant of the American tropics.

Life facts

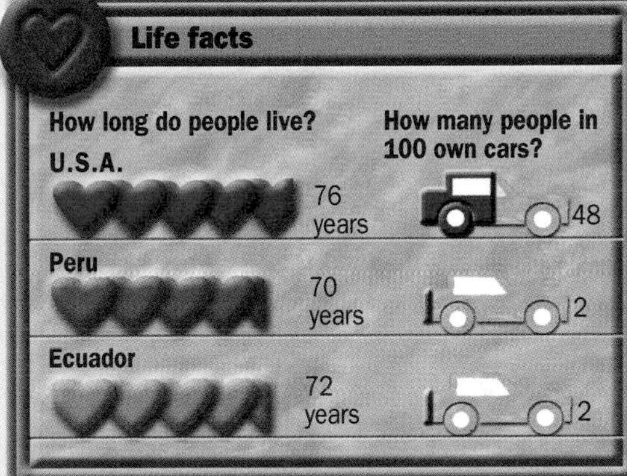
How long do people live?
How many people in 100 own cars?
U.S.A.
76 years
48
Peru
70 years
2
Ecuador
72 years
2

Search and find

Peru

Capital: Lima . . .E5
Arequipa F7
Callao E5
Chiclayo D4
Chimbote D4
Cuzco F6
Huancayo E5
Iquitos C6
Machu Picchu . . .F6
Nazca F6
Piura C4
Trujillo D4

Ecuador

Capital: Quito . .B4
Cuenca B4
Guayaquil B4

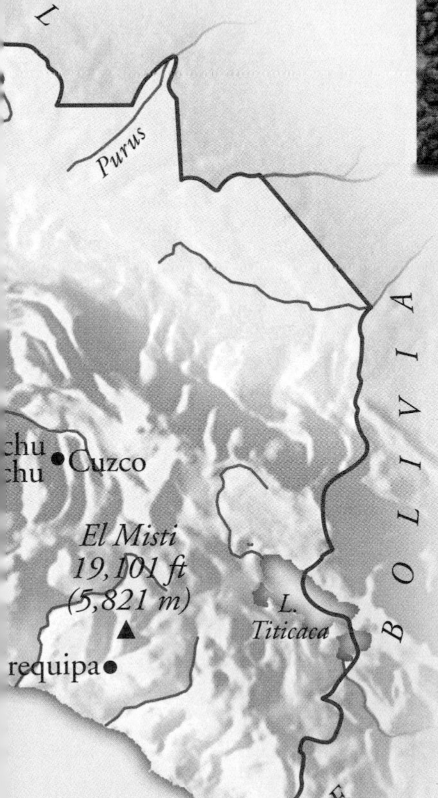
Purus
BOLIVIA
chu
chu
Cuzco
El Misti
19,101 ft
(5,821 m)
L. Titicaca
requipa
CHILE

N
W
E
S

300 miles

500 km

The town of Machu Picchu was built about 500 years ago on a steep ridge 2,000 ft (610 m) above the Urubamba River. It was part of the mighty Inca empire, whose capital was at Cuzco, Peru.

Peru

Ecuador

Country facts

	Area sq mi (sq km)	Population	Language	Religion	Currency
Peru	496,223 (1,285,218)	26,624,582	Spanish	Catholic	New Sol
Ecuador	105,037 (272,046)	12,562,496	Spanish	Catholic	US Dollar

A B C D E F G

Central South America

BOLIVIA, PARAGUAY

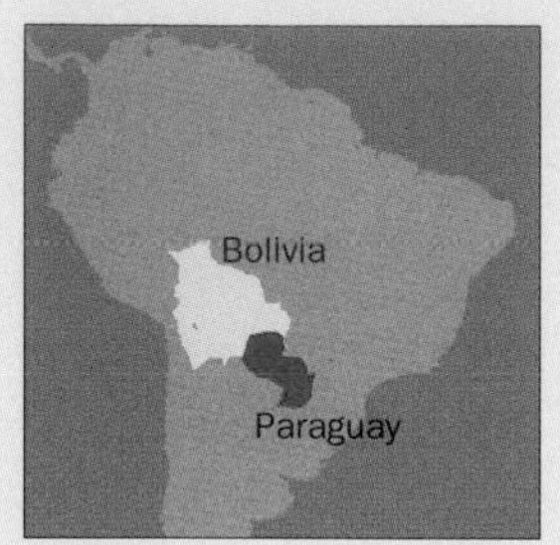
Bolivia
Paraguay

BOLIVIA AND PARAGUAY ARE two landlocked countries occupying the heart of the South American continent. Bolivia has two capitals, La Paz and Sucre, both high in the Andes mountain range, where dazzling snowfields tower above high plateaus and lakes. In these cities, modern high-rise buildings overlook old churches built by Spanish colonists. Country women in the streets wear long, full skirts; shawls and cloaks woven from llama wool; and round derby-style hats. Take a bus into Bolivia's Oriente, or eastern region, and find rough roads plunging down to the Amazon River basin, tropical forests, swamps, and farms producing bananas, coffee, and sugarcane.

The Gran Chaco, a scrub-covered plain that floods in the rainy season, extends into Paraguay. Here, roads are few and far between, and are best traveled on horseback. Most people live east of the Paraguay River, in the large city of Asunción or on the more fertile farmland of the east and south. Almost half of the labor force works on the land. Paraguay depends on its farmers for 90 percent of its exports. Major crops include wheat, cotton, and soybeans. A shrub called the Paraguay holly is grown to make a kind of tea called *yerba maté*, which is widely drunk in parts of South America.

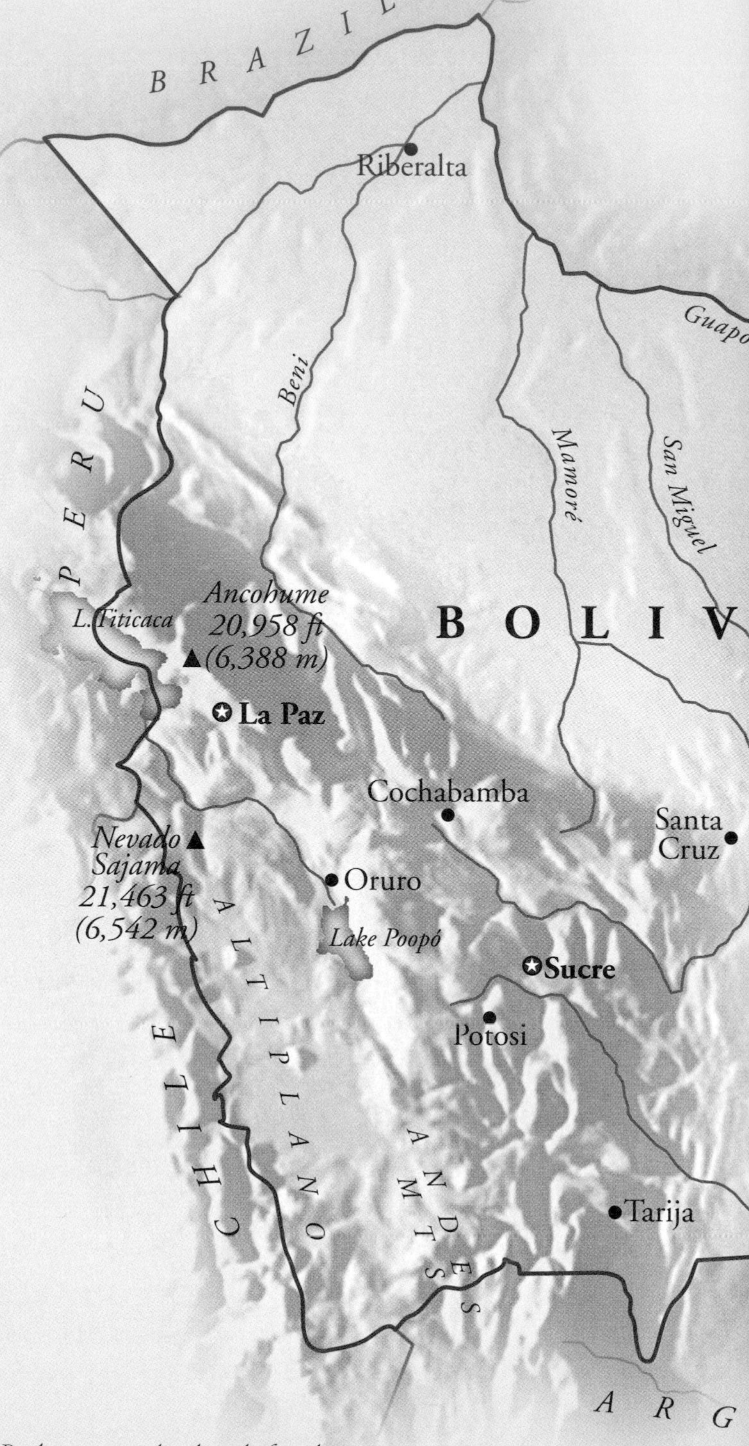
BRAZIL
Riberalta
Beni
Guaporé
Mamoré
San Miguel
PERU
L. Titicaca
Ancohume
20,958 ft
(6,388 m)
BOLIV
La Paz
Cochabamba
Santa Cruz
Nevado Sajama
21,463 ft
(6,542 m)
Oruro
Lake Poopó
ALTIPLANO
Sucre
Potosi
CHILE
ANDES MTS
Tarija
ARG

DISCOVER MORE

- *Paraguayan lacework is so fine that it is known as* ñandutí, *which means "spider's web" in the Guarani language.*
- *The Itaipu Dam on the Paraná River is the world's biggest. The river's flow is used to power great turbines that generate electricity. It is jointly owned by Paraguay and Brazil.*

The Brahman, or zebu, breed of cattle has a humped back, floppy ears, and upturned horns. It originated in southern Asia but now lives in warm, subtropical regions around the world. It is perfectly adapted for life in the warm areas of Bolivia and Paraguay.

Country facts

	Area sq mi (sq km)	Population	Language	Religion	Currency
Bolivia	424,162 (1,098,580)	7,982,850	Spanish/Quechua/Aymara	Catholic	Boliviano
Paraguay	157,046 (406,749)	5,434,095	Spanish/Guarani	Catholic	Guaraní

Bolivia

Paraguay

In Bolivia, the Andes Mountains form two long ranges called the Eastern and Western Cordilleras. Between the two lies the high plateau, or Altiplano. It is a treeless land with lakes and wide salt flats.

B R A Z I L
300 miles
500 km
N
W
E
S
GRAN CHACO
PARAGUAY
B R A Z I L
Verde
Concepción
Paraguay
Pilcomayo
T I N A
Ciudad del Este
Itaipu Dam
Asunción
Paraguay
Alto Paraná

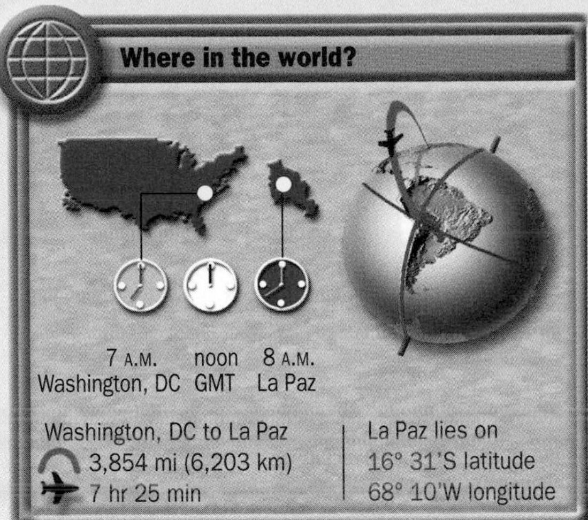

Where in the world?
7 A.M. Washington, DC
noon GMT
8 A.M. La Paz
Washington, DC to La Paz
3,854 mi (6,203 km)
7 hr 25 min
La Paz lies on
16° 31'S latitude
68° 10'W longitude

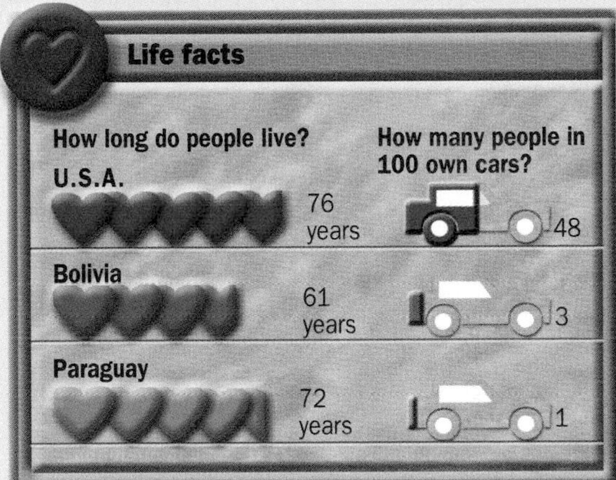

Life facts
How long do people live?
How many people in 100 own cars?
U.S.A.
76 years
48
Bolivia
61 years
3
Paraguay
72 years
1

Women rest and talk after a day visiting La Paz. Native peoples such as the Quechua and Aymara make up two-thirds of the Bolivian population.

Search and find

Bolivia
Capitals: La Paz (Administrative) . . C4
Sucre (Legislative) . . . D5
Cochabamba . . D5
Oruro D4
Potosi D5
Riberalta B5
Santa Cruz . . . D6
Tarija E5

Paraguay
Capital: Asunción F8
Ciudad del Este . F9
Concepción . . . F8

Southern Andes

ARGENTINA, CHILE, URUGUAY

Chile
Uruguay
Argentina

THE JAGGED RIDGES and volcanoes of the Andes run southward from the tropics toward bleak, frozen coasts. The continent breaks up into ragged islands around Tierra del Fuego. Great gray-green seas power their way past Cape Horn.

West of the Andes lies Chile, a long, narrow country. Visitors remember it for its sunny vineyards and the crowds in Santiago, the capital. Few visit the deserts of the north, or the wilderness of the far south.

East of the Andes lie the farmland and cattle country of Argentina and Uruguay, on either side of the broad estuary of La Plata. Spanish invaders and settlers from Europe drove most of the people from these lands and founded the cities of Montevideo in Uruguay and Buenos Aires in Argentina, which is the home of a dramatic Latin dance called the tango.

The lasting image of Argentina is of cowboys called *gauchos* galloping across vast, lonely grasslands of the pampas. Times have changed, but gaucho folklore lives on whenever Argentineans barbecue beef on an open fire. Grapevines are grown in the fertile lands around Mendoza, but the remote, windswept grasslands of Patagonia are best suited for raising sheep.

500 miles
500 km

Arica
Iquique
Antofagasta
ATACAMA DESERT
BOLIVIA
PARAGUAY
GRAN CHACO
Bermejo
Salta
San Miguel de Tucumán
Formosa
Resistencia
Corrientes
Posad
Ojos del Salado 22,575 ft (6,880 m)
Santiago del Estero
Catamarca
SIERRA DE CORDOBA
Salado
Paraná
MESOPOTAMIA
Mar Chiquita
Coquimbo
Punta Lengua de Vaca
Córdoba
Concordia
San Juan
Santa Fé
Paraná
Cerro Aconcagua
Mendoza
Río Cuarto
Rosario
Valparaiso
Santiago
San Rafael
Buenos Aires
Rancagua
La Plata
PAMPAS
PACIFIC OCEAN
Talca
Chillán
ARGENTINA
ANDES MOUNTAINS
Mar del Plata
Concepción
Punta Lavapié
Bahia Blanca
CHILE
Colorado
Blanca Bay
Temuco
Neuquén
Negro
Valdivia
Punta de la Galera
Limay
San Matías Gulf
Osorno
PATAGONIA
Puerto Montt
Valdés Peninsula
Chiloé I.
Chubut
Cape Quilán
Chico
CHONOS ARCHIPELAGO
Comodoro Rivadavia
San Jorge Gulf
L. Buenos Aires
Cape Tres Puntas
Deseado
Gulf of Penas
Chico
FALKLAND ISLANDS (U.K.)
Santa Cruz
Wellington I.
Grande Bay
Stanley
West Falkland
East Falkland
REINA ADELAIDA ARCHIPELAGO
Strait of Magellan
Punta Arenas
Tierra del Fuego
Cape San Diego
Santa Inés I.
Ushuaia
Cape Horn

> **DISCOVER MORE**
>
> • *Chile's Atacama Desert is the driest place on earth, with no rainfall.*
>
> • *The monkey puzzle tree, or Chile pine, can produce cones the size of a coconut. It grows in the southern Andes, often in bleak landscapes of volcanic ash and rocks.*

The fishing port of Ushuaia is built at the southern limits of the Americas. This remote spot attracts visitors interested in seeing penguins and other wildlife.

N
W
E
S

Highest mountains

Cerro Aconcagua
22,831 ft
(6,959 m)
Mount McKinley
20,320 ft
(6,194 m)

Where in the world?

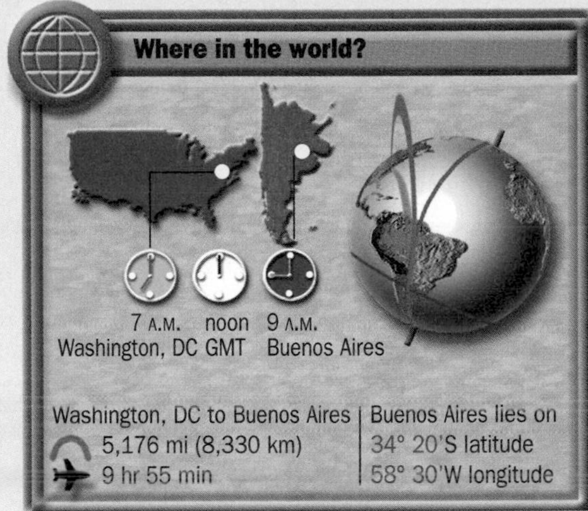

7 A.M.
noon
9 A.M.
Washington, DC GMT
Buenos Aires

Washington, DC to Buenos Aires
5,176 mi (8,330 km)
9 hr 55 min

Buenos Aires lies on
34° 20'S latitude
58° 30'W longitude

AZIL

UAY
ontevideo
Plata

The Atacama Desert is bone-dry and barren, but it is rich in nitrates, iodine, iron ore, and copper.

Life facts

	How long do people live?	How many people in 100 own cars?
U.S.A.	76 years	48
Argentina	75 years	13
Chile	75 years	6
Uruguay	76 years	14

TLANTIC
OCEAN

Argentina

Chile

Uruguay

The folklore of the gauchos, Argentina's wild cowboys of the 1800s, lives on at a modern cattle roundup. Beef is still an important export.

Country facts

	Area sq mi (sq km)	Population	Language	Religion	Currency
Argentina	1,057,518 (2,738,972)	36,737,664	Spanish	Catholic	Peso
Chile	292,258 (756,948)	14,973,843	Spanish	Catholic	Peso
Uruguay	68,039 (176,221)	3,308,523	Spanish	Catholic	Peso

Search and find

Atlantic Ocean
and Islands

THE ATLANTIC OCEAN DIVIDES EUROPE AND AFRICA from the Americas. Its salty waters fill the hot and humid lagoons of Africa's Guinea Coast and sparkle off the Florida Keys. In mid-ocean its white-crested waves may tower to terrifying heights.

The Atlantic is the world's second-largest ocean, covering an area of about 31,744,015 square miles (82,217,000 sq km). The North Atlantic spreads into the freezing Arctic Ocean. It flows eastward to form the North, Baltic, and Mediterranean seas, and westward to form the Caribbean Sea. With an average depth of 11,729 feet (3,575 m), in the Puerto Rico Trench it plunges to an awesome, pitch-black 30,223 feet (9,212 m). The South Atlantic merges with the Pacific and Indian oceans.

Running north to south, the Mid-Atlantic Ridge is a crack in the ocean floor. Molten rock bursts through, creating underwater volcanoes. Islands, many of them volcanic, rise from the ocean—Iceland, the Azores and Madeira, the Canaries, St. Helena, Tristan da Cunha, and Ascension.

In the extreme north and south, the ocean exchanges cold polar waters with warm tropical waters through a system of currents. The cool Benguela Current sweeps down southern Africa, while the Americas are warmed by the Brazil Current and the Gulf Stream. The North Atlantic Drift warms the shores of northwestern Europe.

The trade winds (used by merchant ships in the days of sail) blow in from the northeast and southeast toward the equator, where there is a large windless area called the doldrums. Westerly winds circle the far north and south. In the South Atlantic they join the roaring forties, powerful winds of the Southern Atlantic Ocean—the waters of the South Pacific, South Atlantic, and Indian Ocean, which surround Antarctica.

DISCOVER MORE

- *The islanders of Tristan da Cunha live in one of the most remote places in the world. Their home is 1,513 mi (2,435 km) from the island of St. Helena and 1,702 mi (2,740 km) from Africa.*

Funchal is the chief city on the island of Madeira, which is grouped with the African continent but governed as a part of Portugal, in Europe. It rises from a fine, natural harbor.

Baffin Bay
Greenland (DENMARK)
Cape Chidley
LABRADOR SEA
NORTH AMERICA
Newfoundland
Cape Race
Sable I.
Cape Sable
Cape Cod
Cape Fear
Bermuda (U.K.)
Gulf of Mexico
CARIBBEAN SEA
SOUTH AMERICA
PACIFIC OCEAN
Cape Corrientes
Cape Blanco
Falkland Is (U.K.)
Cape Horn
SCOTIA SEA

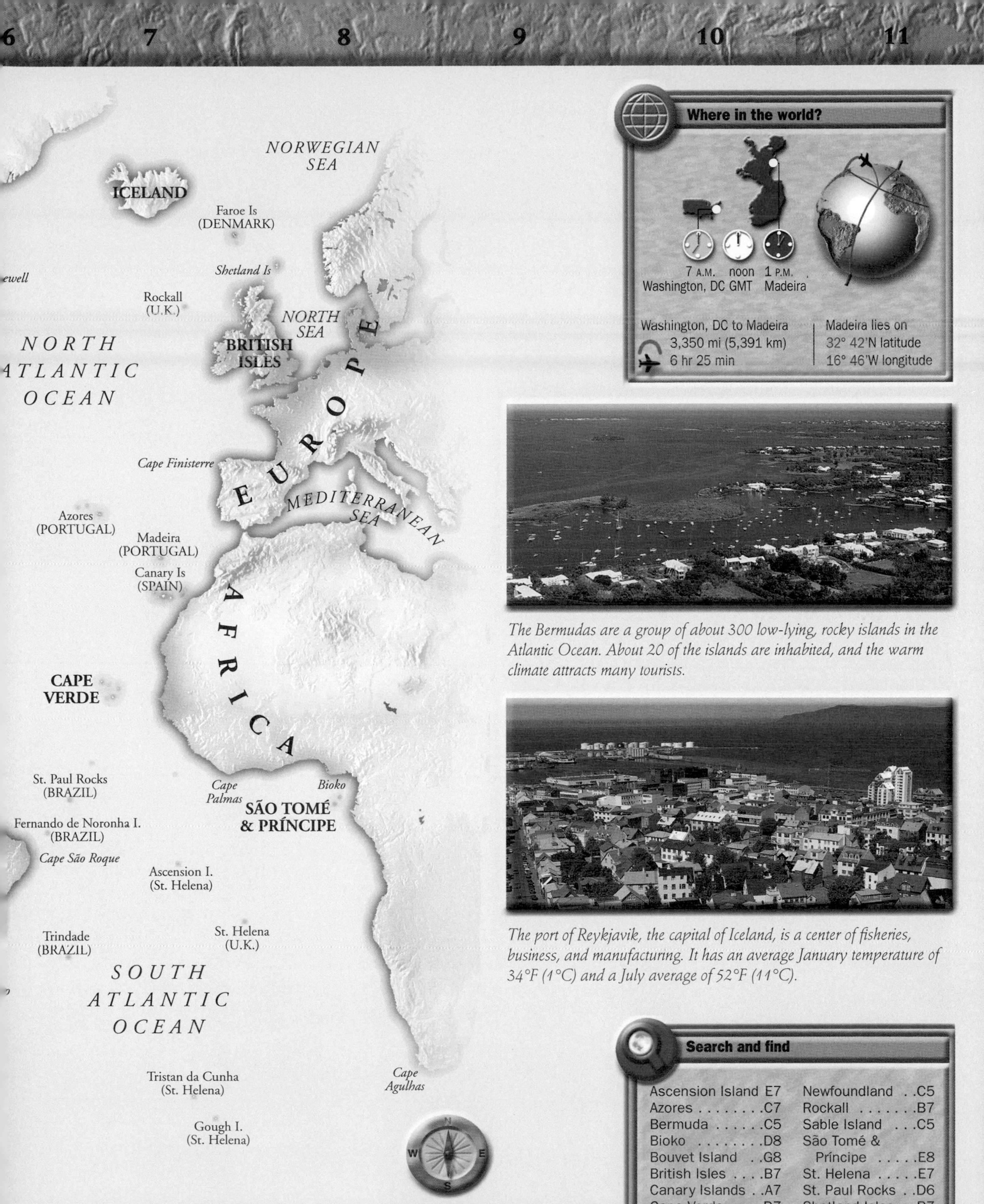

NORWEGIAN SEA
ICELAND
Faroe Is (DENMARK)
Shetland Is
Rockall (U.K.)
NORTH SEA
NORTH ATLANTIC OCEAN
BRITISH ISLES
EUROPE
Cape Finisterre
MEDITERRANEAN SEA
Azores (PORTUGAL)
Madeira (PORTUGAL)
Canary Is (SPAIN)
AFRICA
CAPE VERDE
St. Paul Rocks (BRAZIL)
Cape Palmas
Bioko
SÃO TOMÉ & PRÍNCIPE
Fernando de Noronha I. (BRAZIL)
Cape São Roque
Ascension I. (St. Helena)
Trindade (BRAZIL)
St. Helena (U.K.)
SOUTH ATLANTIC OCEAN
Tristan da Cunha (St. Helena)
Cape Agulhas
Gough I. (St. Helena)
uth Georgia (U.K.)
Bouvet I. (NORWAY)
South Sandwich Is (U.K.)
1,000 miles
3,000 km
Where in the world?
7 A.M. Washington, DC
noon GMT
1 P.M. Madeira
Washington, DC to Madeira
3,350 mi (5,391 km)
6 hr 25 min
Madeira lies on
32° 42'N latitude
16° 46'W longitude

The Bermudas are a group of about 300 low-lying, rocky islands in the Atlantic Ocean. About 20 of the islands are inhabited, and the warm climate attracts many tourists.

The port of Reykjavik, the capital of Iceland, is a center of fisheries, business, and manufacturing. It has an average January temperature of 34°F (1°C) and a July average of 52°F (11°C).

Search and find

Europe

Europe is a small continent, but one of great variety. In wintry Finland, spruce forests and frozen lakes may be blanketed with thick snow, while parts of Spain are so hot that they are becoming desert. Northern France and the United Kingdom have a mild and moist climate, with green fields and woodlands.

The Netherlands are as flat as a pancake, while towering mountain ranges run through southern Europe, including the Pyrenees, the Alps, the Carpathians, and the Caucasus Mountains, where Elbrus rises to 18,510 feet (5,642 m) above sea level.

The European continent belongs to the same landmass as Asia, and together the two continents are often called Eurasia. They are, however, set apart by their different way of life and historical traditions. The dividing line between the two continents runs along the Russian Federation's Ural Mountains, and then follows the Caucasus range, between the Black and Caspian seas. The Strait of Gibraltar, between Morocco and Spain at the western end of the Mediterranean Sea, separates Europe from Africa.

The 47 European countries range in size from the Russian Federation which is by far the largest country, extending across Asia, to the Vatican City which is the smallest. A growing number of countries belong to a close political and economic alliance called the European Union, which provides common economic and other policies for all member countries.

ICELAND
NORWEGIAN SEA
Faroe Is (DENMARK)
SWEDEN
Gulf of Bothn
Shetland Is
NORWAY
Hebrides
Orkney Is
BALTIC SEA
Scotland
Northern Ireland
NORTH SEA
Skagerrak
IRELAND
UNITED KINGDOM
DENMARK
Kaliningra (RUSSIAN FED
Wales
England
NETHERLANDS
POLAND
BELGIUM
GERMANY
LUXEMBOURG
CZECH REPUBLIC
LIECHTENSTEIN
SLOVAK
Bay of Biscay
FRANCE
AUSTRIA
SWITZERLAND
HUNGAR
SLOVENIA
CROATIA
PORTUGAL
BOSNIA-HERZEGOVINA
SLAVIA
ANDORRA
MONACO
SAN MARINO
SPAIN
Corsica (FRANCE)
ITALY
Balearic Is
ALBANIA
Sardinia (ITALY)
VATICAN CITY
Strait of Gibraltar
Gibraltar (U.K.)
MEDITERRANEAN
Sicily

DISCOVER MORE

- *Europe has a longer coastline in proportion to its physical size than any other continent. This is because it has so many inlets, bays, and peninsulas.*
- *The Alps are the highest mountains in western Europe.*

The gondola is the traditional Venice boat. It is poled along the city's canals. Today, gondolas are mostly used by tourists who also use the motor boats and ferries around the waterways.

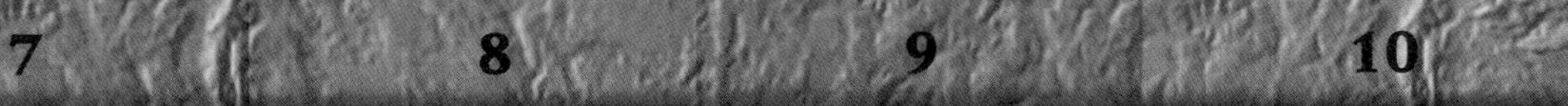

6
7
8
9
10
11

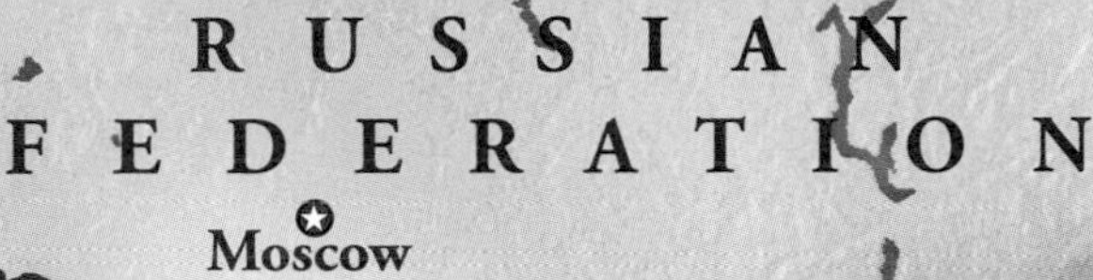

RUSSIAN FEDERATION
Moscow

Kolguyev I.

FINLAND

ESTONIA

LATVIA

LITHUANIA

BELARUS

UKRAINE

MOLDOVA

ROMANIA

BULGARIA

MACEDONIA

GREECE

Crete

SEA

BLACK SEA

CASPIAN SEA

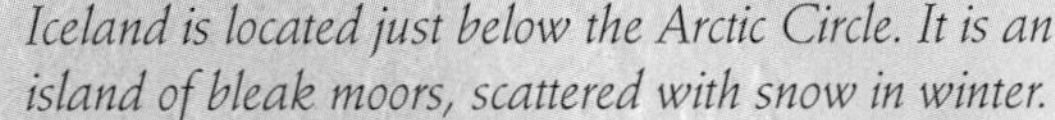

Iceland is located just below the Arctic Circle. It is an island of bleak moors, scattered with snow in winter.

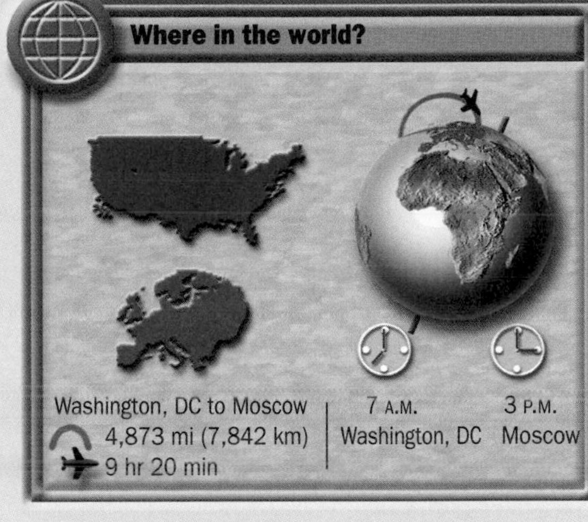

Where in the world?
Washington, DC to Moscow
4,873 mi (7,842 km)
9 hr 20 min
7 A.M.
Washington, DC
3 P.M.
Moscow

Search and find

Albania E6
Andorra E4
Austria D5
Balearic Islands .E4
Belarus D7
Belgium D4
Bosnia-Herzegovina . .E6
Bulgaria E7
Corsica E4
Crete F6
Croatia E5
Czech Republic .D5
Denmark C5
Estonia C6
Faroe Islands . . .B4
Finland B6
France D4
Germany D5
Gibraltar F3
Greece F6
Hebrides C4
Hungary E6
Iceland B4
Ireland C4
Italy E5
Kolguyev Island .A7
Latvia C6
Liechtenstein . . .D5
Lithuania C6
Luxembourg D5
Macedonia E6
Moldova D7
Monaco E4
Moscow C7
Netherlands D5
Norway B5
Orkney Islands . .C4
Poland D6
Portugal E3
Romania E6
Russian Federation . . .C8
San Marino E5
Sardinia E5
Shetland Islands B4
Sicily F5
Slovakia D6
Slovenia E5
Spain E3
Sweden B5
Switzerland D5
Ukraine D7
United Kingdom .C4
Vatican City E5
Yugoslavia E6

N
E
S
W

300 miles
500 km

The Parthenon in Greece was built between 447 and 432 B.C., and was dedicated to Athena, the patron goddess of the city of Athens.

Continent facts

	Area sq mi (sq km)	% of Earth's area	Population	Largest country by area sq mi (sq km)	Largest country by population
Europe	4,015,000 (10,400,000)	6.6	508,285,000	Ukraine* 233,089 (603,700)	Germany* 82,087,361

*largest country entirely in Europe

A

B

C

D

E

F

G

Scandinavia

SWEDEN, FINLAND, NORWAY, ICELAND, DENMARK

A trawlerman repairs nets on a small island off the coast of southern Iceland. The fishing industry is important, but like other nearby countries, Iceland faces decline in stocks of fish because of pollution and overfishing.

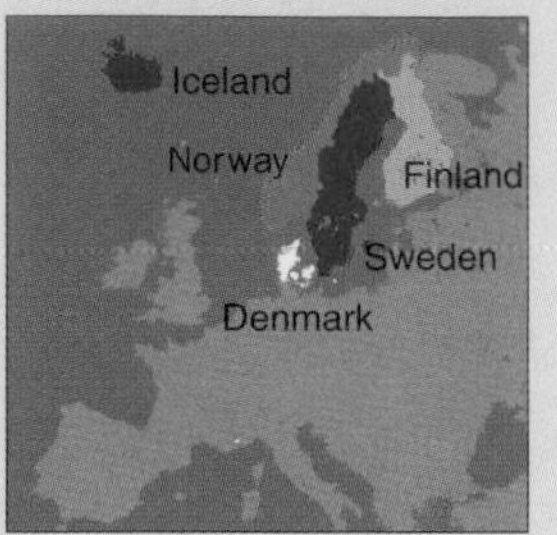
Iceland
Norway
Finland
Sweden
Denmark

THE NORTH SEA AND THE Baltic Sea can be blue and sparkling on summer days, but they are often gray and stormy during the cold winters.

To the south of the Skagerrak strait is Denmark, which is made up of the Jutland Peninsula and some of the neighboring islands. Here the farmland is flat and dotted with wind turbines. Most Danes are city-dwellers. Seagulls squabble on the old docks of the capital, Copenhagen, a lively port whose Danish name means "merchants' harbor."

North of the Skagerrak, the mountainous Scandinavian peninsula stretches far beyond the Arctic Circle, the home of Saami reindeer herders. Norway, with its ragged coastline carved into fjords by the movements of ice, is in the western part of the peninsula. To the east is Sweden, a land of lakes and green forests, with heavy winter snows but milder summers. Most Norwegians and Swedes live in southern or coastal regions, often in large cities such as Oslo or Stockholm, where the climate is less severe. The Scandinavian peninsula is linked to the Russian Federation by Finland, whose snowy forests provide a rich resource of timber.

The people of Iceland, far away in the North Atlantic, are of Scandinavian descent. Their fascinating island is a land of bleak moors, fiery volcanoes, and hot springs.

Grimsey
Olafsfjördhur
Ísafjördhur
Húsavik
Akureyri
Mývatn
ICELAND
Ólafsvik
Eskifjördhur
Borgarnes
Hvítá
Hvítá
Thórsá
VATNAJÖKULL
Reykjavik
Höfn
Keflavik
Hvannadalshnúkur 6,952 ft (2,119 m)
Heimaey
Vik
Surtsey
1 inch to 130 miles
Tromsø
VESTERÅLEN IS
LOFOTEN IS
Narvik
Mt Kebnekaise 6,926 ft (2,111 m)
Bodø
Ume
ATLANTIC OCEAN
Trondheim
Örnsköldsvik
Kristiansund
Östersund
Ålesund
Galdhøpiggen 8,100 ft (2,469 m)
Sundsvall
SWEDEN
NORWAY
Søderhamn
Voss
Lillehammer
Gävle
Bergen
Gjøvik
Falun
Oslo
Haugesund
Uppsala
Västerås
Stavanger
Drammen
Karlstad
Örebro
Skien
Fredrikstad
L. Vänern
Södertälje
NORTH SEA
Norrköping
Kristiansand
Skagerrak
Linköping
Göteborg
L. Vättern
Västervik
Borås
Jönköping
Ålborg
Växjö
Borgholm
Randers
Kattegat
Halmstad
Århus
Helsingborg
Karlshamn
DENMARK
Karlskron
Esbjerg
Copenhagen
Lund
Kolding
Odense
Malmö
GERMANY
BORNHOLM (DENMARK)

The Little Mermaid overlooks Copenhagen's harbor. This much-loved statue honors Hans Christian Andersen (1805–75), who wrote such famous children's tales as The Ugly Duckling, The Snow Queen, and The Little Mermaid.

DISCOVER MORE

- *Northern Scandinavia is often called the "Land of the Midnight Sun" because it stays light all night long in summer. During the bitter winters, it stays dark all day.*
- *Sweden has at least 90,000 lakes. They were created when great sheets of ice scarred and pitted the land during the Ice Age, more than 10,000 years ago.*

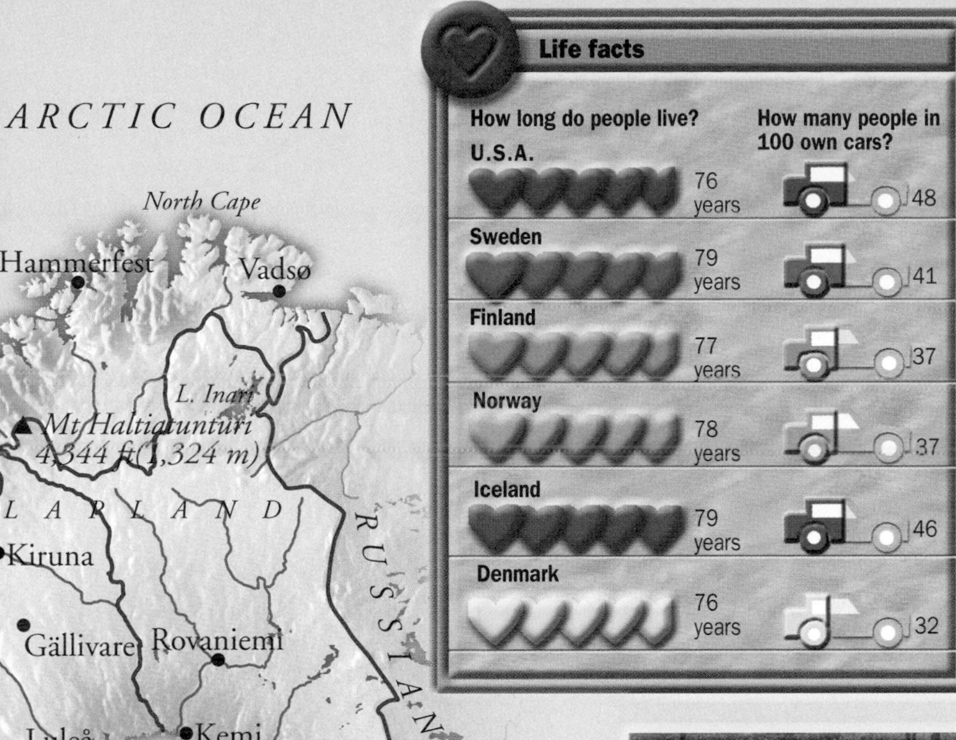

ARCTIC OCEAN
North Cape
Hammerfest
Vadsø
L. Inari
Mt Haltiatunturi 4,344 ft (1,324 m)
LAPLAND
Kiruna
Gällivare
Rovaniemi
Luleå
Kemi
Piteå
Oulu
Skellefteå
RUSSIAN FEDERATION
Umeå
Kokkola
Kuopio
Gulf of Bothnia
Vaasa
FINLAND
Jyväskylä
Tampere
Saimaa
Pöri
Lahti
Hämeenlinna
ÅLAND IS (FINLAND)
Turku
Kotka
Espoo
Helsinki
Mariehamn
tockholm
BALTIC SEA
OTLAND
Visby

Life facts

	How long do people live?	How many people in 100 own cars?
U.S.A.	76 years	48
Sweden	79 years	41
Finland	77 years	37
Norway	78 years	37
Iceland	79 years	46
Denmark	76 years	32

Chain saws and powerful machinery make light work of logging in the conifer forests of Finland. The timber is used in building, furniture manufacture, and papermaking.

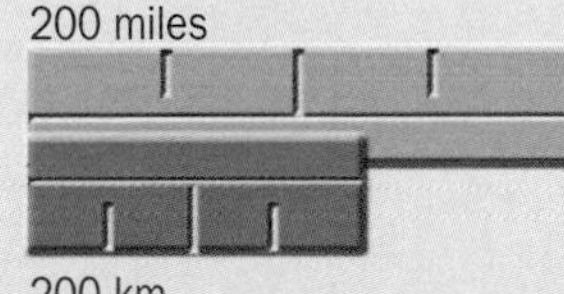

N
W
E
S
200 miles
200 km

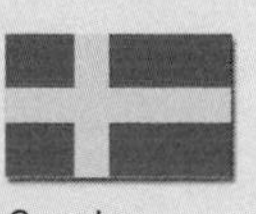
Sweden

Finland

Norway

Iceland

Denmark

Country facts

	Area sq mi (sq km)	Population	Language	Religion	Currency
Sweden	173,731 (449,963)	8,911,296	Swedish	E/Lutheran*	Krona
Finland	130,127 (337,029)	5,158,372	Finnish	E/Lutheran*	Markka
Norway	125,181 (324,219)	4,438,547	Norwegian	E/Lutheran*	Krone
Iceland	39,699 (102,819)	272,512	Icelandic	E/Lutheran*	Krona
Denmark	16,639 (43,095)	5,356,845	Danish	E/Lutheran*	Krone

* Evangelical/Lutheran

Where in the world?

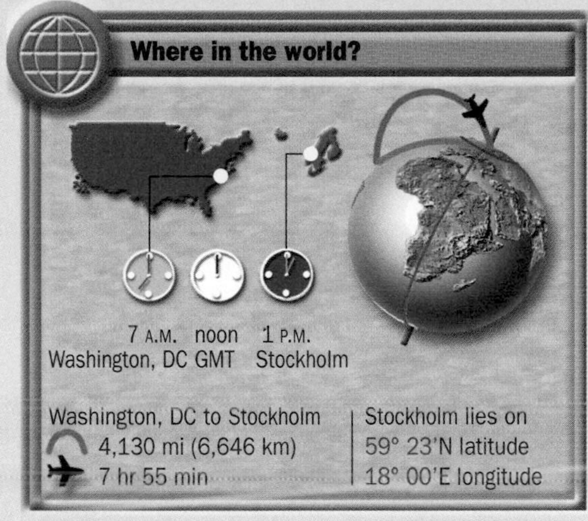

7 A.M. Washington, DC
noon GMT
1 P.M. Stockholm

Washington, DC to Stockholm
4,130 mi (6,646 km)
7 hr 55 min

Stockholm lies on
59° 23'N latitude
18° 00'E longitude

Search and find

Sweden
Capital:Stockholm .E6
Borås F5
Borgholm F6
Falun E6
Gällivare C6
Gävle E6
Göteborg F5
Halmstad F5
Helsingborg F5
Jönköping F5
Karlshamn F5
Karlskrona F6
Karlstad E5
Kiruna B6
Linköping F6
Luleå C6
Lund F5
Malmö F5
Norrköping E6
Örebro E5
Örnsköldsvik . . .D6
Östersund D5
Piteå C6
Skellefteå C6
Søderhamn E6
Södertälje E6
Sundsvall D6
Umeå D6
Uppsala E6
Västerås E6
Västervik F6
Växjö F5
Visby F6

Finland
Capital: Helsinki .E7
Espoo E7
Hämeenlinna . . .E7
Jyväskylä D7
Kemi C7
Kokkola D7
Kotka E7
Kuopio D7
Lahti E7
Mariehamn E6
Oulu C7
Pöri D7
Rovaniemi C7
Tampere D7
Turku E7
Vaasa D6

Norway
Capital: Oslo . . .E5
Ålesund D4
Bergen E4
Bodø C5
Drammen E5
Fredrikstad E5
Gjøvik E4
Hammerfest . . .B6
Haugesund E4
Kristiansand . . .E4
Kristiansund . . .D4
Lillehammer E5
Narvik B6
Skien E5
Stavanger E4
Tromsø B6
Trondheim D5
Vadsø B7
Voss E4

Iceland
Capital:Reykjavik .C4
Akureyri B4
Borgarnes C4
Eskifjördhur C5
Höfn C5
Húsavik B4
Isafjördhur B3
Keflavík C3
Olafsfjördhur . . .B4
Ólafsvik C3
Vik C4

Denmark
Capital:
Copenhagen . .F5
Ålborg F5
Århus F5
Esbjerg F4
Kolding F4
Odense F5
Randers F5

British Isles

UNITED KINGDOM, REPUBLIC OF IRELAND

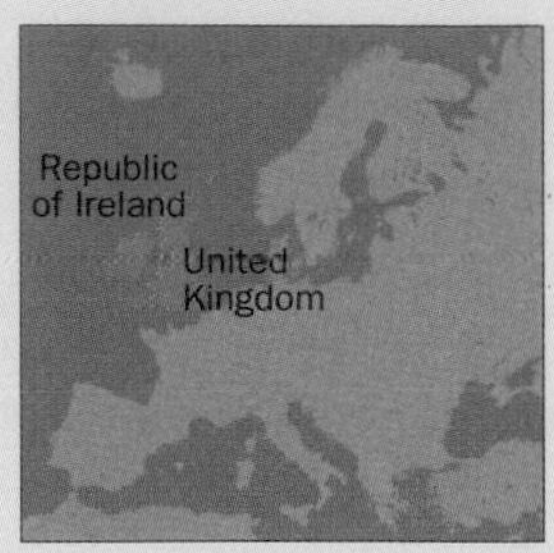
Republic of Ireland
United Kingdom

BATTERED BY THE ATLANTIC Ocean, the coastline of northwest Europe breaks up into the numerous channels and islands of the British Isles. The western shores have a mild, often rainy, climate as a result of the oceans and winds. The inhabitants of these islands include English, Scots, Welsh, and Irish, and large numbers of people of Asian and Afro-Caribbean descent.

The capital of the United Kingdom is London, England, a large city on the Thames River. Red buses and black taxis roar past street markets, fountains, theaters, old churches, royal palaces, and green parks. Beyond London lie wheat fields, rocky shores bordering coastlines, the moors and lakes of northern England, and the mountains of Wales and Scotland, England's partner countries in Great Britain. The British countryside is dotted with historic villages and castles, but there are also large, sprawling cities such as Birmingham, Liverpool, Manchester, and Glasgow.

Across the Irish Sea, Northern Ireland is ruled as part of the United Kingdom, but the Republic of Ireland is an independent country. Its capital is the historic city of Dublin, through which the Liffey River flows. The Irish countryside is peaceful, with lush farmland, peat bogs, and rocky cliffs which tower above the rolling Atlantic surf.

DISCOVER MORE

- *About 10,000 years ago, the British Isles were joined with France. However, the sea gradually flooded the low-lying land to form the English Channel. They were not linked again until a rail tunnel was opened in 1994.*

N W E S

100 miles

150 km

A
B
C
D
E
F
G

SHETLAND IS
Foula
Fair Isle
ORKNEY IS
Kirkwall
John o'Groats
Cape Wrath
Thurso
Butt of Lewis
OUTER HEBRIDES
Stornoway
Lewis
North Minch
NORTHWEST HIGHLANDS
Moray Firth
St. Kilda
North Uist
Skye
Inverness
South Uist
Loch Ness
Spey
Don
Barra
Rhum
Ben Nevis 4,406 ft (1,343 m)
GRAMPIAN MTS
Aberdeen
Dee
Coll
Tiree
Mull
Oban
Perth
Dundee
Tay
ATLANTIC OCEAN
SCOTLAND
Firth of Forth
Forth
Glasgow
Edinburgh
Islay
Clyde
Malin Head
Tory I.
Arran
Ayr
Tweed
Rathlin I.
NORTH CHANNEL
Nith
CHEVIOT HILLS
Aran I.
Londonderry
Stranraer
Donegal
NORTHERN IRELAND
Carlisle
Tyne
Donegal Bay
Lough Neagh
Belfast
Lake District
Sligo
Lower Lough Erne
Isle of Man
Achill Head
Lough Allen
Upper Lough Erne
Douglas
Bradford
Dundalk
IRISH SEA
Blackpool
Lough Mask
Lough Ree
Lough Corrib
Manchester
IRELAND
Liffey
Dublin
Holyhead
Liverpool
Galway
Dun Laoghaire
ARAN IS
Snowdon 3,560 ft (1,085 m)
Shannon
Lough Derg
Wrexham
Loop Head
Limerick
Tipperary
Wolverhampton
Aberystwyth
Birmingham
Gt Blasket I.
Waterford
Cardigan Bay
Killarney
GALTY MTS
WALES
Wye
Severn
Dingle Bay
Carrauntouhill 3,415 ft (1,041 m)
Cork
Hook Head
ST. GEORGE'S CHANNEL
Gloucester
Carmarthen
Newport
Mizen Head
Swansea
Cardiff
Bristol
Lundy
Stonehenge
Bournemouth
Exeter
Lyme Bay
Portland Bill
Penzance
Plymouth
ISLES OF SCILLY
Lands End
ENGLISH
Alderney
CHANNEL IS
Guernsey
Jersey

1 2 3 4 5

erwick

NORTH SEA

ly I.

ewcastle upon Tyne
urham
Middlesbrough
Flamborough Head
eds Hull
Spurn Head
heffield
NGLAND
Nottingham
Derby
eicester
Peterborough
Norwich
Coventry
Cambridge
Northampton
Ipswich
Oxford Luton
Colchester
London
Thames
Canterbury
Reading
Dover
lisbury
Folkestone
outhampton
Brighton
Portsmouth
of Wight
HANNEL

Edinburgh Castle stands on top of a large rocky hill overlooking the city.

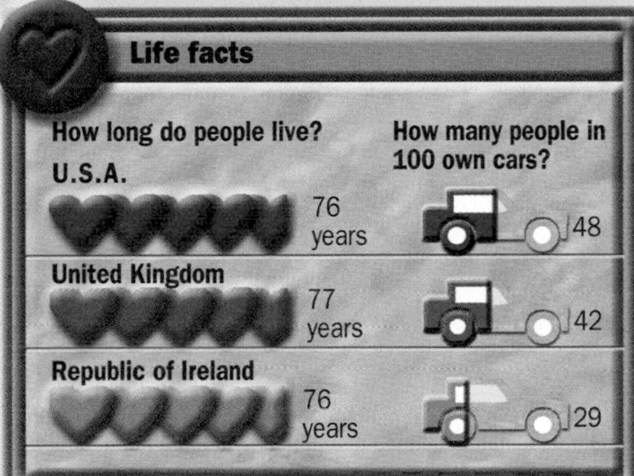
Life facts
How long do people live?
How many people in 100 own cars?
U.S.A.
76 years
48
United Kingdom
77 years
42
Republic of Ireland
76 years
29

The prehistoric pillars of Stonehenge rise from the rolling fields and grassland of Salisbury Plain, in southern England. The site was in use from about 3100 to 1100 B.C.

United Kingdom

Republic of Ireland

Country facts

	Area sq mi (sq km)	Population	Language	Religion	Currency
United Kingdom	94,525 (244,820)	59,113,439	English	Anglican	Pound
Republic of Ireland	27,135 (70,280)	3,632,944	English	Catholic	Irish Pound

Where in the world?

7 A.M. Washington, DC
noon GMT
noon London

Washington, DC to London
3,674 mi (5,913 km)
7 hr 5 min

London lies on
51° 30'N latitude
00° 07'W longitude

Search and find

United Kingdom
Capital: London .F7
Aberdeen C6
Aberystwyth E5
Ayr D5
Belfast D4
Birmingham E6
Blackpool E5
Bournemouth . . .F6
Bradford E6
Brighton F7
Bristol F6
Cambridge F7
Canterbury F7
Cardiff F5
Carlisle D5
Carmarthen F5
Colchester F7
Coventry E6
Derby E6
Douglas D5
Dover F7
Dundee C5
Durham D6
Edinburgh C5
Exeter F5
Folkestone F7
Glasgow C5
Gloucester F6
Holyhead E5
Hull E6
Inverness C5
Ipswich F7
Kirkwall B5
Leeds E6
Leicester E6
Lerwick A6
Liverpool E5
Londonderry . . .D4
Luton F7
Manchester E6
Middlesbrough . .D6
Newcastle upon Tyne D6
Newport F5
Northampton . . .F6
Norwich E7
Nottingham E6
Oban C5
Oxford F6
Penzance G4
Perth C5
Peterborough . . .E6
Plymouth F6
Portsmouth F5
Reading F6
Salisbury F6
Sheffield E6
Southampton . . .F6
Stornoway B4
Stranraer D5
Swansea F4
Thurso B5
Wolverhampton .E6
Wrexham E5

Republic of Ireland
Capital: Dublin . .E4
Cork F4
Donegal D4
Dun Laoghaire . .E4
Dundalk E4
Galway E3
Killarney F3
Limerick E3
Sligo D4
Tipperary E4
Waterford F4

A

Low Countries

NETHERLANDS, BELGIUM, LUXEMBOURG

Netherlands
Belgium
Luxembourg

B

ONLY SEA WALLS AND RIVER barriers prevent the stormy North Sea from flooding into the Netherlands, for large areas of the country are below sea level. The best way to travel is by bicycle, because there are very few hills. Canals and rivers cross the flat farmland. Many fields are grazed by black-and-white Holstein cows, whose milk is used to make Dutch cheeses. In spring, other fields are brilliant with tulips. Many cities have elegant merchants' houses built in the 1600s. The Netherlands is still a center of business and trade, and Rotterdam is the world's busiest seaport. The capital is Amsterdam, but the center of government is at The Hague.

C

Belgium is another low-lying, mostly flat country with a rich history. It is a major industrial and commercial power, which is also famous for its handmade chocolates and lace. Southern Belgium rises to the hills of the Ardennes, which become the fields and woods of tiny Luxembourg.

D

The city of Luxembourg is an international center of finance. Brussels, the Belgian capital, and the city of Luxembourg are the headquarters of many of the institutions of the European Union (EU). Although Luxembourg is a small country, it has its own language, called Letzeburgish. Many people speak it there, in addition to French or German.

E

The Dutch landscape is still dotted with beautiful old windmills, which were once used to power pumps for draining waterlogged fields. Many are still in working order today.

Wearing traditional costume, a Belgian woman moves bobbins skillfully across a pillow to make delicate patterns of lace. Fine lace has been made in the city of Bruges since the Middle Ages.

Zeebrugge
Ostend
Bruges
Roeselare
Kortrijk
Tournai

F

DISCOVER MORE

- *Over 40 percent of the Netherlands has been created by people. It is mostly polder—land that has been reclaimed from the sea and drained.*
- *The Belgian town of Spa has health-enhancing mineral springs, which were discovered more than 600 years ago. They became so famous that health resorts all over the world are now called spas.*

G

Amsterdam is built on marshy land, which lies just below sea level. More than 100 canals cross the city, helping to drain the land. The city's name means "dam of the Amstel"—referring to a dam that was built in the 13th century.

Netherlands

Belgium

Luxembourg

Country facts

	Area sq mi (sq km)	Population	Language	Religion	Currency
Netherlands	16,033 (41,525)	15,807,641	Dutch	Catholic	Guilder
Belgium	11,780 (30,510)	10,182,034	Flemish/French	Catholic	Franc
Luxembourg	999 (2,587)	429,080	French	Catholic	Franc

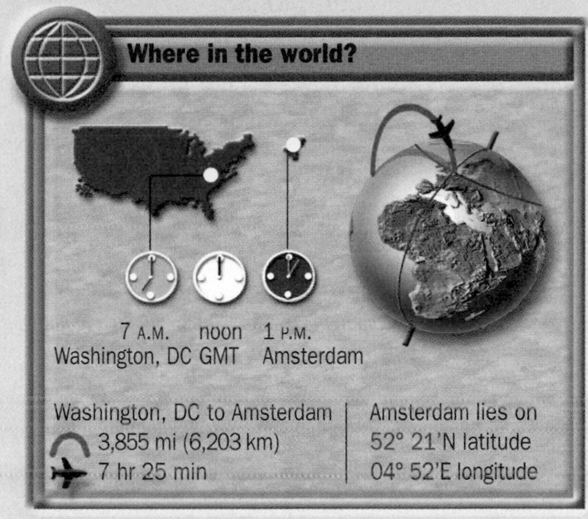

Where in the world?
7 A.M.
Washington, DC
noon
GMT
1 P.M.
Amsterdam
Washington, DC to Amsterdam
3,855 mi (6,203 km)
7 hr 25 min
Amsterdam lies on
52° 21'N latitude
04° 52'E longitude

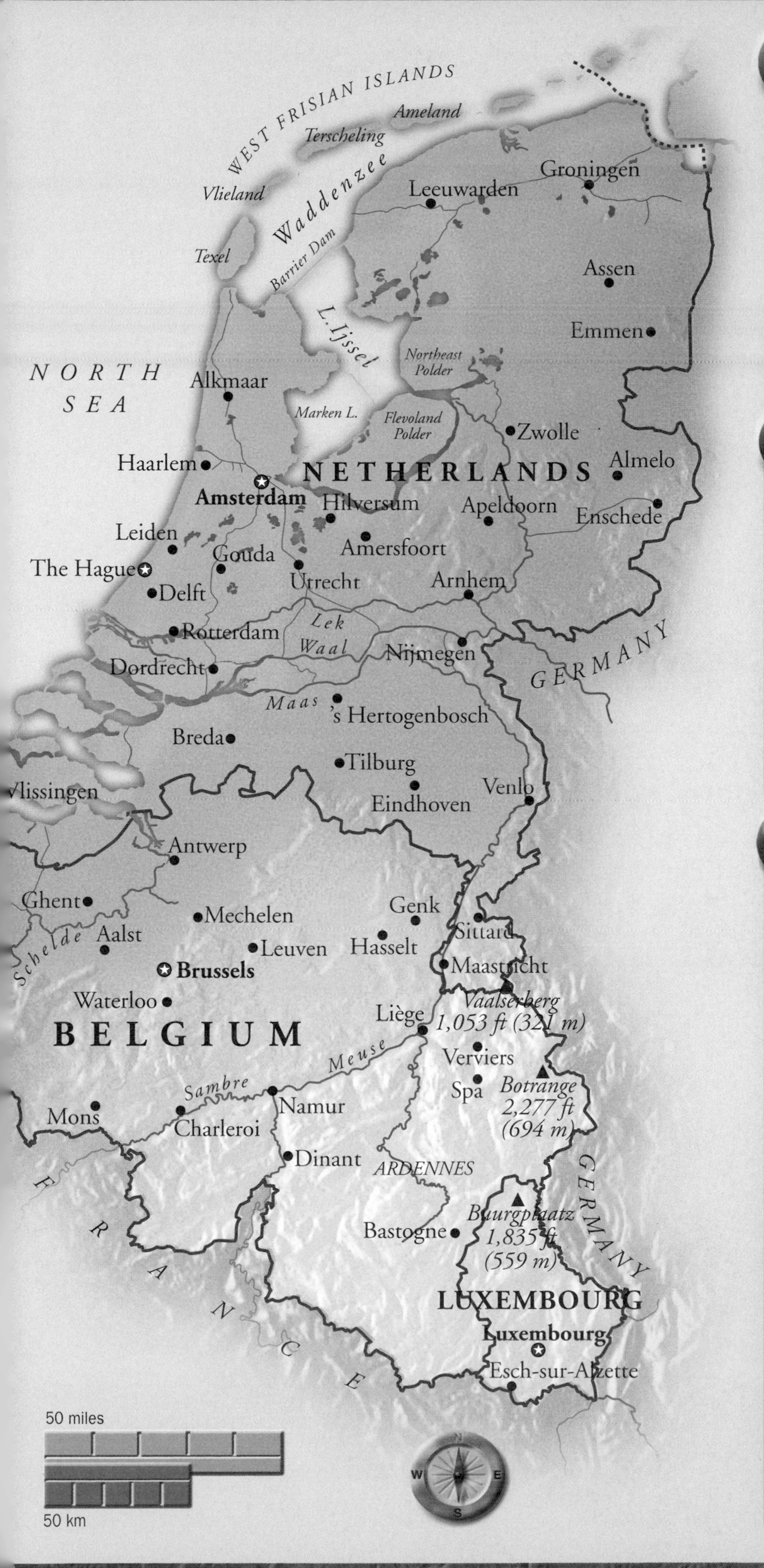

Life facts
How long do people live?
How many people in 100 own cars?
U.S.A.
76 years
48
Netherlands
78 years
36
Belgium
77 years
42
Luxembourg
78 years
54

Search and find

Netherlands

Capitals:

- Amsterdam . . C7
- The Hague . . C7
- Alkmaar B7
- Almelo C9
- Amersfoort C8
- Apeldoorn C8
- Arnhem C8
- Assen B9
- Breda D7
- Delft C7
- Dordrecht C7
- Eindhoven D8
- Emmen B9
- Enschede C9
- Gouda C7
- Groningen A9
- Haarlem C7
- Hilversum C8
- Leeuwarden A8
- Leiden C7
- Maastricht E8
- Nijmegen C8
- Rotterdam C7
- Sittard E8
- 's Hertogenbosch . D8
- Tilburg D8
- Utrecht C7
- Venlo D8
- Vlissingen D6
- Zwolle B8

Belgium

Capital: Brussels E7

- Aalst E6
- Antwerp D7
- Bastogne F8
- Bruges D6
- Charleroi E7
- Dinant F7
- Genk E8
- Ghent E6
- Hasselt E8
- Kortrijk E6
- Leuven E7
- Liège E8
- Mechelen E7
- Mons E6
- Namur E7
- Ostend D5
- Roeselare E6
- Spa E8
- Tournai E6
- Verviers E8
- Waterloo E7
- Zeebrugge D6

Luxembourg

Capital:

- Luxembourg . . F9
- Esch-sur-Alzette . G8

France and Its Neighbors

FRANCE, ANDORRA, MONACO

Southeastern France includes the western end of the Alps, the highest mountain range in western Europe.

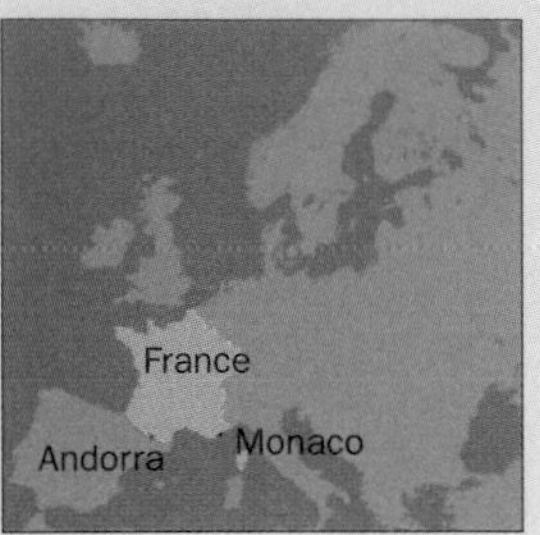
France
Andorra
Monaco

THE CITY OF PARIS, CAPITAL OF France, is built on the islands and banks of the Seine River, which winds across France's northern plain. On land, traffic pours though the city, along broad, tree-lined avenues to the grand memorial, the Triumphal Arc.

Here in Paris you can see the soaring iron arches of the Eiffel Tower. You will find the world-famous art museum of the Louvre, and the arts complex of the Beaubourg Center. There is also the ancient cathedral of Nôtre Dame, and the old artists' quarter of Montmartre, with its fashionable crowds and small restaurants serving *haute cuisine*—fine cooking.

France lies at the heart of western Europe. Its cool north coast is on the English Channel. Its west coast is formed by the stormy Bay of Biscay, but its sunny south coast borders the Mediterranean Sea. Mountains make up its eastern border—from the Vosges and Jura to the icy peaks and glaciers of the Alps. The Rhône River forms a valley running north to south almost through the center of France.

Although French is spoken everywhere, several other languages may be heard too. They include Breton, Catalán, Basque, and Arabic.

Two tiny independent states border France. Monaco, on the Mediterranean coast, is famous for its casinos and automobile racing. The mountain state of Andorra, high in the Pyrenees, attracts thousands of skiers and walkers.

DISCOVER MORE

- *Corsica is a French island in the Mediterranean Sea. It was the birthplace of Napoleon Bonaparte, the French general and emperor.*
- *The world's toughest bicycle race is the Tour de France. It includes mountains and plains and has exceeded 3,540 mi (5,700 km).*

France

Andorra

Monaco

Country facts

	Area sq mi (sq km)	Population	Language	Religion	Currency
France	211,208 (547,029)	58,978,172	French	Catholic	Franc
Andorra	181 (469)	65,939	Catalán	Catholic	Franc/Peseta
Monaco	0.75 (1.95)	32,149	French	Catholic	Franc

7
8
9
10
11

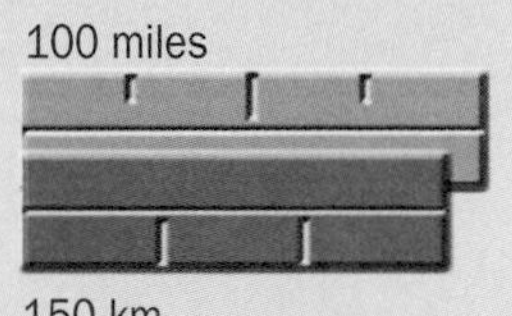

100 miles
150 km

N
W
E
S

LUXEMBOURG
Meuse
Verdun
Châlons-sur-Marne
Metz
Strasbourg
Nancy
LORRAINE
VOSGES MTS
Rhine
GERMANY
Mulhouse
Saône
Dijon
Besançon
SWITZERLAND
JURA MTS
Mâcon
Bourg-en-Bresse
Chamonix
Rhône
Mont Blanc
Lyon
Chambéry
St.-Étienne
ALPS
Grenoble
ITALY
Valence
Montélimar
Durance
Avignon
MONACO
Monaco
Nîmes
Nice
Antibes
Aix-en-Provence
Cannes
Marseille
St.-Tropez
Toulon
Lion
TERRANEAN SEA

Cape Corse
Bastia
CORSICA
Gulf of Sagone
Ajaccio
Strait of Bonifacio

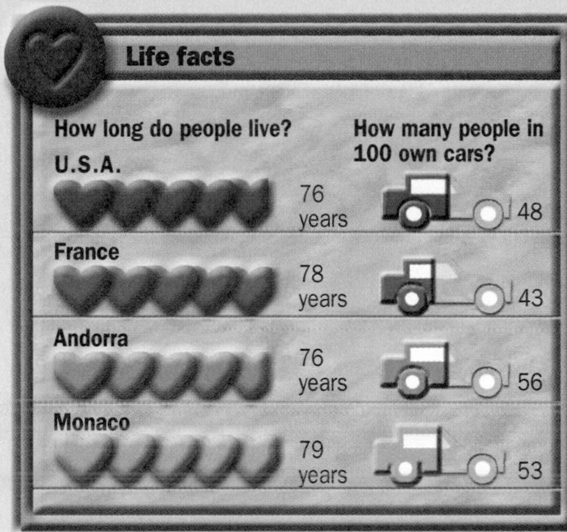

Life facts
How long do people live?
How many people in 100 own cars?
U.S.A.
76 years
48
France
78 years
43
Andorra
76 years
56
Monaco
79 years
53

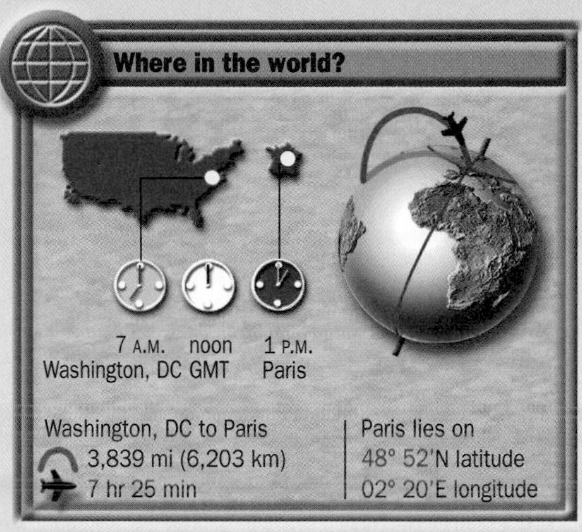

Where in the world?
7 A.M. Washington, DC
noon GMT
1 P.M. Paris
Washington, DC to Paris
3,839 mi (6,203 km)
7 hr 25 min
Paris lies on
48° 52'N latitude
02° 20'E longitude

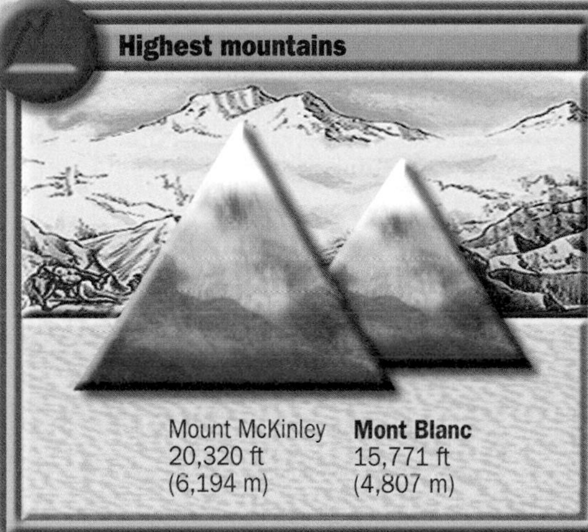

Highest mountains
Mount McKinley
20,320 ft
(6,194 m)
Mont Blanc
15,771 ft
(4,807 m)

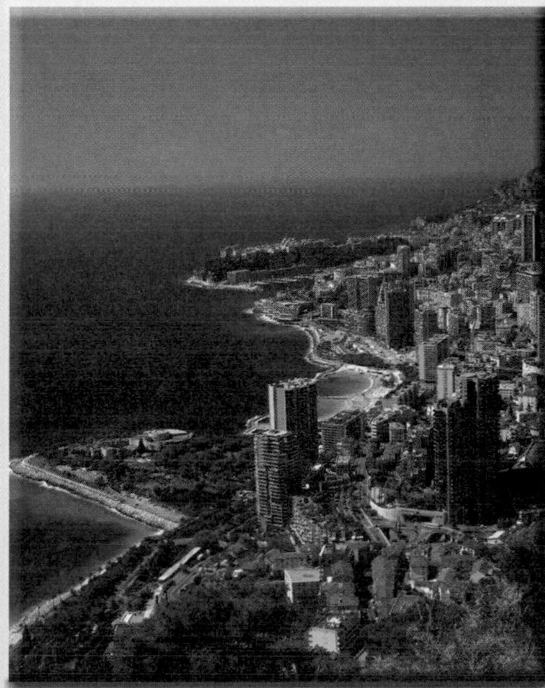

Monte Carlo basks in the warm Mediterranean sunshine. This wealthy, built-up residential area takes up most of the tiny principality of Monaco.

Search and find

France
Capital: Paris. . . C5
Aix-en-Provence . F7
Amiens. B5
Angers D4
Angoulême E4
Antibes F7
Arles. F6
Auxerre. D6
Avignon. E6
Bayonne F4
Bergerac. E5
Besançon D7
Béziers F6
Bordeaux E4
Boulogne B5
Bourg-en-Bresse D7
Bourges D5
Brest C3
Caen C4
Calais B5
Cannes F7
Carcassonne . . . F5
Castres. F5
Châlons-sur-Marne. C6
Chambéry E7
Chamonix D7
Chartres C5
Cherbourg. C4
Clermont-Ferrand E6
Cognac E4
Dieppe B5
Dijon D6
Douai B5
Dunkerque B5
Fontainebleau . . C5
Grenoble. E7
La Rochelle. . . . D4
Le Havre. C5
Le Mans C5
Lille B5
Limoges D5
Lorient C3
Lourdes F4
Lyon. E6
Mâcon D6
Marseille. F7
Metz C7
Montauban E5
Montélimar E6
Montluçon. D5
Montpellier F6
Mulhouse C7
Nancy. C7
Nantes D4
Nice F7
Nîmes. F6
Orléans C5
Pau F4
Périgueux E5
Perpignan F5
Poitiers. D5
Quimper C3
Reims C6
Rennes. C4
Roubaix B6
Rouen C5
Sète F6
St.-Denis. C5
St.-Étienne E6
St.-Malo C4
St.-Nazaire D4
St.-Quentin B6
St.-Tropez F7
Strasbourg C7
Tarbes F4
Toulon. F7
Toulouse F5
Tours D5
Troyes C6
Valence. E6
Valenciennes . . . B6
Verdun C6
Versailles C5

Andorra. F5
Capital: Andorra la Vella F5

Monaco F7
Capital: Monaco F7

Corsica
Ajaccio G7
Bastia. F7

Iberian Peninsula

SPAIN, PORTUGAL

The Torre de Belém guards the entrance to Lisbon's harbor. When it was built in 1520, Portugal was building up a South American empire. That is why today more than 165 million Brazilians speak the Portuguese language.

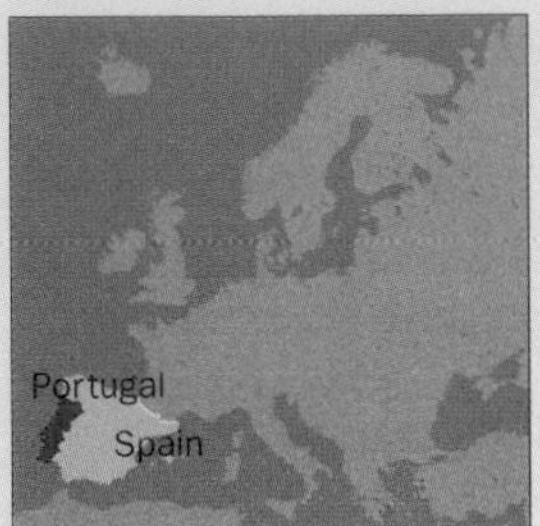
Portugal
Spain

SOUTHWESTERN EUROPE IS A great area of land called the Iberian Peninsula, which sweeps around from the Bay of Biscay into the Atlantic Ocean. The sheer rock face of Gibraltar, just 8 miles (13 km) from the African coast, guards the western approach to the Mediterranean Sea. Spain's northern coast is green and moist, but the southern region of Andalusia is extremely hot in summer. It is a land of red soil and brown rock, with cactuses, olive groves, orange trees, and whitewashed villages. Central Spain is a dry, dusty plateau known as the Meseta. This is framed by the peaks of the Cantabrian, Pyrenees, and Sierra Nevada mountains.

Spain is a land of distinct cultural regions, with the Basque, Catalán, and Galician peoples all retaining their own languages and customs. The country is famous for its fiery, foot-stamping flamenco dances, for its bullfighting, and for colorful Christian processions in which statues of saints are carried through village streets.

In Portugal, the white buildings and red-tiled roofs of many towns face the Atlantic Ocean. One-third of the population lives in cities, such as Lisbon, Coimbra, and Porto. However, most people are country dwellers. Portugal is a land of hills, cork-oak forests, and vineyards, descending to coastal inlets and river estuaries. The rivers provide irrigation and hydroelectric power.

Cape Ortegal
Cape Peñas
Bay of Biscay
El Ferrol
Gijón
Santander
La Coruña
Oviedo
CANTABRIAN MOUNTAINS
Bilbao
Lugo
Sil
Santiago de Compostela
Vitória/Gasteiz
León
Ebro
Logroñ
ATLANTIC OCEAN
Vigo
Miño
Orense
SIERRA CABRERA
Esla
Palencia
Burgos
Braga
Tua
Zamora
Valladolid
Duero
Soria
Porto
Tormes
SPAIN
Douro
Salamanca
Segovia
Guadalaja
Aviero
Ávila
Madrid
Alcalá
Henar
Coimbra
SIERRA DE GREDOS
Tajo
Aranjuez
PORTUGAL
Toledo
Cáceres
Tagus
MONTES DE TOLEDO
Guadiana
Ciudad Real
Lisbon
Évora
Badajoz
Mérida
Setúbal
Puertollano
Valdepeñ
Ardila
SIERRA MORENA
Linares
Guadiana
Chança
Guadalquivir
Córdoba
Jaén
Mulhacé
11,411
(3,479
Lagos
Huelva
Seville
Puente Genil
Genil
Faro
Morón de la Frontera
Antequera
Granada
Cape St. Vincent
Gulf of Cádiz
Jerez de la Frontera
Arcos
Ronda
SIERRA NEVADA
Málaga
Motri
SIERRA DE RONDA
Cádiz
Marbella
Costa del S
Algeciras
Gibraltar (U.K.)
Strait of Gibraltar
Ceuta (SPAIN)
Melilla (SPAIN)

DISCOVER MORE

• *During the annual San Fermín festival in Pamplona, Spain, six bulls are released into the streets each morning. They chase the crowds of people, who try to show off their daring and escape the bulls' sharp horns.*

The massive Rock of Gibraltar towers over the narrow entrance to the Mediterranean Sea. It is linked to the Spanish mainland by a neck of low lying sand.

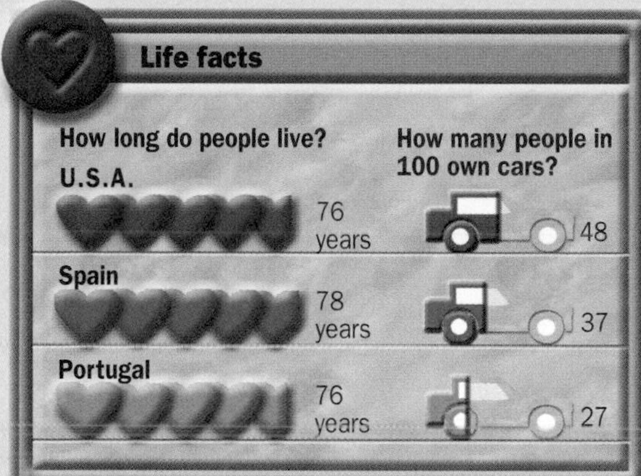

Life facts
How long do people live?
How many people in 100 own cars?
U.S.A.
76 years
48
Spain
78 years
37
Portugal
76 years
27

In swirling, traditional dress, young girls learn how to dance to the flamenco music of the Andalusia region. The occasion is the Feria, a spectacular festival held each April in the city of Seville.

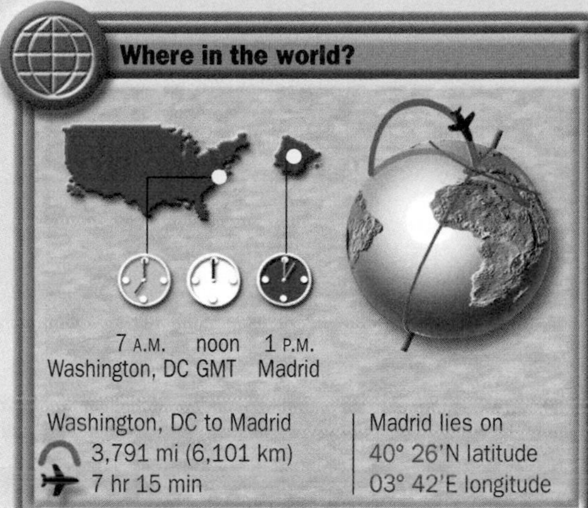

Where in the world?
7 A.M. Washington, DC
noon GMT
1 P.M. Madrid
Washington, DC to Madrid
3,791 mi (6,101 km)
7 hr 15 min
Madrid lies on
40° 26'N latitude
03° 42'E longitude

San Sebastián
FRANCE
PYRENEES
ANDORRA
Pamplona
Arga
Pico de Aneto
11,168 ft
(3,405 m)
Gállego
Cinca
Lleida
Girona
Manresa
Tarrasa
Mataró
Costa Brava
Saragossa
Ebro
Reus
Barcelona
Jalón
Tarragona
Costa Dorada
Tortosa
Cape Tortosa
Tajo
Morella
Teruel
Castellón de la Plana
Costa del Azahar
Cuenca
Turia
Sagunto
Menorca
Mallorca
Palma
Valencia
Gulf of Valencia
Júcar
Ibiza
Ibiza
BALEARIC IS
Albacete
Alcoy
Formentera
Segura
Alicante
Elche
Costa Blanca
Murcia
Cartagena
Cape Palos
Lorca
MEDITERRANEAN SEA
Almería
Cabo de Gata

200 miles

300 km

Olive trees dot the rolling red earth near Córdoba in southern Spain. This part of Spain has hot, dry summers and mild winters.

Spain

Portugal

Search and find

Spain

Capital: Madrid . . .D5
Albacete E6
Alcalá de Henares . .D6
Alcoy E7
Algeciras F5
Alicante E7
Almería F6
Antequera F5
Aranjuez D5
Arcos F4
Ávila D5
Badajoz E4
Barcelona C8
Bilbao B6
Burgos C5
Cáceres D4
Cádiz F4
Cartagena E7
Castellón de la Plana D7
Ceuta F5
Ciudad Real E5
Córdoba E5
Cuenca D6
El Ferrol B4
Elche E7
Gijón B5
Girona C8
Granada F5
Guadalajara D6
Huelva F4
Ibiza E8
Jaén E5
Jerez de la Frontera .F4
La Coruña B3
León C5
Lleida C7
Linares E5
Logroño C6
Lorca E6
Lugo B4
Málaga F5
Manresa C8
Marbella F5
Mataró C8
Melilla G6
Mérida E4
Morella D7
Morón de la Frontera F5
Motril F5
Murcia E7
Orense C4
Oviedo B4
Palencia C5
Palma D8
Pamplona C6
Puente Genil F5
Puertollano E5
Reus C7
Ronda F5
Sagunto D7
Salamanca D5
San Sebastián . . .B6
Santander B5
Santiago de Compostela . . .C3
Saragossa C7
Segovia D5
Seville F4
Soria C6
Tarragona C7
Tarrasa C8
Teruel D7
Toledo D5
Tortosa D7
Valdepeñas E6
Valencia D7
Valladolid C5
Vigo C3
Vitória C6
Zamora C5

Portugal

Capital: Lisbon . .E3
Aviero D3
Braga C3
Coimbra D3
Évora E4
Faro F4
Lagos F3
Porto C3
Setúbal E3

Country facts

	Area sq mi (sq km)	Population	Language	Religion	Currency
Spain	195,364 (505,993)	39,167,744	Spanish	Catholic	Peseta
Portugal	35,672 (92,390)	9,918,040	Portuguese	Catholic	Escudo

Germany

Small towns and villages sit beneath peaks dusted with snow. They are popular for exploring the lakes and forests of the Alps.

Germany

CRANES TOWER OVER THE LEAFY avenues of the German capital, Berlin. New glass buildings rise on the skyline, as the city is rebuilt after long years in which Germany was divided into separate countries, East Germany and West Germany. Berlin lies on a great plain, which stretches from eastern Germany to the Russian Federation. It has cold, snowy winters, while the warm summers are ideal for swimming in the woodland lakes.

Germany has sandy coasts on the North and Baltic seas. In the west, the Rhine River winds through steep-sided valleys, where sunny slopes are covered in vineyards. Central Germany is mountainous, but the country's highest peaks are in the Bavarian Alps in the south. Germany has many large cities and factories producing chemicals, electrical goods, and cars.

Although the German language is spoken everywhere, there are many different dialects and accents because it is such a large country. There are also immigrants from Turkey and Eastern Europe. The German people have a very strong sense of region, with each part of the country having its own way of preparing food and drink, its own newspapers, and its own way of celebrating traditional festivals. Carnival, the week before the Christian period of Lent, is marked by wild parties and fancy dress.

Sylt I.
Schleswig
Helgoland I.
EAST FRISIAN IS
Cuxhaven
Bremerhaven
Wilhelmshaven
Hamburg
Bremen
Oldenburg
Weser
Aller
NETHERLANDS
Ems
Osnabrück
Hannover
Hameln
Bielefeld
TEUTOBURGER FOREST
Münster
Hamm
Rhine
Duisburg
Dortmund
Paderborn
Leine
Krefeld
Essen
Düsseldorf
Wuppertal
Kassel
Solingen
Leverkusen
GERMAN
Cologne (Köln)
Aachen
Bonn
Siegen
Fulda
BELGIUM
Koblenz
Wetzlar
Moselle
Wiesbaden
Frankfurt am Main
Trier
Offenbach
Mainz
HUNSRÜCK
LUXEMBOURG
Worms
Darmstadt
Ludwigshafen
Mannheim
Saar
Kaiserslautern
Heidelberg
Saarbrücken
Karlsruhe
Heilbronn
Pforzheim
Baden-Baden
Stuttgart
FRANCE
Tübingen
BLACK FOREST
Reutlingen
SWABIAN JURA
Ulm
Freiburg
L. Constance
SWITZERLAND

DISCOVER MORE

- *Germany produces 1,500 different types of sausage.*
- *The spire of Ulm cathedral soars to 528 ft (161 m). It is the tallest in the world.*
- *The Black Forest, in southwest Germany, is named after the dark rows of fir trees that cover higher ground. Beech and oak trees cover the lower-lying ground.*

The tall granite turrets of Neuschwanstein date back to 1869, when it was built for King Ludwig II of Bavaria, which is now a state in southeastern Germany.

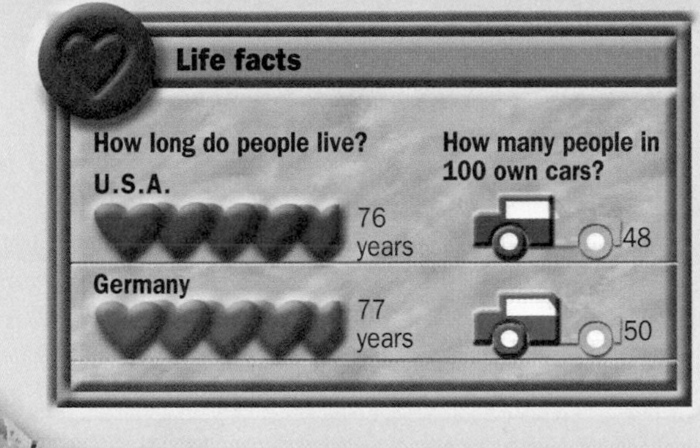
Life facts
How long do people live?
U.S.A.
76 years
Germany
77 years
How many people in 100 own cars?
48
50

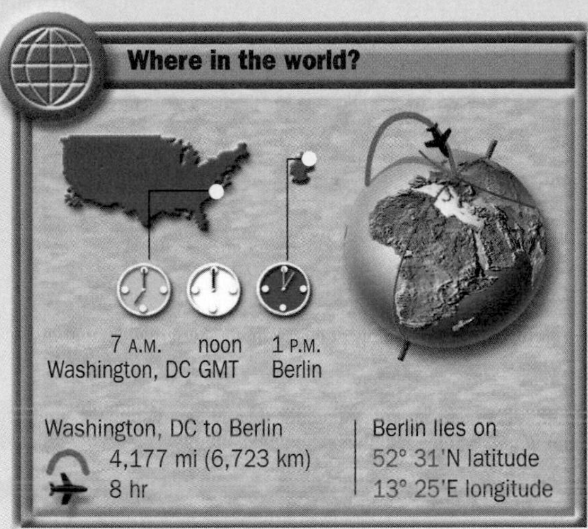
Where in the world?
7 A.M. Washington, DC
noon GMT
1 P.M. Berlin
Washington, DC to Berlin
4,177 mi (6,723 km)
8 hr
Berlin lies on
52° 31'N latitude
13° 25'E longitude

The pretty medieval town of Rothenburg ob der Tauber was once famous for its textile industry. It lies to the south of Würzburg, in southern Germany. It is visited by tourists from all over the world.

Germany

100 miles

150 km

This tollhouse, on an island, was built in 1326 for ships passing up and down the Rhine. This river remains a busy commercial waterway today.

Search and find

Country facts

	Area sq mi (sq km)	Population	Language	Religion	Currency
Germany	137,803 (356,910)	82,087,361	German	Protestant/Catholic	Mark

The Alps

AUSTRIA, SWITZERLAND, LIECHTENSTEIN

Switzerland
Austria
Liechtenstein

IN SUMMER THE ALPS ARE A world of sunny meadows filled with wildflowers, dark forests, lakeshores, and villages of broad-roofed, wooden chalets. The air is filled with the clanking of cowbells and the rush of waterfalls. Glistening peaks form the skyline. In winter all this is transformed: Snow fills the valleys, attracting skiers and snowboarders.

The Alpine region of Europe has famous cities, too. In Switzerland there is Geneva, headquarters of the International Committee of the International Red Cross and Crescent Movement (ICRC), the World Health Organization (WHO), and the World Trade Organization (WTO); and Zürich, a world center of banking. In Austria, Salzburg's music festival celebrates the composer Wolfgang Amadeus Mozart. Vienna, Austria's capital, is a grand city on the Danube River. It is renowned for its theaters, cafés, museums, parks and gardens.

Switzerland is famous for its cheeses, its precision instruments, and its clocks, while Austria produces timber, paper, steel, and glass. Liechtenstein, a tiny nation set between these two countries, relies on tourism. It uses Swiss currency, and its lenient tax laws attract many companies to register there.

The Alps are a meeting place between northern and southern Europe, and the region is shared by several peoples with different cultures and languages.

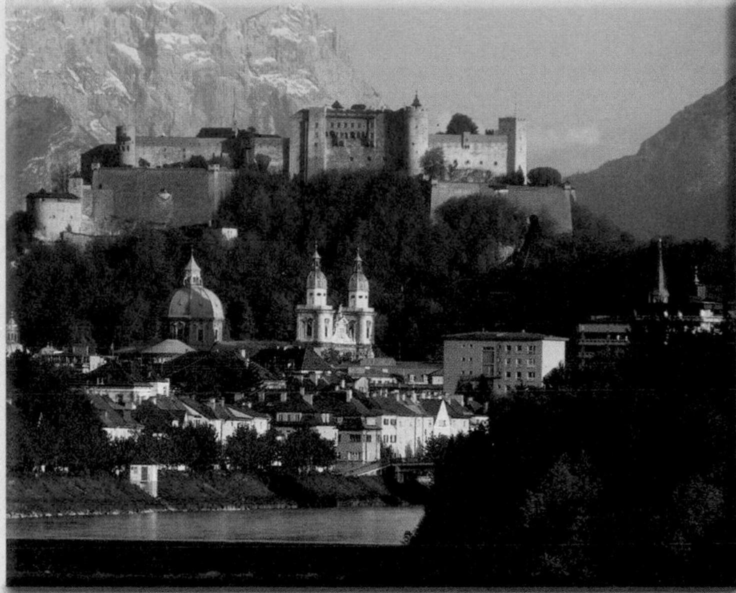

Salzburg was the birthplace of the great composer Wolfgang Amadeus Mozart (1756–91). It is a fine old Austrian city on the banks of the Salzach River, dominated by the towers of Hohensalzburg Castle.

DISCOVER MORE

- *The Austrian composer Johann Strauss the Younger (1825–99) wrote over 400 waltzes, romantic dances which were pop hits of his day. The most famous was called "The Blue Danube," after the Danube River that flows through Vienna.*

The Matterhorn rises in the Alps on Switzerland's border with Italy. Its distinctive peak, 14,688 ft (4,478 m) above sea level, has claimed many lives.

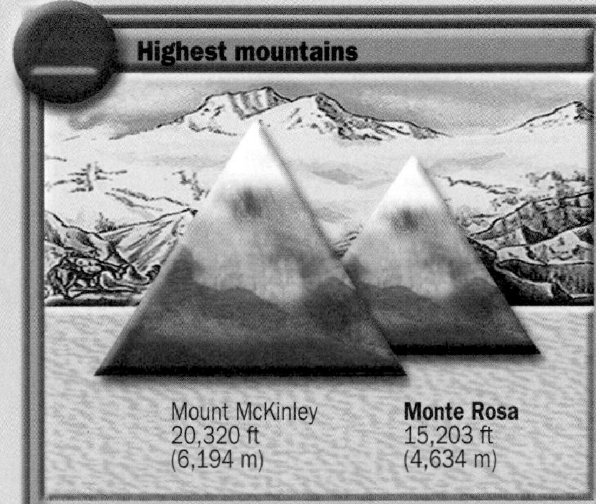
Highest mountains
Mount McKinley
20,320 ft
(6,194 m)
Monte Rosa
15,203 ft
(4,634 m)

Once the winter snows have melted, tall grasses and wildflowers grow in sunny meadows high in the Swiss Alps.

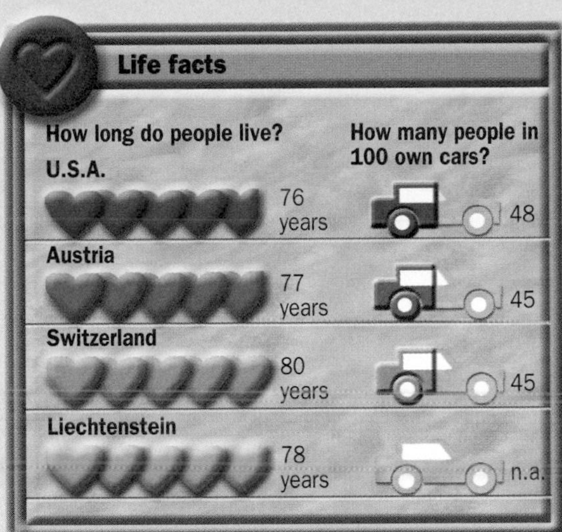

Life facts

	How long do people live?	How many people in 100 own cars?
U.S.A.	76 years	48
Austria	77 years	45
Switzerland	80 years	45
Liechtenstein	78 years	n.a.

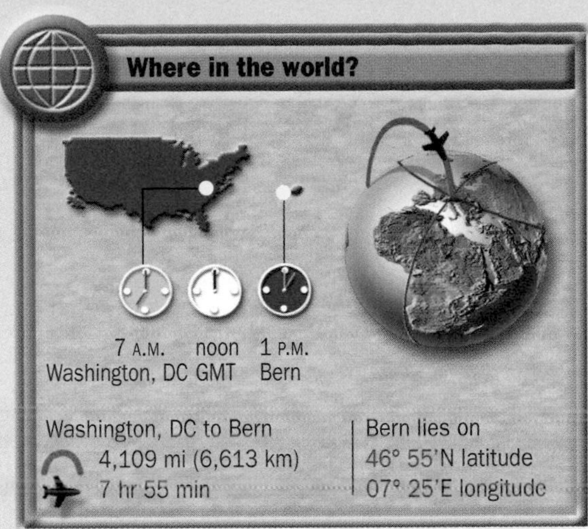

Where in the world?

7 A.M. Washington, DC
noon GMT
1 P.M. Bern

Washington, DC to Bern
4,109 mi (6,613 km)
7 hr 55 min

Bern lies on
46° 55'N latitude
07° 25'E longitude

CZECH REPUBLIC
SLOVAKIA
HUNGARY
SLOVENIA
ITALY
GERMANY
AUSTRIA
Zwettl Stadt
Krems
Klosterneuburg
Vienna
Linz
Danube
Wels
Braunau
Sankt Pölten
Amstetten
Bruck
Baden
Steyr
Neusiedler L.
Salzburg
Gmunden
Wiener Neustadt
Bad Ischl
Hallein
Kufstein
Inn
Enns
Leoben
Kapfenberg
Kitzbühel
Schwaz
NIEDERE TAUERN
Knittelfeld
Salzach
Gleisdorf
Graz
HOHE TAUERN
Judenburg
Mur
Grossglockner
12,457 ft
(3,797 m)
Köflach
Wolfsberg
Spittal
Klagenfurt
Villach
Drau

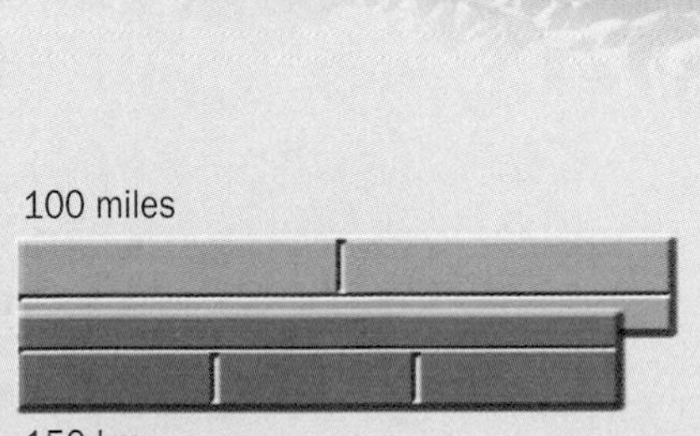

100 miles
150 km

Search and find

Austria

Switzerland

Liechtenstein

Country facts

	Area sq mi (sq km)	Population	Language	Religion	Currency
Austria	32,374 (83,849)	8,139,299	German	Catholic	Schilling
Switzerland	15,942 (41,290)	7,275,467	German/French/Italian	Catholic/Protestant	Franc
Liechtenstein	62 (161)	32,057	German	Catholic	Swiss Franc

Italy and Its Neighbors

ITALY, MALTA, SAN MARINO, VATICAN CITY

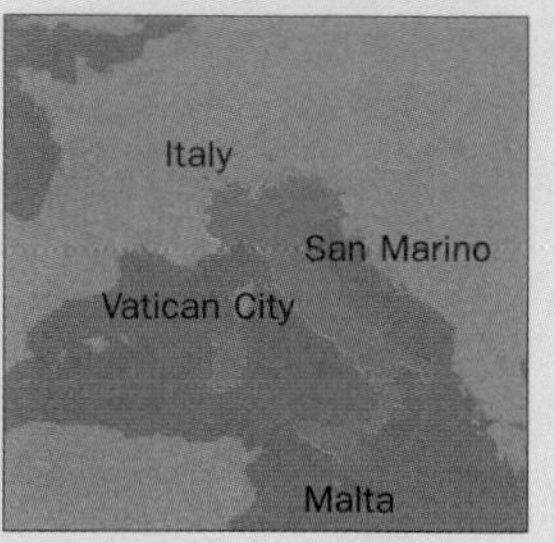
Italy
San Marino
Vatican City
Malta

TRUCKS AND CARS ENTER Italy through the road tunnels of the Alps, emerging into a region of high peaks and shining lakes. They descend to the floodplain of the Po River, a flat patchwork pattern of open fields. Northern cities include wealthy, industrial Milan and beautiful Venice, built on the lagoons and islands of the Adriatic coast.

The Apennine Mountains run down the center of the Italian peninsula. The regional hilltop towns date from the Middle Ages. Grapevines are cultivated on the lower slopes. The Italian capital, Rome, is built beside the Tiber River. Its ruins are a reminder that Roman rule once stretched from Egypt to the British Isles. To the south is Naples and the fertile surrounding region. The south is poorer than the north, dry and dusty with hot summers.

Vatican City is a district of Rome which is recognized internationally as an independent state. It is the headquarters and center of the Roman Catholic Church. The tiny republic of San Marino is completely surrounded by Italy, lying on the slopes of the Apennine Mountains of northeastern Italy.

Beyond the volcanic island of Sicily are the islands of Malta, an independent state whose main industries are tourism and clothing manufacturing.

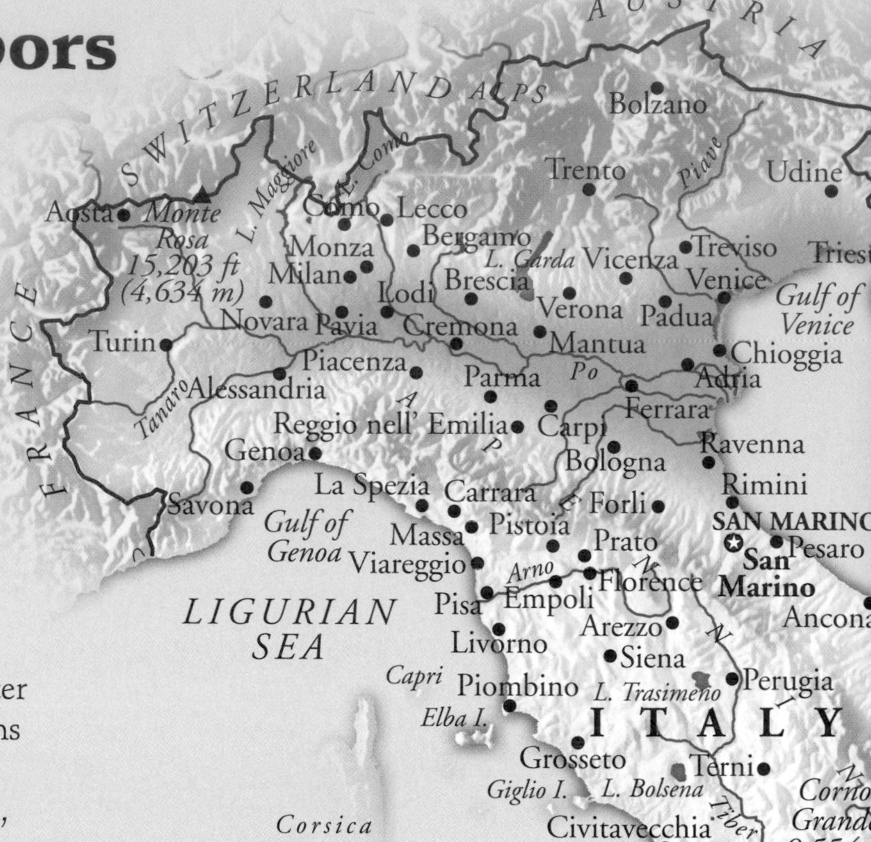
AUSTRIA
SWITZERLAND
ALPS
FRANCE
Bolzano
Trento
Piave
Udine
L. Maggiore
L. Como
Aosta
Monte Rosa
15,203 ft
(4,634 m)
Como
Lecco
Bergamo
Monza
Milan
L. Garda
Vicenza
Treviso
Triest
Lodi
Brescia
Venice
Gulf of Venice
Novara
Pavia
Cremona
Verona
Padua
Turin
Mantua
Chioggia
Piacenza
Parma
Po
Adria
Tanaro
Alessandria
Ferrara
Reggio nell' Emilia
Carpi
Genoa
Bologna
Ravenna
Savona
La Spezia
Carrara
Forli
Rimini
Gulf of Genoa
Massa
Pistoia
Prato
SAN MARINO
San Marino
Pesaro
Viareggio
Arno
Florence
LIGURIAN SEA
Pisa
Empoli
Ancona
Livorno
Arezzo
Siena
Capri
Piombino
L. Trasimeno
Perugia
Elba I.
ITALY
Grosseto
Terni
Giglio I.
L. Bolsena
Tiber
Corsica
(FRANCE)
Civitavecchia
VATICAN CITY
(in Rome)
Rome
Latina
Strait of Bonifacio
Asinara
Gulf of Asinara
Sassari
TYRRHENIAN SEA
Tirso
Nuoro
Sardinia
San Pietro
Cagliari
Gulf of Cagliari

Valletta is the capital and chief seaport of Malta. The city's stone ramparts date back to wars between Christians and Turkish Muslims in the 1500s.

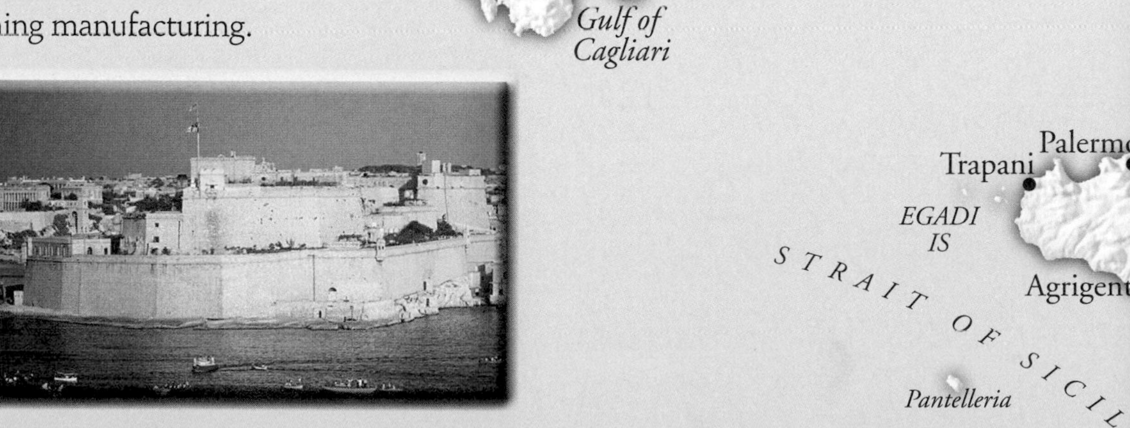
Palermo
Trapani
EGADI IS
Agrigento
STRAIT OF SICILY
Pantelleria

DISCOVER MORE

- *Italy produces more wine than any other country in the world.*
- *San Marino is one of the smallest states in the world. It claims to be the oldest state in Europe.*

Country facts

	Area sq mi (sq km)	Population	Language	Religion	Currency
Italy	116,305 (301,230)	56,735,130	Italian	Catholic	Lira
Malta	124 (321)	381,603	Maltese/English	Catholic	Lira
San Marino	23 (60)	25,061	Italian	Catholic	Italian Lira
Vatican City	0.17 (0.44)	860	Italian/Latin	Catholic	Vatican Lira/Italian Lira

The Colosseum has stood in Rome since A.D. 80. In ancient times this was an amphitheater, where crowds came to watch gladiators fight to the death or wild animals being slaughtered.

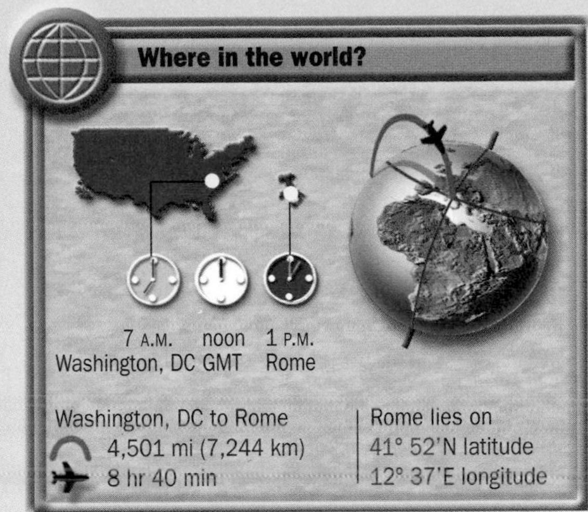

Where in the world?
7 A.M. Washington, DC
noon GMT
1 P.M. Rome
Washington, DC to Rome
4,501 mi (7,244 km)
8 hr 40 min
Rome lies on
41° 52′N latitude
12° 37′E longitude

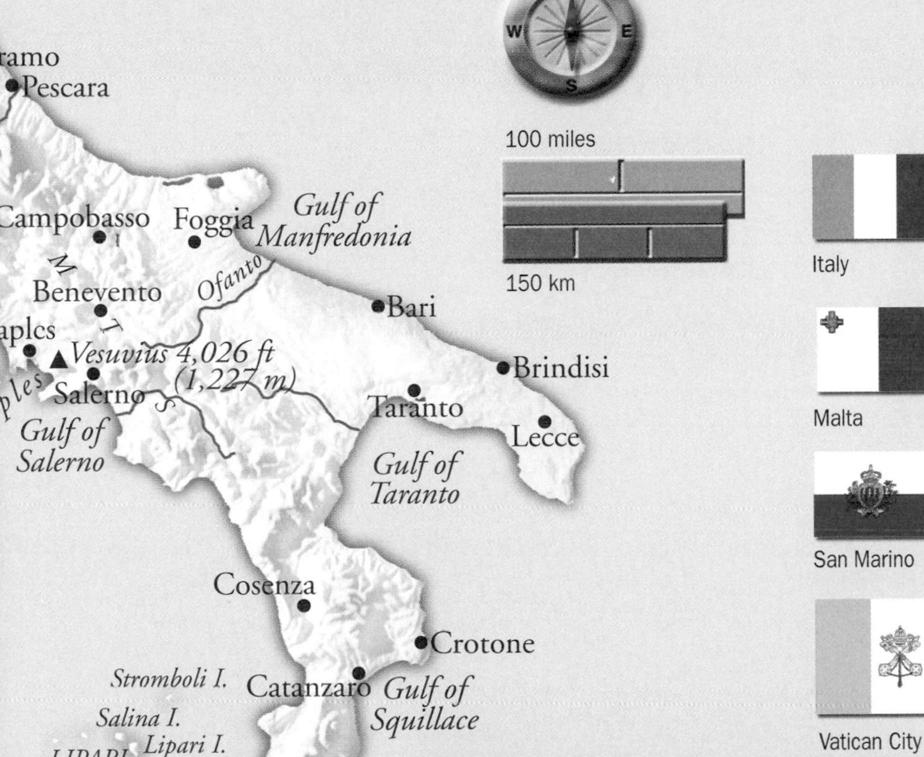

ADRIATIC SEA
N
W
E
S
100 miles
150 km
Italy
Malta
San Marino
Vatican City
Pescara
Campobasso
Foggia
Gulf of Manfredonia
Ofanto
Benevento
Bari
Vesuvius 4,026 ft (1,227 m)
Brindisi
Salerno
Taranto
Lecce
Gulf of Salerno
Gulf of Taranto
Cosenza
Crotone
Stromboli I.
Catanzaro
Gulf of Squillace
Salina I.
Lipari I.
LIPARI IS
Vulcano I.
Messina
Reggio di Calabria
Mt Etna 10,958 ft (3,340 m)
Catania
Gulf of Catania
Caltanissetta
Sicily
Siracusa
Ragusa
Gulf of Gela
MALTA CHANNEL
Valletta
MALTA

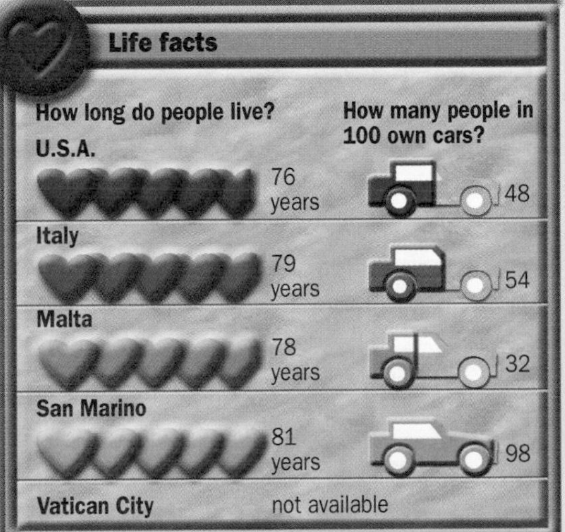

Life facts

	How long do people live?	How many people in 100 own cars?
U.S.A.	76 years	48
Italy	79 years	54
Malta	78 years	32
San Marino	81 years	98
Vatican City	not available	

Search and find

Italy
Capital: Rome . . D5
Adria B5
Agrigento F6
Alessandria B4
Ancona C6
Aosta A3
Arezzo C5
Bari D7
Benevento D6
Bergamo A4
Bologna B5
Bolzano A5
Brescia B5
Brindisi D8
Cagliari E4
Caltanissetta . . . F6
Campobasso . . . D7
Carpi B5
Carrara B4
Catania F7
Catanzaro E7
Chioggia B5
Civitavecchia . . . C5
Como B4
Cosenza E7
Cremona B4
Crotone E8
Empoli C5
Ferrara B5
Florence C5
Foggia D7
Forli B5
Genoa B4
Grosseto C5
La Spezia B4
Latina D6
Lecce D8
Lecco A4
Livorno C5
Lodi B4
Mantua B5
Massa B5
Messina F7
Milan B4
Monza A4
Naples D6
Novara B4
Nuoro D4
Padua B5
Palermo F6
Parma B5
Pavia B4
Perugia C5
Pesaro B5
Pescara C6
Piacenza B4
Piombino C5
Pisa C5
Pistoia B5
Prato C5
Ragusa F7
Ravenna B5
Reggio di Calabria F7
Reggio nell' Emilia B5
Rimini B5
Salerno D7
Sassari D4
Savona B4
Siena C5
Siracusa F7
Taranto D8
Teramo C6
Terni C5
Trapani F5
Trento A5
Treviso A5
Trieste A6
Turin B4
Udine A6
Venice B5
Verona B5
Viareggio C5
Vicenza B5

Malta
Capital: Valletta . G6

San Marino
Capital: San Marino B5

Vatican City . . D5

Northern Central Europe

POLAND, CZECH REPUBLIC, SLOVAKIA

Bridge after bridge crosses the Vltava River in Prague, capital of the Czech Republic.

Czech Republic
Poland
Slovakia

SOUTH OF THE BALTIC COAST, a wide, level plain stretches across central and eastern Europe, broken only by broad rivers such as the Oder and Vistula, by lakes, and by evergreen forests, whose branches bend under the weight of winter snows. Farmers work in the flat fields, digging up sugar beets or potatoes. In the center of this region is the city of Warsaw, capital of Poland.

South of the city of Kraków, which has many beautiful buildings dating back to the 1300s, lie wooded hills, where in summer, farming families rake out hay in the fields beside large, wood-shingled houses. Farther south, high mountains rise along Poland's southern border. For a wedding in these highland regions, traditional costume is worn. Dancing to fiddle music, the men wear vests over their clothes, and round felt hats, while the women wear embroidered bodices and swirling skirts.

The Czech Republic is bordered by the Sudeten Mountains in the north and the Bohemian Forest in the west. There is good farmland here, around the Elbe and Vltava rivers, and industrial areas produce steel and glass. The capital is historic Prague. Slovakia, between the Tatra Mountains and the Danube River, is a center of farming and mining.

Poles, Czechs, and Slovaks all belong to the Slavic group of peoples, and the region is also home to many Roma, commonly known as Gypsies.

BALTIC SEA
Gdańsk
Vistula
Nogat
Szczecin
GERMANY
Oder
Notéc
Bydgoszcz
Warta
Poznań
POLAN
Łódź
Wrocław
Warta
SUDETEN MTS
Oder
Częstochowa
Liberec
Ústí nad Labem
Karlovy Vary
Hradec Králové
Bytom
Zabrze
Sosnow
Gliwice
Katowice
Prague
Elbe
Pardubice
Plzeň
CZECH REPUBLIC
Ostrava
Vltava
BOHEMIAN FOREST
Jihlava
Olomouc
České Budějovice
Brno
Zlin
Žilina
TATRA MTS
Martin
Morava
AUSTRIA
Váh
SLOVA
Tribec
Banská Bystrica
Trnava
Nitra
Levice
Bratislava
Danube
Komárno
HUNG

DISCOVER MORE

- *Every day, a trumpeter blows a lament from the tower of the Mariacki Church in Kraków, Poland. This ancient custom dates back more than 700 years, when a watchman on the tower was hit by the arrow of a Tartar invader.*

A Polish horse-drawn wagon comes in from the fields piled high with hay. Twenty-two percent of the Polish labor force works on the land.

6 7 8 9 10 11

N
W
E
S
100 miles
100 km
KALININGRAD
RUSSIAN FEDERATION
LITHUANIA
BELARUS
Białystok
Narew
Bug
Warsaw
D
Pilica
Vistula
Bug
Lublin
Vistula
San
raków
UKRAINE
Gerlachovsky Peak
Prešov
Košice
A

Highest mountains

Mount McKinley
20,320 ft
(6,194 m)
Gerlachovsky Peak
8,711 ft
(2,655 m)

Where in the world?

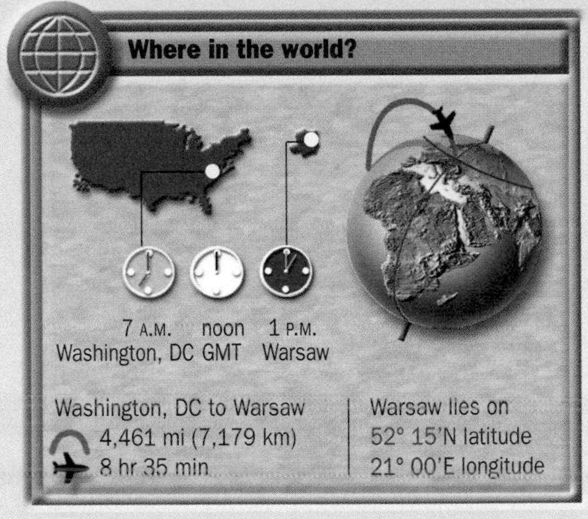

7 A.M. Washington, DC
noon GMT
1 P.M. Warsaw
Washington, DC to Warsaw
4,461 mi (7,179 km)
8 hr 35 min
Warsaw lies on
52° 15'N latitude
21° 00'E longitude

A castle towers over Bratislava, the Slovakian capital. Originally built in the Middle Ages, it was rebuilt several times, up until the eighteenth century.

Life facts

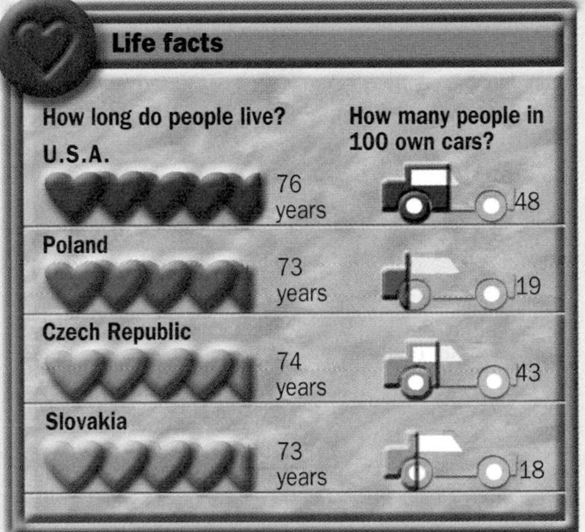

How long do people live?
How many people in 100 own cars?
U.S.A.
76 years
48
Poland
73 years
19
Czech Republic
74 years
43
Slovakia
73 years
18

Poland

Czech Republic

Slovakia

This city square, in Warsaw, Poland, is often filled with street performers and horse-drawn carriages.

Search and find

Poland
Capital: Warsaw .D6
Bialystok C7
Bydgoszcz C5
Bytom E5
Częstochowa . . .E5
Gdańsk B5
Gliwice E5
Katowice E5
Kraków E6
Łódź D6
Lublin E7
Poznań D5
Sosnowiec E5
Szczecin C4
Wroclaw E5
Zabrze E5

Czech Republic
Capital: Prague .E4
Brno F4
České Budějovice F4
Hradec Králové .E4
Jihlava F4
Karlovy Vary E3
Liberec E4
Olomouc F5
Ostrava E5
Pardubice E4
Plzeň E3
Ústí nad Labem .E3
Zlin F5

Slovakia
Capital: Bratislava F5
Banská Bystrica .F5
Komárno G5
Košice F7
Levice F5
Martin F5
Nitra F5
Prešov F6
Trnava F5
Žilina F5

Country facts

	Area sq mi (sq km)	Population	Language	Religion	Currency
Poland	120,727 (312,683)	38,608,929	Polish	Catholic	Zloty
Czech Republic	30,387 (78,702)	10,280,513	Czech	Catholic	Koruna
Slovakia	18,859 (48,845)	5,396,193	Slovak	Catholic	Koruna

A B C D E F G

6 7 8 9 10 11

The Lower Danube

Romania, Bulgaria, Hungary

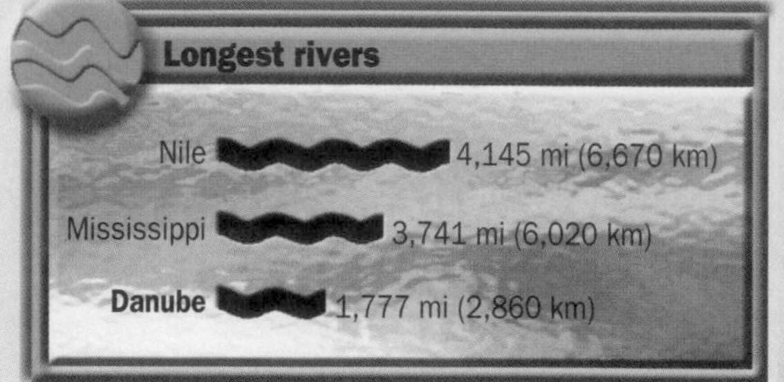
Longest rivers
Nile 4,145 mi (6,670 km)
Mississippi 3,741 mi (6,020 km)
Danube 1,777 mi (2,860 km)

Hungary
Romania
Bulgaria

The broad, swift Danube River runs like a silver thread through Central Europe. It crosses Hungary, loops through Yugoslavia, and runs along the borders of Romania and Bulgaria. Finally the thread unravels, the river dividing into a delta as it joins the Black Sea.

The Hungarian capital, Budapest, is a grand city on the banks of the Danube. To its west are highlands, forests, and Lake Balaton. To the east are the plains where the soil is fertile and the climate is mild enough to support vineyards and orchards, as well as wheat, corn, potatoes, and sugar beets.

Romania's two forested mountain ranges, the Carpathians and the Transylvanian Alps, form a great horseshoe. They ring a high plateau but descend in the east and south to the plains near the capital, Bucharest. South of Romania is Bulgaria, a part of the Balkan peninsula. Here, the northern and central plains are divided by the Balkan Mountains, and the high Rhodope range in the southwest. The capital, Sofia, lies in the west. Rose petals, used to make perfumes, are one of the region's best-known crops.

Living in this part of Europe are Hungarian Magyars, Turks, Bulgarian Slavs, Romanians, and Roma (Gypsies). The Romanian language is partly derived from Latin, which was spoken in this region 1,800 years ago when the Roman Empire extended to the Black Sea.

SLOVAKIA
AUSTRIA
Miskolc
Nyíregyháza
Győr
Budapest
Tisza
Debrecen
Szombathely
Székesfehérvár
HUNGARY
Kecskemét
Orad
SLOVENIA
L. Balaton
Danube
Pécs
Szeged
Arad
CROATIA
Timişoara
YUGOSLAVI

The eroded, rocky spires of the Belogradchik crags rise to heights of 330 ft (100 m). They can be seen near the River Danube in northwestern Bulgaria.

DISCOVER MORE

- *Hungary has many health resorts, or spas, where people can bathe in mineral water from hot springs. Some hot springs, such as those near Miskolc in the north of the country, are found inside caves.*

The Hungarian parliament meets in the capital, Budapest, beside the Danube River. The parliament building is also home to a public library and various art treasures.

A farmer plows his fields in Transylvania. This region of Romania is made up of forested mountains and fertile valleys. Crops include grain and grapes.

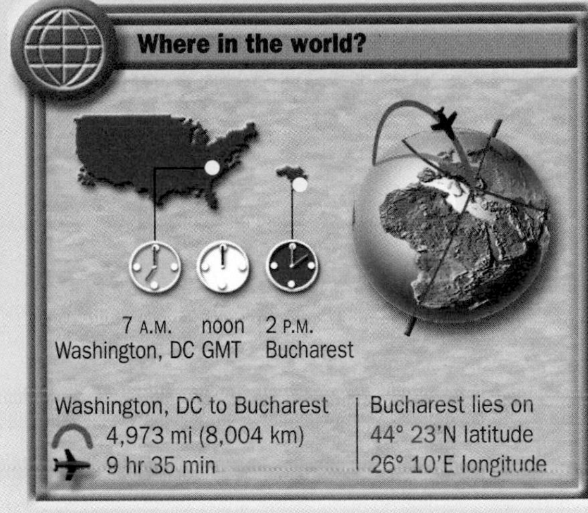

Where in the world?
7 A.M. Washington, DC
noon GMT
2 P.M. Bucharest
Washington, DC to Bucharest
4,973 mi (8,004 km)
9 hr 35 min
Bucharest lies on
44° 23'N latitude
26° 10'E longitude

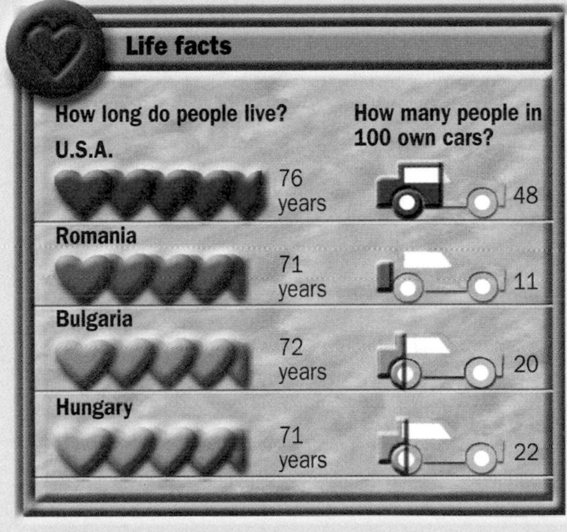

Life facts
How long do people live?
How many people in 100 own cars?
U.S.A.
76 years
48
Romania
71 years
11
Bulgaria
72 years
20
Hungary
71 years
22

UKRAINE
Satu Mare
Someş
CARPATHIAN MTS
MOLDOVA
Iaşi
Prut
Cluj-Napoca
Bacău
Târgu Mureş
Siret
Mureş
ROMANIA
Sibiu
Braşov
Galaţi
TRANSYLVANIAN ALPS
Brăila
Tulcea
Olt
Ploiesti
Jiu
Pitesti
Craiova
Bucharest
Constanţa
Danube
Ruse
BLACK SEA
Dobrich
Pleven
Varna
Iskŭr
BULGARIA
BALKAN MOUNTAINS
Sliven
Sofia
Burgas
Musala Peak 9,596 ft (2,924 m)
Plovdiv
Stara Zagora
Maritsa
Struma
RHODOPE MTS
TURKEY
GREECE
N
W
E
S
200 miles
300 km
Romania
Bulgaria
Hungary

Search and find

Romania
Capital: Bucharest D8
Arad C6
Bacău C8
Brăila D8
Braşov D8
Cluj-Napoca C7
Constanţa D9
Craiova D7
Galati D8
Iaşi C8
Oradea C6
Piteşti D7
Ploiesti D8
Satu Mare B6
Sibiu D7
Timişoara D6
Târgu Mureş . . .C7
Tulcea D9

Bulgaria
Capital: Sofia . . .E7
Burgas E8
Dobrich E8
Pleven E7
Plovdiv F7
Ruse E8
Sliven E8
Stara Zagora . . .F7
Varna E9

Hungary
Capital: Budapest C5
Debrecen C6
Győr B4
Kecskemét C5
Miskolc B5
Nyíregyhaza B6
Pécs C4
Szeged C5
Székesfehérvár .C4
Szombathely . . .C4

Country facts

	Area sq mi (sq km)	Population	Language	Religion	Currency
Romania	91,699 (237,423)	22,334,312	Romanian	Romanian Orthodox	Leu
Bulgaria	42,822 (110,909)	8,194,772	Bulgarian	Non-religious	Lev
Hungary	35,919 (93,030)	10,186,372	Hungarian	Catholic	Forint

A

South Central Europe

Croatia, Bosnia-Herzegovina, Slovenia

White-water rivers and rushing streams are common sights in the mountains of Bosnia. Many pass through old, pretty villages.

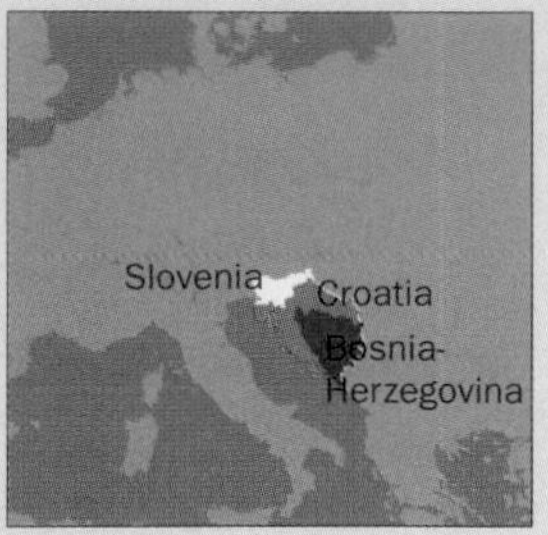
Slovenia
Croatia
Bosnia-Herzegovina

South Central Europe is a region of forested mountains, limestone crags, and caves full of stalactites and stalagmites, pillars of limestone formed by dripping water. The mountains plunge abruptly into the warm, blue Adriatic Sea. Offshore there is a maze of islands.

B

The region is rich in minerals, including iron and coal. There are vineyards and fields of sunflowers. The sunny Dalmatian Coast and islands attract tourists from northern Europe, and major road and rail routes between Greece and Western Europe pass through here.

C

Slovenia borders the high mountain passes of the Austrian and Italian Alps, while Croatia forms a U-shape, with the Pannonian Plains in the north and the Dinaric Alps running through the coastal region of Dalmatia. To the east, Bosnia is mountainous and Herzegovina has hills and plains. These two form a single country.

D

The inhabitants of the Lower Danube belong to many different ethnic groups and religions. In Croatia, the people are mainly Roman Catholic Croats. In Slovenia, Roman Catholic Slovenes make up almost 90 percent of the population. In Bosnia, the majority of people are Bosnian Muslims; however, Serbian Orthodox Serbs also make up a significant proportion of the population.

E

The Balkan region, the poorest part of Europe's Mediterranean coast, has a long history of conquest—by Romans, Byzantines, Turks, Austrians, and Germans. It was an assassination in Sarajevo (capital of Bosnia-Herzegovina) that triggered World War I in 1914.

AUSTRIA
ITALY
Triglav
9,393 ft
(2,863 m)
Kranj
Maribor
Celje
Sava
Ljubljana
SLOVENIA
Novo Mesto
Zagreb
Koper
Kupa
Karlovac
Rijeka
Krk
Pula
Cres
Una
Bihac
DINARIC
Lošinj
Gospić
Dugi Otok
Zadar
ADRIATIC SEA
Šibenik
Dalmation Coast
Vis
N
W
E
S
100 miles
150 km

F

DISCOVER MORE

• *Slovenia is known for its beautiful beaches, lakes and ski resorts. However, it is also an important industrial center. It lies on the main road and rail routes between Western Europe and the Balkans.*

G

Zagreb is a manufacturing city on the Sava River. Since 1991 it has been capital of independent Croatia.

A cable car climbs to dizzying heights. Slovenia flanks the eastern limits of Western Europe's Alpine ranges.

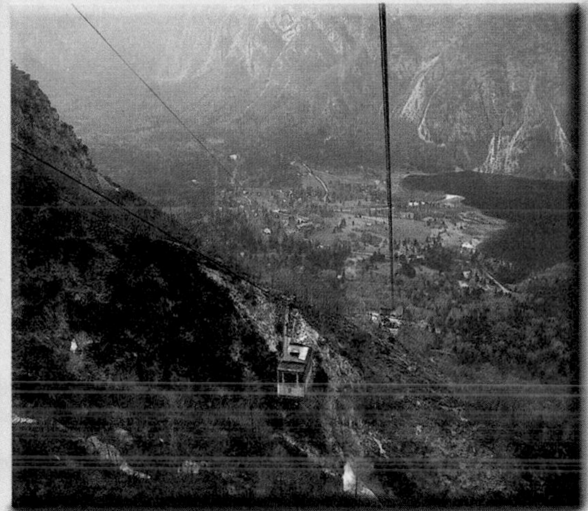

Where in the world?

7 A.M. Washington, DC	noon GMT	1 P.M. Zagreb

Washington, DC to Zagreb
4,505 mi (7,251 km)
8 hr 40 min

Zagreb lies on
45° 48'N latitude
15° 58'E longitude

Varaždin
HUNGARY
Bjelovar
CROATIA
Drava
Sisak
Osijek
Slavonski Brod
Sava
Prijedor
Vrbas
Bosna
Brčko
Banja Luka
Bijeljina
BOSNIA-HERZEGOVINA
Tuzla
YUGOSLAVIA
Zenica
Srebrenica
LPS
Livno
Sarajevo
Drina
Split
Foča
Brac
Mostar
Hvar
Korcula
Neum
Lastovo
Mljet
Dubrovnik

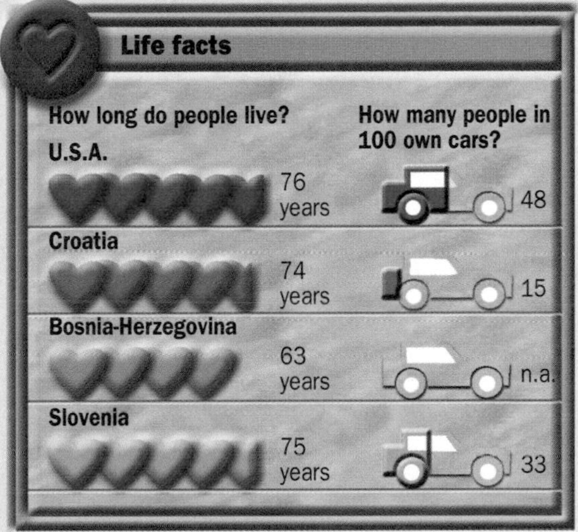

Life facts

	How long do people live?	How many people in 100 own cars?
U.S.A.	76 years	48
Croatia	74 years	15
Bosnia-Herzegovina	63 years	n.a.
Slovenia	75 years	33

Croatia

Bosnia-Herzegovina

Slovenia

Search and find

Croatia
Capital: Zagreb .C6
Bjelovar .C6
Dubrovnik .F8
Gospić .D5
Karlovac .C5
Osijek .C8
Pula .D4
Rijeka .C5
Sibenik .E6
Sisak .C6
Slavonski Brod .D7
Split .E6
Varaždin .B6
Zadar .E5

Bosnia-Herzegovina
Capital: Sarajevo E8
Banja Luka .D7
Bihac .D6
Bijeljina .D8
Brčko .D8
Foča .E8
Livno .E7
Mostar .F7
Neum .F7
Prijedor .D6
Srebrenica .E9
Tuzla .D8
Zenica .E7

Slovenia
Capital: Ljubljana .C5
Celje .B5
Koper .C4
Kranj .B4
Maribor .B6
Novo Mesto .C5

Country facts

	Area sq mi (sq km)	Population	Language	Religion	Currency
Croatia	21,829 (56,537)	4,676,865	Croatian	Catholic	Kuna
Bosnia-Herzegovina	19,781 (51,233)	3,370,000	Serb and Croat	Sunni Islam/Serbian Orthodox/Catholic	Marka
Slovenia	7,821 (20,256)	1,970,570	Slovenian	Catholic	Tolar

Central Balkans

YUGOSLAVIA, ALBANIA, MACEDONIA

Yugoslavia
Albania
Macedonia

THESE SMALL CENTRAL NATIONS lie between the western Balkans, Bulgaria, and Greece. The northernmost of these nations is Yugoslavia, and it is made up of the territories of Serbia, Montenegro, and the southern region of Kosovo. Its full name is the Former Yugoslav Republic of Macedonia. People of different ethnic origins and religious beliefs live scattered throughout the different areas of the country. Muslims form 19 percent of the total population.

Albania has long been a very poor country. Recently, exploiting resources such as iron, natural gas, and oil is helping to increase the country's wealth.

The constant changes that have affected the Balkan region for centuries have taken place against a backdrop of snowy winter mountains and sunbaked summer fields and orchards. Plums are used to make a brandy called *slivovitz*. Tractors and horses still haul farm carts.

Villages with tiled roofs cluster around old stone bridges. There are minarets of mosques and domed churches, too, for this region is home to both Muslims and Christians. Major cities such as Belgrade, Skopje, and Tiranë have suffered from earthquakes, for this region lies on the border of two sections of the earth's crust: the Turkish-Aegean plate and the Eurasian plate.

DISCOVER MORE

- *Albania has twice the altitude of the average European country, with about 70% of the country being mountainous.*
- *Beautiful Lake Ohrid, 938 ft (286 m) deep, lies on the highland border between Albania and Macedonia. It is famous for its clear waters. It is possible to see down to a depth of 65 ft (20 m).*

A patchwork of fields rises to folds of barren rock. Much of Albania is mountainous, and agriculture is difficult in many regions.

Many of the villages in Macedonia are situated in the Vardar basin, a region given over to agriculture and dairy farming.

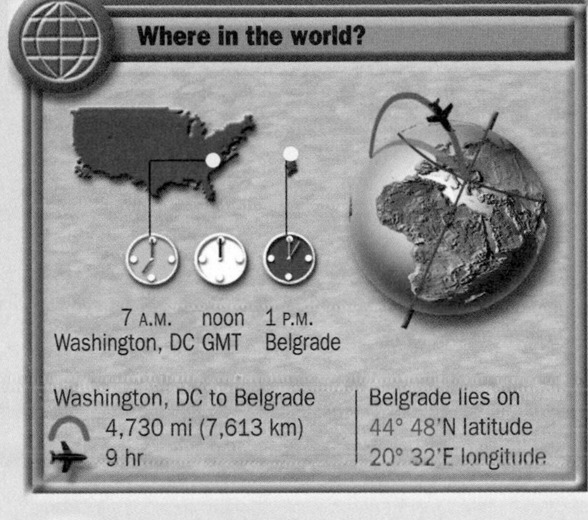
Where in the world?
7 A.M. Washington, DC
noon GMT
1 P.M. Belgrade
Washington, DC to Belgrade
4,730 mi (7,613 km)
9 hr
Belgrade lies on
44° 48'N latitude
20° 32'E longitude

The minaret of a mosque forms part of the Belgrade skyline along with skyscrapers and industrial buildings.

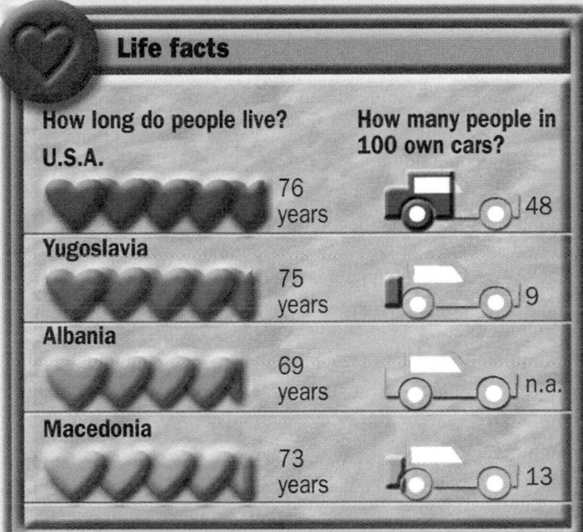
Life facts
How long do people live?
How many people in 100 own cars?
U.S.A.
76 years
48
Yugoslavia
75 years
9
Albania
69 years
n.a.
Macedonia
73 years
13

Negotin
ajecar
Nis
Leskovac
Vranje
manovo
BULGARIA
ONIA
C E
N
W
E
S
100 miles
150 km

Sunflowers open up in the Serbian summer sunshine. They are cultivated in many parts of the Balkans. The flowers are densely packed with edible seeds, which can be processed into margarine or cooking oil.

Search and find

Yugoslavia
Capital: Belgrade B5
Bar E4
Čačak C5
Cetinje E4
Dakovica E5
Ivangrad D5
Kosovska Mitrovica D5
Kragujevac C5
Kruševac C6
Leskovac D6
Negotin C6
Nikšic D4
Nis D6
Novi Pazar D5
Novi Sad B5
Pancevo B5
Peć D5
Podgorica D4
Priština D6
Prizren E5
Šabac B5
Smederevo B5
Smederevska Palanka C5
Subotica A5
Užice C5
Valjevo C5
Vranje D6
Zajecar C6
Zrenjanin B5

Albania
Capital: Tiranë . .E5
Durrës F4
Elbasan F5
Korçë F5
Shkodër E4
Vlorë F4

Macedonia
Capital: Skopje . .E6
Bitola F6
Kumanovo E6
Prilep F6

Country facts

	Area sq mi (sq km)	Population	Language	Religion	Currency
Yugoslavia	39,517 (102,349)	11,206,847	Serb	Serbian Orthodox	ND*/DM**
Albania	11,100 (28,749)	3,364,571	Albanian	Muslim	Lek
Macedonia	9,781 (25,333)	2,022,604	Macedonian	Mac Orthodox***	Denar

*New Dinar **Deutsche Mark ***Macedonian Orthodox

Yugoslavia

Albania

Macedonia

Greece

The Erechtheion is one of several ancient temples built on the Acropolis, the great rock of Athens. It dates back to about 420 B.C. The roof is supported by columns, shaped like women, called caryatids.

Greece

THIS SMALL COUNTRY OCCUPIES the southern part of the Balkan peninsula. Its major industries include tourism, shipping, foodstuffs, and oil refining.

Greece is a land of rugged mountains rising from dusty plains and olive groves, very hot in summer and mostly mild in winter. The mainland is almost divided in two by the Gulf of Corinth, with an earthquake-prone peninsula in the south. Chains of rocky islands are scattered across dark blue seas. Whitewashed villages and tourist cafés surround fishing harbors.

Ferries travel between the islands and Piraeus, south of Athens. The Greek capital is a sprawling city, noisy with honking cars. In its squares one may see old men arguing about politics, bearded Greek Orthodox priests in tall black hats, children buying comics from a newsstand, and vendors of traditional foods such as pretzel rings. Looking out over the city is the great rock of the Acropolis, topped by ancient buildings, including the Parthenon, completed around 438 B.C. At that time, Greece was a center of civilization, home to great sculptors, architects, writers, and thinkers.

MACEDONIA
ALBANIA
GREECE
Palikastron
Sérr
Edessa
Vardar
Kilkís
Florina
Náousa
Yiannitsa
Kastoria
Ptolemaïs
Veroia
Thessaloní
Kozáni
Aliakmon
Kateríni
Gulf of Salonika
Mt Olympus
9,570 ft
(2,917 m)
PINDUS MTS
Metéora
Stómion
Kérkira
Corfu
Ioánnina
Tríkala
Piniós
Larissa
Párga
Kardhitsa
Vólos
Arta
Akhelóös
Préveza
Skiat
Lamía
Lím
Levkás
Agriníon
Mt Parnassus
8,061 ft
(2,456 m)
Thérmon
L. Trichonis
Cephalonía
Ithaca
Mesalóngion
Sámi
Gulf of Corinth
Thebes
Pátrai
Aíyion
Mega
Peloponnese
Corinth
Amaliás
Lambia
Salam
Corinth Canal
Zákinthos
Pyrgos
Olympia
Árgos
Nauplia
Trípolis
Alpheus
Megalópolis
TAIYETOS MTS
Sparti
Kalamata
Neápo
Kíthira

Windmills rise above the whitewashed houses of Mykonos, a tiny island just off the coast of mainland Greece. In the last 30 years this small Greek island has become a major international tourist destination.

DISCOVER MORE

- *After the battle of Marathon in 490 B.C., tradition says a messenger ran 25 mi (40 km) to Athens to tell of the Athenians' victory over the Persians. He died on arrival, but the name for the race was born.*
- *The Corinth Canal, with its sheer walls of rock, is the deepest cut ever made by engineers. Opened in 1893, the canal reaches a depth of 1,505 ft (459 m) and is 4 mi (6.3 km) long.*

Greece

Country facts

	Area sq mi (sq km)	Population	Language	Religion	Currency
Greece	50,942 (131,940)	10,707,135	Greek	Greek Orthodox	Drachma

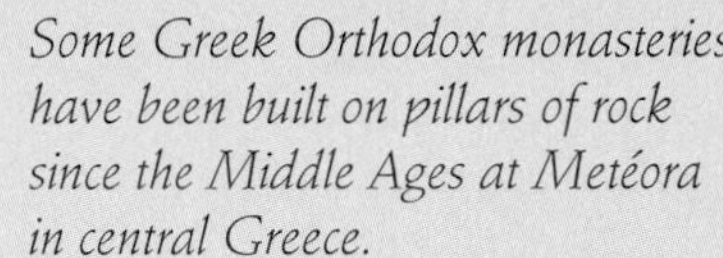

Some Greek Orthodox monasteries have been built on pillars of rock since the Middle Ages at Metéora in central Greece.

BULGARIA
Orestiás
TURKEY
Drama
Xánthi
Komotiní
Kavála
Alexandroúpolis
Thásos

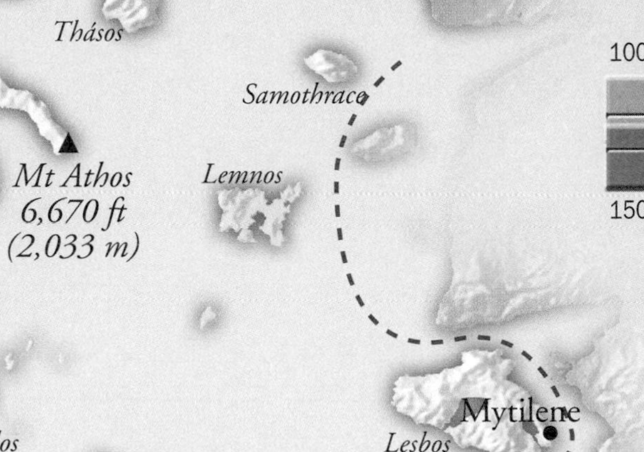

Samothrace
Mt Athos
6,670 ft
(2,033 m)
Lemnos
100 miles
150 km

Mytilene
Lesbos
Skíros
Kími
AEGEAN SEA
Khíos
Chios
Káristos
Andros
Sámos
Vathí
TURKEY
Kéa
Tínos
Ikaría
Kíthnos
Syros
Mykonos
Pátmos
Sérifos
Páros
Náxos
Leros
Kálimnos
Sífnos
Kos
Amorgos
Melos
Íos
Astipálaia
Tílos
Rhódos
Thíra
Rhodes
Lindos
SEA OF CRETE
Kárpathos
Iráklion
Réthimnon
Áyios Nikólaos
Crete
N
W
E
S

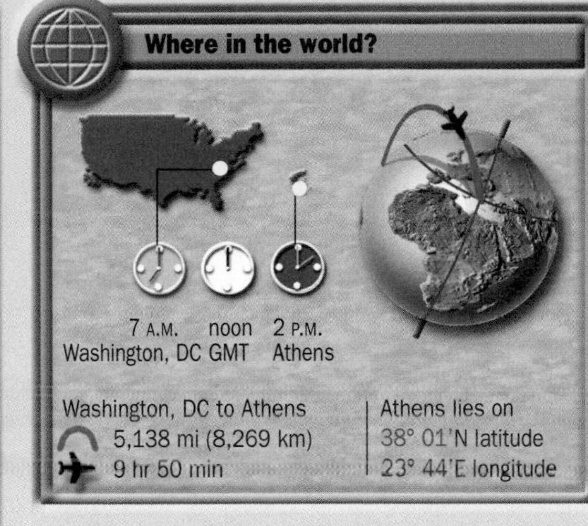

Where in the world?
7 A.M. Washington, DC
noon GMT
2 P.M. Athens
Washington, DC to Athens
5,138 mi (8,269 km)
9 hr 50 min
Athens lies on
38° 01'N latitude
23° 44'E longitude

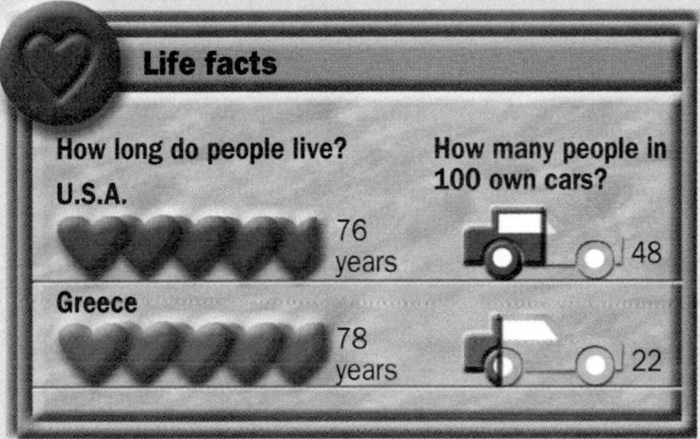

Life facts
How long do people live?
How many people in 100 own cars?
U.S.A.
76 years
48
Greece
78 years
22

Search and find

Greece
Capital: Athens .E6
Agriníon D4
Aíyion D5
Alexandroúpolis .B8
Amaliás E4
Árgos E5
Arta D4
Áyios Nikólios . .G7
Corinth E5
Drama B7
Edessa B5
Florina B5
Ioánnina C4
Iráklion G7
Kalamata E5
Kardhitsa D5
Káristos E7
Kastoría C4
Kateríni C5
Kavála B7
Kérkira C3
Khalkís D6
Khaniá G6
Khiós E8
Kilkís B5
Kími D6
Komotiní B7
Kozáni C5
Lambia E5
Lamía D5
Larissa C5
Límni D6
Lindos F9
Marathon E6
Megalópolis E5
Megara E6
Mesalóngion . . .D4
Mytilene D8
Náousa C5
Nauplia E5
Náxos F7
Neápolis F5
Olympia E5
Orestiás B8
Palikastron B5
Párga D4
Pátrai E5
Piraeus E6
Préveza D4
Ptolemaïs C5
Pyrgos E4
Réthimnon G7
Rhódos F9
Salamis E6
Sámi D4
Sérrai B6
Sparti E5
Stómion C5
Thebes D6
Thérmon D5
Thessaloníki . . .C6
Tríkala C5
Trípolis E5
Vathí E8
Veroia C5
Vólos D6
Xánthi B7
Yiannitsa B5

Baltic States

LITHUANIA, LATVIA, ESTONIA

Estonia
Lithuania
Latvia

CHILLY WINDS BLOW ACROSS the Baltic Sea and the gulfs of Finland and Riga. The eastern Baltic coast is fringed by chains of islands and pale sand dunes. Inland from the coast are three small independent nations, Estonia, Latvia, and Lithuania, which border the Russian Federation in the east. A small enclave, or pocket, of territory around the seaport of Kaliningrad is Russian territory.

The peoples of the region love choral music, folk dance, and festivals, and many of these celebrate regional languages and costumes. The three countries are largely Christian, represented by the Roman Catholic, Protestant, and Orthodox churches. Russians, Belarusians, and Ukrainians also live in the Baltic states, alongside Estonians, Latvians (also known as Letts), and Lithuanians.

Estonia is a low-lying land of farms, peat bogs, and forests, part of the great plain that extends eastward across Russia. Lake Peipus lies on Estonia's eastern border. Latvia, too, lies on the plain, and here, farmers raise pigs and dairy cattle. Many Latvians work in factories, but there are few local resources, and fuel has to be imported from Russia. The lakes, moors, and pine forests of Lithuania lie to the south, extending toward the capital, Vilnius, and the borders of Poland and Belarus. Winters are extremely cold and snowy, while summers are mostly mild and moist.

The Daugava River flows through the Latvian capital, 8 mi (13 km) above its mouth on the Gulf of Riga. In the Middle Ages, Riga was part of a Baltic trading network called the Hansa, and the city still contains many fine buildings from that period.

Kärdla
Hiiumaa
Saaremaa
Kuressaare
Ruhnu
BALTIC SEA
Ventspils
Venta
Auce
Liepāja
N
W
E
S
100 miles
300 km
Klaipeda
Kaliningrad
(RUSSIAN FEDERATION
Kaliningrad
P O L A

DISCOVER MORE

- *The Baltic coasts have long been famous for their fine amber. The fossilized resin from plants comes in beautiful browns and yellows and is used to make jewelry. Some amber contains insects from prehistoric times trapped in the sticky sap.*
- *Despite its small size, Lithuania has no fewer than 3,000 small lakes.*

A cluster of domed roofs in Tallinn, the Estonian capital, shows Russian influence. Many Estonian Christians belong to the Eastern Orthodox Church, but the great majority are Lutheran Protestants.

6 7 8 9 10 11
A B C D E F G
Gulf of Finland
Narva
Kohtla-Järve
Tallinn
ESTONIA
L. Peipus
RUSSIAN FEDERATION
aapsalu
Viljandi
Tartu
Pärnu
L. Vórts
Vóru
Kihnu I.
Valmiera
Gulf of Riga
Gauja
Cesis
LATVIA
Riga
Ergli
Jūrmala
Daugava
Jelgava
Daugavpils
Šiauliai
Panevėžys
LITHUANIA
BELARUS
Nemunas
Kaunas
Vilnius
Alytus
D
Lithuania
Latvia
Estonia
Where in the world?
7 A.M. Washington, DC
noon GMT
2 P.M. Vilnius
Washington, DC to Vilnius
4,530 mi (7,842 km)
9 hr 20 min
Vilnius lies on
55° 45'N latitude
37° 37'E longitude
Life facts
How long do people live?
How many people in 100 own cars?
U.S.A.
76 years
48
Lithuania
69 years
18
Latvia
67 years
11
Estonia
69 years
24
Search and find
Lithuania
Capital: Vilnius . . .F8
Alytus F7
Kaunas F7
Klaipėda E5
Panevėžys E7
Šiauliai E6
Latvia
Capital: Riga . . .D7
Cesis C7
Daugavpils E8
Ergli D7
Jelgava D6
Jūrmala D6
Liepāja D5
Valmiera C7
Ventspils D5
Estonia
Capital: Tallinn . .A7
Haapsalu B6
Kärdla B5
Kohtla-Järve A8
Kuressaare C5
Narva A8
Pärnu B7
Tartu B8
Viljandi B7
Vóru C8
Kaliningrad (Russian Federation)
Kaliningrad F5
6 7 8 9 10 11

Country facts

	Area sq mi (sq km)	Population	Language	Religion	Currency
Lithuania	25,174 (65,201)	3,584,966	Lithuanian	Catholic	Litas
Latvia	24,749 (64,100)	2,353,874	Latvian/Russian	Lutheran/NR*	Lat
Estonia	17,462 (45,227)	1,408,523	Estonian	Lutheran/NR*/EO**	Kroon

*Non-religious **Estonian Orthodox

Eastern Europe

UKRAINE, BELARUS, MOLDOVA

Belarus
Ukraine
Moldova

BELARUS IS PART OF THE GREAT plain that stretches eastward from Germany into the Russian Federation. The flat lands rise to low hills in the center of the country, drained by the Dnieper and Pripyat' rivers. There are marshes, too, and dark forests. Winter snows weigh down the trees' boughs, but summers are warm and sunny. Men and women work in the fields, growing potatoes and beets, but most Belarussians are town dwellers. Many work in industrial cities, such as Minsk.

Ukraine, too, is an industrial country. The capital, Kiev, lies on bluffs above the Dnieper River. Southern Ukraine is a land of rolling steppes where wheat is grown in the rich, black earth. In the south, Ukraine borders the warm waters of the Black Sea. The ports of Odessa and Yalta, on the Crimean Peninsula, are popular resorts for tourists, many of whom are from eastern Europe.

Moldova is a small country, situated between Ukraine and Romania. Its forests and hills descend to the western edge of the steppes. Most Moldovans belong to the same ethnic group as their neighbors, the Romanians, and they speak the same language.

LATVIA
LITHUANIA
RUSSIA
Vitsyebsk
Dnieper
Mahilyow
Minsk
Hrodna
BELARUS
Hoymel'
POLAND
Pripyat' Marshes
Pripyat'
Desna
Bug
Kiev
Lviv
Vinnytsya
UKI
Dniester
SLOVAKIA
HUNGARY
MOLDOVA
ROMANIA
Chişinău
Tiraspol
Prut
Odessa
BLAC

DISCOVER MORE

- *Optimisticekaja ("optimists' cave") in Ukraine is the second-longest cave system in the world, with 125 mi (201 km) mapped so far.*
- *Ukraine is the largest nation to lie entirely within the European continent.*

A Belarussian woman lights a candle in an Eastern Orthodox church. Sixty percent of the Belarussian population follows the Orthodox form of Christianity. Other Christians include Roman Catholics and Protestants.

Ferries moor on the banks of the Dnieper River, in Kiev, capital of Ukraine. This is a large industrial city which produces textiles, machinery, chemicals, and processed foods.

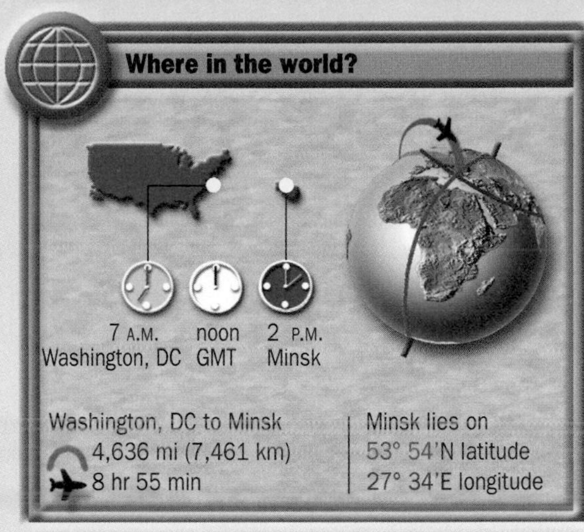
Where in the world?
7 A.M.
Washington, DC
noon
GMT
2 P.M.
Minsk
Washington, DC to Minsk
4,636 mi (7,461 km)
8 hr 55 min
Minsk lies on
53° 54'N latitude
27° 34'E longitude

Life facts
How long do people live?
How many people in 100 own cars?
U.S.A.
76 years
48
Ukraine
66 years
9
Belarus
68 years
8
Moldova
64 years
4

Search and find
Ukraine
Capital: Kiev . . .D5
Dnipropetrovs'k .D7
Donetsk E8
Kharkiv D7
Kherson F6
Kryvyy Rih E7
Lviv D3
Mariupol E8
Odessa F6
Poltava D7
Sevastopol F7
Vinnytsya D5
Yalta F7
Zaporizhzhya . . .E7
Belarus
Capital: Minsk . .B4
Homyel' C5
Hrodna B3
Mahilyow B5
Vitsyebsk B5
Moldova
Capital: Chişinău E5
Tiraspol F5

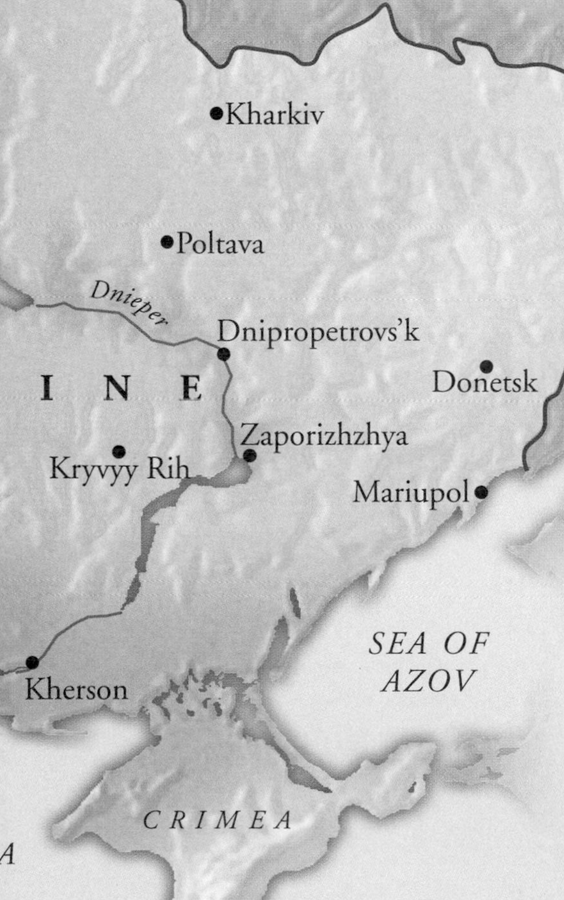
FEDERATION
Kharkiv
Poltava
Dnieper
Dnipropetrovs'k
AINE
Donetsk
Zaporizhzhya
Kryvyy Rih
Mariupol
SEA OF AZOV
Kherson
CRIMEA
EA
Sevastopol
Yalta

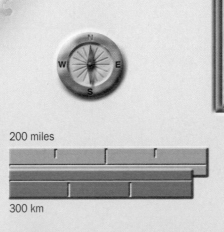

200 miles

300 km

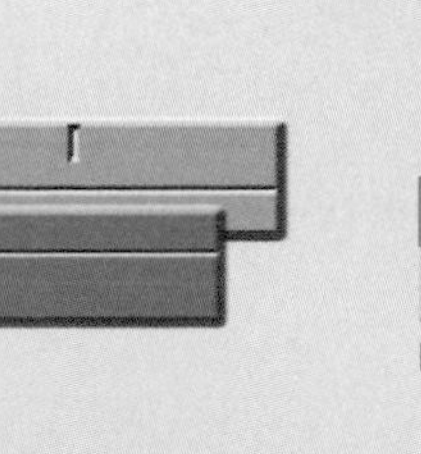
Ukraine

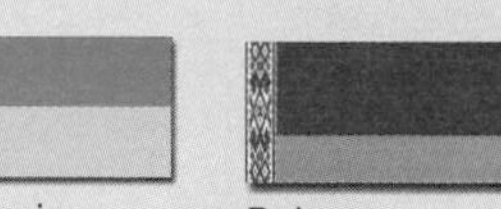
Belarus

Moldova

Country facts

	Area sq mi (sq km)	Population	Language	Religion	Currency
Ukraine	233,089 (603,701)	49,811,174	Ukrainian	NR*/Russian Orthodox	Hryvnya
Belarus	80,154 (207,599)	10,235,000	Belarussian/Russian	NR*/ Orthodox	Ruble
Moldova	13,012 (33,701)	4,460,838	Moldovan	NR*/Romanian Orthodox	Leu

*Non-religious

Western Russia

Western Russia

The ornate, onion-shaped domes of St. Basil's cathedral rise from Red Square, at the heart of Moscow.

RED SQUARE LIES AT THE HEART of Moscow, capital of the Russian Federation. The square is dominated by the red walls of the Kremlin, a medieval fortress that towers over the Moscow River and distant skylines of apartment blocks and factory chimneys. The Kremlin's walls surround government buildings and splendid Russian Orthodox churches with golden domes. Outside the walls are the colorful onion-shaped domes of St. Basil's Cathedral. Away from the river and square, the Kremlin is flanked by wooded slopes, where children go to toboggan in the snow.

Moscow's winters are extremely cold. Outdoors, people in the Moscow crowds are well wrapped and wear fur hats for protection against the icy wind. One way to escape the wind is to travel on the city's elegant, old-fashioned subway, or metro. Visitors come to the city from the Caucasus region, far to the south, from the Arctic north, and from distant Siberia.

The Russian Federation is the largest country in the world. Its western part lies in Europe, but its eastern part stretches across northern Asia. European Russia is a vast plain, with seemingly endless forests of spruce and birch. The region is crossed by great rivers such as the Don and the Volga. Most people live in big cities. Russia's second-largest city is St. Petersburg, which was founded in the 1700s. It has grand palaces, the world's biggest art gallery, a famous opera and ballet theater, factories, and shipbuilding yards.

Gulf of Finland
ESTONIA
LATVIA
L. Ladoga
St. Petersburg
RUSSIAN
BELARUS
Smolensk
Tver'
Bryansk
Moscow
Tula
Ryazan
Volga
UKRAINE
Lipetsk
Don
Voronezh
Penza
Saratov
Volga
SEA OF AZOV
Rostov-na-Donu
Volgograd
BLACK SEA
Krasnodar
Stavropol
CAUCASUS MTS
Mt Elbrus
Astrakhan
Grozny
GEORGIA
AZERBAIJAN
CASPIAN SEA

DISCOVER MORE

- *Moscow's subway system is the world's busiest. It carries about 3.2 billion passengers each year.*
- *Russia's chief Arctic port, Arkhangel'sk, freezes over in winter. From November to May, icebreakers must be used to keep the shipping lanes open.*

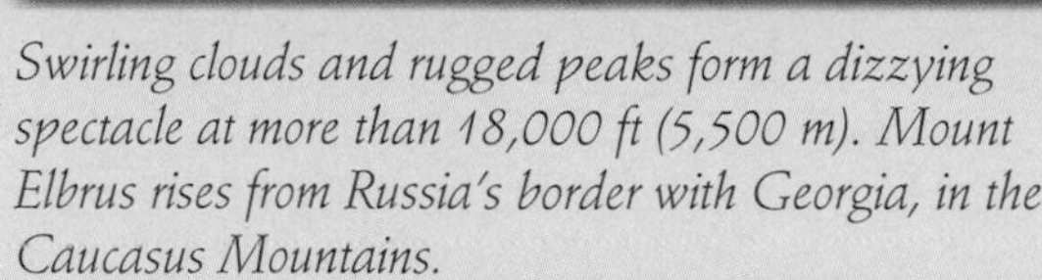
Swirling clouds and rugged peaks form a dizzying spectacle at more than 18,000 ft (5,500 m). Mount Elbrus rises from Russia's border with Georgia, in the Caucasus Mountains.

6 7 8 9 10 11

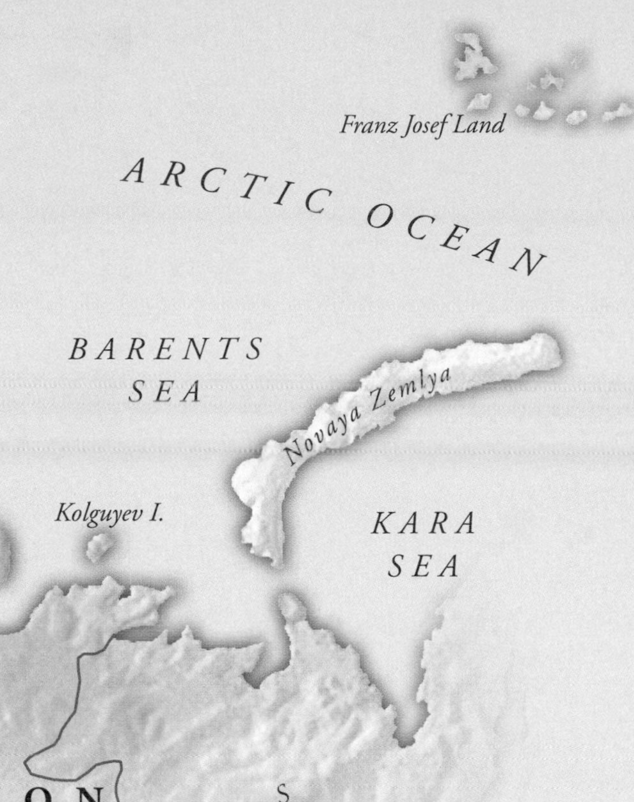

Franz Josef Land
ARCTIC OCEAN
BARENTS SEA
Murmansk
Kola Peninsula
Novaya Zemlya
Kolguyev I.
KARA SEA
WHITE SEA
Arkhangel'sk
FEDERATION
Severnaya Dvina
Pechora
URAL MOUNTAINS

Where in the world?

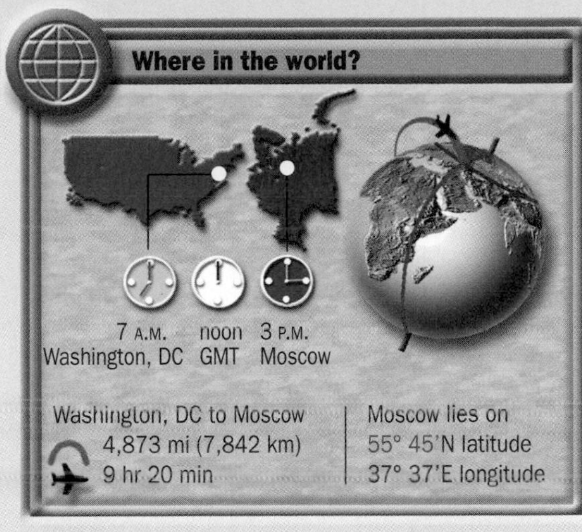

7 A.M. Washington, DC
noon GMT
3 P.M. Moscow
Washington, DC to Moscow
4,873 mi (7,842 km)
9 hr 20 min
Moscow lies on
55° 45'N latitude
37° 37'E longitude

Life facts

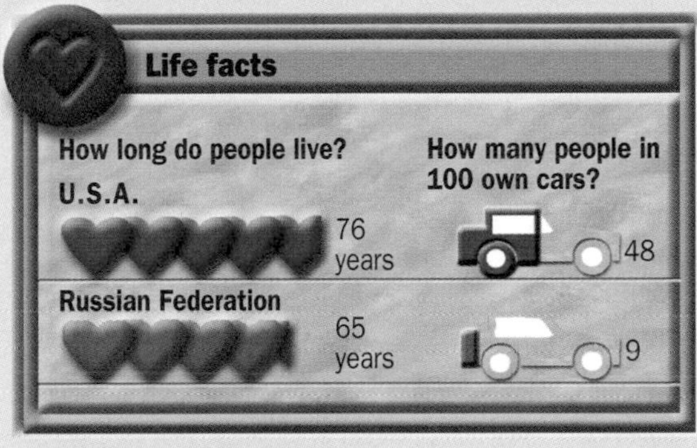

How long do people live?
U.S.A.
76 years
Russian Federation
65 years
How many people in 100 own cars?
48
9

Highest mountains

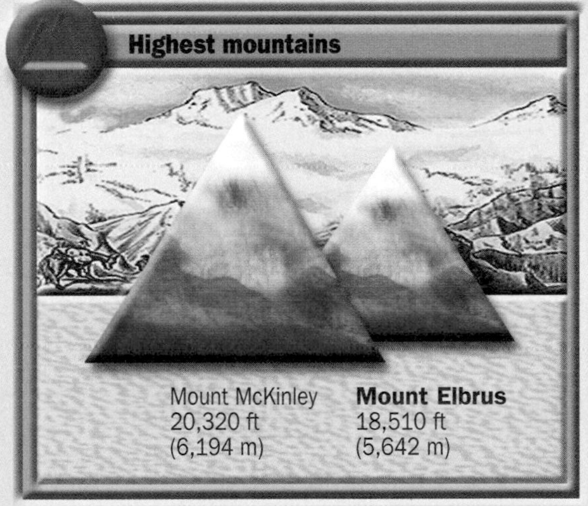

Mount McKinley
20,320 ft
(6,194 m)
Mount Elbrus
18,510 ft
(5,642 m)

Kirov
Perm
Izhevsk
Kazan
Kama
Ufa
Tolyattigrad
Samara

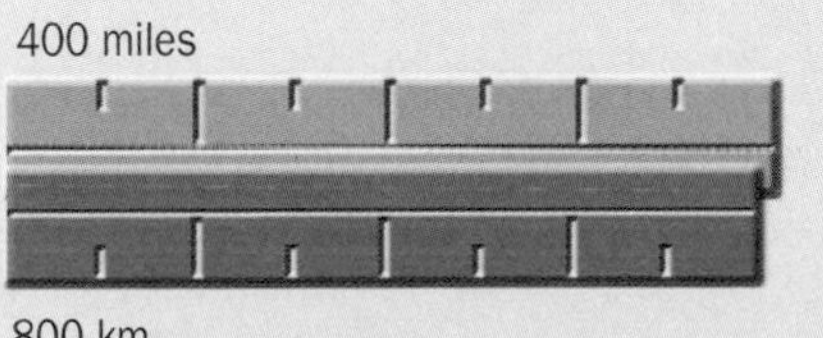

400 miles
800 km

Magnitogorsk
Orenburg
Ural
Orsk
KAZAKHSTAN

Russian Federation

Nizhniy Novgorod, although a modern manufacturing center, has many ancient churches.

Country facts

	Area sq mi (sq km)	Population	Language	Religion	Currency
Russian Federation	6,592,800 (17,075,352)	146,393,569	Russian	Russian Orthodox	Ruble

Search and find

Western Russia

Capital: Moscow D5
Arkhangel'sk . . . C7
Astrakhan F5
Bryansk D4
Grozny F5
Izhevsk D7
Kazan E6
Kirov D6
Krasnodar F4
Lipetsk D5
Magnitogorsk . . . E7
Murmansk B7
Nizhniy Novgorod . . . D6
Orenburg F6
Orsk F7
Penza E5
Perm E7
Rostov-na-Donu . E4
Ryazan D5
Rybinsk D5
Samara E6
Saratov E5
Simbirsk E6
Smolensk D5
St. Petersburg . . C5
Stavropol F4
Tolyattigrad E6
Tula D5
Tver' D5
Ufa E7
Volgograd E5
Voronezh E5
Yaroslavl' D5

A B C D E F G

7 8 9 10 11

Asia

With its beautiful coat and muscular body, the Siberian tiger is an impressive sight. There are now less than 500 living in the wild.

FROM THE TOP OF THE HIGHEST POINT IN THE WORLD, Mount Everest, on the borders of China and Nepal, range after range of snow-white peaks fade into the blue distance. Far below lies Asia, the largest continent on Earth. It takes up one-third of the planet's land area, stretching from the Mediterranean Sea to the Pacific Ocean, from the pack ice of the Arctic to the tropical beaches of the Timor Sea. It is part of the vast Eurasian landmass, bordering the continent of Europe along the Ural and Caucasus mountains and separated from Africa only by the Suez Canal. Asia includes desolate wildernesses, from the frozen wastes of Siberia to the fierce heat of Saudi Arabia's Empty Quarter, but it also has fertile lands, such as the lush green rice paddies of the Mekong River and the rich farmland of China's Huang River valley.

These lands gave birth to ancient civilizations and most of the world's major religions, including Hinduism, Buddhism, Judaism, Christianity, and Islam. Craft workers still produce fine Iranian carpets, Japanese pottery, and Chinese and Indian silk, using traditional skills, while people in modern factories manufacture cars and computers.

About one-third of all Asians live in towns. Millions pour into crowded cities such as Bombay, Calcutta, Shanghai, and Tokyo. The continent has a population of 3.6 billion, and that is expected to double within 50 years.

ARCTI
RUS
FEDE
MEDITERRANEAN SEA
BLACK SEA
TURKEY
GEORGIA
ARMENIA
AZERBAIJAN
CASPIAN SEA
KAZAKHSTAN
ARAL SEA
UZBEKISTAN
TURKMENISTAN
KYRGYZSTAN
TAJIKISTAN
CYPRUS
LEBANON
SYRIA
ISRAEL
JORDAN
IRAQ
IRAN
KUWAIT
AFGHANISTAN
RED SEA
SAUDI ARABIA
BAHRAIN
QATAR
U.A.E.
Gulf of Oman
PAKISTAN
NEPAL
YEMEN
OMAN
ARABIAN SEA
INDIA
Bay
SRI LANKA
MALDIVES
INDIAN OCEAN

DISCOVER MORE

- *Ninety percent of the world's rice is grown in Asia.*
- *More than one-fifth of all the people in the world live in China.*
- *Northern Asia has the largest area of conifer forest in the world, in the Russian region of Siberia.*
- *Asia is home to the highest and lowest points on Earth: Mount Everest and the Dead Sea.*

Vast areas of southwest Asia form a hot, barren wilderness of sand. The southeastern region of Saudi Arabia is called Rub'al-Khali, the Empty Quarter.

6
7
8
9
10
11

OCEAN

SEA OF OKHOTSK

SIAN

ATION

MONGOLIA

SEA OF JAPAN

JAPAN

NORTH KOREA

TOKYO

SOUTH KOREA

CHINA

EAST CHINA SEA

PACIFIC OCEAN

600 miles

1,000 km

BHUTAN

BANGLADESH

TAIWAN

MYANMAR (BURMA)

LAOS

Bengal

THAILAND

VIETNAM

CAMBODIA

SOUTH CHINA SEA

PHILIPPINES

CELEBES SEA

BRUNEI

MALAYSIA

SINGAPORE

INDONESIA

BANDA SEA

EAST TIMOR

JAVA SEA

TIMOR SEA

A B C D E F G

Where in the world?

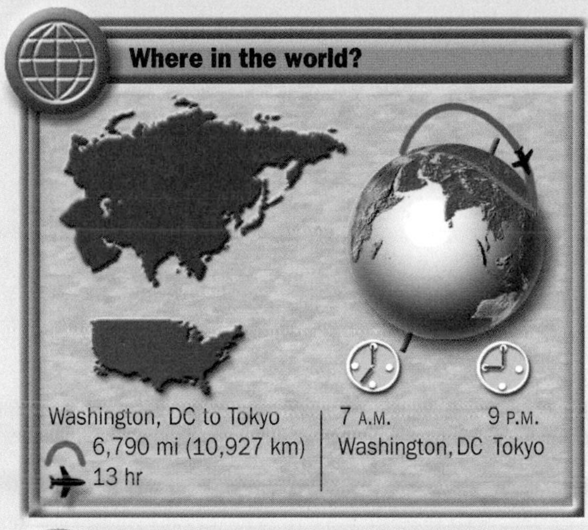

Washington, DC to Tokyo
6,790 mi (10,927 km)
13 hr
7 A.M.
9 P.M.
Washington, DC
Tokyo

Search and find

Afghanistan	D5	Mongolia	C7
Armenia	C4	Myanmar	E7
Azerbaijan	C4	Nepal	E6
Bahrain	D4	North Korea	D8
Bangladesh	E6	Oman	E4
Bhutan	E6	Pakistan	D5
Brunei	F8	Philippines	E8
Cambodia	E7	Qatar	D4
China	D7	Russian Federation	B6
Cyprus	C3	Saudi Arabia	D4
East Timor	F8	Singapore	F7
Georgia	C4	South Korea	D8
India	E5	Sri Lanka	F5
Indonesia	F8	Syria	C4
Iran	D4	Taiwan	E8
Iraq	D4	Tajikistan	D5
Israel	D3	Thailand	E7
Japan	C8	Tokyo	D8
Jordan	D3	Turkey	C3
Kazakhstan	C5	Turkmenistan	D5
Kuwait	D4	U.A.E.	E4
Kyrgyzstan	D5	Uzbekistan	D5
Laos	E7	Vietnam	E7
Lebanon	C4	Yemen	E4
Malaysia	F7		
Maldives	F4		

Throughout Asia, religion plays a key part in people's lives. In Thailand, more than 95 percent of the population is Buddhist. Beautiful temples dedicated to Buddhism can be seen throughout the country.

Continent facts

	Area sq mi (sq km)	% of Earth's area	Population	Largest country by area sq mi (sq km)	Largest country by population
Asia	17,400,000 (45,066,000)	30.1	3,527,969,000	Russian Fed. 6,592,800 (17,075,352)	China 1,250,066,000

Eastern Russia

The gray wolf thrives in the wilderness of Siberia, where it has survived thousands of years of being hunted. It lives in tundra and forest regions, gathering in packs of up to 30 during the harsh winters.

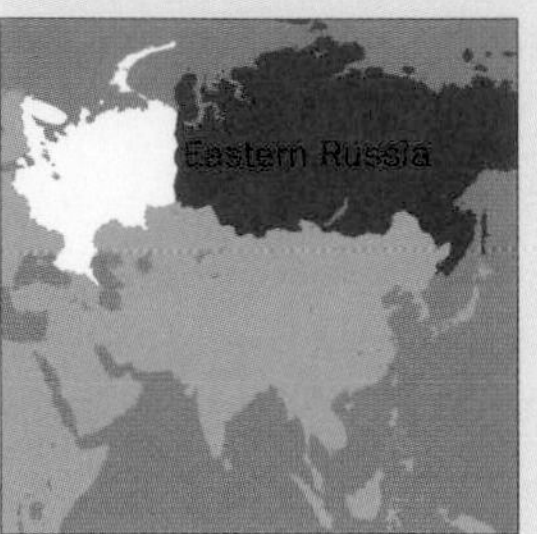
Eastern Russia

In the west of Russia, at Moscow's Yaroslavsky Station, passengers board an eastbound train on the world's longest railroad, the Trans-Siberian. Once past the Ural Mountains, the train enters the region of Siberia, in the Asian part of the Russian Federation. It halts at sprawling industrial cities such as Omsk and rushes past small villages of wooden houses, their carved roof gables hung with icicles in winter. Borscht—beet soup—is served in the dining car.

Vast forests continue eastward, and many westbound locomotives may be seen hauling loads of timber. At Lake Baykal the track divides, southward to Mongolia or eastward to the Pacific coast and the seaport of Vladivostok, more than six days from Moscow, traveling at 35 mph (60 km/h).

Western Siberia forms a great plain, drained by the Ob River. Beyond the Yenisey River is the Central Siberian Plateau, bordered to the east and south by high mountains. Asian Russia has vast mineral wealth, but its great distance from the industrial cities in the west makes transportation expensive. The most fertile region is southwest of Siberia.

Siberian winters are among the most severe on Earth. Milk is delivered in solid blocks, and trucks use frozen rivers as highways. Siberia is sparsely populated, but it is home to many ethnic groups—Kets, Khants, Mani, Yakuts, Evenks, Koryaks, and Chukchi, as well as Russians. Some Arctic groups live by hunting, fishing, and reindeer herding.

Severnaya Zemlya
LAPTE
Nordvik
Dikson
Central Siberian Plateau
URAL MOUNTAINS
Salekhard
Ob
Siberian Lowland
RUSSIAN F
Yenisey
Lower Tunguska
Surgut
Nizhniy Tagil
Tobol
Tyumen'
Tobol'sk
Yekaterinburg
Chelyabinsk
Kurgan
Angara
Omsk
Tomsk
Kemerovo
Novosibirsk
Krasnoyarsk
Bratsk
KAZAKHSTAN
Novokuznetsk
Irkutsk
Barnaul
SAYAN MTS
MONGO

DISCOVER MORE

- *Siberian temperatures have been known to drop to below –140°F (–60°C).*
- *Lake Baykal is the world's oldest surviving lake, dating back over 25 million years. Many of its plant and animal species, such as the rare Baykal seal, are found nowhere else on earth.*

Yakutsk is located by the Lena River, in remote Siberia. It experiences bitterly cold winters, but is home to about 200,000 people.

ARCTIC OCEAN
Wrangel I.
EAST SIBERIAN SEA
BERING SEA
Anadyr
New Siberian Is
Delta of the Lena
Indigirka
Kolyma
Kolyma Lowland
KOLYMA MTS
Komandorskiye I.
CHERSKIY RANGE
Kamchatka Peninsula
Lena
VERKHOYANSKIY MTS
Magadan
Petropavlovsk-Kamchatskiy
DZHUGDZHUR MTS
Okhotsk
Yakutsk
SEA OF OKHOTSK
DERATION
Olekminsk
Lensk
Aldan Plateau
Sakhalin I.
STANOVOY MTS
Tatar Strait
Amur
SIKHOTE-ALIN MTS
Yuzhno-Sakhalinsk
YABLONOVYY MTS
Khabarovsk
L. Baykal
CHINA
SEA OF JAPAN
Ulan-Ude
Vladivostok
N
W
E
S
500 miles
500 km
Russian Federation

Where in the world?

7 A.M. Washington, DC | noon GMT | 10 P.M. Vladivostok

Washington, DC to Vladivostok
6,507 mi (10,471 km)
12 hr 30 min

Vladivostok lies on
43° 06'N latitude
131° 47'E longitude

Life facts

How long do people live?

U.S.A. 76 years

Russian Federation 65 years

How many people in 100 own cars?

U.S.A. 48

Russian Federation 9

Search and find

Eastern Russia

Anadyr A8
Barnaul E4
Bratsk D6
Chelyabinsk D3
Dikson C5
Irkutsk E6
Kemerovo E5
Khabarovsk D8
Krasnoyarsk E5
Kurgan D4
Lensk D6
Magadan C8
Nizhniy Tagil D3
Nordvik B6
Novokuznetsk . . E5
Novosibirsk E4
Okhotsk C8
Olekminsk D7
Omsk E4
Petropavlovsk-Kamchatskiy . . C9
Salekhard C4
Surgut D4
Tobol'sk D4
Tomsk D5
Tyumen' D3
Ulan-Ude E6
Vladivostok E8
Yakutsk C7
Yekaterinburg . . D3
Yuzhno-Sakhalinsk D9

A cone of gray rock called andestite, striped with snow, rises from clouds on Russia's Kamchatka Peninsula. Like many other parts of the Pacific Rim, Kamchatka is a region of intense volcanic activity.

Country facts

	Area sq mi (sq km)	Population	Language	Religion	Currency
Russian Federation	6,592,800 (17,075,352)	146,393,569	Russian	Russian Orthodox	Ruble

The Caucasus

AZERBAIJAN, GEORGIA, ARMENIA

Georgia
Armenia
Azerbaijan

DAZZLING WHITE SNOWFIELDS can be seen above forests in the Caucasus range, which rises to some of Europe's highest peaks. Melting snows feed mountain streams and fast-flowing rivers, and these drain westward into the Black Sea. Eastward they drain into the Caspian Sea—a lake holding the largest volume of fresh water in the world.

The region is known as Trans-Caucasia, and the Caucasus Mountains form a meeting point between Europe and Asia, with the continental border passing through northern Georgia.

Armenia, known as the Land of Stones, contains very dry areas. However, river valleys and the warmer mountain foothills offer fertile land. Lowland crops include grapes, peaches, and figs. At higher altitudes, wheat, tobacco, and potatoes grow.

Trans-Caucasian factories produce chemicals, machinery, textiles, and leather goods. Azerbaijan has seen its oil industry thrive and decline over the years, but it seems likely that the Caspian Sea still has large reserves of oil to be exploited. Oil production is based around Baku, the best situated but most polluted harbor on the Caspian Sea.

More than 500 different ethnic groups live on the slopes of the Caucasus Mountains. Most people in Azerbaijan are Muslims, while Armenia and Georgia hold ancient Orthodox Christian traditions.

Gagra
Mt Elbrus
18,510 ft
(5,642 m)
RUSSIA
Sukhumi
BLACK SEA
Ochamchira
Zugdidi
GEORGIA
Rioni
Kutaisi
Poti
Kura
Batumi
Tbilisi
TURKEY
Vanadzor
Gyumri
Ejmiadzin
Yerevan
Araks

Georgian national costume may still be worn for special festivals. Men wear high leather boots, tunics, and round caps or hats of sheepskin.

DISCOVER MORE

- *The Caucasus range has more than 2,000 glaciers.*
- *Horseback riders gallop at breakneck speed in a Georgian game called* tskhenburi, *which is rather like polo. Teams of players hit a ball with a long racket.*
- *Oil reserves in Baku, the capital of Azerbaijan, once supplied half the world's oil.*

High-rise apartments tower over farmland on the outskirts of Yerevan, Armenia. The city is close to the Turkish border, a region prone to earthquakes.

With banners held high, priests of the Armenian Church lead a procession through the ancient town of Ejmiadzin to celebrate Easter. Armenia was the first country in history to make Christianity its state religion.

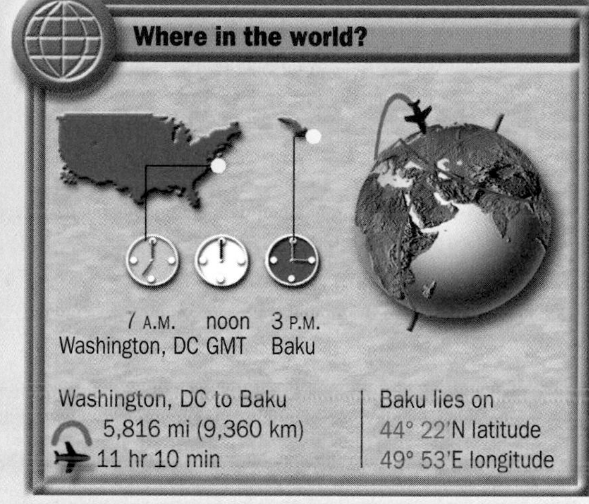
Where in the world?
7 A.M. Washington, DC
noon GMT
3 P.M. Baku
Washington, DC to Baku
5,816 mi (9,360 km)
11 hr 10 min
Baku lies on
44° 22'N latitude
49° 53'E longitude

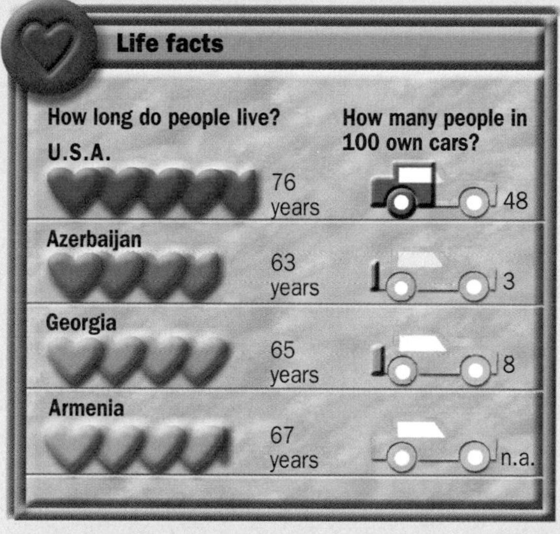
Life facts
How long do people live?
How many people in 100 own cars?
U.S.A.
76 years
48
Azerbaijan
63 years
3
Georgia
65 years
8
Armenia
67 years
n.a.

FEDERATION
MTS
Alazani
Rustavi
Kuba
CASPIAN SEA
Şäki
Mingäçevir
Gyandzha
AZERBAIJAN
Sumgait
Baku
L. Sevan
Nagorno-Karabakh
Kura
Qazimämmäd
Stepanakert
Salyan
Araks
ERBAIJAN
Naxçivan
IRAN
Lenkoran'
N
W
E
S

The Caucasus Mountains are home to the highest point in Europe, Mount Elbrus. Many geographers consider the Caucasus range to be the dividing line between Europe and Asia.

300 miles

400 km

Azerbaijan · Georgia · Armenia

Country facts

	Area sq mi (sq km)	Population	Language	Religion	Currency
Azerbaijan	33,4367 (86,599)	7,908,224	Azeri	Shia Muslim	Manat
Georgia	26,911 (69,911)	5,066,499	Georgian	Georgian Orthodox	Lavi
Armenia	11,506 (29,801)	3,409,234	Armenian	Armenian Apostolic	Dram

Search and find

Azerbaijan
Capital: Baku . . .D9
Gyandzha C7
Kuba C8
Lenkoran' E8
Mingäçevir C7
Naxçivan E6
Qazimämmäd . .D9
Şäki C7
Salyan D8
Stepanakert . . .D7
Sumgait C9

Georgia
Capital: Tbilisi . .C6
Batumi C4
Gagra A3
Kutaisi B5
Ochamchira B4
Poti B4
Rustavi C6
Sukhumi A4
Zugdidi B4

Armenia
Capital: Yerevan .D6
Dilizhan C6
Ejmiadzin D5
Gyumri C5
Vanadzor D5

Central Asia

KAZAKHSTAN, TURKMENISTAN, UZBEKISTAN, KYRGYZSTAN, TAJIKISTAN

A little boy tries the reins of a horse in Kyrgyzstan. Most Kyrgyz people live by farming and herding in rural areas.

Kazakhstan
Uzbekistan
Kyrgyzstan
Turkmenistan
Tajikistan

CENTRAL ASIA STRETCHES from the salty waters of the Caspian Sea to high mountain ranges such as the Pamirs, on the border with western China. Although the region lies at the heart of the Eurasian landmass, it is thinly populated. Its rocky plateaus and empty deserts are freezing in winter, but shimmer in the extreme heat of summer. These are crossed by two-humped Bactrian camels, as they pad and snort along ancient trading routes. There are wide, open, windswept grasslands called steppes, shallow lakes, and bleak mountain passes.

The newly independent nations of Central Asia take their names from the Muslim peoples of the region—the Kazakhs, Turkmen, Uzbeks, Tajiks, and Kyrgyz. Some of these people still lead a nomadic life, pitching tents wherever their goats and sheep can graze. Turkmen women make wool into beautiful, intricately patterned carpets. Some people are farmers, harvesting cotton, grain, melons, or wheat from irrigated land. Others work in a growing industry that is rapidly opening up the region—oil and natural gas.

RUSSI
Aqtöbe
CASPIAN SEA
Baykonu
KAZA
ARAL SEA
TURANIAN PLATEAU
Syr Darya
Dashhowuz
UZBEKISTAN
TURKMENISTAN
Shymke
Ashkhabad
Bukhara
Samarkand
Tashk
Amu Dar'ya
Dushanb
TAJI
IRAN
AFGHANISTAN

DISCOVER MORE

- *The Aral Sea, on the Kazakh-Uzbek border, is vanishing fast. Today, it covers barely one-third of its original area. This is mainly because, huge amounts of water have been drained away to irrigate crops.*

A young woman sets to work at a carpet factory in Ashkhabad, the capital of Turkmenistan. Central Asia and the Middle East have been a center of carpet making for thousands of years.

Kazakhstan

Turkmenistan

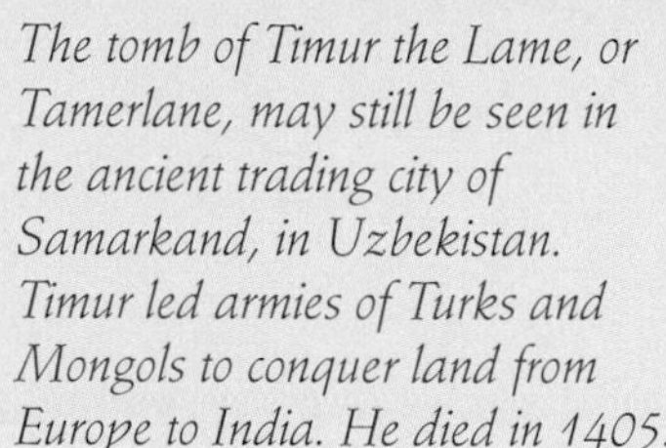

The tomb of Timur the Lame, or Tamerlane, may still be seen in the ancient trading city of Samarkand, in Uzbekistan. Timur led armies of Turks and Mongols to conquer land from Europe to India. He died in 1405.

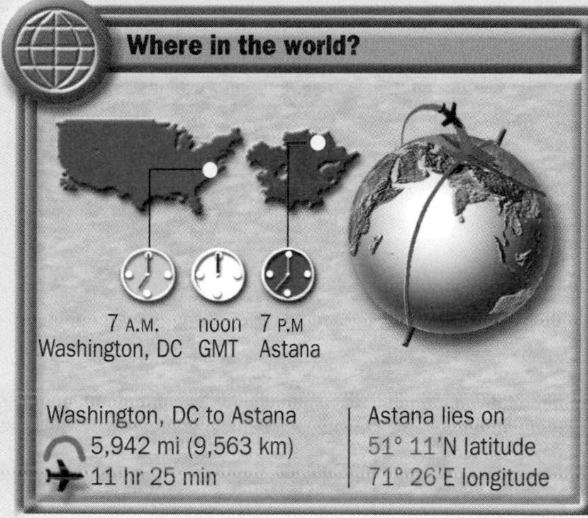

Where in the world?
7 A.M.
Washington, DC
noon
GMT
7 P.M
Astana
Washington, DC to Astana
5,942 mi (9,563 km)
11 hr 25 min
Astana lies on
51° 11'N latitude
71° 26'E longitude

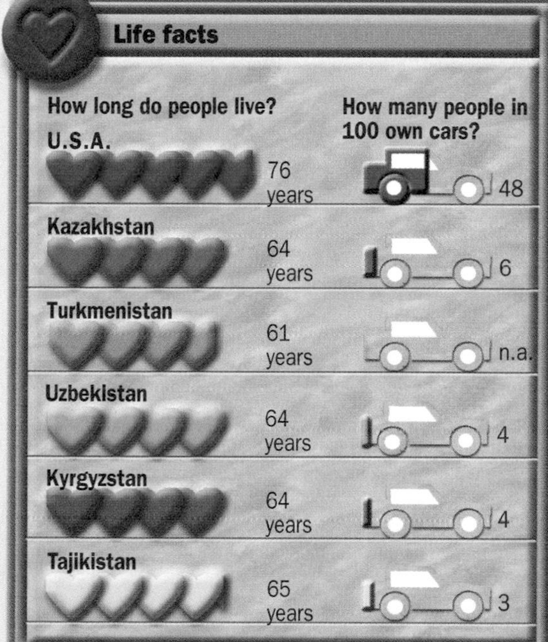

Life facts
How long do people live?
How many people in 100 own cars?
U.S.A.
76 years
48
Kazakhstan
64 years
6
Turkmenistan
61 years
n.a.
Uzbekistan
64 years
4
Kyrgyzstan
64 years
4
Tajikistan
65 years
3

Search and find
Kazakhstan
Capital: Astana .C7
Almaty E7
Aqtöbe C4
Baykonur D5
Qaraghandy D7
Shymkent E6
Turkmenistan
Capital:
Ashkhabad . . .F4
Dashhowuz E4
Uzbekistan
Capital: Tashkent F6
Bukhara F5
Namangan F6
Samarkand F5
Kyrgyzstan
Capital: Bishkek .E7
Tajikistan
Capital:
Dushanbe F5

N FEDERATION

Ishim

Irtysh

Astana

Qaraghandy

ISTAN

ETPAQDALA DESERT

L. Balkhash

CHINA

Almaty

Bishkek

KYRGYZSTAN

TIAN SHAN

TAN

AMIRS

300 miles

500 km

Country facts

	Area sq mi (sq km)	Population	Language	Religion	Currency
Kazakhstan	1,052,100 (2,724,939)	16,824,825	Kazakh/Russian	Sunni Muslim/NR*	Tenge
Turkmenistan	188,455 (488,098)	4,366,383	Turkmen	Muslim	Manat
Uzbekistan	172,741 (447,399)	24,102,473	Uzbek	Sunni Muslim	Som
Kyrgyzstan	76,641 (198,500)	4,546,055	Kyrgyz	Sunni Muslim	Som
Tajikistan	55,251 (143,100)	6,102,854	Tajik	Sunni Muslim	Ruble

*Non-religious

Uzbekistan

Kyrgyzstan

Tajikistan

Northwest Asia

TURKEY, CYPRUS

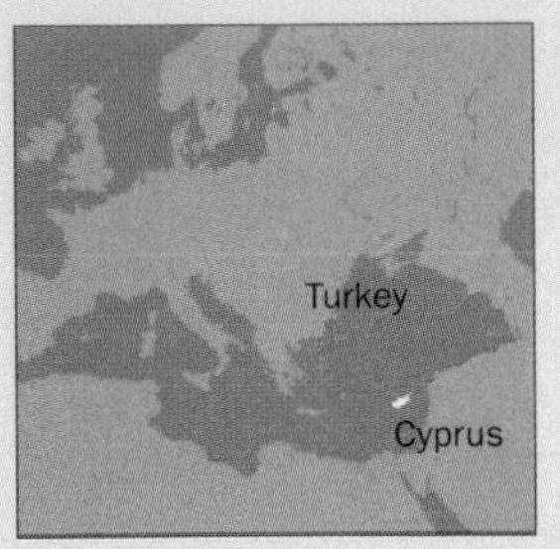
Turkey
Cyprus

A LONG, GRACEFUL SUSPENSION bridge crosses the narrow, windy stretch of sea called the Bosporus. It separates the small European part of Turkey from the broad Anatolian plateau, known since ancient times as Asia Minor. Clustered on the steep, western shores of the Bosporus is the walled city of Istanbul. The beautiful domes of the Blue Mosque and Hagia Sophia mark its skyline. The covered bazaar is a maze of alleys where shops sell gleaming copper pots and carpets. Black tea and coffee are drunk wherever business is done; the coffee is served thick and very strong. Topkapi, the old palace of the Turkish rulers, or sultans, looks out over blue seas.

Anatolia's sunny coasts, with their fishing villages and ancient ruins, attract many tourists. Inland, dusty plains stretch eastward to Iran. Hot in summer but freezing in winter, they are broken by saltwater lakes and mountains. Ankara is Turkey's capital and second-largest populated city.

The beautiful Mediterranean island of Cyprus rises from a plateau to the Troodos Mountains in the southwest. The country is divided between its Greek and Turkish populations.

The landscape of Cappadocia, in the Turkish region of Anatolia, was created more than 8 million years ago by volcanic eruptions. Lava and ash were eroded by the weather into rocky pinnacles. Homes were later built into the rock face.

BULGARIA
GREECE
Edirne
BLACK SEA
Bosporus
Bartin
Zonguldak
Karabük
Istanbul
Tekirdağ
Sea of Marmara
Izmit
Adapazari
Gerede
Kizil
Çoru
Bursa
Sakarya
Ankara
Balikesir
Eskişehir
Porsuk
Kirikkale
Kütahya
Manisa
Uşak
ANATOLIAN PLATEAU
Tuz L.
Izmir
Cappadoc
Aydin
Nazilli
Denizli
Isparta
Konya
Bodrum
TAURUS MOUNTAIN
Ada
Antalya
Tarsus
Mersin
MEDITERRANEAN SEA
Nicosia
CYPRUS
TROODOS MTS
Larnaca
Limassol

DISCOVER MORE

- *Millions of birds belonging to about 200 species use Cyprus as a stopping point on their annual migrations. They are attracted by the wetlands of Cyprus's lakes.*
- *Turkey is known for its ancient* hamams, *or public baths, containing steam rooms, washrooms, and massage rooms for men and women.*

This village in the center of the island of Cyprus lies on the eastern edge of the Troodos mountain range.

Highest mountains
Mount McKinley
20,320 ft
(6,194 m)
Mount Ararat
17,011 ft
(5,186 m)

Ice-capped Mount Ararat is the highest point in Turkey, near the frontiers with Armenia and Iran. Ararat is an extinct volcano.

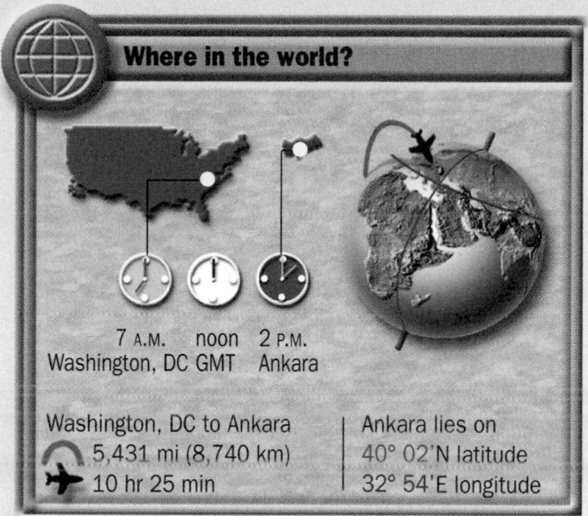

Where in the world?
7 A.M.
Washington, DC
noon
GMT
2 P.M.
Ankara
Washington, DC to Ankara
5,431 mi (8,740 km)
10 hr 25 min
Ankara lies on
40° 02'N latitude
32° 54'E longitude

100 miles
150 km
N
S
E
W
Samsun
Ordu
Trabzon
GEORGIA
PONTIC MOUNTAINS
Çoruh
Kelkit
Kars
ARMENIA
Sivas
Kizil
Erzincan
Erzurum
Mt Ararat
AZER.
TURKEY
Murat
Kayseri
Malatya
Elâziğ
Van
L. Van
IRAN
Adiyaman
Diyarbakir
Batman
Tigris
Osmaniye
Euphrates
Urfa
Gaziantep
IRAQ
Antakya
SYRIA

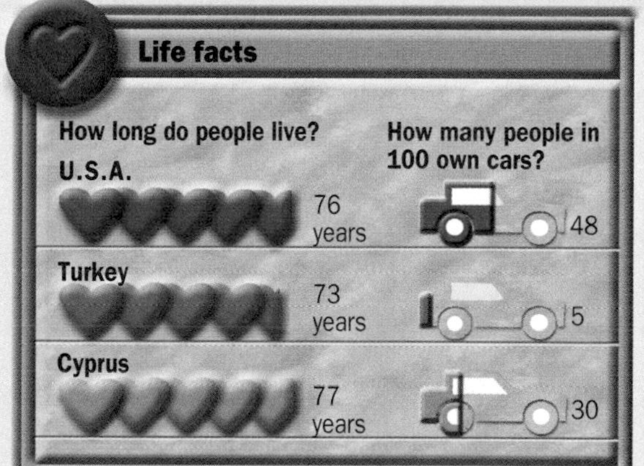

Life facts
How long do people live?
How many people in 100 own cars?
U.S.A.
76 years
48
Turkey
73 years
5
Cyprus
77 years
30

Search and find

Turkey
Capital: Ankara .D5
Adana E6
Adapazari C4
Adiyaman E7
Antakya E6
Antalya E4
Aydin E4
Balikesir D4
Bartin C5
Batman E8
Bodrum E3
Bursa D4
Çorum D6
Denizli E4
Diyarbakir E8
Edirne C3
Elâziğ D7
Erzincan D7
Erzurum D8
Eskişehir D4
Gaziantep E7
Isparta E4
Istanbul C4
Izmir D3
Izmit C4
Karabük C5
Kars D9
Kayseri D6
Kirikkale D5
Konya E5
Kütahya D4
Malatya D7
Manisa D3
Mersin E6
Nazilli E4
Ordu C7
Osmaniye E6
Samsun C6
Sivas D6
Tarsus E6
Tekirdağ C3
Trabzon C7
Urfa E7
Uşak D4
Van D9
Zonguldak C5

Cyprus
Capital: Nicosia .F5
Larnaca F5
Limassol F5

A group of Turkish women ride in a tractor-trailer on their way to work in the fields. Forty-five percent of the Turkish labor force is employed in agriculture.

Turkey

Cyprus

Country facts

	Area sq mi (sq km)	Population	Language	Religion	Currency
Turkey	301,382 (780,579)	65,599,206	Turkish	Sunni Muslim	Lira
Cyprus	3,571 (9,249)	754,064	Greek/Turkish	Greek Orthodox/Sunni Muslim	Pound

Western Asia

SYRIA, LEBANON

Lebanon's long, green Bekáa Valley lies at an altitude of 3,247 ft (990 m). About 12 mi (20 km) across, it is bordered in the west by the Lebanon Mountains. Often streaked with snow, the mountains rise to 10,115 ft (3,083 m) above sea level.

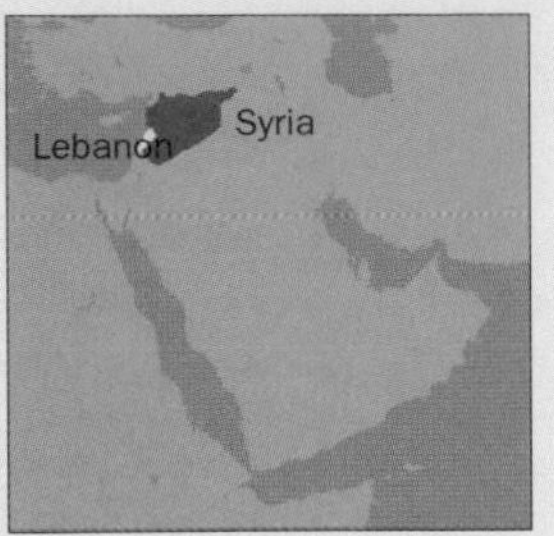
Lebanon
Syria

LEBANON'S COAST ROAD RUNS alongside the warm, blue Mediterranean Sea, through the ancient ports of Tyre and Sidon, and northward to the white apartment blocks and bright lights of the capital, Beirut. The city is being rebuilt after long years of war, and some districts remain badly damaged or ruined. Beirut hopes to regain its reputation for style and entertainment, attracting new tourists and investment. Roads cross the Lebanon Mountains and the fertile Bekáa Valley to the Anti-Lebanon Mountains on the Syrian border.

Syria and Lebanon include many Christians and Druze (a religious movement that broke away from Islam), but most people of the region are Muslim Arabs. Calls to prayer are broadcast five times daily from the loudspeakers of mosques in Damascus, the Syrian capital. They echo and boom around modern high-rise buildings, bustling covered markets, and narrow alleys. Syria extends westward to the orchards of the Mediterranean coast and eastward to the wheat and cotton fields of the fertile valley of the Euphrates River. Much of the country is hot, sandy desert, crossed by camel herders.

This man is a Druze. About one-half million of these people live in Lebanon, Syria, and Israel.

DISCOVER MORE

- *Damascus is the oldest capital city in the world. People have lived there for at least 4,500 years.*
- *Lebanese cedar was used by crafts people in ancient Egypt and Israel. Today very few cedars have survived, so millions of the trees are being grown to replace the forests. The cedar of Lebanon appears on the national flag.*

Al Bāb
Aleppo
Asad
MEDITERRANEAN SEA
Latakia
Orontes
Apamea
Hamāh
Krak des Chevaliers
Tartus
Homs
Palmyra
Kebir
Tripoli
Qurnatas as Sawdā
10,115 ft
(3,083 m)
LEBANON
Asi
Beirut
LEBANON MTS
BEKÁA VALLEY
ANTI-LEBANON MTS
Damascus
Sidon
Litani
Al Kiswah
Syria
Tyre
Al Qunaytirah
ISRAEL
Golan Heights
Shahbā
Dar'ā
As Suwayda
Busrā ash-Shām
JORDAN

In the heart of the city of Damascus, Syria, shops open directly onto the street. They are often festooned with all kinds of produce and household goods to tempt customers. Many of the women wear the long, dark robes and veils of the Islamic religion.

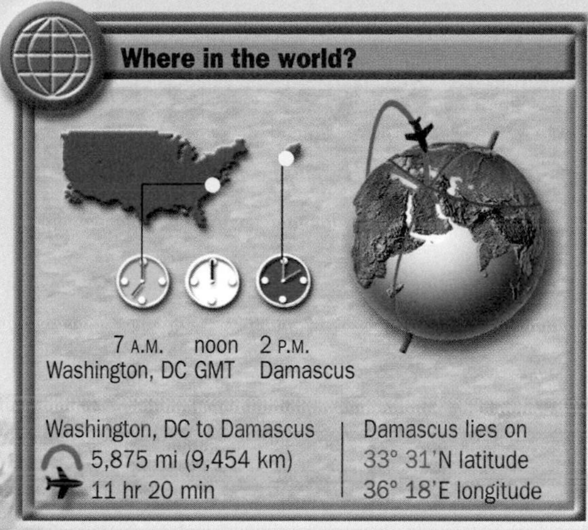

Where in the world?
7 A.M.
Washington, DC
noon
GMT
2 P.M.
Damascus
Washington, DC to Damascus
5,875 mi (9,454 km)
11 hr 20 min
Damascus lies on
33° 31'N latitude
36° 18'E longitude

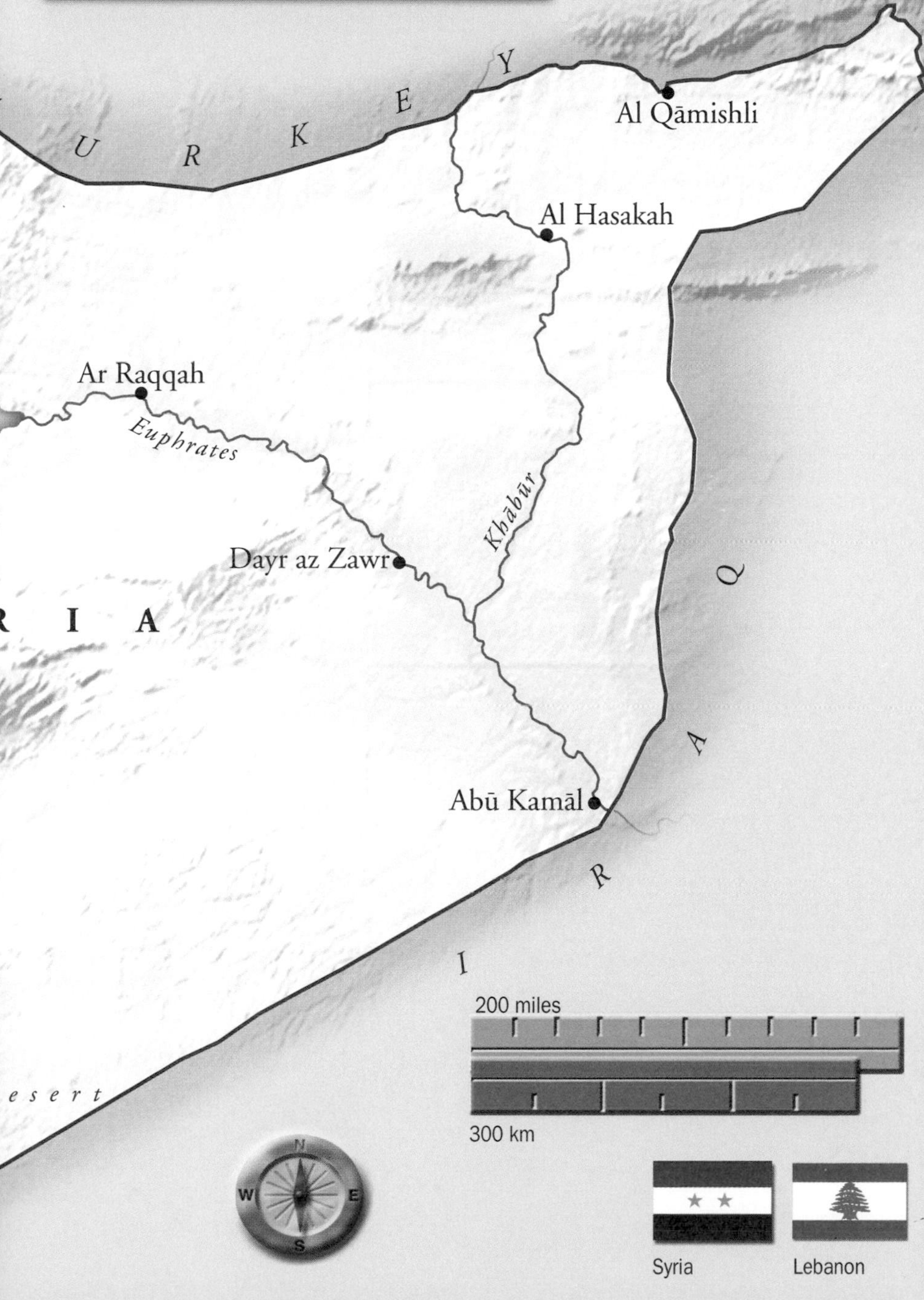

6
7
8
9
10
11
A
B
C
D
E
F
G
T U R K E Y
Al Qāmishli
Al Hasakah
Ar Raqqah
Euphrates
Khābūr
Dayr az Zawr
R I A
I R A Q
Abū Kamāl
e s e r t
200 miles
300 km
N
E
S
W
Syria
Lebanon

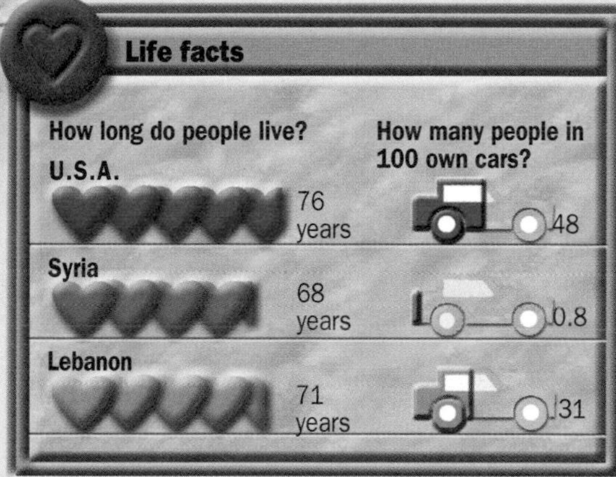

Life facts
How long do people live?
How many people in 100 own cars?
U.S.A.
76 years
48
Syria
68 years
0.8
Lebanon
71 years
31

Cedars of Lebanon spread their ancient branches against the evening sky in Lebanon. The trees are evergreen conifers with a fragrant wood.

Search and find

Syria
Capital:
Damascus . . .F4
Abū Kamāl E8
Al Bāb C5
Aleppo C5
Al Hasakah C8
Al Kiswah F4
Al Qāmishli B9
Al Qunaytirah . . .F4
Ar Raqqah D7
As Suwayda G4
Busrā ash-Shām G4
Dar'ā G4
Dayr az Zawr . . .D8
Hamāh D5
Homs E5
Latakia D4
Shahbā G4
Tartus E4

Lebanon
Capital: Beirut . .F4
Sidon F3
Tripoli E4
Tyre F3

Country facts

	Area sq mi (sq km)	Population	Language	Religion	Currency
Syria	71,498 (185,180)	17,213,871	Arabic	Sunni Muslim	Pound
Lebanon	4,015 (10,399)	3,562,699	Arabic	Muslim	Pound

Southwest Asia

JORDAN, ISRAEL

These Jews are worshipping at the Western Wall in Jerusalem. The stone blocks supported the Second Temple built by King Herod more than 2,000 years ago. It was destroyed by Roman troops in A.D. 70.

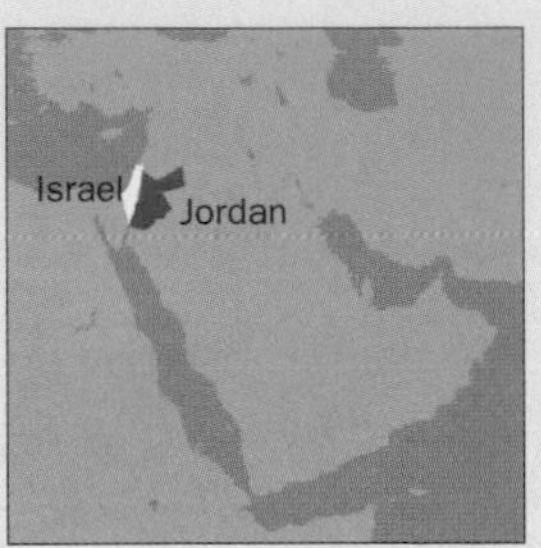
Israel
Jordan

JERUSALEM IS A HOLY CITY TO three faiths. Jews worship at the 2,000-year-old Western Wall, while Christian pilgrims sing hymns as they follow the route along which Jesus Christ is believed to have walked to his crucifixion. The golden Dome of the Rock is a magnificent mosque where it is believed the prophet Muhammad rode to heaven on a winged horse.

Israel is a land of orange, olive, and cypress trees, beside the warm shores of the eastern Mediterranean Sea. Much of the soil is very dry and has to be irrigated to produce crops. The south of the country is occupied by the sand dunes and rocks of the Negev Desert. Eight out of ten Israelis are Jews, many of them settlers who have come from other parts of the world. Most of the rest are Palestinian Arabs.

To the east is Jordan, a Muslim Arab kingdom. This country, too, has many ancient monuments, such as the beautiful city of Petra, carved from rock about 2,400 years ago. The land is mostly desert, where camels pad over rippling sand and four-wheel-drive vehicles kick up dust. Only the valley of the Jordan River is fertile enough to produce fruit and vegetables.

LEBANON
MEDITERRANEAN SEA
Golan Heights
Nahariyya
Acre
Sakhnin
Haifa
Tiberias
Sea of Galilee
Nazareth
'Afula
Irbid
Hadera
Janin
Netanya
Tul Karm
Jordan
Ajlun
Al-Mafr
Herzliyya
Nābulus
Zarqa
Tel Aviv
West Bank
Az-Zarq
Salt
Rishon le-Ziyyon
Rām Allāh
Ammān
Rehovot
Ashdod
Jerusalem
Jericho
Ma'dabā
Ashqelon
Bethlehem
DEAD SEA
Gaza Strip
Gaza
Hebron
Dhībān
Mujib
Khan Yunis
Al-Mazra'ah
Beersheba
Al-Karak
ISRAEL
JO
Dimona
Wadi al Hasa
JEBA
At-Tafilah
Negev Desert
Ard
EGYPT
Wadi al Arabah
Petra
Ma'ān
Yotvata
Elat
'Aqaba
Gulf of 'Aqaba
SAUDI ARABIA

DISCOVER MORE

- *The Dead Sea is actually a lake. Its shores form the deepest exposed depression on Earth, lying some 1,300 ft (400 m) below sea level. The floor of the lake itself plunges to 2,390 ft (728 m) below sea level. The Dead Sea is eight times as salty as other seawater.*
- *Israel has no shortage of sunshine. The country is a world leader in solar energy research, and many houses now use the power of the sun to heat their water.*

A young pupil walks to Koranic school to learn the holy scriptures of Islam. He is from Gaza, a self-governing territory, which is home to about one million Palestinian Arabs.

6
7
8
9
10
11

Israel's Sea of Galilee is also known as Lake Tiberias. The lake lies about 690 ft (210 m) below sea level and is filled and drained by the Jordan River.

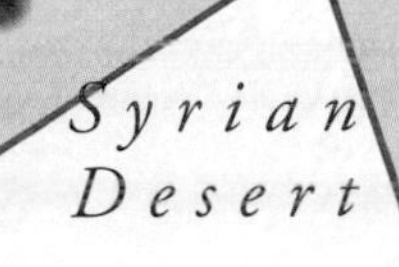
Syrian
Desert

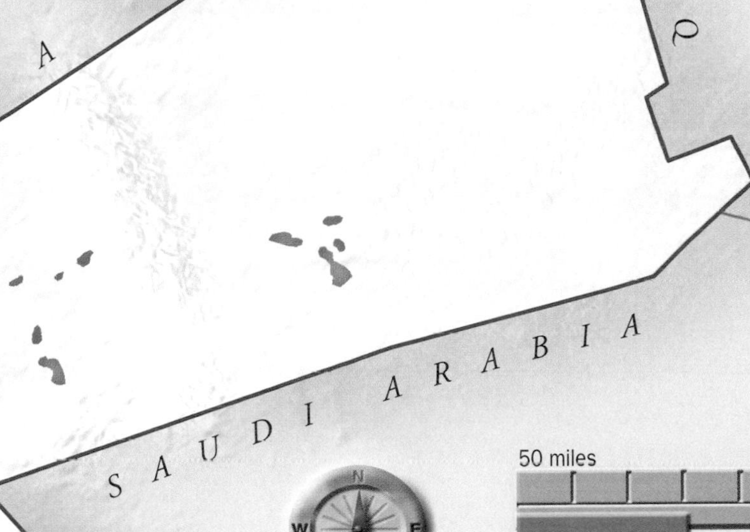
IRAQ
SAUDI ARABIA

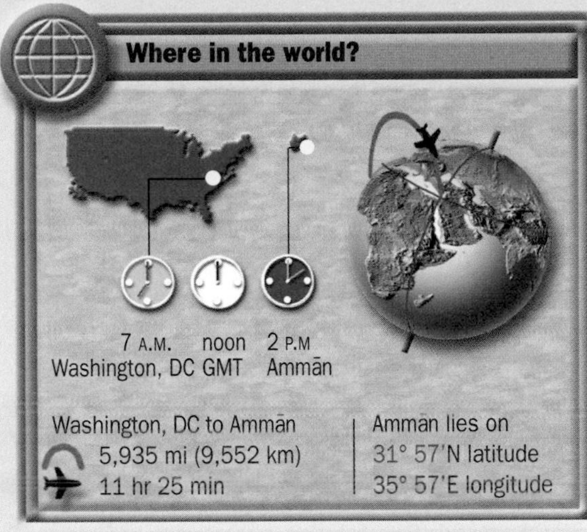
Where in the world?
7 A.M. Washington, DC
noon GMT
2 P.M Ammān
Washington, DC to Ammān
5,935 mi (9,552 km)
11 hr 25 min
Ammān lies on
31° 57′N latitude
35° 57′E longitude

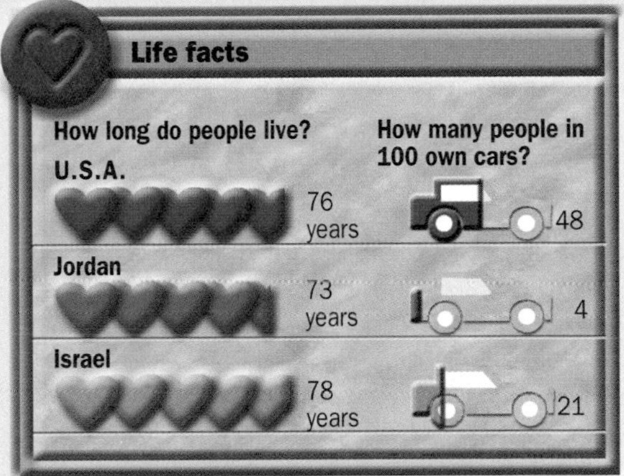
Life facts
How long do people live?
How many people in 100 own cars?
U.S.A.
76 years
48
Jordan
73 years
4
Israel
78 years
21

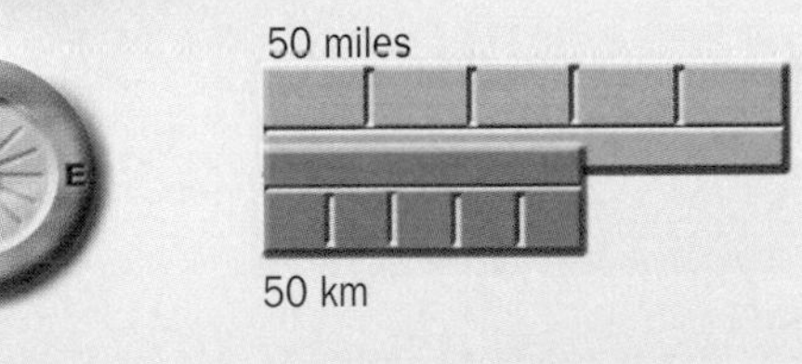
N
W
E
S
50 miles
50 km

Jordan Israel

Petra is a desert city. In ancient times, it controlled the trade route between the Mediterranean region and the Indian Ocean.

Search and find

Jordan
Capital: Ammān . . . D5
Ajlun C5
Al-Karak E5
Al-Mafraq C6
Al-Mazra'ah D5
At-Tafīlah E5
'Aqaba G4
Az-Zarqā C5
Dhībān D5
Irbid C5
Ma'ān F5
Ma'dabā D5
Salt C5

Israel
Capital:
Jerusalem . . D4
Acre B4
'Afula C5
Ashdod D4
Ashqelon D4
Beersheba D4
Bethlehem D4
Dimona E4
Elat G4
Gaza D4
Hadera C4
Haifa B4
Hebron D4
Herzliyya C4
Janin C5
Jericho D5
Khan Yunis D3
Nābulus C4
Nahariyya B4
Nazareth C5
Netanya C4
Rām Allāh D4
Rehovot D4
Rishon le-Ziyyon . D4
Sakhnin B4
Tel Aviv C4
Tiberias C5
Tul Karm C4
Yotvata F4

Country facts

	Area sq mi (sq km)	Population	Language	Religion	Currency
Jordan	34,445 (89,213)	4,561,147	Arabic	Sunni Muslim	Dinar
Israel	7,876 (20,400)	5,749,760	Hebrew	Jewish	New Shekel

Northern Arabia

SAUDI ARABIA, KUWAIT

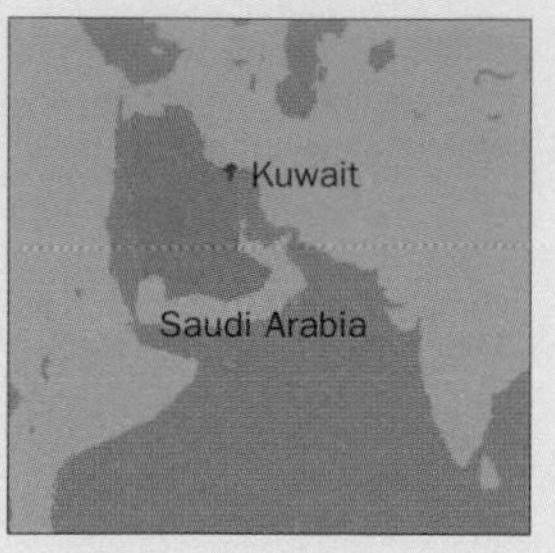
Kuwait
Saudi Arabia

WITH A HEADDRESS AND flowing robes, a Saudi Arabian talks to his brother about hunting with birds of prey. A hooded falcon fidgets on his gloved hand. Inside his car parked on a desert highway, his wife is hidden within black robes. She wears a face veil, revealing only her eyes. Many women in Islamic countries cover their faces, believing that it frees them from the unwelcome attention of men. Other women think that remaining uncovered gives them freedom to carry out everyday work and feel comfortable.

Oil wells rise from the horizon, for Saudi Arabia has become rich through petroleum. This "black gold" has funded the building of modern cities, royal palaces, hospitals, and airports. However, vast areas of Saudi Arabia remain lonely, empty desert, crossed only by nomadic camel herders, many of whom remain poor.

The city of Mecca, in western Saudi Arabia, is the birthplace of the prophet Muhammad, and is visited by tens of thousands of white-robed Muslims from all over the world, during the annual pilgrimage, known as the *hajj*.

Kuwait, Saudi Arabia's neighbor on the Persian Gulf coast, is also a desert country that relies on oil for its wealth. Its people, too, are Muslim Arabs.

IRAQ
JORDAN
Gulf of Aqaba
Al Jawf
Sakākah
Nafud Desert
Buraydah
Shaqra
NEJD
HEJAZ
Medina
RED SEA
SAUDI
Jidda
Mecca
Taif
ASIR
Tihama
Jīzān

DISCOVER MORE

- *One part of Saudi Arabia is so barren and remote that it is known simply as the "Rub 'al-Khali," the "Empty Quarter." Here there are no plants, just gravel and endlessly shifting dunes.*
- *King Khalid airport, Riyadh, is the biggest international aiport in the world, covering an area of 87 sq mi (225 sq km).*

These Saudi Arabian nomads have spread rugs on the ground outside their tent. The elderly man sips strong coffee. He wears a headdress called a ghutra. *The woman wears a black robe and silver jewelry.*

The desert landscape of Kuwait is dominated by the oil industry. Petroleum and other related products account for more than 90 percent of this small country's exports. Since 1946, oil production has transformed Kuwait from a country of little means into one of the world's most prosperous nations.

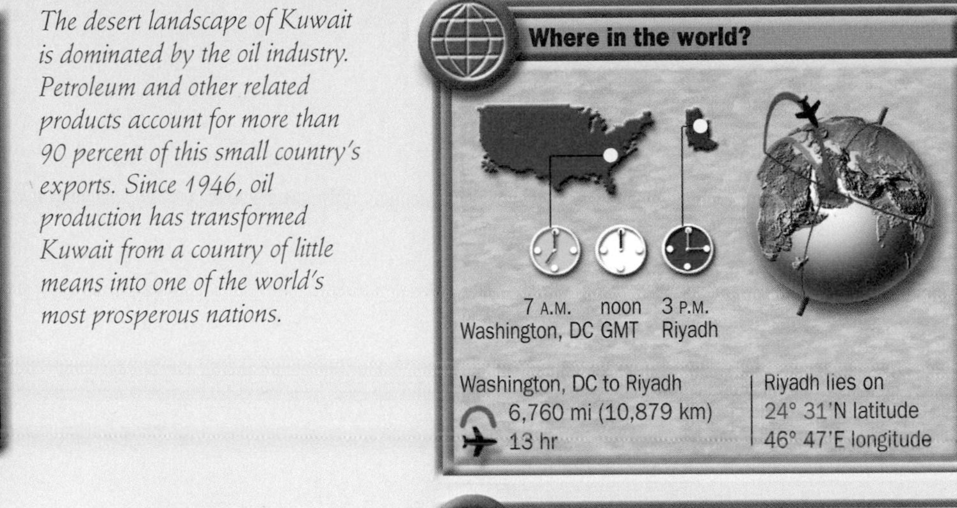

Where in the world?
7 A.M. Washington, DC
noon GMT
3 P.M. Riyadh
Washington, DC to Riyadh
6,760 mi (10,879 km)
13 hr
Riyadh lies on
24° 31'N latitude
46° 47'E longitude

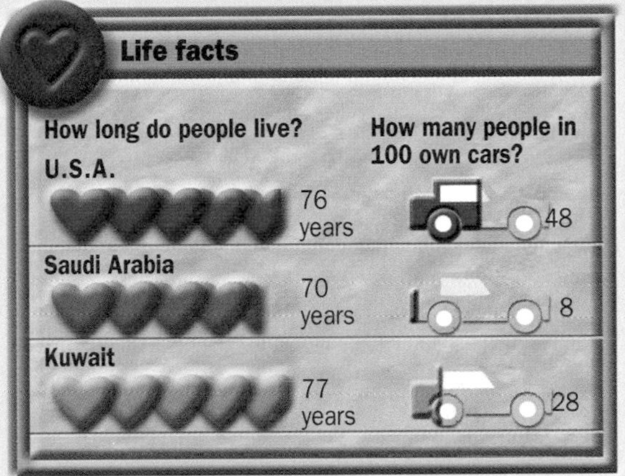

Life facts
How long do people live?
How many people in 100 own cars?
U.S.A.
76 years
48
Saudi Arabia
70 years
8
Kuwait
77 years
28

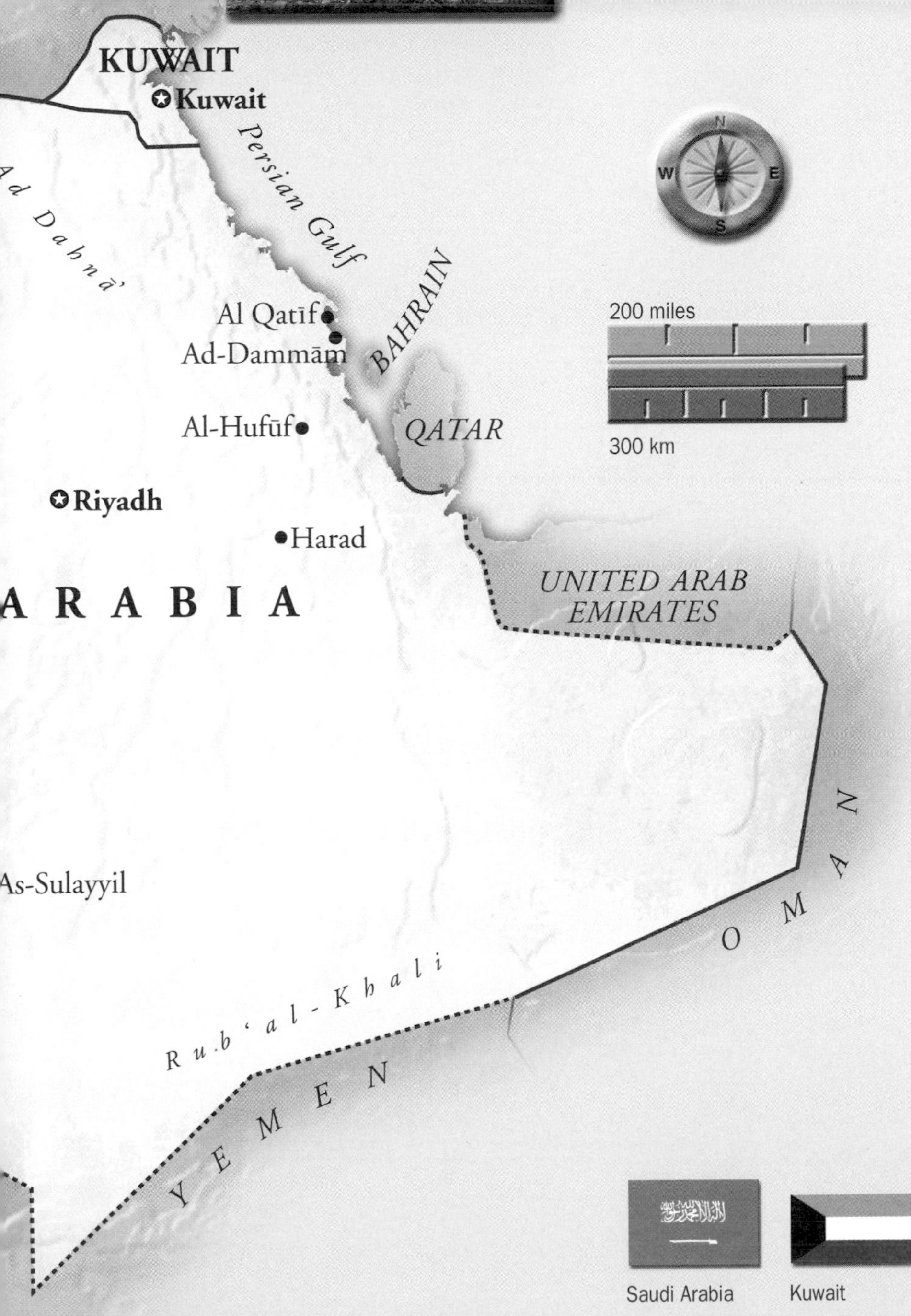

KUWAIT
Kuwait
Persian Gulf
Ad Dahnā
Al Qatīf
Ad-Dammām
BAHRAIN
Al-Hufūf
QATAR
Riyadh
Harad
ARABIA
UNITED ARAB EMIRATES
As-Sulayyil
OMAN
Rub' al-Khali
YEMEN
N
W
E
S
200 miles
300 km
Saudi Arabia
Kuwait

It is the dream of every Muslim to make the pilgrimage to Mecca at least once in a lifetime. Beside the Great Mosque of this Saudi Arabian city is a small, square building called the Kaaba. Set into its eastern corner is the Black Stone, to which Muslims all over the world turn when they pray.

Country facts

	Area sq mi (sq km)	Population	Language	Religion	Currency
Saudi Arabia	864,000 (2,240,350)	21,504,613	Arabic	Sunni Muslim	Riyal
Kuwait	6,880 (17,819)	1,991,115	Arabic	Sunni Muslim	Dinar

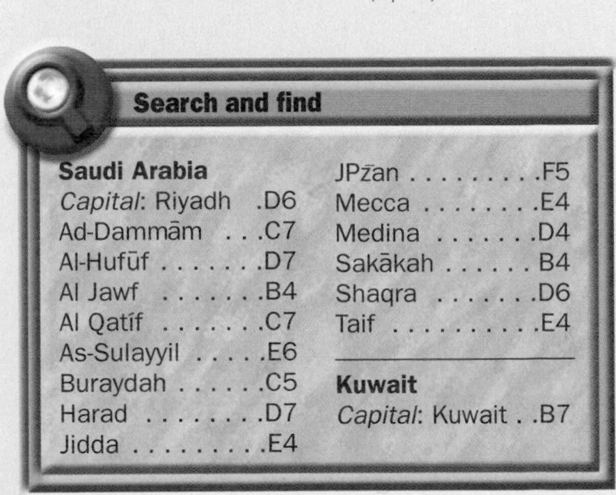

Search and find

Saudi Arabia
Capital: Riyadh .D6
Ad-Dammām . . .C7
Al-Hufūf D7
Al Jawf B4
Al Qatīf C7
As-Sulayyil E6
Buraydah C5
Harad D7
Jidda E4
JPzān F5
Mecca E4
Medina D4
Sakākah B4
Shaqra D6
Taif E4

Kuwait
Capital: Kuwait . .B7

Southern Arabia

YEMEN, OMAN

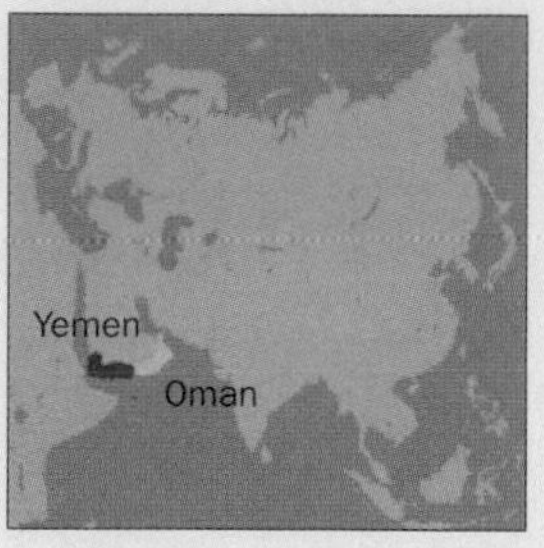
Yemen
Oman

CAMEL CARAVANS HEADING south from the deserts of Saudi Arabia enter the baking, rocky plateaus and mountain ranges of Yemen. Descending from the highlands, the slopes become greener, for they catch moist winds from the Indian Ocean. Coffee and cotton can be grown at this level. The coastal plains beside the Red Sea and the Gulf of Aden shimmer in a heat haze. Yemen's capital is Sanaa, where minarets, the slender towers of mosques, soar above rectangular, four-story buildings built of mud brick trimmed with white, looking like slabs of iced gingerbread.

Oman, too, is a land of mountains and gravelly deserts, beneath a blazing sun. Its territory includes several offshore islands and an enclave, or separate patch of territory, on the Musandam Peninsula, which extends into the Strait of Hormuz. Camels and goats graze on the scrub of the interior. Most nomadic herders belong to the Jebali of the southern region. The only cultivated area of any size is in the far north, where dates are grown. Fishermen sail large wooden boats out of coastal ports. Oil tankers make up most of the sea traffic between the Gulf of Oman and the port of Aden.

Maṭraḥ was an ancient trading center that outgrew the Omani capital until the two towns merged into a single urban area.

SAUDI
RED SEA
Sanaa
YEMEN
Tarīm
Al-Ḥudaydah
Ḥaḍramau
Al Mukallā
Ta'izz
Shaqrā'
Aden
Babel-Mandeb
Gulf of Aden

DISCOVER MORE

- *Southern Arabia and the Horn of Africa were the original home of the coffee plant. It was later introduced to India, Southeast Asia, East Africa, and Central and South America.*
- *Desert valleys called wadis have no rainfall for years and, baked by the sun, they become as hard as concrete. When it does rain, the water cannot soak into the ground, and can form a violent flash flood.*

This old Yemeni palace in Sanaa perches on top of an eroded pillar of rock. Over the ages, desert landscapes have been worn down into strange and fantastic shapes by windborne sand.

Strait of Hormuz
Musandam Peninsula
Persian Gulf
Gulf of Oman
UNITED ARAB EMIRATES
Şuḩār
Maţraḩ
Muscat
Jabal ash Sham 9,957 ft (3,035 m)
Nizwā
Şūr
OMAN
Khaluf
Maşīrah
Ras al Madrakah
ARABIAN SEA
A R A B I A
Salālah
Kuria Muria Is
Ras Fartak
N
W
E
S
200 miles
300 km
Socotra
Abd al-Kuri
INDIAN OCEAN
Yemen
Oman

Where in the world?

7 A.M. Washington, DC
noon GMT
3 P.M. Sanaa

Washington, DC to Sanaa
7,102 mi (11,430 km)
13 hr 40 min

Sanaa lies on
15° 27′N latitude
44° 12′E longitude

Life facts

	How long do people live?	How many people in 100 own cars?
U.S.A.	76 years	48
Yemen	60 years	1
Oman	71 years	9

When they go out, most Yemeni Muslim women wear long, dark robes and a veil that covers their faces, with only their eyes showing. However, country women do not normally cover their faces when they are working on the land.

Country facts

	Area sq mi (sq km)	Population	Language	Religion	Currency
Yemen	207,286 (536,871)	16,942,230	Arabic	Muslim	Rial
Oman	118,150 (306,009)	2,446,645	Arabic	Ibadhi Muslim	Rial Omani

Search and find

Yemen		Oman	
Capital: Sanaa	E4	*Capital*: Muscat	B8
Aden	F4	Khaluf	C8
Al-Hudaydah	E4	Maţraḩ	B9
Al Mukallā	E6	Nizwā	C8
Shaqrā'	F5	Salālah	D7
Ta'izz	F4	Şuḩār	B8
TarPm	E5	Şūr	C9

Gulf States

United Arab Emirates, Qatar, Bahrain

Bahrain
Qatar
United Arab Emirates

Fly into the gleaming, air-conditioned international airports of Abu Dhabi or Dubayy, and the landscape below the plane makes up flat patterns of yellow-brown and emerald-blue. Desert lands stretch westward into the sandy, stony wilderness of Saudi Arabia. The blue is the water of the Persian Gulf, which separates the Arabian Peninsula from Iran. The salt flats, islands, and peninsulas of the Persian Gulf's southern shore are occupied by three small countries—Qatar, Bahrain, and a federation of six tiny states and one large state, Abu Dhabi, called the United Arab Emirates (U.A.E.). An emirate is a region ruled by an emir, or prince. The people are mostly Muslim Arabs.

The Persian Gulf coast is mostly barren, but oil has brought wealth to the region, with giant supertankers carrying the precious fuel eastward through the Strait of Hormuz. Oil has paid for the building of modern cities and for the development of other industries such as fish processing. It has also paid for a factory that removes salt from seawater, an expensive but useful way of producing vital drinking water and irrigating the desert region.

Qatar occupies a peninsula, while Bahrain is an island country, made up of more than thirty different small islands.

This Bahraini girl wears elaborate jewelery and traditional robes. The people of the island of Bahrain are mostly Arabs. They belong to both the Sunni and Shia branches of the Islamic religion.

Manama
BAHRAIN
QATAR
Ad-Dawhah
Persian
SAUDI ARABIA

DISCOVER MORE

- *The world's largest natural gas reserve, North Field, lies off the shores of Qatar.*
- *Camel racing is a popular sport in the United Arab Emirates. Dromedaries (single-humped camels) ridden by jockeys are raced over courses at speeds of more than 12 mph (20 km/h).*
- *The Gulf region contains more than half of the world's supply of oil and gas.*

Traditional wooden ships anchor in Dubayy creek, an inlet of the Persian Gulf that winds through the modern high-rise offices and hotels of Dubayy, the chief port and business center of the U.A.E.

This traditional mosque, a Muslim house of worship, is in Dubayy. People flock here daily to pray. Dubayy is one of the small emirates bordering the Persian Gulf. Ninety-six percent of the population in the U.A.E. is Muslim.

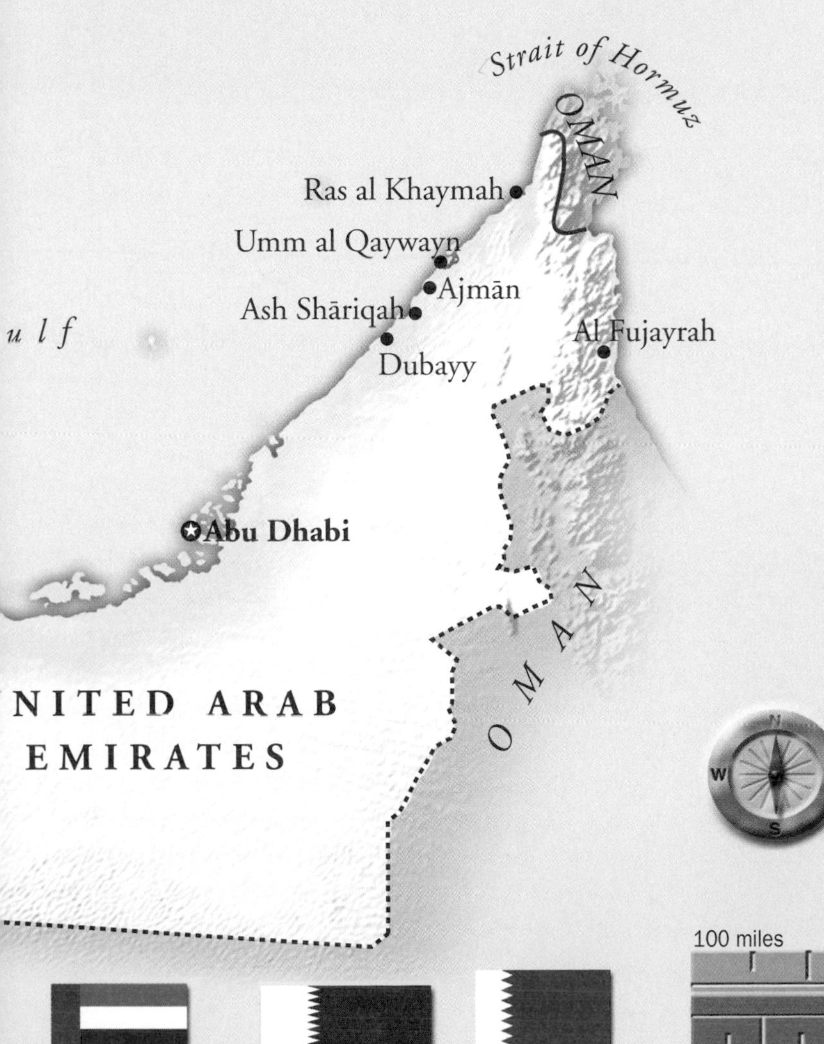
Strait of Hormuz
OMAN
Ras al Khaymah
Umm al Qaywayn
Ajmān
Ash Shāriqah
Dubayy
Al Fujayrah
u l f
Abu Dhabi
OMAN
NITED ARAB
EMIRATES
N
W
E
S

United Arab Emirates | Qatar | Bahrain

100 miles
100 km

Country facts					
	Area sq mi (sq km)	Population	Language	Religion	Currency
U.A.E.	32,000 (82,880)	2,344,402	Arabic	Sunni Muslim	Dirham
Qatar	4,416 (11,437)	723,542	Arabic	Sunni Muslim	Riyal
Bahrain	268 (694)	629,090	Arabic	Shia Muslim	Dinar

Where in the world?

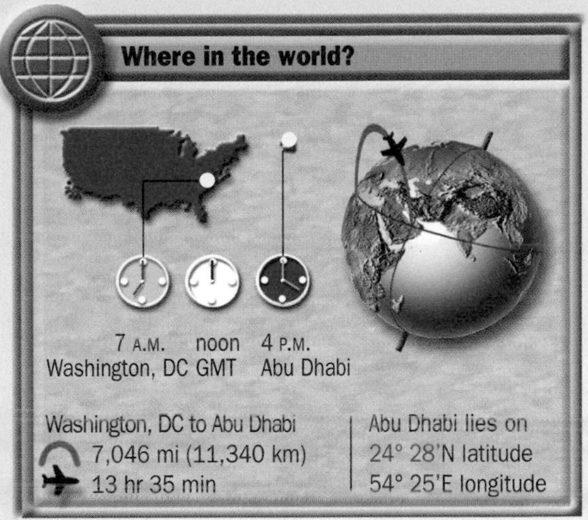
7 A.M. Washington, DC
noon GMT
4 P.M. Abu Dhabi

Washington, DC to Abu Dhabi
7,046 mi (11,340 km)
13 hr 35 min

Abu Dhabi lies on
24° 28'N latitude
54° 25'E longitude

Life facts

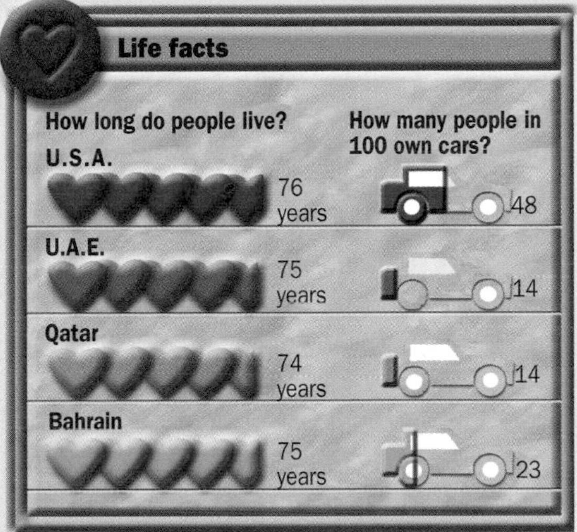

How long do people live?		How many people in 100 own cars?
U.S.A.	76 years	48
U.A.E.	75 years	14
Qatar	74 years	14
Bahrain	75 years	23

Cannons guard the gate of an old fortress in Abu Dhabi. The pirate ships that once sailed along the Gulf Coast have today been replaced by oil tankers.

Search and find

U.A.E.
Capital:
Abu Dhabi E7
Ajmān D8
Al Fujayrah D8
Ash Shāriqah . . .D8
Dubayy D8
Ras al Khaymah .D8
Umm al Qaywayn D8

Qatar
Capital:
Ad-Dawhah . . D4

Bahrain
Capital: Manama D4

The Middle East

IRAN, IRAQ

Iraq
Iran

IN THE HOLY CITY OF Mashhad, in eastern Iran, a group of turbaned travelers wait for a kettle to boil on glowing embers. It is a cold morning, and soon they are gulping down hot, sweet, black tea. A baker brings out round loaves of flat bread. With the sun risen, a bus takes the travelers westward across flat desert, toward snowy mountains and the hot, bustling streets of the capital, Tehrān. During the day the bus stops several times to allow people to climb out to pray. As in other strict Islamic countries, women are expected to wear a veil and men to wear beards, according to religious tradition.

Iraq is another Islamic country. Its capital, Baghdad, is one of the ancient trading centers of the Arab world. Once famous for its camel caravans and bazaars, it is now built of concrete and is noisy with traffic. The Tigris and Euphrates rivers flow through green lands, fringed with date palms and traditional villages of flat-roofed, mud-brick dwellings. Beyond the river valleys lie deserts. In the mountains of the north, stretching across the border into Turkey and Iran, lies the traditional homeland of a people called the Kurds. Iraq and Iran are oil-producing countries.

Men gather for Friday prayers in Tehrān, capital of Iran. Ninety-five percent of Iranians belong to a branch of Islam called Shia, while four percent belong to the Sunni branch.

ARMENIA
AZER.
AZERBAIJAN
Aras
CASPIAN SEA
Tabrīz
L. Urmia
TURKEY
Rasht
ELBURZ
Mosul
Arbīl
Tehrān
Kirkūk
SYRIA
Tigris
Hamadān
Qom
Bākhtarān
Kāshān
Euphrates
Baghdad
ZAGROS MOUNTAINS
Syrian Desert
IRAQ
Eşfahān
JORDAN
Karbalā'
Ahvāz
An Nasiriya
SAUDI ARABIA
Basra
Abādan
KUWAIT
Persian Gulf
Būshehr

DISCOVER MORE

- *A rare kind of sturgeon from the Caspian Sea, called the beluga, weighs up to 2,200 lb (1,000 kg). The black eggs of this fish are used to make a delicacy called caviar.*
- *The Marsh Arabs live in the wetlands of southern Iraq. Their large houses are made of reeds and are built on artificial islands of reeds.*

At the center of Eşfahān, Iran's third-largest populated city, stands the impressive Royal Mosque. It is covered with beautiful enameled tiles, and dates back to the 1600s.

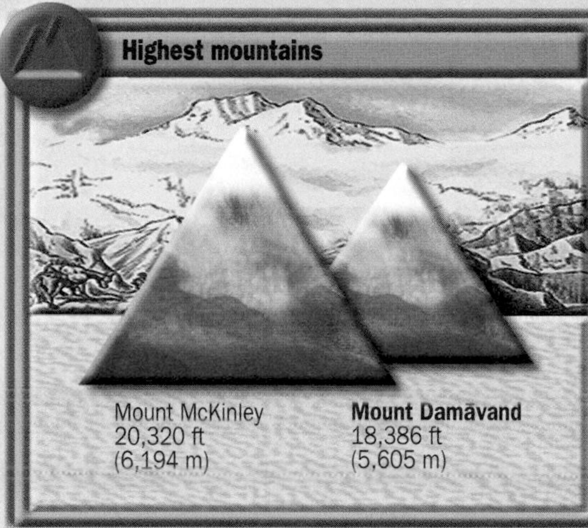
Highest mountains
Mount McKinley
20,320 ft
(6,194 m)
Mount Damāvand
18,386 ft
(5,605 m)

A carpet gradually lengthens on the loom, as an Iranian woman skillfully weaves in the elaborate pattern. Her craft dates back at least 2,500 years, but she is paid less than the equivalent of $1 a day.

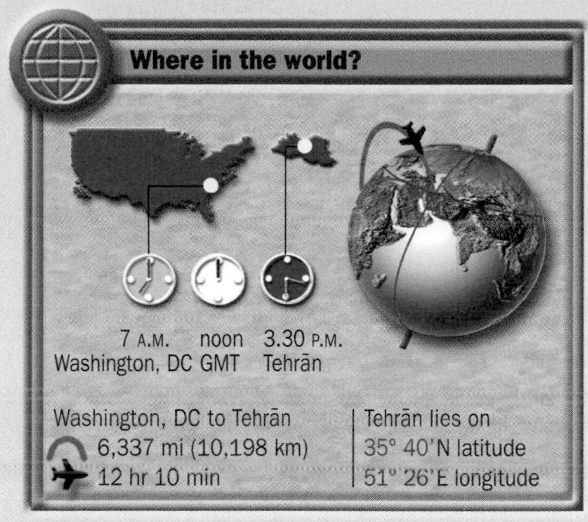
Where in the world?
7 A.M. Washington, DC
noon GMT
3.30 P.M. Tehrān
Washington, DC to Tehrān
6,337 mi (10,198 km)
12 hr 10 min
Tehrān lies on
35° 40′N latitude
51° 26′E longitude

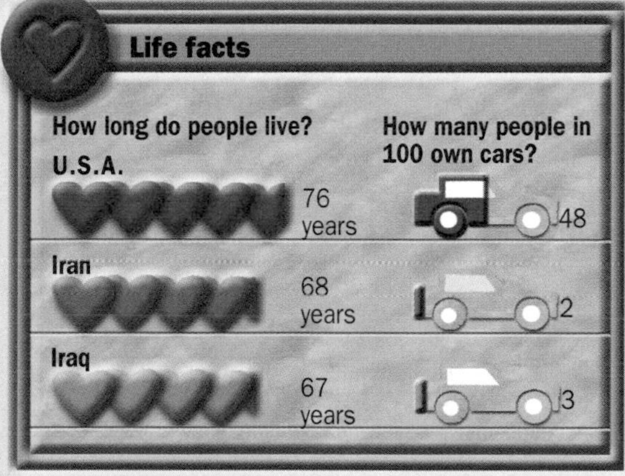
Life facts
How long do people live?
How many people in 100 own cars?
U.S.A.
76 years
48
Iran
68 years
2
Iraq
67 years
3

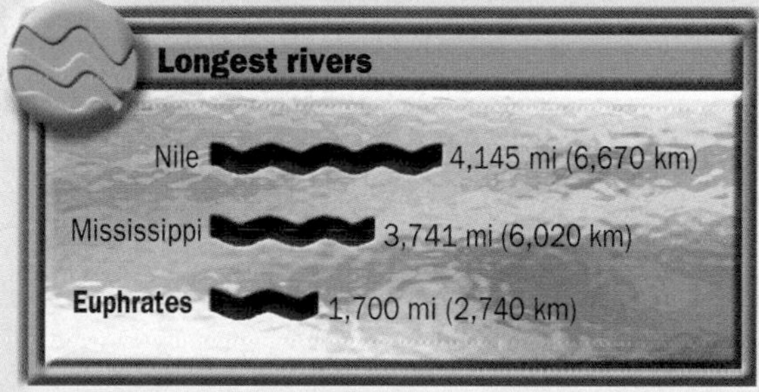
Longest rivers
Nile 4,145 mi (6,670 km)
Mississippi 3,741 mi (6,020 km)
Euphrates 1,700 mi (2,740 km)

TURKMENISTAN
Bābol
MTS
Mt Damāvand
Mashhad
Dasht-e-Kavīr
IRAN
AFGHANISTAN
Yazd
Dasht-e-Lut
Kermān
Shīrāz
Zāhedān
PAKISTAN
Bandar 'Abbās
Bandar-e Lengeh
Strait of Hormuz
Jāsk

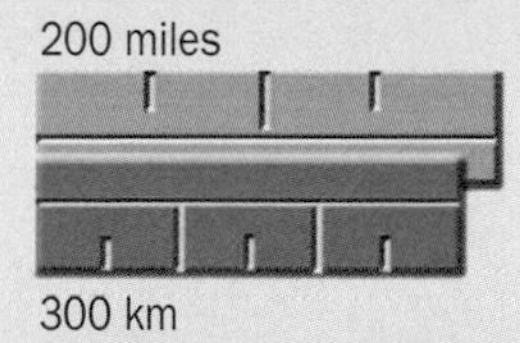
200 miles
300 km

Iran

Iraq

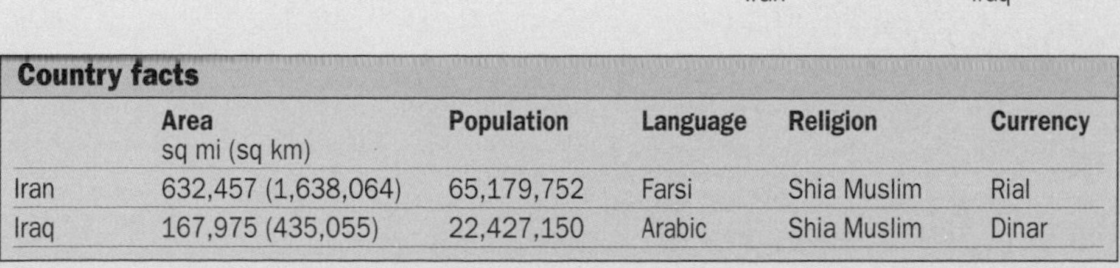

Country facts

	Area sq mi (sq km)	Population	Language	Religion	Currency
Iran	632,457 (1,638,064)	65,179,752	Farsi	Shia Muslim	Rial
Iraq	167,975 (435,055)	22,427,150	Arabic	Shia Muslim	Dinar

Search and find

Iran
Capital: Tehrān . . D6
Abādan E5
Ahvāz E5
Bābol C6
Bākhtarān D5
Bandar 'Abbās . . F7
Bandar-e Lengeh F7
Būshehr E6
Eşfahān D6
Hamadān D5
Jāsk F7
Kāshān D6
Kermān E7
Mashhad C8
Qom D6
Rasht C5
Shīrāz E6
Tabrīz C5
Yazd D7
Zāhedān E8

Iraq
Capital: Baghdad D4
An Nasiriya . . . E5
Arbīl C4
Basra E5
Karbalā' D4
Kirkūk D4
Mosul C4

Kabul to the Indus

PAKISTAN, AFGHANISTAN

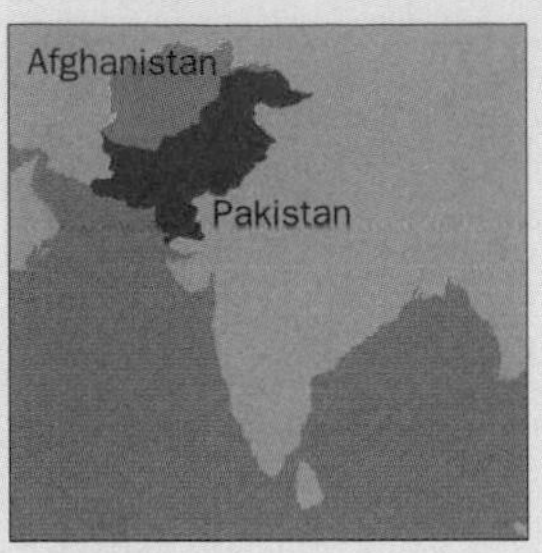
Afghanistan
Pakistan

THE KHYBER PASS IS AN ancient route through rock-strewn hills, on the border between Afghanistan and Pakistan. Old-fashioned trucks, decorated in bright colors, line up at the frontier. The drivers—tall, bearded men with baggy trousers and round felt hats—chat with one another. Following local Islamic custom, Afghan women wear heavy robes and veils, with just a mesh section in front of their eyes to see through.

Northbound trucks are soon lurching around hairpin bends above dizzying gorges. The Afghan capital, Kabul, is surrounded by mountains, which are cold and snowy in winter. Roads lead north to the Hindu Kush range and loop westward to the cities of Qandahār and Herāt. This is a land of mud-brick forts, bazaars, and mosques.

Neighboring Pakistan, too, is a land of snow-covered peaks and deserts. One highway climbs through the bleak Karakoram Range to China. Rivers flow south across a plain to join the mighty Indus River. Wheat, rice, and cotton are grown on the plain. Railroads link large industrial cities such as Karachi and Lahore. City streets are hot and crowded. Men cycle by, wearing white tunics over loose trousers. A group of girls comes out of school, each one wearing brightly colored trousers, with a shawl over her thick braid of hair.

UZBEKISTAN
TURKMENISTAN
Sheberghān
Mazār-e Shar
HINDU KUSH
IRAN
Herāt
Hari Rud
AFGHANISTAN
Farāh
Qandahār
Helmand
Rīgestān Desert
Quetta
IRAN
PAKISTAN
Shikarpu
Sukku
Larkana
KIRTHAR RANGE
Baluchistan Plateau
Indus
Hyderaba
Gwadar
ARABIAN SEA
Karachi

DISCOVER MORE

- *Until 2001 massive statues of Gautama Buddha, founder of the Buddhist faith, towered over a valley 80 mi (130 km) northwest of Kabul. They were first mentioned by a Chinese monk who traveled to see them 1,370 years ago.*

A flute seller demonstrates his wares on the busy streets of Karachi, in Pakistan. Wind instruments, including a wide range of bamboo flutes known as bansuri, *are a very important part of the traditional music of Pakistan and northern India.*

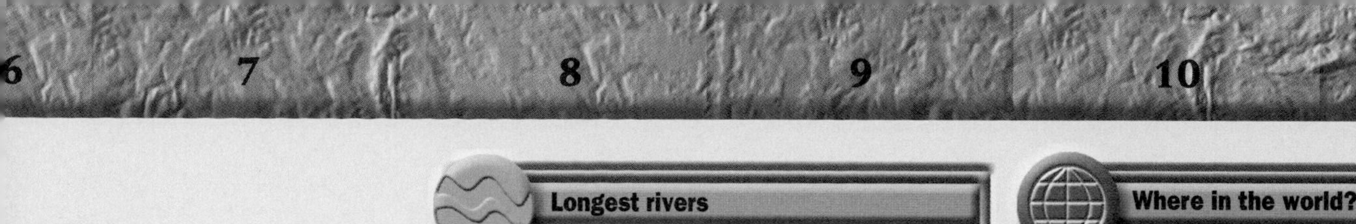
6
7
8
9
10
11

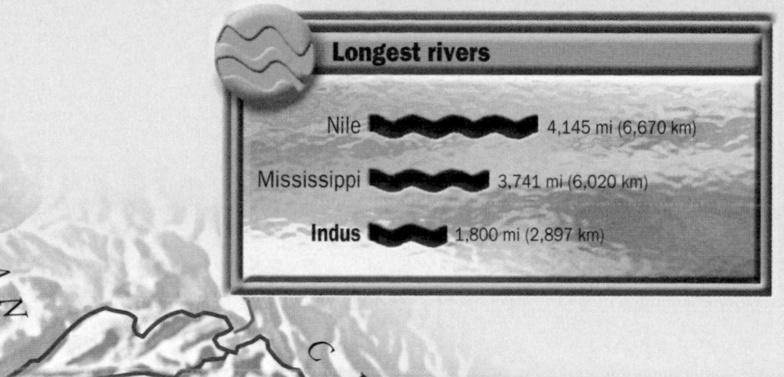
Longest rivers
Nile 4,145 mi (6,670 km)
Mississippi 3,741 mi (6,020 km)
Indus 1,800 mi (2,897 km)

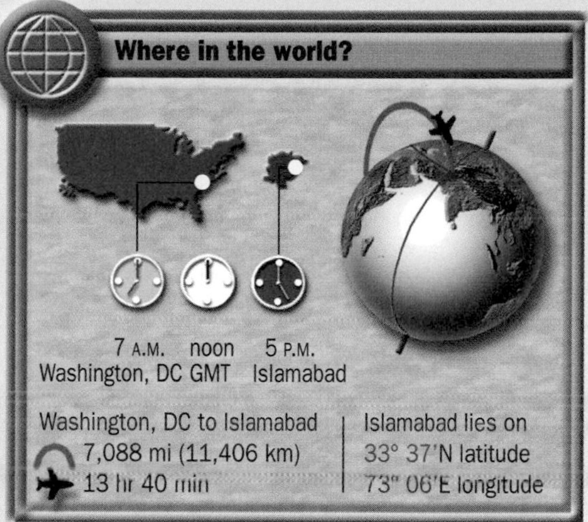
Where in the world?
7 A.M. Washington, DC
noon GMT
5 P.M. Islamabad
Washington, DC to Islamabad
7,088 mi (11,406 km)
13 hr 40 min
Islamabad lies on
33° 37'N latitude
73° 06'E longitude

TAJIKISTAN
CHINA
K2
KARAKORAM RANGE
DISPUTED AREA

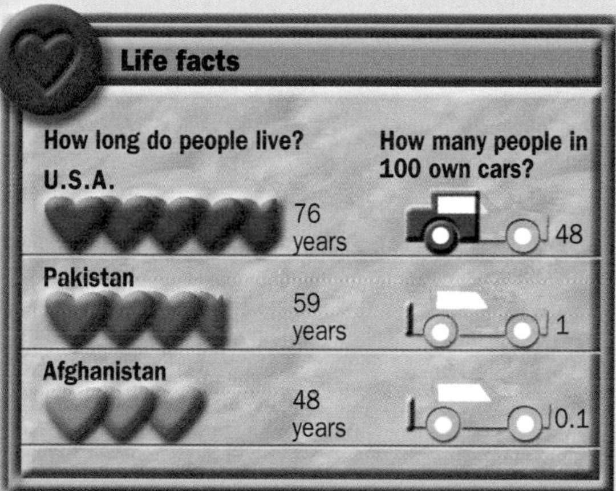
Life facts
How long do people live?
How many people in 100 own cars?
U.S.A.
76 years
48
Pakistan
59 years
1
Afghanistan
48 years
0.1

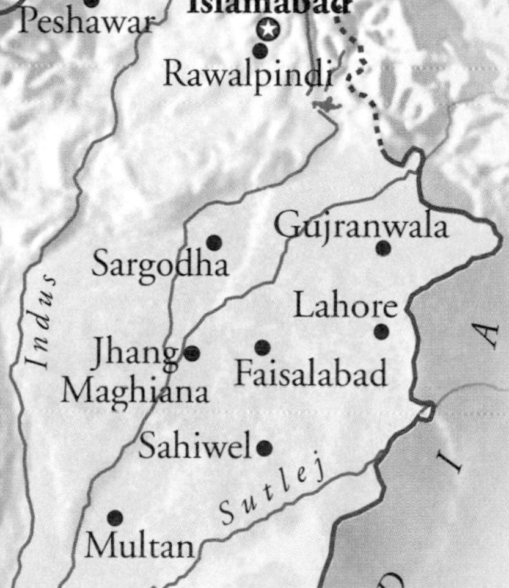
Kabul
Mardan
Khyber Pass
Peshawar
Islamabad
Rawalpindi
SULAIMAN RANGE
Indus
Sargodha
Gujranwala
Lahore
Jhang Maghiana
Faisalabad
Sahiwel
Sutlej
Multan
Bahawalpur
INDIA

N
W
E
S

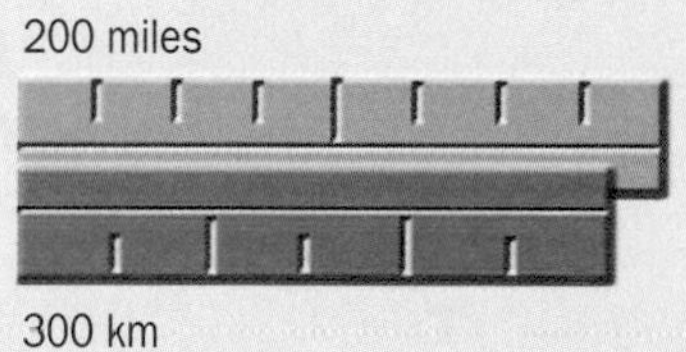
200 miles
300 km

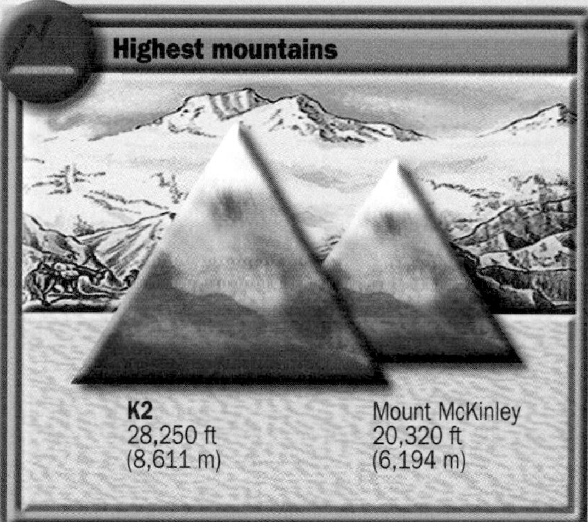
Highest mountains
K2
28,250 ft
(8,611 m)
Mount McKinley
20,320 ft
(6,194 m)

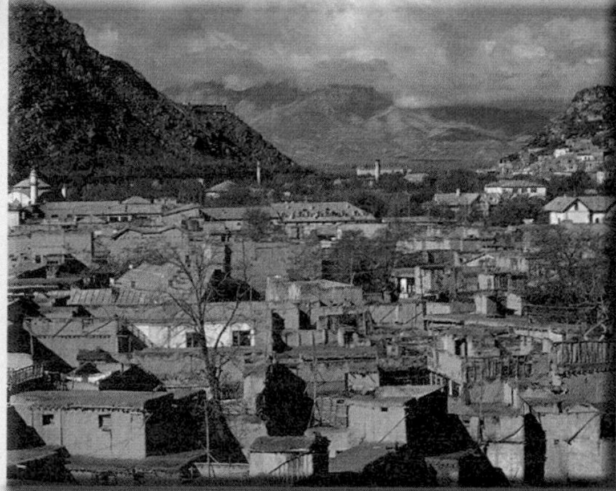

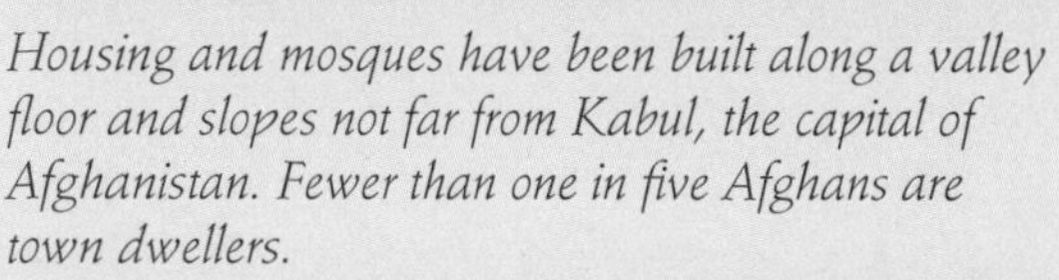
Pakistan
Afghanistan
Mirpur Khas

Housing and mosques have been built along a valley floor and slopes not far from Kabul, the capital of Afghanistan. Fewer than one in five Afghans are town dwellers.

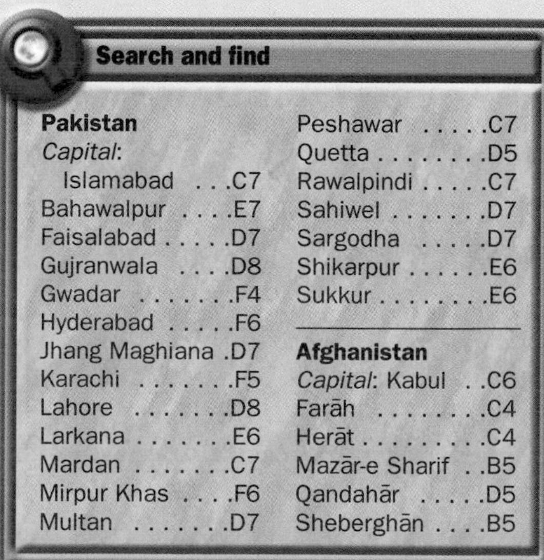

Search and find

Pakistan
Capital:
Islamabad . . .C7
Bahawalpur E7
Faisalabad D7
Gujranwala D8
Gwadar F4
Hyderabad F6
Jhang Maghiana . .D7
Karachi F5
Lahore D8
Larkana E6
Mardan C7
Mirpur Khas F6
Multan D7
Peshawar C7
Quetta D5
Rawalpindi C7
Sahiwel D7
Sargodha D7
Shikarpur E6
Sukkur E6

Afghanistan
Capital: Kabul . .C6
Farāh C4
Herāt C4
Mazār-e Sharif . .B5
Qandahār D5
Sheberghān B5

Country facts

	Area sq mi (sq km)	Population	Language	Religion	Currency
Pakistan	307,374 (796,099)	138,123,359	Urdu	Sunni Muslim	Rupee
Afghanistan	251,825 (652,227)	25,824,882	Pashto	Sunni Muslim	Afghani

A
B
C
D
E
F
G

7 8 9 10 11

Southern Asia

India, Nepal, Sri Lanka, Bhutan

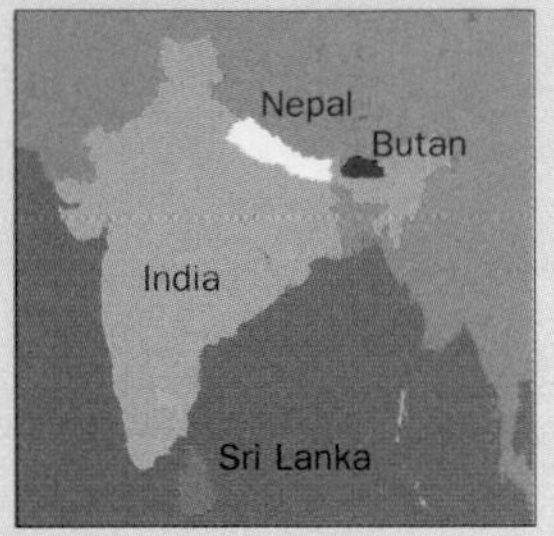
Nepal
Butan
India
Sri Lanka

A Buddhist shrine rises from the outskirts of Kathmandu, the capital of Nepal. Its golden tower is decorated with four pairs of eyes, staring north, south, east, and west. They face north to the Himalayas, the world's highest mountain range, pink in the dawn. They face eastward to the terraced fields of the small mountain kingdom of Bhutan. They face west and south to the sacred Ganges River as it winds its way across the vast plains of northern India.

India is a large and beautiful country of many different peoples and faiths. It has a long tradition of fine crafts, sculpture, dance, music, and poetry. The land is parched by a burning sun and drenched by monsoon rains. This is a land of dusty villages and overcrowded cities, of heavy industry and aged railroads. On every street there is noise from shouting street vendors, and motor-tricycle taxis buzz like hornets. There are the brilliant colors of the women's saris and the smells of exotic spices and fruits sold in outdoor markets.

Southern India's coastal mountains, surrounding the Deccan plateau, converge to a point. Across the Palk Strait are the tropical forests and peaks of Sri Lanka.

This woman comes from northwestern India where women wear silver jewelry and colorful dresses embroidered with mirror sequins.

DISCOVER MORE

- *There are more than 400 different languages spoken throughout India.*
- *India is the world's largest democracy. More than 300 million people vote in the general elections.*
- *Elephants, decorated with electric lightbulbs, glow in the dark during the Esala Perahera festival held each year in Kandy, Sri Lanka. This festival is held to honor the Sacred Tooth of the Buddha, a relic preserved in a temple on the island.*

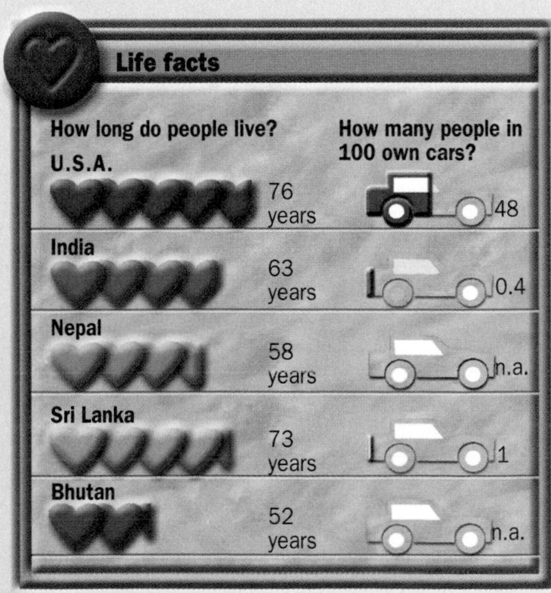

Life facts

	How long do people live?	How many people in 100 own cars?
U.S.A.	76 years	48
India	63 years	0.4
Nepal	58 years	n.a.
Sri Lanka	73 years	1
Bhutan	52 years	n.a.

Srinagar, Sutlej, Ludhiana, PAKISTAN, Delhi, Ganges, Yamuna, Agra, Jaipur, Jodhpur, Ajmer, Kanpur, Udaipur, Lalitpur, Gulf of Kachchh, Ahmadabad, Jamnagar, Vadodara, Indore, Bhopal, Jabalpur, Bhavnagar, Narmada, Surat, INDIA, Gulf of Khambhat, Nagpur, Kalyan, Mumbai (Bombay), DECCAN, Poona, ARABIAN SEA, Godavari, Solapur, Kolhapur, Hyderabad, Krishna, Vijayawada, WESTERN GHATS, EASTERN GHATS, Hubli-Dharwar, Kurnool, Nellore, Bangalore, Chennai (Madras), Mysore, Calicut, Coimbatore, Tiruchchirappalli, Cochin, Madurai, Palk Strait, Jaffna, INDIAN OCEAN, Gulf of Mannar, Trincomalee, SRI LANKA, Colombo, Kandy, Galle

N
W
E
S
300 miles
500 km
CHINA
NEPAL
Annapurna
Mt Everest
Kathmandu
Biratnagar
Thimphu
BHUTAN
Phuntsholing
CHINA
ASSAM
NAGA HILLS
Guwahati
Imphal
MYANMAR (BURMA)
BANGLADESH
Lucknow
Allahabad
Varanasi
Patna
Ganges
Jamshedpur
Haora
Calcutta
Mouths of the Ganges
Jaipur
Mahanadi
Cuttack
Bay of Bengal
Vishakhapatnam
ANDAMAN IS (INDIA)
NICOBAR IS (INDIA)

Highest mountains

Mount Everest	Mount McKinley
29,028 ft (8,848 m)	20,320 ft (6,194 m)

Where in the world?

7 A.M. Washington, DC — noon GMT — 5:30 P.M. Delhi

Washington, DC to Delhi
7,480 mi (12,038 km)
14 hr 25 min

Delhi lies on
28° 54'N latitude
77° 13'E longitude

Longest rivers

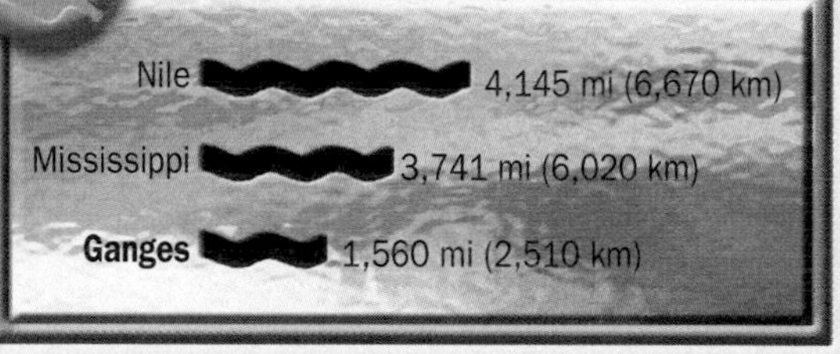

Nile	4,145 mi (6,670 km)
Mississippi	3,741 mi (6,020 km)
Ganges	1,560 mi (2,510 km)

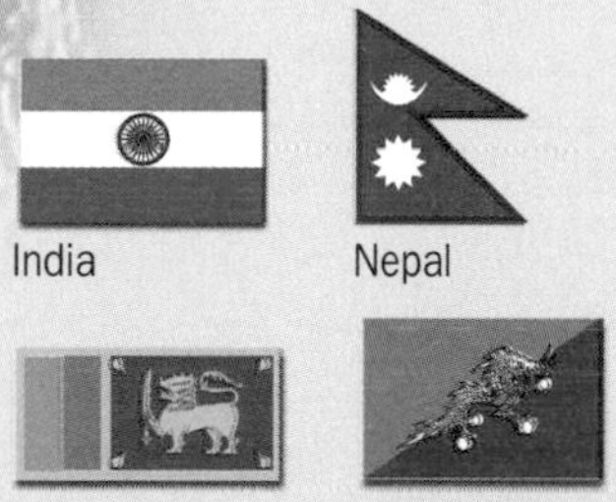

India | Nepal | Sri Lanka | Bhutan

Country facts

	Area sq mi (sq km)	Population	Language	Religion	Currency
India	1,222,243 (3,165,609)	1,000,848,550	Hindi	Hindu	Rupee
Nepal	56,827 (147,182)	24,302,653	Nepali	Hindu	Rupee
Sri Lanka	25,332 (65,610)	19,144,875	Sinhala	Buddhist	Rupee
Bhutan	18,417 (47,000)	1,951,965	Dzongkha	Lamaistic Buddhist	Ngultrum

The Taj Mahal was built in India at Agra by Emperor Shāh Jāhan for his wife in the 1600s. It took over 20,000 workers 23 years to build.

Search and find

Bay of Bengal

MYANMAR, BANGLADESH

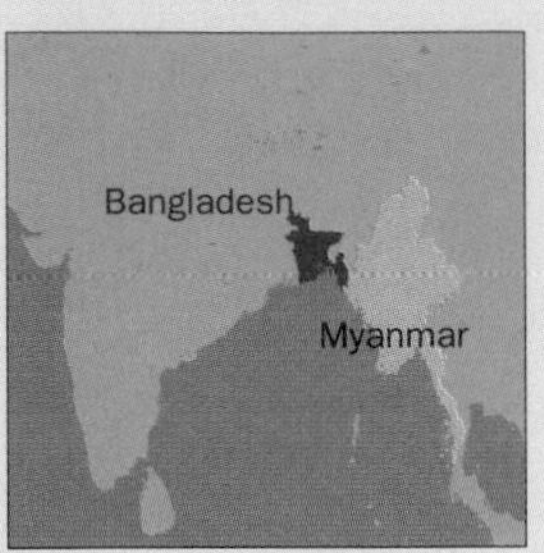
Bangladesh
Myanmar

GREAT RIVERS CARRYING meltwater from the Himalayas spills across low-lying plains before entering the Bay of Bengal. In Bangladesh, the Ganges and Brahmaputra rivers merge and form a maze of waterways and small islands. Tropical storms called cyclones rage across the Bay of Bengal, and large areas of land are often flooded.

Bangladesh is a hot, humid country, with lush, fertile land. It is very crowded, and its people struggle to make a living by growing jute, tea, and rice. Most are Bengali, who follow the Islamic faith.

Myanmar, formerly known as Burma, lies to the east of Bangladesh. The Irrawaddy River flows north to south through the country and forms a broad delta where it meets the sea. Here, many of the wooden houses are built on stilts above the water. Rice, sugarcane, and rubber trees grow in this warm, wet region, and teak forests cover the cooler northern hills. Myanmar exports oil, natural gas, and gemstones. The golden-roofed Shwe Dagon pagoda in Yangon is one of the holiest temples of the Buddhist faith. Most of the population are Burmese, but minority peoples include the Chin, Kachin, Shan, and Karen.

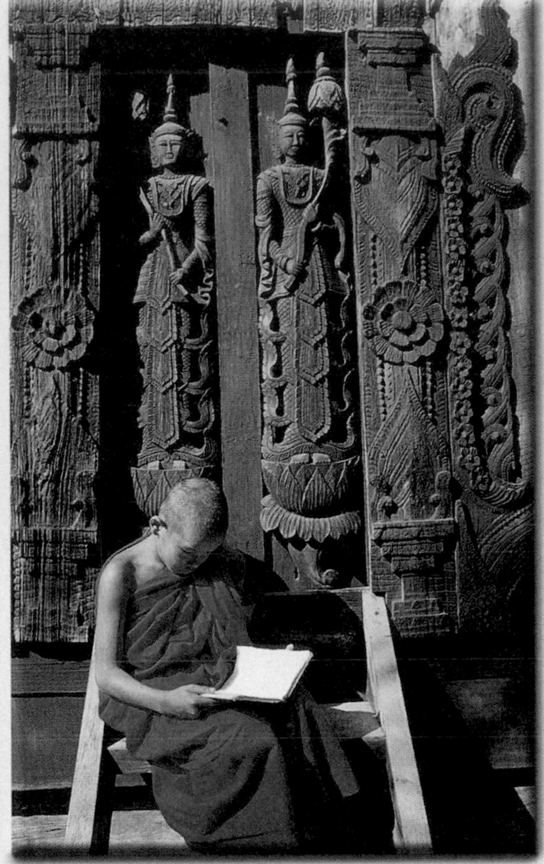

A monk reads in front of ancient statues at a Buddhist monastery in Mandalay. The ornate carvings are made from teak, a precious tropical hardwood grown in the forests of Myanmar.

N
W
E
S

200 miles

300 km

DISCOVER MORE

- *The Brahmaputra and Ganges rivers form the world's largest delta region, occupying about 29,000 sq mi (75,000 sq km).*
- *More than half of Bangladesh can be under water at times of severe flooding. Three-quarters of the country is less than 9 ft (3 m) above sea level.*
- *Every five days on a lake in central Myanmar, farmers, craftworkers, and other people gather in boats. They trade items such as rice cakes, farm tools, silk, fish, fruits, and vegetables.*

In Bangladesh and other coastal regions of the Bay of Bengal, it is often hard to know where the land ends and the water begins. Tropical storms and monsoon rains often create disastrous floods.

Country facts

	Area sq mi (sq km)	Population	Language	Religion	Currency
Myanmar	261,969 (678,500)	48,081,302	Burmese	Buddhist	Kyat
Bangladesh	55,598 (143,999)	127,117,967	Bengali	Sunni Muslim	Taka

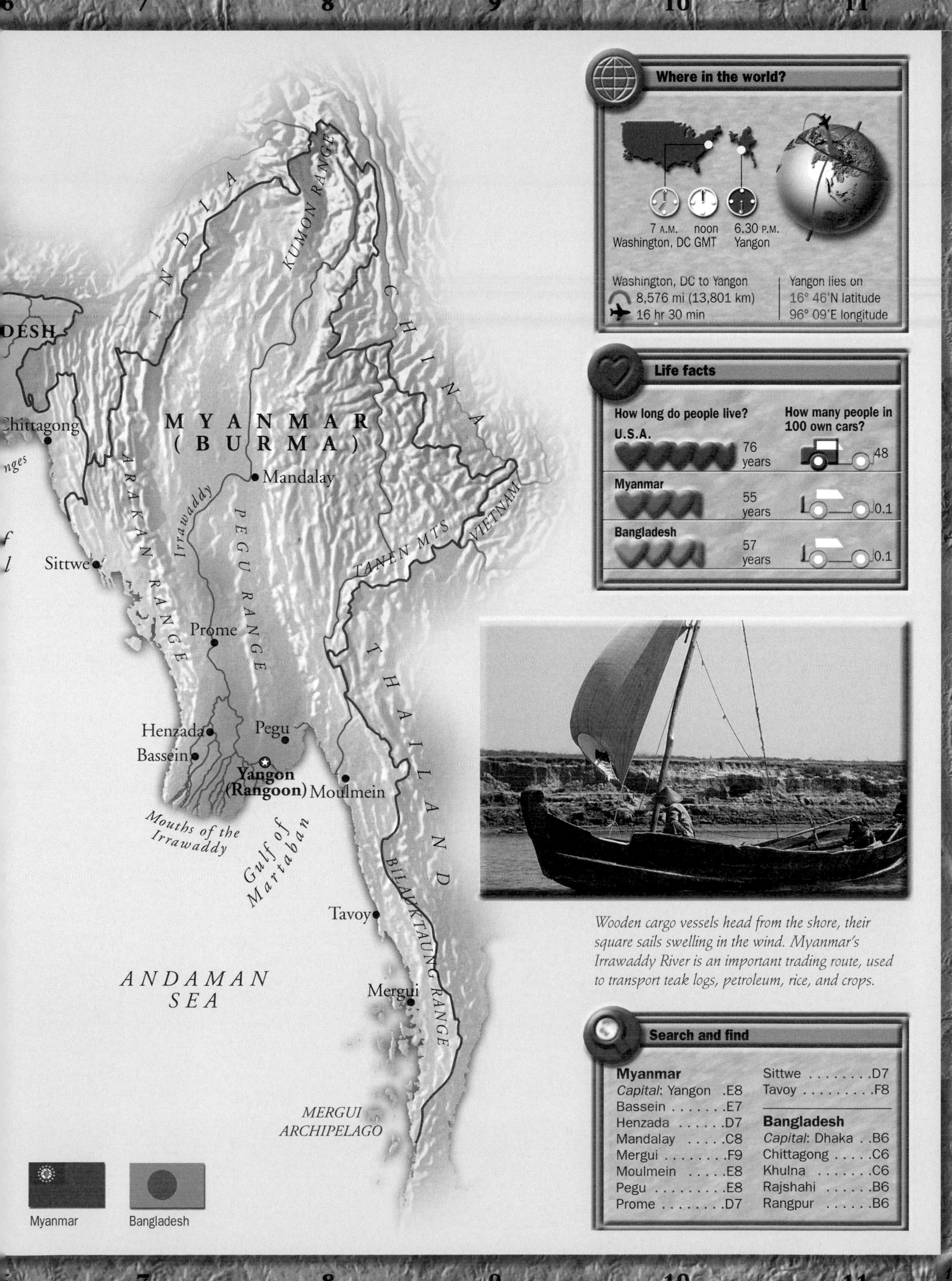

Where in the world?
7 A.M. Washington, DC
noon GMT
6.30 P.M. Yangon
Washington, DC to Yangon
8,576 mi (13,801 km)
16 hr 30 min
Yangon lies on
16° 46'N latitude
96° 09'E longitude
Life facts
How long do people live?
How many people in 100 own cars?
U.S.A.
76 years
48
Myanmar
55 years
0.1
Bangladesh
57 years
0.1
Search and find
Myanmar
Capital: Yangon .E8
Bassein E7
Henzada D7
Mandalay C8
Mergui F9
Moulmein E8
Pegu E8
Prome D7
Sittwe D7
Tavoy F8
Bangladesh
Capital: Dhaka . .B6
Chittagong C6
Khulna C6
Rajshahi B6
Rangpur B6
MYANMAR (BURMA)
INDIA
CHINA
THAILAND
VIETNAM
DESH
KUMON RANGE
ARAKAN RANGE
PEGU RANGE
TANEN MTS
BILAUKTAUNG RANGE
Irrawaddy
Chittagong
Mandalay
Sittwe
Prome
Henzada
Pegu
Bassein
Yangon (Rangoon)
Moulmein
Tavoy
Mergui
Mouths of the Irrawaddy
Gulf of Martaban
ANDAMAN SEA
MERGUI ARCHIPELAGO
Myanmar
Bangladesh

Wooden cargo vessels head from the shore, their square sails swelling in the wind. Myanmar's Irrawaddy River is an important trading route, used to transport teak logs, petroleum, rice, and crops.

Southeast Asia

THAILAND, VIETNAM, LAOS, CAMBODIA

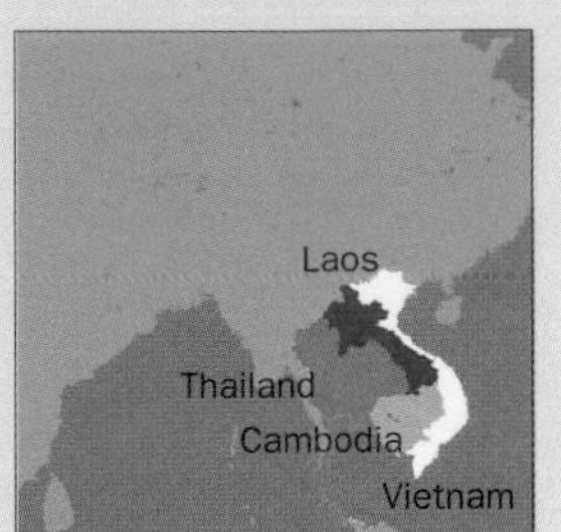
Laos
Thailand
Cambodia
Vietnam

SOUTH OF CHINA AND EAST OF Myanmar, the Asian continent bulges out, forming a long peninsula in the west. This hot and sometimes humid area is occupied by Thailand and the countries sometimes grouped together as "Indochina"—Laos, Cambodia, and Vietnam.

This part of Asia is home to many different peoples, including Thais, Karen, Shan, Hmong, Lao, Khmer, Chinese, and Vietnamese. In the lush river valleys and plains, men and women work in flooded rice paddies. Many wear broad straw hats to keep off the hot sun or the monsoon rains. In the mountains and hills, villagers grow sweet potatoes and hunt in the forests.

There are big cities, too, such as Bangkok, Phnom Penh, Ho Chi Minh City, and Hanoi. Here there are noisy motorcycles and minibuses, street markets, and canal-side boats selling tropical fruits. Among the crowds are orange-robed, shaven-headed Buddhist monks.

Many tourists now come to the region. Some of them are here to visit the ancient ruins of Cambodia's Khmer civilization, others come to see the turquoise seas and limestone rocks that form part of the Thai coast.

DISCOVER MORE

- *The Black River, which flows through northern Vietnam, has carved out a narrow, sheer-sided gorge about 2,600 ft (800 m) deep. The light of day barely reaches the gloomy floor of the Laichau Canyon.*
- *Limestone caves in southwest Thailand are home to the world's smallest mammal, Kitt's hog-nosed bat. It is also called the bumblebee bat because of its tiny size: about 1 in (3 cm) long, with a wingspan of about 5½ in (14 cm).*

Two Cambodians, wearing the saffron-colored robes of Buddhist monks, sit in the ancient temple of Angkor Wat. Situated to the northwest of the Cambodian capital, Phnom Penh, the temple is one of many dating back to the thousand-year-old Khmer civilization.

TANEN MTS
Luang
Chiang Mai
DAWNA RANGE
MYANMAR
Khon Kaen
THAILAND
Nakhon Ratchasima
BILAUKTAUNG RANGE
Bangkok
Gulf of Thailand
Nakhon Si Thammarat
Phuket
Songkhla
Hat Yai
MALAYSIA

6 7 8 9 10 11
A B C D E F G
I N A
Thai Nguyen
aichau
anyon
Hanoi
Haiphong
Nam Dinh
Gulf of Tonkin
Vinh
Mekong
Hue
Savannakhet
Da Nang
SOUTH CHINA SEA
Ubon Ratchathani
AEK MTS
VIETNAM
Qui Nhon
CAMBODIA
Tonle Sap L.
Kampong Cham
Nha Trang
Phnom Penh
Ho Chi Minh City
Can Tho
Mouths of the Mekong
N
W
E
S
200 miles
300 km
Thailand
Vietnam
Laos
Cambodia

Longest rivers

Nile	4,145 mi (6,670 km)
Mississippi	3,741 mi (6,020 km)
Mekong	2,600 mi (4,180 km)

In the Far East, small wooden boats may be used for fishing or carrying goods to market. They are called sampans—these boats are in Vietnam.

Where in the world?

7 A.M. Washington, DC
noon GMT
7 P.M. Bangkok

Washington, DC to Bangkok
8,799 mi (14,160 km)
16 hr 55 min

Bangkok lies on
13° 50'N latitude
100° 29'E longitude

Life facts

	How long do people live?	How many people in 100 own cars?
U.S.A.	76 years	48
Thailand	69 years	3
Vietnam	68 years	0.1
Laos	54 years	0.1
Cambodia	48 years	0.1

Search and find

Thailand
Capital: Bangkok D5
Chiang Mai B4
Hat Yai G5
Khon Kaen C6
Nakhon Ratchasima . .D5
Nakhon Si Thammarat . . .F5
Phuket F4
Songkhla G5
Ubon Ratchathani D7

Vietnam
Capital: Hanoi . .B7
Can Tho E7
Da Nang C8
Haiphong B7
Ho Chi Minh City E7
Hue C7
Nam Dinh B7
Nha Trang E8
Qui Nhon D8
Thai Nguyen A7
Vinh B7

Laos
Capital: Vientiane C6
Luang Prabang . .B6
Savannakhet . . .C6

Cambodia
Capital: Phnom Penh . .E6
Battambang D6
Kampong Cham .E7

Country facts

	Area sq mi (sq km)	Population	Language	Religion	Currency
Thailand	198,455 (513,998)	61,210,000	Thai	Buddhist	Baht
Vietnam	127,243 (329,559)	77,311,210	Vietnamese	Buddhist	Dong
Laos	91,428 (236,799)	5,407,453	Lao	Buddhist	Kip
Cambodia	69,900 (181,041)	10,750,000	Khmer	Theravada Buddhist	Riel

Eastern Seas

INDONESIA, MALAYSIA, EAST TIMOR BRUNEI, SINGAPORE

Malaysia
Brunei
Singapore
Indonesia
East Timor

SOUTHEAST ASIA IS mostly made up of islands, the majority forming part of Indonesia or Malaysia. A small motorbike is a good way to get around on the Indonesian island of Bali. Roads pass through green, terraced rice fields fringed with palm trees, forests with waterfalls and monkeys, and villages of thatched wooden houses. Craft workers carve wood or produce beautiful textiles, woven with dyed yarns or dyed with a wax method called batik. Young girls take lessons in graceful, swaying dance movements. Ducks swim in the moats of palaces and ornate temples that celebrate the Hindu beliefs of the Balinese people. Most other Indonesians are Muslims.

East Timor broke away from Indonesia in 2000. The small, oil-rich state of Brunei is located on the north coast of Borneo. While Southeast Asia contains vast areas of remote forest, it also includes centers of international business, with soaring skyscrapers, such as Kuala Lumpur (capital of Malaysia) and the port of Singapore, a city that is an independent state in its own right.

THAILAND
Kuala Terengganu
Ipoh
Medan
Kelang
Kuala Lumpur
Strait of Malacca
MALAYSIA
Johor Baharu
SINGAPORE
Natuna Is
Bandar Se
BRUN
Sarawak
Kapuas
Pontianak
Borneo
Sumatra
Padang
Hari
Jambi
Bangka
BARISAN MTS
Palembang
Belitung
JAVA SEA
Jakarta
Semarang
Bandung
Java
Surabaya
Malang

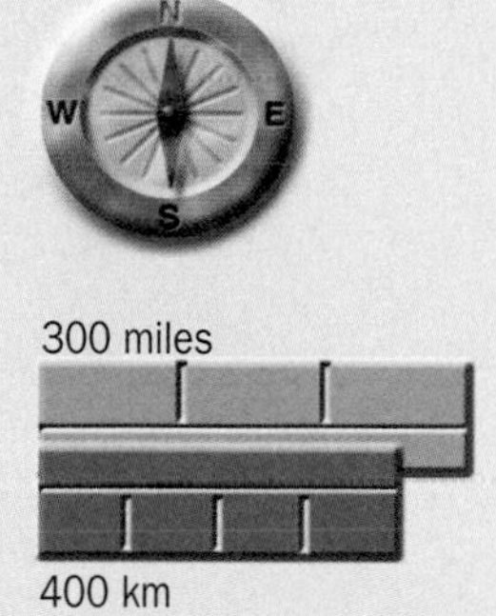
N
W
E
S
300 miles
400 km

DISCOVER MORE

- *When the twin Petronas Towers building in Kuala Lumpur, Malaysia, was opened in 1996, it became the world's tallest building, at 1,483 ft (452 m).*
- *The Komodo dragon, a monitor lizard growing to 8 ft (2.5 m) in length, is the largest reptile in the world. It lives on several Indonesian islands, including the island of Komodo.*
- *The Indonesian archipelago is the biggest on Earth. It is made up of more than 17,000 islands.*

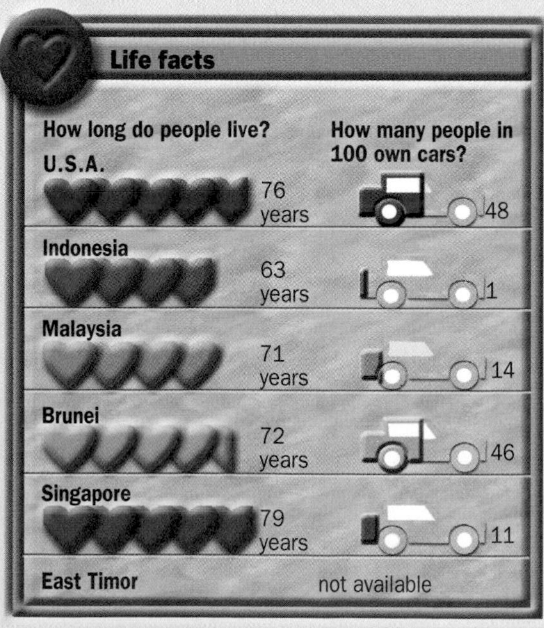
Life facts
How long do people live?
How many people in 100 own cars?
U.S.A.
76 years
48
Indonesia
63 years
1
Malaysia
71 years
14
Brunei
72 years
46
Singapore
79 years
11
East Timor
not available

Highest mountains
Mount McKinley
20,320 ft
(6,194 m)
Puncak Jaya
16,503 ft
(5,031 m)

6 7 8 9 10 11

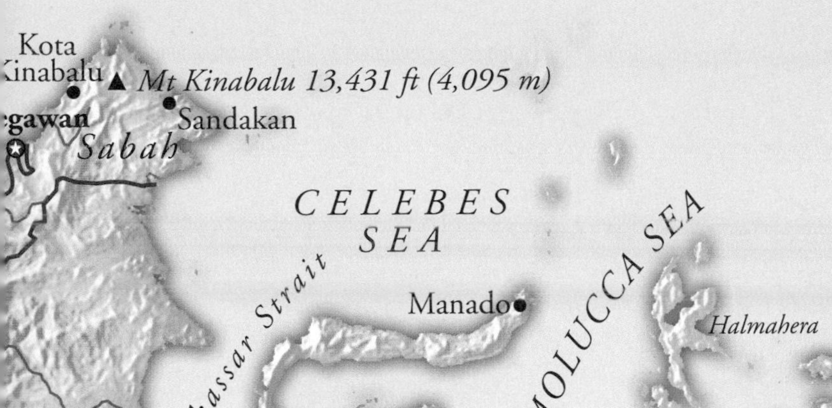

Kota Kinabalu
Mt Kinabalu 13,431 ft (4,095 m)
Sandakan
Sabah
CELEBES SEA
Makassar Strait
Manado
MOLUCCA SEA
Halmahera

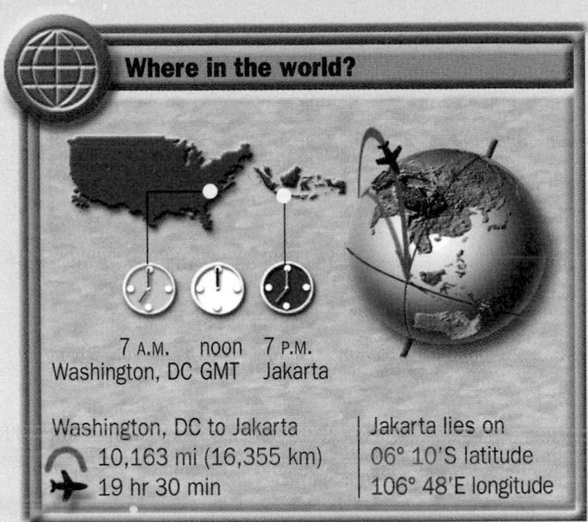

Where in the world?
7 A.M. Washington, DC
noon GMT
7 P.M. Jakarta
Washington, DC to Jakarta
10,163 mi (16,355 km)
19 hr 30 min
Jakarta lies on
06° 10'S latitude
106° 48'E longitude

Balikpapan
Palu
Sorong
Jayapura
CERAM SEA
Irian Jaya

Barito
Sulawesi
INDONESIA
Ceram
Ambon
Buru
PAPUA NEW GUINEA
Banjarmasin
Puncak Jaya
Ujungpandang
Baubau
BANDA SEA
Aru Is
Digul
FLORES SEA
Wetar
Tanimbar Is
Bali
Lombok
Komodo
Flores
Dili
EAST TIMOR
ARAFURA SEA
Mataram
Sumbawa
Ende
Timor
Kupang
Sumba

Search and find

Indonesia
Capital: Jakarta .D5
Ambon .C8
Balikpapan .C6
Bandung .D5
Banjarmasin .C6
Baubau .C8
Ende .D7
Jambi .C4
Jayapura .C11
Kupang .D8
Malang .D6
Manado .B8
Mataram .D6
Medan .B3
Padang .C4
Palembang .C4
Palu .C7
Pontianak .C5
Semarang .D5
Sorong .C9
Surabaya .D6
Ujungpandang .C7

Malaysia
Capital: Kuala Lumpur .B4
Ipoh .B4
Johor Baharu .B4
Kelang .B4
Kota Kinabalu .A6
Kuala Terengganu .B4
Sandakan .A6

East Timor
Capital: Dili .D8

Brunei
Capital: Bandar Seri Begawan .B6

Singapore .B4

The skyscrapers of Singapore's business district rise from a small island, which is linked to the Malay Peninsula by a causeway over the Johore Strait. The population of Singapore is a mixture of peoples of Chinese, Malay, and Indian descent.

Indonesia

Malaysia

East Timor

Brunei

Singapore

Country facts

	Area sq mi (sq km)	Population	Language	Religion	Currency
Indonesia	735,309 (1,904,450)	202,110,000	Javanese	Sunni Muslim	Rupiah
Malaysia	127,316 (329,748)	20,932,901	Malay	Sunni Muslim	Ringgit
East Timor	5,743 (14,874)	845,000	Tetum	Catholic	Escudo
Brunei	2,228 (5,771)	315,292	Malay	Sunni Muslim	Dollar
Singapore	250 (648)	3,490,356	Chinese	Buddhist	Dollar

A

Philippines

Philippines

SOUTHEAST ASIA'S BORDER with the wide Pacific Ocean is formed by a scattering of more than 7,000 tropical islands made of coral and volcanic rocks. These make up a nation called the Philippines. The Filipino people, as they are called, include more than 100 different ethnic groups, many of them from Malaysia. Most of them share Christian beliefs, and many are Roman Catholics.

The Philippine climate is warm and humid, but pleasantly fresh in the mountains. Coconut palms bend during violent storms, and monsoon rains drench the islands between June and October each year. Some of the islands have volcanoes that erupt from time to time, filling the air with choking fumes and showering ash over the countryside. The islands often experience earthquakes, too.

The Philippine landscape is very beautiful. Water buffalo plow the terraced rice paddies, which snake around lush green hillsides. Some Filipinos live in the country, but most live in the hustle and bustle of the towns and cities. Manila, the capital, is on the island of Luzon. The city has many manufacturing industries, which include textiles, garments, electrical goods, cane ("rattan") furniture, and food processing.

Rice has been grown on flooded terraces, cut from hillsides on the largest island, Luzon, for more than 2,000 years. It remains the chief crop and a major part of the inhabitants' diet.

On a hot day in Manila, street vendors sell jasmine flowers to churchgoers attending a Holy Week service. Eighty-three percent of Filipinos are Roman Catholic, while the rest are Protestant or Muslim.

SOUT
CHIN
SEA
Palawan Passage
Palawan
Puerto Princesa
Balabac
Balabac Strait

DISCOVER MORE

- *Pineapples are a major crop in the Philippines and are not harvested only for their fruit. Their fiber is used to weave a fabric that is made into the embroidered shirts worn by many men at the religious festivals for which the islands are famous.*
- *Mount Mayon, in the south of Luzon, is one of the world's most beautiful and most dangerous volcanoes. Its perfect cone shape was spoiled by a massive eruption in 1993.*

CANADIAN STAR
SARAO

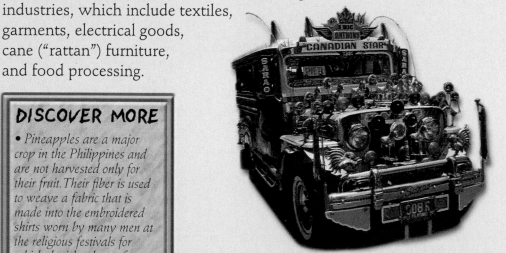

Public transportation in Manila is often provided by customized "jeepneys." Half-jeep, half-bus, they sparkle with polished chrome, mirrors, and every imaginable kind of accessory.

Philippines

Country facts

	Area sq mi (sq km)	Population	Language	Religion	Currency
Philippines	115,830 (300,000)	79,345,812	Pilipino	Catholic	Peso

Highest mountains

Mount McKinley
20,320 ft
(6,194 m)

Mount Apo
9,692 ft
(2,954 m)

100 miles

100 km

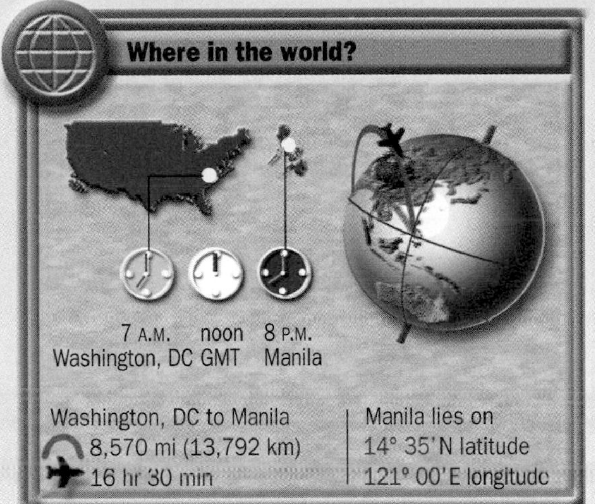

Where in the world?
7 A.M.
Washington, DC
noon
GMT
8 P.M.
Manila
Washington, DC to Manila
8,570 mi (13,792 km)
16 hr 30 min
Manila lies on
14° 35'N latitude
121° 00'E longitude

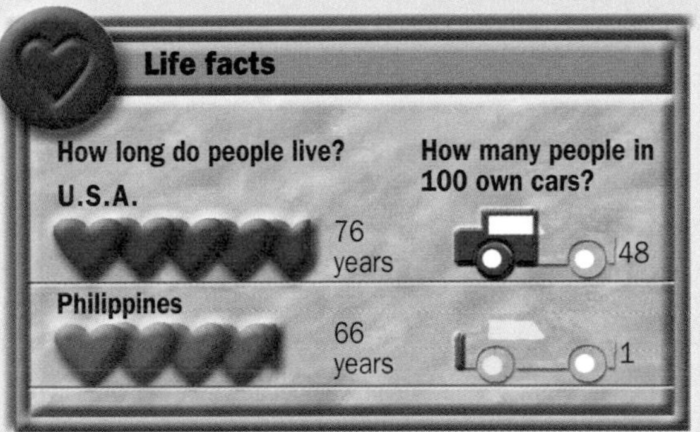

Life facts
How long do people live?
U.S.A.
76 years
Philippines
66 years
How many people in 100 own cars?
48
1

This woman is gathering pumice stone from the volcano Mount Pinatubo. Pumice is a porous rock made from frothy lava. It serves as an abrasive, or rubbing material, and may be used to clean the skin.

Search and find

Philippines			
Capital: Manila	C7	General Santos	F9
Aparri	A7	Gingoog	E8
Bacolod	D7	Ilagan	B7
Batangas	C7	Iloilo	D7
Butuan	E9	Jolo	F7
Cabanatuan	B7	Laoag	A6
Cadiz	D8	Legazpi	C8
Cagayan de Oro	E8	Mati	F9
Calapan	C7	Naga	C8
Calbayog	D8	Olongapo	C6
Cebu	E8	Ormoc	D8
Cotabato	F8	Pagadian	F8
Daet	C7	Puerto Princesa	E6
Dagupan	B6	Quezon City	C7
Davao	F9	San Pablo	C7
Dipolog	E8	Tacloban	D8
Dumaguete	E8	Vigan	B6
		Zamboanga	F7

Mongolia

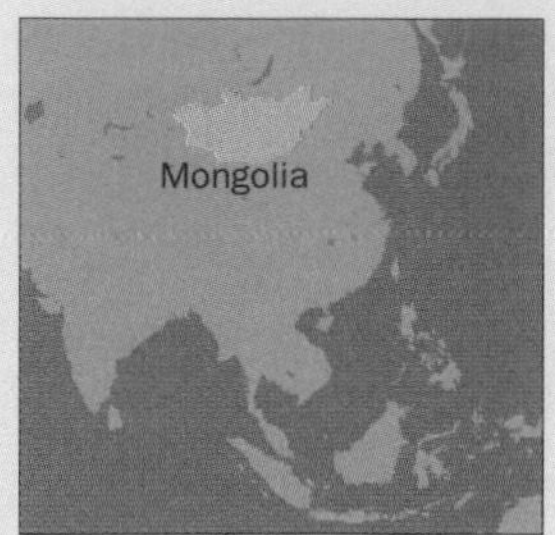
Mongolia

A TRAIN FROM RUSSIA ON ITS journey southward to the Chinese border pulls in at the sprawling apartment blocks and factories that make up Ulaanbaatar, the Mongolian capital. Old men stand by the gray-and-white station entrance, wearing traditional Mongol dress—high boots with upturned toes, woolen tunics with sashes. From the capital, a four-wheel-drive vehicle or a galloping horse takes a rider out into the emptiest landscape imaginable.

This is a vast expanse of bare, rolling hills and grasslands, bordering the wasteland of the Gobi Desert. The summer sun produces average temperatures of 70°F (21°C), while winter temperatures average –16°F (–27°C). Two-humped Bactrian camels, with their shaggy coats, are well suited to this harsh climate. So is the *ger*, the circular tent of Mongol sheep herders. It is made of thick felted wool and sometimes canvas, placed over a wooden frame. Inside, mutton stew may simmer slowly on the stove. Today the family may be watching television, but many people still take part in traditional sports such as wrestling, archery, and horseracing, having learned these skills as children.

The carpeted interior of this Mongolian ger *is as warm and comfortable as a house. Tents similar to this may be seen across Central Asia and are often known as yurts.*

SAYAN MTS
Hövsgöl Nuur
Hatgal
Ulaangom
Selenge
Hyargas Nuur
Erdenet
Hovd
Har Us Nuur
Uliastay
ALTAI MOUNTAINS
Altay
Bayanhongor
CHINA
MONG
Dalandzadgad

These Mongolian children learn to ride at a very early age. Horses were first tamed by humans on the steppe grasslands of Asia.

DISCOVER MORE

- *Mongolia is the most sparsely populated country in Asia, with just five people per sq mi (two people per sq km).*
- *The deserts of Mongolia are famous for fossils of dinosaurs, such as* Protoceratops. *It was here that American scientists discovered dinosaur eggs and nests during an expedition in 1922.*

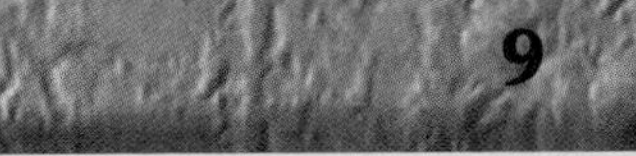

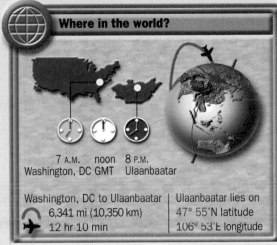

A Mongolian woman provides water for Bactrian camels at a well. These tough animals are used for transporting goods and people. They can withstand the extreme temperatures of the Gobi Desert.

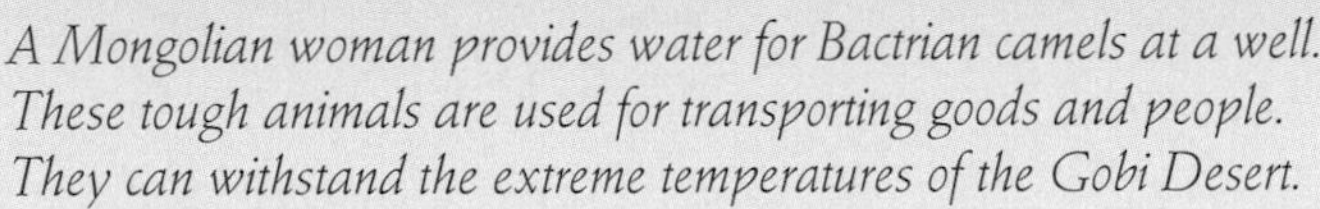

Where in the world?

7 A.M. Washington, DC | noon GMT | 8 P.M. Ulaanbaatar

Washington, DC to Ulaanbaatar
6,341 mi (10,350 km)
12 hr 10 min

Ulaanbaatar lies on
47° 55′N latitude
106° 53′E longitude

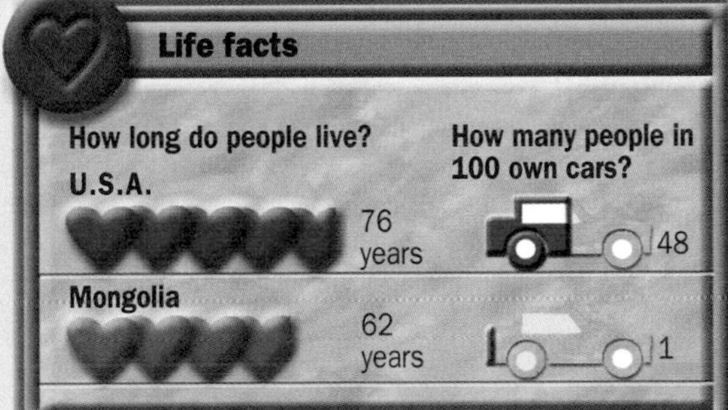
Life facts
How long do people live?
U.S.A.
76 years
Mongolia
62 years
How many people in 100 own cars?
48
1

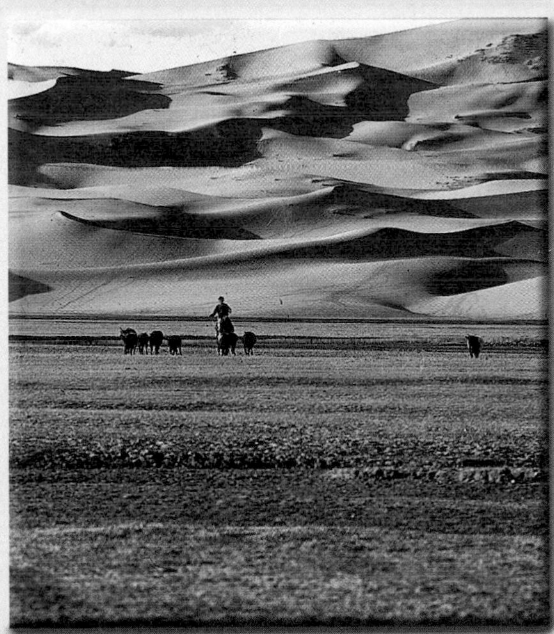

Cattle are brought in over grasslands, against a backdrop of sand dunes near Hyargas Nuur, along a distance of 150 miles (240 km).

RUSSIAN FEDERATION
Darhan
Orhon
HENTIYN MOUNTAINS
Kerulen
Choybalsan
Buyr Nuur
Ulaanbaatar
L I A
Saynshand
Gobi Desert
CHINA
N
W
E
S
200 miles
300 km
Mongolia

Country facts					
	Area sq mi (sq km)	Population	Language	Religion	Currency
Mongolia	604,247 (1,565,000)	2,617,379	Khalka Mongol	Tibetan Buddhist	Tugrik

Search and find
Mongolia
Capital:
Ulaanbaatar . . D6
Altay E4
Bayanhongor . . . E6
Choybalsan D8
Dalandzadgad . . F6
Darhan D6
Erdenet D6
Hatgal D5
Hovd D3
Saynshand E7
Ulaangom D3
Uliastay D4

Western China

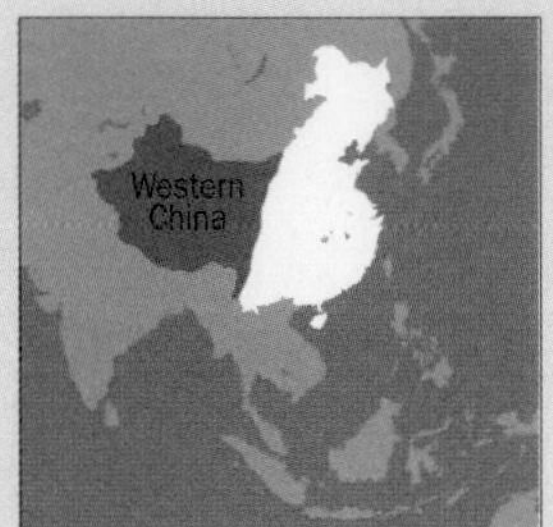
Western China

SLOWLY ACROSS THE WORLD'S highest plateaus, shaggy oxen called yaks meander like black dots in distant fields of snow. Trucks jolt past jagged mountain ranges, glaciers, and trackless sand dunes. They follow the ancient trading routes leading westward from China into Central and Western Asia.

The western half of China is made up of three vast but sparsely populated regions. The far west is a good source of minerals and timber, and the parched lowlands of the Turpan Depression have been irrigated to allow the production of crops such as grapes and melons.

A great many people in the west of the country do not belong to the Chinese ethnic group, although many people from the east are now beginning to settle in these remote regions too. Uygur, Kazakh, and Uzbek farmers and herders all live in the Xinjiang region in the northwest. They are Muslim peoples, speaking languages that are related to Turkish. The Tibetan people follow Buddhist beliefs. Their mountaintop monasteries and shrines are filled with the deep chanting of monks, and are lit by the flickering flames from yak-butter lamps. The Tibetan city, Lhasa, is dominated by the awe-inspiring palace of the Potala.

DISCOVER MORE

- *Mount Everest, on the Tibet-Nepal border, is the world's highest peak at 29,078 ft (8,863 m) above sea level. Tibet is often called "Roof of the World."*
- *One name for the Xinjiang desert is Taklimakan, which means "enter and never return"—a name that has often proved to be appropriate.*

Tajik people inhabit the far west of China and also the neighboring countries of Tajikistan and Afghanistan. Many of them herd sheep, goats, and camels in remote, bleak valleys. They live in large, round tents called yurts.

Country facts

	Area sq mi (sq km)	Population	Language	Religion	Currency
China	3,696,527 (9,573,998)	1,250,066,000	Mandarin Chinese	Atheist	Renminbi

7
8
9
10
11
A
B
C
D
E
F
G
Hami
Yumen
QILIAN MTS
Qinghai L.
Xining
A
Huang He
Gyaring L.
Ngoring L.
BAYAN HAR MTS
Chang Jiang
TANGGULA MTS
Qamdo
Mekong
Salween
INDIA
MYANMAR (BURMA)
Xiaguan
LAOS
China
200 miles
300 km
N
W
E
S

Highest mountains

Mount Everest
29,078 ft
(8,863 m)
Mount McKinley
20,320 ft
(6,194 m)

Where in the world?

7 A.M. Washington, DC
noon GMT
8 P.M. Lhasa

Washington, DC to Lhasa
7,652 mi (12,314 km)
14 hr 45 min

Lhasa lies on
29° 41'N latitude
91° 12'E longitude

Life facts

	How long do people live?	How many people in 100 own cars?
U.S.A.	76 years	48
China	70 years	0.4

High on the Tibetan plateau, the Potala palace towers over the city of Lhasa. Approached by 1,000 steps, it was formerly the home of Tibet's chief religious leaders, the Dalai Lamas.

Search and find

Western China

Aksu	C4	Qamdo	E7
Hami	C6	Ürümqi	B5
Hotan	D4	Xiaguan	F8
Karamay	B5	Xigazê	F5
Kashi	C3	Xining	C8
Lhasa	E6	Yining	B4
		Yumen	C7

Eastern China

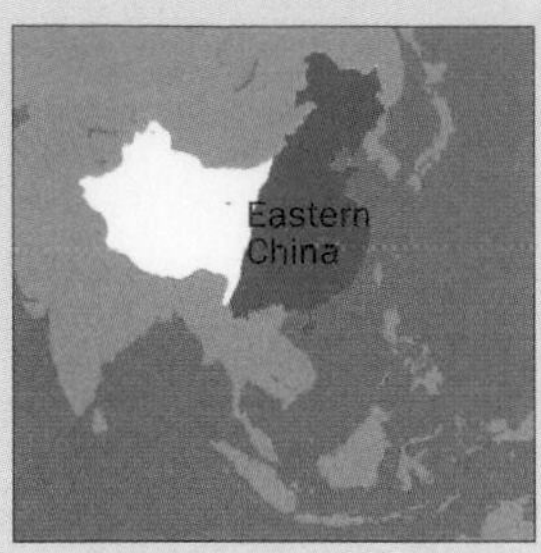
Eastern
China

At dawn, groups of Chinese people gather in the peaceful Park of Tiantan to practice the graceful exercises known as tai chi. Later, schoolchildren stop to watch a man fly a paper kite in the gusting wind. Their teacher takes them into the Hall of Good Harvests, where in the old days the emperors came to pray. The wooden roof and pillars dazzle the eye with patterns of scarlet, gold, blue, and green. Outside the park, minibuses and bicycles pass the high-rise buildings of Beijing, China's capital.

China is the most populous country in the world, and most of its people live in the eastern region. These lands contain cold forests, grasslands, misty valleys, and lakes. The fertile plains of the east are crossed by great rivers. The Huang He (Yellow River) winds through northern China, taking its name from the windblown soil that clouds its waters. The Chang Jiang River enters the sea near the port of Shanghai. The south is hot and humid, with paddy fields of rice. Here is the seaport of Guangzhou, the skyscrapers of Hong Kong—a center of international business—and the Portuguese colonial buildings of Macao.

Small offshore islands include another state called Taiwan. Its people are of Chinese origin. Rice terraces are carved from the island's mountain slopes, but two-thirds of the islanders live in the coastal towns.

Running across the north of China is the Great Wall, built originally to keep out invaders about 2,220 years ago. Its main course alone is about 2,260 mi (3,640 km) in length, which makes it the longest such structure on Earth.

DISCOVER MORE

- *More people speak standard Mandarin Chinese than any other language in the world.*
- *Shanghai is China's biggest city. It is the world's largest non-capital city, with a total population of 13.5 million.*

The tiled roofs of the old Imperial Palace give way to modern skyscrapers in Beijing. The palace became known as the Forbidden City because it was out-of-bounds to Chinese citizens for 500 years.

N FEDERATION
AN RANGE
Harbin
Mudanjiang
Jilin
Changchun
Tonghua
Fushun
Shenyang
NORTH KOREA
Anshan
Dalian
Korea Bay
Bo Gulf
Weihai
Yantai
YELLOW SEA
Zibo
Qingdao
Weishan L.
EAST CHINA SEA
Xuzhou
Nanjing
Shanghai
Chao L.
Zhoushan I.
Shaoxing
Hangzhou
Poyang L.
Nanchang
Fuzhou
Taiwan Strait
Taipei
TAIWAN
Zhangzhou
Xiamen
P'eng-hu Is
Kao-hsiung
Shantou
Guangzhou
Hong Kong
Macao
SOUTH CHINA SEA

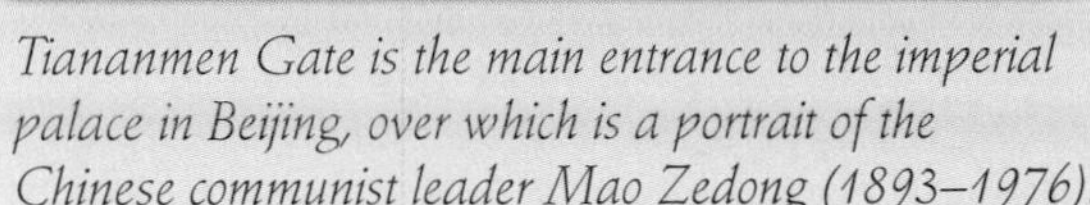

Tiananmen Gate is the main entrance to the imperial palace in Beijing, over which is a portrait of the Chinese communist leader Mao Zedong (1893–1976).

Longest rivers
Nile 4,145 mi (6,670 km)
Chang Jiang 3,964 mi (6,380 km)
Mississippi 3,741 mi (6,020 km)

The city of Hong Kong spreads over a number of small islands and part of the mainland, linked by tunnels and ferries. Most of its high-rise offices were built when the city was a British colony, before 1997.

N
W
E
S

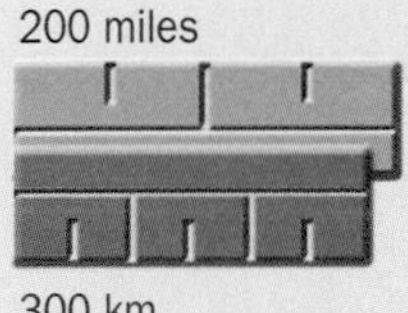

200 miles
300 km

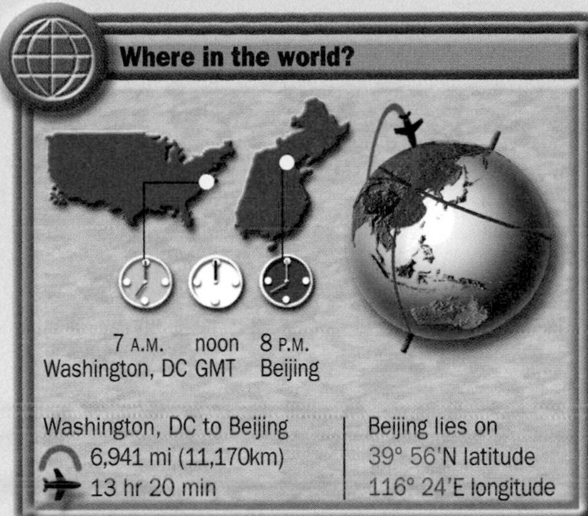

Where in the world?
7 A.M. Washington, DC
noon GMT
8 P.M. Beijing
Washington, DC to Beijing
6,941 mi (11,170km)
13 hr 20 min
Beijing lies on
39° 56'N latitude
116° 24'E longitude

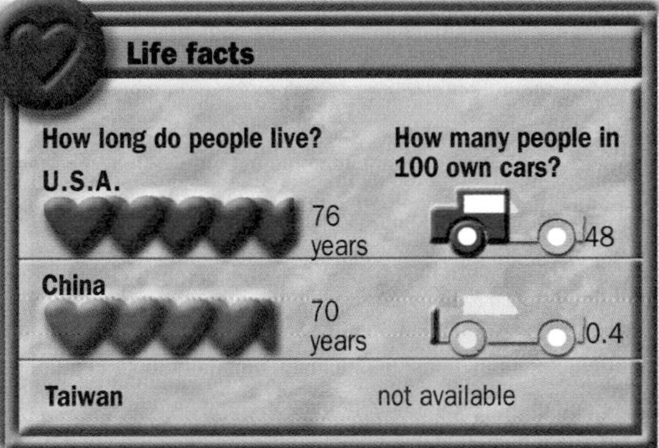

Life facts
How long do people live?
How many people in 100 own cars?
U.S.A.
76 years
48
China
70 years
0.4
Taiwan
not available

Search and find

Eastern China
Capital: Beijing . . C5
Anshan C6
Baotou C5
Changchun B6
Changsha E6
Chengdu E4
Chongqing E5
Dalian C6
Fushun C6
Fuzhou E7
Guangzhou F6
Guiyang F5
Haikou G6
Hangzhou E7
Harbin B6
Hengyang F6
Hong Kong F6
Jilin B6
Jinan D6
Kunming F4
Lanzhou D4
Leshan F4
Liuzhou F5
Luzhou F5
Macao F6
Mudanjiang B7
Nanchang E6
Nanjing D6
Nanning F5
Pingxiang G5
Qingdao D6
Qiqihar B6
Shanghai D7
Shantou F7
Shaoxing E7
Shenyang C6
Shijiazhuang . . . D5
Taiyuan D5
Tianjin C6
Tonghua C7
Weihai D7
Wuhan E6
Xi'an D5
Xiaguan F4
Xiamen F7
Xining D4
Xuzhou D6
Yantai C6
Yichang E5
Zhangzhou F7
Zhanjiang G6
Zhengzhou D5
Zibo D6

Taiwan
Capital: Taipei . . E7
Kao-hsiung F7

China

Taiwan

Country facts

	Area sq mi (sq km)	Population	Language	Religion	Currency
China	3,696,527 (9,573,998)	1,250,066,000	Mandarin Chinese	Atheist	Renminbi/HK Dollar
Taiwan	13,969 (36,179)	22,113,250	Min/Mandarin Chinese	Daoism/Buddhist	Taiwan Dollar

Korean Peninsula

North Korea, South Korea

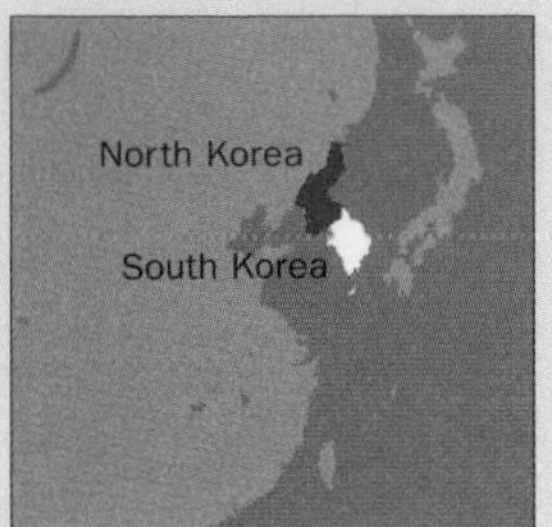
North Korea
South Korea

The Korean Peninsula extends from northeastern China toward Japan. It divides the Sea of Japan from the Yellow Sea. The land is occupied by a single people, the Koreans, but today is divided into two separate countries.

North Korea is a land of mountains, descending to plains around the capital, P'yŏngyang. The rocks are rich in silver, iron ore, and uranium. In the bitterly cold winters, snow drives across the crumpled, brown landscape. In summer the land thaws out and becomes green, with high temperatures and heavy rains—ideal conditions for growing rice.

The mountains continue into South Korea. Most people live in the west and south, where the ragged coast breaks up into thousands of small islands. The South Korean landscape is a patchwork of fields growing rice or soybeans. Cities are linked with the capital, Seoul, by expressways and railroads. Palaces and temples from the ancient Chosŏn kingdom can still be seen around Seoul. South Korea is a major international economic power, with factories producing computers, electrical goods, and cars.

The industrial city of Seoul is the capital of South Korea. It is built in the valley of the Han River and is served by the coastal port of Inch'ŏn, on the Yellow Sea.

Laborers plant rice in the flooded paddy fields, their heads shaded against the heat of the Sun.

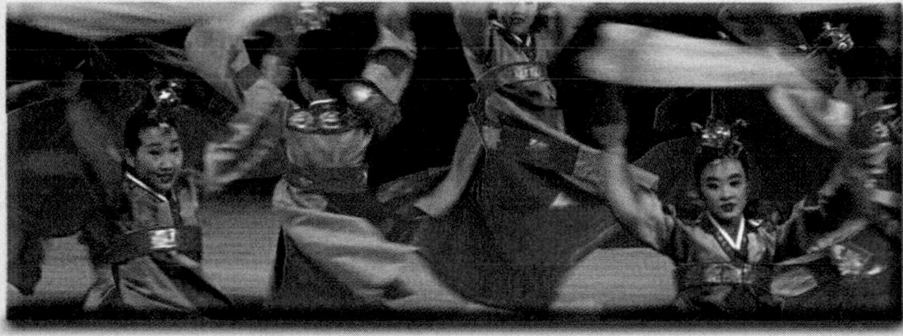

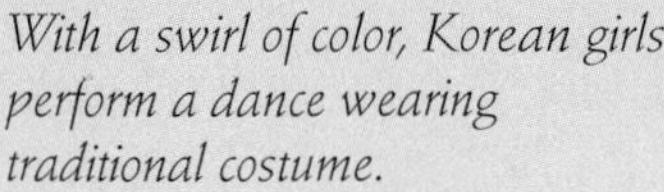

With a swirl of color, Korean girls perform a dance wearing traditional costume.

DISCOVER MORE

- *The Korean Peninsula is surrounded by over 3,000 small islands. Most of them are uninhabited.*
- *Two-thirds of the Korean Peninsula is covered by forest.*

North Korea

South Korea

Country facts

	Area sq mi (sq km)	Population	Language	Religion	Currency
North Korea	46,540 (120,539)	21,386,109	Korean	Non religious/traditional beliefs	Won
South Korea	38,023 (98,480)	46,884,800	Korean	Non religious/Buddhist	Won

6
7
8
9
10
11
A
B
C
D
E
F
G
Where in the world?
7 A.M. Washington, DC
noon GMT
9 P.M. Seoul
Washington, DC to Seoul
6,950 mi (11,186 km)
13 hr 20 min
Seoul lies on
37° 35'N latitude
127° 3'E longitude
Life facts
How long do people live?
How many people in 100 own cars?
U.S.A.
76 years
48
North Korea
51 years
n.a.
South Korea
74 years
15
Search and find
North Korea
Capital: P'yŏngyang C7
Anju C7
Ch'ongjin B9
Haeju D7
Hamhŭng C8
Hŭngdŏki C8
Hyesan B8
Kaesŏng D7
Kanggye B7
Kapsan B8
Kilchu B9
Kosong D8
Najin A9
Namp'o D7
Sariwŏn D7
Sinp'o C8
Sinŭiju C6
Sunch'ŏn C7
Tanch'ŏn C8
Tokch'ŏn C7
Wŏnsan C8
Yŏnghŭng C8
South Korea
Capital: Seoul . .D7
Andong E8
Cheju G7
Chinju F8
Chŏngju E8
Chonju F7
Ch'ŏrwŏn D8
Ch'unch'ŏn D8
Ch'ungju E8
Inch'ŏn D7
Kunsan F7
Kwangju F7
Masan F8
Mokp'o F7
P'ohang E9
Puch'ŏn E7
Pusan F8
Samch'ŏk E8
Sangju E8
Suwŏn D7
Taegu F8
Taejon E8
Ulsan F9
Yanggu D8
Yŏndŏk E9
C H I N A
RUSSIAN FED.
Najin
Ch'ŏngjin
Hyesan
Kapsan
Kilchu
Kanggye
NANGNIM MTS
Changjin
Tanch'ŏn
Sinp'o
Sinŭiju
Hamhŭng
Hŭngdŏki
Tokch'ŏn
Anju
Yŏnghŭng
Sunch'ŏn
NORTH KOREA
Korea Bay
Wŏnsan
P'yŏngyang
Namp'o
Sariwŏn
Imjin
Kosŏng
SEA OF JAPAN
Haeju
Kaesŏng
Ch'ŏrwŏn
Yanggu
Ch'unch'ŏn
Puch'ŏn
Seoul
Inch'ŏn
Suwŏn
Han
Ullung I.
Samch'ŏk
Ch'ungju
SOUTH KOREA
Chŏngju
Andong
Anmyŏn I.
Yŏndŏk
Taejon
Sangju
YELLOW SEA
Kunsan
P'ohang
Chonju
Taegu
Naktong
Ulsan
Chinju
Kwangju
Masan
Pusan
Mokp'o
Korea Strait
Chin I.
Cheju Strait
Cheju
Cheju I.
100 miles
150 km
N
W
E
S

Japan

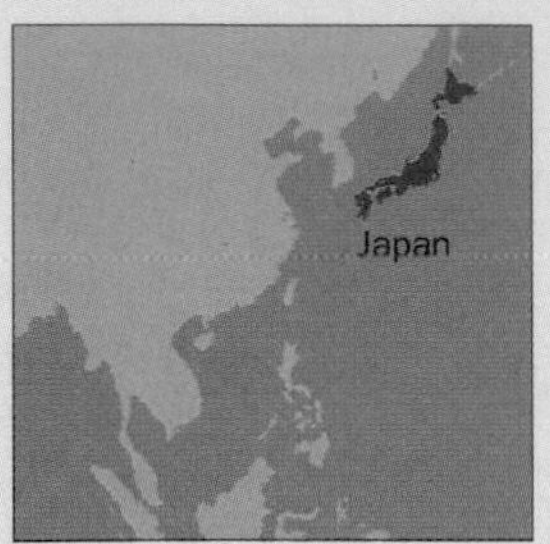
Japan

Some old Japanese paintings and woodcuts show beautiful islands set in blue seas, the snowy slopes of Mount Fuji, or cherry blossoms in the spring. Others depict glowing paper lanterns, temples and shrines, or simply furnished but beautiful wooden houses. People dressed in silk robes, called *kimonos*, or farmers planting rice are shown in still other paintings and woodcuts.

A photographer visiting Japan today is able to record many of the same scenes. However, modern additions might include the bright lights of Tokyo; flashing pinball arcades; a high-speed train streaking across the landscape; factories assembling cars and computers; traders at a busy fish market; or a suited businessman eating a packed lunch of cold rice, pork, egg, and pickles with chopsticks.

Japan, snowy in the far north and semitropical in the far south, is made up of a chain of islands on the earthquake-prone rim of the Pacific Ocean. It is a mountainous land, and most of its people live in the cities of the narrow lowlands near the coasts.

Two traditional crops, rice and tea, remain important today. Japan has few mineral resources, and must import large amounts of oil for its industries. Japanese-owned companies operate worldwide.

Japanese religions include Shinto and various forms of Buddhism. Many beautiful temples can be seen throughout the country.

Owls and bears make up just one of the figures sculpted from snow at a festival in Sapporo, on the northern island of Hokkaido, which experiences harsh winters.

Oki Is
Matsue
Korea Strait
Okayama
Tsushima
Hiroshima
Takamatsu
Tokushima
Kitakyūshū
Fukuoka
Matsuyama
Shikoku
Sasebo
Bungo Channel
Kochi
Oita
Nagasaki
Kumamoto
Amakusa Is
Kyushu
Koshiki Is
Miyazaki
Kagoshima
Tanega I.
Yaku I.

DISCOVER MORE

- *Emperor Akihito of Japan is the 125th ruler in the same Japanese royal family, or dynasty, which dates back more than 2,000 years.*
- *The Seikan Tunnel passes underneath the Tsugaru Strait, linking the Japanese islands of Honshu and Hokkaido. At 33 mi (54 km), it is the world's longest rail tunnel.*

Japan has been in the forefront of developing high-speed locomotives such as the famous Bullet train. Current track speeds can reach 186 mph (300 km/h).

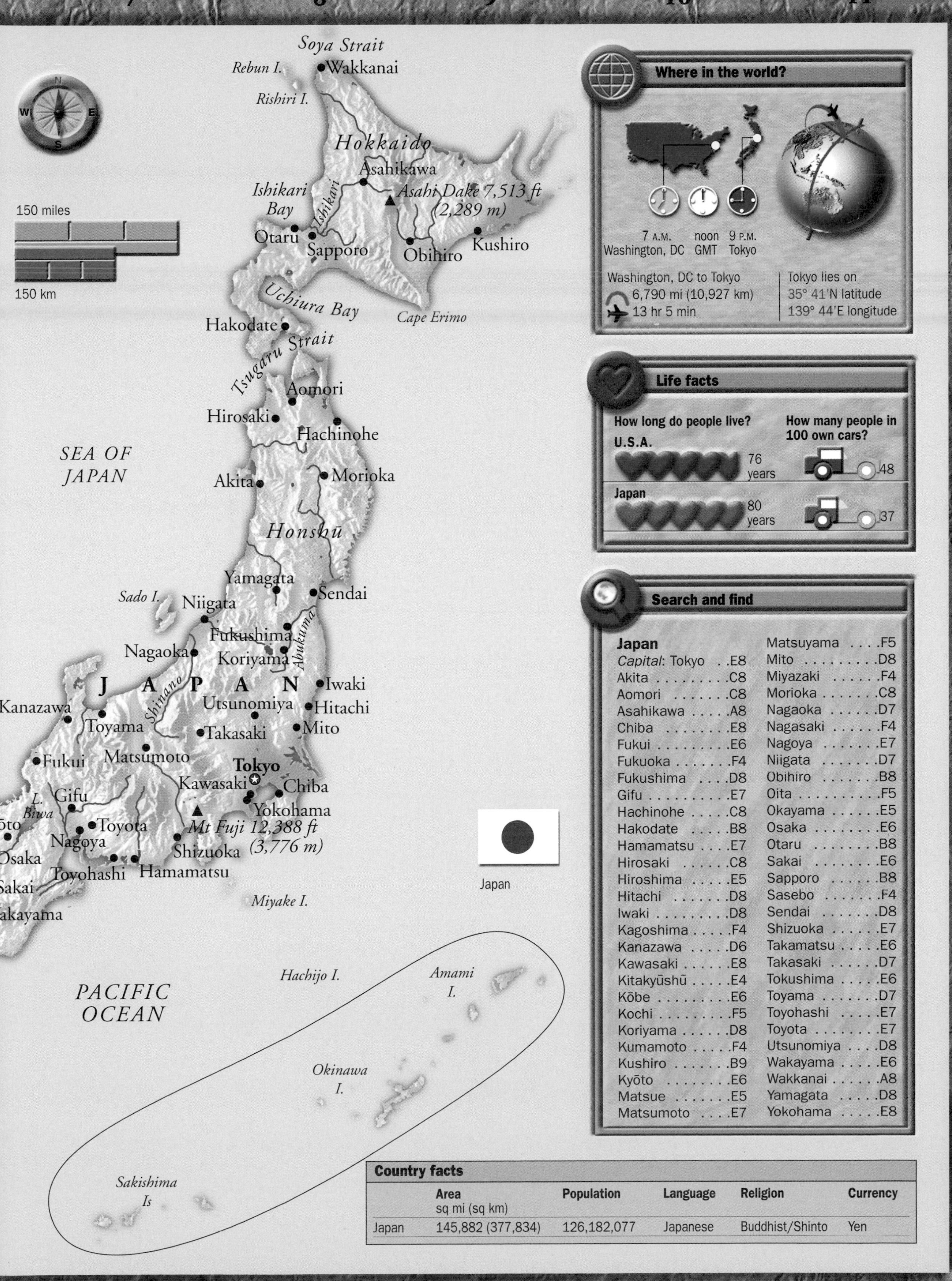

6
7
8
9
10
11
A
B
C
D
E
F
G
N
W
E
S
150 miles
150 km
Soya Strait
Rebun I.
Wakkanai
Rishiri I.
Hokkaido
Asahikawa
Ishikari Bay
Ishikari
Asahi Dake 7,513 ft (2,289 m)
Otaru
Sapporo
Obihiro
Kushiro
Uchiura Bay
Cape Erimo
Hakodate
Tsugaru Strait
Aomori
Hirosaki
Hachinohe
SEA OF JAPAN
Akita
Morioka
Honshu
Yamagata
Sendai
Sado I.
Niigata
Fukushima
Nagaoka
Koriyama
Abukuma
J A P A N
Shinano
Iwaki
Kanazawa
Utsunomiya
Hitachi
Toyama
Takasaki
Mito
Fukui
Matsumoto
Tokyo
Kawasaki
Chiba
Gifu
L. Biwa
Yokohama
Toyota
Mt Fuji 12,388 ft (3,776 m)
Nagoya
Shizuoka
Osaka
Toyohashi
Hamamatsu
Sakai
Miyake I.
Hachijo I.
Amami I.
PACIFIC OCEAN
Okinawa I.
Sakishima Is
Japan

Where in the world?

7 A.M. Washington, DC | noon GMT | 9 P.M. Tokyo

Washington, DC to Tokyo
6,790 mi (10,927 km)
13 hr 5 min

Tokyo lies on
35° 41'N latitude
139° 44'E longitude

Life facts

How long do people live?

U.S.A. 76 years

Japan 80 years

How many people in 100 own cars?

U.S.A. 48

Japan 37

Search and find

Japan
Capital: Tokyo . . E8
Akita C8
Aomori C8
Asahikawa A8
Chiba E8
Fukui E6
Fukuoka F4
Fukushima D8
Gifu E7
Hachinohe C8
Hakodate B8
Hamamatsu . . . E7
Hirosaki C8
Hiroshima E5
Hitachi D8
Iwaki D8
Kagoshima F4
Kanazawa D6
Kawasaki E8
Kitakyūshū E4
Kōbe E6
Kochi F5
Koriyama D8
Kumamoto F4
Kushiro B9
Kyōto E6
Matsue E5
Matsumoto . . . E7
Matsuyama F5
Mito D8
Miyazaki F4
Morioka C8
Nagaoka D7
Nagasaki F4
Nagoya E7
Niigata D7
Obihiro B8
Oita F5
Okayama E5
Osaka E6
Otaru B8
Sakai E6
Sapporo B8
Sasebo F4
Sendai D8
Shizuoka E7
Takamatsu E6
Takasaki D7
Tokushima E6
Toyama D7
Toyohashi E7
Toyota E7
Utsunomiya . . . D8
Wakayama E6
Wakkanai A8
Yamagata D8
Yokohama E8

Country facts

	Area sq mi (sq km)	Population	Language	Religion	Currency
Japan	145,882 (377,834)	126,182,077	Japanese	Buddhist/Shinto	Yen

Indian Ocean
and Islands

The world's third biggest ocean covers an area of 28,350,500 square miles (73,427,000 sq km), meeting the Atlantic Ocean off South Africa and merging with the Pacific Ocean off Southeast Asia and Australia. The long, thin arm of the Red Sea is linked to the Mediterranean Sea by the Suez Canal. The Indian Ocean is tropical, washing over coral reefs and white sands bordered by coconut palms. Moisture from the ocean is picked up by seasonal winds called monsoons and falls as torrential rain over southern Asia.

Madagascar, off Africa's east coast, is the fourth largest island in the world. Its people are partly of Southeast Asian origin and partly African. It is a land of mountains and plateaus, and its forests are home to many unique wild animals, such as lemurs. Smaller African islands have been created by volcanic activity or by coral formation. They include the Comoros, the Seychelles, Mauritius, and Réunion.

Asian islands include the Laccadive Islands and the Maldives, a long necklace of coral islands strung across the ocean, southwest of India. They are so low-lying that any future rise in the level of the ocean would submerge most of them. In the northeastern Indian Ocean are the Andaman and Nicobar islands, while far to the southeast lie Christmas Island and the Cocos Islands, which are territories of Australia.

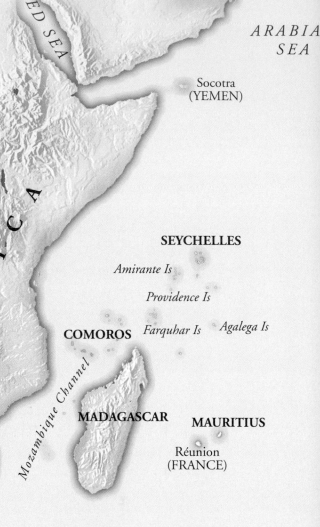

RED SEA
ARABIA SEA
Socotra (YEMEN)
AFRICA
SEYCHELLES
Amirante Is
Providence Is
Farquhar Is
Agalega Is
COMOROS
Mozambique Channel
MADAGASCAR
MAURITIUS
Réunion (FRANCE)
Prince Edward Is (SOUTH AFRICA)
Crozet Is (FRANCE)
Kerguelen (FRANCE

DISCOVER MORE

- *The Indian Ocean plunges to an amazing depth of 23,376 ft (7,125 m) in the Java Trench.*
- *Monsoon rains from the Indian Ocean are the heaviest on Earth. The island of Réunion received the rainfall record for one day, 74 in (1,870 mm).*
- *The island of Madagascar is home to the strange aye-aye, an endangered animal that is similar in appearance to a lemur.*

Coconut palms line the beach on La Digue Island in the Seychelles. Located in the Indian Ocean, this group of 115 islands makes up an independent African nation. The economy is based upon tourism, copra (dried coconut), spices, fruit, and small industries.

N
W
E
S

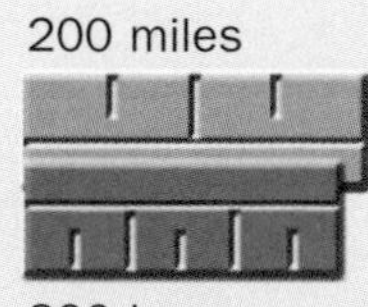
200 miles
300 km

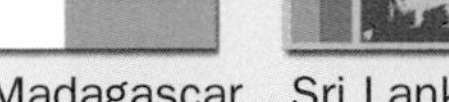

Madagascar Sri Lanka Mauritius Comoros Seychelles Maldives

ASIA

Bay of Bengal

Andaman Is (INDIA)

Laccadive Is (INDIA)

SRI LANKA

Nicobar Is (INDIA)

MALDIVES

Chagos Archipelago (U.K.)

Christmas I. (AUSTRALIA)

Cocos Is (AUSTRALIA)

INDIAN OCEAN

AUSTRALIA

Amsterdam I. (FRANCE)

St. Paul I. (FRANCE)

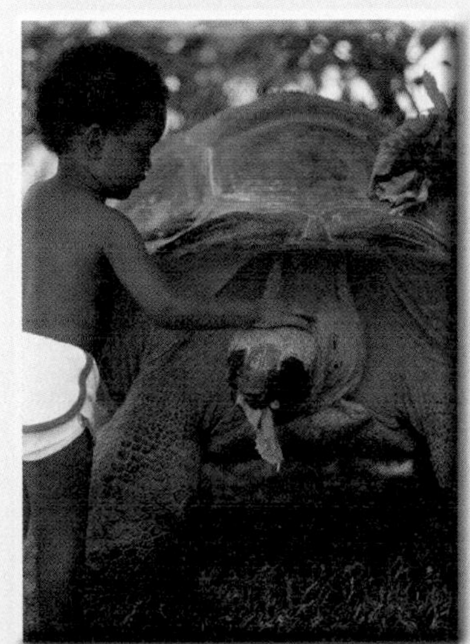

Some of the world's biggest tortoises live on the Indian Ocean islands of Mauritius and the Seychelles. Males have been known to weigh over 660 lb (300 kg).

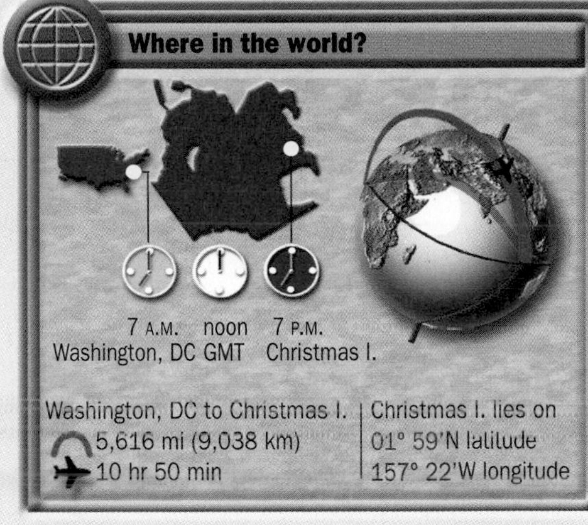
Where in the world?
7 A.M. Washington, DC
noon GMT
7 P.M. Christmas I.
Washington, DC to Christmas I.
5,616 mi (9,038 km)
10 hr 50 min
Christmas I. lies on
01° 59'N latitude
157° 22'W longitude

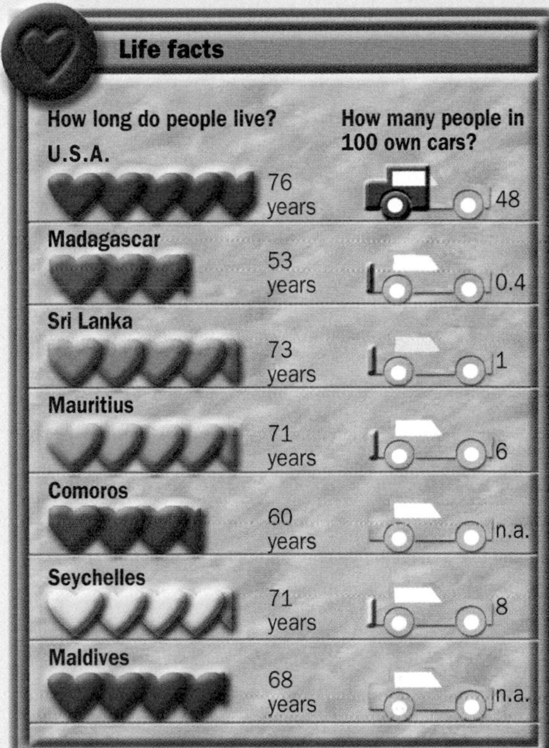
Life facts
How long do people live?
How many people in 100 own cars?
U.S.A. 76 years 48
Madagascar 53 years 0.4
Sri Lanka 73 years 1
Mauritius 71 years 6
Comoros 60 years n.a.
Seychelles 71 years 8
Maldives 68 years n.a.

Country facts

	Area sq mi (sq km)	Population	Language	Religion	Currency
Madagascar	226,656 (587,039)	14,873,387	Malagasy	IB*	Franc
Sri Lanka	25,332 (65,610)	18,933,558	Sinhali	Buddhist	Rupee
Mauritius	788 (2,041)	1,182,212	English	Hindu	Rupee
Comoros	719 (1,862)	562,723	Arabic	Sunni Muslim	Franc
Seychelles	176 (456)	76,164	English	Catholic	Rupee
Maldives	116 (300)	300,220	Divehi	Sunni Muslim	Rufiyaa

*Indigenous beliefs

Search and find

Agalega Islands .D5
Amirante Islands D5
Amsterdam Island F6
Andaman Islands B7
Chagos Archipelago . .D6
Christmas Island D8
Cocos Islands . .D8
Comoros D4
Crozet Islands . .G5
Farquhar Islands D5
Kerguelen Islands G5
Laccadive Islands C6
Madagascar E4
Maldives C6
Mauritius E5
Nicobar Islands .C8
Prince Edward Islands G4
Providence Islands D5
Réunion E5
Seychelles C5
Socotra B5
Sri Lanka C7
St. Paul Island . .F7

Africa

MEDITERRA
TUNISIA
MOROCCO
ALGERIA
LI
Western Sahara
CAPE VERDE
MAURITANIA
MALI
NIGER
SENEGAL
GAMBIA
GUINEA-BISSAU
GUINEA
BURKINA FASO
SIERRA LEONE
LIBERIA
IVORY COAST
GHANA
TOGO
BENIN
NIGERIA
EQUATORIAL GUINEA
CAMEROON
SÃO TOMÉ & PRÍNCIPE
GABON
REP. OF CONGO
N
W
E
S
500 miles
500 km
ATLANTIC OCEAN
AN
NAMIBIA

A SMALL BOY IS RUNNING, SPINNING ALONG A hoop he has made from a bent bicycle wheel and hammered straight. He runs past a market where stalls are heaped with mangoes. He cuts across the palm-lined beach, calling to the fishermen as they haul up their boats. He crosses the dusty main road, swerving between honking buses, then sprints out of the sunshine into a shady back alley. Africa is a continent of young people—44 percent of the population is under fifteen years of age. Many people live in the big, bustling cities, but others still live in small villages, following ancient customs and learning to herd, hunt, cook, and farm in the traditional way. Africa is the world's second largest continent and lies between the Atlantic and Indian oceans and the Mediterranean Sea. It has huge deserts, such as the Sahara and the Kalahari, dripping tropical rain forests, and great rivers such as the Nile and the Congo. Snowcapped mountains rise on the equator. Africa is the home of many of the last big wild animals on Earth—lions hunt zebra on the grasslands, while crocodiles and hippotamuses feed in the lakes.

Many parts of Africa are poor, and some have suffered for many years from natural disasters, such as the spread of the Sahara desert southward. However, the continent also has many rich resources, including diamonds, gold, and oil.

DISCOVER MORE

- *The Great Rift Valley is a huge crack in the earth's crust which runs through Ethiopia to Mozambique. It is more than 4,350 mi (7,000 km) long and, in places, more than 6,000 ft (1,829 m) deep.*
- *The Victoria Falls, on the Zambezi River between Zambia and Zimbabwe, form a wall of white water 5,495 ft (1,675 m) high.*

A zebra foal gallops with its mother across the savanna, the dry grassland of East Africa. Wildlife reserves protect spectacular herds of wildlife and attract tourists from all over the world.

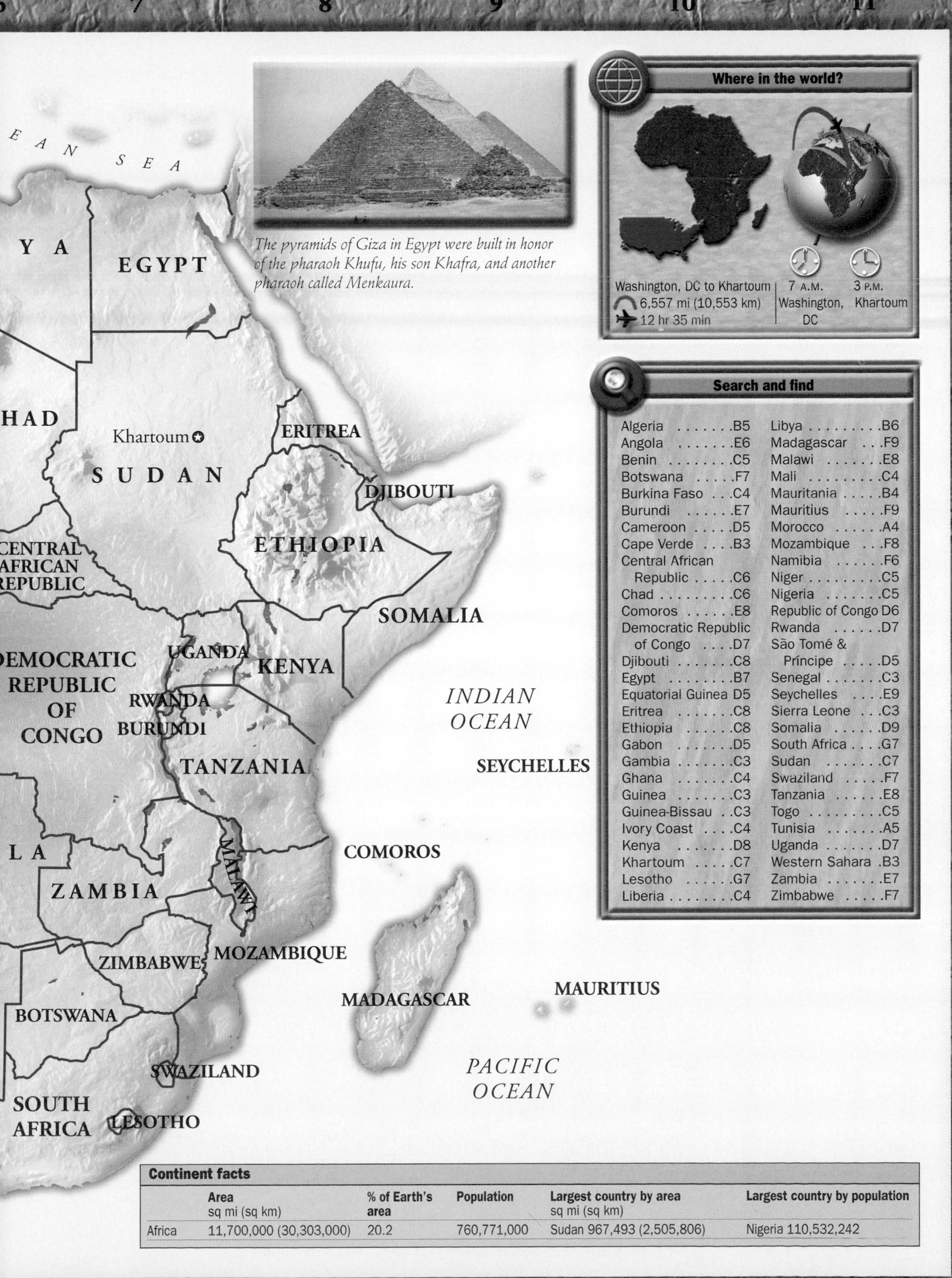
6
7
8
9
10
11
A
B
C
D
E
F
G
EAN SEA
YA
EGYPT
HAD
Khartoum
SUDAN
ERITREA
DJIBOUTI
ETHIOPIA
CENTRAL AFRICAN REPUBLIC
SOMALIA
DEMOCRATIC REPUBLIC OF CONGO
UGANDA
KENYA
RWANDA
BURUNDI
INDIAN OCEAN
TANZANIA
SEYCHELLES
LA
COMOROS
MALAWI
ZAMBIA
MOZAMBIQUE
ZIMBABWE
MADAGASCAR
MAURITIUS
BOTSWANA
PACIFIC OCEAN
SWAZILAND
SOUTH AFRICA
LESOTHO

The pyramids of Giza in Egypt were built in honor of the pharaoh Khufu, his son Khafra, and another pharaoh called Menkaura.

Where in the world?

Washington, DC to Khartoum	7 A.M. Washington, DC	3 P.M. Khartoum
6,557 mi (10,553 km) 12 hr 35 min		

Search and find

Algeria	B5	Libya	B6
Angola	E6	Madagascar	F9
Benin	C5	Malawi	E8
Botswana	F7	Mali	C4
Burkina Faso	C4	Mauritania	B4
Burundi	E7	Mauritius	F9
Cameroon	D5	Morocco	A4
Cape Verde	B3	Mozambique	F8
Central African Republic	C6	Namibia	F6
Chad	C6	Niger	C5
Comoros	E8	Nigeria	C5
Democratic Republic of Congo	D7	Republic of Congo	D6
Djibouti	C8	Rwanda	D7
Egypt	B7	São Tomé & Príncipe	D5
Equatorial Guinea	D5	Senegal	C3
Eritrea	C8	Seychelles	E9
Ethiopia	C8	Sierra Leone	C3
Gabon	D5	Somalia	D9
Gambia	C3	South Africa	G7
Ghana	C4	Sudan	C7
Guinea	C3	Swaziland	F7
Guinea-Bissau	C3	Tanzania	E8
Ivory Coast	C4	Togo	C5
Kenya	D8	Tunisia	A5
Khartoum	C7	Uganda	D7
Lesotho	G7	Western Sahara	B3
Liberia	C4	Zambia	E7
		Zimbabwe	F7

Continent facts

	Area sq mi (sq km)	% of Earth's area	Population	Largest country by area sq mi (sq km)	Largest country by population
Africa	11,700,000 (30,303,000)	20.2	760,771,000	Sudan 967,493 (2,505,806)	Nigeria 110,532,242

Northeast Africa

LIBYA, EGYPT

Many tourists visit Luxor, a city on the Nile River in southern Egypt, to see the ancient temples of Luxor and Karnak.

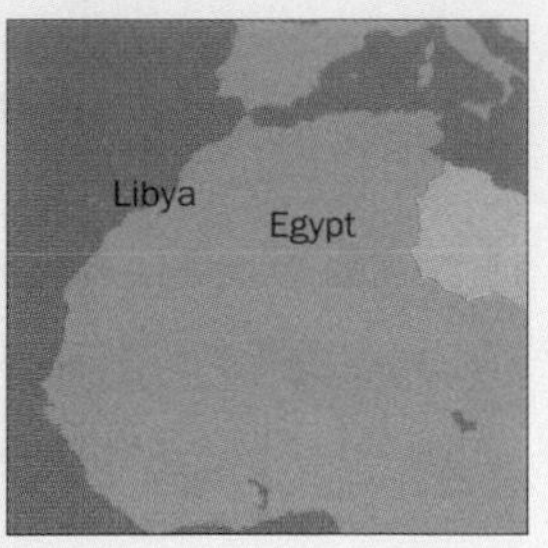
Libya
Egypt

WELCOME TO THE SEAPORT OF Alexandria, in Egypt. White buildings and domes rise up above the harbor. Bustling crowds pack the dockside as passengers step ashore. Many of the men wear long white shifts, while women wear gowns of black or patterned cotton. They are Muslims and wear long headscarves as a mark of their faith.

A train takes travelers south across the delta of the Nile River. This is lush farmland, crisscrossed by waterways. In the narrow streets of Cairo, Egypt's capital, old men drink coffee and students argue about religion and politics. There are fine old mosques alongside modern hotels and offices. On the edge of the city are the pyramids, massive royal tombs built more than 4,500 years ago.

Upstream, southward from Cairo, the Nile flows past ancient temples and industrial towns until it reaches the Aswān Dam. Wooden sailing ships float by. The Nile is bordered by a wide strip of green fields and date palms, beyond which lies a vast desert. It stretches eastward to the Red Sea and westward into Libya.

The sweltering deserts of Libya record some of the fiercest temperatures on Earth. Crops are grown at a few water sources, called oases, but most farming takes place along the coast. The chief source of wealth is oil. Most Libyans live in coastal cities such as Tripoli and Benghazi. The people are Muslim Arabs.

MEDIT
Sabrata
Tripoli
Az-Zāwiyah
Misurata
Benghazi
Gulf of Sidra
Surt
TUNISIA
Ghadāmis
ALGERIA
LIBYA
S a h a
NIGER
CHAD

DISCOVER MORE

- *At 100 mi (162 km), the Suez Canal is one of the longest canals in the world built to carry large ships. It links the Mediterranean with the Red Sea.*
- *The world's highest temperature, 136°F (58°C) taken in the shade, was recorded at Al Azizyah in Libya in 1922.*

Food is sold at this stall in the back streets of Cairo. Egyptian food includes mashi *(a mixture of various vegetables including tomatoes, cabbage, and stuffed eggplants),* fuul *(beans),* hummus *(chickpea paste), macaroni, lamb, and fish.*

About 2,000 years ago, Libya and Egypt were part of the Roman Empire, which controlled vast areas of Europe, western Asia, and North Africa. Roman ruins such as Coastal Curia at Sabrata can still be seen.

RANEAN SEA
Derna
Alexandria
El Mahalla El Kubra
Port Said
Tanta
Cairo
Suez Canal
Suez
Giza
Qattara Depression
Great Sand Sea
ISRAEL
Sinai Peninsula
Gulf of Suez
Gulf of 'Aqaba
Tell el-'Amârna
Asyūt
Nile
LIBYAN DESERT
EGYPT
Luxor
RED SEA
Western Desert
Aswān
L. Nasser
SUDAN

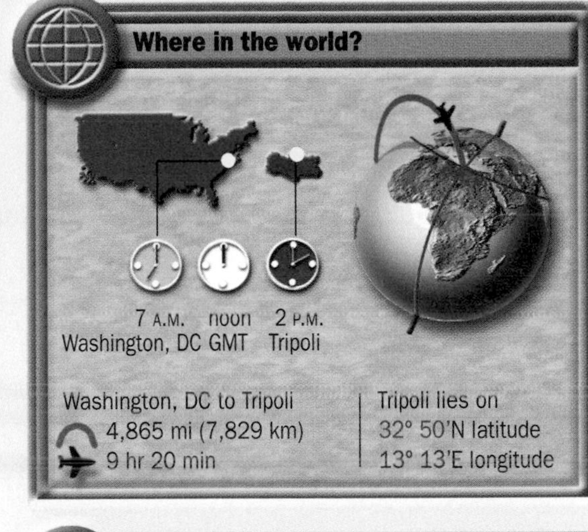

Where in the world?
7 A.M. Washington, DC
noon GMT
2 P.M. Tripoli
Washington, DC to Tripoli
4,865 mi (7,829 km)
9 hr 20 min
Tripoli lies on
32° 50'N latitude
13° 13'E longitude

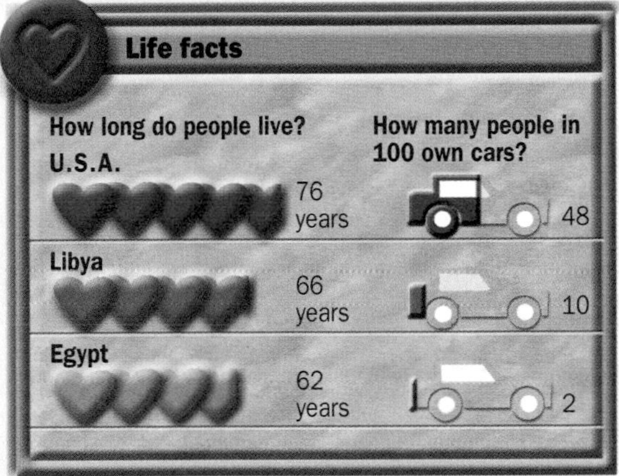

Life facts
How long do people live?
How many people in 100 own cars?
U.S.A.
76 years
48
Libya
66 years
10
Egypt
62 years
2

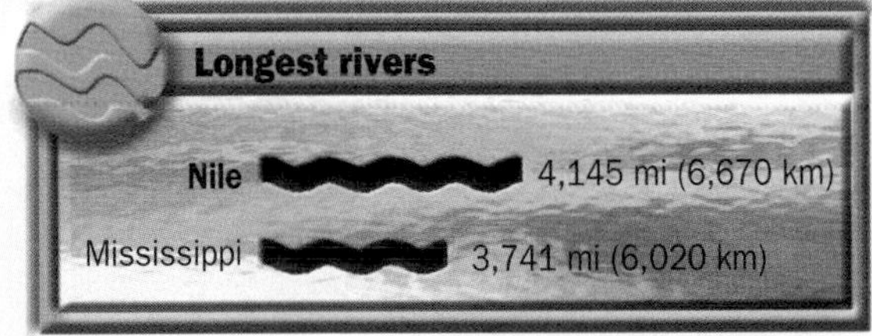

Longest rivers
Nile
4,145 mi (6,670 km)
Mississippi
3,741 mi (6,020 km)

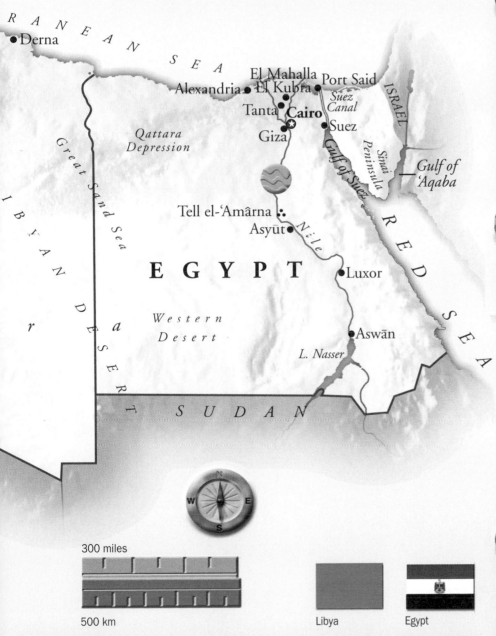

Nefertiti, a queen of ancient Egypt, died in 1340 B.C. This bust was found by archaeologists at Tell el-'Amârna. It shows her wearing cosmetics and a royal crown.

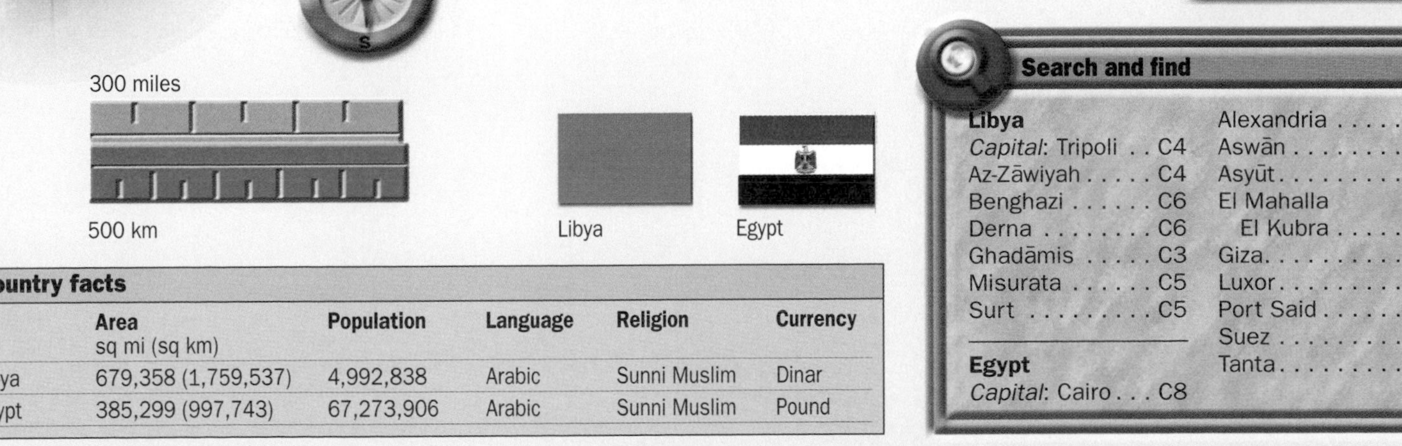

300 miles
500 km
Libya
Egypt

Country facts

	Area sq mi (sq km)	Population	Language	Religion	Currency
Libya	679,358 (1,759,537)	4,992,838	Arabic	Sunni Muslim	Dinar
Egypt	385,299 (997,743)	67,273,906	Arabic	Sunni Muslim	Pound

Search and find

Northwest Africa

ALGERIA, MOROCCO, TUNISIA

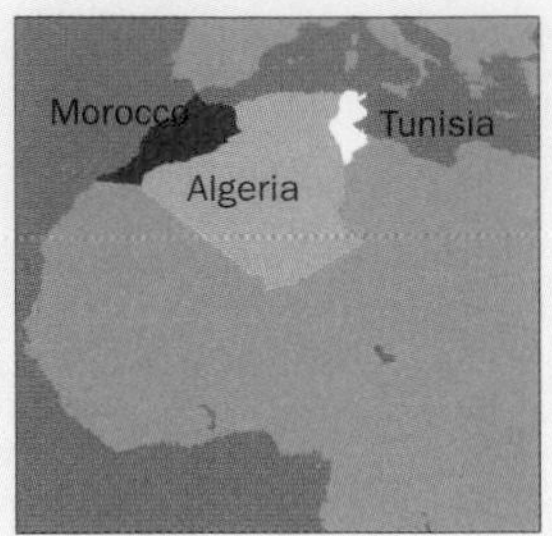

Morocco
Tunisia
Algeria

Algeria is Africa's second largest country, after Sudan. Eighty percent of the land area is the Sahara Desert, where rocks blasted with windblown sand have been eroded into unusual shapes.

THE SUN IS HIGH OVER THE square of Jemaa el-Fna, in the Moroccan city of Marrakech. Countrywomen sell finely woven baskets, while a street vendor in a broad-brimmed hat sells cupfuls of cool, refreshing water from his goatskin flask. There are people selling oranges, dates, pumpkins, and beans. There are dancers, drummers, boxers, fortune-tellers, snake charmers, and performing monkeys. As evening approaches, the sun sets behind the Koutoubia mosque. Lanterns are lit and stalls sell sizzling snacks of fish and lamb.

The Arabs call Morocco *Maghreb*, which means "the west," a term that is now extended to include the neighboring countries of Algeria, Tunisia, and the small state of Western Sahara (claimed by Morocco). The Maghreb lands are also home to another people, named the Berbers.

Africa's Mediterranean coast, just 8 miles (13 km) south of Spain across the Strait of Gibraltar, is a land of olive groves, whitewashed villages, and large ports such as Oran, Algiers, and Tunis. The land rises through foothills to the crumpled rocks and snow-streaked ridges of the Atlas Mountains. Beyond, camel caravans and four-wheel-drive vehicles follow tracks into the endless, baking wasteland of the Sahara Desert, where rocks, gravel, and high, windblown sand dunes stretch toward Central Africa.

SPAIN
Strait of Gibraltar
Tangier
Tétouan
Kenitra
Rabat
Fez
Oujda
Casablanca
Meknès
MOROCCO
Safi
Marrakech
ATLANTIC OCEAN
Mt Toubkal
ATLAS MTS
Agadir
Canary Is (SPAIN)
Tarfaya
El Aaiún
Tindouf
Adrar
Western Sahara
Dakhla
MAURITANIA
MALI
N
W
E
S
200 miles
300 km

DISCOVER MORE

- *The fennec fox, native to the Sahara Desert, is the world's smallest fox, standing just 8 in (20 cm) at the shoulder. Its enormous ears, which help it to lose body heat, add almost another 6 in (15 cm) to its height.*

In the medina, or old city center, in Marrakech, Morocco, this souk, or market, sells an enormous variety of olives.

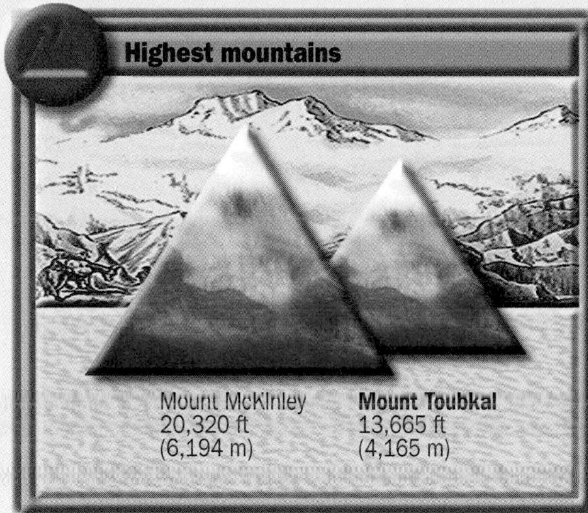
Highest mountains
Mount McKinley
20,320 ft
(6,194 m)
Mount Toubkal
13,665 ft
(4,165 m)

This Berber girl comes from the Atlas Mountains of Morocco. The Berbers are North African people.

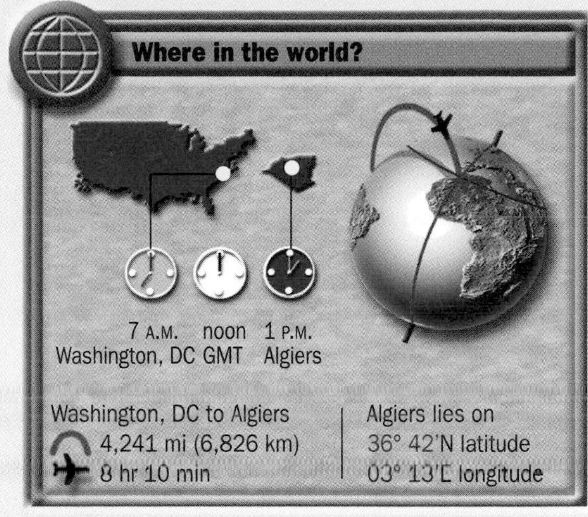
Where in the world?
7 A.M. Washington, DC
noon GMT
1 P.M. Algiers
Washington, DC to Algiers
4,241 mi (6,826 km)
8 hr 10 min
Algiers lies on
36° 42'N latitude
03° 13'E longitude

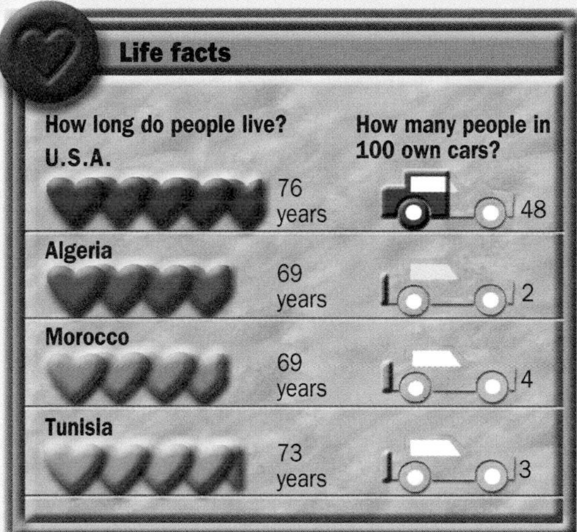
Life facts
How long do people live?
How many people in 100 own cars?
U.S.A.
76 years
48
Algeria
69 years
2
Morocco
69 years
4
Tunisia
73 years
3

Search and find
Algeria
Capital: Algiers .C7
Adrar E6
Annaba C8
Batna C8
Béchar D6
Bejaïa C7
Blida C7
Constantine C8
Ech-Cheliff C7
Ghardaïa D7
In Salah E7
Oran C6
Sidi Bel Abbès . .C6
Skikda C8
Tamanrasset . . .F7
Tindouf E4
Morocco
Capital: Rabat . .C5
Agadir D4
Casablanca C5
Fez C5
Kenitra C4
Marrakech D4
Meknès D5
Oujda C6
Safi D4
Tangier C5
Tarfaya E4
Tétouan C5
Tunisia
Capital: Tunis . . .C8
Bizerte C8
Kairouan C8
Sfax C8
Sousse C8
Western Sahara
Dakhla E3
El Aaiún E3

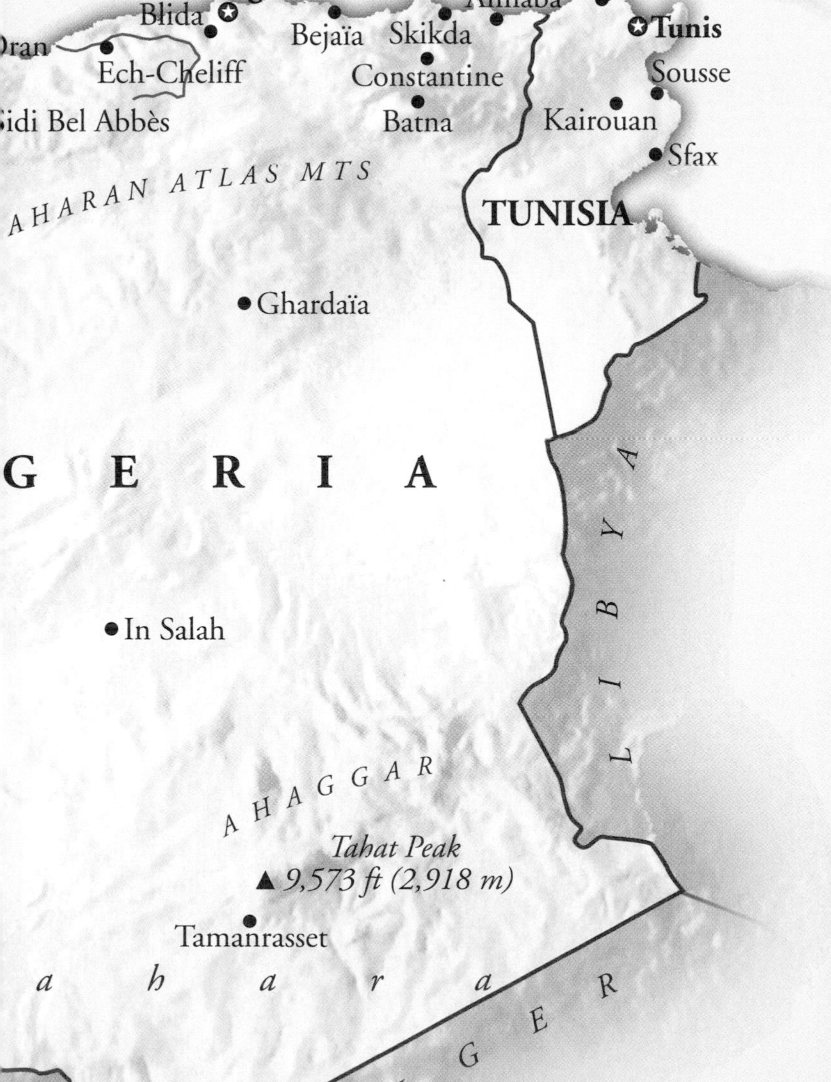
MEDITERRANEAN SEA
Algiers
Blida
Oran
Ech-Cheliff
Sidi Bel Abbès
Bejaïa
Skikda
Annaba
Constantine
Batna
Bizerte
Tunis
Sousse
Kairouan
Sfax
TUNISIA
SAHARAN ATLAS MTS
Ghardaïa
GERIA
LIBYA
In Salah
AHAGGAR
Tahat Peak
9,573 ft (2,918 m)
Tamanrasset
ahara
NIGER

Algeria

Morocco

Tunisia

Country facts

	Area sq mi (sq km)	Population	Language	Religion	Currency
Algeria	919,595 (2,381,751)	31,133,486	Arabic	Sunni Muslim	Dinar
Morocco	177,117 (458,733)	29,661,636	Arabic	Sunni Muslim	Dirham
Tunisia	63,170 (163,610)	9,513,603	Arabic	Sunni Muslim	Dinar

West Africa

NIGER, MALI, MAURITANIA, NIGERIA, IVORY COAST, BURKINA FASO, GUINEA, GHANA, SENEGAL, BENIN, LIBERIA, SIERRA LEONE, TOGO, GUINEA-BISSAU, GAMBIA, CAPE VERDE

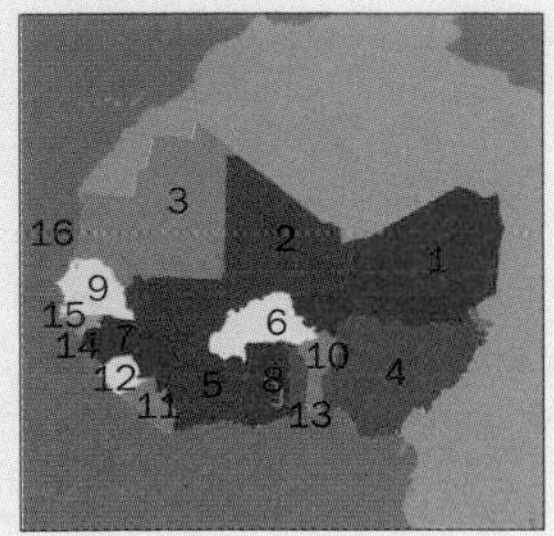
3
16
2
1
9
15
14
7
6
10
12
5
8
4
11
13

1 Niger
2 Mali
3 Mauritania
4 Nigeria
5 Ivory Coast
6 Burkina Faso
7 Guinea
8 Ghana
9 Senegal
10 Benin
11 Liberia
12 Sierra Leone
13 Togo
14 Guinea-Bissau
15 Gambia
16 Cape Verde

A WEST AFRICAN JOURNEY MIGHT START on the Gulf of Guinea, where Atlantic surf pounds sandy beaches lined with palms. The Guinea coast is naturally covered in tropical forest, and remains so around the oil fields of the Niger River delta. Elsewhere it is taken up by plantations producing cocoa, peanuts, natural rubber, or palm oil.

On the coast are large, modern cities; Lagos, Nigeria, is one. This city is extremely hot and humid, and is often jammed solid with traffic. Transportation north might be a crowded train or an overloaded minibus or truck, painted with humorous or religious motifs and slogans.

To the north, the landscape changes, with cultivated grasslands becoming drier and drier toward the plateaus and desert fringes of the north. A cool, seasonal desert wind, the *harmattan*, blows dust southward from the Sahara Desert over dried-up riverbeds and towns of dried mud brick.

Hundreds of different ethnic groups live in West Africa—among them the Ashante, Ibo, Yoruba, Hausa, and Fulani.

Western Sahara
ALGERIA
Sahara
Des
MAURITANIA
Nouakchott
MALI
Tombouctou (Timbuktu)
CAPE VERDE
Praia
Senegal
Thiès
Dakar
SENEGAL
Banjul
GAMBIA
Niger
Ségou
BURKINA FASO
Niamey
Maradi
Bissau
GUINEA-BISSAU
GUINEA
Bamako
Sikasso
Bobo Dioulasso
Ouagadougou
Conakry
Kankan
BENIN
Zaria
Kaduna
Freetown
SIERRA LEONE
IVORY COAST
Tamale
GHANA
TOGO
Ilorin
Abuja
Bouaké
L. Volta
Ogbomosho
Oshogbo
Monrovia
Harbel
Daloa
Kumasi
Porto-Novo
Ibadan
Abeokuta
LIBERIA
Yamoussoukro
Lagos
Onitsha
Abidjan
Accra
Lomé
Cotonou
Cape Palmas
Gulf of Guinea
Bight of Benin
Port Harcourt

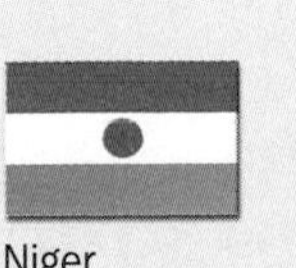
Niger

Mali

Mauritania

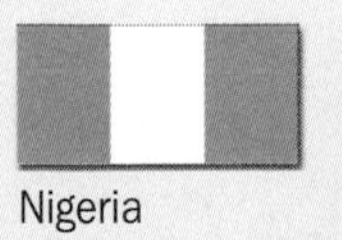
Nigeria

Ivory Coast

Burkina Faso

Guinea

Ghana

Senegal

Benin

Liberia

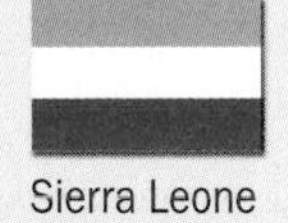
Sierra Leone

Togo

Guinea-Bissau

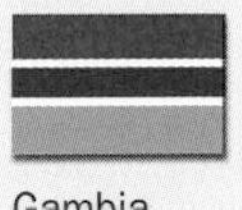
Gambia

Cape Verde

Country facts

	Area sq mi (sq km)	Population	Language	Religion	Currency
Niger	496,900 (1,286,971)	9,962,242	Hausa	Muslim	CFA Franc
Mali	428,077 (1,108,719)	10,429,124	Babara	Muslim	CFA Franc
Mauritania	397,953 (1,030,698)	2,581,738	Arabic	Muslim	Ouguiya
Nigeria	356,668 (923,770)	113,828,587	Hausa	Muslim	Naira
Ivory Coast	124,502 (322,460)	15,818,068	French	Muslim	CFA Franc
Burkina Faso	105,869 (274,201)	11,575,898	Mossi	Muslim	CFA Franc
Guinea	94,927 (245,861)	7,538,953	Fulani	Muslim	Franc
Ghana	92,100 (238,539)	18,887,626	Hausa	Indigenous	Cedi
Senegal	75,749 (196,190)	10,051,930	Wolof	Muslim	CFA Franc
Benin	43,483 (112,621)	6,305567	Fon	Indigenous	CFA Franc
Liberia	38,250 (99,068)	2,923,725	Creole	Traditional	Dollar
Sierra Leone	27,699 (71,740)	5,296,651	Creole	Muslim	Leone
Togo	21,927 (56,791)	5,080.413	Ewe	Indigenous	CFA Franc
Guinea-Bissau	13,946 (36,120)	1,234,555	Portuguese	Indigenous	CFA Franc
Gambia	4,363 (11,300)	1,336,320	Malinke	Muslim	Dalasi
Cape Verde	1,556 (4,030)	405,748	Creole/ Portuguese	Catholic	Escudo

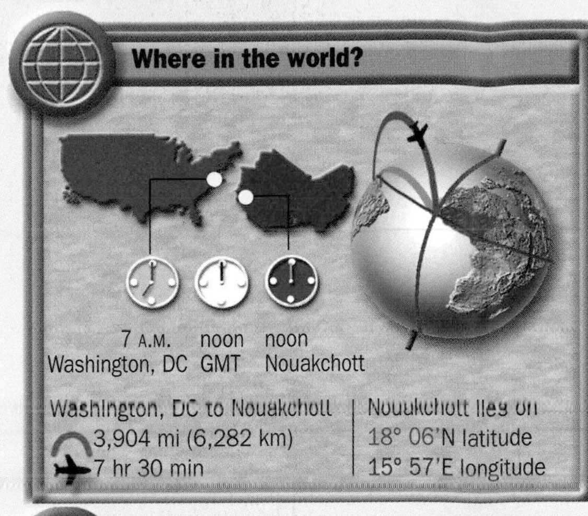

Where in the world?
7 A.M. Washington, DC
noon GMT
noon Nouakchott
Washington, DC to Nouakchott
3,904 mi (6,282 km)
7 hr 30 min
Nouakchott lies on
18° 06'N latitude
15° 57'E longitude

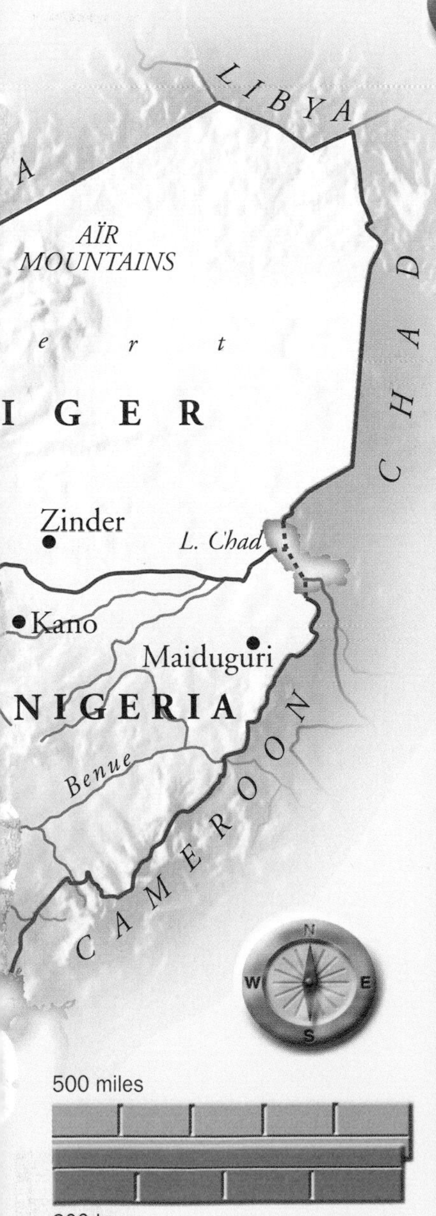

LIBYA
AÏR MOUNTAINS
e r t
IGER
CHAD
Zinder
L. Chad
Kano
Maiduguri
NIGERIA
Benue
CAMEROON
N
W
E
S
500 miles
800 km

Search and find

Niger
Capital: Niamey .E5
Maradi E6
Zinder E6

Mali
Capital: Bamako .E4
Ségou E4
Sikasso E4
Tombouctou (Timbuktu) . . .D4

Mauritania
Capital: Nouakchott D2

Nigeria
Capital: Abuja . . .F6
Abeokuta F5
Ibadan F5
Ilorin F5
Kaduna E6
Kano E6
Lagos F5
Maiduguri F7
Ogbomosho F5
Oshogbo F6
Onitsha F6
Port Harcourt . .G6
Zaria F6

Ivory Coast
Capital: Yamoussoukro .F4
Abidjan F4
Bouaké F4
Daloa F4

Burkina Faso
Capital: Ouagadougou . .E4
Bobo Dioulasso .E4

Guinea
Capital: Conakry F3
Kankan F3

Ghana
Capital: Accra . . .F5
Kumasi F4
Tamale F5

Senegal
Capital: Dakar . .E2
Thiès E2

Benin
Capitals: Cotonou F5
Porto-Novo . . .F5

Liberia
Capital: Monrovia F3
Harbel F3

Sierra Leone
Capital: Freetown F3

Togo
Capital: Lomé . . .F5

Guinea-Bissau
Capital: Bissau .E2

Gambia
Capital: Banjul . .E2

Cape Verde
Capital: Praia . . .D1

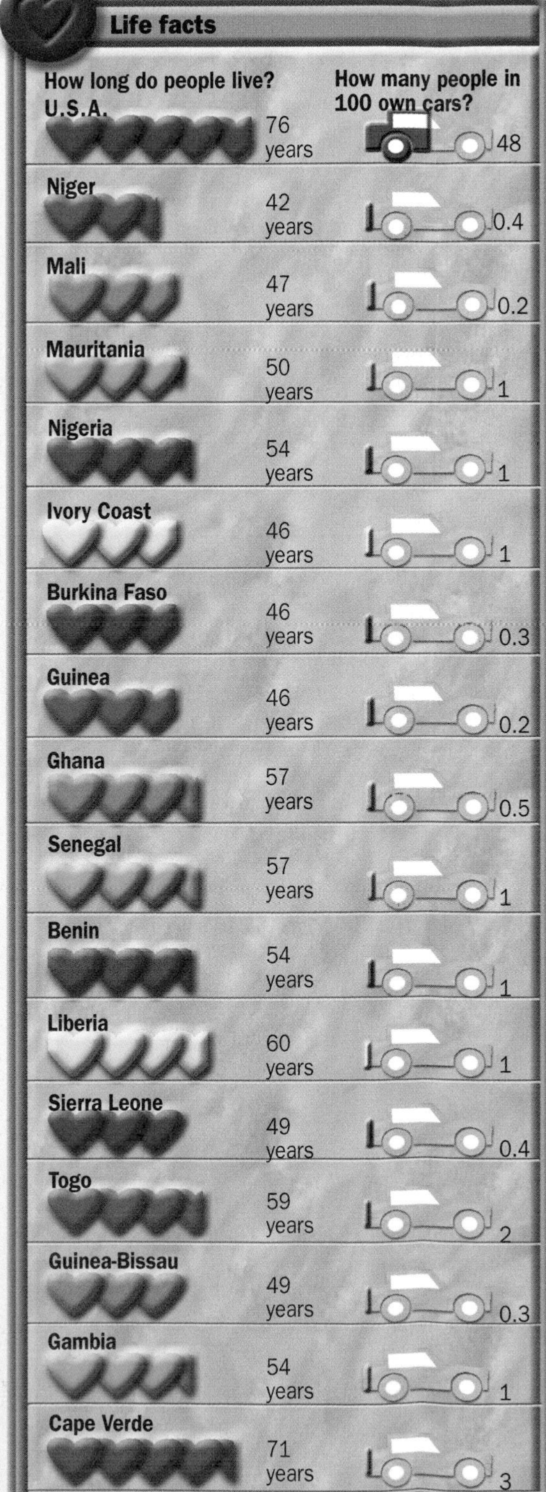

Life facts
How long do people live?
How many people in 100 own cars?
U.S.A. 76 years 48
Niger 42 years 0.4
Mali 47 years 0.2
Mauritania 50 years 1
Nigeria 54 years 1
Ivory Coast 46 years 1
Burkina Faso 46 years 0.3
Guinea 46 years 0.2
Ghana 57 years 0.5
Senegal 57 years 1
Benin 54 years 1
Liberia 60 years 1
Sierra Leone 49 years 0.4
Togo 59 years 2
Guinea-Bissau 49 years 0.3
Gambia 54 years 1
Cape Verde 71 years 3

Northern Central Africa

SUDAN, CHAD, CENTRAL AFRICAN REPUBLIC, CAMEROON

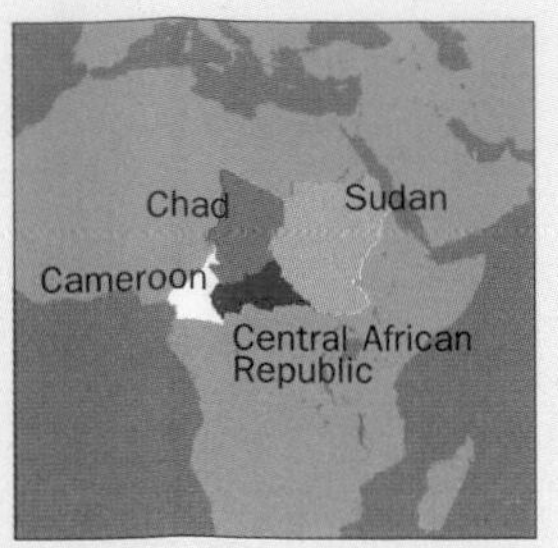
Chad
Sudan
Cameroon
Central African Republic

These court musicians from Cameroon blow long horns. The musical tradition of Africa is rich, with a wide range of drums, flutes, bells, xylophones, and stringed instruments.

ARRIVING AT WADI HALFA OFF the Lake Nasser steamer, travelers board dusty train coaches to cross the scorching Nubian Desert. Khartoum, the Sudanese capital, is built where two rivers, the Blue and White Nile, join to form the single Nile River. Sudan is an Islamic country, of mosques and camel markets, of long-robed, turbanned men sipping tea or coffee, of old colonial buildings and flat-roofed mud-brick dwellings. However, many days' journey onward through Africa's largest country, by gear-grinding truck or by rusty Nile riverboat from the town of Kosti, lead to the swamps of the Sudd and the southern mountains. Here, in the lands of the Dinka, Nuer, and Shilluk peoples, the villages consist of round thatched huts, with stockades for cattle. Customs in the southern part of Sudan are African or Christian, a world away from the Islamic north.

Chad, too, has an Islamic north and a Christian south. Thin savanna grasslands border Chad's desert, a poverty-stricken zone where drought and famine are common. More fertile lands border the Chari and Logone rivers and the shallow waters of Lake Chad. Savanna extends southward into the Central African Republic (C.A.R.) and the plateaus of Cameroon, on the Atlantic coast. The far south of this region includes the great rain forests of central Africa. These extend from southern Cameroon and southwestern C.A.R. across the basin of the Congo River.

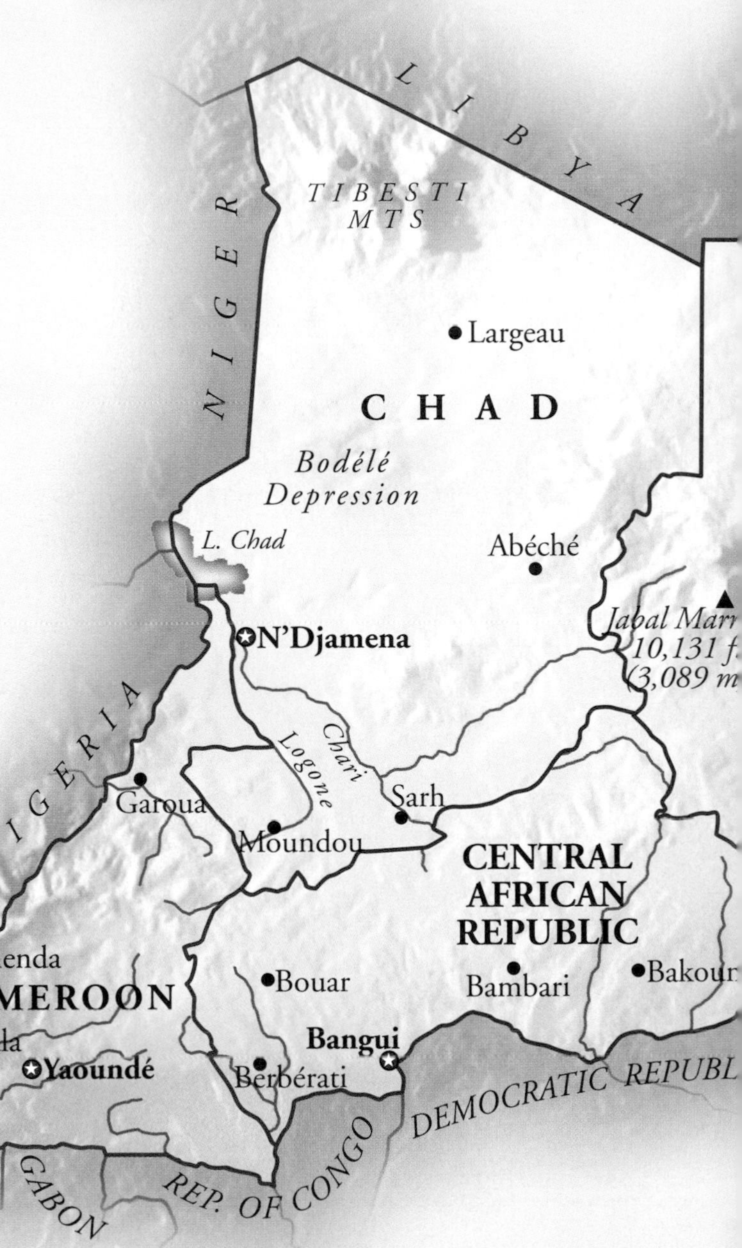
LIBYA
TIBESTI MTS
NIGER
Largeau
CHAD
Bodélé Depression
L. Chad
Abéché
Jabal Marr
10,131 f
(3,089 m
N'Djamena
Chari
Logone
NIGERIA
Garoua
Sarh
Moundou
CENTRAL AFRICAN REPUBLIC
Bamenda
CAMEROON
Bouar
Bambari
Bakour
Mt Cameroon
13,353 ft
(4,071 m)
Douala
Yaoundé
Bangui
Berbérati
DEMOCRATIC REPUBL
EQUATORIAL GUINEA
GABON
REP. OF CONGO

DISCOVER MORE

* *The Sudd, in southern Sudan, is a vast swamp of 6,370 sq mi (16,500 sq km). Its area is doubled each year when the White Nile floods. Tangled with water hyacinth roots and papyrus reeds, it is home to crocodiles and hippopotamuses.*

In the center of Omdurman is the tomb of Sudan's national hero, Sheik Muhammed Ahmed, known as the Mahdi.

A B C D E F G

Fulani cattle herders collect water from a well in Kanem, a region of northwest Chad that borders the Sahara Desert. The Fulani people, known in some areas as Fulbe or Peul, live across a broad band of Central and West Africa.

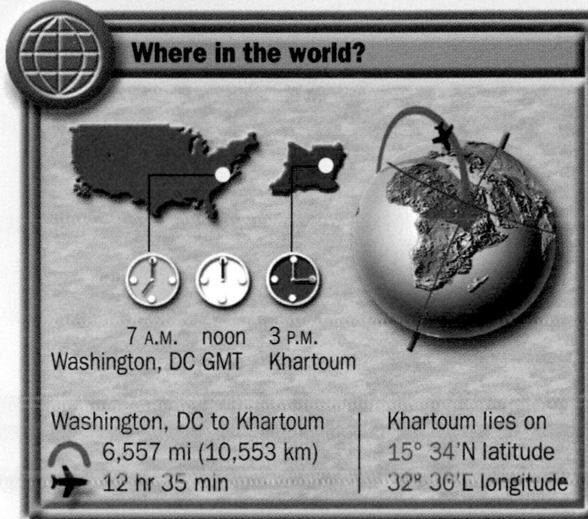

Where in the world?
7 A.M. Washington, DC
noon GMT
3 P.M. Khartoum
Washington, DC to Khartoum
6,557 mi (10,553 km)
12 hr 35 min
Khartoum lies on
15° 34'N latitude
32° 36'E longitude

EGYPT
Libyan Desert
Wadi Halfa
Nubian Desert
RED SEA
Nile
Port Sudan
Merowe
Atbara
SUDAN
Atbara
Kassala
ERITREA
Omdurman
Khartoum
Wad Medani
El Obeid
Blue Nile
Kosti
Nyala
ETHIOPIA
Malakal
Bahr al-Ghazal
Sudd
White Nile
Juba
CONGO
UGANDA
KENYA

300 miles
500 km

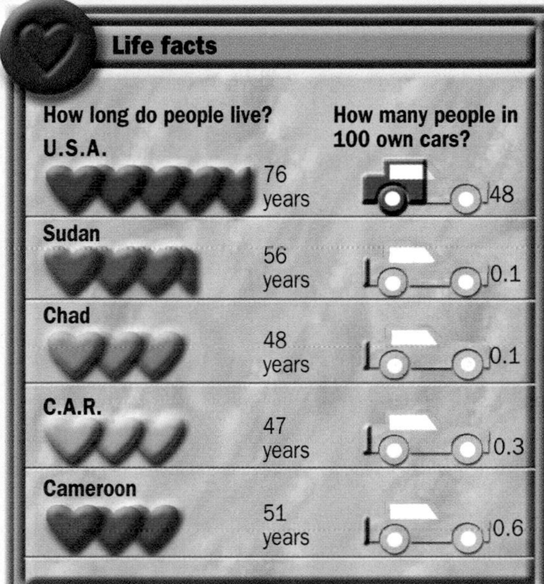

Life facts
How long do people live?
How many people in 100 own cars?
U.S.A.
76 years
48
Sudan
56 years
0.1
Chad
48 years
0.1
C.A.R.
47 years
0.3
Cameroon
51 years
0.6

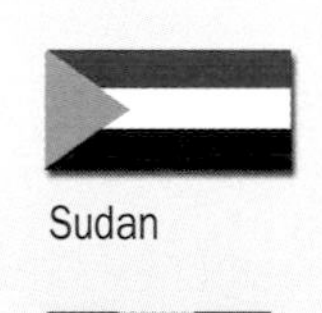
Sudan

Chad

C.A.R.

Cameroon

Search and find

Sudan
Capital: Khartoum C7
Atbara C8
El Obeid D7
Juba E7
Kassala C8
Kosti D7
Malakal E7
Merowe C7
Nyala D6
Omdurman C7
Port Sudan C8
Wadi Halfa B7
Wad Medani . . .D8

Chad
Capital: N'Djamena D4
Abéché D5
Largeau C5
Moundou D4
Sarh D5

C.A.R.
Capital: Bangui .E5
Bakouma E5
Bambari E5
Berbérati E4
Bouar E4

Cameroon
Capital: Yaoundé E3
Bamenda E3
Douala E3
Garoua D4

There are three main national parks in the Central African Republic. International conservation groups are working with local people to preserve threatened wildlife species, including rhinoceroses.

Country facts

	Area sq mi (sq km)	Population	Language	Religion	Currency
Sudan	967,493 (2,505,807)	34,475,690	Arabic	Sunni Muslim	Pound
Chad	495,752 (1,283,998)	7,557,436	Sara	Sunni Muslim	CFA Franc
C.A.R.	240,533 (622,980)	3,444,951	Sango/French	Trad/Bap/Cath*	CFA Franc
Cameroon	183,567 (475,439)	15,456,092	Fang/Murri/French	Cath/Trad**	CFA Franc

* Traditional beliefs/Baptist/Catholic **Catholic/Traditional beliefs

The Horn of Africa

ETHIOPIA, SOMALIA, ERITREA, DJIBOUTI

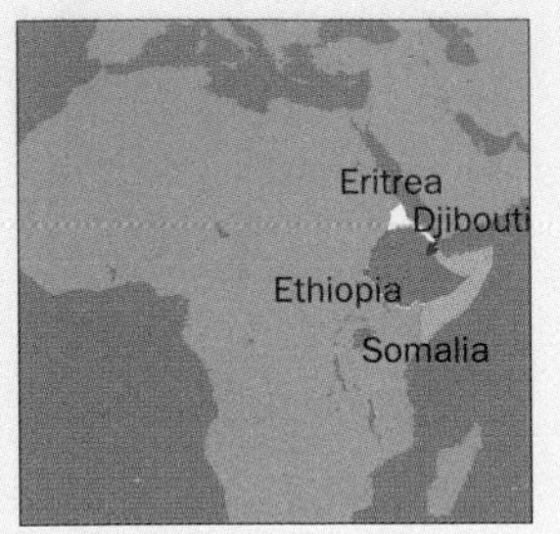
Eritrea
Djibouti
Ethiopia
Somalia

An Ethiopian mother sits with her young daughter. Most Ethiopians live on the land, and the climate is moderate. However, droughts are common, causing harvests to fail and people to go hungry.

IN A ROUND THATCHED HOUSE made of mud and straw, an Ethiopian family rests after a hard day's work plowing the land with oxen. The evening is cold in the highlands, and the farmer pulls a woolen cloak around his body for warmth. His wife tends a stew pot that is simmering on the hearth and stacks up *injera,* pancakes of sour bread. These are made from a grain called teff.

Ethiopia is a land of mountains, rocky plateaus, and deserts, crossed by part of the Great Rift Valley and by the Blue Nile River, which tumbles over the spectacular Tisissat Falls, southeast of Lake Tana. Ethiopia has ancient palaces and rock-hewn Christian churches. Today, its modern capital, Addis Ababa, is the largest city of the region, with a population of three million. It is the headquarters of the Organization of African Unity (O.A.U.), whose member states aim to promote peace and prosperity across the continent. The city is also famous for its silverwork and other crafts.

The Horn of Africa, the peninsula that juts out south of the Red Sea, is occupied by three countries: Eritrea , Djibouti, and Somalia. All three consist largely of desert, scrub, and mountain. These lands are crossed by herders of goats and camels. Most of the population inhabits seaports on the Indian Ocean. The region includes Muslims and, in Ethiopia and Eritrea, Christians.

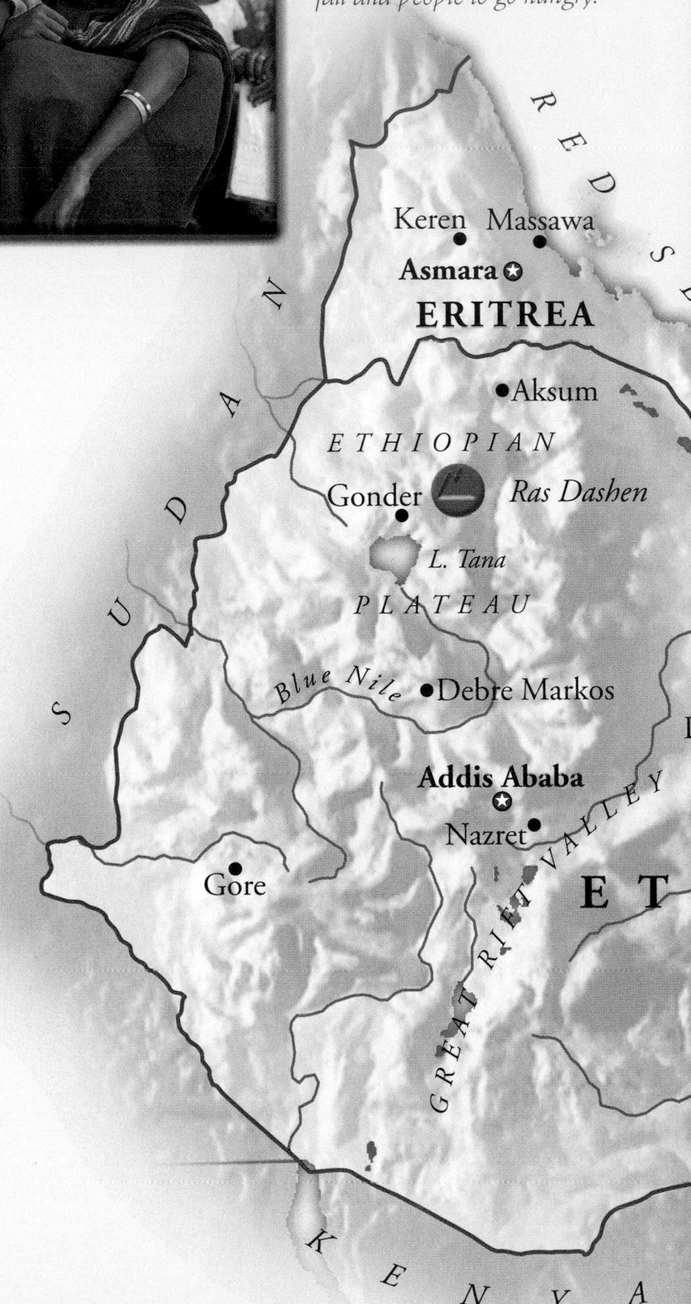
RED SE
Keren
Massawa
Asmara
ERITREA
SUDAN
Aksum
ETHIOPIAN
Gonder
Ras Dashen
L. Tana
PLATEAU
Blue Nile
Debre Markos
Addis Ababa
Nazret
GREAT RIFT VALLEY
Gore
ET
KENYA

DISCOVER MORE

- *Lake Assal, in Djibouti, is the lowest point in Africa, 512 ft (156 m) below sea level. Its waters evaporate in the hot, dry air, leaving behind islands made of salt.*
- *Nearly 100 different languages are spoken in Ethiopia. The country's official language is Amharic, which is spoken by about half of the population.*

Traditional circular thatched huts are found mostly in the south of Somalia, where there is enough rain to support farming. In the dry desert regions, nomadic herders use portable, dome-shaped shelters instead.

Highest mountains

Mount McKinley
20,320 ft
(6,194 m)
Ras Dashen
15,158 ft
(4,620 m)

Eritrean girls gather at a well to fill containers with fresh water. Water is a precious resource in this dry country. Supplies are replenished by seasonal rains in the Ethiopian highlands.

Where in the world?

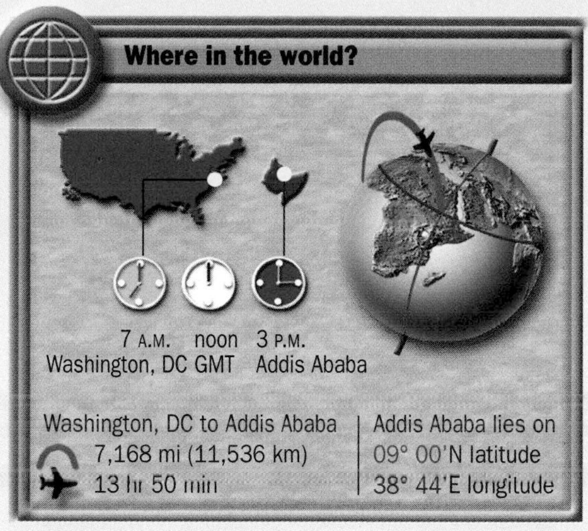
7 A.M. Washington, DC
noon GMT
3 P.M. Addis Ababa
Washington, DC to Addis Ababa
7,168 mi (11,536 km)
13 hr 50 min
Addis Ababa lies on
09° 00'N latitude
38° 44'E longitude

Asseb
DJIBOUTI
ssab
Djibouti
Gulf of Aden
Cape Caseyr
Berbera
awa
Hargeisa
Harer
SOMALIA
IOPIA
Eyl
OGADEN
Shebelē
INDIAN OCEAN
Jubba
Baydhabo
Mogadishu
Marka
Baraawe
Kismaayo
N
W
E
S
200 miles
300 km

Life facts

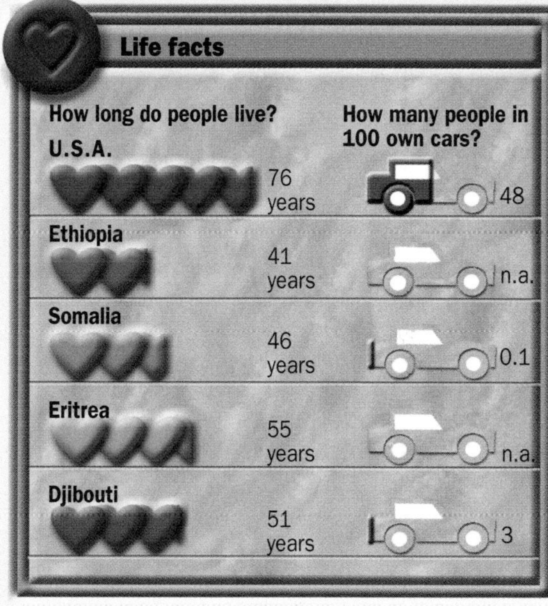
How long do people live?
How many people in 100 own cars?
U.S.A.
76 years
48
Ethiopia
41 years
n.a.
Somalia
46 years
0.1
Eritrea
55 years
n.a.
Djibouti
51 years
3

Ethiopia

Somalia

Eritrea

Djibouti

Search and find

Ethiopia
Capital:
Addis Ababa . . D5
Aksum C5
Debre Markos . . D5
Dire Dawa D6
Gonder C5
Gore D4
Harer D6
Nazret D5

Somalia
Capital:
Mogadishu . . . F7
Baydhabo F7
Baraawe F7
Berbera D7
Eyl D8
Hargeisa D7
Kismaayo G6
Marka F7

Eritrea
Capital: Asmara . B5
Asseb C6
Keren B5
Massawa B5

Djibouti
Capital: Djibouti . C6

Country facts

	Area sq mi (sq km)	Population	Language	Religion	Currency
Ethiopia	435,184 (1,127,127)	59,680,383	Amharic/Oromo	EO*/Sunni Muslim	Birr
Somalia	246,201 (637,661)	7,140,643	Somali	Sunni Muslim	Shilling
Eritrea	46,842 (121,321)	3,984,723	Tigrinya	Sunni Muslim	Nakfa
Djibouti	8,494 (21,999)	447,439	French	Muslim	Franc

*Ethiopian Orthodox

East Africa

Tanzania, Kenya, Uganda, Burundi, Rwanda

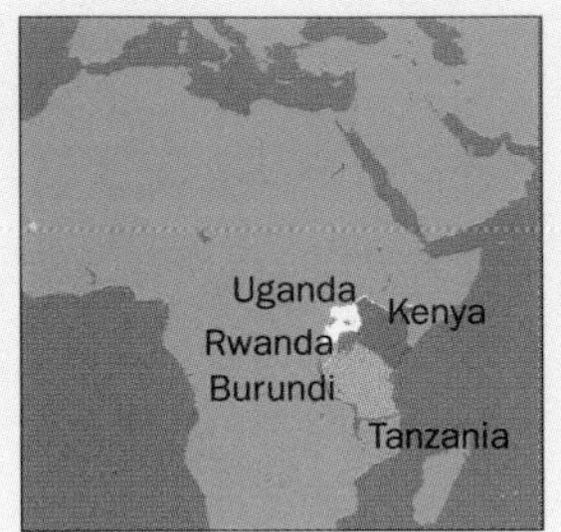
Uganda
Kenya
Rwanda
Burundi
Tanzania

In the far west, volcanic mountain ranges and forests descend to the lands of Rwanda, Burundi, and Uganda. These small countries lie among Africa's great lakes: Edward, Albert, Kivu, Kyoga, Victoria, and Tanganyika. Huts and houses are scattered over hillsides, where shady, green banana leaves contrast with the rich, red soil.

In Kenya, northern deserts around Lake Turkana give way to misty highlands, spread out beneath the jagged peaks of Mount Kenya. Sprawling modern cities, such as Nairobi, attract tourists, businesspeople, and poor country dwellers in search of work.

Beyond the Great Rift Valley, from Kenya across the border into Tanzania, are sweeping savanna grasslands dotted with acacia trees, with the snowcapped peaks of Kilimanjaro in the distance. In these huge, tawny landscapes, beneath blue skies and billowing white clouds, all the big animals seem very much at home.

Off the East African coast, wooden sailing ships called dhows sail between islands such as Zanzibar and Pemba, famous for their fragrant cloves. Cargo ships sail into big seaports such as Dar es Salaam and Mombasa.

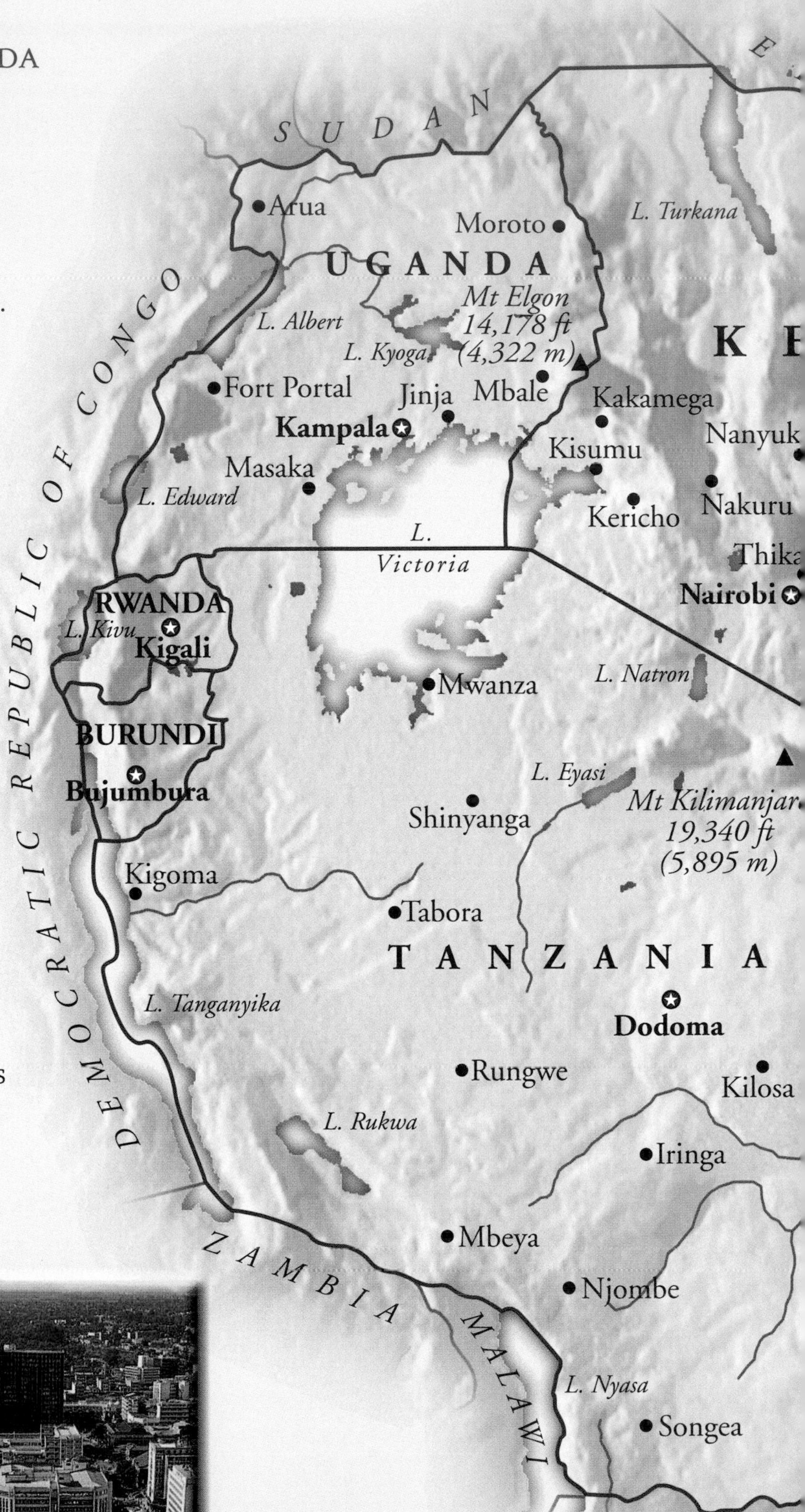

DISCOVER MORE

- *Lake Victoria, within Uganda, Kenya, and Tanzania, is Africa's biggest lake, with a total area covering 26,590 sq mi (68,880 sq km). Its waves can be as high as those of the ocean.*
- *Tanzania's Kilimanjaro is the highest mountain in Africa, reaching 19,340 ft (5,895 m) above sea level. The first European explorers on first sight could scarcely believe that mountains near the equator could be covered in snow.*

Nairobi is the capital of Kenya and the chief commercial center of East Africa. In the city center, modern office and hotel buildings rise from broad, tree-lined avenues. Beyond the sprawling suburbs there are cool, green hills and, to the south and east, hot savanna grasslands.

SUDAN
UGANDA
Arua
Moroto
L. Turkana
L. Albert
Mt Elgon 14,178 ft (4,322 m)
L. Kyoga
Fort Portal
Jinja
Mbale
Kakamega
Kampala
Kisumu
Nanyuk
Masaka
L. Edward
Kericho
Nakuru
L. Victoria
Thika
Nairobi
RWANDA
L. Kivu
Kigali
Mwanza
L. Natron
BURUNDI
Bujumbura
L. Eyasi
Shinyanga
Mt Kilimanjaro 19,340 ft (5,895 m)
Kigoma
Tabora
TANZANIA
DEMOCRATIC REPUBLIC OF CONGO
L. Tanganyika
Dodoma
Rungwe
Kilosa
L. Rukwa
Iringa
Mbeya
ZAMBIA
Njombe
MALAWI
L. Nyasa
Songea
MOZA
W E S
200 miles
300 km

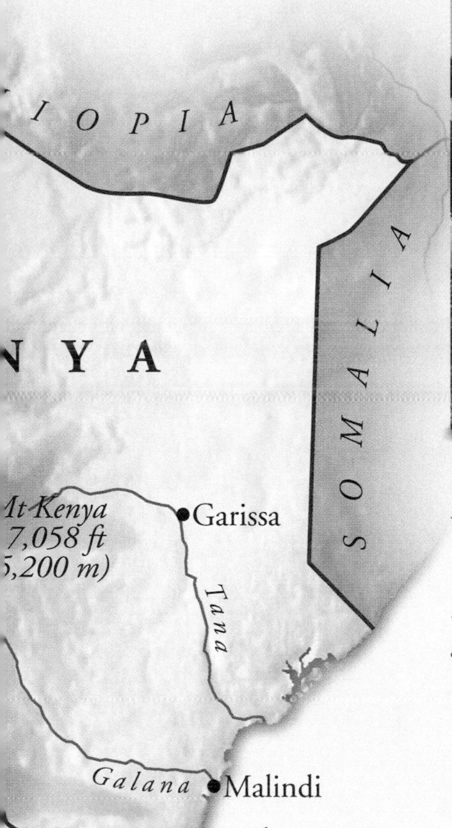
IOPIA
NYA
SOMALIA
Mt Kenya
7,058 ft
5,200 m)
Garissa
Tana

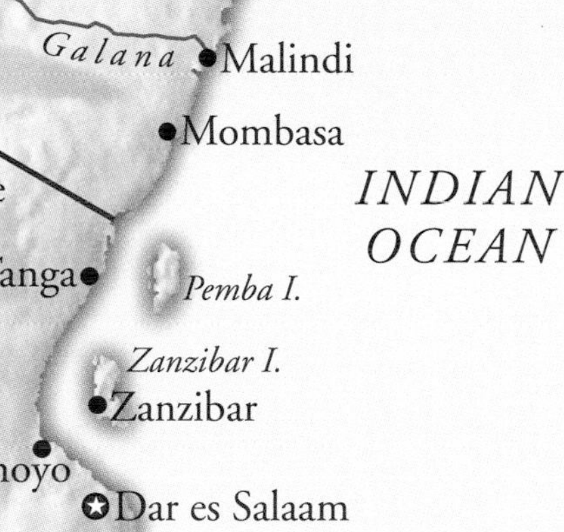
Galana
Malindi
Mombasa
Same
INDIAN
OCEAN
Tanga
Pemba I.
Zanzibar I.
Zanzibar
agamoyo
Dar es Salaam

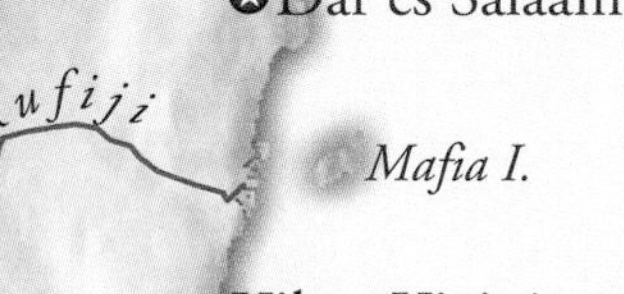
ufiji
Mafia I.

Kilwa Kivinje
Lindi
Mtwara
Ruvuma
IQUE

The clouds clear to reveal snowcapped Kibo and Mawenzi, the two highest points of the Kilimanjaro massif. They tower above the flat-topped acacia trees of the East African savanna. The slopes of Kilimanjaro rise through farmland, forest, mountain grasses, and snowfields.

A high collar of beaded necklaces adorns this woman of the Turkana people. The Turkana live in the arid lands of northwestern Kenya and also across the border in Sudan.

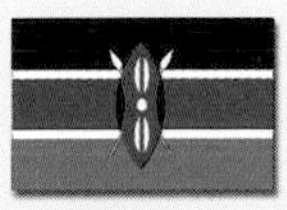

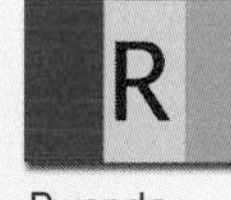

Tanzania Kenya Uganda Burundi Rwanda

Country facts

	Area sq mi (sq km)	Population	Language	Religion	Currency
Tanzania	364,899 (945,088)	31,270,8209	Swahili	Trad*/Sunni Muslim	Shilling
Kenya	224,961 (582,649)	28,808,658	Swahili	Cath/Prot/Trad**	Shilling
Uganda	93,070 (241,051)	22,804,973	Swahili/Ganda	Protestant/Catholic	Shilling
Burundi	10,745 (27,830)	5,735,937	Rundi	Catholic	Franc
Rwanda	10,170 (26,340)	8,154,933	Rwanda	Catholic	Franc

*Traditional beliefs **Catholic/Protestant/Traditional beliefs

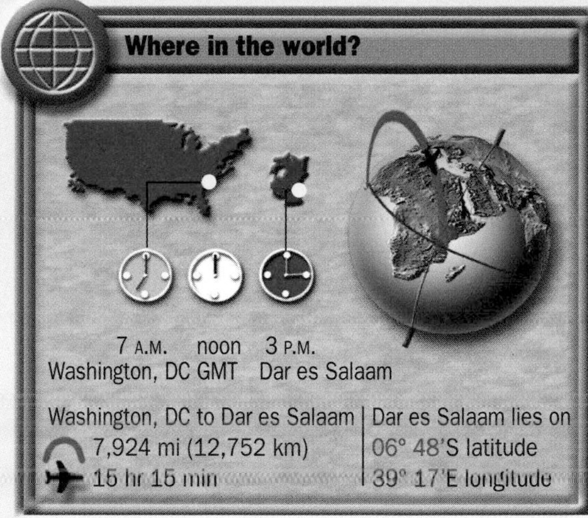
Where in the world?
7 A.M. Washington, DC
noon GMT
3 P.M. Dar es Salaam
Washington, DC to Dar es Salaam
7,924 mi (12,752 km)
15 hr 15 min
Dar es Salaam lies on
06° 48'S latitude
39° 17'E longitude

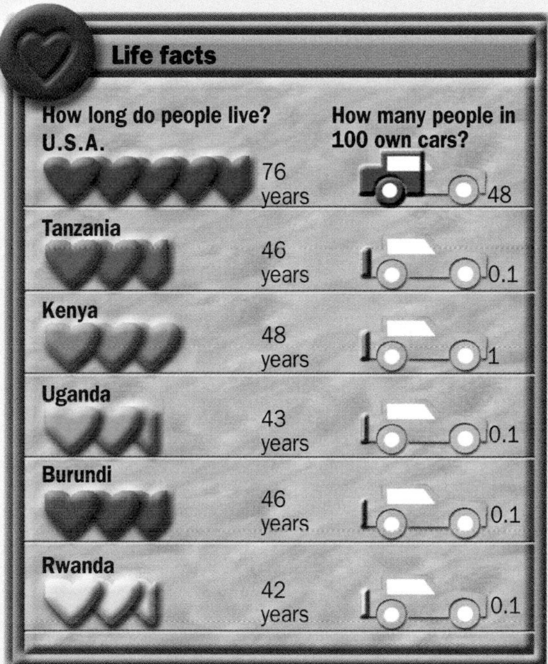
Life facts
How long do people live?
How many people in 100 own cars?
U.S.A. 76 years 48
Tanzania 46 years 0.1
Kenya 48 years 1
Uganda 43 years 0.1
Burundi 46 years 0.1
Rwanda 42 years 0.1

Search and find

Tanzania
Capitals: Dar es Salaam (Administrative) . .E7
Dodoma (Legislative) D5
Bagamoyo E7
Iringa E5
Kigoma D3
Kilosa E6
Kilwa Kivinje . . .E7
Lindi F7
Mbeya E5
Mtwara F7
Mwanza C5
Njombe F5
Rungwe E5
Same D6
Shinyanga D5
Songea F5
Tabora D4
Tanga D7
Zanzibar D7

Kenya
Capital: Nairobi .C6
Garissa C7
Kakamega B5
Kericho C5
Kisumu B5
Malindi C7
Mombasa D7
Nakuru C6
Nanyuki B6
Thika C6

Uganda
Capital: Kampala B4
Arua B4
Fort Portal B4
Jinja B4
Masaka C4
Mbale B5
Moroto B5

Burundi
Capital: Bujumbura . . .D3

Rwanda
Capital: Kigali . .C4

Equatorial Africa

DEMOCRATIC REPUBLIC OF CONGO, ANGOLA, ZAMBIA, REPUBLIC OF CONGO, GABON, EQUATORIAL GUINEA, SÃOTOMÉ & PRÍNCIPE

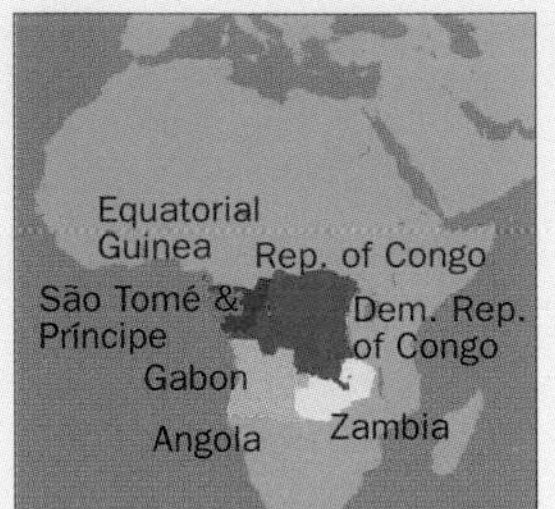
Equatorial Guinea
Rep. of Congo
São Tomé & Príncipe
Dem. Rep. of Congo
Gabon
Angola
Zambia

A CROWDED RIVERBOAT, MADE up of barges hauled by a tug boat, slowly churns its way up the muddy flood of the Congo River. On deck, a woman washes out a cotton dress in a plastic bowl, while another cooks a fish stew on a stove. Radios blare out the intricate electric guitar rhythms of the late, great Franco or the sweet, lilting voice of Mbilia Bel—the king and queen of Congolese pop music. The Congo, the greatest river of Central Africa, winds between the cities of Brazzaville and Kinshasa, forming the international boundary between the Republic of Congo and the Democratic Republic of Congo.

The heart of the African continent is dense rain forest, drained by countless streams and rivers. Small bands of hunters, such as the slightly built Mbuti, live in the forest, but most people of the region are farmers or city dwellers. The forest extends westward into Gabon and Equatorial Guinea, and southward into Angola, where it gives way to plateaus, highlands, and desert.

Part of Equatorial Guinea is made up of islands. The hot, humid islands of São Tomé make up a separate country, 125 miles (200 km) west of Gabon.

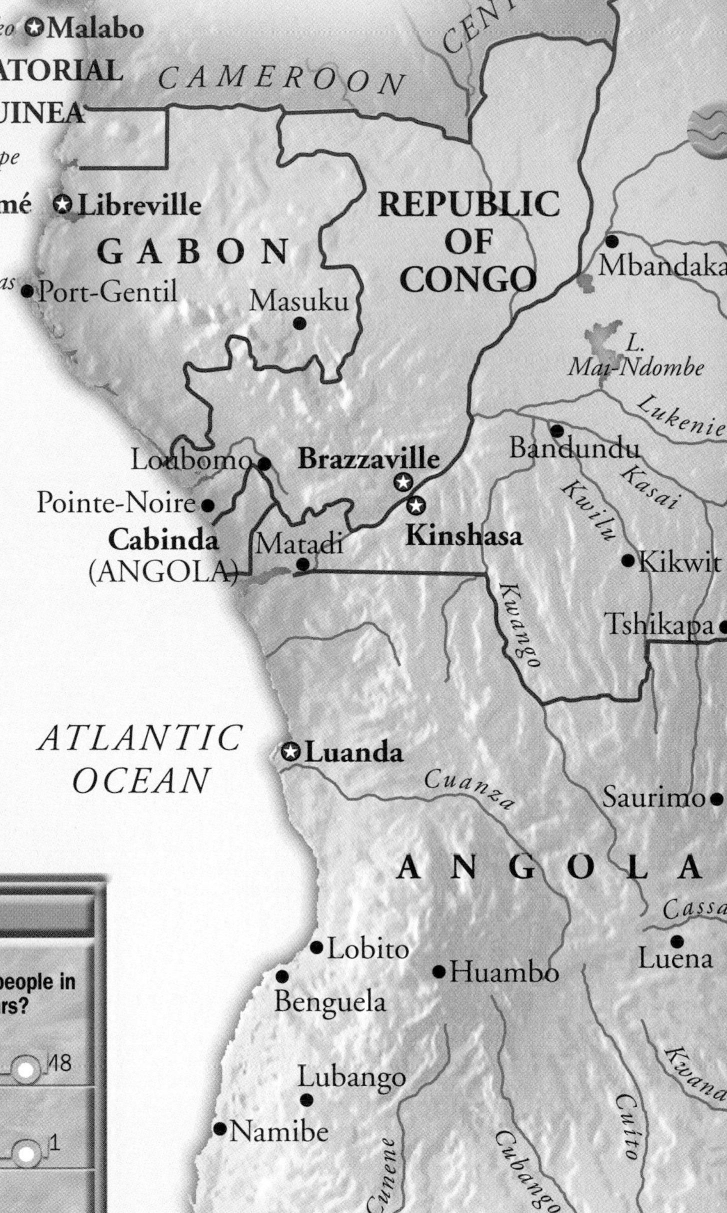
CENTRAL AFRICA
Bioko
Malabo
EQUATORIAL GUINEA
CAMEROON
SÃO TOMÉ & PRÍNCIPE
Príncipe
São Tomé
São Tomé
Libreville
GABON
REPUBLIC OF CONGO
Mbandaka
Cape Esterias
Port-Gentil
Masuku
L. Mai-Ndombe
Lukenie
Loubomo
Brazzaville
Bandundu
Kasai
Pointe-Noire
Kwilu
Cabinda (ANGOLA)
Matadi
Kinshasa
Kikwit
Kwango
Tshikapa
ATLANTIC OCEAN
Luanda
Cuanza
Saurimo
ANGOLA
Cassa
Lobito
Huambo
Luena
Benguela
Kwando
Lubango
Namibe
Cuito
Cunene
Cubango
NAMIBIA

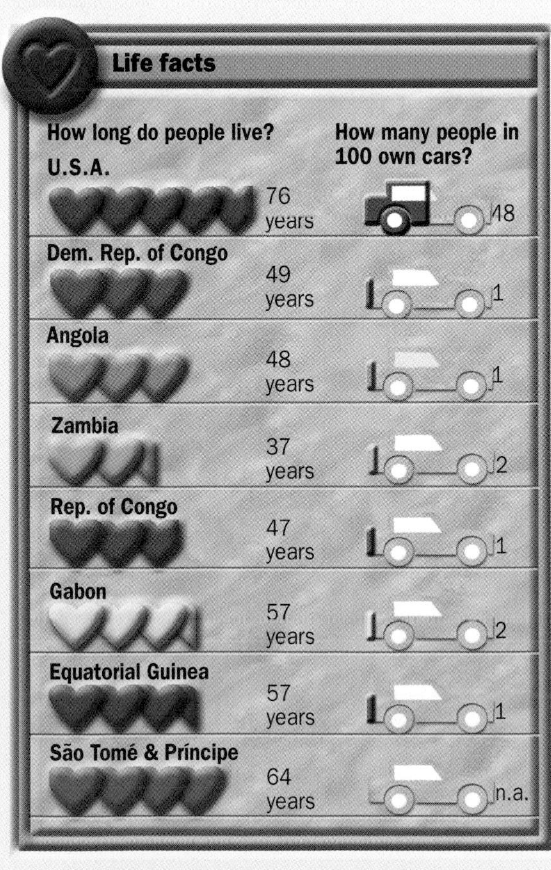
Life facts
How long do people live?
How many people in 100 own cars?
U.S.A. 76 years 48
Dem. Rep. of Congo 49 years 1
Angola 48 years 1
Zambia 37 years 2
Rep. of Congo 47 years 1
Gabon 57 years 2
Equatorial Guinea 57 years 1
São Tomé & Príncipe 64 years n.a.

DISCOVER MORE

- *The Congo River is the second longest in Africa, covering 2,900 mi (4,667 km) from its source to the Atlantic Ocean.*
- *The Congo region has one of the finest artistic traditions in Africa. The elongated and distorted features of its carved wooden masks inspired some of the world's great twentieth-century artists, such as Henri Matisse and Pablo Picasso.*

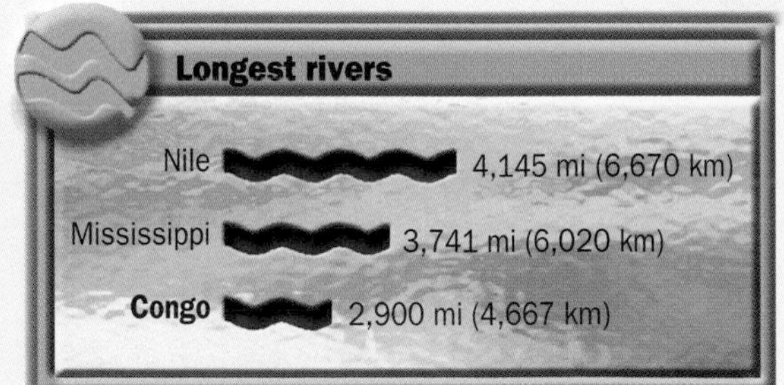
Longest rivers
Nile 4,145 mi (6,670 km)
Mississippi 3,741 mi (6,020 km)
Congo 2,900 mi (4,667 km)

6
7
8
9
10
11

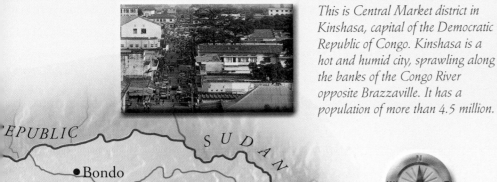

This is Central Market district in Kinshasa, capital of the Democratic Republic of Congo. Kinshasa is a hot and humid city, sprawling along the banks of the Congo River opposite Brazzaville. It has a population of more than 4.5 million.

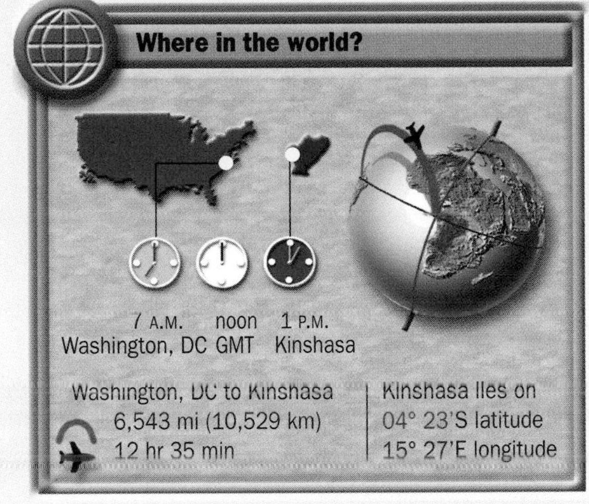

Where in the world?
7 A.M.
Washington, DC
noon
GMT
1 P.M.
Kinshasa
Washington, DC to Kinshasa
6,543 mi (10,529 km)
12 hr 35 min
Kinshasa lies on
04° 23'S latitude
15° 27'E longitude

N
W
E
S

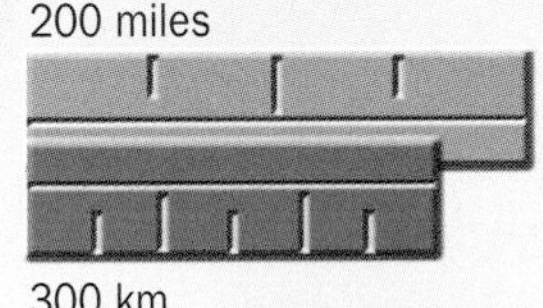

200 miles
300 km

REPUBLIC
SUDAN
Bondo
Uele
Watsa
Congo
UGANDA
Bunia
Basoko
Kisangani
L.Edward
DEMOCRATIC REPUBLIC OF CONGO
L.Kivu
RWANDA
Bukavu
BURUNDI
Lualaba
Lomami
TANZANIA
Kananga
Mbuji-Mayi
Kalemie
Kasai
Lubilash
L. Tanganyika
Kamina
Bukama
L. Mweru
Mbala
Kolwezi
Likasi
Kasama
Lubumbashi
L. Bangweulu
MALAWI
Mufulira
Kitwe
Ndola
Chipata
ZAMBIA
Kabwe
Zambezi
Lusaka
MOZAMBIQUE
Kafue
ZIMBABWE
Livingstone

Dem. Rep. of Congo

Angola

Zambia

Rep. of Congo

Gabon

Equatorial Guinea

São Tomé & Príncipe

Search and find

Democratic Republic of Congo
Capital: Kinshasa C5
Bandundu C5
Basoko B7
Bondo B7
Bukama D7
Bukavu C8
Bunia B8
Kalemie D8
Kamina D7
Kananga D6
Kikwit D5
Kisangani B7
Kolwezi E7
Likasi E7
Lubumbashi E7
Matadi D4
Mbandaka B5
Mbuji-Mayi D7
Tshikapa D6
Watsa B8

Angola
Capital: Luanda .D4
Benguela E4
Huambo E5
Lobito E4
Lubango E4
Luena E6
Namibe E4
Saurimo D6

Zambia
Capital: Lusaka .F7
Chipata E8
Kabwe E8
Kasama E8
Kitwe E7
Livingstone F7
Mbala D8
Mufulira E7
Ndola E8

Republic of Congo
Capital: Brazzaville C5
Loubomo C4
Pointe-Noire C4

Gabon
Capital: Libreville B4
Masuku C4
Port-Gentil C4

Equatorial Guinea
Capital: Malabo .B4

São Tomé & Príncipe
Capital: São Tomé B3

A
B
C
D
E
F
G

Country facts

	Area sq mi (sq km)	Population	Language	Religion	Currency
D.R. of Congo	905,563 (2,345,408)	50,481,305	French/Lingala	Catholic	Congolese Franc
Angola	481,351 (1,246,699)	11,177,537	Portuguese/Umbundu	Cath/Trad*	Kwanza
Zambia	290,583 (752,610)	9,663,535	English/Bemba	Prot/Trad/Cath**	Kwacha
R. of Congo	132,046 (341,999)	2,716,814	French/Monokutuba	Catholic	CFA Franc
Gabon	103,347 (267,669)	1,225,853	French/Fang	Christian/IB***	CFA Franc
Eq. Guinea	10,830 (28,050)	465,746	Fang/Spanish	Catholic	CFA Franc
S. Tomé & Prín.	371 (961)	154,878	Portuguese	Catholic	Dobra

*Catholic/Traditional beliefs **Protestant/Traditional beliefs/Catholic ***Indigenous beliefs

6 7 8 9 10 11

Namibia to Mozambique

NAMIBIA, MOZAMBIQUE, BOTSWANA, ZIMBABWE, MALAWI

Malawi
Zimbabwe
Namibia
Botswana
Mozambique

THE GRAVEL AND SAND DUNES of the hot Namib Desert lie on the southwest African coast, bordered by the cold currents of the Atlantic Ocean. Rain is very rare, but at night sea mists roll inland, providing just enough moisture for desert plants. Few people live in Namibia's harsh landscapes, which are rich in minerals—uranium, lead, and cadmium.

The Okavango River spills over northeastern Botswana, forming vast wetlands which are the haunt of thousands of animals and birds. Southeastern Botswana is occupied by another desert, the Kalahari. The San people, who live here, are experts at desert survival. They have lived in southern Africa longer than any other people. A central plateau gives way to eastern grasslands, where most of the Tswana people live. Cattle ranching and diamond mining are the major industries.

Zimbabwe lies on a plateau to the south of the Zambezi River. Farmers grow tobacco and vegetables, often struggling during long periods of drought. The capital, Harare, is one of the major cities of southern Africa. The Zambezi River flows eastward, to enter the Indian Ocean in central Mozambique. Its capital, Maputo, has the second largest harbor in Africa. Its port also serves the landlocked nations to the east.

To the north, Malawi lies on the edge of a split in the earth's crust called the Great Rift Valley. A system of rift valleys extend throughout much of eastern Africa.

Windhoek, the Namibian capital, is a busy, modern city. Its industries include the cutting and polishing of semi-precious stones and diamonds, and meat canning.

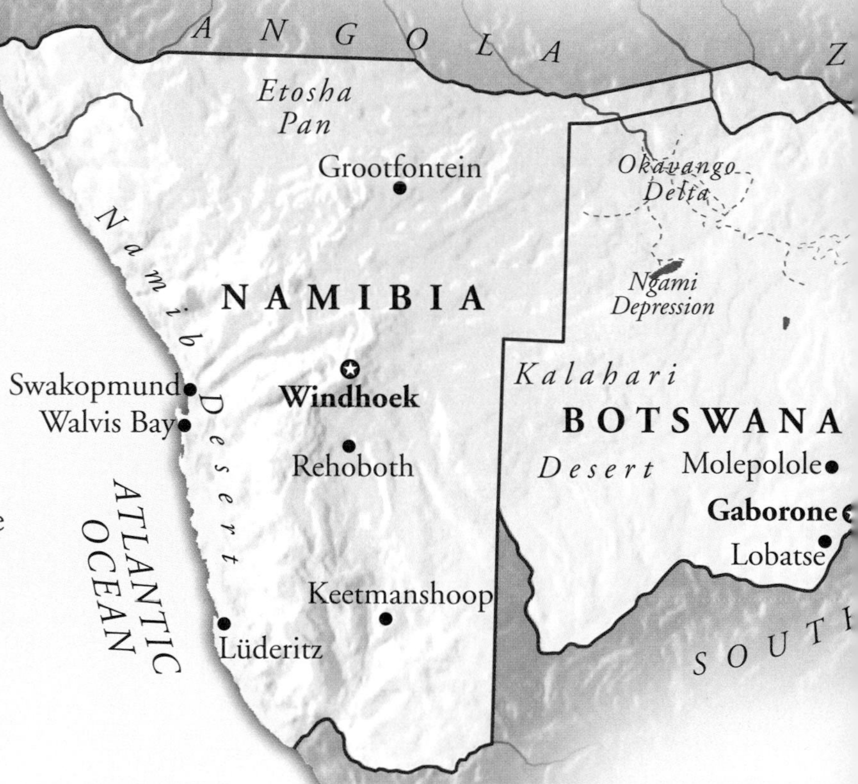
ANGOLA
Cape Fria
Etosha Pan
Grootfontein
Okavango Delta
Ngami Depression
Namib Desert
NAMIBIA
Swakopmund
Walvis Bay
Windhoek
Rehoboth
Kalahari Desert
BOTSWANA
Molepolole
Gaborone
Lobatse
ATLANTIC OCEAN
Keetmanshoop
Lüderitz
SOUTH

Namibia

Mozambique

Botswana

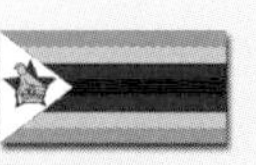
Zimbabwe

Malawi

DISCOVER MORE

• *The Okavango is a river that never reaches the sea. It forms the world's largest swamp, over 10,810 sq mi (28,000 sq km) in area. Ninety percent of its water is lost through evaporation.*

Country facts

	Area sq mi (sq km)	Population	Language	Religion	Currency
Namibia	318,694 (825,417)	1,648,270	Ovambo/English	Lutheran	Rand
Mozambique	309,494 (801,589)	19,124,335	Portuguese/Makua	Indigenous Beliefs	Metical
Botswana	224,607 (581,732)	1,464,167	English/Tswana	Traditional Beliefs/AC*	Pula
Zimbabwe	150,803 (390,580)	11,163,160	English/Shona	Ang**/Traditonal Beliefs	Dollar
Malawi	45,745 (118,480)	10,000,416	English/Chichewa	Sunni Islam/Catholic/PB	Kwacha

*African Churches **Anglican

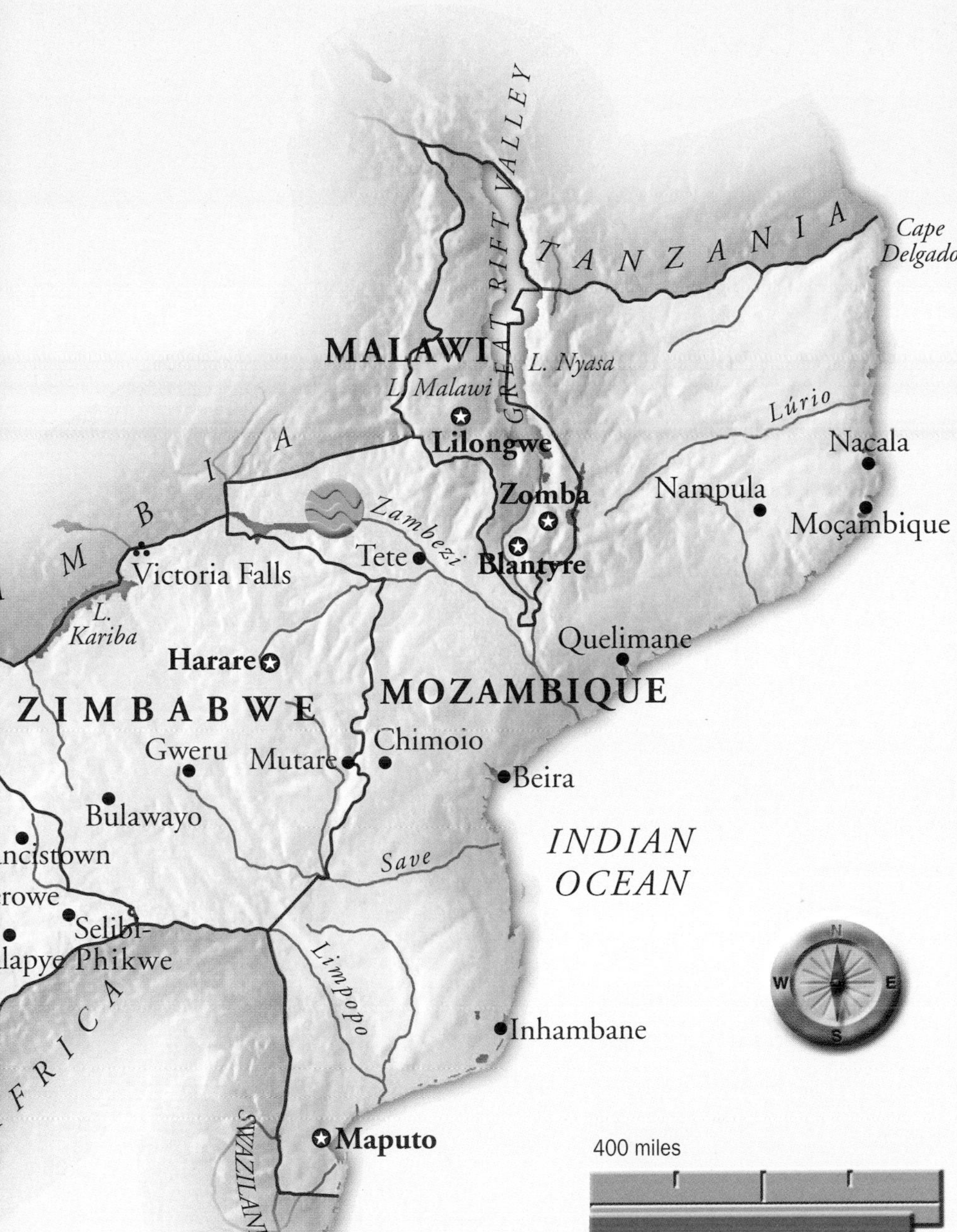

TANZANIA
GREAT RIFT VALLEY
Cape Delgado
MALAWI
L. Nyasa
L. Malawi
Lilongwe
Lúrio
Nacala
ZAMBIA
Zomba
Nampula
Zambezi
Moçambique
Victoria Falls
Tete
Blantyre
L. Kariba
Quelimane
Harare
ZIMBABWE
MOZAMBIQUE
Chimoio
Gweru
Mutare
Beira
Bulawayo
INDIAN OCEAN
Francistown
Save
Serowe
Selibi-Phikwe
Palapye
Limpopo
AFRICA
Inhambane
SWAZILAND
Maputo

Where in the world?

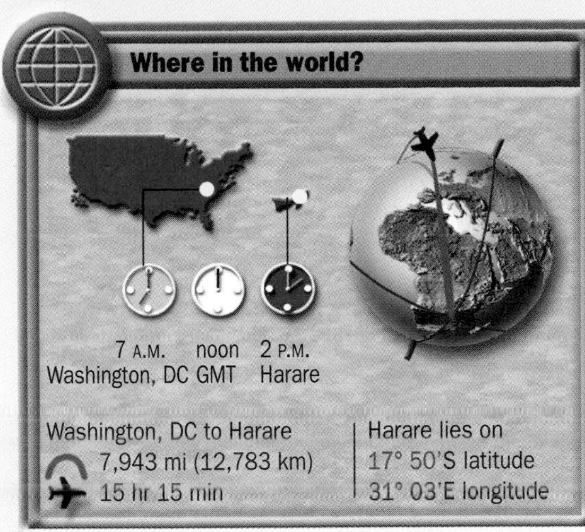

7 A.M. Washington, DC
noon GMT
2 P.M. Harare

Washington, DC to Harare
7,943 mi (12,783 km)
15 hr 15 min

Harare lies on
17° 50'S latitude
31° 03'E longitude

Life facts

	How long do people live?	How many people in 100 own cars?
U.S.A.	76 years	48
Namibia	41 years	4
Mozambique	45 years	0.5
Botswana	40 years	6
Zimbabwe	39 years	2
Malawi	37 years	0.5

400 miles

600 km

Longest rivers

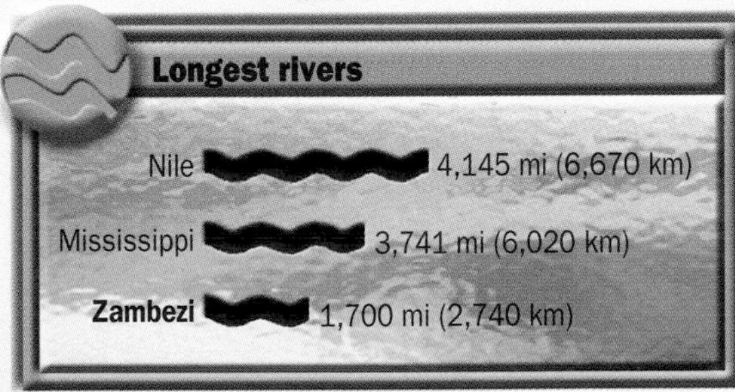

Nile 4,145 mi (6,670 km)
Mississippi 3,741 mi (6,020 km)
Zambezi 1,700 mi (2,740 km)

The thundering waters of the Victoria Falls, on the Zimbabwe-Zambia border, are at their most impressive between June and October, when the Zambezi River is in flood.

Search and find

Namibia
Capital:
Windhoek D4
Grootfontein . . .C4
Keetmanshoop . .E4
Lüderitz E4
Rehoboth D4
Swakopmund . . .D4
Walvis Bay D4

Mozambique
Capital: Maputo .E7
Beira C8
Chimoio C8
Inhambane D8
Moçambique . . .B9
Nacala B9
Nampula B9
Quelimane C8
Tete C8

Botswana
Capital: Gaborone D6
Francistown D6
Lobatse D6
Molepolole D6
Palapye D6
Selibi-Phikwe . . .D7
Serowe D6

Zimbabwe
Capital: Harare .C7
Bulawayo C7
Gweru C7
Mutare C7

Malawi
Capitals:
Lilongwe B8
Blantyre C8
Zomba B8

South Africa and Its Neighbors

SOUTH AFRICA, LESOTHO, SWAZILAND

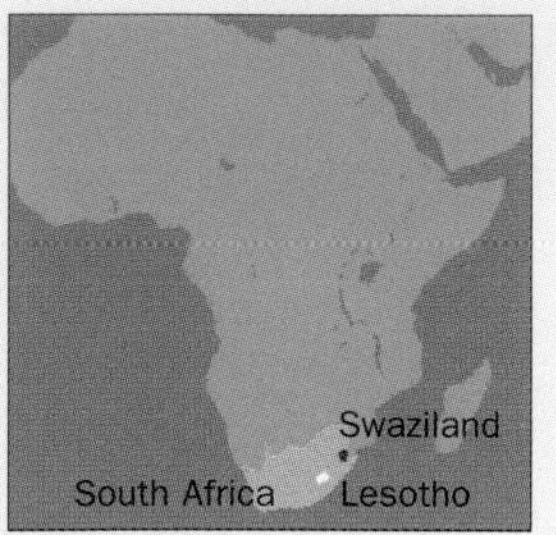
Swaziland
South Africa
Lesotho

PASSENGERS SAILING INTO CAPE Town stare at the skyline instead of the harbor, for looming above South Africa's third largest city is the awesome sight of Table Mountain, a massive slab wreathed in white clouds beneath a blue sky.

South Africa, the continent's richest country, is a land of contrasts. There are vineyards and orchards growing in the warm sunshine of the Cape Province—on the Cape of Good Hope—dusty velds (grassland), the fortresslike walls of the Drakensberg Mountains, and deep underground shafts where miners drill for gold. There are the modern, wealthy cities of Pretoria and Johannesburg, but there are also sprawling townships such as Soweto, where young black people seek to educate themselves despite desperately poor housing conditions and little chance of employment.

South Africa is a land of many peoples. There are Zulu, Xhosa, and Ndebele, and many other black African groups. There are people of Asian and mixed descent, English-speaking city dwellers and Afrikaner farmers, who are descendants of the Dutch settlers.

South African territory surrounds two small independent kingdoms, home of the Sotho and Swazi peoples. Lesotho is a land of mountains and plateaus, grazed by sheep, while the veld of Swaziland is used for corn and cattle farming.

A Swazi carries the traditional weapons of the warrior. The Swazi people live in Swaziland. They speak a language called siSwati, which is related to Zulu.

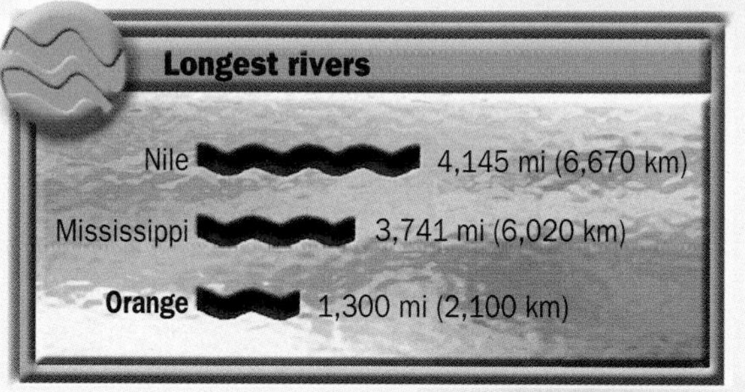
Longest rivers
Nile 4,145 mi (6,670 km)
Mississippi 3,741 mi (6,020 km)
Orange 1,300 mi (2,100 km)

BOT
Kalahari Desert
Kuruman
NAMIBIA
Upington
Alexander Bay
Namib Desert
Orange
Port Nolloth
Springbok
Kenhardt
Hart
Dougl
SOUTH AFRICA
ATLANTIC OCEAN
Carnarvon
Calvinia
Victoria West
Great Karoo
Clanwilliam
Beaufort West
Malmesbury
Cape Town
Worcester
Oudtshoorn
Paarl
Cape of Good Hope
False Bay
Hermanus
Mosselbaai
Cape Agulhas

DISCOVER MORE

- *Many South African languages include clicking sounds, which outsiders find very hard to pronounce. The Xu! language includes 48 different types of click.*
- *The fossilized footprints of three different types of dinosaur can still be seen on the bank of the Subeng River in Lesotho.*

Miners drill for ore in a South African gold mine. Many miners come from neighboring countries, such as Lesotho, as well as from South Africa itself. South Africa is the world's biggest producer of gold.

The world's biggest bird is the ostrich. It cannot fly and so runs at high speed on long, powerful legs. In South Africa, ostriches are farmed for their meat and feathers.

Highest mountains
Mount McKinley
20,320 ft
(6,194 m)
Thabana Ntlenyana
11,425 ft
(3,482 m)

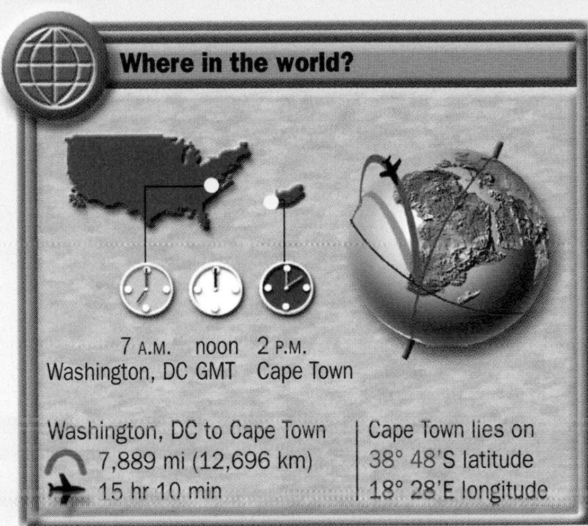
Where in the world?
7 A.M.
Washington, DC
noon
GMT
2 P.M.
Cape Town
Washington, DC to Cape Town
7,889 mi (12,696 km)
15 hr 10 min
Cape Town lies on
38° 48'S latitude
18° 28'E longitude

ZIMBABWE
BOTSWANA
MOZAMBIQUE
Limpopo
Messina
Louis Trichardt
Pietersburg
Potgietersrust
Sun City
Mafikeng
Pretoria
Middelburg
Krugersdorp
Johannesburg
Soweto
Mbabane
Vryburg
Sasolburg
Vereeniging
Manzini
Vaal
Vaaldam
SWAZILAND
Welkom
Kimberley
Thabana Ntlenyana
Ladysmith
Bloemfontein
Maseru
Empangeni
LESOTHO
Pietermaritzburg
Mafeteng
Durban
Orange
Aliwal North
DRAKENSBERG MTS
Port Shepstone
Burgersdorp
Umtata
INDIAN OCEAN
Gt. Fish
Kirkwood
East London
Grahamstown
Port Elizabeth
South Africa
Lesotho
Swaziland
N
W
E
S
200 miles
300 km

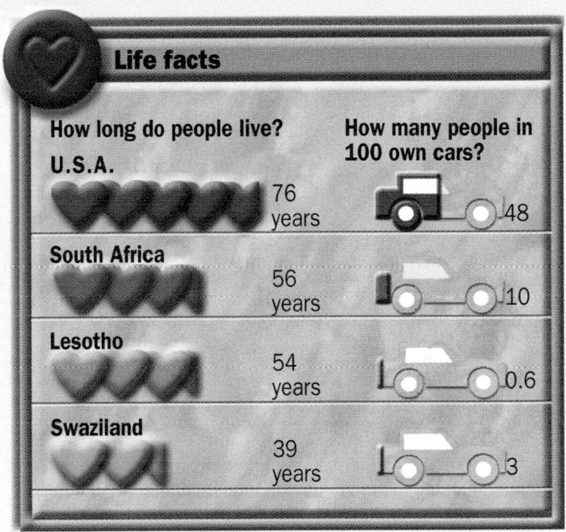
Life facts
How long do people live?
How many people in 100 own cars?
U.S.A.
76 years
48
South Africa
56 years
10
Lesotho
54 years
0.6
Swaziland
39 years
3

Search and find

South Africa
Capitals: Cape Town
(Legislative) F4
Pretoria
(Administrative) . .D7
Alexander Bay . .E4
Aliwal North F7
Beaufort West . .F5
Bloemfontein . . .E7
Burgersdorp F7
Calvinia F5
Carnarvon F5
Clanwilliam F4
Douglas E6
Durban E8
East London F7
Empangeni E8
Grahamstown . . .F7
Hermanus G4
Johannesburg . .D7
Kenhardt E5
Kimberley E6
Kirkwood F6
Krugersdorp . . .D7
Kuruman D6
Ladysmith E8
Louis Trichardt . .C8
Mafikeng D6
Malmesbury F4
Messina C8
Middelburg D8
Mosselbaai G5
Oudtshoorn F5
Paarl F4
Pietermaritzburg .E8
Pietersburg C8
Port Elizabeth . . .F6
Port Nolloth E4
Port Shepstone .F8
Potgietersrust . .C7
Sasolburg D7
Soweto D7
Springbok E4
Sun City D7
Umtata F7
Upington E5
Vereeniging D7
Victoria West . . .F5
Vryburg D6
Welkom E7
Worcester F4

Lesotho
Capital: Maseru .E7
Mafeteng E7

Swaziland
Capital:
Mbabane D8
Manzini D8

Country facts

	Area sq mi (sq km)	Population	Language	Religion	Currency
South Africa	471,008 (1,219,911)	43,426,386	Eng/Zulu/Xhosa	Trad/LCC*	Rand
Lesotho	11,718 (30,350)	2,128,950	Sesotho	Cath/Trad**	Loti
Swaziland	6,703 (17,361)	985,335	siSwati	LCC/Trad*	Lilangeni

*Traditional beliefs/local Christian churches **Catholic/Traditional beliefs

Oceania

OCEANIA IS THE SMALLEST OF ALL THE CONTINENTS, and most of its area is made up of deep, blue ocean, known mainly to sharks and swooping frigate birds. Even so, Oceania takes up a huge area of our planet, including Australia and the island of Papua New Guinea—the second largest island in the world. There are hundreds of smaller islands to be found within this vast expanse of water, but those most notable in size include New Zealand, the Solomon Islands, Vanuatu, and New Caledonia.

The largest country is Australia. It was first settled by Aboriginal peoples more than 50,000 years ago, but their descendants are greatly outnumbered by people of European (especially British) and Asian descent. Most Australians live in the big cities, for much of the back country consists of vast sheep and cattle stations, tropical forests, or empty desert.

The tropical island of New Guinea lies across the Torres Strait. Its western half is part of Indonesia, but its eastern half is an independent state, Papua New Guinea.

The islands of New Zealand, far across the Tasman Sea, are cool and green, largely given over to farming and raising sheep. Most New Zealanders are of European descent, or belong to a Polynesian people called the Maoris.

The didgeridoo is a traditional musical instrument played by the Australian Aborigines. It is made of a long wooden tube. Rhythmic sucking and blowing produce an eerie, reverberating sound.

Guam (U.S.A.)
PALAU
Irian Jaya
(INDONESIA)
PAPUA
NEW
GUINEA

ARAFURA SEA

AUSTRALIA

GREAT DIVIDING RANGE

Great Barrier

Great Australian Bight

DISCOVER MORE

- *It is estimated that more languages are spoken in Papua New Guinea than in any other country—at the latest count, 817.*
- *Pitcairn is a tiny island about halfway between Australia and South America. Its inhabitants are descended from the crew of a British naval ship called the* Bounty. *The sailors settled here in 1790 after organizing a mutiny.*
- *The Solomon Islands have 39 endangered or threatened animal species. As in many Pacific nations, they include corals, turtles, and shells.*

N
W
E
S

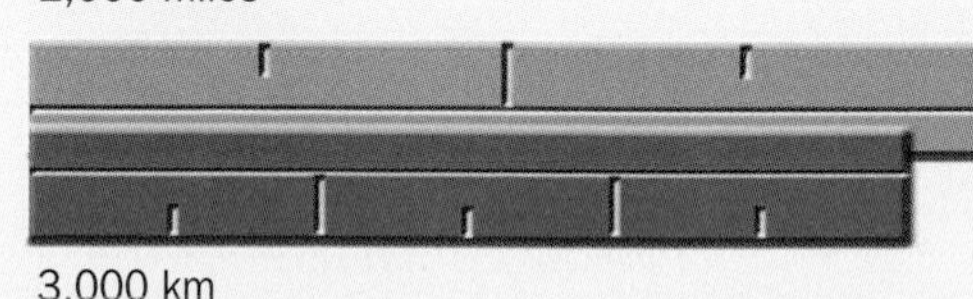
2,000 miles
3,000 km

The flightless emu is Australia's biggest bird. It weighs about 88 lb (40 kg) and has long, very powerful legs. It pecks the ground for seeds, berries, flowers, and insects.

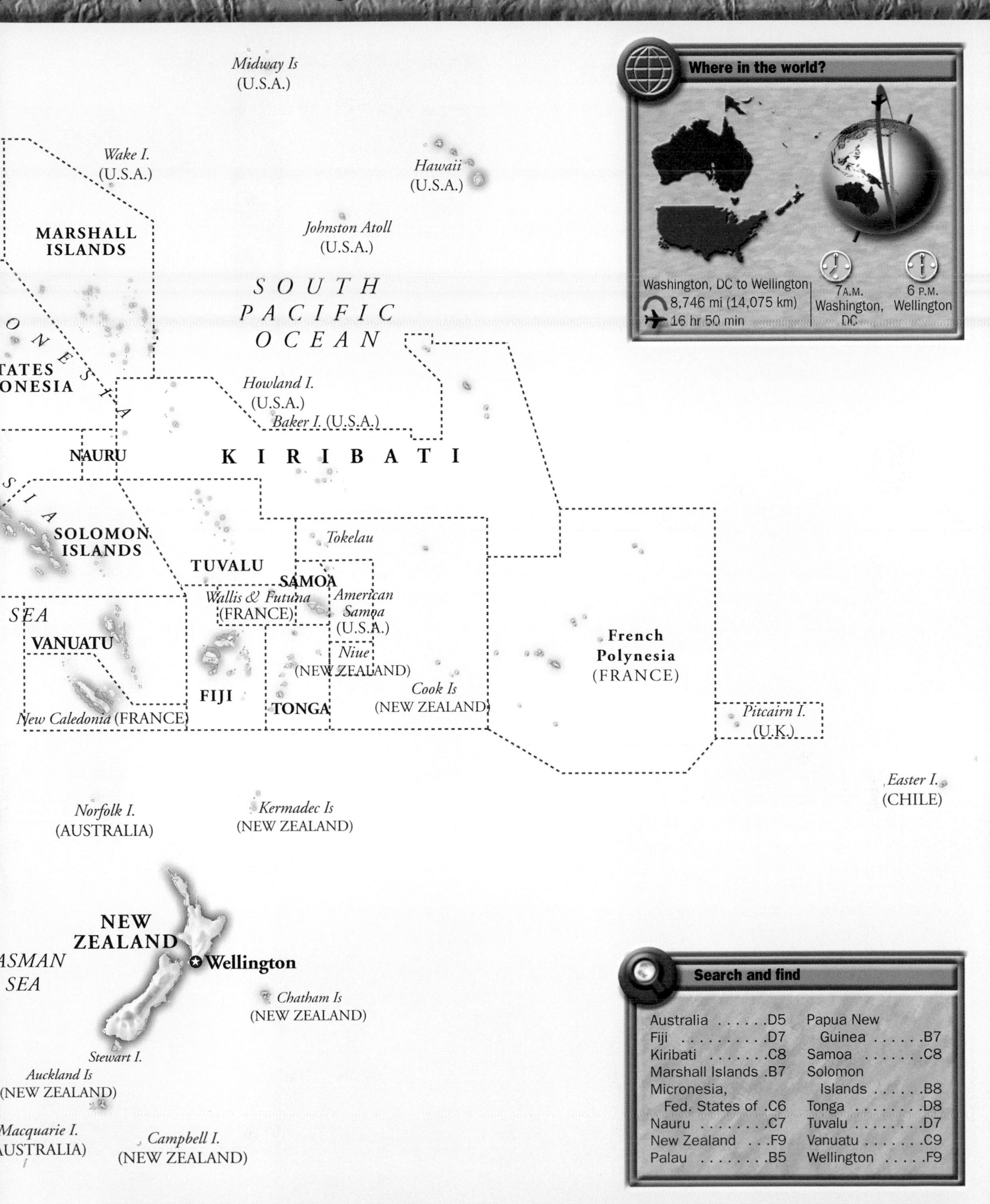

Midway Is
(U.S.A.)
Wake I.
(U.S.A.)
Hawaii
(U.S.A.)
MARSHALL ISLANDS
Johnston Atoll
(U.S.A.)
SOUTH PACIFIC OCEAN
TATES
RONESIA
Howland I.
(U.S.A.)
Baker I. (U.S.A.)
NAURU
KIRIBATI
SOLOMON ISLANDS
Tokelau
TUVALU
SAMOA
Wallis & Futuna
(FRANCE)
American Samoa
(U.S.A.)
SEA
VANUATU
Niue
(NEW ZEALAND)
French Polynesia
(FRANCE)
Cook Is
(NEW ZEALAND)
FIJI
TONGA
New Caledonia (FRANCE)
Pitcairn I.
(U.K.)
Easter I.
(CHILE)
Norfolk I.
(AUSTRALIA)
Kermadec Is
(NEW ZEALAND)
NEW ZEALAND
Wellington
ASMAN SEA
Chatham Is
(NEW ZEALAND)
Stewart I.
Auckland Is
(NEW ZEALAND)
Macquarie I.
AUSTRALIA)
Campbell I.
(NEW ZEALAND)
Where in the world?
Washington, DC to Wellington
8,746 mi (14,075 km)
16 hr 50 min
7 A.M. Washington, DC
6 P.M. Wellington
Search and find
Australia D5
Fiji D7
Kiribati C8
Marshall Islands .B7
Micronesia, Fed. States of .C6
Nauru C7
New Zealand . . .F9
Palau B5
Papua New Guinea B7
Samoa C8
Solomon Islands B8
Tonga D8
Tuvalu D7
Vanuatu C9
Wellington F9

Continent facts

	Area sq mi (sq km)	% of Earth's area	Population	Largest country by area sq mi (sq km)	Largest country by population
Oceania	3,300,000 (8,547,000)	5.7%	29,659,000	Australia 2,967,893 (7,686,843)	Australia 18,613,087

Western Australia

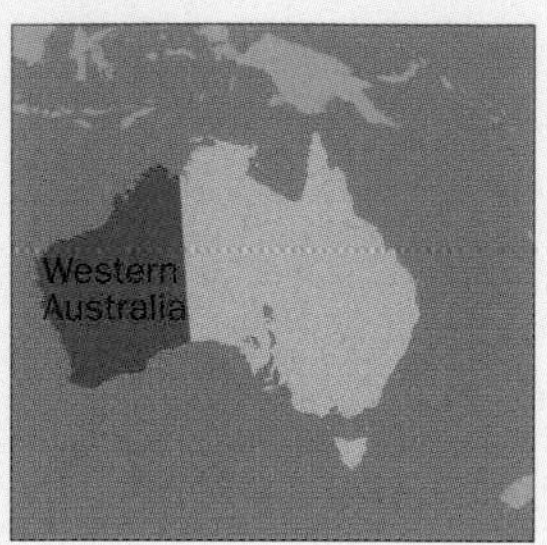
Western Australia

ALONG A DESERT TRACK, A mining truck roars, kicking up a cloud of dust. A lizard, basking in the hot sunshine, scuttles for cover. A dog barks by a shack, waiting for an Aborigine child to throw sticks.

The state of Western Australia is a very thinly populated region, which takes in storm-battered coasts on the Indian Ocean, the Great Sandy Desert, the Gibson Desert, and the Great Victoria Desert. In the north are remote cattle stations and the amazing gorges of the Purnululu (or Bungle Bungle) National Park; in the south, the flat, vast expanse of the Nullarbor Plain. The far southwest is forested, and types of eucalyptus trees known as *jarah* and *karri* are felled for their hardwood. Off the coast of North West Cape is the Ningaloo Reef, an underwater spectacle of corals and fishes. The state's mineral wealth includes gold, industrial diamonds, iron ore, bauxite, coal, and oil.

Highways converge on the state capital, Perth, and its port of Fremantle, which together are home to more than one million people. The skyscrapers are a world away from the deserts of the Australian interior, known as the "outback." In the southwest, the mild climate allows fruit, grapevines, and wheat to be grown and sheep to be raised.

The skyscrapers of downtown Perth tower over green parkland. Perth, on the Swan River, has been called the world's most remote city because it is so far from other major centers of population.

N
W
E
S

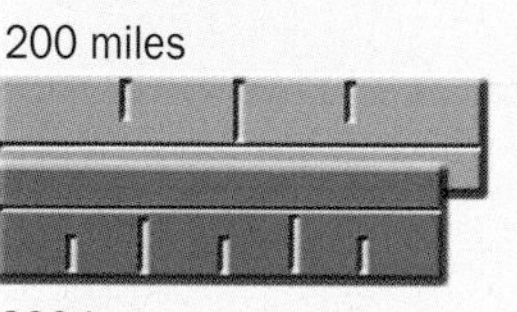
200 miles
300 km

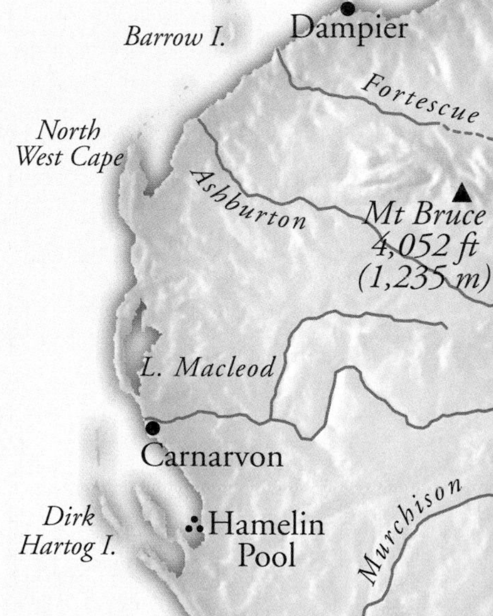
INDIAN OCEAN
Port Hedland
Dampier
Barrow I.
Fortescue
North West Cape
Ashburton
Mt Bruce 4,052 ft (1,235 m)
L. Macleod
Carnarvon
Dirk Hartog I.
Hamelin Pool
Murchison
Geraldton
Northam
Perth
Fremantle
Mandurah
Bunbury
Cape Naturaliste
Busselton
Cape Leeuwin

DISCOVER MORE

- *The Nullarbor Plain is a railroad engineer's dream. One stretch of track between West and South Australia runs absolutely straight for 297 mi (478 km).*
- *What seem to be rocks on the shore at Hamelin Pool in Western Australia are in fact stromatolites—colonies of tiny bacteria. They have been called living fossils, and are believed to be descended from the first organisms ever to develop on Earth.*

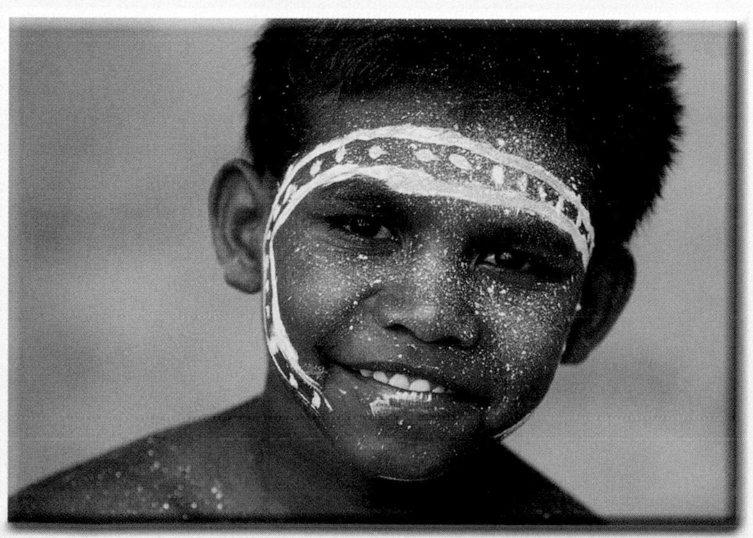

This young Aborigine comes from the Kimberley Plateau, a remote highland region in northwestern Australia. Many Australian Aborigines decorate their faces and bodies for ceremonies and dances.

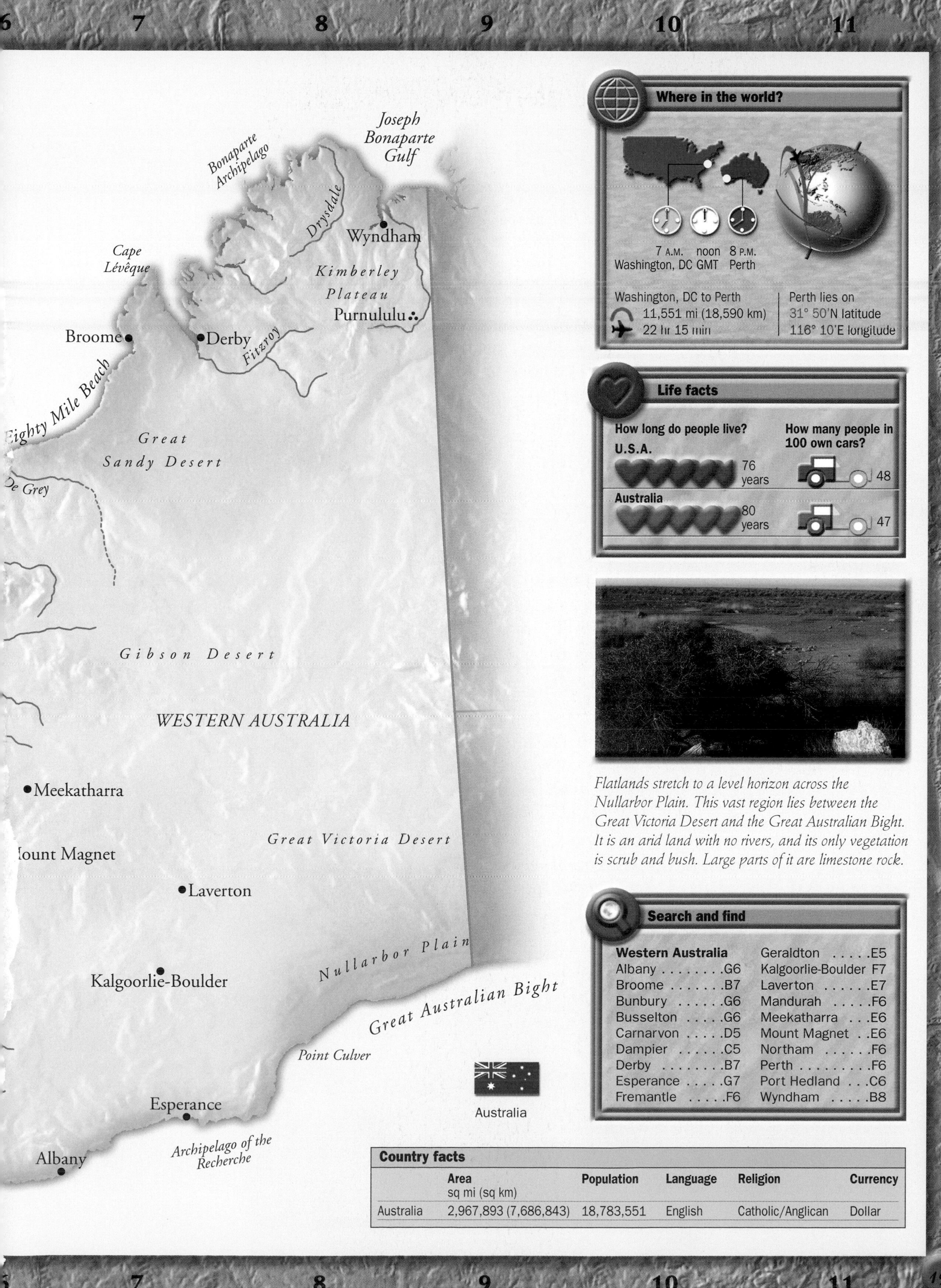
6 7 8 9 10 11
A
B
C
D
E
F
G
Joseph Bonaparte Gulf
Bonaparte Archipelago
Drysdale
Wyndham
Cape Lévêque
Kimberley Plateau
Purnululu
Broome
Derby
Fitzroy
Eighty Mile Beach
Great Sandy Desert
De Grey
Gibson Desert
WESTERN AUSTRALIA
Meekatharra
Mount Magnet
Great Victoria Desert
Laverton
Nullarbor Plain
Kalgoorlie-Boulder
Great Australian Bight
Point Culver
Esperance
Archipelago of the Recherche
Albany
Australia
Where in the world?
7 A.M. Washington, DC
noon GMT
8 P.M. Perth
Washington, DC to Perth
11,551 mi (18,590 km)
22 hr 15 min
Perth lies on
31° 50'N latitude
116° 10'E longitude
Life facts
How long do people live?
U.S.A.
76 years
Australia
80 years
How many people in 100 own cars?
48
47

Flatlands stretch to a level horizon across the Nullarbor Plain. This vast region lies between the Great Victoria Desert and the Great Australian Bight. It is an arid land with no rivers, and its only vegetation is scrub and bush. Large parts of it are limestone rock.

Search and find

Country facts

	Area sq mi (sq km)	Population	Language	Religion	Currency
Australia	2,967,893 (7,686,843)	18,783,551	English	Catholic/Anglican	Dollar

Eastern Australia

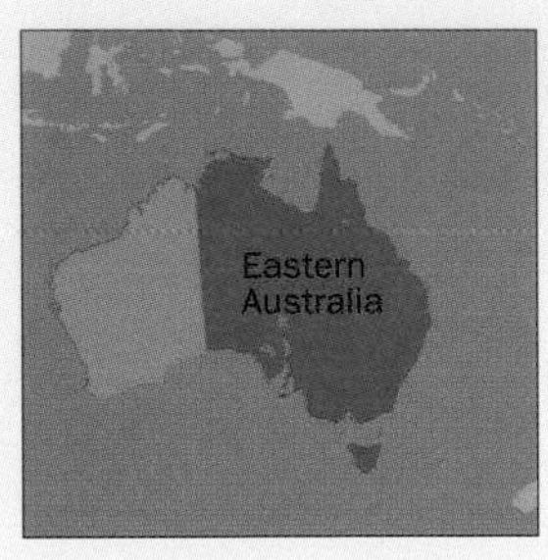
Eastern
Australia

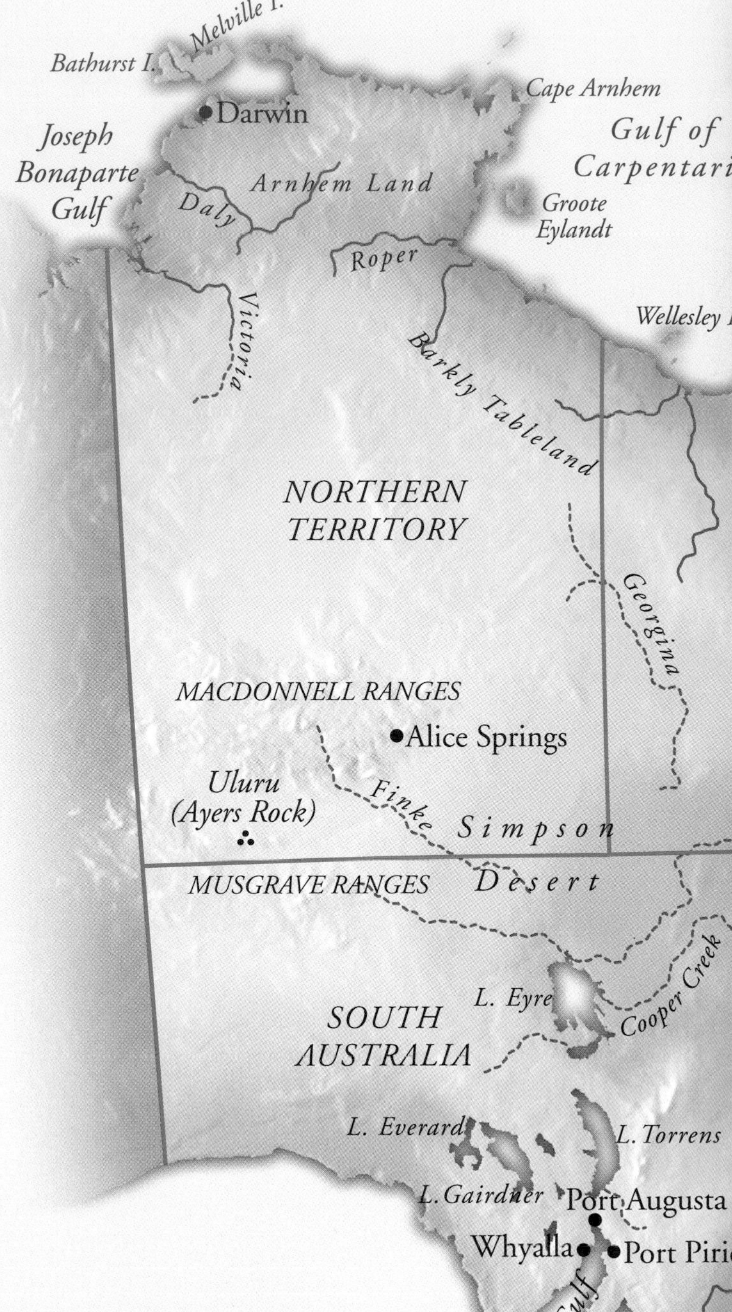
Melville I.
Bathurst I.
Darwin
Cape Arnhem
Gulf of
Carpentari
Joseph
Bonaparte
Gulf
Arnhem Land
Daly
Groote
Eylandt
Roper
Victoria
Wellesley
Barkly Tableland
NORTHERN
TERRITORY
Georgina
MACDONNELL RANGES
Alice Springs
Uluru
(Ayers Rock)
Finke
Simpson
MUSGRAVE RANGES
Desert
L. Eyre
Cooper Creek
SOUTH
AUSTRALIA
L. Everard
L. Torrens
L. Gairdner
Port Augusta
Whyalla
Port Piri
Spencer Gulf
Adelaid
Port Lincoln
Kangaroo I.
Mount Gambier

A NIGHT FLIGHT ACROSS Australia reveals very few lights. The vast landmass remains dark and mysterious. However, as the sun rises and the plane descends over Sydney, a large, sprawling city comes into view, clustered around the blue waters of its famous harbor. Most Australians live in the coastal cities of the east and south—Brisbane, Sydney, Melbourne, and Adelaide. They look outward to sandy beaches and rolling surf, rather than inland to the sparsely populated "outback." Some coastal cities have a look of London, England, about them, for modern Australia was founded by British settlers who seized the land from its original inhabitants, the Aborigines. Many of today's Australians come from other ethnic backgrounds: Greek, Italian, Lebanese, Vietnamese, and Thai.

Eastern Australia stretches from the tropical creeks and sugarcane fields of Queensland to the vineyards of South Australia, and south to the forests and cool, rocky shores of the island of Tasmania. Eastern Australia is rimmed with the mountains of the Great Dividing Range and the Australian Alps, the source of the Murray and Darling river system. The highlands enclose large areas of grassland (grazed by kangaroos and huge numbers of sheep and cattle), stands of gray-barked, fragrant eucalyptus, burning desert, and rock.

DISCOVER MORE

- *The Great Barrier Reef, running parallel to Australia's Pacific coast, is the longest coral reef in the world. Teeming with underwater life, it is more than 1,200 mi (2,000 km) long.*
- *South Australia has the world's biggest sheep station, covering more than 3,860 sq mi (10,000 sq km). Australia is the world's biggest producer of wool.*

Sydney's Opera House rises like a series of sails beside the city's harbor. The beautiful building, which was completed in 1973, has become the most familiar landmark in Oceania.

Torres Strait
Cape York
Great Barrier Reef
Cape York Peninsula
GREAT DIVIDING RANGE
Mitchell
Cairns
Gilbert
Norman
Burdekin
Townsville
PACIFIC OCEAN
Flinders
QUEENSLAND
Mackay
Diamantina
Thomson
Belyando
Cape Townsend
Rockhampton
Great Artesian Basin
Barcoo
Bundaberg
Fraser I.
Warrego
Sunshine Coast
Toowoomba
Brisbane
Gold Coast
Barwon
Grafton
NEW SOUTH WALES
Darling
GREAT DIVIDING RANGE
Maitland
Dubbo
Newcastle
Lachlan
Gosford
Wagga Wagga
Sydney
Murray
Canberra
Wollongong
Albury
AUSTRALIAN CAPITAL TERRITORY
Mt Kosciusko
Bendigo
AUSTRALIAN ALPS
VICTORIA
Ballarat
Melbourne
Geelong
Morwell
Cape Otway
Wilson's Promontory
TASMAN SEA
King I.
Bass Strait
Flinders I.
Cape Barren I.
Burnie
Devonport
Launceston
Queenstown
TASMANIA
Hobart
South East Cape

200 miles
300 km

Highest mountains

Mount McKinley
20,320 ft
(6,194 m)

Mount Kosciusko
7,310 ft
(2,229 m)

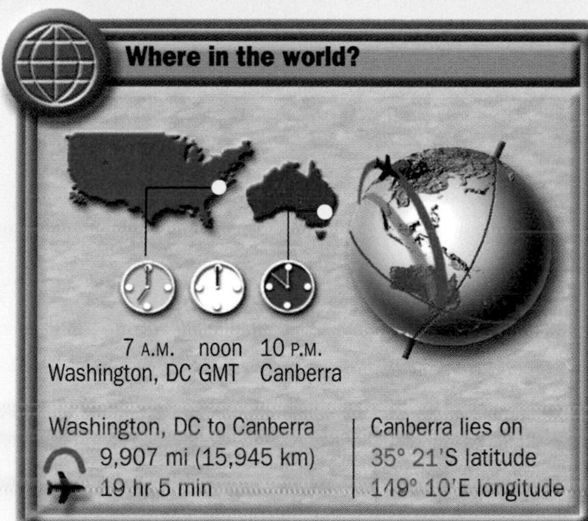
Where in the world?
7 A.M. Washington, DC
noon GMT
10 P.M. Canberra
Washington, DC to Canberra
9,907 mi (15,945 km)
19 hr 5 min
Canberra lies on
35° 21'S latitude
149° 10'E longitude

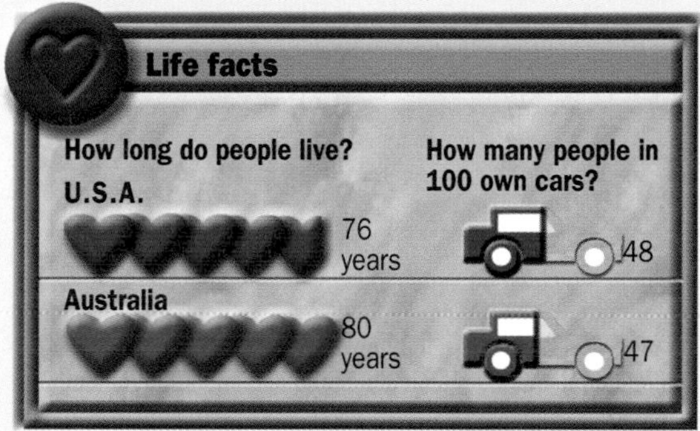
Life facts
How long do people live?
U.S.A.
76 years
Australia
80 years
How many people in 100 own cars?
48
47

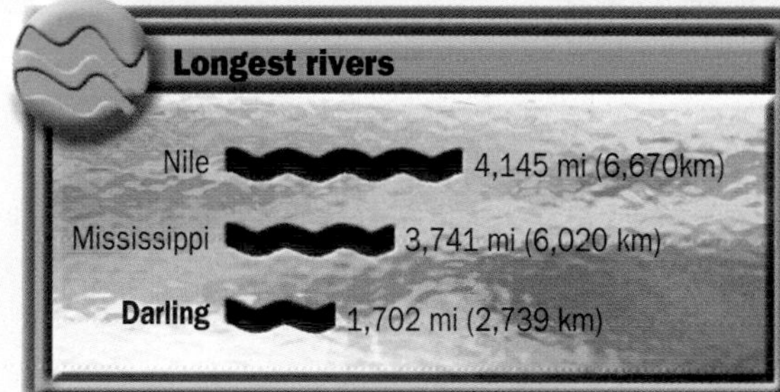
Longest rivers
Nile 4,145 mi (6,670km)
Mississippi 3,741 mi (6,020 km)
Darling 1,702 mi (2,739 km)

Search and find

Eastern Australia
Capital: Canberra F7

Adelaide	E6	Launceston	G7
Albury	E7	Mackay	C7
Alice Springs	C5	Maitland	E8
Ballarat	F6	Melbourne	F7
Bendigo	F7	Morwell	F7
Brisbane	D8	Mount Gambier	F6
Bundaberg	D8	Newcastle	E8
Burnie	G7	Port Augusta	E5
Cairns	B7	Port Lincoln	E5
Darwin	A4	Port Pirie	E5
Devonport	G7	Queenstown	G7
Dubbo	E7	Rockhampton	C8
Geelong	F7	Sunshine Coast	D8
Gold Coast	D8	Sydney	E8
Gosford	E8	Toowoomba	D8
Grafton	E8	Townsville	C7
Hobart	G7	Wagga Wagga	F7
		Whyalla	E5
		Wollongong	E8

Australia

Country facts

	Area sq mi (sq km)	Population	Language	Religion	Currency
Australia	2,967,893 (7,686,843)	18,783,551	English	Catholic/Anglican	Dollar

New Zealand

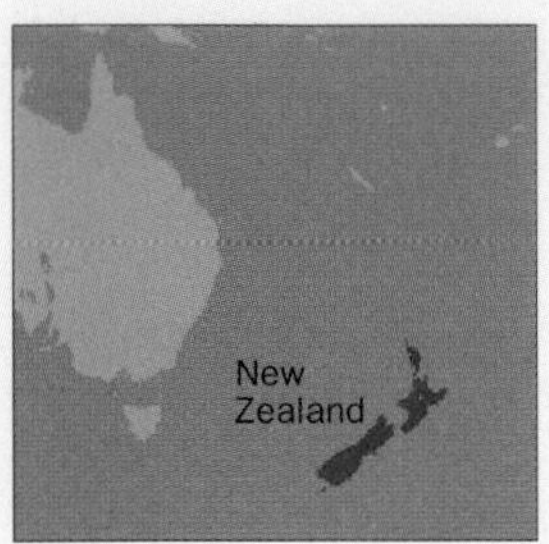
New Zealand

SET SAIL SOUTHEASTWARD from Australia, across the swell of the Tasman Sea, and after some 1,240 miles (2,000 km), high, clouded peaks rise on the horizon. These are the Southern Alps, snowy mountains, whose glaciers have carved deep sea inlets into the coastline. The highest peak, Mount Cook, towers over South Island, the largest of the island group that makes up New Zealand. The Pacific Ocean ports of Christchurch and Dunedin lie on its east coast, serving the fertile Canterbury Plains and the Central Otago plateau. Most people work on the land, fruit farming or sheep-shearing.

Most New Zealanders live across Cook Strait on North Island, many of them in the cities of Wellington or Auckland. Like many other Pacific islands, New Zealand has volcanic origins. The proof lies in North Island's bubbling hot springs and gushing geysers, plumes of water turned into steam by intense heat below the surface. The energy of these natural forces is harnessed to generate power.

New Zealanders are often nicknamed "Kiwis," after a flightless bird that lives in the forests. The original New Zealanders are the Maoris, a Polynesian people who retain many of their ancient traditions, including elaborate wood carving, choral singing, and dancing. Many New Zealanders are of European, mostly British, descent. The remainder come from Asia or other Pacific islands. The Cook Islands, Niue, and the Tokelau Islands are also governed by New Zealand.

A Maori dancer wearing traditional facial markings bares his tongue as a sign of respect. New Zealand's Polynesian people have retained a strong interest in their social and cultural traditions.

Auckland, with its modern skyline, is New Zealand's biggest city. It is a seaport, built in northern North Island between the harbors of Manukau and Waitemata.

DISCOVER MORE

- *New Zealanders have a passion for rugby. Their national team is called the All Blacks. It starts all international games with an ancient Maori war dance, the* hakka.
- *New Zealand has 15 sheep for every human.*

White Island rises from New Zealand's Bay of Plenty like an angry monster, its volcanic interior rumbling and spewing out plumes of smoke.

TASMAN SEA
Cape Foulw
Greymout
Mt Cook
SOUTHERN ALP
Jackson Head
Mt Aspiring 9,957 ft (3,036 m)
Timar
Waitaki
L. Wakatipu
L. Te Anau
Oamar
Clutha
CENTRAL OTAGO
Dunedi
Cape Providence
Invercargill
Foveaux Strait
Stewart I.

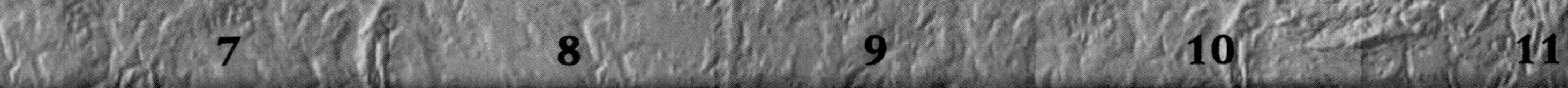
6
7
8
9
10
11

North Cape
Whangerei
Gt Barrier I.
Hauraki Gulf
Auckland

The tuatara lives on islands off the New Zealand coast. It is the only surviving species from a group of reptiles that died out about 100 million years ago.

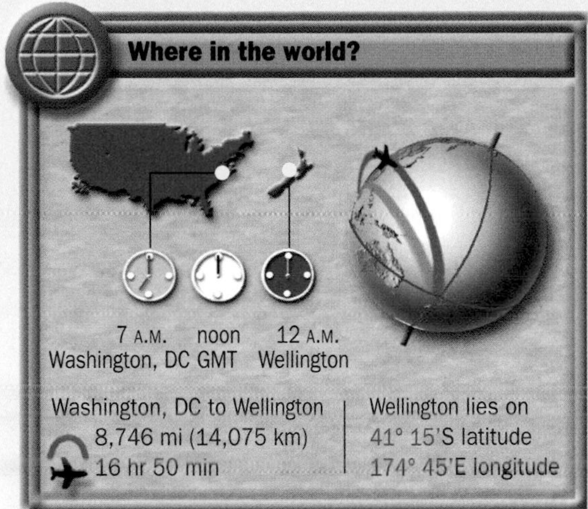
Where in the world?
7 A.M. Washington, DC
noon GMT
12 A.M. Wellington
Washington, DC to Wellington
8,746 mi (14,075 km)
16 hr 50 min
Wellington lies on
41° 15'S latitude
174° 45'E longitude

A

B

Bay of Plenty
Hamilton
Tauranga
East Cape
Rotorua
Waikato
RAUKUMARA RANGE
Gisborne
L. Taupo
New Plymouth
Ruapehu
9,175 ft
(2,797 m)
L. Waikaremoana
Poverty Bay
Cape Egmont
Wanganui
Hawke Bay
Mahia Peninsula
Napier
Hastings
NORTH ISLAND

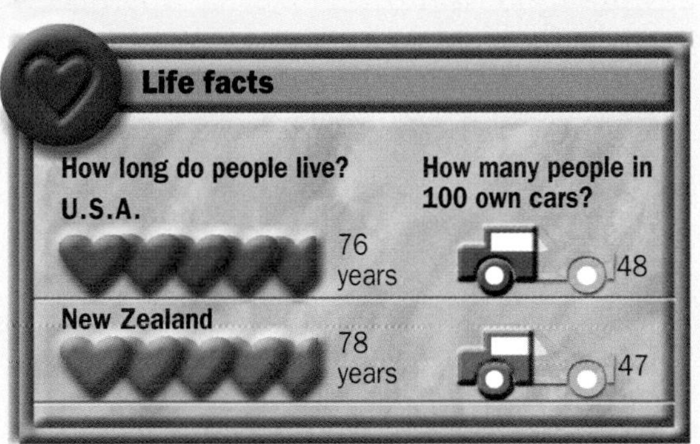
Life facts
How long do people live?
U.S.A.
76 years
New Zealand
78 years
How many people in 100 own cars?
48
47

C

Cape Farewell
Golden Bay
Tasman Bay
Nelson
Cook Strait
Palmerston North
PACIFIC OCEAN
Wellington
Blenheim
Cape Palliser
Westport
Tapuaenuku
9,465 ft (2,886 m)
SOUTH ISLAND
Pegasus Bay
Christchurch
Canterbury Plains
Banks Peninsula
Canterbury Bight

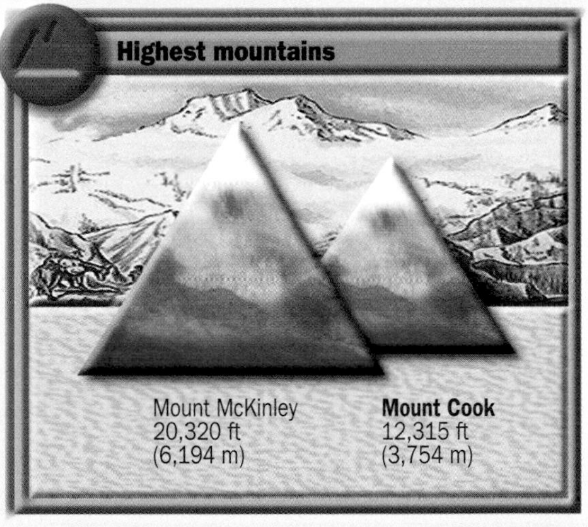
Highest mountains
Mount McKinley
20,320 ft
(6,194 m)
Mount Cook
12,315 ft
(3,754 m)

D

E

New Zealanders are proud of their sheep-shearing skills. They have plenty of practice. Wool is among the country's chief exports.

Search and find

New Zealand
Capital:
Wellington . . .D7
Auckland B7
Blenheim D7
Christchurch . . .E7
Dunedin F6
Gisborne C9
Greymouth E6
Hamilton B8
Hastings C8
Invercargill G5
Napier C8
Nelson D7
New Plymouth . .C7
Oamaru F6
Palmerston North D8
Rotorua C8
Tauranga B8
Timaru F6
Wanganui D8
Westport D6
Whangerei B7

F

N
W
E
S

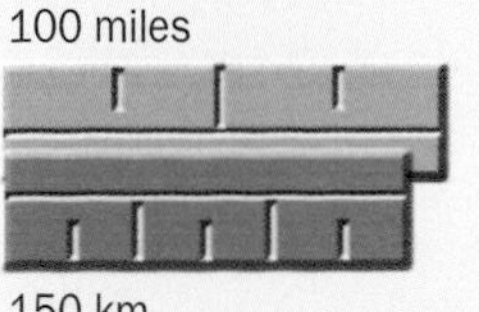
100 miles
150 km

New Zealand

Country facts

	Area sq mi (sq km)	Population	Language	Religion	Currency
New Zealand	107,737 (279,039)	3,662,265	English	NR/Ang/Pres*	Dollar

*Non-religious/Anglican/Presbyterian

G

6 7 8 9 10 11

Pacific Ocean
and Islands

FLYING FISH SKIM OVER THE BLUE OCEAN SWELL, WHILE DEEP below the surface, giant squid propel themselves through inky black waters. Extending from the Arctic in the north to the Antarctic in the south, from Asia to the west and the Americas to the east, the Pacific Ocean is circled by a "ring of fire," a danger zone for earthquakes and volcanoes. These may trigger gigantic waves called tsunamis. Covering 64,186,300 square miles (1,662,425,000 sq km), the Pacific Ocean is the largest ocean in the world.

Volcanoes and coral reefs form chains of tiny islands across the Pacific Ocean. Pacific peoples may be grouped into three main cultures: Polynesians, Melanesians, and Micronesians. There are also people of European and South Asian descent. Island crafts include carving in stone and wood, basketry, and matting. The islanders are famous for their love of song and dance.

Papua New Guinea and its islands have copper mines, and tea and coffee plantations. There are also forests, mountains, and valleys where warriors dress for festivals. Eastward are the sugarcane fields of Fiji, the barren landscape of Nauru, wasted by phosphate mining, and small islands exporting copra (dried coconut). People live by growing taro (a tuber crop), fishing, or farming.

Travel and communication between so many tiny, remote, and reef-encircled islands can be very difficult.

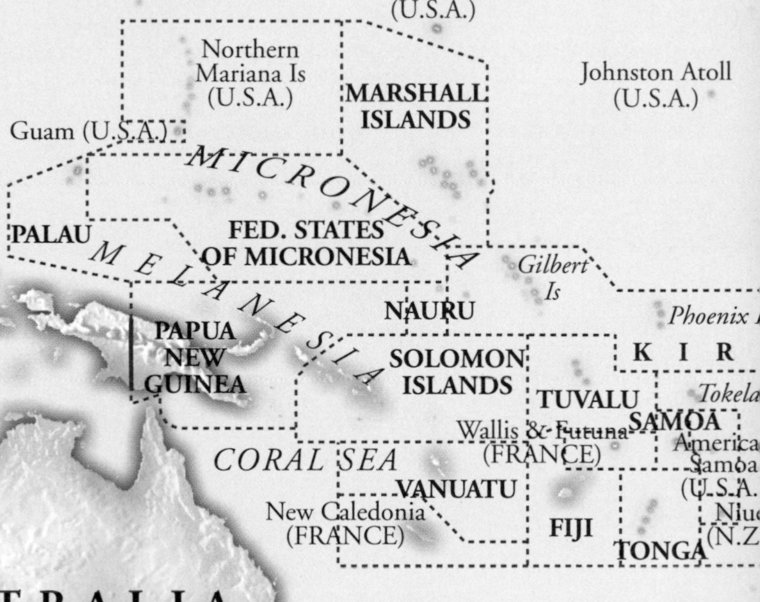

BERING SEA
Aleutian Is
ASIA
NORTH PACIFIC OCEAN
Midway Is (U.S.A.)
Wake I. (U.S.A.)
Northern Mariana Is (U.S.A.)
Johnston Atoll (U.S.A.)
MARSHALL ISLANDS
Guam (U.S.A.)
MICRONESIA
PALAU
FED. STATES OF MICRONESIA
MELANESIA
Gilbert Is
NAURU
Phoenix
PAPUA NEW GUINEA
SOLOMON ISLANDS
KIR
TUVALU
Tokela
SAMOA
Wallis & Futuna (FRANCE)
America Samoa (U.S.A.)
CORAL SEA
VANUATU
New Caledonia (FRANCE)
FIJI
TONGA
Niu (N.Z.)
AUSTRALIA
Norfolk I. (AUSTRALIA)
Gt Barrier I.
NEW ZEALAND
Chatham Is (N.Z.)
Stewart I.
Auckland Is (N.Z.)
Campbell I. (N.Z.)

DISCOVER MORE

- *Easter Island is famous for the huge statues carved from stone and erected by Polynesian people between A.D. 1000–1600. We do not know why they were made.*
- *The longest atoll on earth is Kwajalein. It is situated in the Marshall Islands, and is 175 mi (283 km) long.*

Yachts anchor in Opunohu Bay, on the island of Moorea, 12 mi (19 km) northwest of Tahiti, in French Polynesia. Moorea's warm climate makes it possible to produce coffee, vanilla, and copra.

6
7
8
9
10
11

A B C D E F G

Papua New Guinea | Solomon Islands | Fiji | Vanuatu

Samoa | Kiribati | Tonga | Micronesia

Palau | Marshall Islands | Nauru | Tuvalu

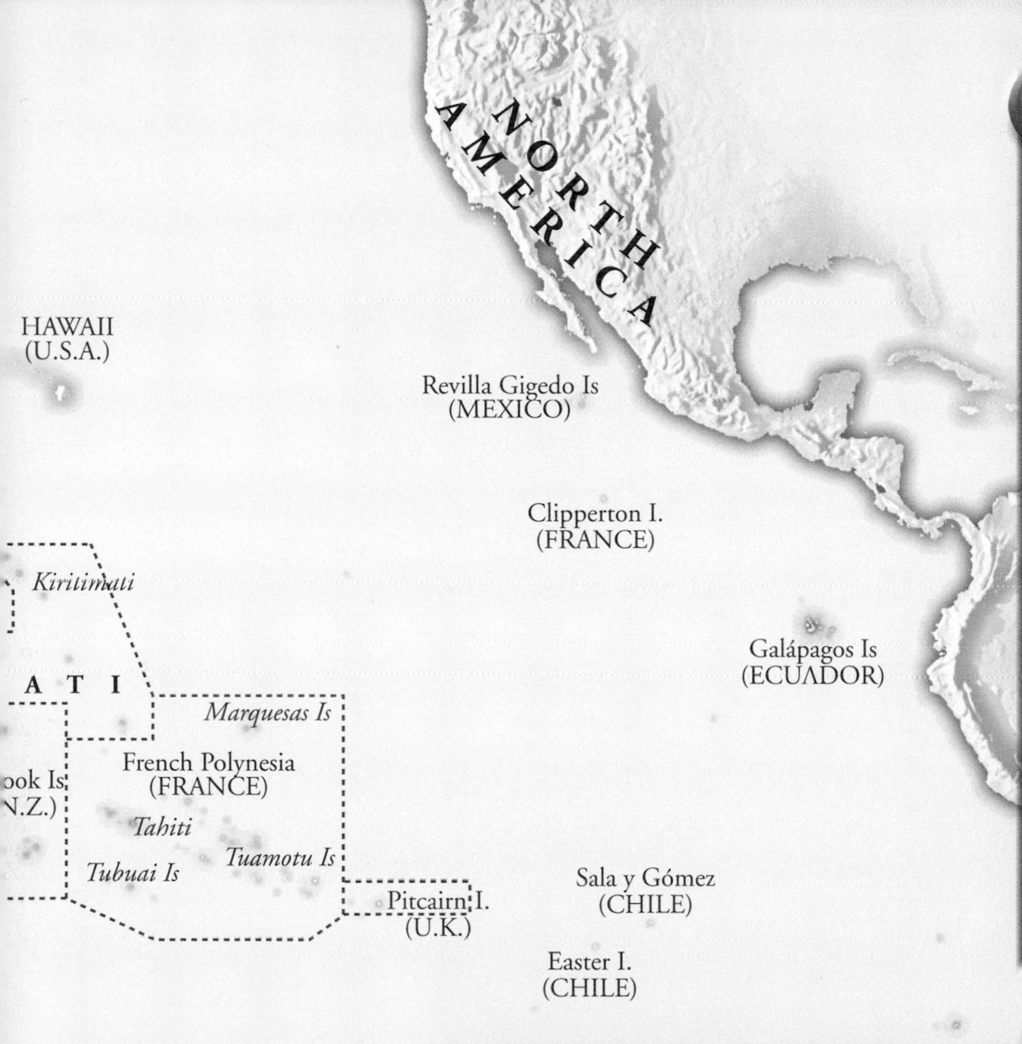

Where in the world?

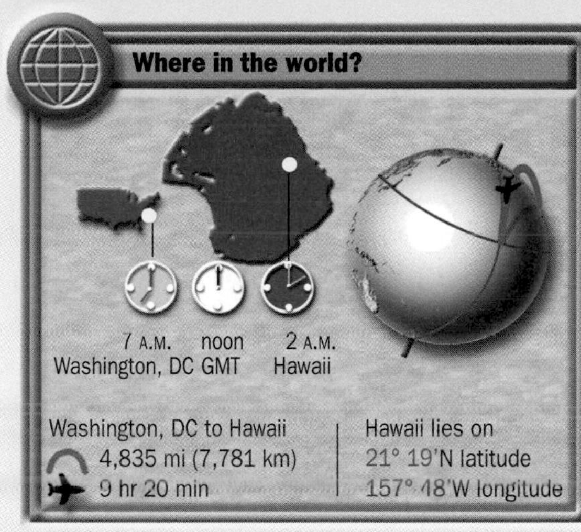

7 A.M.
Washington, DC
noon
GMT
2 A.M.
Hawaii

Washington, DC to Hawaii

4,835 mi (7,781 km)

9 hr 20 min

Hawaii lies on

21° 19'N latitude

157° 48'W longitude

NORTH AMERICA

HAWAII (U.S.A.)

Revilla Gigedo Is (MEXICO)

Clipperton I. (FRANCE)

Galápagos Is (ECUADOR)

Kiritimati

ATI

Marquesas Is

French Polynesia (FRANCE)

ook Is (N.Z.)

Tahiti

Tuamotu Is

Tubuai Is

Pitcairn I. (U.K.)

Sala y Gómez (CHILE)

Easter I. (CHILE)

SOUTH PACIFIC OCEAN

Search and find

Country facts

	Area sq mi (sq km)	Population	Language	Religion	Currency
Papua New Guinea	178,703 (462,841)	4,599,785	PidginEnglish/English	Catholic/Lutheran	Kina
Solomon Islands	10,985 (28,451)	441,039	English/PidginEnglish	Anglican	Dollar
Fiji	7,054 (18,270)	802,611	Fijan/English/Hindi	Hindu/Methodist	Dollar
Vanuatu	4,707 (12,191)	185,204	Bislama	Presbyterian	Vatu
Samoa	1,104 (2,859)	224,713	Samoan	Mormon/Cong*	Tala
Kiribati	313 (811)	83,976	English/Kiribati	Catholic	Australian Dollar
Tonga	289 (749)	108,207	Tongan	Free Wesleyan	Pa'anga
Micronesia	271 (702)	129,658	English/Chuukese	Catholic/Cong*	US Dollar
Palau	188 (487)	18,110	Palauan/English	Catholic/Trad***	US Dollar
Marshall Islands	70 (181)	63,031	Marshallese/English	Cong*/NR**/Catholic	US Dollar
Nauru	21 (54)	10,501	Nauruan	Cong*	Australian Dollar
Tuvalu	10 (26)	10,444	Tuvaluan	Church of Tuvalu	Australian Dollar

*Congregational **Non-religious ***Tradional beliefs

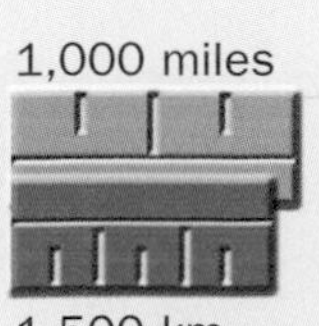

1,000 miles
1,500 km

N
W
E
S

Antarctica

NOBODY LIVES HERE. VISITING SCIENTISTS have set up bases to study the ice, the rocks, and the climate (which in recent years has become warmer). But this is still the coldest and windiest place on Earth, a frozen wilderness where nobody would want to settle. Blizzards howl over the mountain ridges, glaciers and the great shelves of permanent ice that extend from parts of the coast. Penguins huddle together for warmth on the shores, but no wild animals survive in the interior. During the southern winter (when the northern part of the world is experiencing summer), gloom and darkness settle over the landscape. In summer, the snowfields dazzle the eye, and huge icebergs drift out to sea.

The Antarctic continent is surrounded by the southern Atlantic, Indian, and Pacific Oceans, with the Ross and Weddell seas biting in deep toward the center of the landmass and the world's most southerly point, the South Pole. Mountain ranges run across the center. In this land of ice, a fiery volcano, Mount Erebus, rises from the Ross Sea.

Many countries claim Antarctic territory, largely because of the mineral wealth that lies hidden deep beneath the ice and the rich fishing offered by its oceans. However, the future of the continent is to be decided by the international community—and no decisions have been made yet.

ATLANTIC OCEAN
South Orkney Is
South Shetland Is
Cape Norvegia
Coats Land
WEDDELL SEA
Graham Land
Antarctic Peninsula
Halley (U.K.)
Palmer Archipelago
Palmer (U.S.A.)
Palmer Land
Berkner I.
Alexander I.
Ronne Ice Shelf
Charcot I.
PENSACOLA MTS
BELLINGSHAUSEN SEA
Ellsworth Land
Vinson Massif 16,864 ft (5,141 m)
Walgreen Coast
WEST ANTARCTICA
Thurston I.
AMUNDSEN SEA
Marie Byrd Land
Siple I.
Roosevelt I.
Cape Colbeck
PACIFIC OCEAN
Scott I.

DISCOVER MORE

- *The thickest parts of the Antarctic ice cap are more than 3 mi (5 km) thick.*
- *Seventy percent of the world's freshwater is locked up in the ice of Antarctica.*
- *The coldest temperature ever recorded was –192°F (–89°C), at the Vostok base in Antarctica in 1983.*

In Antarctica, one can still get some idea of what the world must have been like before its habitation by plants, animals, and people.

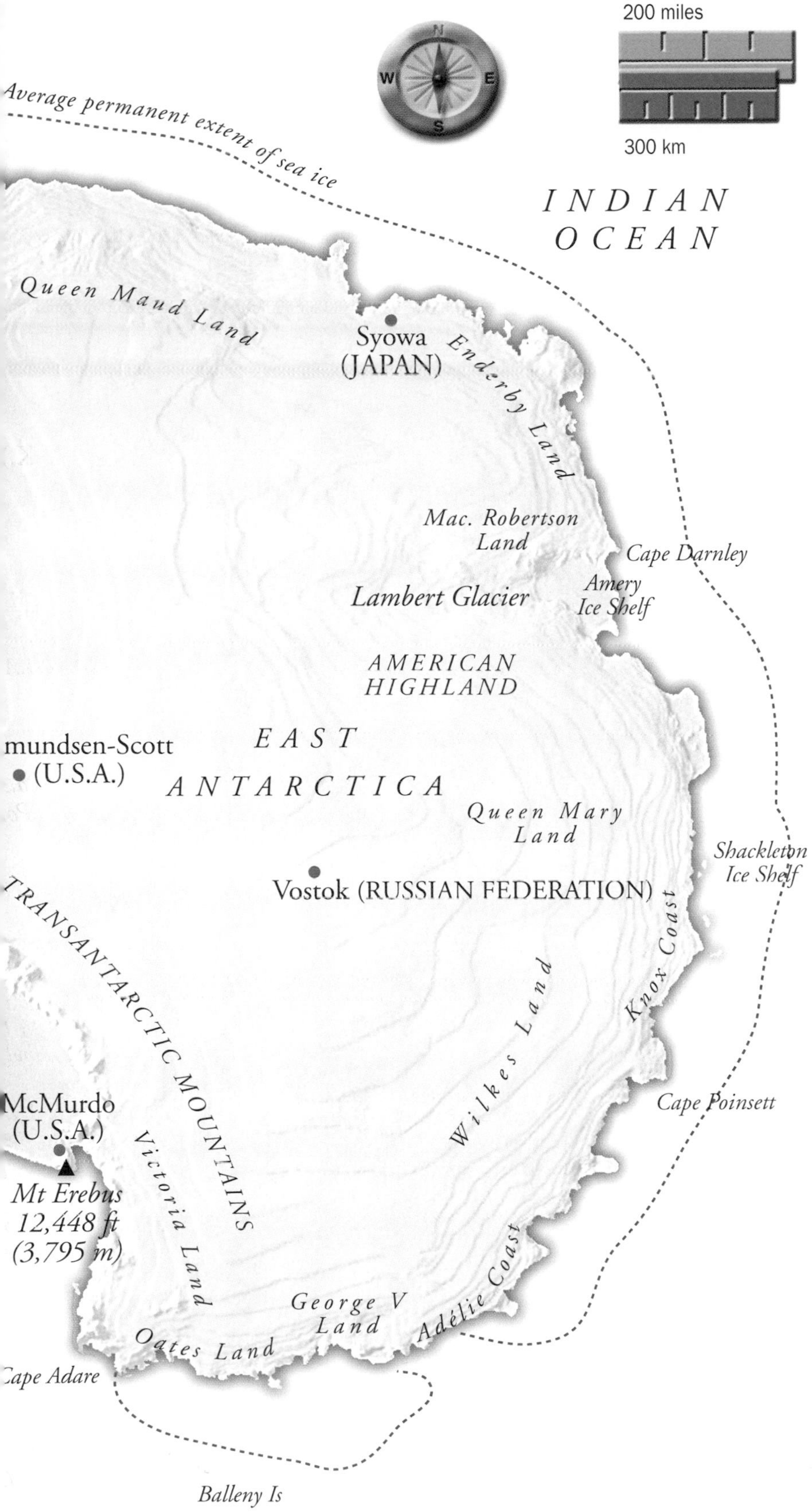

200 miles

300 km

Average permanent extent of sea ice

INDIAN OCEAN

Queen Maud Land

Syowa (JAPAN)

Enderby Land

Mac. Robertson Land

Cape Darnley

Lambert Glacier

Amery Ice Shelf

AMERICAN HIGHLAND

mundsen-Scott (U.S.A.)

EAST ANTARCTICA

Queen Mary Land

Shackleton Ice Shelf

Vostok (RUSSIAN FEDERATION)

TRANSANTARCTIC MOUNTAINS

Knox Coast

Wilkes Land

Cape Poinsett

McMurdo (U.S.A.)

Victoria Land

Mt Erebus 12,448 ft (3,795 m)

George V Land

Adélie Coast

Oates Land

Cape Adare

Balleny Is

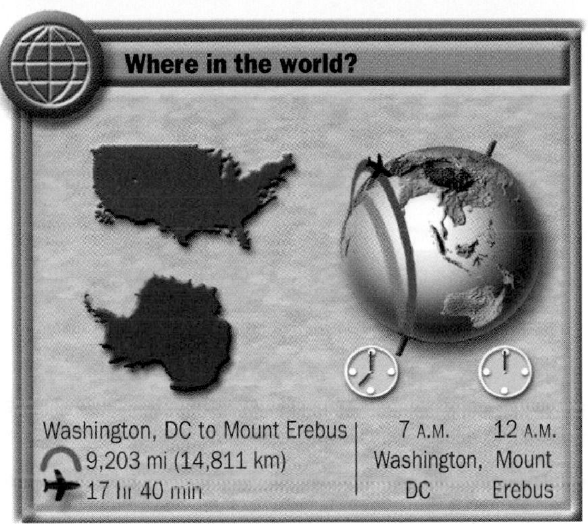
Where in the world?
Washington, DC to Mount Erebus
9,203 mi (14,811 km)
17 hr 40 min
7 A.M. Washington, DC
12 A.M. Mount Erebus

Emperor penguins form large colonies around the ice-bound Antarctic coast. The adult birds recognize the call of their own chicks when they return after a long swimming expedition in search of food.

Search and find

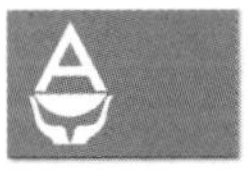

Antarctica

Continent facts	Area sq mi (sq km)	% of Earth's area	Population
Antarctica	5,400,000 (13,986,000)	9.3	uninhabited

Arctic Ocean
and Islands

An explorer battles across the Arctic ice, heading for the North Pole. His feet drag with exhaustion, his beard is rimed with frost. He is not crossing land, but the thick ice of the Arctic Ocean. Here it is so cold that the sea is permanently frozen over. Summer nights remain bright, while winter days are dark, lit only by the flickering patterns of the Northern Lights.

The edges of the great ice cap break up into floes, which drift in bitterly cold waters. Arctic seas are home to whales, fish, walrus, and seals, hunted by polar bears. In recent years, the world's climate has become warmer, and scientists fear that the ice cap is melting and that arctic wildlife will possibly soon be threatened.

Arctic Ocean islands include nine in the Norwegian territory of Svalbard. Greenland is a land of ice, settled only in coastal areas. Belonging to the North American continent, it is a self-governing Danish territory. The arctic mainland is made up of Alaska, Canada, Scandinavia, and Russia. Most of it is tundra, a deep-frozen, treeless plain, covered in snow and ice for most of the year.

Over the ages, humans have settled these harsh lands and learned to survive by hunting or by herding reindeer. They include the Inuit and related peoples of North America, the Saami of Scandinavia, the Nenets, Chukchi, and other peoples of Arctic Russia.

In recent years many Arctic peoples have had to adapt to a more modern way of life but at the same time try to protect their traditions. They have demanded greater control over their own affairs.

ALASKA (U.S.A.)
Bering Strait
CHUKCHI SEA
Barrow
Point Barrow
CANADA
BEAUFORT SEA
Cape Bathurst
Banks I.
M'Clure Strait
Victoria I.
Melville I.
Prince of Wales I.
North Magnetic Pole
Devon I.
Ellesmere I.
LINCOLN SEA
Foxe Basin
Baffin I.
Baffin Bay
Davis Strait
GREENLAND (DENMARK)
Denmark Strait
ICELAND

DISCOVER MORE

- *Greenland is generally considered to be the biggest island in the world, with an area of 840,000 sq mi (2,175,600 sq km). That's nearly one-quarter the size of the United States. Beneath its 1.8-mi (3-km)-thick cap of ice, Greenland is actually made up of three islands of rock.*

Arctic icebergs break off, or calve, from glaciers in Alaska and Greenland and float out to sea. They pose a danger to ships sailing in the area.

6
7
8
9
10
11

200 miles
300 km

Ambarchik
EAST SIBERIAN SEA
RUSSIAN FEDERATION
New Siberian Is
LAPTEV SEA
ARCTIC OCEAN
Nordvik
Severnaya Zemlya
North Pole
Dikson
Franz Josef Land
Average permanent extent of sea ice
KARA SEA
Novaya Zemlya
Svalbard
BARENTS SEA
GREENLAND SEA
North Cape
Murmansk
NORWEGIAN SEA
NORWAY
SWEDEN
FINLAND
Arctic Circle

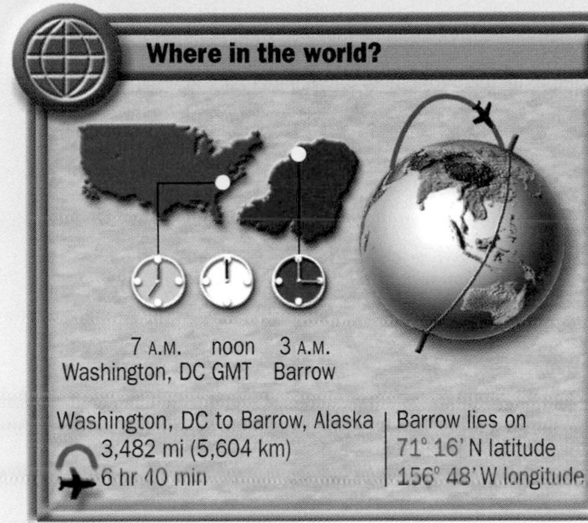

Where in the world?
7 A.M. Washington, DC
noon GMT
3 A.M. Barrow
Washington, DC to Barrow, Alaska
3,482 mi (5,604 km)
6 hr 40 min
Barrow lies on
71° 16′ N latitude
156° 48′ W longitude

Search and find

Ambarchik B7	New Siberian Islands B7
Baffin Island . . .D4	Nordvik C8
Banks Island . . .C5	Novaya Zemlya .D8
Barrow C6	Prince of Wales Island C4
Devon Island . . .D5	Svalbard E7
Dikson D8	Svernaya Zemlya C7
Ellesmere Island D5	Victoria Island . .C4
Franz Josef Land D7	
Melville Island . .C5	
Murmansk E7	

At the top of the world, the sun is still shining at midnight in midsummer.

The polar bear, an excellent swimmer, is perfectly adapted to its environment, with its thick, white coat.

A
B
C
D
E
F
G

6 7 8 9 10 11

Dependencies

A dependency is a territorial unit under the jurisdiction of another state, but not formally annexed to it. Some territories are too small to appear on the atlas maps. Their approximate positions are given here.

Territory	Administered by	Area sq mi (sq km)	Population	Language	Religion	Currency	Page number
American Samoa	U.S.A.	77 (199)	62,100	Samoan/English	Congregationalist	Dollar	191, 198
Anguilla	U.K.	37 (96)	12,400	English/Creole	Anglican	East Caribbean dollar	60 mi NW of St. Kitts & Nevis (73)
Aruba	Netherlands	75 (193)	89,000	Dutch/Papiamento	Catholic	Aruban florin	41, 73
Ashmore & Cartier Is	Australia	2 (5)	uninhabited	–	–	–	off N coast of western Australia (193)
Bermuda	U.K.	21 (54)	62,100	English	Anglican/Methodist	Bermuda dollar	41, 88
Bouvet I.	Norway	23 (59)	uninhabited	–	–	–	89
British Indian Ocean Territory	U.K.	23 (60)	2,900 (military)	English	–	Dollar	Indian Ocean (124)
British Virgin Is	U.K.	59 (153)	16,800	English	Anglican/Catholic/ Methodist	Dollar	60 mi E of Puerto Rico (41)
Cayman Is	U.K.	100 (259)	35,000	English	Anglican/Catholic	Cayman Is dollar	72
Christmas I.	Australia	52 (135)	2,500	English/Chinese	Buddhist/Taoist	Australian dollar	169
Clipperton I.	France	3 (7)	uninhabited	–	–	–	199
Cocos Is	Australia	6 (14)	590	English/Malay	Sunni Islam	Australian dollar	169
Cook Is	New Zealand	92 (237)	18,000	English/Cook Islands Maori	Cook Is Christian Church	New Zealand dollar	191, 196, 199
Coral Sea Is Territory	Australia	5 (8)	3*	–	–	–	off NE coast of Australia (195)
Falkland Is	U.K.	4,698 (12,170)	2,600	English	Anglican	Falkland pound	75, 86, 88
Faroe Is	Danish	540 (1,399)	43,800	Faeroese/Danish	Evangelical Lutheran	Faeroese krona	89, 90
French Guiana	France	33,399 (86,503)	169,000	French/Creole	Catholic	French franc	74, 79
French Polynesia	France	1,544 (4,000)	228,000	French/Tahitian	Evangelical Church of Polynesia	French Pacific franc	191, 199
Gibraltar	U.K.	2.5 (6.5)	27,100	English	Catholic	Gibraltar pound	90, 100
Greenland	Denmark	840,000 (2,175,600)	56,300	Greenland Inuit/ Danish	Evangelical Lutheran	Danish krona	41, 88
Guadeloupe	France	687 (1,779)	434,000	French/Creole	Catholic	French franc	41, 68, 73
Guam	U.S.A.	209 (541)	148,000	English/Chamorro/ Filipino	Catholic	Dollar	190, 198
Guernsey	U.K.	30 (79)	61,700	English	Anglican/Catholic	Pound	94
Heard & McDonald Is	Australia	161 (417)	uninhabited	–	–	–	310 mi SE of Kerguelen I. (168)
Howland, Baker & Jarvis Is	U.S.A.	2 (5)	–	–	–	–	NW and E of Phoenix Is (198)
Isle of Man	U.K.	221 (572)	72,600	English	Anglican	Pound	94
Jersey	associated with U.K.	45 (116)	85,600	English/French patois	Anglican	Pound	94
Johnston Atoll	U.S.A.	0.5 (1.3)	1,200 (service personnel)	–	–	–	191, 198
Kingman Reef	U.S.A.	0.1 (0.3)	uninhabited	–	–	–	500 mi NW of Christmas I. (169)
Martinique	France	436 (1,129)	399,000	French/Creole	Catholic	French franc	41, 73
Mayotte	France	145 (376)	128,000	French/Mahorian	Sunni Islam	French franc	168
Midway I.	U.S.A.	2 (5)	military	–	–	–	191, 198
Montserrat	U.K.	38 (98)	3,500	English	Anglican/Methodist	East Caribbean dollar	41, 73
Navassa I.	U.S.A.	2 (5)	uninhabited	–	–	–	90 mi E of Jamaica (73)
Netherlands Antilles	Netherlands	309 (800)	213,000	Dutch/Papiamento/ English	Catholic	Netherlands Antilles guilder or florin	41, 73

Territory	Administered by	Area sq mi (sq km)	Population	Language	Religion	Currency	Page number
New Caledonia	France	7,172 (18,576)	204,000	French/Melanesian	Catholic	French Pacific franc	191, 198
Niue	New Zealand	100 (259)	1,710	English/Niuean	Cong. Niue Church	New Zealand dollar	191, 198
Norfolk I.	Australia	13 (34)	1,770	English/Norfolk Island	Anglican	Australian dollar	191, 198
Northern Mariana Is	U.S.A.	184 (477)	66,600	English/Chamorro/ Filipino	Catholic	Dollar	190, 198
Pitcairn I.	U.K.	5 (14)	44	English/Pitkern	Seventh Day Adventist	New Zealand dollar	191, 199
Puerto Rico	U.S.A.	3,515 (9,104)	3,808,610	Spanish/English	Catholic	Dollar	73
Réunion	France	982 (2,542)	692,000	French/Creole	Catholic	French franc	168
St. Helena	U.K.	159 (411)	7,040	English	Anglican/Baptist	Pound (local issue)	89
St. Pierre & Miquelon	France	93 (242)	6,800	French	Catholic	French franc	40 mi S of Newfoundland (65)
South Georgia & South Sandwich Is	U.K.	1,580 (4,091)	military	–	–	–	88, 89
Tokelau	New Zealand	5 (13)	1,500	English	Congregationalist	New Zealand dollar	191, 198
Turks & Caicos Is	U.K.	166 (430)	13,800	English	Anglican/Methodist	Dollar	72
Virgin Is of the U.S.A.	U.S.A.	136 (352)	118,000	English/Spanish	Baptist/Catholic	Dollar	41, 73
Wake I.	U.S.A.	3 (8)	military	–	–	–	191, 198
Wallis & Futuna Is	France	106 (274)	14,100	French/Wallisian/ Futunian	Catholic	French Pacific franc	191, 198

*meteorological station

Disputed and other territories

The following are dependencies that are disputed. Various states claim them.

Territory	Claimed by	Area sq mi (sq km)	Population	Language	Religion	Currency	Page number
Argentine Antarctic Territory	Argentina	475,314 (1,231,064)	research bases	–	–	–	200
Australian Antarctic Territory	Australia	2,333,500 (6,043,700)	research bases	–	–	–	200
British Antarctic Territory	United Kingdom	700,000 (1,800,000)	research bases	–	–	–	200
Chilean Antarctic Territory	Chile	490,240 (1,269,723)	research bases	–	–	–	200
French Southern and Antarctic Territories	France	169,806 (439,797)	research bases	–	–	–	200
Golan Heights	Syria/Israel	444 (1,150)	29,000	Hebrew/Arabic	Sunni Islam/Jewish	New Israeli shekel	134, 136
Paracel Is	China/ Vietnam	62 (160)	military	–	–	–	220 mi E of Vietnam (153)
Peter I Island	Norway	69 (180)	–	–	–	–	200
Queen Maud Land	Norway	–	research bases	–	–	–	200
Ross Dependency	New Zealand	282,000 (730,000)	research bases	–	–	–	200
Spratly Is	China/Vietnam/ Philippines/Taiwan/ Brunei/Malaysia	undefined	–	–	–	–	250 mi NW of Brunei (154)
Sovereign Military Order of Malta	Sovereign Roman Catholic Order	2 acres (1.2 hectares)	30	Italian	Catholic	Scudo	106
Western Sahara	Morocco/Polisario guerilla movement	97,344 (252,120)	281,000	Arabic	Sunni Islam	Moroccan dirham	170, 174
The following statistics relate to territory controlled by the Palestinian Authority on July 23, 2000							
Palestinian Entity	–	10,160 (26,314)	2,897,000	Arabic/Hebrew	Sunni Islam	New Israeli shekel	136

Glossary

altitude the height of land above sea level.

archipelago a group of islands that are close together.

basin 1. a bowl-shaped area of land that is lower than the surrounding area. 2. an area of land through which a river flows.

bay an inlet in the coastline of an ocean or lake, normally eroded by the waves.

bayou a shallow stretch of water that flows very slowly through a marshy or boggy area.

bluff a steep cliff.

border 1. the edge of an area of land or vegetation. 2. the area between two countries. 3. a boundary.

boundary an imaginary line that separates one country or area of land from another.

butte a steep-sided rock that stands on its own and rises sharply above the land around it.

canal a human-made waterway used for transportation or irrigation.

canyon a deep valley, with steep sides, which often has a river flowing through it.

cape a large region of land that projects from the coastline into a sea or ocean.

capital a location officially designated as the chief city of a nation, state, province, or territory, often the center of government.

channel a narrow stretch of water between two areas of land.

cinder cone a cone-shaped volcano that is made from layers of dust and tiny pieces of rock.

climate the pattern of weather conditions normally recorded in any one place or region.

coast the land that borders a sea or ocean.

compass rose the points of the compass, as displayed on a map.

continent a landmass or part of a landmass, making up one of the seven major geographical divisions of the world.

coral hard rock that is made from the shells and skeletons of tiny sea creatures.

crag a steep, rough rock formation.

crater 1. a large opening or depression at the top of a volcano. 2. a hollow in the land caused when a meteor crashes to Earth.

crust the thin layer of rock that covers Earth's surface.

current the movement of water over long distances in seas, oceans, and rivers.

delta an area in which a river splits into several separate waterways before entering the sea. It is normally created by deposits of mud or sand. The name comes from the triangular shape of such a region, which looks like the Greek letter delta (Δ).

desert an area of land that has very little or no rain.

divide a ridge or line of crests separating two drainage areas.

earthquake a shaking of the ground that happens when sections of Earth's crust move.

elevation the height above sea or ground level.

Equator an imaginary horizontal line around the middle of the globe, halfway between the North Pole and the South Pole.

estuary a river mouth, where freshwater meets and mixes with the salt water from an ocean or sea.

ethnic group a group of people sharing common descent, language, or culture.

fault line a fracture in Earth's surface along which sections of crust are forced together, or slide past each other, sometimes causing earthquakes.

fjord a long, deep-sea inlet, formed by glaciers in prehistoric times.

floodplain the flat land on either side of a river that is covered by water when the river floods.

forest any large area of dense woodland.

geyser jets of hot water and steam that gush up into the air. They are formed when rainwater seeps into the rocks and is heated by volcanic forces deep underground.

glacier a large body of ice that moves slowly along a valley or down a mountain.

gorge a narrow valley, with steep rocky sides, through which a river runs.

Greenwich mean time the mean solar time of the Greenwich Meridian, used throughout the world as the basis of standard time.

Greenwich Meridian the line of longitude (0°) from which distances to the east or west are measured. It passes through Greenwich, England. Also called the Prime Meridian.

grid a crisscross network of lines used to locate places on a map.

gulf an area of seawater that reaches into the land. A gulf is usually wide, with a narrow opening into the sea.

harbor a natural or human-made sea inlet that protects boats at their moorings.

hemisphere the globe divided into two halves, either north and south or east and west.

hill land that rises from the ground around it but is not as high as a mountain.

iceberg a large chunk of ice that floats in seas and oceans. Most of the iceberg lies hidden beneath the water's surface.

inlet a narrow stretch of water that cuts into the land from a sea or a river.

International Date Line an imaginary line drawn north to south across the Pacific Ocean, which notes where one day ends and another begins. For instance, if it were Monday on the west side of the line, it would be Sunday on the east side of the line.

island an area of land completely surrounded by water.

isthmus a narrow stretch of land connecting two larger bodies of land.

lagoon a body of salt water that is separated from the sea by a strip of land.

lake a body of water that is surrounded by land.

landlocked surrounded by land on all sides, with no coastline.

latitude the location of a place north or south of the Equator, that is measured in degrees. Measurements are determined using imaginary horizontal lines that circle the globe, parallel to the Equator.

lava the hot liquid rock that pours out of a volcano during an eruption.

levee a wall that is built along a riverbank to stop the river from flooding.

longitude the location of a place east or west of the Greenwich Meridian, measured in degrees. Measurements are determined using imaginary vertical lines, called meridians, which run from the North Pole to the South Pole.

marsh an area of very wet land that is usually low lying.

mesa a rocky hill or mountain with a flat top and steep sides.

mineral a natural substance that is formed inside the earth, for example gold and copper.

monsoon a strong wind that brings heavy rains in the summer months in the Indian Ocean and southern Asia.

moor an area of rough, open, high ground, often boggy.

mountain a very high area of land.

mountain pass a passageway from one side of a mountain to the other.

mountain range a chain of high peaks and ridges.

mountain system a chain of mountain ranges, or ranges sharing the same geological origins.

oasis a place in the desert where there is water and some vegetation.

ocean a very large area of salt water on Earth's surface.

paddy a flooded field in which rice plants are grown.

pampas the grasslands of South America.

peak the highest point of a mountain.

peninsula a strip of land that sticks out into the sea and is almost completely surrounded by water.

pinnacle a column of rock, eroded to a slender point.

plain a large area of flat land.

plateau an area of high ground that is usually very flat.

population the people or the number of individuals living in a given place.

prairie the flat, grass-covered lands of North America.

rain forest forests with dense, evergreen vegetation fed by very high rainfall. The term normally refers to tropical forests, but can also be applied to similar forests in temperate regions.

reef a platform of rocks or coral just below the surface of the sea.

ridge a long, thin stretch of high ground.

rift valley a long valley created by movement along a fault line in Earth's crust.

river a moderate to large body of water draining off the land and normally flowing between banks toward the sea or ocean.

salt flat a large area of flat land that is covered with crystals of salt.

sand dune a hill of sand that is formed by the wind.

savanna a wide grassy plain with a few scattered trees.

scale a distance on a map shown in proportion to the real distance.

scrub an area of land that is thickly covered with low-growing trees and shrubs.

sea a body of salt water, making up an arm or region of an ocean.

solar energy energy that is produced using the sun's rays.

steppe a wide area of flat grass-covered land in eastern Europe and central Asia.

strait a narrow stretch of water connecting two larger bodies of water.

subtropics the regions bordering the tropics.

swamp an area of wet and muddy land.

territory 1. an area of land that does not have the status of an independent nation. 2. a province or region within a nation.

time zone a large area where every place has the same time. The world is divided into 24 different time zones. The time in each zone is one hour behind or in front of the time in the neighboring zones.

tree line the point above which trees do not grow due to poor soil and climate conditions.

tributary a stream or river that flows into another one during its journey to the ocean.

Tropic of Cancer a line of latitude (23.5° north of the Equator) marking the northernmost point reached by the overhead sun on July 21.

Tropic of Capricorn a line of latitude (23.5° south of the Equator) marking the southernmost point reached by the overhead sun on December 22.

tropics the warm regions between the Tropic of Cancer and the Tropic of Capricorn near the Equator.

tundra cold bare land where the soil is frozen for long periods of each year. Only small, low-lying plants can grow on the tundra.

valley a low-lying area, eroded from the land by a river or glacier between two hills or mountains.

veldt the open, grassy plains of southern Africa.

volcano a weak point in the Earth's crust, where molten lava bursts through the surface. Past eruptions of lava may build up to form a mountain.

wetland an area of wet ground.

Index

Numbers in **bold** type refer to main entries. Numbers in *italics* refer to illustrations.

D

H

I

N

O

P

Credits

The publishers would like to thank the following sources for the use of their photographs: Page 10 (c) Ann Ronan Picture Library, (b/c) Michael Maslan Historic Photographs/Corbis; 15 (t/c) N.A.S.A.; 16 (c) Galen Rowell/Corbis, (b/r) Hanan Isachar/Corbis; 17 (c) James L. Amos/Corbis, (b/l) Andrey Zvoznikov/Hutchison Library, (b/r) Yann Arthus Bertrand/Corbis; 19 (c/r) AFP/Corbis; 20 (t/r) Ralph White/Corbis; 21 (b/l) Paul A. Souders/Corbis; 24 (b/l) Peter Lillie/Gallo Images/Corbis; 25 (b/l) Jim McDonald/Corbis; 26 (t/r) The Purnell Team/Corbis, (t/r) Craig Lovell/Corbis, (b/l) Philip Gould/Corbis; 27 (b/l) James Marshall/Corbis; 28 (t/r) Yann Arthus Bertrand/Corbis, (t/r) Paul Almasy/Corbis; 29 (c) Yann Arthus Bertrand/Corbis; 30 (c) Eric Lawrie/Hutchison Library, (b/r) Andrey Zvoznikov/Hutchison Library; 31 (t/r) Nigel Smith/Hutchison Library, (c/r) David Muench/Corbis; 33 (t/l) Jo Brewer, (t/l) Richard Hamilton Smith/Corbis, (t/l) Robert Francis/Hutchison; 34 (c/r) Hulton-Deutch Collection/Corbis, (c/r) Nik Wheeler/ Corbis; 35 (t/r) Keren Su/Corbis, (c) Chicago Department of Aviation, (c/r) Roger Ressmayer/Corbis, (b/l) Steve Chen/Corbis; 45 (t) Peter Finger/Corbis, (c/r) James P. Blair/Corbis; 46 (t/r) Nathan Benn/Corbis, (b/r) Farrell Grehan/Corbis; 47 (b/l) Bob Krist/Corbis, (c/l) Richard T. Nowitz/Corbis; 51 (b/l) Bill Ross/Corbis; 52 (b/c) Buddy Mays/Corbis; 54 (b) Sandy Felsenthal/Corbis; 55 (t/l) Dallas & John Heaton/Corbis, (c) Kevin Morris/Corbis; 57 (c/r) Dean Conger/Corbis; 60 (t/r) Lowell Georgia/Corbis; 68 (b) Robert Frerck/Odyssey/Chicago/Robert Harding Picture Library; 70 (b/c) Galen Rowell/Corbis; 71 (t/c) J.G. Fuller/Hutchison Library; 73 (t/l) Robert Harding Picture Library, (b/r) Robert Francis/Hutchison Library; 75 (b/r) Charles Bowman/Robert Harding Picture Library; Cover, 77 (b/r) Jeremy Horner/Corbis; 78 (b/c) J. Henderson/Hutchison Library; 79 (t/l) Adam Woolfitt/ Corbis; 82 (b) Roman Soumar/Corbis; Cover, 83 (c) Owen Franken/Corbis; 84 (b/l) Buddy Mays/Corbis; 85 (t/l) Graham Neden/Ecoscene/Corbis, (b/r) Bettman/Corbis; 86 (b/l) Dave G. Houser/Corbis; 87 (c) R. McLeod/Robert Harding Picture Library, (b/l) Pern/Hutchison Picture Library; 88 (b) Tony Aruzza/Corbis; 89 (t/r) Corbis, (c/r) D. Lomax/Robert Harding Picture Library; 92 (t/r) Kim Hart/Robert Harding Picture Library; 93 (c) Bernard Regent/Hutchison Picture Library; 96 (c/r) Sancez/Explorer/Robert Harding Picture Library; 98 (t/r) G. Hellier/Robert Harding Picture Library; 100 (b/c) Charles Bowman/Robert Harding Picture Library; 101 (t/c) Robert Frerck/Robert Harding Picture Library, (b/c) Michael Russelle/Robert Harding Picture Library; 102 (t/r) Gavin Hellier/Robert Harding Picture Library; 103 (t/c) Nigel Blythe/Robert Harding Picture Library, (b/c) Bob Krist/Corbis; 106 (b/c) Charles & Josette Lenars/Corbis; 108 (b/c) Norman Froggard/Hutchison Library; 109 (c) Adam Woolfitt/Corbis, (b/c) Gavin Hellier/Robert Harding Picture Library; 110 (c) Sandra Vanninil/Corbis, (b/c) Regent/Hutchison Library; 112 (t/r) Hans Georg Roth/Corbis; 113 (t/c) Crispin Hughes/Hutchison Library; 114 (b/c) Arne Hodalic/Corbis; 115 (t/c) AFP/Corbis, (c) Melanie Friend/Hutchison Library, (b/c) Jeremy Horner/Panos Pictures; 118 (b/c) Ludovic Maisant/Corbis; 120 (b/c) Reuters Newmedia Inc./Corbis; 121 (t/c) Nik Wheeler/Corbis; 122 (b/c) Dean Conger/Corbis; 123 (b/c) Dean Conger/Corbis; 124 (b/c) Arthur Thévenart/Corbis; 126 (b/c) Dean Conger/Corbis; 127 (b/l) Wolfgang Kaehler/Corbis; Cover, 128 (c) John Egan/ Hutchison Library, (b/c) Brian Goddard/Panos Pictures; 129 (t/c) J.C. Tordai/Hutchison Library; 130 (t/r) Janet Wishnetsky/ Corbis, (b/l) Audrey Zvoznikov/Hutchison Library; 131 (t/c) Brian Vikander/Corbis; 132 (t/r) Adam Woolfitt/Robert Harding Picture Library, (b/c) Philip Wolmuth/ Hutchison Library; 133 (t/r) Robert Harding Picture Library, (b/l) Hutchison Library; 134 (t/r) Paolo Koch/Robert Harding Picture Library; Cover, 134 (c) K.M. Westermann/Corbis; 135 (t/l) K.M. Westerman/Corbis, (b/r) Paolo Koch/Robert Harding Picture Library; 136 (b/l) J.C. Tordai/Panos Pictures; 137 (t/l) E. Simanor/Robert Harding Picture Library; 138 (b/l) T. Maugher/Robert Harding Picture Library; 139 (t/l) Robert Harding Picture Library, (b/r) Mohamed Amin/Robert Harding Picture Library; 140 (t/r) Juliet Highet/Hutchison Library; Cover, 142 (t/r) Adam Woolfitt/Corbis; 143 (b/r) Charles & Josette Lenars/Corbis; 144 (t/r) David Lomax/Robert Harding Picture Library, (b/c) Lister/Hutchison Library; 145 (t/c) Trygve Bolstad/Panos Pictures; 146 (b/l) David Cumming/Corbis; 147 (b/r) Charles & Josette Lenars/Corbis; 148 (t/r) Hutchison Library; 150 (t/r) Jean-Leo Dugast/Panos Pictures, (b/r) Trygve Bolstad/Panos Pictures; 151 (b/r) Richard Bickel/Corbis; 152 (b/c) Jermey Horner/Hutchison Library; 153 (t/c) Steve Raymer/ Corbis; 155 (b/l) Robert Harding Picture Library; 156 (c/r) Caroline Penn/Panos Pictures, (b/c) John Watt/Hutchison Library; 157 (c/r) Chris Stowers/ Panos Pictures; 158 (t/r) Adam Woolfitt/Corbis, (b/l) Hutchison Library; 159 (t/l) Robert Harding Picture Library, (b/r) Hutchison Library; 160 (b/l) John R. Jones, Papilio/Corbis; 162 (b/l) Wolfgang Koehler/Corbis; 163 (t/c) Wolfgang Koehler/Corbis, (c) Nocholas Hall/Robert Harding Picture Library; 164 (b/l) Stephanie Maze/Corbis; 166 (t/r) Paul Quayle/Panos Pictures, (b/l) Craig Lovell/Corbis; 168 (b/l) The Stock Market; 169 (b/l) Nik Wheeler/ Corbis; 172 (b/c) Liba Taylor/Hutchison Library; 173 (t/l) Sandro Vannini/Corbis; 174 (b/c) Jeremy Horner/Hutchison Library; 175 (t/c) M. Jelliffe/ Hutchison Library; 178 (t/r) Michael & Patricia Fogden/Corbis, (b/l) Paul Almasy/Corbis; 179 (t/l) Jacques Jangoux/Tony Stone Images; Cover, 180 (t/r) Sarah Errington/Hutchison Library, (b/c) Liba Taylor/Hutchison Library; 181 (t/c) Coroline Penn/Corbis; 182 (b/l) Pemberton/Hutchison; Cover, 183 (c) Adrian Arbib/Corbis; 185 (t/l) Marc Schlossman/Panos Pictures; 186 (t/r) Yann Arthus-Bertrand/Corbis; 188 (t/r) Philip Perry/Frank Lane Picture Agency/Corbis, (b/c) Hutchison Library; 189 (t/l) Charles O'Rear/Corbis; 190 (t/r) Charles & Josette Lenars/Corbis; 192 (t/r) John Lamb/Tony Stone Images; Cover, 192 (b/c) Paul Chesley/Tony Stone Images; 193 (c/r) Roger Garwood & Trish Ainslie/Corbis; 196 (t/r) The Stock Market, (c/r) The Stock Market, (b/c) AFP/Corbis; 197 (t/c) Kevin Schafer/Corbis, (b/c) Jack Fields/Corbis; 198 (b/c) The Stock Market. All other photographs from MKP Archives. In addition the publisher would like to thank: The Flag Institute; and the following artists for their contribution – Rob Jakeway and Martin Saunders.

The publisher has made every effort to contact all copyright holders, but apologize if any source remains unacknowledged.